GW01425107

WORLD REFERENCE FACTS & ATLAS

WORLD REFERENCE FACTS & ATLAS

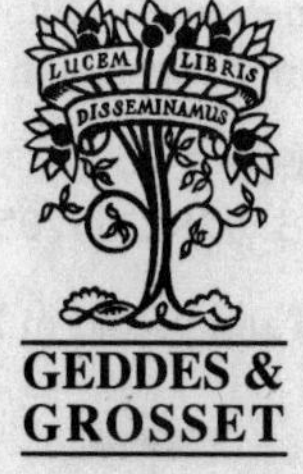
LUCEM
LIBRIS
DISSEMINAMUS
GEDDES &
GROSSET

Published 2005 by Geddes & Grosset, David Dale House,
New Lanark, ML11 9DJ

Mapping based upon data owned by
Lovell Johns Ltd., Oxford, UK
+44 (0)1993 883161, www.lovelljohns.com

First printed 2005

ISBN 10: 1 84205 330 2
ISBN 13: 978 1 84205 330 0

Printed and bound in Poland

POLSKABOOK

Contents

Geographical Information 7
The Planet Earth 7
The Solar System 10
The Earth's Structure 12
The Atmosphere 14
Seas and Oceans 17
The Sun 19
The Moon 21
World Facts 23
Atlas 237
Index 239
Maps 321

Geographical Information

This introductory section, by use of illustrated and informative text, concisely summarizes recent scientific discoveries and conclusions about our physical world: our place in the universe; our neighbours in space; the origin, structure and dynamics of our planet; its enveloping atmosphere; and its vast oceans of water, so crucial to life on earth.

The Planet Earth

Earth is the planet which we inhabit, a nearly spherical body which every twenty-four hours rotates from west to east round an imaginary line called its axis. This axis has at its extremities, the north and south poles—and in the course of a year it completes one revolution round the sun.

The Earth is nearly 4600 million years old, and most probably took over 100 million years to form into a ball of rock, at which time the surface cooled to form the crust, with the first tiny signs of growth appearing some 3500 million years ago. Life as we know it has evolved over the last 40 to 50 million years.

Volcanic eruptions produced gases which formed the Earth's atmosphere—the layer of air surrounding the Earth containing mainly the gases oxygen, nitrogen, carbon dioxide and water vapour. The atmosphere is approximately 1000 km (620 miles) thick. This layer shields the Earth from the harmful ultraviolet rays emanating from the sun and protects it from extremes of temperature.

These eruptions also produced huge volumes of water vapour which condensed to fill the hollows in the Earth's crust to form the seas and oceans.

The Earth's surface layer of rock is known as the crust, around 65 km (40 miles) deep in areas of land mass, and 6 km (4 miles) deep under the oceans.

Beneath the crust is the mantle; a rock layer some 2900 km (1800 miles) thick.

The core of the Earth has two further layers; the outer core, and the inner core. The outer core is made up of molten iron, around 2000 km (1240 miles) deep.

The inner core is of solid iron and nickel, a great ball at the centre of the Earth. To an observer, the visible part of the Earth appears as a circular and horizontal expanse. Accordingly, in remote antiquity, the Earth was regarded by man as a flat, circular body, floating on the waters. But gradually the spherical form of the Earth began to be suspected. The mere fact that the Earth could be circumnavigated did not prove it to be globular. Its surface, land and ocean, were explored and accurately mapped, and the relative distances and directions found to be consistent only with its possessing a spherical shape.

The Earth is not, however, an exact sphere, but is very slightly flattened at the poles, so as to have the form known as an oblate spheroid. In this way the polar diameter, or diameter from pole to pole, is shorter than the diameter at right angles to this—the equatorial diameter. The most accurate measurements make the polar diameter almost 42 km (27 miles) less than the equatorial, the equatorial diameter being 12,756 km (7926.7 miles), and the polar 12,714 km (7900 miles). The Earth is regarded as divided into two halves—the northern and the southern hemispheres—by the equator, an imaginary line going right round it midway between the poles. In order to indicate with precision the position of places on the Earth, additional circles are traced upon the surface in such a way that those of the one set all pass through both poles, while those of the other are drawn parallel to the equator. The former are called meridians, the latter parallels of latitude, and by reference to them we can state the latitude and longitude, and thus the exact position, of any place.

The surface of the Earth covers 511,000,000 sq km (196,900,000 sq miles) of which about 30% is dry land, the remaining 70% being water. The land is arranged into masses of irregular shape and size, the greatest connected mass being in the eastern hemisphere. The chief masses receive the name of continents, detached masses of smaller size being islands. The surface of the land is variously diversified, mountains, valleys, plains, plateaux and deserts. The water area of the Earth is divided into oceans, seas, bays, gulfs, etc., while rivers and lakes are regarded as features of the land surface. The great phenomena of the oceans are the currents and tides. The Earth's seas and oceans have an average depth of 3.5 km (2.2 miles).

The Earth, is one of nine planets which circle around the sun, completing its revolution in about 365 days and 6 hours. The orbit of the Earth is an ellipse.

Earth is the third planet from the sun and the only one which we know that supports life. Scientists and astronomers estimate that there could be as many as 10,000 million galaxies which form the universe. The Sun is but one of around 100,000 million stars in our galaxy.

The Earth's daily motion about its own axis takes place in twenty-three hours, fifty-six minutes, and four seconds of mean time. This revolution brings about

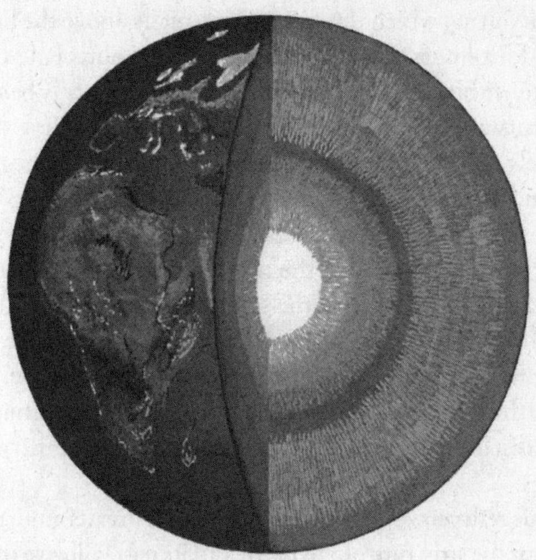

This cut-out diagram shows the inner structure of the Earth. The thickness of the Earth's crust may be likened proportionally to the skin of an apple. Beneath it lie the rocks of the mantle and the two-layered core, which is mostly liquid iron.

The core has a diameter of 6740 km (4200 miles). The outer core is 2000 km (1250 miles) thick, the inner core is 1370 km (850 miles) thick. The top 15 km (9.5 miles) of the crust is mostly made up of igneous rocks (those formed from molten magna) and metamorphic rocks (igneous or sedimentary rocks which have been changed by physical or chemical action). The dominant feature of landmass surface is sedimentary rock.

the alternation of day and night. As the axis on which the Earth rotates is inclined towards the plane of its path about the sun at an angle of 66.5°, and the angle between the plane of the ecliptic and the plane of the Earth's equator is therefore 23.5°, the sun ascends as seen from our northern latitudes, from 21st March to 21st June (the summer solstice), to about 23.5° above the celestial equator, and descends again towards the equator from 21st June to 23rd September. It then sinks till 22nd December (the winter solstice), when it is about 23.5° below the equator, and returns again to the equator by 21st March. This arrangement is the cause of the seasons, and the unequal measure of day and night during them.

For all places removed from the equator, day and night are equal only twice in the year (at the equinoxes). At the summer solstice in the northern hemisphere, the north pole of the Earth is turned towards the sun, and the south pole away from it, and for places within 23.5° of the North Pole there is a period of longer or shorter duration during which the sun is continually above the horizon throughout the twenty-four hours of each day. Round the South Pole there is an equal extent of surface within which the sun for similar periods is below the horizon. The reverse occurs at the winter solstice. The circles bounding these regions are called respectively the arctic and the antarctic circles, and the regions themselves the polar or frigid zones. Throughout a region extending to 23.5° on each side of the equator the sun is directly overhead at any place twice in the year. The circles which bound this region are called the tropics, that in the northern hemisphere being the tropic of Cancer, that in the southern the tropic of Capricorn, while the region between is the torrid zone. The regions between the tropics and the polar circles are the north and south temperate zones respectively.

The term 'earth sciences' has entered our vocabulary, covering a synthesis of the traditional disciplines of geology, geophysics, geochemistry, oceanography and meteorology.

This new focus reflects worldwide concern that a greater understanding of the global elements of the structure of the Earth and its past will give the most valuable insight as to how the Earth's resources can be best sustained.

In comparison to the age of the Earth, man's relatively short existence has caused alarming levels of pollution, and the environment is under increasing stress.

Ozone forms a key layer in the upper atmosphere and there is concern over damage to it, caused by chlorofluorocarbons—chemicals, used by man which release chlorine into the upper atmosphere, destroying the ozone.

The World sustains more than 5,000 million people—a population which has doubled since the early 1950's, and it is believed by many experts that the population could double again within the next half-century. We must learn to sustain this growth, and face the growing ecological crisis.

The Solar System

The first astronomers, long ago, noticed five special 'stars' that gradually moved through the constellations. The Greeks called them planetoi, the wanderers, from which came our word planet. Planets shine with a steady light, but real stars often twinkle. This is because a planet is, in fact, a disc of light, whereas a star is so distant that it is always just a point of light. The light from a point source shimmers as it passes through the Earth's atmosphere.

Planets are not like stars at all. The Sun is a typical star. It radiates heat and light of its own, but the planets shine only by the light they reflect from the Sun. Most stars are much larger than planets. The Sun is a thousand times more massive than the biggest planet, Jupiter. The twinkling stars are other suns, much farther away from Earth than any planet.

All the planets visible in the night sky are members of the Sun's family, or solar system. The five planets that can be seen without the aid of a telescope are Mercury, Venus, Mars, Jupiter and Saturn. Mercury is closest to the Sun. It is not easy to pick out because it is never far from the Sun in the sky. Venus is also closer to the Sun than is the Earth. This brilliant planet is seen at its best at dawn or dusk and so it is often called the morning star or evening star. Mars is the 'Red Planet,' so named because of its colour. Jupiter and Saturn, both of them giant planets, can often be seen shining with a steady yellow light.

After the invention of the telescope, astronomers found three, more distant planets. Uranus was discovered in 1781. Neptune in 1846 and Pluto in 1930. All nine planets travel in orbits around the Sun. They all journey in the same direction. The planets closest to the Sun take the least time in orbit. Mercury, nearest to the Sun, makes a circuit in only 88 days, Earth takes a year, and Jupiter almost 12 years.

Studying the motion of the planets, the German astronomer Johannes Kepler discovered in 1609 that the orbits of the planets are slightly stretched circles, called ellipses. An ellipse has two focal points. For each planetary orbit the Sun is at one of the focuses. This means that the distances of the planets from the Sun change slightly as they travel in their orbits.

Kepler found out how the planets move, but it was Isaac Newton, the seventeenth-century English mathematician, who realized that gravitational force holds the planets in their orbits. The Earth's gravity makes objects that are dropped fall to the ground. If the Sun's gravity did not constantly keep tugging at the planets, they would fly off into the depths of space.

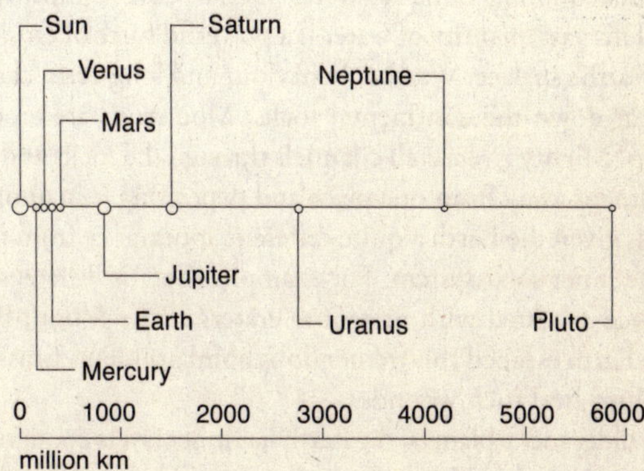
Sun
Saturn
Venus
Neptune
Mars
Jupiter
Earth
Uranus
Pluto
Mercury
0
1000
2000
3000
4000
5000
6000
million km

The Solar System

The Sun's family has other members apart from planets. Swarming between Mars and Jupiter are thousands of asteroids or minor planets. Comets with their streaming tails approach the Sun from the farthest parts of the solar system. In addition, dust is scattered in the space between the planets, as well as stones called meteoroids. These space rocks burn up if they crash through the Earth's atmosphere, creating a meteor trail, or shooting star. Many of the planets have moons orbiting them, rather like miniature solar systems. Jupiter has at least sixteen moons, four of which can be seen with a small telescope. Gravitation holds the moons in their orbits around their planets, just as it keeps the whole of the Sun's family together.

The exploration of most of the planets in the solar system is a major scientific achievement of the twentieth century. Men in space have landed on the Moon, and brought back samples from its surface. The five planets that are visible to the naked eye — along with other moons from those of Mars to the satellites of Saturn—have been investigated and photographed by unmanned spacecraft.

The Earth's Structure

Man has been able to study the surface of his own planet for as long as the Earth has been inhabited. Yet it is strange to think that before orbiting spacecraft had actually returned colour photographs of Earth, nobody had predicted accurately what it would look like from space. Now the Earth can be seen and photographed as a beautiful blue and white planet. From beneath the spiralling patterns of brilliant white clouds, the shapes of the continents come into view.

Many factors make the Earth unique in the solar system. It is the only planet with substantial amounts of liquid water. Oceans cover almost three-quarters of the surface. This vast quantity of water is a powerful force of erosion–the wearing away of the Earth's surface. Weather behaviour and long-term changes in climate gradually wear down the continental rocks. Mountains are eroded by glaciers, wind and rain. Mighty rivers etch channels through the rocks and lowland plains, carrying sediment away from one place and depositing it in another.

Erosion has given the Earth a quite different appearance from that of the other planets in the inner solar system. For example, there is little evidence now that Earth was once as pitted with meteorite craters as the Moon. But it is hard to imagine that Earth escaped this tremendous bombardment. Erosion by wind and water has helped heal such wounds.

Unlike the older rocky planets, the Earth has inner layers containing tremendous forces that are very active. Volcanoes and earthquakes, for example, permit Earth to let off pressure from friction and heat that build up inside as the great plates

THE PLANETS

Name	Distance from the Sun		Distance from the Sun compared to the Earth	Time to orbit the Sun in years	Mass compared to the Earth	Radius c ompared to the Earth
Mercury	58	(36)	0.39	0.24	0.06	0.38
Venus	108	(67)	0.72	0.62	0.82	0.95
Earth	149.5	(93)	1.00	1.00	1.00	1.00
Mars	228	(142)	1.52	1.88	0.11	0.53
Jupiter	778.5	(484)	5.20	11.86	318.00	11.00
Saturn	1427	(887)	9.54	29.46	95.00	9.00
Uranus	2870	(1783)	19.18	84.00	15.00	4.00
Neptune	4497	(2794)	30.06	165.00	17.00	4.00
Pluto	5900	(3706)	39.44	248.00	0.0024	0.28–0.34

This table lists the nine planets in the order of their distances from the Sun. Together with their moons, the asteroids and comets, these planets make up the solar system. Distance from the Sun is measured in millions of kilometres (miles). The comparisons of the characteristics of the other planets to those of the Earth are given in decimal ratio, that is, Mars is 1.52 times farther from the

of rock comprising the Earth's surface slowly slide about. Earthquakes, sudden, unpredictable and lethal though they may be, teach geologists about the inner structure of the Earth. Vibrations spreading out from an earthquake are measured and analyzed by scientific instruments all over the globe. These vibrations reveal that Earth is made of several layers. On top is a thin crust of rock that is nowhere more than 65km (40 miles) thick. The crust lies atop a thick layer of rock 2900km (1800 miles) deep called the mantle. Inside that, there is a liquid core of hot iron 225 km (1400 miles) in diameter. Possibly the central part of this core is solid because of the immense pressure created by the weight of the overlying material.

Magnetism is generated by electric currents flowing through the liquid iron in the interior. On most planets a magnetic compass would be of no use for ending north. The compass works here because the Earth has its own magnetic field of influence. A compass needle lines up with the Earth's magnetism and points to the north.

Compared with most of the other rocky worlds in the solar system, Earth is a hive of geological activity. Mountains are constantly being thrust up, earthquakes make the globe tremble and volcanoes cough out liquid rock. Even the continents are slowly gliding about. Only Io, a moon of Jupiter, shows similar activity. Why does the Earth differ from Venus and Mars?

The answer is that the crust of the Earth consists of several large plates that will not keep still. Beneath the oceans and continents there is a rock layer that moves. According to theory, heat flowing from underneath the plates causes this motion, which is like that of a conveyor belt. The heat comes partly from the decay of radioactive rocks. In certain places the plates push into each other, and cause tremendous buckling. This crumpling of two continental plates has caused the formation of the Alps and Himalayas. Along the west coast of North and South America the continental plates are being forced against the oceanic plates and this has formed a great range of coastal mountains from Alaska to southern Chile.

Another effect of these rock movements is to generate friction. This may melt the rock below the surface; molten material works its way upward through cracks and erupts as a volcano.

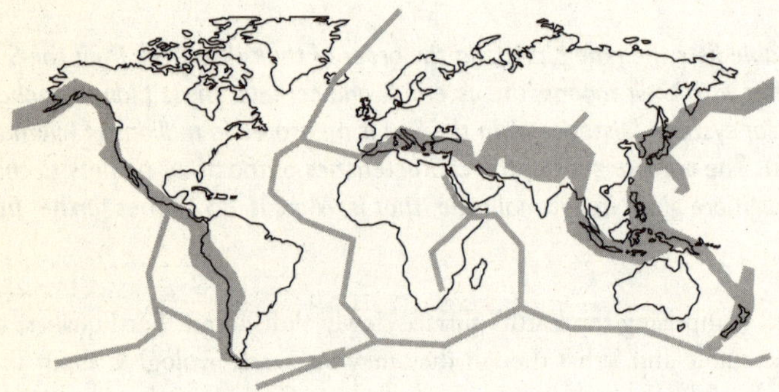

Areas of Earthquake Activity

The motion of continental and oceanic plates is not noticeable in a human lifetime. But it is fast enough to change the face of the Earth. For example, all the present continents resulted when two enormous land masses shattered about 200 million years ago. South America and Africa are still moving about but a look at a map shows how they once fitted together.

The Atmosphere

The atmosphere, which surrounds and sustains life, is the stage setting within which the drama of weather is played. Extending from the Earth's surface to perhaps 965 km (600 miles) or more into space, the atmosphere divides into several layers, each comprised of gases in varying quantities and densities. The predominant gases in the lowest layer, the troposphere, are oxygen, nitrogen, traces (about 0.03 per cent) of carbon dioxide and–most important for the weather–water vapour.

Virtually all of the weather as we know it–with constant changes from wet to dry, clear to cloudy, hot to cold, windy to still–and vice versa–takes place in the troposphere. This is mainly because all but the tiniest traces of water vapour –the stuff of which fog, clouds, rain and all other forms of precipitation is made–occur in the troposphere. Without this water vapour there would be no life.

The troposphere varies in thickness, from about eight kilometres over the Poles to about 16 km (10 miles) over the Equator. Above the troposphere there is very little water vapour. This is called the stratosphere, where supersonic aircraft fly with little danger of colliding with an ice crystal, which could do enormous damage. This atmospheric layer contains almost no clouds. Here too, oxygen and most of the other life-sustaining gases thin out.

As the altitude changes, so too does the temperature. This happens because the Earth and the water vapour in the troposphere act as radiators, absorbing and giving off the Sun's heat.

Beyond the troposphere, neither the Earth's heat nor water vapour is a factor in determining atmospheric temperature. In the stratosphere the temperature becomes warmer with increased altitude because of the dominance of solar radiation. Then in the next layer, the mesosphere, the temperature turns cold again, in part because of the reaction of a gas called ozone that blocks out the Sun's ultraviolet rays. The temperature continues to drop until it reaches 85°C or more below zero. Then, at perhaps 80 km (50 miles) over the Earth, where the thermosphere begins, the gases–under the direct influence of the Sun–become so thinly concentrated that they all but disappear.

Although these upper layers contain no weather in the popular use of the term, they affect events in the troposphere by shielding the Earth from the searing rays of the Sun. In addition these upper layers together contribute about 25 per cent of the atmospheric weight that presses down upon the Earth's surface.

The troposphere contributes the other 75 per cent of the atmosphere's weight, through the presence of the relatively dense gases–including water vapour. Vapour enters the atmosphere by evaporation from oceans, seas, and lakes, and to a lesser extent from wet ground and vegetation (transpiration). Heat is needed for evaporation to occur, and this heat is taken from the surrounding atmosphere and the surface of the Earth, which therefore becomes cooler.

This heat is not lost, but is stored in the vapour as hidden, or latent, heat. The vapour is carried by winds to higher levels of the atmosphere and to different parts of the world. As a result, water vapour may be found throughout the troposphere and over all regions, oceans and continents. Eventually, water vapour condenses into liquid water or solid ice and falls to the ground as precipitation–rain, snow or hail. In condensing, it releases its latent heat to the atmosphere. Thus if water evaporates into the air from a tropical ocean and winds then carry it to a temperate continent, where it condenses and falls as rain, this provides a very effective means of carrying not only water but also heat from places that have plenty to places that are short of both.

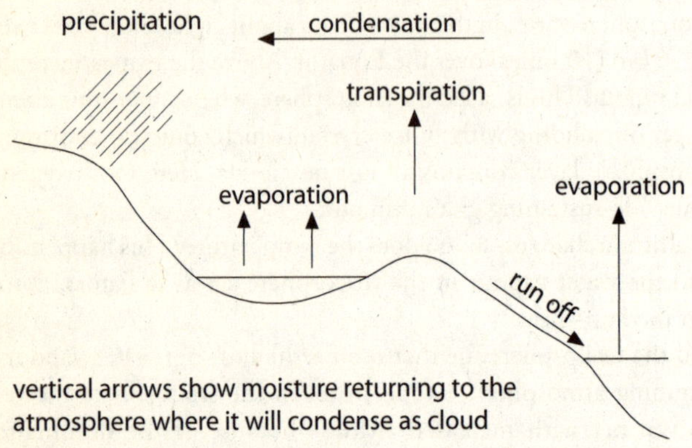
precipitation
condensation
transpiration
evaporation
evaporation
run off
vertical arrows show moisture returning to the
atmosphere where it will condense as cloud

The Hydrological Cycle

In the air around us, the temperature, pressure and moisture content are affected by the fourth critical ingredient that makes up our weather; the wind. As we know, wind is the name for a moving mass of air. Nearly everyone is familiar with winds that blow from north, south, east or west–that is across the Earth's surface, or horizontally. But winds also blow vertically–as bird-watchers know from seeing gulls or crows sail upwards on rising currents of warm air, or from watching a hawk sink down rapidly on a descending cold current.

Most vertical air currents are much gentler than horizontal winds. But they are vitally important, because they can generate many different types of weather. When air rises it expands, because the pressure on it becomes less. As it rises, the air cools. Because it cools, its moisture content increases. Eventually the rising air may reach a level at which it becomes saturated with moisture. If it rises still further, water vapour starts condensing to form clouds. nearly all clouds and rain originate in up-currents of air.

One reason why air starts to rise is because of temperature differences from place to place. Such differences are very marked on sunny days over land, when the air above some surfaces, such as asphalt or bare soil, becomes warmer than that over adjacent surfaces, such as trees or lakes. The warmer masses of air, which can be called bubbles, then start to rise. The air between the rising bubbles sinks to compensate. This type of air movement is called convection.

Once a bubble of air has started to rise, it will continue to do so as long as it remains warmer than its surroundings. As it rises, it cools, initially at a rate of 15°C per 90 metres. But its surroundings also cool with height. Eventually the bubble will reach its condensation level and clouds will start to form. The condensation in such clouds releases latent heat, making the rising air even warmer. This increases the difference in temperature between the rising air and the surrounding air. The atmosphere is then said to be unstable. As long as the atmosphere remains unstable, the bubble will grow bigger and rise further, producing a tall cloud. This cloud may become so saturated with moisture that rain or snow begins to fall from it.

On the other hand, if the rate of decrease of the temperature in the air surrounding the bubble is quite small, or if the temperature actually rises with height–as it sometimes does –then the rising air bubble will soon become colder than its surroundings. The bubble will then stop rising. In this situation the atmosphere is said to be stable. Bubbles may never reach their condensation level, in which case no clouds will form–or the bubble will produce only small, shallow clouds. When clouds do form, condensation may stop before the air becomes so saturated that precipitation begins. This is typically the case in stable air.

Seas and Oceans

The water on the Earth's surface that now fills the oceans got there as part of a process that started with the origin of the Earth itself. This is the opinion of most Earth-scientists today. To understand that process, we need to know something about the origin of the solar system. The material from which the Earth and the other planets were later to be formed probably began as a cloud of gases spinning around the sun. These gases gradually condensed, making solid particles. Many of them collided, and built up larger and larger concentrations of matter.

The part that was eventually to become the Earth seems to have cooled and begun solidifying about 4.6 billion years ago, and as the spinning movement shaped matter into a ball, it contracted even further. Under these pressures, matter at the centre of the newly formed Earth began to heat up again and became molten. When this happened, water that had been contained inside the Earth was released to the surface as vapour and was added to the primitive atmosphere.

When it cooled and condensed, it fell to the surface as rain and eventually formed the first oceans. We do not know how much of the water in the oceans came from this source. Estimates range from a third to almost all of it–there is no way we can determine the exact amount. Neither can we tell when this happened, but some indication comes from rocks. The oldest rock discovered so far on the Earth's surface is from Greenland and is 3.8 billion years old. It is a kind of rock formed from pebbles laid down under water and later compressed. This shows that water must already have condensed and fallen to Earth during the 800 million years that had passed since the Earth was formed.

The rest of the water in the oceans also came from the interior of the Earth, but was forced to the surface by volcanic eruptions and hot springs. There are many volcanoes and hot springs on land and even more in parts of the ocean, and they are still spewing out water. Only a small proportion of this water is new, or juvenile, water coming from deep inside the Earth for the first time. Most of it is groundwater or seawater that seeped down into the Earth, heated up through contact with hot rocks and then returned to the surface in a volcanic eruption or a hot spring. Although only a small proportion of this water is juvenile, the total amount of new water brought to the surface in the billions of years this process has been going on has been enough to help fill the oceans.

Was the water that came from the Earth's interior to fill the oceans the same salty seawater we know today? As far as we can tell, the oceans never had fresh water. Salt, or salinity, comes from gases and other substances dissolved in the water. When water first rose to the surface of the Earth as steam, it contained gases, some of which dissolved in the original oceans. Since then, volcanoes have supplied other gases along with water and added them to the oceans. Other substances in seawater reached and still reach the ocean by a different process. They come from rocks on land which slowly break down to produce tiny fragments that flow in rivers into the oceans.

Although the ocean, like the atmosphere, had very little oxygen up to about 1.9 billion years ago and had differing amounts of gases and metals in the past, the total amount of all dissolved substances in the ocean–and salinity–was probably similar to the present. And about 1 billion years ago the oceans reached a composition very similar to what it is today.

Just as substances are being added to seawater, so also are they being removed. If they were not, the concentration would go on building up. Water is still being added to the oceans by volcanoes, rain and rivers, and is being lost again by evaporation. The salinity of seawater remains at the same level because some of the solids sink to the bottom or are thrown into the air in sea spray. Salt particles attract water in the atmosphere and droplets grow on them, some of which are blown away over the land as rain. By these means, water and solids are recycled through the atmosphere, rivers, sediments, seawater, rock, and the Earth's interior to maintain the overall composition, of the oceans.

The Sun

To the planets, animals and peoples of the Earth, the Sun is a unique and vital star. Every living thing on the Earth owes its existence to the fact that the Sun is nearby and keeps shining, and has done so for about five billion years. The energy from the burning of coal, oil and natural gas was once sun-energy. These fuels are the remains of plants and animals that grew in the warmth of sun-energy millions of years ago. The nearest star, apart from the Sun, is 300,000 times farther away, and the weak star energy we receive from it cannot possibly replace sun energy.

The Sun is far larger than the Earth and also a great deal more massive. One hundred and nine Earth-planets placed side by side would stretch from one side of the Sun to the other. Its volume is 1.3 million times greater than the Earth and the mass 330,000 times as much.

The distance from Earth to Sun is about 150 million km (93 million miles). Light and heat take eight minutes and twenty seconds to race across interplanetary space and reach the Earth from this distance. Although this seems a great separation, only a handful of stars exists within a million times this distance from the solar system.

The Sun's gravity pulls much harder than the Earth's gravity. A person who could venture to the surface of the Sun would weigh about one and a half tons. However, this is an impossible adventure since the Sun has no solid surface and the temperature there is about 10,000°F. This exceeds the melting temperature of every known substance. The temperature of the surface seems high, but inside the Sun it is much hotter. Its entire globe is a glowing mass of gas. At the centre the temperature is about 27 million degrees Fahrenheit.

The gas inside the Sun is three-quarters hydrogen, the lightest gas. Deep inside the hot Sun, hydrogen atoms crowd together. In the jostling a group of them collides so violently with another group that they fuse together and make a completely different substance, helium. Each second, 650 million tons of hydrogen become helium. A small part of this mass of material is transformed in the process and reappears as pure energy, as Einstein has predicted would be the case. In one second, the Sun's mass falls by four million tons. In fifty million years the lost mass is equal to the mass of the Earth.

The Sun

Flashes of energy burst forth as the hydrogen turns to helium. The great density of matter traps the energy flashes inside the Sun. They wander through the interior for a million years or so before reaching the surface. The energy then streams off into space.

Along with the heat and light, the Sun emits radiation that can be harmful to living creatures. Ultraviolet rays and X-rays damage the cells in plants and animals. The Earth's blanket of atmosphere soaks up almost all of this radiation, although the small amount that reaches the ground on a fine day will make fair skin tan, or cause painful sunburn if exposure is too long. Astronauts journeying into space have to be protected from the Sun's harmful rays.

Sunspots look like holes in the fiery surface of the Sun. In fact they are areas that are about 3000°F cooler than the surrounding surface. This makes their temperature roughly 7000°F. Something that hot is actually extremely brilliant: sunspots only look dark because they are cooler and dimmer than the rest of the Sun. If a sunspot could be plucked from the Sun and examined separately it would seem a hundred times brighter than the full Moon. An average spot is 32,000 km (20,000 miles) across; most spots are more or less as big as the Earth, and huge spots span 145,000 km (90,000 miles.)

The chromosphere, the cool layer of atmosphere— above the yellow surface, can be seen readily only during total eclipses. The temperature in this thin layer is about 8000°F. Above the chromosphere is the intensely hot and invisible corona, where the temperature soars to an amazing two million degrees Fahrenheit. The gas in the corona is boiling away into space. This gas rush is called solar wind.

The Moon

Moon soil is not all like Earth soil, it is made entirely from finely pulverized rock–the dust from meteoroid crashes. Moon soil has no water, decaying plant material or life. But it does contain something beautiful and unusual. Moon soil has many glass beads, emerald green and orange-red in colour, shaped like jewels and teardrops. These are made when a meteoroid impact sprays liquid rock in every direction. When the droplets of rock solidify, they turn glassy.

On the surface of the Moon a man weighs only one-sixth of his Earth weight. This is because the Moon's mass is a mere one-eightieth of the Earth's, so the gravitational pull is considerably smaller.

It was once feared that if a spacecraft landed on the Moon it would rapidly sink without trace into the deep dust layers. However, the lunar soil is well packed down to provide a reasonably firm surface. The main hazard of Moon travel is finding a smooth place to land. At close quarters the surface looks much like a bomb site, with small craters everywhere.

Moon rocks are distinctly different from Earth rocks. A geologist could easily tell them apart. The difference between them suggests that the Moon was once hotter than the Earth has ever been, and emphasizes the fact that the Moon has no air and no water. The oldest rocks found on the Moon are 4.6 billion years old. In comparison, the most aged rock yet discovered on Earth dates from only 3.8 billion years ago.

Astronauts left scientific apparatus on the Moon, including sensors that have detected numerous 'moonquakes' as well as the impacts of meteoroids, some spacecraft and man-made debris slamming into the surface. Several small reflectors, like those on a car or bicycle, were placed on the Moon. Scientists can now measure the Moon's distance to within an inch or so by aiming a powerful laser beam at these reflectors and timing the beam's round trip from Earth to Moon and back again. This distance on the average is 385,000 km (240,000 miles.)

Geological maps of most of the surface are now available, a possibility undreamed of before about 1960. Samples mainly from the Apollo program, have been sent to laboratories throughout the world for very detailed examination. Nevertheless, this analysis of lunar material has shown that the surface has never supported life in the past. However, astronauts brought back to the Earth a piece of the Moon lander, *Surveyor 3*, which had landed on the Moon three years previously. Bacteria on this craft were still alive after several years of exposure to the harsh lunar environment. These bacteria did not flourish, but neither did they die. Thus there is a faint, extremely remote possibility that spacecraft are contaminating the Moon, planets and deep space with microscopic life from Earth even though the equipment is given a complete cleaning before its launch.

The Moon

Two or three times a year, the full Moon moves into the Earth's shadow, and the Moon is eclipsed. During this so-called lunar eclipse, the shadowed part of the Moon looks dimly red because of Earth's atmosphere scatters reddish sunlight into the Earth's shadow. Eclipses do not take place every month because the Moon's orbit is tilted at an angle to the Earth's path around the Sun.

The Moon's gravitational pull has the important effect of creating ocean tides. The water surrounding the solid Earth is distorted into the shape of a squashed ball under the influence of the Moon's attraction. As the Earth spins on it axis, the bulges in the water seem to sweep around the Earth, causing two tides each day in most places. The Sun, too, influences the tides. When the Moon and the Sun are both pulling from the same direction, the highest tides are formed.

World Facts

How to use this section

World Facts contains up-to-date geographical information on the world's countries, and its important natural features. The entries are arranged alphabetically. Where a place name has a commonly used English language form, e.g. Seoul, Soul, the commonly used form is listed first with the local spelling, or an alternative transliteration, given in brackets. Natural features such as rivers and mountains are listed with the specific name given first, e.g. Nile, River or Everest, Mount. Place names containing 'St' (denoting saint), e.g. St Petersburg, are listed under 'St' rather than 'Saint'. Where the form is generally spelled in full, e.g. Saint John it is listed under 'Saint'.

Entries on countries contain details of the geographical structure and economic nature of the country with information on area and population (the most recent figure available, whether based on census results or estimated). The capital city and other major cities are listed, as are the type of government in general terms, the major religions, and the form of currency. In addition, there is a key map indicating the part of the continent in which the country is situated to aid reference to the maps in the World Maps section.Entries on natural features list physical details – length in miles and kilometres of rivers, height in feet and metres of mountains, etc. There are also entries on places of historical interest.

A

Aberdeenshire a council area in northern Scotland, with its administrative centre in the city of Aberdeen. (2,439 sq miles/6,319 sq km; pop. 227,000)

Abruzzi a region of southern central Italy; its capital is L'Aquila. (Pop. 1,298,000)

Abu Dhabi (Abu Zabi) the largest sheikhdom of the United Arab Emirates, of which the city of Abu Dhabi is the capital. (26,000 sq miles/67,350 sq km; pop. emirate 1,211,000/city 520,000)

Aconcagua the highest mountain of the Andes, Argentina. (22,835 ft/6,960 m)

Adana a city and province in southern Turkey. (Pop. city 1,162,000)

Adirondack Mountains a mountain range in New York State, USA. The highest peak is Mount Marcy at 5,344 feet (1,629 metres).

Adriatic Sea a branch of the Mediterranean Sea, between Italy, Slovenia, Croatia and Albania.

Aegean Sea a branch of the Mediterranean Sea between Greece and Turkey.

Afghanistan a landlocked country in southern Asia. The greater part of the country is mountainous with a central mass of huge mountain ranges. Many of the peaks rise to enormous heights, the greatest being Nowshak at 24,557 feet (7,845 metres). The climate is generally arid with great extremes of temperature. There is considerable snowfall in winter, which may remain on the mountain summits all year round. The country experiences many earthquakes, and periods of severe drought. Its main exports have been fruit and nuts, carpets, wool, and opium. Afghanistan has suffered from ongoing conflict during its modern history to the extent that its economy and infrastructure have been severely affected After the Russian withdrawal from Afghanistan in 1989, the country was troubled by mainly ethnic conflict. In 1996, the Taleban, a fundamentalist Islamic group, took control of Afghanistan. Their extreme version of Islam attracted widespread criticism, and their refusal to hand over Osama bin Laden (accused by the US of masterminding the bombing of their embassies in Africa in 1998 and the attacks on the US on 11 September) led to a series of US-initiated aerial attacks. These attacks paved the way for opposition groups within the country to drive the Taleban from power (although fighting continued in a small area of the country still controlled by Taleban forces). In December 2001,

Afghan groups signed a two-stage deal (involving an Interim Authority and a Transitional Authority) aimed at setting up a fully representative government within three years. Successful presidential elections were held in 2004 but the country was still far from stable.

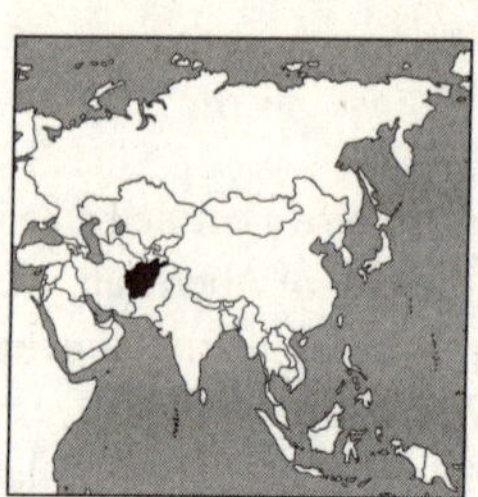

Area: 251,772 sq miles/652,225 sq km
Population: 20,833,000
Capital: Kabul
Other major cities: Herat, Kandahar, Mazar-i-Sharif
Form of government: Administration by Interim and Transitional Authorities (2002)
Religions: Sunni Islam, Shia Islam
Currency: Afghani

Africa the second largest continent in the world, with the Mediterranean Sea to the north, the Atlantic Ocean to the west and the Indian Ocean to the east. There are 53 nations within Africa, excluding Western Sahara. (11,700,000 sq miles/ 30,300,000 sq km; pop. 805,000,000)

Ajman the smallest emirate of the United Arab Emirates. (96 sq miles/250 sq km; pop. emirate 155,000/town 149,000)

Alabama a state in southern USA. The state capital is Montgomery. (51,606 sq miles/ 133,667 sq km; pop. 4,482,000)

Alaska the largest and most northerly state of the USA. The state capital is Juneau. (586,400 sq miles/1,518,800 sq km; pop. 643,000)

Albacete a town and province of southeastern Spain. (Pop. town 153,000)

Albania a small, mountainous country in the Balkan region of southeastern Europe. Its immediate neighbours are Greece, Serbia and Montenegro, and Macedonia, and it is bounded to the west by the Adriatic Sea. The climate is typically Mediterranean and although most rain falls in winter, severe thunderstorms frequently occur on the plains in summer. Winters are severe in the highland areas and heavy snowfalls are common. All land is state-owned, with the main agricultural areas lying along the Adriatic coast and in the Korce Basin with about a fifth of the land being arable. Industry is also nationalized and output is small. The principal industries are agricultural product processing, textiles, oil products, cement, iron, and steel. There is also potential for producing hydroelectricity, with the country's many mountain streams. Albania has been afflicted by severe economic problems and, in late 1996, public dissatisfaction with the government erupted into civil unrest, leading to a major revolt by citizen militias during which the government forces lost control. By March 1997, the country was on the brink of collapse and large numbers of refugees were leaving. The situation was reversed, however, when ethnic cleansing of Albanian inhabitants of the Kosovo region of Serbia in 1999 led to a flood of refugees into Albania (and elsewhere) before NATO bombing ended the cleansing and Kosovar Albanians were able to return home.

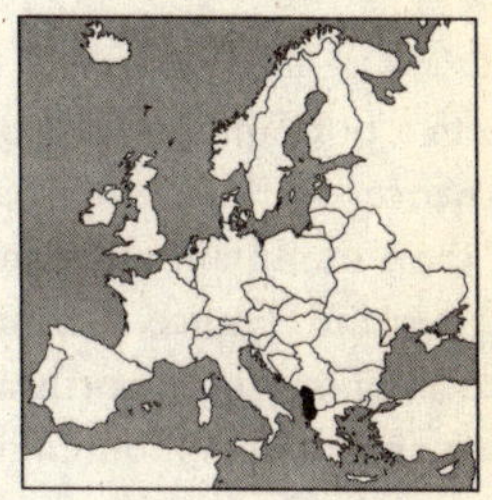

Area: 11,100 sq miles/28,748 sq km
Population: 3,200,000
Capital: Tirana (Tiranè)
Other cities: Durrès, Shkodèr, Elbasan
Form of government: Socialist Republic
Religions: Sunni Islam, Orthodox, RC
Currency: Lek

Albert, Lake in the Great Rift Valley, is shared between Uganda and Democratic Republic of Congo. Formerly known as Lake Mobuto Sésé Seko. (2,000 sq miles/5,180 sq km)

Alberta a province of western Canada; Edmonton is its capital. (255,285 sq miles/661,190 sq km; pop. 3,162,000)

Al Fujayrah (Fujairah) one of the seven United Arab Emirates, in the Persian Gulf. (502 sq miles/1,300 sq km; pop. emirate 99,000/town 43,000)

Algarve the southern province of Portugal. (Pop. 393,000)

Algeria a huge country in northern Africa that fringes the Mediterranean Sea in the north. Over four-fifths of Algeria is covered by the Sahara Desert to the south. Near the north coastal area the Atlas Mountains run east-west in parallel ranges. The Chelif, at 450 miles (724 kilometres) long, is the country's main river, rising in the Tell Atlas and flowing to the Mediterranean. The climate in the coastal areas is warm and temperate with most of the rain falling in winter. The summers are dry and hot with temperatures rising to over 89°F (32°C). Inland beyond the Atlas Mountains conditions become more arid and temperatures range from 120°F (49°C) during the day to 50°F (10°C) at night. Most of Algeria is unproductive agriculturally, but it does possess one of the largest reserves of natural gas and oil in the world. Algeria's main exports are oil-based products, fruit, vegetables, tobacco, phosphates, and cork, while imports include textiles, foodstuffs, machinery, iron, and steel. In recent years, the country has been wracked by civil strife and terrorist attacks, with the various opposing forces unable to agree peace proposals.

Area: 919,595 sq miles/2,381,741 sq km
Population: 29,168,000
Capital: Algiers (El Djazair, Alger)
Other major cities: Oran, Constantine, 'Annaba
Form of government: Republic
Religion: Sunni Islam
Currency: Algerian Dinar

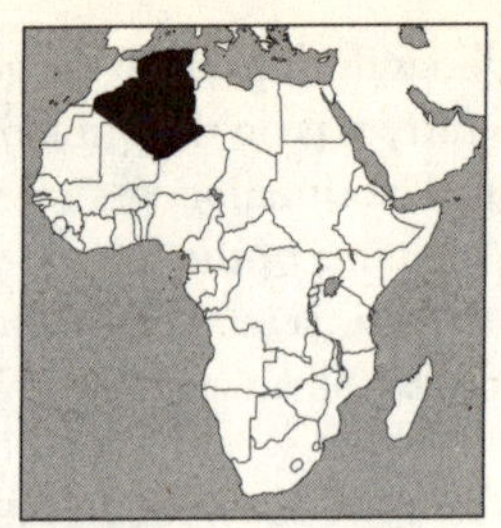

Alicante a port and popular beach resort, and also the name of the surrounding province, on the Mediterranean coast of Spain. (Pop. town 251,400)

Alps, the a mountain range in southern central Europe that spans the borders of Switzerland, France, Germany, Austria, Slovenia, Italy and Liechtenstein.

Alsace a region in the northeast of France.

Altai an area of high mountain ranges in central Asia on the borders of China and the Russian Federation at the western end of Mongolia.

Amazon (Amazonas) the world's second longest river, it rises in the Andes of Peru and flows east through Brazil to the Atlantic Ocean. (Length 4,000 miles/ 6,440 km)

Ambon (Amboina) an island and the capital of the so-called Spice Islands in the Maluku group in eastern central Indonesia. (314 sq miles/813 sq km; pop. city 262,000)

America the continent lying between the Atlantic and Pacific Oceans, divided into three zones: North America, consisting of USA, Canada, Mexico and Greenland (9,000,000 sq miles/23,500,000 sq km; pop. 347,000,000); Central America, consisting of the area between the southern Mexico border and the Panama-Colombia border with the Caribbean (714,000 sq miles/1,849,000 sq km; pop. 137,000,000); and South America, consisting of the area south of the Panama-Colombia border (6,800,000 sq miles/17,600,000 sq km; pop. 307,000,000).

Amudar'ya a central Asian river forming much of the border between Tajikistan and Afghanistan before flowing through Uzbekistan into the Aral Sea. Its ancient name was Oxus. (Length 1,630 miles/2,620 km)

Amundsen Sea an arm of the South Pacific in Antarctica.

Amur (Heilong Jiang) a river which runs along the border between China and the Russian Federation, flowing east into the Pacific Ocean. (Length 2,800 miles/ 4,510 km)

Anatolia the historical name for the Asian part of Turkey.

Andalusia (Andalucía) a region of southwestern Spain, with a coast on the Mediterranean and Atlantic.

Andaman and Nicobar Islands two groups of islands in the Bay of Bengal, administered by India. (Pop. 363,000)

Andaman Sea a branch of the Bay of Bengal, lying between the Andaman Islands and Myanmar.

Andes a high mountain range that runs down the entire length of the western coast of South America. The highest peak is Mount Aconcagua, in Argentina at 22,835 feet (6,960 metres).

Andhra Pradesh a state in southeast India. The capital is Hyderabad. (106,184 sq miles/275,088 sq km; pop. 77,207,000)

Andorra a tiny state, situated high in the eastern Pyrénées, between France and Spain. The state consists of deep valleys and high mountain peaks which reach heights of 9,843 feet (3,000 metres). Although only 12 miles (20 kilometres) wide and 19 miles (30 kilometres) long, the spectacular scenery and climate attract many tourists. About 10 million visitors arrive each year, during the cold weather when heavy snowfalls make for ideal skiing, or in summer when the weather is mild and sunny and the mountains are used for walking. Tourism and the duty-free trade are now Andorra's chief sources of income. Sheep and cattle are raised on the high pastures. Although Andorra has no airport or railroad, there is a good road system. In 1993, an Andorran government was elected and has its own parliament after 715 years of being ruled by France's leader and the Spanish Bishop of Urgel.

Area: 175 sq miles/453 sq km
Population: 65,900
Capital: Andorra la Vella
Form of government: Principality
Religion: RC
Currency: Euro

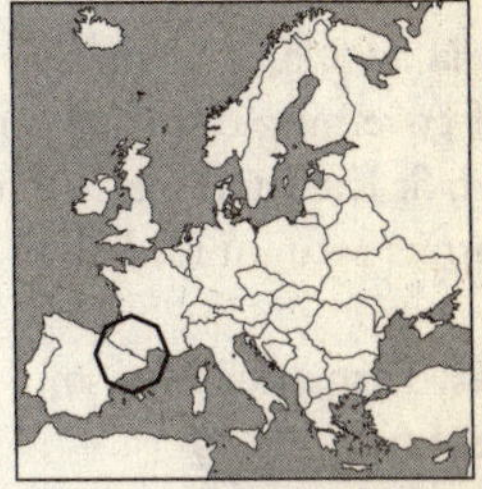

Andros the largest of the islands of the Bahamas (1,600 sq miles/4,144 sq km; pop. 8,000)

Angara a river in the Russian Federation flowing from Lake Baikal into the Yenisey River. (Length 1,135 miles/1,825 km)

Angel Falls a narrow band of water falling 3,212 feet (979 metres) from a high plateau in southeastern Venezuela to form the world's highest waterfall.

Anglesey an island off the northwestern tip of Wales, also a council area of Wales, with its administrative centre in Llangefni (278 sq miles/720 sq km; pop. 69,000)

Angola situated on the Atlantic coast of southern Africa, Angola lies about 10° south of the equator. It shares borders with Congo, Democratic Republic of Congo, Zambia, and Namibia. Its climate is tropical with temperatures constantly between 68°F (20°C) and 77°F (25°C). The rainfall is heaviest in inland areas where there are vast equatorial forests. The country is also rich in minerals, however deposits of manganese, copper, and phosphate are as yet unexploited. Diamonds are mined in the northeast and oil is produced near Luanda. Oil production is the most important aspect of the economy, making up about 90 per cent of exports which have traditionally included diamonds, fish, coffee, and palm oil. Around 70 per cent of the workforce are engaged in agriculture. Since independence from Portugal in 1975, the United States is the main recipient of the country's exports. However, the Angolan economy has been severely damaged by the civil war of the 1980s and early 1990s.

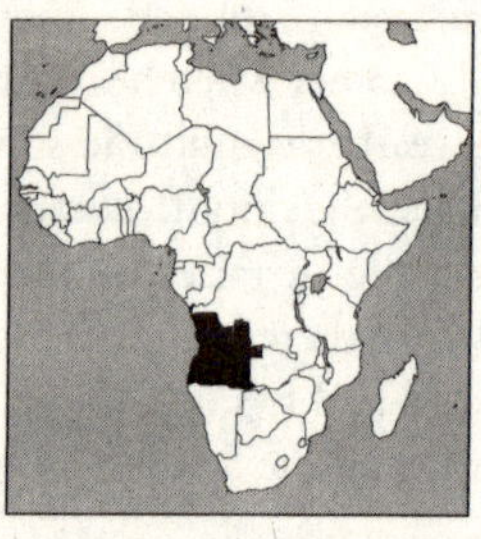

Area: 481,354 sq miles/1,246,700 sq km
Population: 11,185,000
Capital: Luanda
Other major cities: Huambo, Lobito, Benguela
Form of government: People's Republic
Religions: RC, traditional African religions
Currency: Kwanza

Anguilla an island in the Leeward Islands group of the Caribbean Sea, now a self-governing British dependency. From 1967 until 1980, it was in federation with St Kitts and Nevis. The country's main source of revenue is tourism, and lobsters account for half of the island's exports.

Area: 37 sq miles/96 sq km
Population: 12,400
Capital: The Valley
Form of government: British Overseas Territory
Religion: Christianity
Currency: East Caribbean Dollar

Angus a council area in east Scotland, with its administrative centre in the town of Forfar. (842 sq miles/2,181 sq km; pop. 111,000)

Anhui (Anhwei) a province of eastern China. Its capital is Hefei. (50,000 sq miles/130,000 sq km; pop. 60,596,000)

Anjou a former province of western France, in the valley of the River Loire.

Annapurna a mountain of the Himalayas, in Nepal. (26,810 ft/8,172 m)

Antarctica an ice-covered continent around the South Pole consisting of a plateau and mountain ranges reaching a height of 15,000 feet (4,500 metres). It is uninhabited apart from temporary staff at research stations. (5,100,000 sq miles/ 14,000,000 sq km)

Antarctic Circle latitude 66° 32' south. At the southern winter solstice, the sun does not rise, nor does it set at the summer solstice, at this line, or in higher latitudes.

Antarctic Ocean (Southern Ocean) the waters that surround Antarctica, made up of the southern waters of the Atlantic, Indian and Pacific Oceans.

Antigua and Barbuda located on the eastern side of the Leeward Islands, Antigua and Barbuda is a tiny state comprising three islands: Antigua, Barbuda and the uninhabited rocky islet of Redonda. Antigua's strategic position was recognized by the British in the 18th century when it was an important naval base, and later by the USA who built the island's airport during World War II to defend the Caribbean and the Panama Canal. Although mainly low-lying, the country's highest point is Boggy Peak at 1,329 feet (405 metres). The climate is tropical although its average rainfall of 4 inches (100 millimetres) makes it drier than most of the other islands of the West Indies. Tourism is the main industry as its numerous sandy beaches make it an ideal destination. Barbuda is surrounded by coral reefs and the island is home to a wide range of wildlife. Cotton, sugar cane, and fruits are cultivated and fishing is an important industry. Great damage was inflicted on Antigua and Barbuda in 1995 by Hurricane Luis when over 75 per cent of property was destroyed or damaged.

Area: 171 sq miles/442 sq km
Population: 66,000
Capital: St. John's
Form of government: Constitutional Monarchy
Religion: Christianity (mainly Anglicanism)
Currency: East Caribbean Dollar

Antilles a major chain of islands in the Caribbean, divided into two groups: the Greater Antilles (which includes Cuba and Puerto Rico) to the west; the Lesser Antilles (including Martinique and Barbados) to the east.

Antrim (1) a historical county in northeast Northern Ireland. (1,200 sq miles/ 3,100 sq km) (2) a district council area in Co. Antrim. (160 sq miles/415 sq km; pop. 44,516)

Apennines (Appennino) the mountain range which forms the 'backbone' of Italy. The highest peak is Monte Corno at 9,554 feet (2,912 metres).

Apia the capital of Samoa. (Pop. 36,000)

Appalachian Mountains a chain of mountains which stretches 1,600 miles (2,570 kilometres) down eastern North America from Canada to Alabama in the USA. The highest peak is Mount Mitchell at 6,684 feet (2,037 metres).

Aquitaine a region and former kingdom of southwestern France.

Arabian Sea a branch of the Indian Ocean between India and Arabia.

Arafura Sea a stretch of the Pacific Ocean between New Guinea and Australia.

Aragon (Aragón) a region and former kingdom of northeast Spain.

Aral Sea a large, salty lake, to the east of the Caspian Sea, on the border between Uzbekistan and Kazakhstan. (25,000 sq miles/64,750 sq km)

Aran Islands (Oileáin Arann) three small islands, Inishmore, Inishmaan and Inisheer, off County Galway in the Republic of Ireland. (18 sq miles/44 sq km; pop. 1,380)

Ararat, Mount (Büjük Agri Dagi) the mountain peak in eastern Turkey where Noah's Ark is said to have come to rest. (17,000 ft/5,165 m)

Arauca a major tributary of the Orinoco River which forms part of the border between Colombia and Venezuela. (Length 620 miles/1,000 km)

Arctic the regions that lie to the north of the Arctic Circle.

Arctic Circle latitude 66° 32' north. The sun does not set above this line at the northern summer solstice, nor does it rise above this line at the winter solstice.

Arctic Ocean the ice-laden sea to the north of the Arctic Circle. (5,440,000 sq miles/ 14,100,000 sq km)

Ardennes a hilly and forested region straddling the borders of Belgium, Luxembourg and France.

Ards a district council area in Co. Down. (142 sq miles/368 sq km; pop. 65,000)

Arequipa a city and department of Peru. (Pop. city 734,000)

Argentina the world's eighth largest country, which stretches from the Tropic of Capricorn to Cape Horn on the southern tip of the South American continent. To the west a massive mountain chain, the Andes, forms the border with Chile. The climate ranges from warm temperate over the Pampas in the central region, to a more arid climate in the north and west, while in the extreme south conditions although also dry are much cooler. The vast fertile plains of the Pampas are the main agricultural area and produce cereals and wheat, while in other irrigated areas sugar cane, fruit, and grapes for wine are raised. Meat processing, animal products, and livestock production are major industries and also feature prominently in export trade. A series of military regimes and ongoing political and economic crises have resulted in an unstable economy which fails to provide reasonable living standards for the population.

Area: 1,073,518 sq miles/2,780,400 sq km
Population: 35,220,000
Capital: Buenos Aires
Other major cities: Córdoba, Rosaria, Mendoza, La Plata
Form of government: Republic
Religion: RC
Currency: Peso

Argyll and Bute a council area in west Scotland, with its administrative centre in the town of Lochgilphead. (2,676 sq miles/6,930 sq km; pop. 90,000)

Arizona a state in the southwest of the USA. The capital is Phoenix. (113,902 sq miles/295,024 sq km; pop. 5,484,000)

Arkansas a state in the south of the USA. The state capital is Little Rock. (53,104 sq miles/137,539 sq km; pop. 2,711,000)

Arkansas a tributary of the River Mississippi in the USA, flowing from the Rocky Mountains through the states of Kansas, Oklahoma and Arkansas. (Length 1,450 miles/2,335 km)

Armagh (1) a historical county in south Northern Ireland. (512 sq miles/ 1,326 sq km) (2) a district council area, in Co. Armagh. (258 sq miles/ 667 sq km; pop. 52,000) (3) a town in the Armagh district council area, Co. Armagh. (Pop. 15,000)

Armenia (1) the smallest republic of the former USSR and part of the former kingdom of Armenia. It declared independence from the USSR in 1991. It is a landlocked Transcaucasian republic, and its neighbours are Turkey, Iran, Georgia, and Azerbaijan. The country is very mountainous, with many peaks over 9,900 feet (3,000 metres), the highest being Arragats Lerr at 13,435 feet (4,095 metres). Agriculture is mixed in the lowland areas. The main crops grown are grain, sugar beet, and potatoes, and livestock reared include cattle, pigs, and sheep. Mining of copper, zinc, and lead is important, and to a lesser extent gold, aluminium, and molybdenum, and industrial development is increasing. Hydroelectricity is produced from stations on the River Razdan as it falls 3,281 feet (1,000 metres) from Lake Sevan to its confluence with the River Araks. Territorial conflict with Azerbaijan over Nagorny Karabakh under a ceasefire since 1994 put a brake on economic development for many years.

(2) the former independent kingdom that straddled the borders of modern Turkey, Iran, Georgia, and Azerbaijan.

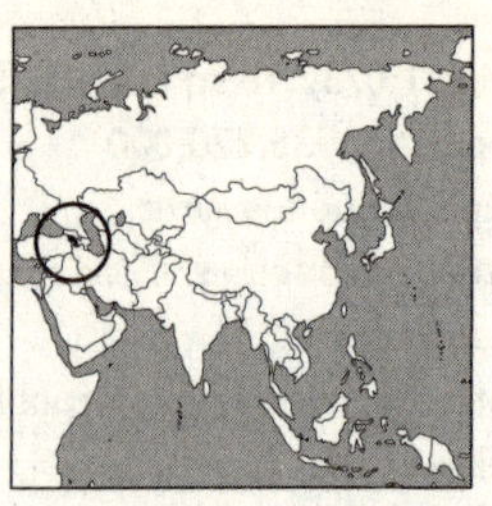

Area: 11,500 sq miles/29,800 sq km
Population: 3,893,000
Capital: Yerevan
Other major city: Kunmayr (Gyumri)
Form of government: Republic
Religion: Armenian Orthodox
Currency: Dram

Arnhem Land an Aboriginal reserve in the Northern Territory of Australia.

Arno the main river of Tuscany in Italy, flowing westward through Florence to Pisa on the coast. (Length 152 miles/245 km)

Aruba a Caribbean island off the coast of Venezuela that was one of the Netherlands Antilles until 1986. It is now a self-governing dependency of the Netherlands. Tourism has been a growing industry since the 1980s.

Area: 75 sq miles/193 sq km
Population: 87,000
Capital: Oranjestad
Form of government: Self-governing Dutch Territory
Religion: Christianity
Currency: Aruban Florin

Arunachal Pradesh a state of northern India, bordering Tibet. The capital is Shillong. (Pop. 1,112,000)

Ascension Island a tiny volcanic island in the South Atlantic Ocean, forming part of the St Helena Dependencies. (Pop. 1,100)

Asia the largest continent, bounded by the Arctic, Pacific and Indian Oceans, plus the Mediterranean and Red Seas. East Asia is taken to mean those countries to the northeast of Bangladesh; South Asia refers to the countries on the Indian subcontinent; and Southeast Asia includes those countries to the southeast of China, including the islands to the west of New Guinea. (16,800,000 sq miles/ 43,600,000 sq km; pop. 3,688,000,000)

Assam a state in northeastern India. (38,476 sq miles/99,680 sq km; pop. 27,159,000)

Asturias a region of northern Spain. The capital is Oviedo. (Pop. 1,071,000)

Athabasca a river in Canada which flows north from the Rocky Mountains to Lake Athabasca. (Length 765 miles/1,231 km)

Athens (Athinai) the historical capital, and the principal city, of Greece. (Pop. 757,000)

Atlantic Ocean the second largest ocean, lying between North and South America, Europe and Africa. (31,700,000 sq miles/82,200,000 sq km)

Atlas Mountains a series of mountain chains stretching across North Africa from Morocco to Tunisia.

Australasia a general term for Australia, New Zealand and neighbouring islands.

Australia the world's smallest continental land mass is a vast and sparsely populated island state in the southern hemisphere and is comprised of seven states. The most mountainous region is the Great Dividing Range, which runs down the entire east coast. Because of its great size, Australia's climates range from tropical monsoon to cool temperate and there are also large areas of desert. The majority of the country's natural inland lakes are salt water and are the remnants of a huge inland sea. The Great Barrier Reef is approximately 1,250 miles (2,000 kilometres) long and is the largest coral formation known in the world. Central and south Queensland are subtropical while north and central New South Wales are warm temperate. Much of Australia's wealth comes from agriculture, with huge sheep and cattle stations extending over large parts of the interior known as the Outback. Australia is the world's leading producer of wool, particularly the fine merino wool. Cereal growing is dominated by wheat. Mining continues to be an important industry and produces coal, natural gas, oil, gold, and iron ore. Australia is the largest producer of diamonds.

Area: 2,988,902 sq miles/ 7,741,220 sq km
Population: 18,871,000
Capital: Canberra
Other major cities: Adelaide, Brisbane, Melbourne, Perth, Sydney
Form of government: Federal Parliamentary State
Religion: Christianity
Currency: Australian Dollar

Australian Capital Territory the small region which surrounds Canberra, the capital of Australia. (939 sq miles/2,432 sq km; pop. 323,000)

Austria a landlocked country in central Europe surrounded by seven nations. The wall of mountains that runs across the centre of the country dominates the scenery. In the warm summers, tourists come to walk in the forests and mountains, and in the cold winters skiers come to the mountains that now boast over 50 ski resorts. The main river is the Danube and there are numerous lakes, principally Lake Constance (Bodensee) and Lake Neusiedler. Agriculture is based on small farms, many of which are run by single families. Dairy products, beef, and lamb from the hill farms contribute to exports. More than 37 per cent of Austria is covered in forest, resulting in the papermaking industry near Graz. There are mineral resources of lignite, magnesium, petroleum, iron ore, and natural gas, and high-grade graphite is exported. Unemployment is very low and its low strike record has attracted multinational companies in recent years. Attachment to local customs is still strong and in rural areas men still wear lederhosen and women the traditional dirndl skirt on feast days and special occasions.

Area: 32,378 sq miles/83,859 sq km
Population: 8,106,000
Capital: Vienna (Wien)
Other major cities: Graz, Linz, Salzburg
Form of government: Federal Republic
Religion: RC
Currency: Euro

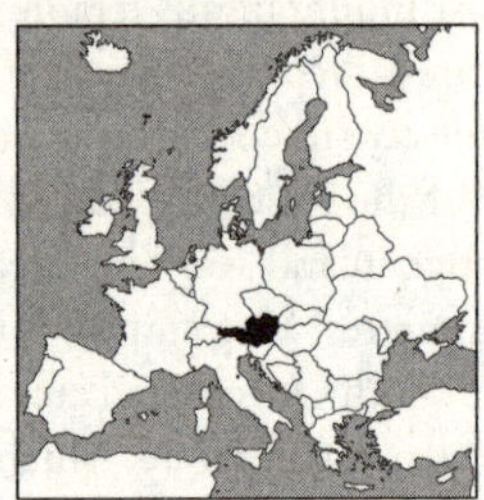

Auvergne a mountainous region of central France.

Avila (Ávila) a town and province in the mountainous central region of Spain, famous as the birthplace of St Teresa (1515–82). (Pop. town 48,000)

Axios a river flowing through the Balkans to Greece and the Aegean Sea. (Length 241 miles/388 km)

Ayers Rock (Uluru) a huge rock, sacred to the Aborigines, rising sharply out of the plains in the Northern Territory of Australia. (1,142 ft/348 m)

Azerbaijan (1) a republic of the former USSR that declared itself independent in 1991. It is situated on the southwest coast of the Caspian Sea and shares borders with Iran, Armenia, Georgia, and the Russian Federation. The Araks River separates Azerbaijan from the region known as Azerbaijan in northern Iran. The country is semi-arid, and 70 per cent of the land is irrigated for the production of cotton, wheat, maize, potatoes, tobacco, tea, and citrus fruits. It has rich mineral deposits of oil, natural gas, iron, and aluminium. The most important mineral is oil, which is found in the Baku area from where it is piped to Batumi on the Black Sea. There are steel, synthetic rubber, and aluminium works at Sumqayit just north of the capital, Baku. However, Azerbaijan is only minimally developed industrially and is hindered by its dispute with Armenia over the Nagorny-Karabakh region. (2) a region of northern

Iran. Its population shares the same language as the people of neighbouring Azerbaijan. (Pop. 6,147,000)

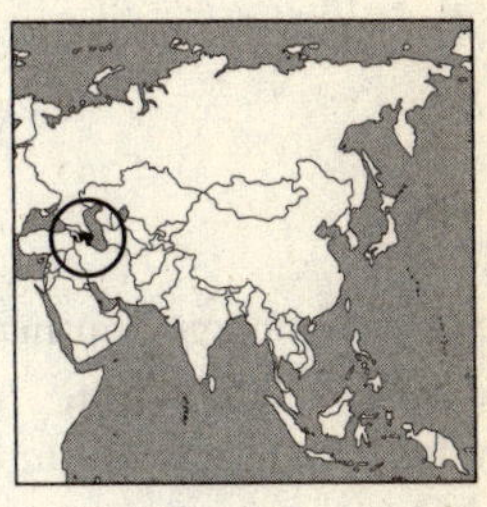

Area: 33,436 sq miles/86,600 sq km
Population: 7,625,000
Capital: Baku
Other major city: Sumqayit
Form of government: Republic
Religions: Sunni Islam, Russian Orthodox
Currency: Manat

Azores (Açores) three groups of small islands in the North Atlantic Ocean, belonging to Portugal. The capital is Ponta Delgada. (901 sq miles/2,335 sq km; pop. 243,000)

Azov, Sea of (Azovskoye More) a shallow, inland sea lying between the Russian Federation and the Ukraine.

B

Baden-Württemberg a southern state of Germany bordering France and Switzerland. (Pop. 10,521,000)

Baffin Bay a huge bay within the Arctic Circle between Baffin Island in Canada and Greenland.

Baffin Island a large, mainly ice-bound island in northeast Canada. (195,927 sq miles/ 507,451 sq km)

Bahamas the Bahamas consist of an archipelago of 700 islands located in the Atlantic Ocean off the southeast coast of Florida. The largest island is Andros (1,600 sq miles/4,144 sq km), and the two most populated are Grand Bahama and New Providence where the capital, Nassau, lies. Winters in the Bahamas are mild and summers warm. Most rain falls in May, June, September, and October, and thunderstorms are frequent in summer. The islands are also subject to hurricanes and other tropical storms. The islands have few natural resources, and for many years fishing and small-scale farming (citrus fruits and vegetables) were the only ways to make a living. Now, however, tourism, which employs almost half the workforce, is the most important industry and has been developed on a vast scale. Offshore banking is also a growing source of income.

Area: 5,358 sq miles/13,878 sq km
Population: 284,000
Capital: Nassau
Other important city: Freeport
Form of government: Constitutional Monarchy
Religion: Christianity
Currency: Bahamian Dollar

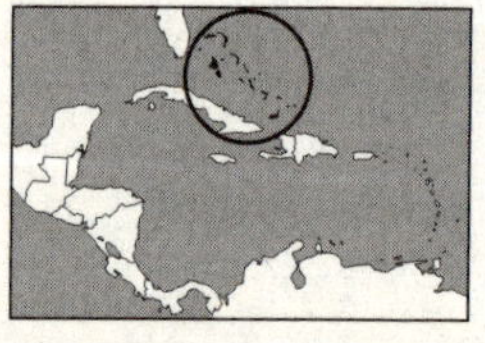

Bahrain a Gulf State comprising 33 low-lying islands situated between the Qatar Peninsula and the mainland of Saudi Arabia. Bahrain Island is the largest and a causeway – the King Fahd Causeway – linking it to Saudi Arabia was opened in 1986. The highest point in the state is only 402 feet (122 metres) above sea level. The climate is pleasantly warm between December and March, but very hot from June to November. Most of Bahrain is sandy and too saline to support crops but drainage schemes are now used to reduce salinity and fertile soil is imported from other islands. Oil was discovered in 1931 and revenues from oil now account for about 80 per cent of the country's total revenue. Bahrain is being developed as a major manufacturing state, the main enterprises being aluminium smelting and the manufacture of clothing, paper products, and consumer goods. Traditional industries include pearl fishing, boat building, weaving, and pottery. Agricultural products include vegetables, dates, and fruits, with artesian wells providing irrigation mainly on the north coast.

Area: 268 sq miles/694 sq km
Population: 599,000
Capital: Al Manamah (Manama)
Form of government: Monarchy (Emirate)
Religions: Shia Islam, Sunni Islam
Currency: Bahraini Dinar

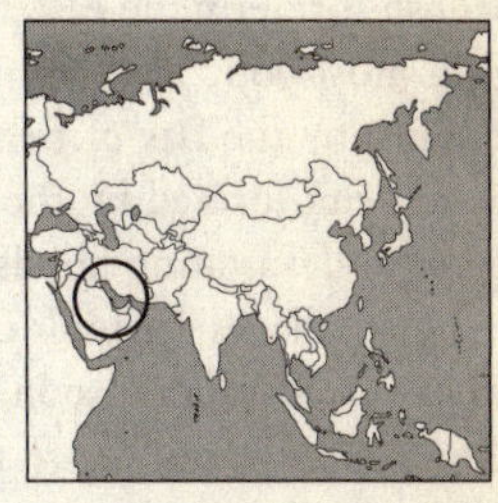

Baikal, Lake (Ozero Baykal) the world's deepest freshwater lake, and the largest by volume, situated in southeast Siberia in the Russian Federation. (12,150 sq miles/31,500 sq km)

Baja California a huge peninsula, some 800 miles (1,300 kilometres) long, belonging to Mexico which stretches south from California in the USA into the Pacific Ocean. (Pop. 2,662,000)

Balaton, Lake a lake in western Hungary. (232 sq miles/601 sq km)

Balearic Islands (Islas Baleares) a group of islands in the western Mediterranean Sea belonging to Spain and famous as tourist resorts. The main islands are Majorca, Minorca, Ibiza, Formentera and Cabrera. (Pop. 896,000; cur. Euro)

Bali a small island off the eastern tip of Java, the only island in Indonesia to have preserved intact a predominantly Hindu culture. The main town and capital is Denpasar. (2,159 sq miles/5,591 sq km; pop. 3,276,000)

Balkans the southeastern corner of Europe, a broad, mountainous peninsula bordered by the Adriatic, Ionian, Aegean and Black Seas. Albania, Bulgaria, Greece, Romania, Slovenia, Croatia, Bosnia-Herzegovina, Macedonia, Serbia and Montenegro, and European Turkey are in the Balkans.

Balkhash, Lake (Ozero Balkhash) a massive lake in Kazakhstan, near the border with China. (8,500 sq miles/22,000 sq km)

Ballymena a district council area in Co. Antrim, central Northern Ireland. (247 sq miles/634 sq km; pop. 57,000)

Ballymoney a district council area in Co. Antrim, north Northern Ireland. (161 sq miles/417 sq km; pop. 24,000)

Baltic Sea a shallow sea in northern Europe, completely surrounded by land masses except for the narrow straits that connect it to the North Sea.

Baluchistan a province of southwestern Pakistan, bordering Iran and Afghanistan. (Pop. 7,216,000)

Banbridge a district council area in Co. Down, south Northern Ireland. (170 sq miles/442 sq km; pop. 34,000)

Banda Sea a part of the Pacific Ocean, in eastern Indonesia.

Bangladesh formerly the eastern province of Pakistan, Bangladesh is the world's eighth most populated country. It is bounded almost entirely by India and to the south by the Bay of Bengal. The country is extremely flat and is virtually a huge delta formed by the Ganges, Brahmaputra, and Meghna Rivers. It is subject to devastating floods and cyclones that sweep in from the Bay of Bengal. Most villages are built on mud platforms to keep them above water. The climate is tropical monsoon with heat, extreme humidity, and heavy rainfall in the monsoon season (April to October) along with accompanying tornadoes. The short winter season is mild and dry. The combination of rainfall, sun, and silt from the rivers makes the land productive, and it is often possible to grow three crops a year. Bangladesh produces about 70 per cent of the world's jute, and the production of jute-related products is a principal industry, with tea being an important cash crop. There are few mineral resources although natural gas, coal, and peat are found.

Area: 55,598 sq miles/143,998 sq km
Population: 120,073,000
Capital: Dhaka (Dacca)
Other cities: Chittagong, Khulna
Form of government: Republic
Religion: Sunni Islam
Currency: Taka

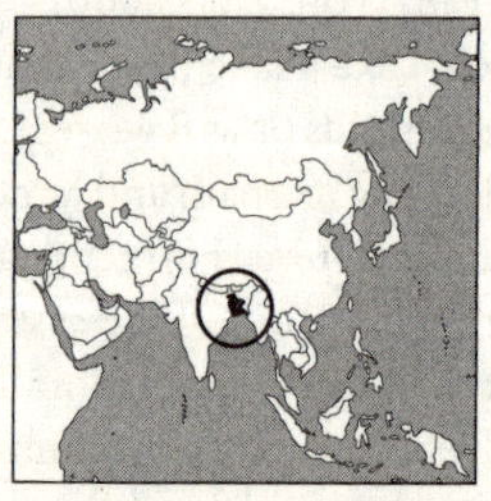

Bangweulu, Lake a large lake in northern Zambia. (3,784 sq miles/9,800 sq km)

Barbados the most easterly island of the West Indies, lying well outside the group of islands that make up the Lesser Antilles. Mainly surrounded by coral reefs, most of the island is low-lying and only in the north does it rise to 1,104 feet (336 metres) at Mount Hillaby. The climate is tropical, but the cooling effect of the northeast trade winds prevents the temperatures rising above 86°F (30°C). There are only two seasons, the dry and the wet, when rainfall is very heavy.

At one time the economy depended almost exclusively on the production of sugar and its by-products, molasses and rum, and although the industry is now declining, sugar is still the principal export. Tourism has now taken over as the main industry, employing approximately 40 per cent of the island's labour force, although there are industries manufacturing furniture, clothing, electrical and electronic equipment. More recently, deposits of natural gas and petroleum have been discovered and fishing is an important activity. The island is surrounded by pink and white sandy beaches and coral reefs that are visited by around 400,000 tourists each year.

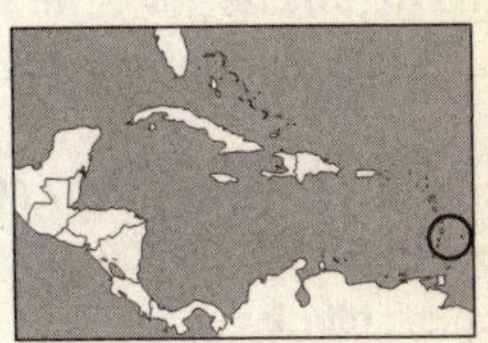

Area: 166 sq miles/430 sq km
Population: 265,000
Capital: Bridgetown
Form of government: Constitutional Monarchy
Religions: Anglicanism, Methodism
Currency: Barbados Dollar

Barents Sea a part of the Arctic Ocean to the north of Norway.

Barossa Valley a wine-producing region in South Australia.

Bashkirya (Baskir Republic) an autonomous republic of the Russian Federation, in the southern Urals. The capital is Ufa. (55,400 sq miles/143,500 sq km; pop. 4,069,000)

Basque Country (Euskadi, País Vasco, Pays Basque) an area straddling the border of Spain and France on the Atlantic coast, the home of the Basque people.

Bass Strait the stretch of water spanning the 180 miles (290 kilometres) which separate the mainland of Australia from Tasmania.

Bavaria (Bayern) the largest state in Germany. (27,241 sq miles/70,553 sq km; pop. 12,155,000)

Beaufort Sea a part of the Arctic Ocean to the north of North America.

Beaujolais a famous wine-producing region of France situated on the River Saône between Lyons and Mâcon.

Bechuanaland the former name of Botswana (until 1966).

Bedfordshire a county in central southern England; the county town is Bedford. (477 sq miles/1,235 sq km; pop. 543,000)

Belarus (Belorussia, Byelorussia) a republic of the former USSR that declared itself independent in 1991, Belarus borders Poland to the west, Ukraine to the south, Latvia and Lithuania to the north, and the Russian Federation to the east. The country consists mainly of a low-lying plain, and forests cover approximately one-third of the land. The climate is continental, with long severe winters and short warm summers. Although the economy is overwhelmingly based on industry, including oil refining, food processing, woodworking, chemicals, textiles, and machinery, output has gradually declined since 1991 and problems persist in the supply of raw materials from other republics that previously were part of the USSR. Agriculture, although seriously affected by contamination from the Chernobyl nuclear accident of 1986, accounts for approximately 20 per cent of employment, the main crops being flax, potatoes, and hemp. The main livestock raised are cattle and pigs. Extensive forest areas also contribute in the supply of raw materials for woodwork and papermaking. Peat is the fuel used to provide power for industry and the country's power plants. Belarus has a good transportation system of road, rail, navigable rivers, and canals.

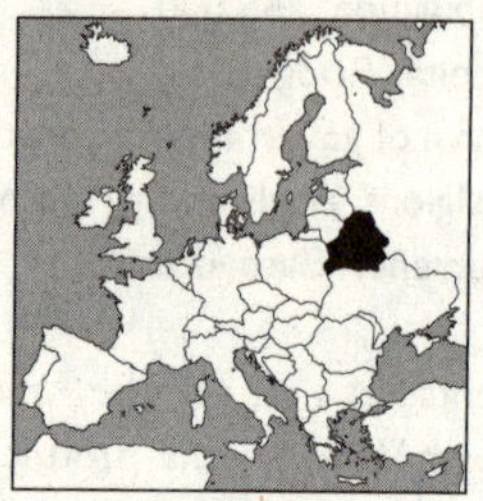

Area: 80,155 sq miles/207,600 sq km
Population: 10,203,000
Capital: Minsk
Other major cities: Homyel' (Gomel'), Vitsyebsk, Mahilyov
Form of government: Republic
Religions: Russian Orthodox, RC
Currency: Rouble

Belfast (1) a city and port on Belfast Lough and the capital of Northern Ireland. (Pop. 279,000) (2) City of a district council area in Co. Antrim and Co. Down, west Northern Ireland. (44 sq miles/115 sq km; pop. 296,000)

Belgium a highly industrialized, relatively small country in northwest Europe with a short coastline on the North Sea. The Meuse River divides Belgium into two distinct geographical regions. To the north of the river the land slopes continuously for 93 miles (150 kilometres) until it reaches the North Sea where the coastlands are flat and grassy. To the south of the river is the forested plateau area of the Ardennes. Between these two regions lies the Meuse valley. Belgium is a densely populated country with few natural resources. Agriculture, which uses about 45 per cent of the land for cultivation or rearing of livestock, employs only 3 per cent of the workforce. About one-fifth of the country is covered with forests, with the wooded areas mainly used for recreation. The metalworking industry, originally based on the small mineral deposits in the Ardennes, is the most important industry, and in the northern cities new textile industries are producing carpets and clothing. Nearly all raw materials are now imported through the main port of Antwerp. There are three officially recognized languages in Belgium – French, German, and Flemish (Dutch).

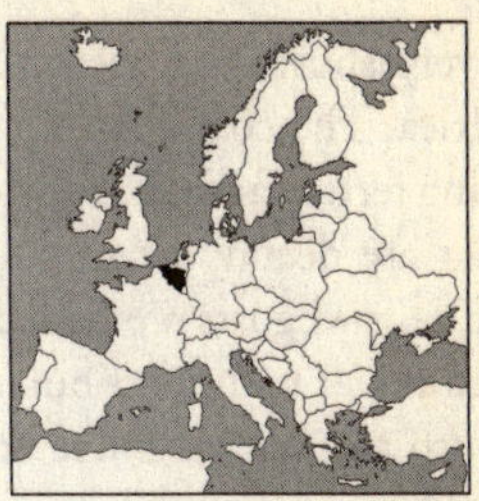

Area: 11,783 sq miles/30,519 sq km
Population: 10,159,000
Capital: Brussels (Brussel, Bruxelles)
Other major cities: Antwerp, Ghent, Charleroi, Liège
Form of government: Constitutional Monarchy
Religion: RC
Currency: Euro

Belize a small Central American country on the southeast of the Yucatan Peninsula in the Caribbean Sea. Its coastline on the Gulf of Honduras is approached through some 342 miles (550 kilometres) of coral reefs and keys (cays). The coastal area and north of the country are low-lying and swampy with dense forests inland. In the south, the Maya Mountains rise to 3,609 feet (1,100 metres). The subtropical climate is warm and humid and the trade winds bring cooling sea breezes. Rainfall is heavy, particularly in the south, and hurricanes may occur in summer. The dense forests that cover most of the country provide valuable hardwoods such as mahogany. Most of the population make a living from forestry, fishing, or agriculture, although only 5 per cent of the land is cultivated. The main crops grown for export are sugar cane, citrus fruits (mainly grapefruit), bananas and coconuts. Industry is very underdeveloped, causing many people to emigrate to find work. The official language is English although many others are spoken, including Mayan, Carib, and Spanish.

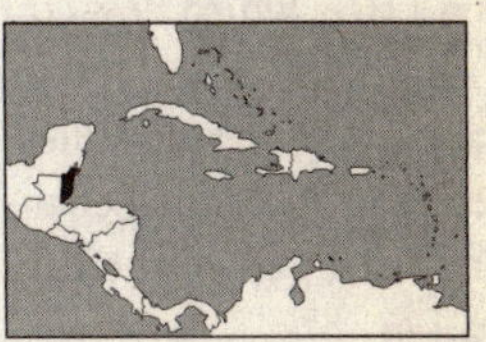

Area: 8,863 sq miles/22,965 sq km
Population: 222,000
Capital: Belmopan
Other major city: Belize City
Form of government: Constitutional Monarchy
Religions: RC, Protestantism
Currency: Belize Dollar

Bellinghausen Sea a part of the Pacific Ocean off Antarctica, due south of South America.

Bengal a former Indian state which was divided in 1947 into two parts: West Bengal in India, and East Pakistan (now Bangladesh).

Bengal, Bay of the massive bay occupying the broad sweep of the Indian Ocean between India and Myanmar, to the south of Bangladesh.

Benin an ice cream cone-shaped country, formerly known as Dahomey, with a very short coastline on the Bight of Benin on the southern coast of West Africa. The coastal area has white sandy beaches backed by lagoons and low-lying fertile lands. In the northwest, the Atakora Mountains are grassy plateaus that are deeply cut into steep forested valleys, and on the grasslands sheep, cattle, and goats are reared. The main rivers of Benin are the Donga, Couffo, and Niger with its tributaries. The climate in the north is tropical and in the south equatorial. There are nine rainy months each year so crops rarely fail. Farming is predominantly subsistence and accounts for around 60 per cent of employment, with yams, cassava, maize, rice, groundnuts, and vegetables forming most of the produce. The country is very poor, although since the late 1980s economic reforms have been towards a market economy and Western financial aid has been sought. The main exports are palm oil, palm kernels, and cotton. Tourism is now being developed but as yet facilities for this are few except in some coastal towns.

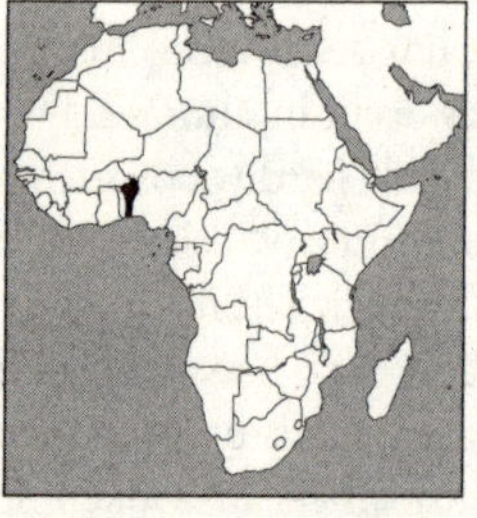

Area: 43,484 sq miles/112,622 sq km
Population: 5,563,000
Capital: Porto Novo
Other major city: Cotonou
Form of government: Republic
Religions: traditional African religions, RC, Sunni Islam
Currency: CFA Franc

Benue a river which flows through Cameroon and Nigeria to the Gulf of Guinea. (Length 865 miles/390 km)

Beqa'a a long, fertile valley running north to south in Lebanon, between the Lebanon and Anti-Lebanon Mountains.

Bering Sea a part of the Pacific Ocean between Alaska and eastern Russian Federation.

Bering Strait the stretch of sea, 55 miles (88 kilometres) wide, that separates the Russian Federation from Alaska in the USA.

Berkshire a historical county of central southern England.

Bermuda a country consisting of a group of 150 small islands in the western Atlantic Ocean. It lies about 572 miles (920 kilometres) east of Cape Hatteras on the coast of the United States. The hilly limestone islands are the caps of ancient volcanoes rising from the sea bed. The main island, Great Bermuda, is linked to the other islands by bridges and causeways. The climate is warm and humid, with rain spread evenly throughout the year but with the risk of hurricanes from June to November. Bermuda's chief agricultural products are fresh vegetables, bananas, and citrus fruit, but 80 per cent of food requirements are imported. Many foreign banks and financial institutions operate from the island, taking advantage of the lenient tax laws. Other industries include ship repair and pharmaceuticals. Its proximity to the USA and the pleasant climate have led to a flourishing tourist industry.

Area: 20 sq miles/53 sq km
Population: 64,000
Capital: Hamilton
Form of government: British Overseas Territory
Religions: Protestantism, RC
Currency: Bermudan Dollar

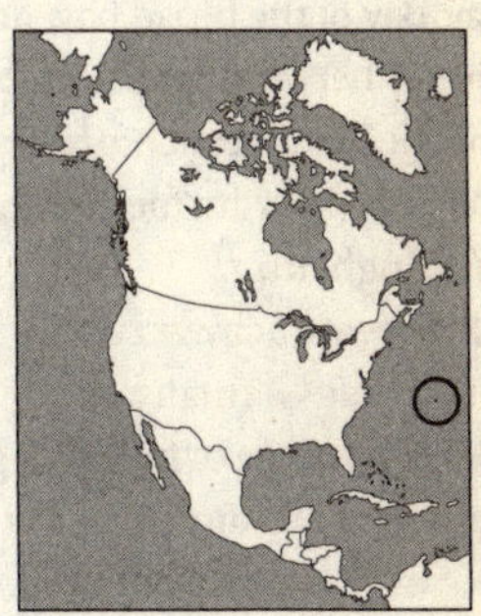

Bhutan surrounded by India to the south and China to the north, Bhutan rises from foothills overlooking the Brahmaputra River to the southern slopes of the Himalayas. The Himalayas, which rise to over 24,600 feet (7,500 metres) in Bhutan, make up most of the country. The climate is hot and wet on the plains but temperatures drop progressively with altitude, resulting in glaciers and permanent snow cover in the north. The valleys in the centre of the country are wide and fertile, and about 95 per cent of the workforce are farmers growing wheat, rice, potatoes, and corn. Fruit such as plums, pears, apples, and also cardamom are grown for export. There are many monasteries, with some 6,000 monks. Yaks reared on the high pasture land provide milk, cheese, and meat. Vast areas of the country still remain forested as there is little demand for new farmland. Bhutan is one of the world's poorest and least developed countries. It has little contact with the rest of the world although tourism has been encouraged in recent years. There are no railways but roads join many parts of the country.

Area: 18,147 sq miles/47,000 sq km
Population: 1,812,000
Capital: Thimphu (Thimbu)
Form of government: Constitutional Monarchy
Religion: Buddhism
Currency: Ngultrum

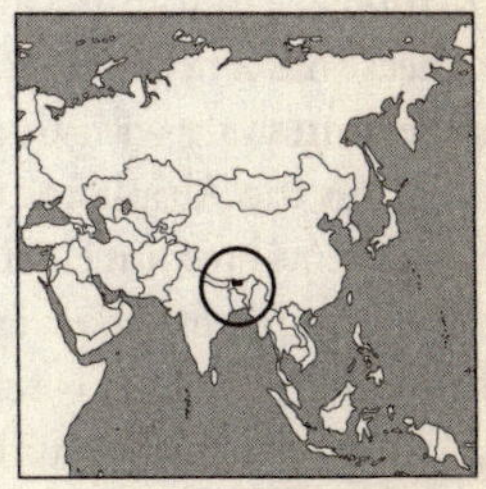

Bikini an atoll in the Marshall Islands, the site of US nuclear weapon tests between 1946 and 1962.

Bihar a state in northeast India. The capital is Patna. (Pop. 81,788,000)

Bioko an island in the Gulf of Guinea (formerly Fernando Po) now governed by Equatorial Guinea. (780 sq miles/2,017 sq km; pop. 125,000)

Biscay, Bay of the broad bay, notorious for its rough weather, formed by the Atlantic Ocean between northern Spain and Brittany in northwest France.

Bismarck Sea a branch of the Pacific Ocean to the north of Papua New Guinea.

Black Country a formerly heavily industrialized area in central England, around Birmingham.

Black Forest (Schwarzwald) an extensive area of mountainous pine forests in southwest Germany.

Black Hills a range of hills rising to 7,242 feet (2,207 metres) on the border between the states of South Dakota and Wyoming in the USA.

Black Sea a sea lying between southeast Europe and western Asia; it is surrounded by land except for the Bosphorus channel, leading to the Mediterranean Sea.

Blaenau Gwent a council area in southeast Wales, with its administrative centre in Ebbw Vale. (42 sq miles/109 sq km; pop. 78,000)

Blue Mountains (1) a range of mountains rising to 3,609 feet (1,100 metres) in New South Wales in Australia, some 40 miles (65 kilometres) from Sydney. (2) the mountains in eastern Jamaica rising to 7,402 feet (2,256 metres) at Blue Mountain Peak. The region produces high-quality coffee.

Bohemia formerly an independent kingdom (9th–13th centuries), now a western region of the Czech Republic which includes the capital, Prague.

Bohol one of the Visayan Islands in the central area of the Philippines. (1,491 sq miles/3,862 sq km; pop. 759,370)

Bolivia a landlocked republic of central South America through which the great mountain range of the Andes runs. It is in the Andes that the highest navigable lake in the world, Lake Titicaca, is found. On the Altiplano, an undulating depression south of the lake, is the highest capital city in the world, La Paz. To the east and northeast of the mountains is a huge area of lowland containing tropical rainforests (the Llanos) and wooded savanna (the Chaco). The northeast has a heavy rainfall while in the southwest the rainfall is negligible. Temperatures vary with altitude, from extremely cold on the mountain summits to cool on the Altiplano, where at least half the population lives. Although rich in natural resources, such as lead, silver, copper, zinc, oil, and tin, Bolivia lacks the funds for their extraction, due to a lack of investment, and political instability. Bolivia is self-sufficient in petroleum and exports natural gas. Agriculture produces soya beans, sugar cane, and cotton for export. Increased production of coca, from which cocaine is derived, has resulted in an illicit economy.

Area: 424,165 sq miles/1,098,581 sq km
Population: 8,140,000
Capital: La Paz (administrative), Sucre (legal)
Other major city: Cochabamba
Form of government: Republic
Religion: RC
Currency: Boliviano

Bonaire a Caribbean island off the coast of Venezuela and part of the Netherland Antilles (111 sq miles/288 sq km; pop. 18,000)

Bondi Beach a famous surfing beach in the suburbs of Sydney, Australia.

Bonin Islands a group of small volcanic islands in the Pacific Ocean belonging to Japan. (Pop. 2,300)

Bophuthatswana one of the ten former South African Homelands, the area is now part of the Free State and North West Provinces.

Bordeaux a major port on the Gironde estuary in southwestern France. The region is famous for its wines. (Pop. 217,000)

Borneo one of the largest islands in the world, now divided between three countries. Most of the island is known as Kalimantan, a part of Indonesia. The northern coast is divided into the two states of Sarawak and Sabah, which are part of Malaysia, and the small independent Sultanate of Brunei. (290,320 sq miles/751,900 sq km)

Bosnia-Herzegovina a republic of former Yugoslavia that was formally recognized as an independent state in March 1992. It is a very mountainous country and includes part of the Dinaric Alps, which are densely forested and deeply cut by rivers flowing northwards to join the Sava River. Half the country is forested, and lumber is an important product of the northern areas. One quarter of the land is cultivated, and corn, wheat, and flax are the principal products of the north. In the south, tobacco, cotton, fruits, and grapes are the main products. Bosnia-Herzegovina has large deposits of lignite, iron ore, and bauxite, and its metallurgical plants create air pollution. Water is also polluted around these plants, with the Sava River being severely affected. Despite its natural resources the economy has been devastated by civil war, which began in 1991 following the secession of Croatia and Slovenia from the former Yugoslavia. Dispute over control of Bosnia-Herzegovina continued, leading to United Nations intervention in an attempt to devise a territorial plan acceptable to all factions. A peace agreement, the Dayton Accord, signed in late 1995 has resulted in the division of the country into two self-governing provinces. The population of the state was significantly diminished when refugees from the civil war fled between 1992 and 1993.

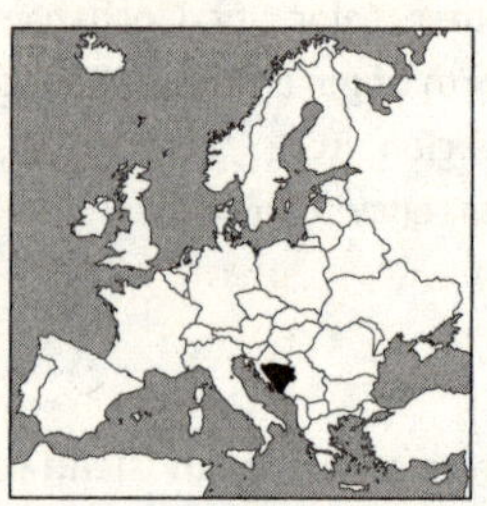

Area: 19,735 sq miles/51,129 sq km
Population: 3,675,000
Capital: Sarajevo
Other major cities: Banja Luka, Tuzla
Form of government: Federal Democratic Republic
Religions: Eastern Orthodox, Sunni Islam, RC
Currency: Dinar

Bosphorus the narrow strip of water, some 18 miles (29 kilometres) long and no more than 2.5 miles (4 kilometres) wide, which provides the navigable link between the Mediterranean and Black Seas by way of the Sea of Marmara. It separates the European part of Turkey from its Asian part.

Botany Bay a bay, now in the suburbs of Sydney, Australia, discovered by Captain James Cook in 1770.

Bothnia, Gulf of the most northerly arm of the Baltic Sea, bordered by Finland and Sweden.

Botswana a landlocked republic in southern Africa that straddles the Tropic of Capricorn. Much of the west and southwest of the country forms part of the Kalahari Desert. In the north, there is a huge area of marshland around the Okavango Delta, which is home to a wide variety of wildlife. With the exception of the desert area, most of the country has a subtropical climate but is subject to drought. In winter, days are warm and nights cold while summer is hot with sporadic rainfall. The people are mainly farmers and cattle rearing is the main activity. After independence in 1966, the exploitation of minerals started. In 1972, the first diamond mine was set up at Orapa, and diamonds quickly became the country's most important export. Copper from the nickel/copper complex at Selebi-Pikwe was also exported. Exploitation of these mineral resources has facilitated a high rate of economic growth within the country. Coal is also mined but the majority is for domestic use. About 17 per cent of the land is set aside for wildlife preservation in national parks, game reserves, game sanctuaries, and controlled hunting areas.

Area: 224,607 sq miles/581,730 sq km
Population: 1,490,000
Capital: Gaborone
Other major cities: Mahalapye, Serowe, Francistown
Form of government: Republic
Religions: traditional African religions, Christianity
Currency: Pula

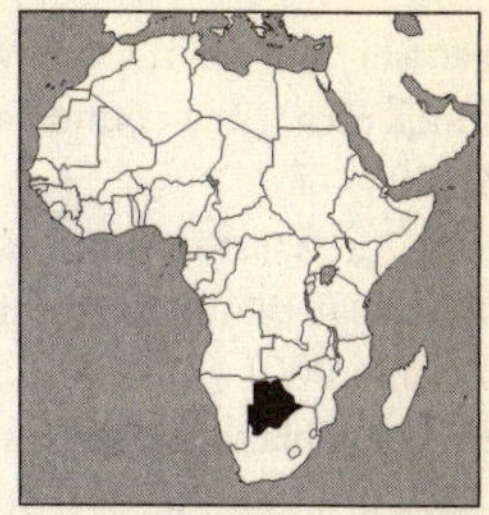

Bougainville the easternmost island belonging to Papua New Guinea, and a part of, though politically separate from, the Solomon Islands.

Boyne a river flowing into the Irish Sea on the east coast of the Republic of Ireland. It was the site of a battle (1690) in which William of Orange defeated James II. (Length 70 miles/115 km)

Boyoma Falls a series of seven cataracts over 56 miles (90 kilometres) where the Lualaba River becomes the Congo River. They were formerly called Stanley Falls after the British explorer Sir Henry Morton Stanley.

Brabant the central province of Belgium around the capital, Brussels. (1,297 sq miles/3,358 sq km; pop. 1,016,000)

Brahmaputra a major river of South Asia, flowing from the Himalayas in Tibet through Assam in northern India to join the River Ganges in Bangladesh. (Length 1,802 miles/2,900 km)

Brazil the fifth largest country in the world, which covers nearly half of South America. The climate is mainly tropical, but droughts may occur in the north-east, where it is hot and arid. Around 14 per cent of the population is employed in agriculture, and the main products exported are coffee, soya beans and cocoa. It is rich in minerals and is the only source of high-grade quartz crystal in commercial quantities.

Area: 3,300,171 sq miles/8,547,403 sq km
Population: 157,872,000
Capital: Brasília
Other major cities: Belo Horizonte, Porto Alegre, Recife, Rio de Janeiro, Salvador, São Paulo
Form of government: Federal Republic
Religion: RC
Currency: Real

Bridgend (1) a town in south Wales, and the administrative centre for the Bridgend council area. (2) a council area in South Wales. (102 sq miles/264 sq km; pop. 131,000)

Bristol (1) a major city and port on the River Avon in southwest England. (Pop. 409,000) (2) a unitary authority in southwest England. (42 sq miles/110 sq km; pop. 374,000)

British Columbia the western seaboard province of Canada. The capital is Victoria. (358,968 sq miles/929,730 sq km; pop. 4,122,000)

British Indian Ocean Territory the Chagos Archipelago, a group of five coral atolls in the middle of the Indian Ocean. (20 sq miles/52 sq km)

British Isles the name given to the group of islands in northwestern Europe formed by Great Britain and Ireland, and the surrounding islands.

Brittany (Bretagne) the region of France which occupies the extreme northwestern peninsula, protruding into the Atlantic.

Brunei a sultanate located on the northwest coast of the island of Borneo in southeast Asia. It is bounded on all sides by the Sarawak territory of Malaysia, which splits the sultanate into two separate parts. Broad tidal swamplands cover the coastal plains, and inland Brunei is hilly and covered with tropical rainforests that occupy almost half the country's land area. The climate is tropical marine, hot and moist, with cool nights. Rainfall is heavy (98 inches/2,500 millimetres) at the coast but even heavier (197 inches/5,000 millimetres) inland. The main crops grown are rice, vegetables, and fruit, but economically the country depends on its oil industry, which employs 7 per cent of the working population. Cloth weaving and metalwork are also small local industries. Oil production began in the 1920s and now oil and natural gas account for almost all exports. Other minor products are rubber, pepper, gravel, and animal hides.

Area: 2,226 sq miles/5,765 sq km
Population: 300,000
Capital: Bandar Seri Begawan
Other major cities: Kuala Belait, Seria
Form of government: Monarchy (Sultanate)
Religion: Sunni Islam
Currency: Brunei Dollar

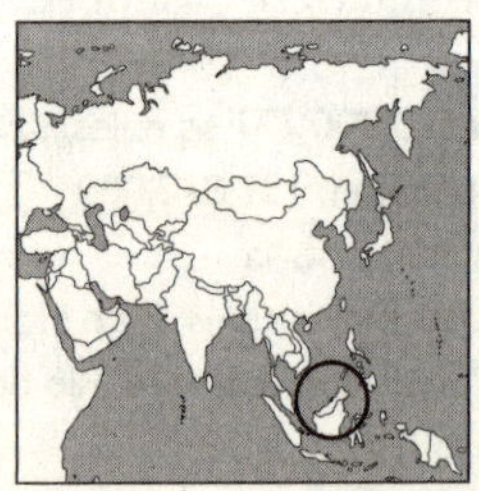

Buckinghamshire a county in central southern England, with its administrative centre in the town of Aylesbury. (727 sq miles/1,883 sq km; pop. 658,000)

Bug a river which flows northwest from the Ukraine, forming the border with

Poland before turning west into Poland and joining the Narew and Vistula Rivers. (Length: 480 miles/813 km)

Bulgaria a southeast European republic located on the east Balkan Peninsula and with a coast on the Black Sea. It is bounded to the north by Romania, to the west by Serbia and the Former Yugoslav Republic of Macedonia, and to the south by Greece and Turkey. The centre of Bulgaria is crossed from west to east by the Balkan Mountains. The south of the country has a Mediterranean climate with hot dry summers and mild winters. Farther north the temperatures become more extreme and rainfall is higher in summer. The main river in Bulgaria is the Danube, and about a third of the country is covered by forests. Traditionally Bulgaria is an agricultural country and a revolution in farming during the 1950s led to great increases in output. This was because of the collectivization of farms and the use of more machinery, fertilizers, and irrigation. Increased mechanization led to more of the workforce being available to work in mines and industry. However, the country suffered very high rates of inflation and unemployment in the early 1990s after the break-up of the former Soviet Union, with whom Bulgaria had very close trade links, and industrial pollution affects its rivers, soils, and the Black Sea coastline, an area that is extremely important for tourism, with over 10,000,000 people visiting the Black Sea resorts annually.

Area: 42,823 sq miles/110,912 sq km
Population: 8,356,000
Capital: Sofia (Sofiya)
Other major cities: Burgas, Plovdiv, Ruse, Varna
Form of government: Republic
Religion: Eastern Orthodox
Currency: Lev

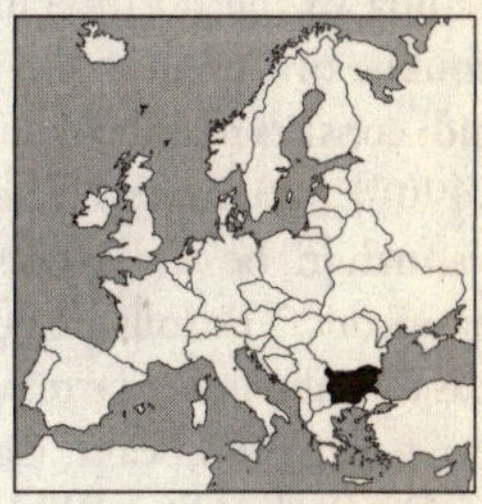

Burgundy (Bourgogne) a region of east central France, famous for its wine.

Burkina Faso a landlocked state in West Africa, Burkina Faso (formerly called Upper Volta) lies on the fringe of the Sahara, to the north. It comprises a plateau region in the north which gives way southwards to an area of plains. The northern part of the country is arid and is more or less an extension of the Sahara Desert. The south is less dry and has savannah-type vegetation and scattered trees. Precipitation is generally low, the heaviest rain falling in the southwest, while the rest of the country is semi-desert. The dusty grey plains in the north and west have infertile soils that have been further impoverished by overgrazing and over-cultivation. Around 85 per cent of the people live by subsistence farming, and food crops include sorghum, millet, pulses, corn, and rice. The main industries are textiles, metal products, and the processing of agricultural products and production of consumer items such as footwear and soap. Cotton is the main export, along with minerals such as gold and animal products. There is great poverty and shortage of work, and many of the younger population go to Ghana and Côte d'Ivoire for employment. During the 1970s, the country was severely affected by drought and this was followed by political instability in the 1980s. The situation has improved since 1992.

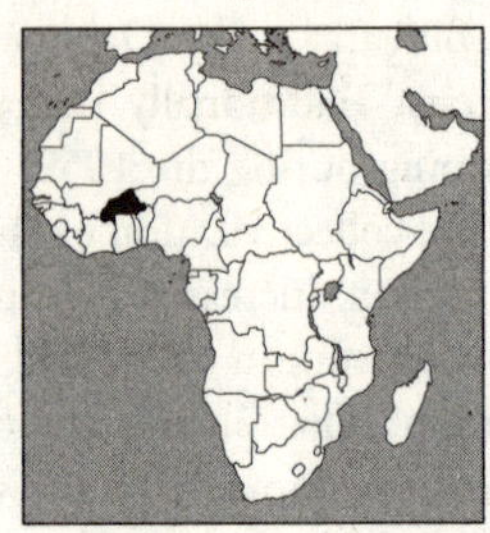

Area: 105,792 sq miles/274,000 sq km
Population: 10,780,000
Capital: Ouagadougou
Other cities: Bobo-Dioulasso, Koudougou
Form of government: Republic
Religions: traditional African religions, Sunni Islam
Currency: CFA Franc

Burma *see* Myanmar

Burundi a small, densely populated country in central east Africa, bounded by Rwanda to the north, Tanzania to the east and south, and the Democratic Republic of Congo to the west. One of the poorest nations in the world, Burundi consists mainly of an upland plateau at an elevation of 4,600–5,900 feet (1,400–1,800 metres). The climate is equatorial but modified by altitude. The savannah in the east is several degrees hotter than the plateau and there are two wet seasons. The soils are not rich but there is enough rain to grow crops in most areas for subsistence farming. The main food crops are bananas, sweet potatoes, peas, lentils, and beans. Cassava is grown near the shores of Lake Tanganyika which is in the Great Rift Valley. The main cash crop is coffee, which accounts for 90 per cent of Burundi's export earnings. Cotton and tea are also cultivated for export. There is a little commercial fishing on Lake Tanganyika, otherwise industry is very basic. Since 1994, Burundi has been afflicted by ethnic conflict between the majority Hutu and minority Tutsi. Between 1994 and 1995 it is estimated that 150,000 were killed as a result of ethnic violence and the political situation remains volatile.

Area: 10,747 sq miles/27,834 sq km
Population: 6,088,000
Capital: Bujumbura
Form of government: Republic
Religion: RC
Currency: Burundi Franc

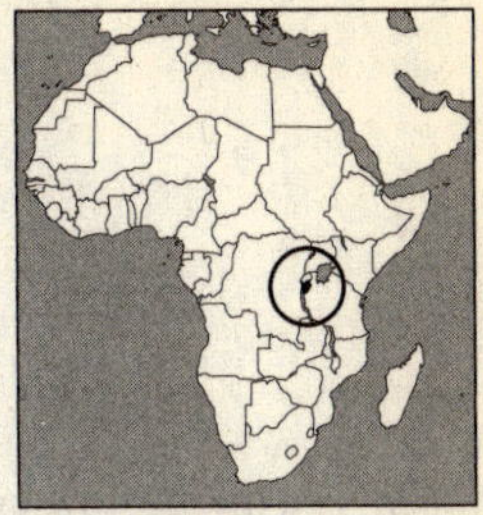

Buryatiya Republic an autonomous republic of the Russian Federation, situated in the southeast, between Lake Baikal and Mongolia. (135,600 sq miles/ 351,300 sq km; pop. 1,014,000)

C

Caerphilly (1) a market town in southeast Wales. (Pop. 28,000) (2) a council area in southeast Wales, with its administrative centre in the town of Hengoed. (106 sq miles/275 sq km; pop. 170,000)

Cairngorms a mountain range forming part of the Grampian Mountains in Scotland.

Calabria the region which occupies the southern 'toe' of Italy. The main town is Reggio Di Calabria. (Pop. 2,072,000)

California the most populous state of the USA on the Pacific coast. The state capital is Sacramento, but Los Angeles is the biggest city. (158,693 sq miles/ 411,015 sq km; pop. 35,140,000)

California, Gulf of (Cortes, Sea of; California, Golfo de) the narrow inlet which separates the mainland part of Mexico from the peninsula of Baja California.

Calvados a department of northern France, a part of the region of Normandy. It is famous for its apple-based liqueur, also called Calvados. (Pop. 665,000)

Camargue the broad, flat area of sea marshes in the delta of the River Rhône in the centre of the Mediterranean coast of France.

Cambodia a southeast Asian state bounded by Thailand, Laos and Vietnam, with its southern coast lying on the Gulf of Thailand. The country was devastated by its involvement in the Vietnam War (1960–75) followed by the brutal regime of the Khmer Rouge under Pol Pot (1975–79). The heart of the country is saucer-shaped, and gently rolling alluvial plains are drained by the Mekong River. The Dangrek Mountains form the frontier with Thailand in the northwest. In general, Cambodia has a tropical monsoon climate and about half the land is tropical forest. During the rainy season the Mekong swells and backs into the Tonlé Sap (Great Lake), increasing its size threefold to about 4,015 square miles (10,400 kilometres). This seasonal flooding means the area is left with rich silt when the river recedes. Crop production depends entirely on the rainfall and floods but production was badly disrupted during the civil war when there was widespread famine, and yields still remain low. The cultivation of rice accounts for about 80 per cent of agricultural land and the other main crop is rubber, which grows in the eastern plateau. Despite the gradual rebuilding of the infrastructure in the early 1990s, Cambodia remains one of the world's poorest nations.

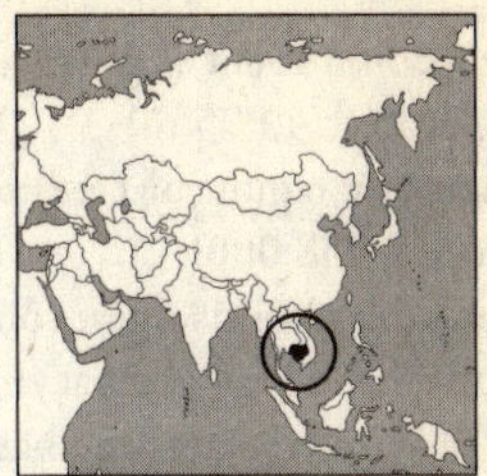

Area: 69,898 sq miles/181,035 sq km
Population: 10,273,000
Capital: Phnom-Penh
Other major cities: Kampong Cham, Battambang
Form of government: People's Republic
Religion: Buddhism
Currency: Riel

Cambrian Mountains a mountain range which forms the 'backbone' of Wales.

Cambridgeshire a county in eastern England, with its administrative centre in Cambridge. (1,350 sq miles/3,409 sq km; pop. 687,000)

Cameron Highlands an upland area of Malaysia where tea and vegetables are grown.

Cameroon a triangular-shaped country of diverse landscapes in west central Africa. It stretches from Lake Chad at its apex to the northern borders of Equatorial Guinea, Gabon and the Congo in the south. The landscape ranges from low-lying lands, through the semi-desert Sahel to dramatic mountain peaks and then to the grassy savannah, rolling uplands, steaming tropical forests, and hardwood plantations. Cameroon's jungles contain not only commercially valuable trees but also an immense diversity of other plants, many of which have been identified as useful for their medicinal properties. Farther south are the volcanoes, including the sporadically active Mount Cameroon, the highest peak at 1,250 feet (4,100 metres), and the palm beaches at Kribi and Limbe. The climate is equatorial with high temperatures and plentiful rain. The majority of the population are farmers who live in the south and in central Cameroon where they grow maize, millet, cassava, and vegetables. In the drier north, where drought and hunger are well known, life is harder and this area is populated by semi-nomadic herders. Bananas, coffee, and cocoa are the major exports although oil, gas, and aluminium are becoming increasingly important.

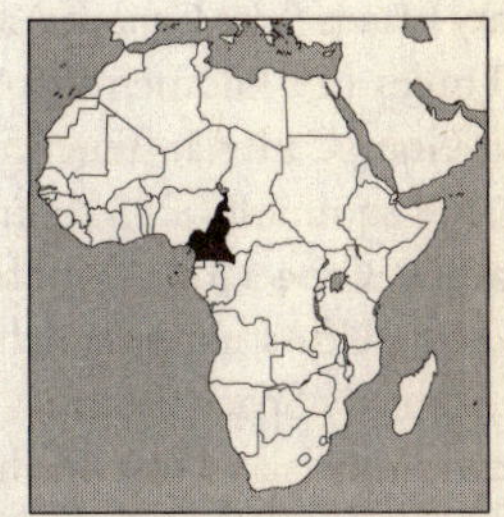

Area: 183,569 sq miles/475,442 sq km
Population: 13,560,000
Capital: Yaoundé
Other major city: Douala
Form of government: Republic
Religions: traditional African religions, RC, Sunni Islam
Currency: CFA Franc

Cameroon, Mount (Cameroun, Mount) an active volcano in west Cameroon. (13,435 ft/4,095 m)

Campania a region of central southern Italy, on the west coast around Naples. (Pop. 5,938,000)

Canada the second largest country in the world and the largest in North America. Canada is a land of great climatic and geographical extremes. It lies to the north of the United States and has Pacific, Atlantic, and Arctic coasts. The country has the highest number of inland waters and lakes in the world, including the Great Lakes on the border with the USA. The Rocky Mountains and Coast Mountains run down the west side, and the highest point, Mount Logan at 19,524 feet (6,050 metres), is in the Yukon. Climates range from polar conditions in the north to cool temperate in the south, with considerable differences from west to east. More than 80 per cent of its farmland is in the prairies that stretch from Alberta to Manitoba. Wheat and grain crops cover three-quarters of the arable land. Canada is rich in forest reserves, which cover more than half the total land area. The most valuable mineral deposits (oil, gas, coal, and iron ore) are found in Alberta. Most industry in Canada is associated with processing its natural resources and it is one of the main exporters of food products.

Area: 3,848,900 sq miles/9,984,670 sq km
Population: 31,414,000
Capital: Ottawa
Other major cities: Toronto, Montréal, Vancouver, Québec
Form of government: Federal Parliamentary State
Religions: RC, United Church of Canada, Anglicanism
Currency: Canadian Dollar

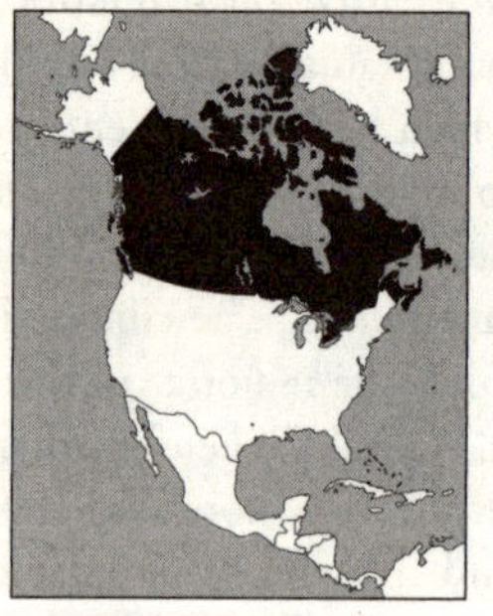

Canary Islands (Islas Canarias) a group of islands belonging to Spain, situated some 60 miles (95 kilometres) off the coast of Western Sahara. The main islands are Gran Canaria, Tenerife, La Palma, Fuerteventura, Gomera, Lanzarote. (2,808 sq miles/7,273 sq km; pop. 1,493,000; cur. Euro)

Canaveral, Cape a long spit of land on the east coast of the state of Florida, USA. It is the USA's main launch site for space missions and the home of the John F. Kennedy Space Centre.

Cancún a tiny island just off the Yucatan coast of Mexico, connected to the mainland by a causeway, and now a popular holiday resort. (Pop. 436,000)

Cape Breton Island part of the province of Nova Scotia lying off the eastern coast of Canada. (3,970 sq miles/10,349 sq km; pop. 170,000)

Cape Verde one of the world's smallest nations, situated in the Atlantic Ocean about 400 miles (640 kilometres) northwest of Senegal. It consists of ten islands and five islets and there is an active volcano on Fogo, one of the islands. The islands are divided into the Windward group and the Leeward group. Over 50 per cent of the population live on São Tiago on which is Praia, the capital. The climate is arid with a cool dry season from December to June and warm dry conditions for the rest of the year. Rainfall is sparse and the islands suffer from periods of severe drought. Agriculture is mostly confined to irrigated inland valleys and the chief crops are coconuts, sugar cane, potatoes, cassava, and dates. Bananas and some coffee are grown for export. Fishing for tuna and lobsters is an important industry but in general the economy is shaky and Cape Verde relies heavily on foreign aid. Because of its lack of natural resources and droughts, large numbers of its people have emigrated for many years. Tourism is being encouraged although the number of visitors is at present relatively low.

Area: 1,557 sq miles/4,033 sq km
Population: 396,000
Capital: Praia
Form of government: Republic
Religion: RC
Currency: Cape Verde Escudo

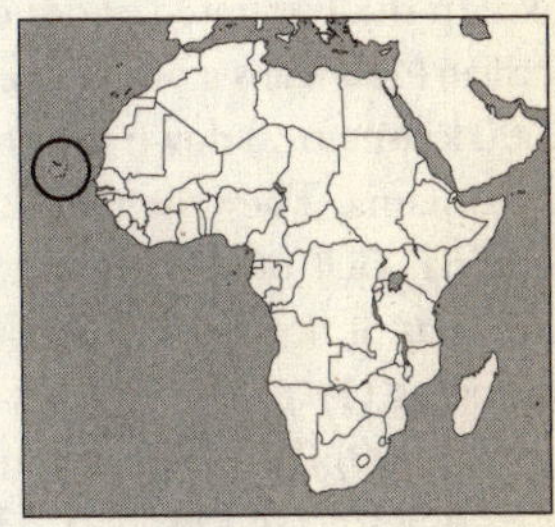

Capri a rocky island at the southern end of the Bay of Naples on the west coast of Italy, famous as a fashionable holiday retreat. (4 sq miles/10.4 sq km; pop. 16,500)

Caprivi Strip a narrow corridor of land, 280 miles (450 kilometres) long, which belongs to Namibia and gives it access to the Zambezi River along the border between Botswana to the south and Angola and Zambia to the north.

Caracas the capital of Venezuela, in the northeast of the country. (Pop. 1,763,000)

Cardamom Mountains a mountain range rising to 5,948 feet (1,813 metres) which lines the coast of Cambodia and separates the interior from the Gulf of Thailand.

Cardiff (Caerdydd) (1) the capital of Wales, situated in southeast Wales, formerly an important port, and the administrative centre for the Cardiff council area.

(Pop. 280,000) (2) a council area in southeast Wales. (54 sq miles/139 sq km; pop. 307,000)

Cardigan Bay the long, curving bay which, as part of the Irish Sea, forms much of the west coast of Wales.

Caribbean, The a term that refers to the islands lying within the compass of the Caribbean Sea.

Caribbean Sea a part of the western Atlantic Ocean, bounded by the east coast of Central America, the north coast of South America, and the West Indies.

Carinthia (Kärnten) the southern state of Austria, which borders Italy and Slovenia. (3681 sq miles/9,533 sq km; pop 560,000)

Carlow a landlocked county in the southeast of the Republic of Ireland. The county town is also called Carlow. (Pop. 43,000)

Carmarthenshire a council area in south Wales, with its administrative centre in the town of Carmarthen. (926 sq miles/2,398 sq km; pop. 169,000)

Carmel, Mount a ridge of land rising to 1,746 feet (528 metres) in northern Israel.

Caroline Islands a scattered group of islands in the western Pacific Ocean which now make up the Federated States of Micronesia and the separate state of Belau.

Carpathian Mountains a broad sweep of mountains stretching for nearly 625 miles (1,000 kilometres) down the border between Slovakia and Poland and into central Romania. They rise to 8,737 feet (2,663 metres) at their highest point.

Carpentaria, Gulf of the broad gulf of shallow sea between the two horn-like peninsulas of northern Australia.

Carrickfergus (1) a town in the Carrickfergus district council area, Co. Antrim. (Pop. 23,000) (2) a district council area in Co. Antrim, east Northern Ireland. (32 sq miles/83 sq km; pop. 33,000)

Cascade Range a range of mountains stretching some 700 miles (1,125 kilometres) parallel to the coast of northern California in the USA and into southern Canada. The highest point is at Mount Rainier (14,410 ft/4,392 m) in Washington State.

Caspian Sea the largest inland (salt) sea in the world, supplied mainly by the River Volga. It lies to the north of Iran, which shares its coasts with Azerbaijan, Georgia, Kazakhstan and Turkmenistan.

Castile (Castilla) a former kingdom of Spain, occupying most of the central area, now divided into two regions, Castilla la Mancha and Castilla y León.

Castlereagh a district council area in Co. Down, east Northern Ireland. (33 sq miles/85 sq km; pop. 61,000)

Catalonia (Cataluña) an autonomous region of Spain, in the northeast, centring on Barcelona. (12,328 sq miles/31,929 sq km; pop. 6,090,000)

Catskill Mountains a range of mountains in New York State, USA, famed for their scenic beauty. The highest peak is Slide Mountain at 4,204 feet (1,282 metres).

Caucasus (Kavkaz) the mountainous region between the Black and Caspian Seas, bounded by the Russian Federation, Georgia, Armenia and Azerbaijan. It contains Europe's highest point, Mount Elbrus at 18,510 feet (5,642metres).

Cavan a county in the north of the Republic of Ireland, part of the ancient province of Ulster; Cavan is also the name of the county town. (730 sq miles/ 1,890 sq km; pop. 55,000)

Cayman Islands a group of three low-lying coral islands in the Caribbean Sea, 150 miles (240 kilometres) south of Cuba and northwest of Jamaica, which form a British Overseas Territory. The group comprises Grand Cayman, by far the largest of the three, Cayman Brac and Little Cayman.

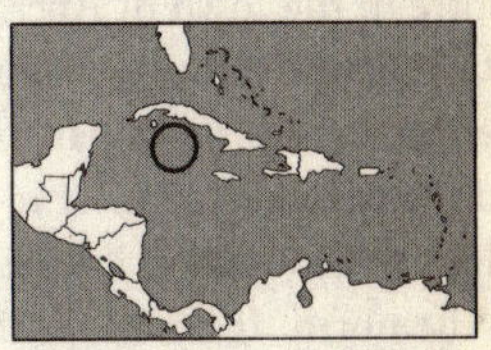

Area: 102 sq miles/264 sq km
Population: 38,000
Capital: George Town, on Grand Cayman
Form of government: British Overseas Territory
Religion: Christianity
Currency: Cayman Islands Dollar

Cebú an island in the central Philippines, forming part of the Visayan group; also the name of its capital city. (1,707 sq miles/4,422 sq km; pop. island 2,092,000/city 688,000)

Celebes Sea a sea between the islands of eastern Indonesia and the Philippines.

Central African Republic a landlocked country in central Africa bordered by Chad in the north, Cameroon in the west, Sudan in the east, and the Congo and Democratic Republic of Congo in the south. The terrain consists of 2,000–3,000 feet (610–915 metres) high undulating plateaux with dense tropical forest in the south and a semi-desert area in the east. The climate is tropical with little variation in temperature throughout the year. The wet months are May, June, October, and November. Floods and tornadoes can occur at the beginning of the rainy season. Most of the population live in the west and in the hot, humid south and southwest. Over 86 per cent of the working population are subsistence farmers and the main crops grown are cassava, groundnuts, bananas, plantains, millet, and maize. Livestock rearing is small-scale. Gems and industrial diamonds are mined, and deposits of uranium, iron ore, lime, zinc, and gold have been discovered, although they remain relatively undeveloped. The country's main exports are coffee, diamonds, cotton, tobacco, and lumber, although this is hampered by the distance from a port. Since the country's independence in

1960, its political and economic fortunes have been mixed, with widespread corruption and violence.

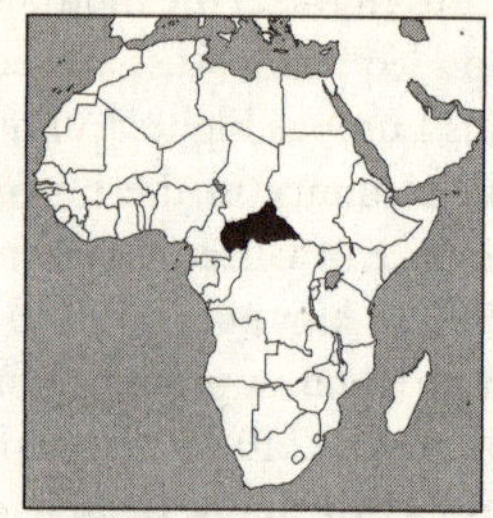

Area: 240,535 sq miles/622,984 sq km
Population: 3,344,000
Capital: Bangui
Form of government: Republic
Religions: traditional African religions, RC
Currency: CFA Franc

Ceredigion a council area in south Wales, on Cardigan Bay, with its administrative centre in the town of Aberaeron. (692 sq miles/1,793 sq km; pop.64,000)

Ceuta a Spanish administered enclave in northern Morocco. (Pop. 78,000)

Cévennes the southern part of the Massif Central in France.

Chad a landlocked country in the centre of northern Africa that extends from the edge of the equatorial forests in the south to the middle of the Sahara Desert in the north. It lies more than 944 miles (1,600 kilometres) from the nearest coast. The climate is tropical, with adequate rainfall in the south, but the north experiences semi-desert conditions. In the far north of the country the Tibesti Mountains rise from the desert sand more than 11,200 feet (3,415 metres). The southern part of Chad is the most densely populated and its relatively well-watered savannah has always been the country's most arable region. Unless there is drought, this area is farmed for cotton (the main cash crop along with livestock exports), millet, sorghum, groundnuts, rice, and vegetables. Fishing is carried out in the rivers and in Lake Chad. Cotton ginning and manufacture of peanut oil are the principal industries. As a result of drought and civil war, Chad remains one of the poorest countries in the world. The country was torn by civil strife for much of the latter part of the 20th century but a ceasefire has been in place since 1994.

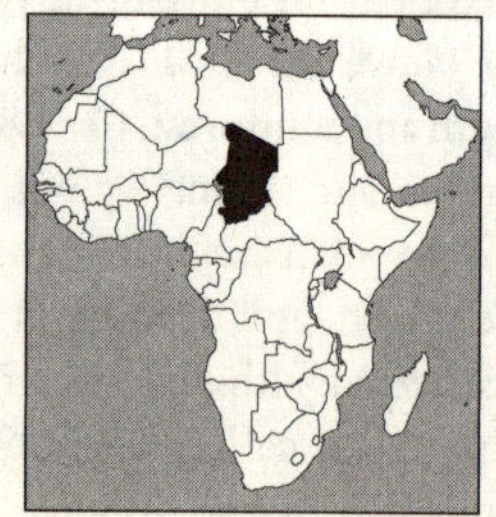

Area: 495,755 sq miles/1,284,000 sq km
Population: 6,515,000
Capital: Ndjamena
Other major cities: Sarh, Moundou
Form of government: Republic
Religions: Sunni Islam, traditional African religions
Currency: CFA Franc

Chad, Lake a large lake in western Chad, on the border with Niger and Nigeria. (10,000 sq miles/26,000 sq km)

Champagne a former region of northeastern France famous for the sparking wine also called champagne. It now forms part of the administrative region called Champagne-Ardenne.

Chang Jiang (Yangtze) the world's third longest river. It rises in Tibet and flows across central China into the East China Sea. (Length 3,965 miles/6,380 km)

Channel Islands a group of islands in the English Channel, close to the coast of France, consisting of Jersey, Guernsey, Alderney, Great Sark, Little Sark, Herm, Jethou, and Lihou (British crown dependencies) and the Roches Douvres and the Îles Chausey (which belong to France). (75 sq miles/194 sq km; pop. 143,000)

Chao Phrya a river running from north to south down the west side of Thailand and through its capital, Bangkok. (Length 62 miles/100 km)

Chapala, Lake the largest lake in Mexico, near Guadalajara. (950 sq miles/ 2,460 sq km)

Chechen-Ingush Republic an autonomous republic of the Russian Federation. (7,450 sq miles/19,300 sq km; pop. 1,204,000)

Cheju Do an island belonging to South Korea, lying some 56 miles (90 kilometres) off its southern tip, and dominated by the sacred volcano, Mount Halla (6,398 ft/1,950 m). (706 sq miles/1,828 sq km; pop. 505,000)

Chengdu the capital of Sichuan Province, China. (Pop. 1,927,000)

Chesapeake Bay an inlet, 195 miles (314 kilometres) long, on the east coast of the USA, shared by the states of Virginia and Maryland.

Cheshire a county in northwest England, with its administrative centre in Chester. (899 sq miles/2,328 sq km; pop. 975,000)

Cheviot Hills a range of hills, 37 miles (60 kilometres) long, which line the border between Scotland and the county of Northumberland in England.

Chianti a winemaking region of central Tuscany, Italy.

Chihuahua a city in northern central Mexico, and the name of the surrounding province, of which it is the capital. (Pop. 678,000)

Chile a country that lies like a backbone down the Pacific coast of the South American continent with the Andes Mountains extending its length. Its Pacific coastline is 2,600 miles (4,184 kilometres) long and the country is liable to volcanic explosions and earthquakes. Because of its enormous range in latitude it has almost every kind of climate, from desert conditions to icy wastes. The north, in which lies the Atacama Desert, is extremely arid. The climate of the central region is Mediterranean and that of the south cool temperate. Sixty per cent of the population live in the central valley where the climate is similar to that of southern California. The land here is fertile and the principal crops grown are grapes, wheat, apples, sugar beet, maize, tomatoes, and potatoes. There is also a significant winemaking industry. It is also in the central valley that the vast copper mine of El Teniente is located. This is one of the largest copper mines in the world and accounts for Chile's most important source of foreign exchange.

Area: 292,135 sq miles/756,626 sq km
Population: 14,419,000
Capital: Santiago
Other major cities: Arica, Concepción, Valparaíso, Viña del Mar
Form of government: Republic
Religion: RC
Currency: Chilean Peso

Chiltern Hills a range of low chalk hills to the northwest of London, England, rising to 850 feet (260 metres).

China the third largest country in the world, which covers a large area of East Asia and also includes over 3,400 islands. In western China, most of the terrain is very inhospitable. In the northwest, there are deserts that extend into Mongolia and the Russian Federation, and much of the southwest consists of the ice-capped peaks of Tibet. The southeast has a green and well-watered landscape comprising terraced hillsides and paddy fields, and its main rivers are the Chang Jiang (Yangtze), Huang He, and Xi Jiang. Most of China has a temperate climate but in such a large country wide ranges of latitude and altitudes produce local variations. China is an agricultural country, and intensive cultivation and horticulture are necessary to feed its population of over one billion. After the death of Mao Tse-tung in 1976 and under the leadership of Deng Xiaoping, China experienced a huge modernization of agriculture and industry as a result of the supply of expertise, capital, and technology from Japan and the West. The country was opened up to tourists and, to a degree, adopted the philosophy of free enterprise, resulting in a dramatic improvement in living standards for a significant proportion of the population. The change towards a market economy, however, created internal political problems. Pro-democracy demonstrations in 1989 resulted in the Tianmen Square massacre, which was condemned throughout the world and raised questions regarding China's approach to human rights.

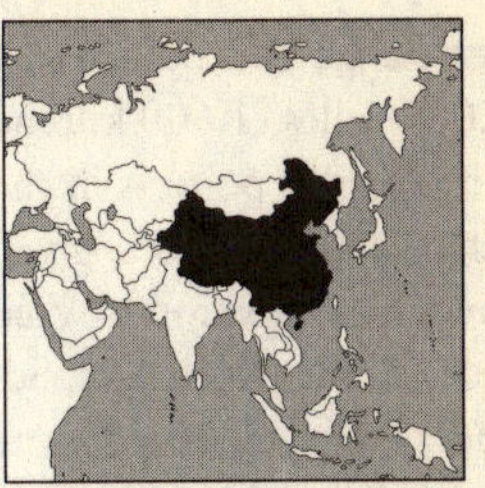

Area: 3,705,408 sq miles/ 9,596,961 sq km
Population: 1,246,872,000
Capital: Beijing (Peking)
Other major cities: Chengdu, Guangzhou, Shanghai, Tianjin, Wuhan
Form of government: People's Republic
Religions: Buddhism, Confucianism, Taoism
Currency: Yuan

China Sea a part of the Pacific Ocean, off the east coast of China.

Chindwin a river in Myanmar, flowing parallel to the northwest border before joining the River Irrawaddy in the centre of the country. (Length 700 miles/ 1,130 km)

Chios (Khios) a Greek island in the Aegean Sea, lying only 5 miles (8 kilometres) from the coast of Turkey. (349 sq miles/904 sq km; pop. 52,900)

Christmas Island (1) an island in the eastern Indian Ocean, 250 miles (400 kilometres) to the south of Java, administered by Australia since 1958. (55 sq miles/ 142 sq km; pop. 3,000) (2) former name for Kiritimati.

Chubu Sangaku a national park in central Honshu Island that contains two of the highest mountains in Japan, Mount Hotaka (10,466 ft/3,190 m) and Mount Yari (10,434 ft/3,180 m)

Churchill a river which flows into the Hudson Bay at the port of Churchill after a journey through Saskatchewan and Manitoba. (Length 1,000 miles/ 1,600 km)

Chuvash Republic an autonomous republic of the Russian Federation. (7,050 sq miles/18,300 sq km; pop. 1,327,000)

CIS *see* **Commonwealth of Independent States.**

Ciskei one of ten former South African Homelands, the area is now part of the Eastern Cape Province, in southeast South Africa.

Citaltépetl a volcanic peak to the southeast of Mexico City, at 18,697 feet (5,699 metres) the highest point in Mexico.

Clackmannanshire a council area in central Scotland, with its administrative centre in the town of Alloa. (55 sq miles/142 sq km; pop. 48,000)

Clare a county on the west coast of the Republic of Ireland; the county town is Ennis. (1,230 sq miles/3,188 sq km; pop. 98,000)

Clermont-Ferrand a city in Auvergne, central France. (Pop. 137,000)

Clyde a river in southwest Scotland which flows northwest to form an estuary 60 miles (100 kilometres) long, called the Firth of Clyde, with the city of Glasgow at its head. (Length 105 miles/170 km)

Coast Range the mountains lining the western coast of the USA, stretching 1,000 miles (1,600 kilometres) from the borders with Canada to Los Angeles. The highest point is in the San Jacinto Mountains (10,831 ft/3,301 m).

Cochin China the name given to the region around the Mekong delta during the French occupation of Vietnam.

Cocos Islands (Keeling Islands) a cluster of 28 small coral islands in the eastern Indian Ocean, equidistant from Sumatra and Australia, and administered by Australia since 1955. (6 sq miles/14 sq km; pop. 1,000)

Cod, Cape a narrow, low-lying peninsula on the coast of Massachusetts, USA, where the Pilgrim Fathers landed in 1620.

Coleraine a district council area in Co. Londonderry, north Northern Ireland. (187 sq miles/485 sq km; pop. 50,000)

Colombia a country situated in the north of South America, most of it lying between the Equator and 10 degrees north. The Andes, which split into three ranges (the Cordilleras) in Colombia, run north along the west coast and gradually disappear towards the Caribbean Sea. Half of Colombia lies east of the Andes, and much of this region is covered in tropical grassland. Towards the Amazon Basin the vegetation changes to tropical forest. The climates in Colombia include equatorial and tropical, according to altitude. Very little of the country is under cultivation although much of the soil is fertile. The range of climates results in an extraordinary variety of crops, of which coffee is the most important, and includes cocoa beans, sugar cane, bananas, cotton, and tobacco. Colombia is rich in minerals such as gold, silver, platinum, and copper, and produces about half of the world's emeralds. It is South America's leading producer of coal, and petroleum is the country's most important foreign revenue earner. However, it has been wracked by violence, involving not only guerrilla groups but also the country's sizable illegal drug trade.

Area: 439,737 sq miles/1,138,914 sq km
Population: 35,626,000
Capital: Bogotá
Other major cities: Barranquilla, Cali, Cartagena, Medellín
Form of government: Republic
Religion: RC
Currency: Colombian Peso

Colorado an inland state of central western USA; the state capital is Denver.

(104,247 sq miles/270,000 sq km; pop. 4,536,000)

Colorado a river which rises in the Rocky Mountains in the state of Colorado, USA, and flows southwest to the Gulf of California, forming the Grand Canyon on its way. (Length 1,450 miles/2,330 km)

Columbia, District of *see* **Washington D.C.**

Columbia a river which flows northwards from its source in British Columbia, Canada, before turning south into Washington State, USA and entering the Pacific Ocean at Portland, Oregon. (Length 1,210 miles/1,950 km)

Commonwealth of Independent States (CIS) an organization created in 1991 to represent the common interests of eleven independent states of the former USSR. The eleven member states are: Armenia, Azerbaijan, Belarus, Kazakhstan, Kyrgyzstan, Moldova, Russian Federation, Tajikistan, Turkmenistan, Ukraine and Uzbekistan. The former Soviet states of Estonia, Latvia, Lithuania and Georgia did not join the CIS on gaining independence.

Comorin, Cape the southern tip of India.

Comoros a country that consists of three volcanic islands in the Indian Ocean, situated between mainland Africa and Madagascar. Physically, four islands make up the group but the island of Mayotte remained a French dependency when the three western islands became a federal Islamic republic in 1975. The islands are mostly forested and the tropical climate is affected by Indian monsoon winds from the north. There is a wet season from November to April that is accompanied by cyclones. Only small areas of the islands are cultivated and most of this land belongs to foreign plantation owners. The chief product was formerly sugar cane but now vanilla, copra, maize, cloves, and essential oils are the most important products. The forests provide lumber for building and there is a small fishing industry. The coelacanth, a primitive bony fish previously thought to have been extinct for millions of years, was discovered living in the seas off the Comoros in 1938.

Area: 720 sq miles/1,865 sq km
Population: 538,000
Capital: Moroni
Form of government: Federal Islamic Republic
Religion: Sunni Islam
Currency: Comorian Franc

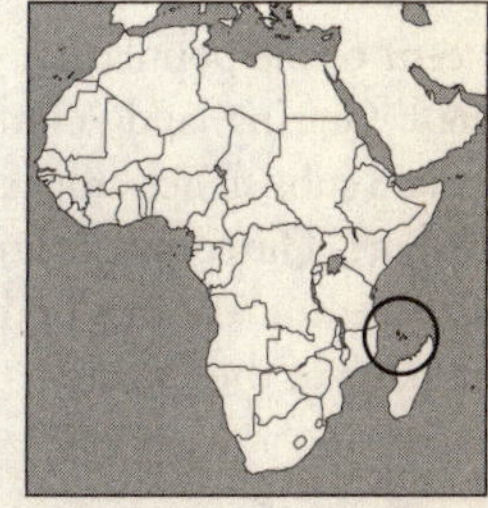

Congo formerly a French colony and now a republic, the Congo is situated in west central Africa where it straddles the equator. The climate is equatorial, with a moderate rainfall and a small range of temperature. The Bateke Plateau has a long dry season but the Congo Basin is more humid and rainfall approaches 9.8 inches (2,500 mm) each year. About 62 per cent of the total land area is covered with equatorial forest from which lumber is produced. Valuable hardwoods, such as mahogany, are exported. Cash crops, such as coffee and cocoa, are mainly grown on large plantations but food crops are grown on small farms usually worked by the women. A manufacturing industry is now growing and oil discovered offshore accounts for about 90 per cent of the Congo's revenues and exports. The remaining exports are wood, cocoa, sugar, coffee, and diamonds.

Area: 132,047 sq miles/342,000 sq km
Population: 2,668,000
Capital: Brazzaville
Other major city: Pointe-Noire
Form of government: Republic
Religion: traditional African religions, Christianity
Currency: CFA Franc

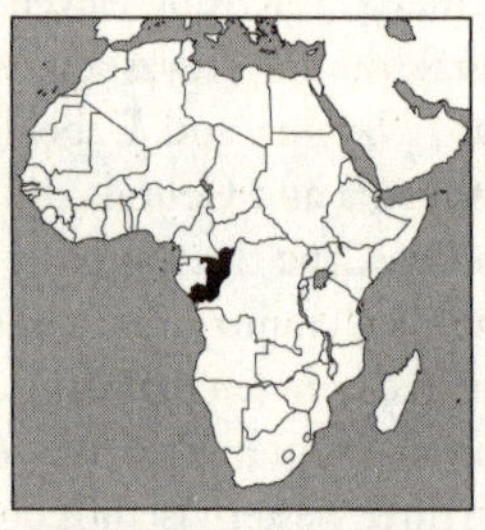

Congo, Democratic Republic of a vast country, formerly known as The Democratic Republic of Congo, situated in west central Africa. It has a short coastline of only 25 miles (40 kilometres) on the Atlantic Ocean. Rainforests, which cover about 55 per cent of the country, contain valuable hardwoods such as mahogany and ebony. The country is drained by the Congo River, which is largely navigable, and its main tributaries. There is enormous potential for hydroelectricity, but this is not yet exploited. Mountain ranges and plateaux surround the Congo basin, and in the east the Ruwenzori Mountains overlook the lakes in the Great Rift Valley. In the central region the climate is hot and wet all year but elsewhere there are well-marked wet and dry seasons. Agriculture employs 75 per cent of the population yet less than 3 per cent of the country can be cultivated. Grazing land is limited by the infestation of the tsetse fly. Cassava is the main subsistence crop, and coffee, tea, cocoa, rubber, and palms are grown for export. The country's huge mineral resources have fuelled the ongoing civil war and ethnic conflict in the region, and the government has no control over large parts of the country.

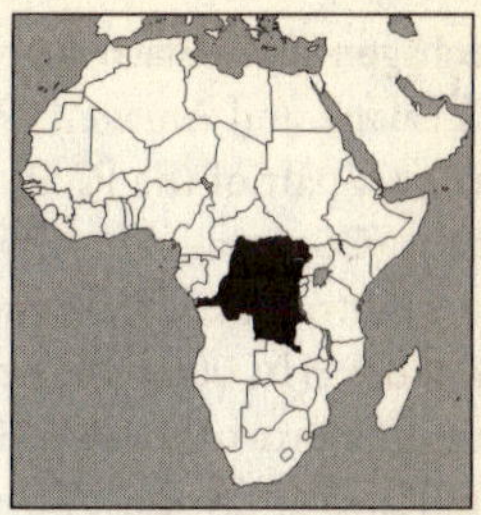

Area: 905,355 sq miles/2,344,858 sq km
Population: 46,812,000
Capital: Kinshasa
Other major cities: Lubumbashi, Mbuji-Mayi, Kananga
Form of government: Republic
Religions: RC, Protestantism, traditional African religions
Currency: Franc

Congo (Zaïre) a major river of central Africa (the second longest river in Africa after the Nile) and, with its tributaries, forming a massive basin. It rises as the Lualaba in the south of the Democratic Republic of Congo, then flows north and northwest, and finally southwest, forming the border between Democratic Republic of Congo and the Congo before entering the Atlantic Ocean. (Length 3,000 miles/4,800 km)

Connacht (Connaught) a province and ancient kingdom of the Republic of Ireland, covering the northwest of the island.

Connecticut a state on the northeastern seaboard of the USA, in New England; the capital is Hartford. (5,009 sq miles/12,973 sq km; pop. 3,445,000)

Connemara a coastal area of Co. Galway on the west coast of Ireland centring upon the distinctive peaks of the Twelve Bens.

Constance, Lake a lake north of the Swiss Alps, surrounded by Germany to the north, Switzerland to the south and Austria to the east. (207 sq miles /536 sq km)

Conwy (1) a market town and holiday resort in north Wales, on the estuary of the River Conwy, also the administrative centre for the Conwy council area. (Pop. 14,000) (2) a council area in north Wales. (436 sq miles/1,130 sq km; pop. 70,000)

Cook Islands a group of 15 islands in the South Pacific, independent since 1965 but associated with New Zealand. The capital is Avarua. (Area 93 sq miles/ 240 sq km; pop. 20,000; cur. Cook Islands Dollar/ New Zealand Dollar)

Cook, Mount the highest mountain in New Zealand, on South Island. (12,316 ft/ 3,753 m)

Cookstown a district council area in Co. Tyrone, central Northern Ireland. (240 sq miles/622 sq km; pop. 31,000)

Cook Strait the strait that separates North Island and South Island of New Zealand, 16 miles (26 kilometres) across at its widest point.

Cooper Creek a river flowing into Lake Eyre in South Australia from its source in central Queensland. The upper stretch is known as the Barcoo River. (Length 800 miles/1,420 km)

Copenhagen (København) a port and the capital of Denmark, located on the islands of Zealand and Amager. (Pop. 1,096,000)

Coral Sea a part of the Pacific Ocean, off the northeast coast of Australia.

Córdoba (Cordova) (1) a city in southern Spain, famous for its cathedral which was built originally as a mosque; also the name of the surrounding province. (Pop. city 316,000) (2) the second city of Argentina, and the name of the surrounding province. (Pop. 1,460,000)

Corfu (Kérkira) the most northerly of the Ionian Islands, in western Greece; the capital is also called Corfu. (229 sq miles/592 sq km; pop. 114,000)

Cork (1) the second largest city in the Republic of Ireland, at the head of a large natural harbour which cuts into the southern coast. (2) the county of which Cork is the county town. (County 2,880 sq miles/7,459 sq km; pop. county 438,000; city 188,000)

Cornwall a county occupying the southwestern tip of England, with its administrative centre in Truro. (1,376 sq miles/3,564 sq km; pop. 480,000)

Coromandel Coast the coast of southeastern India around Madras.

Coromandel Peninsula the central peninsula reaching northwards from North Island, New Zealand.

Corsica (Corse) a large island in the Mediterranean Sea lying to the north of Sardinia, governed by France. The capital is Ajaccio. (3,350 sq miles/8,680 sq km; pop. 263,000)

Costa Brava a strip of coastline to the northeast of Barcelona in Spain, famous for its beaches and popular resorts.

Costa del Sol a strip of coastline in southern Spain, famous for its beaches and popular resorts.

Costa Rica with the Pacific Ocean to the south and west and the Caribbean Sea to the east, Costa Rica is sandwiched between the Central American countries of Nicaragua and Panama. Much of the country consists of volcanic mountain chains that run northwest to southeast. The climate is tropical with a small temperature range and abundant rain. The dry season is from December to April. The most populated area is the Valle Central in which the Spanish settled in the 16th century. The upland areas have rich volcanic soils that are good for coffee growing and the slopes provide lush pastures for cattle. Coffee and bananas are grown commercially and are the major agricultural exports. Costa Rica's mountainous terrain provides hydroelectric power, which makes it almost self-sufficient in electricity, and attractive scenery for its growing tourist industry The country has a high literacy rate (around 92 per cent) and its culture reflects its Spanish heritage.

Area: 19,730 sq miles/51,100 sq km
Population: 3,398,000
Capital: San José
Other major city: Límon
Form of government: Republic
Religion: RC
Currency: Costa Rican Colón

Costa Smeralda the 'emerald coast' on the northeast side of the island of Sardinia in the Mediterranean, famed for its watersports and its upmarket resorts.

Côte d'Azur the coast of southeast France, famous for its beaches and resorts such as St Tropez, Cannes and Nice.

Côte d'Ivoire (Ivory Coast) a former French colony in West Africa, Côte d'Ivoire is located on the Gulf of Guinea with Ghana to the east and Liberia and Guinea to the west. The southwest coast has rocky cliffs but farther east there are coastal plains, which are the country's most prosperous region. The climate is tropical and affected by distance from the sea. The coastal area has two wet seasons, but in the north there is only the one. Côte d'Ivoire is basically an agricultural country with about 55 per cent of the workforce involved in producing cocoa, coffee, rubber, bananas, and pineapples. It is the world's largest producer of cocoa and the fourth largest producer of coffee. These two crops bring in half the country's export revenue although lumber production is also of economic importance. Since independence was achieved in 1960, industrialization has developed rapidly, particularly food processing, textiles, and sawmills. Oil was discovered offshore in the late 1970s and there is mining for gold and diamonds.

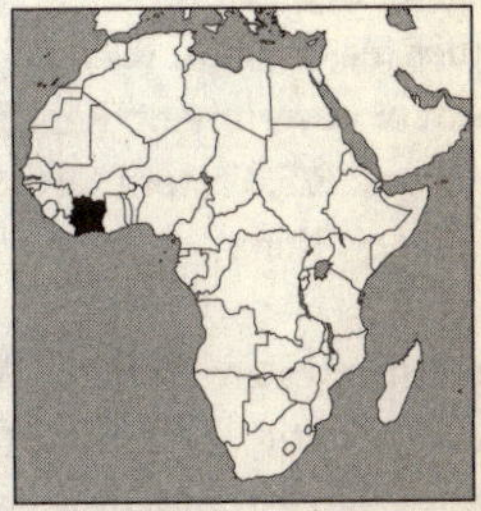

Area: 124,504 sq miles/322,463 sq km
Population: 14,781,000
Capital: Yamoussoukro
Other major cities: Abidjan, Bouaké, Daloa
Form of government: Republic
Religions: traditional African religions, Sunni Islam, RC
Currency: CFA Franc

Cotswold Hills a range of hills in central England, lying east of the River Severn.

Craigavon a district council area in Co. Armagh, central Northern Ireland. (108 sq miles/279 sq km; pop. 78,000)

Crete (Kríti) the largest and most southerly of the islands of Greece, with important ruins of the Minoan civilization at Knossos. The capital is Chania (Khania). (3,229 sq miles/8,366 sq km; pop. 540,000)

Crimea (Krym) a diamond-shaped peninsula jutting out into the northern part of the Black Sea and an autonomous region of the Ukraine. (10,000 sq miles/ 25,900 sq km; pop. 2,073,000)

Croatia a republic of former Yugoslavia that made a unilateral declaration of independence on 25 June 1991. Sovereignty was not formally recognized by the international community until early in 1992. Located in southeast Europe, it is bounded to the west by the Adriatic Sea, to the north by Slovenia and Romania, and to the south by Bosnia-Herzegovina. Western Croatia lies in the Dinaric Alps. The eastern region, drained by the Rivers Sava and Drava, which both flow into the Danube, is low-lying and agricultural. The chief farming region is the Pannonian Plain. Over one-third of the country is forested, with beech and oak trees being predominant, and lumber is a major export. Deposits of coal, bauxite, copper, petroleum, oil, and iron ore are substantial, and most of the republic's industry is based on their processing. In Istria in the northwest and on the Dalmatian coast, tourism was a major industry until Croatia became embroiled in the Serbo-Croat war prior to its secession in 1992. Following the formal recognition of Croatia's independence by the international community, the fighting abruptly ceased; however, the tourism industry continued to suffer from the effects of the ongoing hostilities in other parts of the former Yugoslavia. More recently, tourists are returning although there is a need to rebuild the infrastructure.

Area: 21,824 sq miles/56,538 sq km
Population: 4,501,000
Capital: Zagreb
Other major cities: Rijeka, Split
Form of government: Republic
Religions: RC, Eastern Orthodox
Currency: Kuna

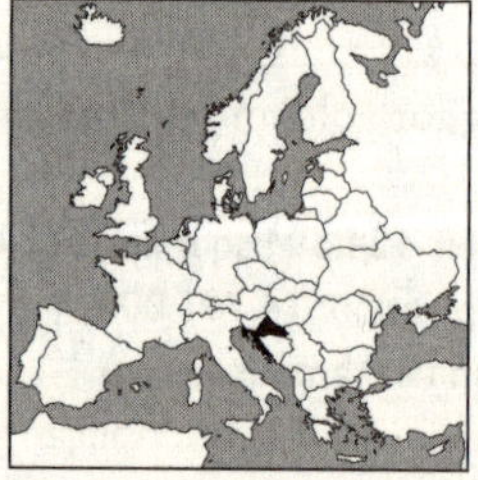

Crozet Islands a group in the Antarctic Ocean, forming part of the French Southern and Antarctic Territories. (116 sq miles/300 sq km)

Cuba the largest and most westerly of the Greater Antilles group of islands in the West Indies. Cuba is strategically positioned at the entrance to the Gulf of Mexico and lies about 87 miles (140 kilometres) south of the tip of Florida. Cuba is as big as all other Caribbean islands put together and is home to a third of the whole West Indian population. The climate is warm and generally rainy, and hurricanes are liable to occur between June and November. It possesses unusual natural subsurface limestone caverns and its rivers tend to be short and unnavigable. The island consists mainly of extensive plains and the soil is fertile. The most important agricultural product is sugar and its byproducts, and the processing of these is the most important industry. Tobacco is also of commercial significance, with Havana cigars being known internationally. Most of Cuba's trade has been with other communist countries, particularly the former USSR, and the country's economy has suffered as a result of a US trade embargo.

Area: 42,804 sq miles/110,861 sq km
Population: 11,019,000
Capital: Havana (La Habana)
Other major cities: Camaguey, Holguín, Santiago de Cuba
Form of government: Socialist Republic
Religion: RC
Currency: Cuban Peso

Cumbria a county in northwest England, with its administrative centre in Carlisle. (2,629 sq miles/6,809 sq km; pop. 493,000)

Curaçao an island in the Caribbean lying just off the coast of Venezuela but a part of the Netherlands Antilles. (171 sq miles/444 sq km; pop. 186,000)

Cyclades (Kikládhes) a group of some 220 islands in the middle of the Aegean Sea belonging to Greece. The capital is Hermoupolis. (Pop. 112,000)

Cyprus an island that lies in the eastern Mediterranean about 53 miles (85 kilometres) south of Turkey. It has a long thin panhandle and is divided from west to east by two parallel ranges of mountains that are separated by a wide central plain open to the sea at either end. The highest point is Mount Olympus (6,401 feet/1,951 metres) in the southwest. The climate is Mediterranean, with very hot dry summers and warm damp winters. This contributes towards the great variety of crops grown, such as early potatoes, vegetables, cereals, tobacco, olives, bananas, and grapes, and these account for about 17 per cent of the land. The grapes are used for the strong wines and sherries for which Cyprus is famous. The main mineral found is copper while asbestos, gypsum, and iron pyrites are also found. Fishing is a significant industry, but above all the island depends on visitors and it is the tourist industry that has led to a recovery in the economy since 1974, when it was invaded by Turkey, which still occupies the northern third of the island. There are no railways on the island although it does possess three international airports.

Area: 3,572 sq miles/9,251 sq km
Population: 756,000
Capital: Nicosia
Other major cities: Limassol, Larnaca
Form of government: Republic
Religions: Greek Orthodox, Sunni Islam
Currency: Cyprus Pound

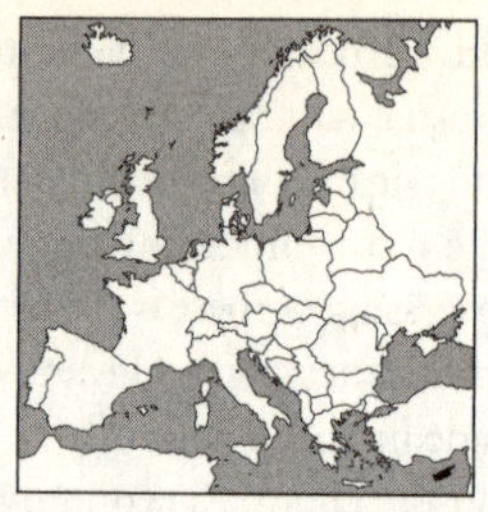

Czechoslovakia a former state in central Europe. In 1993, it separated into two independent republics, the Czech Republic and Slovakia.

Czech Republic a country that was newly constituted on 1 January 1993 with the dissolution of the 74-year-old federal republic of Czechoslovakia. It is land-locked, at the heart of central Europe, bounded by Slovakia, Germany, Poland, and Austria. Natural boundaries are formed by the Sudeten Mountains in the north, the Erzgebirge, or Ore Mountains, to the northwest, and the Bohemian Forest in the southwest. The climate is humid continental, with warm summers and cold winters. Most rain falls in summer and thunderstorms are frequent. Agriculture, although accounting for only a small percentage of the national income, is highly developed and efficient. The main crops are sugar beet, wheat, and potatoes. Over a third of the labour force is employed in industry, which has to import its raw materials and energy. The most important industries are iron and steel, coal, machinery, cement, and paper, but industrialization has caused serious environmental problems. The Czech Republic was considered to be the most polluted country in eastern Europe in the early 1990s. Recently investment has gone into electronics factories and research establishments. Tourism has increased post-Communism, with the country's many resorts, historical cities, and winter sports facilities attracting visitors.

Area: 30,450 sq miles/78,864 sq km
Population: 10,291,900
Capital: Prague (Praha)
Other major cities: Brno, Ostrava, Plzen
Form of government: Republic
Religions: RC, Protestantism
Currency: Koruna

D

Dagestan an autonomous republic of the Russian Federation lying to the west of the Caspian Sea. The capital is Makhachkala. (19,400 sq miles/50,300 sq km; pop. 2,173,000)

Dakota *see* **North Dakota, South Dakota.**

Dal, Lake the most famous of the lakes of Kashmir, India, near Srinagar.

Dalmatia (Dalmacija) a coastal region of west Croatia, on the Adriatic Sea with many offshore islands. The principal tourist centre is Dubrovnik.

Damavand, Mount an extinct volcano, and the highest peak in the Elburz Mountains, Iran. (18,600 ft/5,671 m)

Danube (Donau) the longest river in Western Europe, rising in the Black Forest in Germany, and passing through Austria, Slovakia, Hungary and Serbia, forming much of the border between Bulgaria and Romania before turning north and forming a delta on the Black Sea. (Length 1,770 miles/2,850 km)

Dardanelles the narrow ribbon of water, some 50 miles (80 kilometres) long, in Turkey which connects the Aegean Sea to the Sea of Marmara (and from thence the Black Sea). Gallipoli is on the peninsula to the north. The Dardanelles were known as the Hellespont to the ancient Greeks.

Darién the eastern province of Panama, a narrow neck of land on the border with Colombia, and the only gap in the Pan-American Highway, which otherwise runs from Alaska to Chile.

Darling a river flowing from southern Queensland through New South Wales in Australia before converging with the Murray River. (Length 1,900 miles/3,057 km)

Dartmoor an area of moorland in Devon, England. (365 sq miles/945 sq km)

Davis Strait the broad strait, some 180 miles (290 kilometres) across at its narrowest, separating Baffin Island in Canada and Greenland.

Dead Sea a small sea on the border between Israel and Jordan into which the River Jordan flows and does not exit. It is one of the lowest places on Earth at 1,299 feet (396 metres) below normal sea level, and the body of water with the world's highest salt content. (395 sq miles/1,049 sq km)

Death Valley a desert basin in southeastern California, USA, it contains the lowest point in North America.

Deccan the broad, triangular plateau which forms much of the southern part of India.

Delaware a state on the east coast of the USA, and the second smallest state in the USA after Rhode Island. The capital is Dover. (2,057 sq miles/5,328 sq km; pop. 809,000)

Delphi the ruins of the Temple of Apollo on Mount Parnassos, 102 miles (166 kilometres) northwest of Athens, Greece. It was the seat of the most important oracle of ancient Greece.

Demerara a river in central Guyana which flows through the capital, Georgetown. It has given its name to the type of brown sugar which is grown in the region. (Length 200 miles/320 km)

Denbighshire a council area of north Wales, with its administrative centre in the town of Ruthin. (327 sq miles/844 sq km; pop. 92,000)

Denmark a small European state lying between the North Sea and the entrance to the Baltic. It consists of a western peninsula and an eastern archipelago of more than 400 islands, some 90 of which are inhabited. The country is very low-lying and the proximity of the sea combined with the effect of the Gulf Stream result in warm sunny summers and cold cloudy winters. The scenery is flat and monotonous, and the acidic soils need a great deal of fertilization for a wide variety of crops to be grown. It is an agricultural country and three-quarters of the land is cultivated, mostly by the rotation of grass, barley, oats, and sugar beet. Animal husbandry is, however, a particularly important activity, its produce including the famous bacon and butter. Danish beer and lager are also famous throughout the world. It is estimated that 85 per cent of the population live in the towns and cities. Despite Denmark's limited range of raw materials, it produces a wide range of manufactured goods and is famous for its imaginative design in ceramics, furniture, silverware, and porcelain. Denmark is a wealthy country and the standard of living is high.

Area: 16,639 sq miles/43,094 sq km
Population: 5,262,000 (excluding Faeroe Islands)
Capital: Copenhagen (København)
Other major cities: Ålborg, Århus, Odense
Form of government: Constitutional Monarchy
Religion: Lutheranism
Currency: Danish Krone

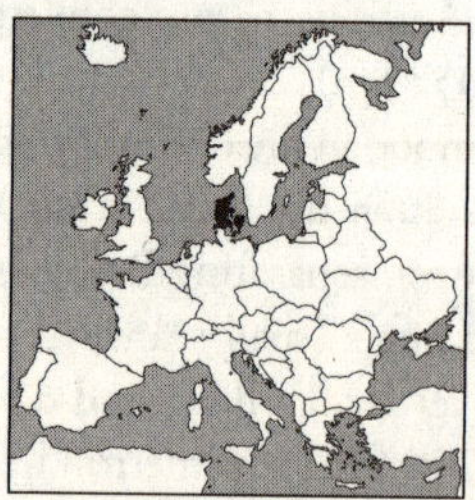

Denmark Strait the arm of the North Atlantic Ocean which separates Iceland from Greenland, some 180 miles (290 kilometres) apart.

Denpasar the capital of the island of Bali, Indonesia. (Pop. 492,000)

Denver the state capital of Colorado, USA. (Pop. 585,000)

Derby (1) a city of Saxon and Danish origins in the county of Derbyshire, England. (Pop. 228,000) (2) a unitary authority in Derbyshire, central England. (30 sq miles/78 sq km; pop.230,000)

Derbyshire a county in north central England, with its administrative centre in Matlock. (1,016 sq miles/2,631 sq km; pop. 954,000)

Derry a district council area in Co. Londonderrry. *See also* **Londonderry.** (149 sq miles/387 sq km; pop. 95,000)

Devon (also called **Devonshire**) a county in southwest England, with its administrative centre in Exeter. (2,593 sq miles/6,715 sq km; pop. 1,053,000)

Dhaulagiri, Mount a peak of the Himalayas in Nepal. (26,810 ft/8,172 m)

Diyarbakir a city on the River Tigris in southeastern Turkey, and the name of the province of which it is the capital. (Pop. 571,000)

Djibouti a country that is situated in northeast Africa and is bounded almost entirely by Ethiopia except in the southeast where it shares a border with Somalia and in the northwest where it shares a border with Eritrea. Its coastline is on the Gulf of Aden. Djibouti was formerly a French Overseas Territory but achieved independence in 1977. The land, which is mainly basalt plains, has some mountains rising to about 5,000 feet (1,500 metres). The climate is hot, among the world's hottest, and extremely dry. Less than a tenth of the land can be farmed even for grazing so it has great difficulty supporting its modest population. The native population is mostly nomadic, moving from oasis to oasis or across the border to Ethiopia in search of grazing land. Crops raised include fruits, vegetables, and dates. Most foodstuffs for the urban population in Djibouti city are imported. The capital is linked to Addis Ababa by a railway. Cattle, hides, and skins are the main exports. There are small deposits of copper, iron ore, and gypsum but these are not mined.

Area: 8,958 sq miles/23,200 sq km
Population: 617,000
Capital: Djibouti
Form of government: Republic
Religion: Sunni Islam
Currency: Djibouti Franc

Dnieper (Dnepr) the third longest river in Europe after the Volga and the Danube, flowing south through the Russian Federation and the Ukraine to the Black Sea via Kiev. (Length 1,420 miles/2,285 km)

Dniester (Dnestr) a river flowing through the Ukraine and Moldova to the Black Sea. (Length 877 miles /1,411 km)

Dodecanese (Dhodhekanisos) Islands a group of twelve islands belonging to Greece in the eastern Aegean Sea near the coast of Turkey. They include Samos, Patmos, Kalimnos, Karpathos, Kos and Rhodes (Rodhos), the largest in the group. They are also called the Southern Sporades. (Pop. 189,000)

Dolomites (Dolomiti) a range of mountains in northeastern Italy, near the border with Austria. The highest point is Mount Marmolada at 10,964 feet (3,342 metres).

Dominica discovered by Columbus, Dominica is the most northerly of the Windward Islands in the West Indies. It is situated between the islands of Martinique and Guadeloupe. The island is very rugged and with the exception of 87 square miles (225 square kilometres) of flat land, it consists of three inactive volcanoes, the highest of which is 4,747 feet (1,447 metres). There are many unnavigable rivers, and Boiling Lake, situated in the south, often gives off sulphurous gases. The climate is tropical and even on the leeward coast it rains two days out of three. The wettest season is from June to October when hurricanes often occur. The steep slopes are difficult to farm but agriculture provides almost all Dominica's exports. Bananas are the main agricultural export, but copra, citrus fruits, cocoa, coconuts, bay leaves, cinnamon, and vanilla are also revenue earners. Industry is mostly based on the processing of the agricultural products.

Area: 290 sq miles/751 sq km
Population: 74,000
Capital: Roseau
Form of government: Republic
Religion: RC
Currency: East Caribbean Dollar

Dominican Republic a country that forms the eastern portion of the island of Hispaniola in the West Indies. It covers two-thirds of the island, the smaller portion consisting of Haiti. The climate is semi-tropical, and occasionally hurricanes occur, causing great destruction. The west of the country is made up of four almost parallel mountain ranges, and between the two most northerly is the fertile Cibao Valley. The southeast is made up of fertile plains. Although well endowed with fertile land, only about 30 per cent is cultivated. Sugar is the main crop and mainstay of the country's economy and is grown mainly on plantations in the southeast plains. Other crops grown are rice, coffee, bananas, cocoa, and tobacco. Mining of gold, silver, platinum, nickel, and aluminium is carried out, but the main industries are food processing and manufacture of consumer goods. Fishing is also carried out but not to any great extent because of lack of equipment and refrigeration facilities. The island has fine beaches and the tourism industry is now very important to the economy.

Area: 18,816 sq miles/48,734 sq km
Population: 8,052,000
Capital: Santo Domingo
Other major city: Santiago de los Caballeros
Form of government: Republic
Religion: RC
Currency: Dominican Republic Peso

Don a river flowing southwards into the Sea of Azov from its source south of Moscow. (Length 1,165 miles/1,870 km)

Donegal the northernmost county of the Republic of Ireland, on the west coast. The county town is also called Donegal. (Pop. 136,000)

Donets Basin (Donbass) a coal-mining region and major industrial area in the eastern Ukraine.

Dongbei (Manchuria) the northeastern region of China, covering part of the Nei Mongol Autonomous Region and the three provinces of Heilongjiang, Jilin and Liaoning. (502,000 sq miles/1,300,000 sq km; pop. 87,962,000)

Dordogne a river of southwestern France which rises in the Massif Central and flows west to the Gironde estuary. (Length 295 miles/475 km)

Dorset a county of southwest England, with its administrative centre in Dorchester. (1,025 sq miles/2,654 sq km; pop. 673,000)

Douro (Duero) a river flowing west from north central Spain across northern Portugal to the Atlantic Ocean. (Length 555 miles/895 km)

Dover, Strait of the stretch of water separating England and France, where the English Channel meets the North Sea. The ports of Dover and Calais are situated on either side of its narrowest point, 21 miles (34 kilometres) across.

Down (1) a historical county in southeast Northern Ireland. (952 sq miles/ 2,466 sq km) (2) a district council area in Co. Down. (250 sq miles/649 sq km; pop. 58,000)

Drakensberg Mountains a range of mountains which stretch 700 miles (1,125 kilometres) across Lesotho and neighbouring regions of South Africa. The highest point is Thabana Ntlenyana at 11,424 feet (3,482 metres).

Drake Passage the broad strait, some 400 miles (640 kilometres) wide, which separates Cape Horn on the southern tip of South America and Antarctica.

Drava (Drau) a river flowing from eastern Austria to Croatia and Serbia, where it forms much of the border with Hungary before joining the Danube. (Length 447 miles/718 km)

Duarte, Pico a mountain peak in central Dominican Republic which is the highest point in the West Indies. (10,417 ft/3,175 m)

Dubai (Dubayy) the second largest of the United Arab Emirates, at the eastern end of the Persian Gulf. Most of the population lives in the capital, also called Dubai. (1,506 sq miles/3,900 sq km; pop. emirate 879,000/city 873,000)

Dublin (Baile Atha Cliath) the capital of the Republic of Ireland, on the River Liffey, and also the name of the surrounding county. Its main port area is at Dun Laoghaire. (Pop. county 1,103,000/city 993,000)

Dumfries and Galloway a council area in southwest Scotland, with its administrative centre in the town of Dumfries. (2,486 sq miles/6,439 sq km; pop. 147,000)

Dundee (1) a city and port, and administrative centre of the City of Dundee council area, on the east coast of Scotland, on the north side of the Firth of Tay. (Pop. 159,000) (2) **City of** a council area of east Scotland. (25 sq miles/ 65 sq km; pop. 167,000)

Dungannon a district council area in Co. Tyrone, south Northern Ireland. (302 sq miles/783 sq km; pop. 46,000)

Durham (1) a city in northeast England, and the administrative centre of Co. Durham. (Pop. 37,000) (2) a county in northeast England. (1051 sq miles/ 2,722 sq km; pop. 875,000)

Dvina the name of two quite separate rivers. The West (Zapadnaya) Dvina flows from its source to the west of Moscow into the Baltic Sea at Riga in Latvia. The North (Severnaya) Dvina flows through the northwest of the Russian Federation to the White Sea at Archangel. (Length West Dvina 635 miles/1,020 km; North Dvina 820 miles/1,320 km)

Dyfed a former county in southwest Wales.

E

East Anglia an old Anglo-Saxon kingdom occupying the bulge of the east coast of England between the Thames estuary and The Wash, and now covered by Norfolk, Suffolk, and parts of Cambridgeshire and Essex.

East Ayrshire a council area in southwest Scotland, with its administrative centre in the town of Kilmarnock. (483 sq miles/1,252 sq km; pop. 123,000)

East Dunbartonshire a council area in central Scotland, with its administrative centre in the city of Glasgow. (66 sq miles/172 sq km; pop. 110,000)

Easter Island (Isla de Pascua) a remote and tiny island in the South Pacific Ocean annexed by Chile in 1888. About 1,000 years ago it was settled by Polynesians who set up over 600 huge stone statues of heads on the island. (46 sq miles/ 120 sq km; pop. 1,300)

Eastern Cape one of South Africa's nine provinces, in southeast South Africa, with its administrative centre in Bisho. (65,458 sq miles/169,580 sq km; pop. 6,482,000)

East Lothian a council area in central Scotland, with its administrative centre in the town of Haddington. (262 sq miles/678 sq km; pop. 86,000)

East Renfrewshire a council area in central Scotland, with its administrative centre in the town of Giffnock. (67 sq miles/173 sq km; pop. 87,000)

East Riding of Yorkshire a county in northeast England, with its administrative centre in Beverley. (704 sq miles/1,819 sq km; pop. 595,000)

East Sussex a county in southeast England, with its administrative centre in Lewes. (693 sq miles/1,795 sq km; pop. 726,000)

East Timor the eastern part of the island of Timor and a small coastal enclave to the west. A former possession of Portugal, it was annexed illegally in 1975 by Indonesia. A referendum in 1999 showed that most of the population favoured independence. Following violent reprisals from Indonesia, East Timor was placed under United Nations protection prior to control being handed over to its own government in May 2002.

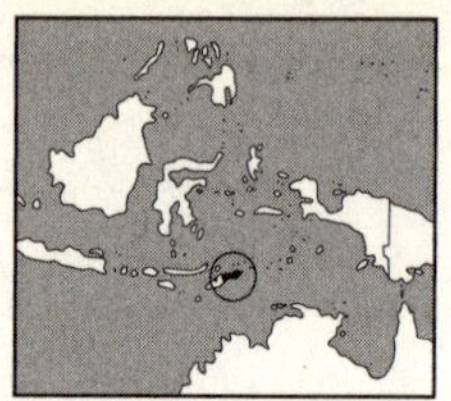

Area: 5,743 sq miles/14,874 sq km
Population: 857,000
Capital: Dili
Form of government: Democratic Republic
Religion: RC
Currency: US dollar

Ebro a river flowing across northeastern Spain, from near the north coast to the Mediterranean Sea south of Tarragona. (Length 565 miles/909 km)

Ecuador an Andean country situated in the northwest of the South American continent. It is bounded to the north by Colombia and to the east and south by Peru. It also includes the Galapagos Islands, which are located about 600 miles (965 kilometres) west of the mainland. The country contains over 30 active volcanoes, with Mount Cotopaxi at 19,340 feet (5,895 metres) the highest active volcano on Earth. Running down the middle of Ecuador are two ranges of the Andes that are divided by a central plateau. The coastal area consists of plains and the eastern area is made up of tropical jungles. The climate varies from equatorial through warm temperate to mountain conditions according to altitude. It is in the coastal plains that plantations of bananas, cocoa, coffee, and sugar cane are found. In contrast to this, the highland areas are adapted to grazing, dairy farming, and cereal growing. The fishing industry is important on the Pacific Coast and processed fish such as tuna and shrimp are main exports. Ecuador is one of the world's leading producers of balsawood. Oil is produced in the eastern region and petroleum is Ecuador's most important export. The official language is Spanish although many people in rural areas speak Quecha, the Incan language.

Area: 109,484 sq miles/283,561 sq km
Population: 11,698,000
Capital: Quito
Other major cities: Guayaquil, Cuenca
Form of government: Republic
Religion: RC
Currency: Sucre

Edinburgh (1) the capital city of Scotland, seat of the Scottish Parliament, and administrative centre for the City of Edinburgh council area, on the Firth of Forth (the estuary of the River Forth) in central Scotland. (Pop. 402,000) (2) **City of** a council area of central Scotland. (101 sq miles/262 sq km; pop. 448,000)

Edmonton the capital of Alberta, Canada. (Pop. 694,000)

Edward (Rutanzige), Lake a lake in the Great Rift Valley, on the border between Uganda and Democratic Republic of Congo. (820 sq miles/2,135 sq km)

Egypt a country situated in northeast Africa, acting as the doorway between Africa and Asia. Its outstanding physical feature is the River Nile, the valley and delta of which cover about 13,737 square miles (35,580 square kilometres). The climate is mainly dry but there are winter rains along the Mediterranean coast. The temperatures are comfortable in winter but summer temperatures are extremely high, particularly in the south. The rich soils deposited by flood waters along the banks of the Nile can support a large population and the Nile delta is one of the world's most fertile agricultural regions. Around 99 per cent of the population live in the delta and Nile valley where the main crops are rice, cotton, sugar cane, maize, tomatoes, and wheat. This concentration makes it one of the most densely populated areas in the world. The main industries are food processing and textiles. The economy has been boosted by the discovery of oil and is enough to supply the country's needs and leave surplus for export. Natural gas production is increasing for domestic use and Egypt has a significant fishing industry, mainly in the shallow lakes and Red Sea. The Suez Canal, shipping, and tourism connected with the ancient sites are also important revenue earners.

Area: 386,662 sq miles/1,001,449 sq km
Population: 60,603,000
Capital: Cairo (El Qâhira)
Other major cities: Alexandria, Port Said
Form of government: Republic
Religions: Sunni Islam, Christianity
Currency: Egyptian Pound

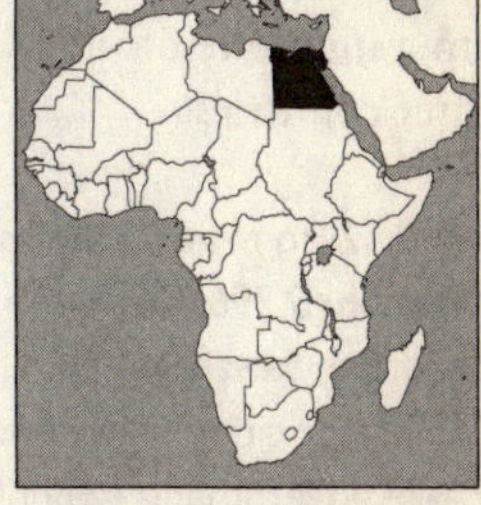

Eifel an upland area of western Germany between the Moselle River and the border with Belgium.

Eiger, The a mountain in southern central Switzerland, renowned among climbers for its daunting north face. (13,025 ft/3.970 m)

Elba an island lying about 6 miles (10 kilometres) off the coast of Tuscany, Italy. (86 sq miles/223 sq km; pop. 28,400)

Elbe a largely navigable river flowing northward from its source in the Czech Republic through Germany to Hamburg, and then into the North Sea. (Length 720 miles/1,160 km)

Elbrus, Mount the highest mountain in Europe, situated in the western Caucasus Mountains, Russian Federation. (18,510 ft/5,642 m)

Elburz Mountains a range of mountains in northern Iran, between Tehran and the Caspian Sea. The highest peak is the extinct volcano, Damavand, at 18,600 feet (5,671 metres).

El Faiyum (Fayum) a large and fertile oasis to the west of the River Nile in Egypt. (Pop. 298,000)

El Gezira a major irrigation scheme in Sudan between the Blue Nile and the White Nile.

El Salvador the smallest and most densely populated state in Central America. It is bounded north and east by Honduras and has a Pacific coast to the south. Two volcanic ranges run from east to west across the country. The Lempa River cuts the southern ranges in the centre of the country and opens as a large sandy delta to the Pacific Ocean. Although fairly near the equator, the climate tends to be warm rather than hot and the highlands have a cooler temperate climate. The country is predominantly agricultural: 32 per cent of the land is used for crops such as coffee (the major crop and revenue earner), cotton, maize, beans, rice, and sorghum, with a slightly smaller area being used for grazing cattle, pigs, sheep, and goats. Fishing is carried out, the most important being shrimp, although tuna, mackerel, and swordfish are also caught. A few industries, such as food processing, textiles, and chemicals, are found in the major towns. The country suffers from a high rate of inflation and unemployment and is one of the world's poorer countries.

Area: 8,124sq miles/21,041 sq km
Population: 5,796,000
Capital: San Salvador
Other major cities: Santa Ana, San Miguel
Form of government: Republic
Religion: RC
Currency: Colón

Emilia-Romagna a region on the east coast of northern central Italy; the capital is Bologna. (8,542 sq miles/22,123 sq km; pop. 3,960,000)

Emmenthal the valley of the River Emme, in Switzerland, famous for its distinctive cheese.

England the country occupying the greater part of the island of Great Britain, and the largest of the countries that make up the United Kingdom. Scotland lies to the north and Wales to the west. The capital is London. (50,331 sq miles/ 130,357 sq km; pop. 50,016,000)

English Channel the arm of the eastern Atlantic Ocean which separates the south coast of England from France.

Eolian (Lipari) Islands a group of small volcanic islands which lie between the north coast of Sicily and mainland Italy. The main islands are Stromboli, Lipari, Salina, Panarea and Vulcano. (Pop. 12,500)

Equatorial Guinea a country that lies about 124 miles (200 kilometres) north of the Equator on the hot humid coast of west Africa. It consists of a square-shaped mainland area (Mbini), with its few small offshore islets, and the islands of Bioko and Pagalu (Annobon). The climate is tropical and the wet season in Bioko and Pagalu lasts from December to February. Bioko is a very fertile volcanic island, and it is here that the capital, Malabo, is situated beside a volcanic crater flooded by the sea. It is also the centre of the country's cocoa production. Coffee and lumber are produced for export on the mainland. The country now relies heavily on foreign aid. Spanish is the official language although a variant of Bantu, Fang, is most commonly used. There is, however, much potential for a tourist industry.

Area: 10,830 sq miles/28,051 sq km
Population: 410,000
Capital: Malabo
Other major city: Bata
Form of government: Republic
Religion: RC
Currency: CFA Franc

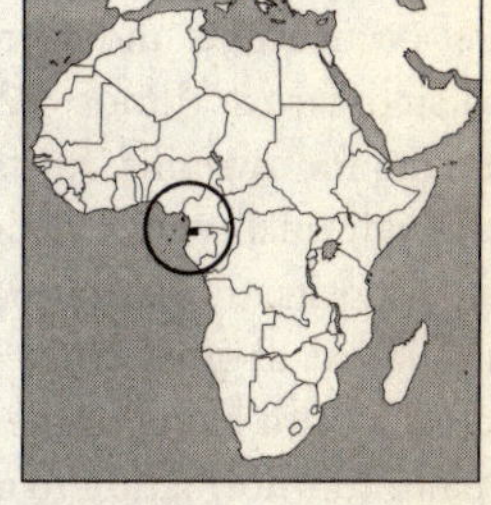

Erfurt a historical town and tourist centre in central Germany. (Pop. 195,000)

Erie, Lake the second smallest of the five Great Lakes, on the border between Canada and the USA. (9,910 sq miles/25,670 sq km)

Eritrea formerly an autonomous province of Ethiopia that gained independence in May 1993, shortly after a landslide vote in favour of sovereignty. Bounded by Djibouti, Sudan, and Ethiopia, Eritrea has acquired Ethiopia's entire coastline along the Red Sea. The small Eritrean port of Aseb, in the southeast corner of the country has, however, been designated a 'free port' guaranteeing the right of access for the now landlocked Ethiopia. Eritrea's climate is hot and dry along its desert coast but is colder and wetter in its central highland regions. Most of the population depend on subsistence farming. Future revenues may come from its developing fishing, tourism, and oil industries. Eritrea's natural resources include gold, potash, zinc, copper, salt, fish, and probably oil. Deforestation and the consequent erosion are partly responsible for the frequent droughts and resultant famines that have blighted this area in recent years. Many of the population have been displaced by famine or continuing war with Ethiopia.

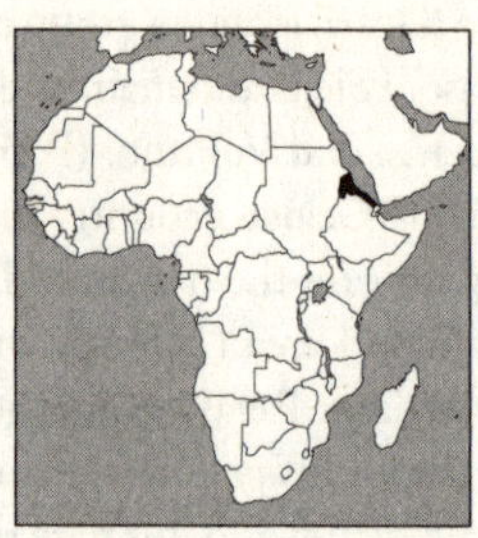

Area: 45,406 sq miles/117,600 sq km
Population: 3,280,000
Capital: Asmara (Asmera)
Other major cities: Mits'iwa, Keren, Assab (Aseb)
Form of government: Republic
Religions: Sunni Islam, Christianity
Currency: Nakfa

Essex a county in southeast England, with its administrative centre in Chelmsford. (1,419 sq miles/3,674 sq km; pop. 1,569,000)

Estonia a country that has over 1,500 islands and lies to the northwest of the Russian Federation. It is bounded to the north by the Gulf of Finland, to the west by the Baltic Sea, and to the south by Latvia and is the smallest of the three previous Soviet Baltic Republics. Agriculture and dairy farming are the chief occupations and there are nearly three hundred agricultural collectives and state farms. Almost 22 per cent of Estonia is forested, and this provides material for sawmills, furniture, match and pulp industries. The country has rich, high-quality shale deposits and phosphorous has been found near Tallinn. Peat deposits are substantial and supply some of the electric power stations. Estonia has about 72 per cent of its population living in urban areas, with almost a third living in the capital city. The economy is currently undergoing a major transformation to a free market system. Tourism and investment from the West have greatly contributed to the country's economy.

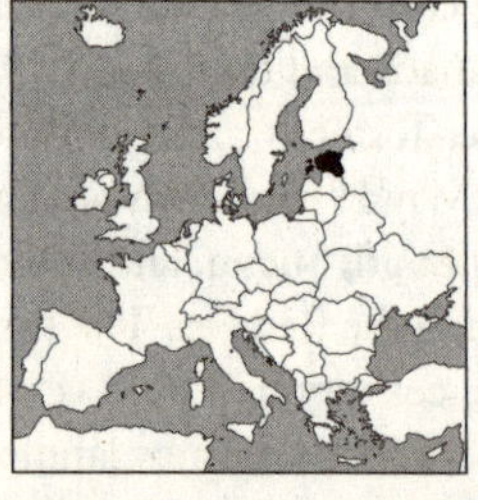

Area: 17,413 sq miles/45,227 sq km
Population: 1,454,000
Capital: Tallinn
Other major cities: Tartu, Narva
Form of government: Republic
Religions: Eastern Orthodox, Lutheranism
Currency: Kroon

Ethiopia a landlocked, East African country with borders with Sudan, Kenya, Somalia, Djibouti and Eritrea. Most of the country consists of highlands that drop sharply toward Sudan in the west. Because of the wide range of latitudes, Ethiopia has many climatic variations between the high temperate plateau and the hot humid lowlands. The country is very vulnerable to drought but in some areas thunderstorms can erode soil from the slopes, reducing the area available for crop planting. Around 80 per cent of the population are subsistence farmers, and there are mineral deposits of copper, iron, petroleum, platinum and gold, which have been exploited. Coffee is the main source of rural income and teff is the main food grain. The droughts in 1989–90 brought much famine. Employment outside agriculture is confined to a small manufacturing sector in Addis Ababa. The country has been racked with environmental, economic and political problems culminating in the loss of the province of Eritrea, which became independent in May 1993.

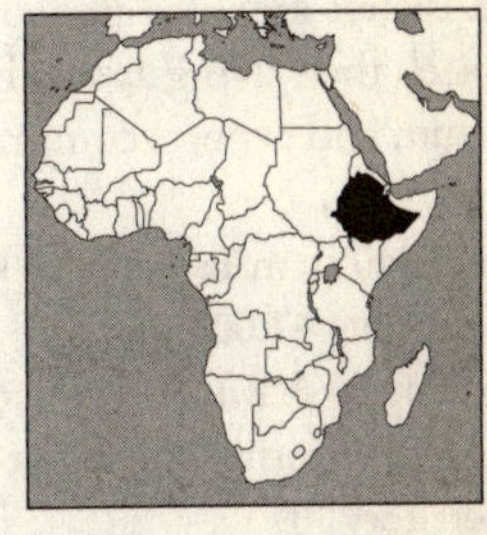

Area: 426,373 sq miles/1,104,300 sq km
Population: 58,506,000
Capital: Addis Ababa (Adis Abeba)
Other cities: Dire Dawa, Gonda, Jima
Form of government: People's Republic
Religions: Ethiopian Orthodox, Sunni Islam
Currency: Ethiopian Birr

Etna, Mount the largest volcano in Europe, situated near the east coast of Sicily, Italy, and still highly active. (10,902 ft/3,323 m)

Euboea (Evvoia) a large Greek island in the Aegean Sea lying close to the east coast of mainland Greece and joined to the mainland by a bridge. (1,411 sq miles/ 3,655 sq km; pop. 220,000)

Euphrates (Al Furat) one of the great rivers of the Middle East, flowing from its source in eastern Turkey, across Syria and central Iraq to the Persian Gulf. (Length 1,690 miles/2,720 km)

Europe a continent that is divided from Asia by a border that runs down the Ural Mountains to the Caspian Sea and then west to the Black Sea. For convenience it is commonly divided into two areas: Eastern Europe (the countries that had Communist governments after the Second World War) and Western Europe. (4,053,300 sq miles/10,498,000 sq km; pop. 728,982,000)

Everest, Mount the highest mountain in the world, situated on the border between Nepal and China in the eastern Himalayas. (29,028 ft /8,848 m)

Everglades a vast area of subtropical swampland on the western side of southern Florida, USA.

Eyre, Lake a large salt lake in South Australia. (3,400 sq miles/8,900 sq km)

F

Faeroe (Faroe) Islands (Føroyar) a self-governing territory of Denmark since 1948 which consists of a group of 18 basaltic islands situated in the North Atlantic, approximately halfway between the Shetland Islands and Iceland. The landscape of these islands is characterized by steep, stepped peaks rising out of the sea to nearly 3,000 feet (900 metres) and glaciated, trough-shaped valleys. Although the islands are inhabited, poor agricultural conditions compel the population to seek their living at sea. Fishing, including some whaling, is the main occupation, and exports comprise fish and associated products.

Area: 540 sq miles/1,399 sq km
Population: 47,000
Capital: Tørshavn
Form of government: Self-governing Danish Territory
Religion: Lutheranism
Currency: Danish Krone

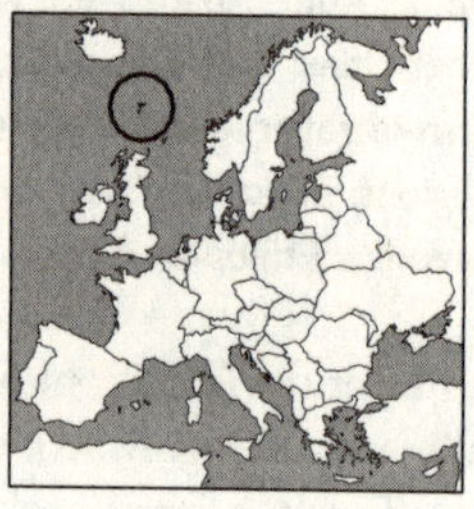

Fair Isle a small island situated between the Orkney and Shetland Islands to the north of Scotland, famous for distinctive, patterned sweaters. (Pop. 75)

Faisalabad (Lyallpur) an industrial city and agricultural centre in northeast Pakistan. (Pop. 2,191,000)

Falkirk (1) a town in central Scotland and the administrative centre of the Falkirk council area. (Pop. 36,000) (2) a council area in central Scotland. (115 sq miles/ 299 sq km; pop. 142,000)

Falkland Islands (Islas Malvinas) a British crown colony situated in the South Atlantic, consisting of two large islands (West and East Falkland), separated by the 10-mile (16-kilometre) wide Falkland Sound and surrounded by some 200 smaller islands. Lying about 410 miles (650 kilometres) east of southern Argentina, which has long laid claim to them, the islands were invaded by Argentina in 1982, but were recaptured by a British marine task force a few months later. The main economic activity is sheep farming, with open grazing on the windswept, treeless, rugged moorland that rises to over 2,295 feet (705 metres) on both main islands. The highest point is Mount Usborne at 2,313 feet (705 metres). Over recent years, substantial income has been gained from the sales of licenses to permit foreign trawlers to fish in the Falklands exclusion zone. There are also considerable offshore oil reserves available.

Area: 4,700 sq miles/12,173 sq km
Population: 2,200
Capital: Port Stanley
Form of government: British Crown Colony
Religion: Christianity
Currency: Falkland Islands Pound

Fermanagh a historical lakeland county, and a district council area in southwest Northern Ireland. (656 sq miles/1,700 sq km; pop. 54,000)

Fife a council area of eastern Scotland, with its administrative centre in Glenrothes. (511 sq miles/1,323 sq km; pop. 351,000)

Fiji one of the largest nations in the western Pacific, consisting of some 800 islands and atolls of which only about 100 are inhabited. It is situated around the 180-degree International Date Line and lies about 17 degrees south of the equator. Fiji has high rainfall, high temperatures, and plenty of sunshine all year round. The two main islands, Viti Levu and Vanua Levu, are extinct volcanoes, and most of the islands in the group are fringed with coral reefs. The southeast of the islands have tropical rainforests but a lot of lumber has been felled and soil erosion is a growing problem. The main cash crop is sugar cane although copra, ginger, and fish are also exported. Tourism is now a major industry and source of revenue although it was adversely affected by political coups in the late 1980s. In 1993, Cyclone Kina caused great destruction to agriculture and the general infrastructure.

Area: 7,056 sq miles/18,274 sq km
Population: 797,000
Capital: Suva
Form of government: Republic
Religions: Christianity, Hinduism
Currency: Fijian Dollar

Finistère the department of France occupying the tip of the Brittany Peninsula. (Pop. 870,000)

Finisterre, Cape the northwest corner of Spain.

Finland a Scandinavian country that shares borders with Sweden, Norway, and the Russian Federation. Its coastline lies along the Gulf of Bothnia and the Gulf of Finland, both of which are arms of the Baltic Sea. Some 30,000 islands and islets line Finland's coast. Finnish Lappland in the north lies within the Arctic Circle. Most of mainland Finland is low-lying, becoming more hilly towards the north. Almost three-quarters of the country is forested, comprising mainly coniferous trees such as spruce and pine, and there are many thousands of lakes. The climate has great extremes between summer and winter. Winter is very severe and lasts about six months (but only for three months in the south). Summers are short but quite warm, with light rain throughout the country. Finland is largely self-sufficient in food and produces great surpluses of dairy produce. Most crops are grown in the southwest. In the north, reindeer are herded and forests yield great quantities of lumber for export. Just under 20 per cent of the electricity was supplied by its hydroelectric power stations in the early 1990s. Major industries are lumber products, wood pulp and paper, machinery, and shipbuilding, which developed because of the country's great need for an efficient fleet of ice-breakers. Finland has an efficient transport system utilizing canals, road, rail, and air services.

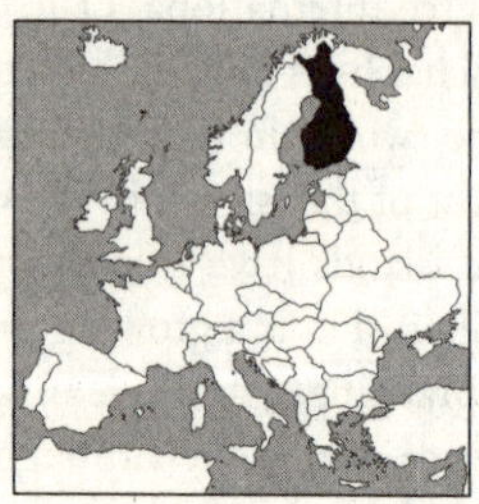

Area: 130,559 sq miles/338,145 sq km
Population: 5,205,000
Capital: Helsinki (Helsingfors)
Other major cities: Turku, Tampere
Form of government: Republic
Religion: Lutheranism
Currency: Euro

Finland, Gulf of the easternmost arm of the Baltic Sea, with Finland to the north, St Petersburg at its eastern end, and Estonia to the south.

Flanders (Vlaanderen, Flandre) a Flemish-speaking coastal region of northern Belgium, now divided into two provinces, East and West Flanders. (2361 sq miles/ 6,115 sq km; pop. 2,499,000)

Flinders Range a range of mountains in the eastern part of South Australia, stretching over 250 miles (400 kilometres). St Mary Peak is the highest (3,898 ft/1,188 m).

Flintshire a council area in northeast Wales, with its administrative centre in the town of Mold. (169 sq miles/437 sq km; pop. 145,000)

Flores a volcanic island in the Lesser Sunda Islands in Indonesia, lying in the chain due east of Java. (6,622 sq miles/17,150 sq km; pop. 803,000)

Flores Sea a stretch of the Pacific Ocean between Flores and Sulawesi.

Florida a state occupying the peninsula in the southeastern corner of the USA. The state capital is Tallahassee. (158,560 sq miles/51,670 sq km; pop. 16,817,000)

Florida, Straits of the waterway which separates the southern tip of Florida, USA, from Cuba some 90 miles (145 kilometres) to the south.

Fly a largely navigable river flowing south from the central mountains in western Papua New Guinea to its broad estuary on the Gulf of Papua. (Length 750 miles/1,200 km)

France the largest country in western Europe, with a coastline on the English Channel, the Mediterranean Sea and on the Atlantic Ocean. The lowest parts of the country are the great basins of the north and southwest from which it rises to the Massif Central and the higher Alps, Jura and Pyrénées. Climate ranges from moderate maritime in the northwest to Mediterranean in the south. Farming is possible in all parts of France, with forestry and fishing also providing some employment. The western shores are ideal for rearing livestock, while the Paris Basin is good arable land. In the southwest around Bordeaux, vineyards produce some of the world's best wines. The main industrial area of France is in the north and east and the main industries are iron and steel, engineering, chemicals, textiles, and electrical goods. France has a long cultural history of art, literature, sculpture, and music, and is famous for its immense Gothic churches.

Area: 212,935 sq miles/551,500 sq km
Population: 58,375,000
Capital: Paris
Other major cities: Bordeaux, Lyons, Marseilles, Toulouse
Form of government: Republic
Religion: RC
Currency: Euro

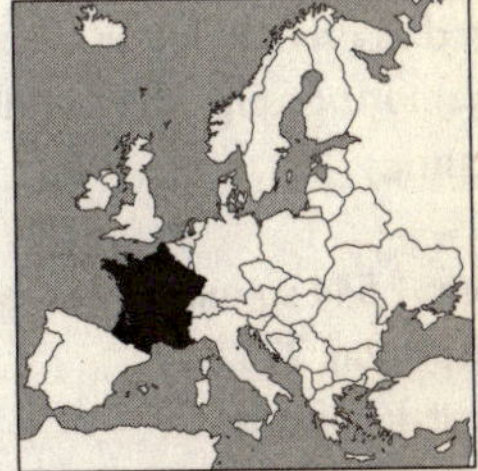

Fraser a river flowing through southern British Columbia, Canada, from its source in the Rocky Mountains to the Strait of Georgia by Vancouver. (Length 850 miles/1,370 km)

Free State one of South Africa's nine provinces, in central South Africa, formerly Orange Free State, with its administrative centre in Bloemfontein. (49,992 sq miles/129,480 sq km; pop. 2,928,000)

French Guiana (Guyane) situated on the northeast coast of South America and still a French Overseas Department, French Guiana is bounded to the south and east by Brazil and to the west by Suriname. The climate is tropical with heavy rainfall. French Guiana's economy relies almost completely on subsidies from France. It has little to export apart from shrimps, and the small area of land that is cultivated produces rice, manioc, and sugar cane. Recently the French have tried to develop the tourist industry and exploit the extensive reserves of hardwood in the jungle interior. This has led to a growing sawmill industry and the export of logs. Natural resources, in addition to lumber, include bauxite, cinnabar (mercury ore), and gold (although this is in scattered deposits). The Ariane rocket launch site of the European Union Space Agency is located at Kourou, on the north coast.

Area: 34,749 sq miles/90,000 sq km
Population: 153,000
Capital: Cayenne
Form of government: French Overseas Department
Religion: RC
Currency: Euro

French Polynesia a total of about 130 islands in the South Pacific Ocean administered as French overseas territories. The islands include the Society Islands, the Tuamotu group, the Gambier group, the Tubual Islands, and the Marquesas Islands.

Area: 1,544 sq miles/4,000 sq km
Population: 223,000
Capital: Papeete
Form of government: Overseas Territory of France
Religions: Protestantism, RC
Currency: Pacific Franc

French Southern and Antarctic Territories a set of remote and widely scattered territories in Antarctica and the Antarctic Ocean administered by France. They include the Crozet Islands and Kerguelen.

Frisian (Friesian) Islands a string of sandy, low-lying islands that line the coasts in the southeastern corner of the North Sea. The West Frisians (including Terchelling and Texel) belong to the Netherlands; the East Frisians (including Borkum and Norderney) belong to Germany; and the North Frisians are divided between Germany and Denmark.

Fuji, Mount (Fujiyama) the highest peak in Japan, a distinctive volcanic cone 62 miles (100 kilometres) to the southwest of Tokyo. (12,389 ft/3,776 m)

Fujian (Fukien) a coastal province in southeast China. The capital is Fuzhou. (46,350 sq miles/120,000 sq km; pop. 36,213,000)

Fundy, Bay of lies between Nova Scotia and New Brunswick, Canada. It has the world's largest tidal range – 50 feet (15 metres) between low and high tide.

Fyn (Fünen) the second largest of the islands of Denmark, in the centre of the country. (1,048 sq miles/2,976 sq km; pop. 478,000)

G

Gabès, Gulf of an inlet of the Mediterranean Sea which, with the Gulf of Sirte to the east, makes a deep indent in the coast of North Africa.

Gabon a small country in west central Africa that straddles the equator. It has a low narrow coastal plain, with the rest of the country comprising a low plateau. Three-quarters of Gabon is covered by dense tropical forest. The climate is hot, humid, and typically equatorial, with little seasonal variation. It was in Lambaréné that Albert Schweitzer, the medical missionary, had his hospital. Until the 1960s lumber was virtually Gabon's only resource and then oil was discovered. By the mid-1980s, it was Africa's sixth largest oil producer, and other minerals, such as manganese, uranium, and iron ore, were being exploited. Deposits of lead and silver have also been discovered. Around two-thirds of the Gabonese people remain subsistence farmers, growing cassava, sugar cane, plantains, and yams. The country has great tourist potential but because of the dense hardwood forests, transport links with the uninhabited interior are very difficult.

Area: 103,347 sq miles/267,668 sq km
Population: 1,106,000
Capital: Libreville
Other major city: Port Gentile
Form of government: Republic
Religions: RC, traditional African religions
Currency: CFA Franc

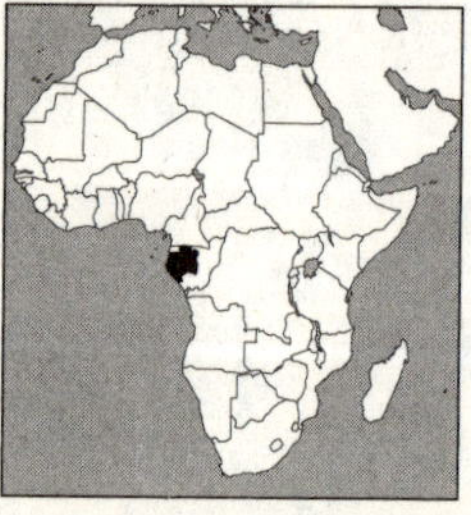

Galapagos Islands a group of 15 islands on the Equator administered by Ecuador, but located some 680 miles (1,100 kilometres) to the west of that country. (3,016 sq miles/7,812 sq km; pop. 16,000)

Galicia a region in the very northwest corner of Spain.

Galilee the most northerly region of Israel, bordering Lebanon and Syria, with the Sea of Galilee (Lake Tiberias) on its eastern side.

Gallipoli (Gelibolu) the peninsula and port on the northern side of the Dardanelles in Turkey.

Galway a county in the central part of the west coast of the Republic of Ireland. The county town is also called Galway, or Galway City. (2,293 sq miles/5,940 sq km; pop. county 197,000/town 60,000)

Gambia (1) the smallest country in Africa, which pokes like a crooked finger into Senegal. The country is divided along its entire length by the River Gambia, which can be crossed at only two main ferry crossings. On the coast, there are pristine beaches and sand cliffs backed by mangrove swamps, with tropical jungle clothing many of the river banks away from the coast. Gambia has two very different seasons. In the dry season there is little rainfall, but then the southwest monsoon sets in, with spectacular storms producing heavy rain for four months. Most Gambians live in villages with a few animals, and grow enough millet and sorghum to feed themselves. Groundnuts are the main and only export crop of any significance. The river provides a thriving local fishing industry, and the white sandy beaches on the coast are becoming increasingly popular with foreign tourists, although a military takeover in 1994 dealt tourism and trade a severe blow. (2) a major river of West Africa, flowing into the Atlantic Ocean from its source in Guinea, through Senegal and Gambia. (Length 300 miles/483 km)

Area: 4,361 sq miles/11,295 sq km
Population: 1,141,000
Capital: Banjul
Form of government: Republic
Religions: Sunni Islam, Christianity
Currency: Dalasi

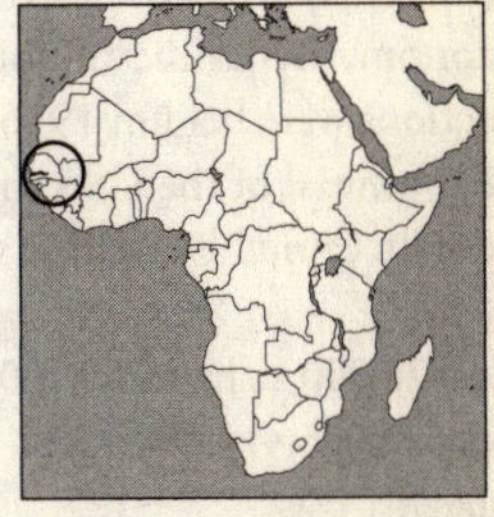

Ganges (Ganga) the holy river of the Hindus, flowing from its source in the Himalayas, across northern India and forming a delta in Bangladesh as it flows into the Bay of Bengal. (Length 1,568 miles/2,525 km)

Gansu a mountainous province in northern central China; the capital is Lanzhou. (170,000 sq miles/450,000 sq km; pop. 27,069,000)

Garonne a major river of southwestern France, flowing north from the central Pyrenees to the Gironde estuary. (Length 355 miles/575 km)

Gascony (Gascogne) the historical name of an area in the southwestern corner of France bordering Spain.

Gauteng one of South Africa's nine provinces, in north central South Africa, once part of the former province of Transvaal, with its administrative centre in Johannesburg. (7,262 sq miles/18,810 sq km; pop. 7,048,000)

Gazankulu one of ten former South African Homelands, the area is now part of the provinces of Mpumalanga and Limpopo in northeast South Africa.

Gaza Strip a strip of coastal land stretching from the Egyptian border to the Mediterranean port of Gaza and bordering with Israel to its east and north. It was administered by Egypt after the creation of Israel in 1948, becoming home to numerous Palestinian refugees, and was taken over by Israel in the Six-Day War of 1967. In 1994, it was placed under the jurisdiction of the Palestinian National Authority. (Pop. 1,054,000)

Georgia (1) a republic in the southwest of the former USSR, occupying the central and western parts of the Caucasus. It shares borders with Turkey, Armenia, Azerbaijan, and the Russian Federation. It is bounded to the west by the Black Sea. Almost 40 per cent of the country is covered by forests. Agriculture, which is the main occupation of the population, includes tea cultivation and fruit growing, especially citrus fruits and viticulture. The republic is rich in minerals, especially manganese, but imports the majority of its energy needs. Industries include coal, lumber, machinery, chemicals, silk, food processing, and furniture. In the past, the Black Sea tourist trade exploited the country's wealth of thermal and mineral springs very successfully, and tourism should again become an economic mainstay. Georgia declared itself independent in 1991. A struggle for regional autonomy by ethnic minorities led to much disruption and violent conflict. Elections were held in 1995, heralding some progress and reform. (2) a state in the southeast of the USA, named after George II by English colonists in 1733; the state capital is Atlanta. (58,876 sq miles/152,490 sq km; pop. 8,584,000)

Area: 26,900 sq miles/69,700 sq km
Population: 5,411,000
Capital: T'bilisi
Other major cities: Kutaisi, Rustavi, Batumi
Form of government: Republic
Religions: Georgian and Russian Orthodox, Sunni Islam
Currency: Lari

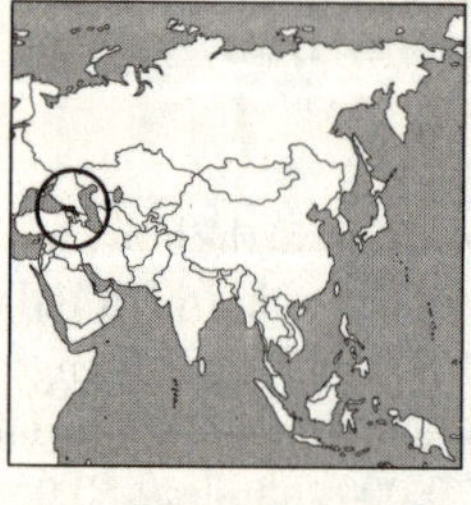

Georgia, Strait of the southern part of the stretch of water which separates Vancouver Island from the coast of British Columbia in Canada.

Germany a large populous country in northern central Europe that comprises the former East and West German Republics, unified in 1990. In the north, is the North German Plain, which merges with the North Rhinelands in the west. Farther south, a plateau that stretches across the country from east to west is divided by the River Rhine. In the southwest, the Black Forest separates the Rhine Valley from the fertile valleys and scarplands of Swabia. More recently, coniferous forests have suffered from acid rain caused by industrial pollution. The Bohemian Uplands and Erz Mountains mark the border with the Czech Republic. Generally the country has warm summers and cold winters. Agricultural products include wheat, rye, barley, oats, potatoes, and sugar beet, although agriculture accounts for only a small percentage of employment and a third of the country's food has to be imported. The main industrial and most densely populated areas are in the Ruhr Valley. Products of the principal manufacturing industries include iron and steel, motor vehicles, mechanical and electrical equipment, aircraft, ships, computers, electronic and technical goods, chemicals and petrochemicals, pharmaceuticals, textiles, clothing and footwear, foods, beer, optical and high precision instruments.

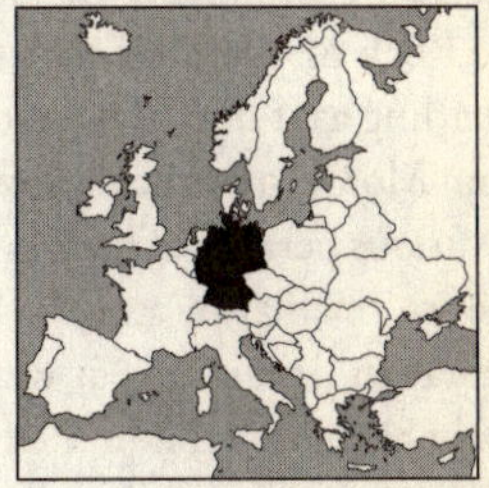

Area: 137,735 sq miles/356,733 sq km
Population: 81,912,000
Capital: Berlin
Other major cities: Cologne, Frankfurt, Hamburg, Leipzig, Munich, Stuttgart
Form of government: Republic
Religions: Lutheranism, RC
Currency: Euro

Ghana a country located on the southern coast of West Africa between Côte d'Ivoire and Togo. In 1957, as the former British Gold Coast, it became the first African state to achieve independence from European colonial rule. It has palm-fringed beaches of white sand along the Gulf of Guinea and where the great River Volta meets the sea there are peaceful blue lagoons. The climate on the coast is equatorial, and towards the north there are steamy tropical evergreen forests which give way in the far north to tropical savannah. The landscape becomes harsh and barren near the border with Burkina Faso. Most Ghanaians are village dwellers whose homes are made of locally available materials. The south of the country has been most exposed to European influence and it is here that cocoa, rubber, palm oil, and coffee are grown. Ghana's most important crop is cocoa and others include coffee, palm kernels, coconut oil, copra, shea nuts, and bananas which are all exported. Fishing is also of major importance and has increased in recent years. Ghana has important mineral resources, notably gold, diamonds, manganese and bauxite. Most of Ghana's towns are in the south.

Area: 92,100 sq miles/238,537 sq km
Population: 17,460,000
Capital: Accra
Other cities: Kumasi, Tamale, Sekondi-Takoradi
Form of government: Republic
Religions: Protestantism, traditional African religions, RC
Currency: Cedi

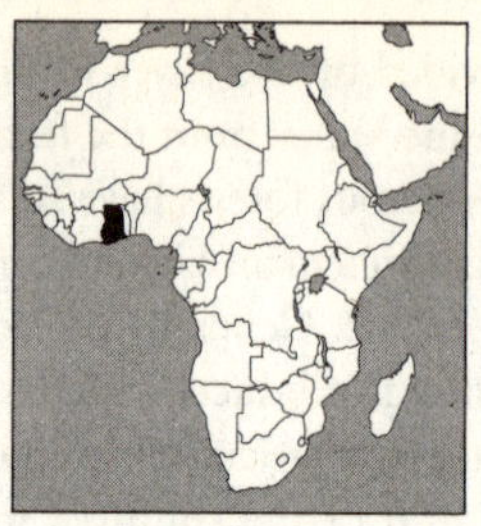

Ghats the two ranges of mountains that line the coasts of the Deccan Peninsula in India: the Eastern Ghats, rising to about 2,000 feet (600 metres), and the Western Ghats rising to 5,000 feet (1,500 metres).

Gibraltar a self-governing former British Crown Colony that is still linked politically with Britain, on the southwestern tip of Spain, where a limestone hill called the Rock of Gibraltar rises to 1,394 feet (425 metres). Its strategic importance, guarding as it does the western approaches to the Mediterranean and separated from Morocco by the narrow Straits of Gibraltar, has resulted in it being occupied at various periods of history by Phoenicians, Carthaginians, Romans, Visigoths, Moors, Spaniards, and the British. In 1713, the Treaty of Utrecht awarded Gibraltar to Britain and it was a British Crown Colony from 1830 to 1969, but Spain has never relinquished its claim to the Rock and relations have at times been difficult. English is the official language, although Spanish is also spoken. The British armed forces, tourism, banking, and construction are the main sources of employment and most imports are from Britain. The Mediterranean climate and many sites of natural and historical interest attract numerous visitors each year. (2.5 sq miles/6.5 sq km; pop. 29,000; cur. Gibraltar Pound)

Gibraltar, Strait of the narrow waterway, 8 miles (13 kilometres) at its narrowest, which connects the Mediterranean Sea to the Atlantic Ocean, with Spain to the north and Morocco to the south.

Gibson Desert a desert of sand and salt marshes in western central Australia, between the Great Sandy Desert and the Victoria Desert.

Gilgit a mountain district in northern Pakistan, noted for its great beauty. The small town of Gilgit perches startlingly beneath a dramatic rock face. (Pop. town 9,000)

Gironde the long, thin estuary stretching some 50 miles (80 kilometres) which connects the Rivers Dordogne and Garonne to the Atlantic coast of southwest France.

Glamorgan a former county of south Wales.

Glasgow (1) a major industrial city and important cultural centre on the River Clyde in central Scotland, also the administrative centre for the City of Glasgow council area. It is the largest city in Scotland. (Pop. 663,000) (2) **City of** a council area in central Scotland. (68 sq miles/175 sq km; pop. 624,000)

Gloucestershire a county in southwest England, with administrative centre in Gloucester. (1,217 sq miles/3153 sq km; pop. 769,000)

Goa a territory on the west coast of India, 250 miles (400 kilometres) south of Bombay, which was captured by Portugal in 1510 and remained under Portuguese control until it was annexed by India in 1961. (1,429 sq miles/ 3,702 sq km; pop. 1,370,000)

Gobi Desert a vast expanse of arid land which occupies much of Mongolia and central northern China. (500,000 sq miles/1,295,000 sq km)

Godavari a river which runs eastwards across the middle of the Deccan Peninsula in India. (Length 910 miles/1,465 km)

Golan Heights a range of high hills in southwest Syria on the border with northern Israel. Under Syrian control until they were taken by Israeli forces in 1967, possession is still disputed between Syria and Israel.

Gold Coast (1) the name given to a string of beach resorts in Australia, on the east coast of Queensland to the south of Brisbane. (2) the former name of Ghana (until 1957).

Golden Triangle the remote and mountainous region where the borders of Thailand, Myanmar and Laos meet, noted in particular for its opium cultivation and as one of the world's main sources of the drug heroin.

Good Hope, Cape of the tip of the narrow Cape Peninsula which extends from the southwestern corner of South Africa.

Gotland a Swedish island in the Baltic Sea off the southeast coast of Sweden. (1,210 sq miles/3,140 sq km; pop. 57,000)

Grampian a former region of northeastern Scotland.

Grampian Mountains a range of mountains that stretch across northern Scotland to the south of Loch Ness. The mountains rise to their highest point at Ben Nevis (4,409 ft/1,344 m), the highest peak in the UK.

Grand Canyon the dramatic gorge of the Colorado River, in places over 1 mile (1.5 kilometres) deep, in northwestern Arizona, USA.

Great Australian Bight the arm of the Antarctic Ocean which forms the deep indentation in the centre of the southern coastline of Australia.

Great Australian Desert the collective word for the deserts that occupy much of the centre of Australia. (1,480,000 sq miles/3,830,000 sq km)

Great Barrier Reef the world's most extensive coral reef which lines the coast of Queensland, Australia, stretching some 1,250 miles (2,000 kilometres).

Great Bear Lake the fourth largest lake in North America, in northwest Canada. It drains into the Mackenzie River. (12,028 sq miles/31,153 sq km)

Great Britain the island shared by England, Scotland and Wales, and which forms the principal part of the United Kingdom of Great Britain and Northern Ireland.

Great Dividing Range a range of mountains which runs down the east coast of Australia, from Queensland in the north, across New South Wales to Victoria in the south, some 2,250 miles (3,600 kilometres) in all. The highest point is Mount Kosciusko at 7,316 feet (2,230 metres).

Greater Sunda Islands a group of islands in the western Malay Archipelago, forming the larger part of the Sunda Islands and consisting of Borneo, Sumatra, Java and Sulawesi.

Great Lakes the largest group of freshwater lakes in the world, drained by the St Lawrence River. There are five lakes, four of which (Lakes Huron, Superior, Erie and Ontario) are on the border of Canada and the USA; the fifth (Lake Michigan) is in the USA.

Great Plains a vast area in North America of flat and undulating grassland east of the Rocky Mountains and stretching from northern Canada to Texas, USA. It includes the Prairies, most of which are now ploughed for cereal and fodder crops.

Great Rift Valley a series of geological faults which has created a depression stretching 4,000 miles/6,400 kilometres) from the valley of the River Jordan across the Red Sea and down East Africa to Mozambique.

Great Salt Lake a salt lake in northwest Utah, USA, lying just to the northwest of Salt Lake City. (2,000 sq miles/5,200 sq km)

Great Sandy Desert the desert region in the north of Western Australia.

Great Slave Lake a lake drained by the Mackenzie River in the southern part of the Northwest Territories of Canada. (11,030 sq miles/28,570 sq km)

Great Smoky Mountains part of the Appalachian Mountains, running along the border between Tennessee and North Carolina, USA. The highest point is Clingmans Dome (6,643 ft/2,025 m).

Great Victoria Desert a vast area of sand dunes straddling the border between Western Australia and South Australia.

Greece the Greek Peninsula is the most southeasterly extension of Europe, and has over 1,400 islands lying off its coast and scattered throughout the Aegean Sea. Mainland Greece shares borders with Albania in the northwest, Macedonia and Bulgaria in the north, and Turkey in the northeast. The northwestern and central regions of the country are rugged and mountainous, the main chain being the Pindus Mountains. About 70 per cent of the land is hilly, with harsh mountain climates and poor soils, and there are few natural resources of economic value although there are deposits of petroleum and natural gas found under the Aegean Sea. The Greek islands and coastal regions have a typical

Mediterranean climate, with mild rainy winters and hot dry summers. Winter in the northern mountains is severe, with deep snow and heavy precipitation. Around 21 per cent of the people are engaged in agriculture, mostly on small family farms. Forestry and fishing are carried out on a small scale. Greece has undergone a rapid process of industrialization since the Second World War, and pollution is a serious problem in some areas. Tourism is a major source of revenue for the country along with shipping.

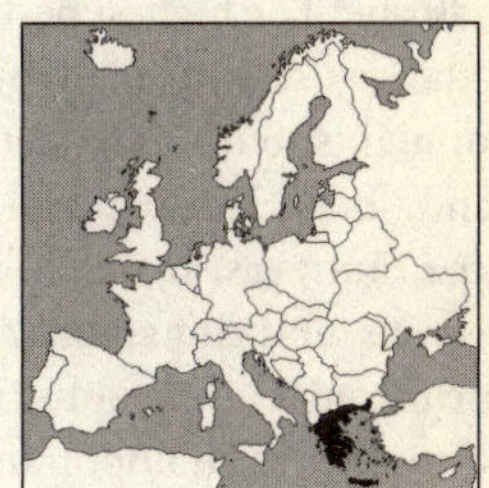

Area: 50,949 sq miles/131,957 sq km
Population: 10,475,000
Capital: Athens (Athínai)
Other cities: Iráklion, Patras, Piraeus, Thessaloníki
Form of government: Republic
Religion: Greek Orthodox
Currency: Euro

Greenland (Kalaallit Nunaat) the largest island in the world (discounting continental land masses). It lies mainly within the Arctic Circle, off the northeast coast of Canada. Its vast interior is mostly covered with a permanent ice cap that has a known thickness of up to 11,000 feet (3,300 metres). The ice-free coastal strips are characterized by largely barren mountains, rising to Gunnbjorn at 12,140 feet (3,700 metres) in the southeast. Glaciers flow into deeply indented fjords which are fringed by many islands, islets and icebergs. Of the small ice-free fringe, only about a third can be classed as being inhabited, mainly in the southwest. The largely Eskimo population is heavily dependent on fishing for its livelihood, and fish account for 95 per cent of exports. There is some sheep farming, and mining of coal and mineral resources as well as iron ore, lead, zinc, uranium, and molybdenum.

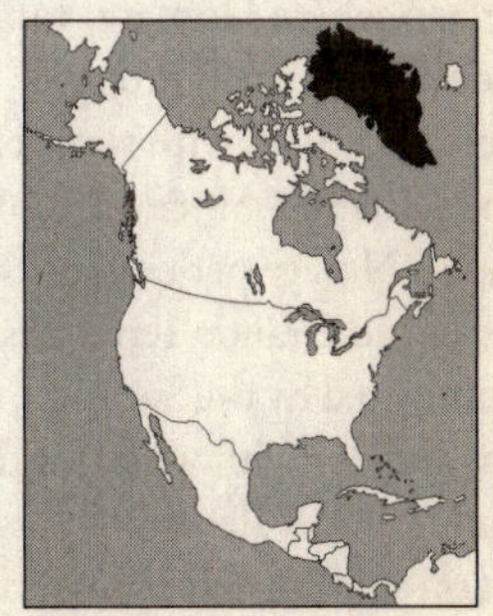

Area: 840,000 sq miles/2,175,600 sq km
Population: 58,200
Capital: Godthåb (Nuuk)
Form of government: Self-governing region of Denmark
Religion: Lutheranism
Currency: Danish Krone

Greenwich a Greater London borough, on the south bank of the River Thames in England. It was the site of the original Royal Observatory, and since 1884 it has been accepted that Greenwich Mean Time is the time at 0° longitude, against which all world time differences are measured.

Grenada the most southerly of the Windward Islands chain in the Caribbean. Its territory includes the southern Grenadine Islands to the north. The main island consists of the remains of extinct volcanoes and has an attractive wooded landscape. The highest peak is Mount St Catherine at 2,750 feet (838 metres). In the dry season, the typical climate is very pleasant, with warm days and cool nights, but in the wet season it is hot day and night. Agriculture is the island's main industry and the chief crops grown for export are citrus fruits, cocoa, nutmegs, bananas, and mace. Other crops grown are cloves, cotton, coconuts, and cinnamon. Apart from the processing of its crops, Grenada has little manufacturing industry. Grenada is a popular port of call for cruise ships, and tourism is an important source of foreign revenue.

Area: 133 sq miles/344 sq km
Population: 92,000
Capital: St George's
Form of government: Independent State within the Commonwealth
Religions: RC, Anglicanism, Methodism
Currency: East Caribbean Dollar

Grenadines a string of some 600 small islands in the Caribbean that lie between St Vincent to the north and Grenada to the south. Most of them belong to St Vincent, but the largest, Carriacou, is divided between St Vincent and Grenada.

Guadalcanal an island in the southwest Pacific, at the southern end of the archipelago where Honiara, capital of the Solomon Islands, is located.

Guadeloupe a small group of islands in the Caribbean lying in the middle of the Lesser Antilles, with some islands in the Leeward Islands and some in the Windward Islands. Since 1946, Guadeloupe has been an French Overseas Department. Ninety per cent of the population live on the two main islands of Basse Terre and Grande Terre. Basse Terre is mountainous, covered with rainforest, and dominated by the Soufrière volcano at 4,318 feet (1,467 metres). Grande Terre is flat and dry with white sandy beaches. The other islands include Marie Galante, La Désirade, Îles des Saints, St Barthélémy, and St Martin. The islands have a warm and humid climate with rainfall heaviest between May and November.

Main exports include bananas, sugar, and rum. (658 sq miles/1,705 sq km; pop. 431,000; cur. Euro)

Guam the most southerly and the largest of the Mariana Islands in the northwest Pacific. It consists mainly of a high, coraline limestone plateau with some low volcanic mountains in the south of the island. Guam's climate is tropical with a rainy season from July to December. An unincorporated territory of the USA, its economy depends to a large extent on government activities and military installations account for some 35 per cent of the land area of the island. Exports include copra, palm oil, and processed fish. The country has also become a financial centre, particularly for mainland and Asian banks, and tourism has come to play an important role in its economy. (212 sq miles/549 sq km; pop. 153,000; cur. US Dollar)

Guangdong a province of southeast China. The capital is Guangzhou (Canton). (81,000 sq miles/210,000 sq km; pop. 74,017,000)

Guangxi-Zhuang an autonomous region of southern China on the border with Vietnam. To the south of the city of Guilin, around the Gui Jiang River, is a famous landscape of towering rock hills which rise up from the watery plains. The regional capital is Nanning. (89,000 sq miles/230,000 sq km; pop. 50,541,000)

Guatemala a country situated between the Pacific Ocean and the Caribbean Sea where North America meets Central America. It is mountainous, with a ridge of volcanoes running parallel to the Pacific coast. It has a tropical climate with little or no variation in temperature and a distinctive wet season. The Pacific slopes of the mountains are exceptionally well watered and fertile, and it is here that most of the population is settled. Coffee growing on the lower slopes dominates the economy, although bananas, sugar, cardamom, petroleum, and shellfish are exported. The forested area of the country, about 36 per cent, plays an important part in the country's economy, and there are also deposits of petroleum and zinc, while lead and silver are mined. Industry is mainly restricted to the processing of the country's agricultural products. Most trade is with the USA. Guatemala is politically unstable and civil conflict has practically destroyed tourism.

Area: 42,042 sq miles/108,889 sq km
Population: 10,928,000
Capital: Guatemala City
Other cities: Cobán, Puerto Barrios, Quezaltenango
Form of government: Republic
Religion: RC
Currency: Quetzal

Guernsey one of the Channel Islands, lying in the centre of the group and some 30 miles (50 kilometres) off the coast of France. The capital is St Peter Port. (30 sq miles/78 sq km; pop. 63,000)

Guinea formerly a French West African territory, Guinea is located on the coast at the 'bulge' in Africa. It is a lush green beautiful country about the same size as the United Kingdom. It has a tropical climate with constant heat and a high rainfall near the coast. Its principal rivers are the Gambia and the Bafing while the River Niger rises in the forests of the Guinea Highlands. Guinea has great agricultural potential, and many of the coastal swamps and forested plains have been cleared for the cultivation of rice, cassava, yams, maize, and vegetables. Around 80 per cent of the population are subsistence farmers. Although the country has eight national languages, the official language is French. Further inland, on the plateau of Fouta Djallon, dwarf cattle are raised, and in the valleys bananas and pineapples are grown. Coffee and kola nuts are important cash crops grown in the Guinea Highlands to the southwest. Minerals such as bauxite, of which there are substantial reserves, iron ore, diamonds, gold, and uranium are mined but further development is hampered by a lack of transport.

Area: 94,926 sq miles/245,857 sq km
Population: 7,518,000
Capital: Conakry
Other major cities: Kankan, Labé
Form of government: Republic
Religion: Sunni Islam
Currency: Guinea Franc

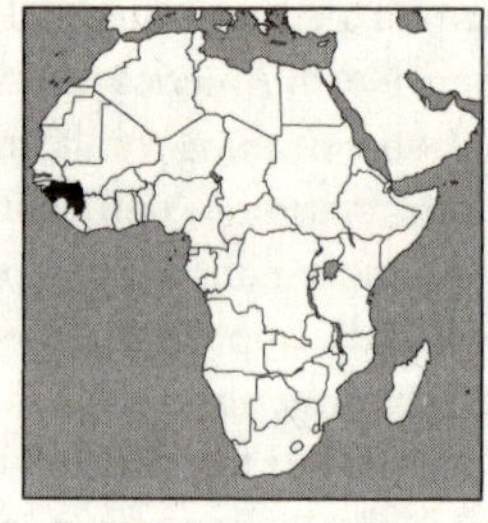

Guinea-Bissau formerly a Portuguese territory but granted independence in 1974, Guinea-Bissau is located south of Senegal on the Atlantic coast of West Africa. The republic's territory includes over 60 coastal islands, including the archipelago of Bijagós. It is a country of stunning scenery and rises from a deeply indented and island-fringed coastline to a low inland plateau and hills on the border with neighbouring Guinea. The climate is tropical, with abundant rain from June to November but hot dry conditions for the rest of the year. Years of Portuguese rule and civil war have left Guinea-Bissau impoverished, and it is one of the poorest West African states. The country's main aim is to become self-sufficient in food, and the main crops grown by the subsistence farmers are rice, groundnuts, cassava, sugar cane, plantains, maize, and coconuts. Fishing is an important export industry although cashew nuts are the principal export.

Peanuts, palm tree products, and cotton are also a source of export revenue.

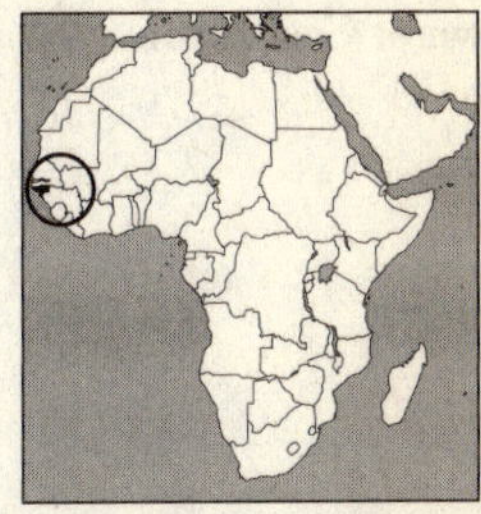

Area: 13,948 sq miles/36,125 sq km
Population: 1,091,000
Capital: Bissau (Bissão)
Form of government: Republic
Religions: traditional African religions, Sunni Islam
Currency: Guinea-Bissau Peso

Guinea, Gulf of the arm of the Atlantic Ocean which creates the deep, right-angled indent in the west coast of Africa.

Guizhou a province of southwest China, between the Rivers Yangtze and Xi. The capital is Guiyang. (170,000 sq km/65,600 sq miles; pop. 38,372,000)

Gujarat a state in northwest India, on the border with Pakistan. The capital is Gandhinagar. (75,665 sq miles/196,024 sq km; pop. 51,585,000)

Guyana the only English-speaking country in South America, situated on the northeast coast of the continent on the Atlantic Ocean. Guyana was formerly called British Guiana but achieved independence in 1966. The country is intersected by many rivers and the coastal area comprises tidal marshes and mangrove swamps. Rice is grown on this narrow coastal area and vast plantations produce sugar. The jungle in the southwest has potential for the production of minerals, hardwood, and hydroelectric power, but 90 per cent of the population live in the coastal area where the climate is moderated by sea breezes. Sugar and its by-products, and rice are the mainstay of the country's economy, while tropical fruits and vegetables, such as coconuts, citrus, coffee, and corn, are grown mainly for home consumption. Large numbers of livestock including cattle, sheep, pigs, and chickens are also raised. Guyana's principal mineral is bauxite, with gold, manganese, and diamonds also being exploited.

Area: 83,000 sq miles/214,969 sq km
Population: 838,000
Capital: Georgetown
Other major city: New Amsterdam
Form of government: Cooperative Republic
Religions: Hinduism, Protestantism, RC
Currency: Guyana Dollar

Guyane *see* **French Guiana.**

Gwynedd a council area in northwest Wales, with its administrative centre in the town of Caernarfon. (869 sq miles/2,550 sq km; pop. 118,000)

H

Hainan Island (Hainan Dao) a large tropical island in the South China Sea belonging to China, and the southernmost extremity of that country. (13,000 sq miles/ 33,670 sq km; pop. 8,035,000)

Haiti occupying the western third of the large island of Hispaniola in the Caribbean, Haiti is a mountainous country consisting of five different ranges, the highest point reaching 8,793 feet (2,680 metres) at Pic La Selle. The mountain ranges are separated by deep valleys and plains. The climate is tropical but semi-arid conditions can occur in the lee of the central mountains. Hurricanes and severe thunderstorms are a common occurrence. Only a third of the country is arable, yet agriculture is the chief occupation, with around 80 per cent of the population concentrated in rural areas. Many farmers grow only enough to feed their own families, and the export crops of coffee, sugar, and sisal are grown on large estates. Severe soil erosion caused by extensive forest clearance has resulted in a decline in crop yields and environmental damage has been caused. The country has only limited amounts of natural resources, bauxite not now being commercially profitable, although deposits of salt, copper, and gold exist. Haiti is the poorest country in the Americas and has experienced many uprisings and attempted coups.

Area: 10,714 sq miles/27,750 sq km
Population: 7,336,000
Capital: Port-au-Prince
Other cities: Cap-Haïtien, Les Cayes, Gonaïves
Form of government: Republic
Religions: RC, Voodooism
Currency: Gourde

Hamersley Range a range of mountains in Western Australia. The highest peak is Mount Bruce (4,052 ft/1,235 m).

Hamhung (Hamheung) a port and industrial city on the east coast of North Korea. (Pop. 821,000)

Hampshire a county of central southern England, with its administrative centre in Winchester. (1,456 sq miles/3,773 sq km; pop. 1,605,000)

Haryana a state in northwest India, formed in 1966. (17,066 sq miles/ 44,212 sq km; pop. 21,495,000)

Harz Mountains a range of mountains, noted for their forests, in central Germany. The highest peak is Brocken (3,747 ft/1,142 m).

Hatteras, Cape the tip of a chain of islands lining the coast of North Carolina, USA, notorious for its violent weather.

Hawaii a group of 122 islands just to the south of the Tropic of Cancer, some 2,300 miles (3,700 kilometres) from the coast of California. Since 1959, they have formed a state of the USA. The main islands are Oahu, Maui and Hawaii Island, which at 4,049 square miles (10,488 square kilometres) is by far the largest. Honolulu, the state capital, is on Oahu. (6,450 sq miles/16,705 sq km; pop. 1,237,000)

Hebei a province in northern China which surrounds (but does not include) Beijing. The capital is Shijiazhuang. (70,000 sq miles/180,000 sq km; pop. 70,421,400)

Hebrides some 500 islands lying off the west coast of Scotland, consisting of the Inner Hebrides to the southeast, whose main islands are Tiree, Jura, Coll, Mull, Eigg and Skye, and the Outer Hebrides to the northwest whose islands include Lewis and Harris, the Uists, Benbecula and Barra.

Heilongjiang a province of Dongbei (Manchuria) in northern China; the capital is Harbin. (179,000 sq miles/464,000 sq km; pop. 38,253,000)

Hejaz (Hijaz) a mountainous region which lines the Red Sea, formerly an independent kingdom but since 1932 a part of Saudi Arabia.

Heligoland (Helgoland) a small island and former naval base in the North Sea off the coast of Germany. (0.5 sq miles/2.1 sq km)

Henan a province of central China; the capital is Zhengzhou. (62,000 sq miles/ 160,000 sq km; pop. 100,845,000)

Herefordshire a county in the west of England, on the border with Wales, with its administrative centre in Hereford. (842 sq miles/2,180 sq km; pop. 167,000)

Hermon, Mount a mountain in southern Lebanon near the borders with Syria and Israel. It is the source of the River Jordan. (9,332 ft/2,814 m)

Hertfordshire a county in southeast England, to the north of London, with its administrative centre in Hertford. (631 sq miles/1,634 sq km; pop. 1,005,000)

Hessen (Hesse) a state in central western Germany. The capital is Wiesbaden. (8,151 sq miles/21,112 sq km; pop. 6,041,000)

Highland a council area in northern Scotland, with its administrative centre in the town of Inverness. (9,710 sq miles/25,149 sq km; pop. 207,000)

Highlands the rugged region of northern Scotland, which includes the Grampian Mountains and the North West Highlands.

Himachal Pradesh a state in northern India, in mountainous country bordering Tibet. (21,490 sq miles/55,673 sq km; pop. 6,196,000)

Himalayas the massive mountain range stretching some 1,500 miles (2,400 km) in a broad sweep from the northern tip of India, across Nepal, Bhutan and southern Tibet to Assam in northeastern India. The average height of the mountains is some 20,000 ft (6,100 m), rising to the world's tallest peak, Mount Everest (29,028 ft/8,848 m).

Hindu Kush a range of mountains which stretches some 370 miles (600 km) at the western end of the Himalayas, straddling the web of borders where Afghanistan, Tajikistan, China, India and Pakistan meet. The highest peak is Tirich Mir (25,229 ft/7,690 m) in Pakistan.

Hispaniola the name of the large Caribbean island that is shared by Haiti and the Dominican Republic. (29,400 sq miles/76,200 sq km)

Hoggar (Ahaggar) a remote mountain range of southern Algeria noted for its rock formations. The highest peak is Tahat (9,573 ft/2,918 m).

Hohe Tauern a part of eastern Alps in southern Austria, rising to the highest point at Grossglockner (12,460 ft/3,798 m), Austria's highest peak.

Hokkaido the most northerly of the main islands of Japan, and the second largest after Honshu Island. The capital is Sapporo. (30,312 sq miles/78,509 sq km; pop. 5,680,000)

Holland a name generally applied to the Netherlands, but in fact the term really applies to the central coastal region which comprise the two provinces of Noord Holland and Zuid Holland.

Holy Island (Lindisfarne) a small island just off the coast of Northumberland in northeast England. It has an 11th-century priory built on the site of a monastery founded in the 7th century.

Honduras a fan-shaped country in Central America that spreads out towards the Caribbean Sea at the Gulf of Honduras. Four-fifths of the country is covered by mountains that are indented with river valleys running towards the very short Pacific coast. There is little change in temperatures throughout the year and rainfall is heavy, especially on the Caribbean coast where temperatures are also higher than inland. The highlands are covered with forests, mainly of oak and pine, while palms and mangroves grow in the coastal areas. The country is sparsely populated and, although agricultural, only about 25 per cent of the land is cultivated. Honduras was once the world's leading banana exporter and that fruit is still its main export, but agriculture is now more diverse. Grains, coffee, and sugar are important crops, and these are grown mainly on the coastal plains of the Pacific and Caribbean. The forestry industry is one of the country's principal industries, producing mahogany, pine, walnut, ebony, and rosewood. Other industries have increased in recent years, with cotton, cement, and sugar products being produced for export.

Area: 43,277 sq miles/112,088 sq km
Population: 6,140,000
Capital: Tegucigalpa
Form of government: Republic
Religion: RC
Currency: Lempira

Hong Kong formerly a British dependent territory, Hong Kong became a special autonomous province of China on 1 July 1997. It is located in the South China Sea and consists of Hong Kong Island (once a barren rock), the peninsula of Kowloon and about 386 square miles (1,000 square kilometres) of adjacent land known as the New Territories. Hong Kong is situated at the mouth of the Pearl River, about 81 miles (130 kilometres) southeast of Guangzhou (Canton). The climate is warm subtropical with cool dry winters and hot humid summers. Hong Kong has no natural resources, even its water comes from reservoirs across the Chinese border. Its main assets are its magnificent natural harbour and its position close to the main trading routes of the Pacific. Hong Kong's economy is based on free enterprise and trade, an industrious work force, and an efficient and aggressive commercial system. Hong Kong's main industries are textiles, clothing, tourism, and electronics.

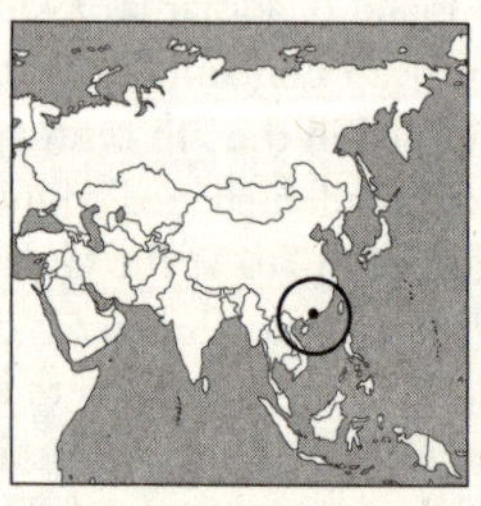

Area: 415 sq miles/1,075 sq km
Population: 6,688,000
Form of government: Special Autonomous Province of China
Religions: Buddhism, Taoism, Christianity
Currency: Hong Kong Dollar

Honshu the central and largest of the islands of Japan. (89,185 sq miles/230,988 sq km; pop. 101,000,000)

Hormuz (Ormuz), Strait of the strait at the mouth of the Persian Gulf between the Musandam Peninsula of Oman to the south, and Iran to the north.

Horn, Cape (Cabo de Hornos) the southern tip of South America, represented by a spattering of remote islands belonging to Chile off Tierra del Fuego.

Huang He (Hwang Ho, Yellow River) the second longest river in China, flowing from the Qinghai Mountains across northern central China to the Yellow Sea, south of Beijing. (Length 3,395 miles/5,464 km)

Huascarán a peak in the Andes in central Peru, and that country's highest mountain at 22,205 feet (6,768 metres).

Hubei a landlocked province of central China. (69,500 sq miles/180,000 sq km; pop. 63,361,000)

Hudson Bay a huge bay in northeastern Canada, hemmed in to the north by Baffin Island, and connected to the Atlantic Ocean by the Hudson Strait.

Hudson River a river flowing from its source in the Adirondack Mountains in New York State, USA, to the Atlantic Ocean at New York City. The Erie Canal joins the Hudson River to link New York to the Great Lakes. (Length 306 miles/492 km)

Hugli (Hoogly) a major branch of the River Ganges which forms at its delta and flows through Calcutta and the surrounding industrial conurbations into the Bay of Bengal. (Length 120 miles/193 km)

Humber the estuary of the Rivers Ouse and Trent which cuts deep into the east coast of England to the north of the Wash. (Length 35 miles/60 km)

Humberside a former county of north England.

Hunan an inland province of southeast China. The capital is Changsha. (210,000 sq km/81,000 sq miles; pop. 63,261,000)

Hungary landlocked in the heartland of Europe, Hungary is dominated by the great plain to the east of the River Danube, which runs north-south across the country. In the west, lies the largest lake in Central Europe, Lake Balaton. Winters are severe, but the summers are warm and although wet in the west, summer droughts often occur in the east. Hungary experienced a modest boom in its economy in the 1970s and 1980s. The government invested money in improving agriculture by mechanizing farms, using fertilizers, and bringing new land under cultivation. Yields of cereals and rice have since soared, and large areas between the Danube and Tisza Rivers are now used to grow vegetables. However, the use of these artificial fertilizers has caused water pollution. Industries have been carefully developed where adequate natural resources exist, such as bauxite, which is the country's main resource. New industries, such as the electronics industry, are now being promoted, and tourism is fast developing around Lake Balaton.

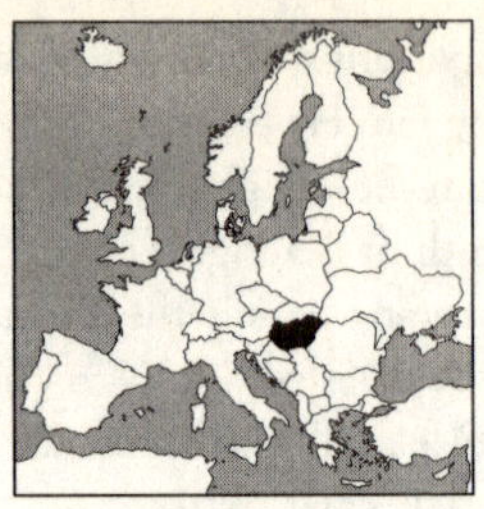

Area: 35,920 sq miles/93,032 sq km
Population: 10,193,000
Capital: Budapest
Other major cities: Debrecen, Miskolc, Pécs, Szeged
Form of government: Republic
Religions: RC, Calvinism, Lutheranism
Currency: Forint

Hunter Valley the valley of the Hunter River, lying 60 miles (100 kilometres) northwest of Sydney, Australia. It is particularly noted for its wine.

Huron, Lake one of the Great Lakes, lying at the centre of the group on the border between Canada and the state of Michigan in the USA. (23,000 sq miles/ 59,570 sq km)

Hydra (Idhra) a small island in the Aegean Sea, off the east coast of the Peloponnese Peninsula, Greece, noted as a haven where motor traffic is prohibited.

I

Iboland a densely populated region of southeastern Nigeria inhabited by the Ibo people. The attempt by the region to break away from Nigeria (1967–70) under the name of Biafra caused a civil war that led to a famine which killed over a million people. (Pop. 10,000,000)

Iceland a large island situated in a tectonically unstable part of the North Atlantic Ocean, just south of the Arctic Circle. The island has over 100 volcanoes, at least one of which erupts every five years. One-ninth of the country is covered by ice and snow fields, and there are about 700 hot springs, which are an important source of central heating, particularly in the volcanic areas. In the capital city, the majority of homes and industries are heated by this method. The climate is cool temperate, but because of the effect of the North Atlantic Drift it is mild for its latitude. Permanent daylight occurs for three months in summer and the beautiful Aurora Borealis (Northern Lights) can be seen from the end of August. The southwest corner is the most densely populated area as the coast here is generally free from ice. Very little of the land can be cultivated and the main crops are root vegetables such as turnip and potatoes. Fishing and fish processing are the mainstay of the Icelandic economy, with much of the catch being exported. Aluminium and ferrosilicon, nitrates for fertilizers, cement, and chemicals are produced for export. Other manufactured goods include paints, textiles, clothing, footwear, and knitted products. Tourism is also of growing importance to the island's economy.

Area: 39,769 sq miles/103,000 sq km
Population: 275,000
Capital: Reykjavík
Form of government: Republic
Religion: Lutheranism
Currency: Icelandic Króna

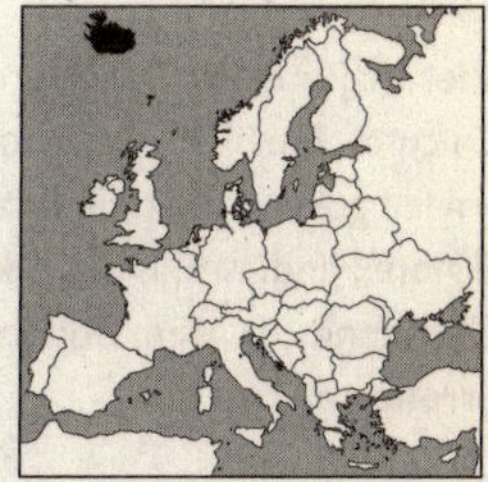

Idaho an inland state in the northwest of the USA. The state capital is Boise. (83,557 sq miles/216,413 sq km; pop. 1,348,000)

IJsselmeer formerly a large inlet of the North Sea known as the Zuiderzee on the northeastern coast of the Netherlands, but after the creation of the dam called the Afsluitdijk across its mouth, it has filled with water from the River IJssel and is now a freshwater lake, bordered by fertile areas of reclaimed land (polders).

Ile de France a region and former province of France with Paris at its centre, now consisting of eight separate departments. (4,638 sq miles/12,012 sq km)

Illinois a state in the Midwest of the USA, bordering Lake Michigan to the north. The capital is Springfield, but Chicago is its main city. (56,400 sq miles/ 46,075 sq km; pop. 12,546,000)

India a vast country in South Asia that is dominated in the extreme north by the world's youngest and highest mountains, the Himalayas, which extend about 1,500 miles (about 2,400 kilometres) along India's northern and eastern borders. The range contains Mount Everest and K2. At the foot of the Himalayas, a huge plain, drained by the Indus and Ganges Rivers, is one of the most fertile areas in the world and the most densely populated part of India. Further south, the ancient Deccan plateau extends to the southern tip of the country. India generally has four seasons, cool, hot, rainy, and dry. About 70 per cent of the population depend on agriculture for their living and the lower slopes of the Himalayas represent one of the world's best tea-growing areas. Rice, sugar cane, and wheat are grown in the Ganges plain, and there is a comprehensive system of irrigation to aid agriculture. India is self-sufficient in all its major food crops, and main exports include precious stones, jewellery, engineering products, clothes, and chemicals. Since becoming a republic in 1950, India has been troubled by internal dissent and external disputes, particularly with Pakistan over the status of Kashmir.

Area: 1,269,346 sq miles/3,287,590 sq km
Population: 970,930,000
Capital: New Delhi
Other major cities: Bangalore, Bombay, Calcutta, Delhi, Hyderabad, Madras
Form of government: Federal Republic
Religion: Hinduism, Islam, Sikhism, Christianity, Jainism, Buddhism
Currency: Rupee

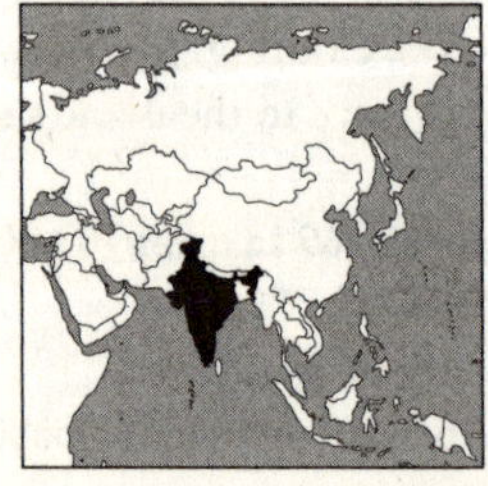

Indiana a state in the Midwest of the USA to the southeast of Lake Michigan. The state capital is Indianapolis. (36,291 sq miles/93,994 sq km; pop. 6,149,000)

Indian Ocean the third largest ocean, bounded by Asia to the north, Africa to the west and Australia to the east. The southern waters merge with the Antarctic Ocean. (28,364,000 sq miles/73,481,000 sq km)

Indonesia a country made up of 13,667 islands that are scattered across the Indian and Pacific Oceans in a huge crescent. It is the world's fourth most highly populated country. Its largest land mass is the province of Kalimantan, which is part of the island of Borneo. Sumatra is the largest individual island. Java, however, is the dominant and most densely populated island. The climate is generally tropical monsoon, and temperatures are high all year round. The country has 130 active volcanoes, and earthquakes are frequent in the southern islands. An underwater earthquake off the coast of Sumatra triggered the December 2004 tsunami that devestated the lives of millions in the region. The city of Banda Aceh alone lost some 200,000 people in just 15 minutes. Complete recovery in the province of Aceh from the effects of the tsunami also requires an end to 30 years of civil conflict in the area. Rice, maize and cassava are the main crops grown. Indonesia has the largest reserves of tin in the world and is one of the world's leading rubber producers. Other mineral resources found are bauxite, natural gas, nickel and copper. The development of the country's economy has been hampered by the devastation caused by the tsunami as well as ongoing political instability, corruption, human rights violations and armed separatist movements in Aceh and Papua.

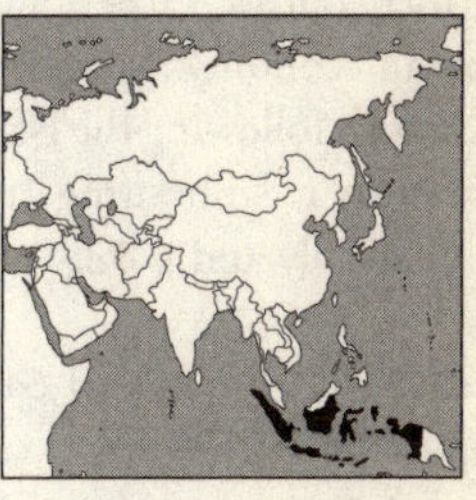

Area: 741,052 sq miles/1,919,317 sq km
Population: 203,000,000
Capital: Jakarta
Other cities: Banda Aceh, Bandung, Medan, Semarang, Surabaya
Form of government: Republic
Religion: Sunni Islam, Christianity, Hinduism
Currency: Rupiah

Indus one of the great rivers of Asia, whose valleys supported some of the world's earliest civilizations, notably at Mohenjo Daro. It flows from its source in Tibet and across the northern tip of India before turning south to run through the entire length of Pakistan to its estuary on the Arabian Sea, south of Karachi. (Length 1,900 miles/3,059 km)

Inverclyde a council area in west central Scotland, with its administrative centre in the town of Greenock. (63 sq miles/162 sq km; pop. 90,000)

Iona a small island off the southwestern tip of Mull, Scotland, where the Irish monk St Columba founded a monastery in AD 563. (3 sq miles/8 sq km)

Ionian Islands (Eptanisos) the seven largest of the islands which lie scattered along the west coast of Greece in the Ionian Sea. They are Corfu, Paxoí, Cephalonia, Levkás, Ithaca, Zákinthos and Kíthira. (Pop. 182,700)

Ionian Sea that part of the Mediterranean Sea between southern Italy and Greece. It is named after Io, a mistress of the Ancient Greek god Zeus.

Iowa a state in the Midwest of the USA bounded on the east and west by the upper reaches of the Mississippi and Missouri Rivers. The capital is Des Moines. (56,290 sq miles/145,791 sq km; pop. 2,921,000)

Iran, Islamic Republic of lying across the Persian Gulf from the Arabian Peninsula and stretching from the Caspian Sea to the Arabian Sea, Iran is a land dominated by mountains in the north and west, with a huge expanse of desert in its centre. The climate is hot and dry, although more temperate conditions are found on the shores of the Caspian Sea. In winter, terrible dust storms sweep the deserts and almost no life can survive. Most of the population live in the north and west, where Tehran is situated. The only good agricultural land is on the Caspian coastal plains, where wheat, barley, potatoes, and rice are grown. Around 5 per cent of the population are nomadic herdsmen who wander in the mountains. Most of Iran's oil is in the southwest, and other valuable minerals include coal, iron ore, copper, and lead. Precious stones are found in the northeast. The country's main exports are fresh and dried fruit, petroleum and petrochemicals, carpets and rugs, textiles, raw cotton, and leather goods. The Iranian economy expanded rapidly as a result of petroleum industry revenue. However, following the Islamic revolution in the late 1970s, and the subsequent war with neighbouring Iraq between 1980 and 1988, the economy slowed dramatically and is only gradually beginning to pick up again.

Area: 634,293,sq miles/1,648,195 sq km
Population: 61,128,000
Capital: Tehran
Other major cities: Esfahan, Mashhad, Tabriz
Form of government: Islamic Republic
Religion: Shia Islam
Currency: Rial

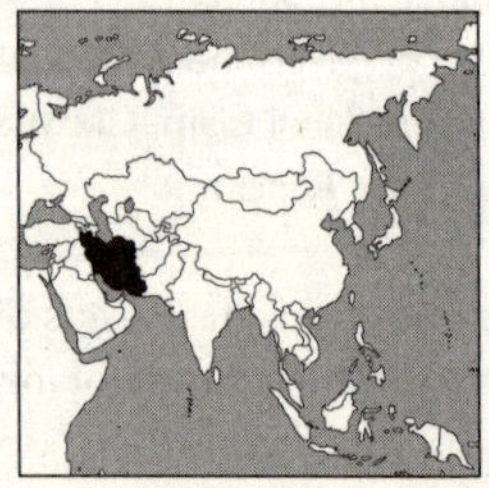

Iraq located in southwest Asia, wedged between the Persian Gulf and Syria, Iraq is almost landlocked except for its outlet to the Gulf at Shatt al Arab. Its two great rivers, the Tigris and the Euphrates, flow from the northwest into the Gulf at this point. The climate is arid, with very hot summers and cold winters. The high mountains on the border with Turkey are snow-covered for six months of the year, and desert covers nearly half the country in the southwest. The only fertile land in Iraq is in the basins of the Tigris and Euphrates. Oil was the main export traditionally providing 95% of foreign exchange earnings. Iraq profited from the great oil boom of the 1970s, but during the war with Iran, oil terminals in the Gulf were destroyed and the Trans-Syrian Pipeline closed. Iraq invaded Kuwait in 1990, leading to the first Gulf War in 1991 in which Iraq was defeated by UN forces. Following this the country's standard of living went from very high to very low, and continued international sanctions kept the economy in a state of crisis. The regime of Saddam Hussein, President of Iraq since 1979, collapsed in April 2003, three weeks into a major US-led military campaign. Coalition forces remain in Iraq amid ongoing violence to facilitate the establishment of a freely elected Iraqi government.

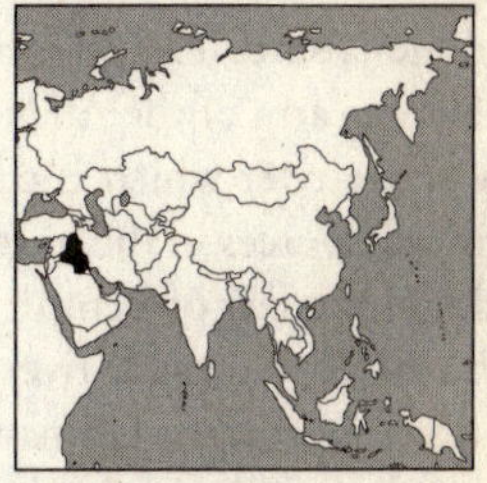

Area: 169,235 sq miles/438,317 sq km
Population: 20,607,000
Capital: Baghdad
Other major cities: Basra (Al-Basrah), Mosul (Al Mawsil)
Form of government: Republic (under Interim Government, 2004)
Religions: Shia Islam, Sunni Islam
Currency: Iraqi Dinar

Ireland an island off the west coast of Great Britain, almost four fifths of which is the independent Republic of Ireland, while the remainder is Northern Ireland, which is part of the UK. (32,588 sq miles/80,400 sq km, pop. 5,525,000)

Ireland, Republic of one of Europe's most westerly countries, situated in the Atlantic Ocean and separated from Great Britain by the Irish Sea. It has an equable climate, with mild southwest winds, which makes temperatures uniform over most of the country. The Republic extends over four-fifths of the island of Ireland, and the west and southwest are mountainous, with the highest peak reaching 3,416 feet (1,041 metres) at Carrauntoohil. The main rivers are the Erne and the Shannon. The central plain is largely limestone covered by boulder clay, which provides good farmland and pasture, with about 80 per cent of the land being under agriculture. Livestock production, including cattle, sheep, pigs, and horses, is the most important agricultural activity. The rural population have tended to migrate to the cities, mainly Dublin, which is the main industrial centre and the focus of radio, television, publishing, and communications. Lack of energy resources and remoteness from major markets did slow industrial development, but by taking full advantage of membership of the European Union the economy has improved markedly in recent years.

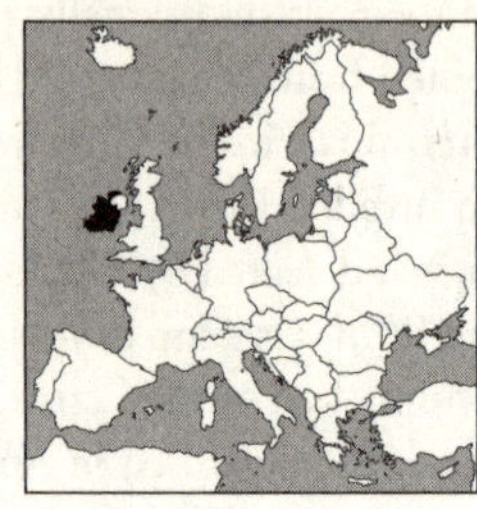

Area: 27,137 sq miles/70,284 sq km
Population: 3,781,000
Capital: Dublin (Baile Atha Cliath)
Other major cities: Cork, Galway, Limerick, Waterford
Form of government: Republic
Religion: RC
Currency: Euro

Irian Jaya the western half of the island of New Guinea, which has been part of Indonesia since 1963. (158,556 sq miles/410,660 sq km; pop. 2,762,000)

Irish Sea the arm of the Atlantic that separates Ireland and Great Britain.

Irrawaddy a river which is the central focus of Myanmar, flowing from its two primary sources in the north of the country to Mandalay and then south to its delta in the Bay of Bengal. (Length 1,250 miles/2,000 km)

Irtysh a largely navigable river flowing northwards from its source near the border between northwest China and Mongolia across the centre of Kazakhstan and through the Siberian city of Omsk to join the River Ob' on its journey to the Arctic Ocean. (Length 2,760 miles/4,440 km)

Israel occupying a long narrow stretch of land in the southeast of the Mediterranean, Israel's eastern boundary is formed by the Great Rift Valley through which the River Jordan flows to the Dead Sea. The south of the country is made up of a triangular wedge of the Negev Desert, which ends at the Gulf of Aqaba. The Negev has mineral resources, such as copper, phosphates, and manganese, plus commercial amounts of natural gas and petroleum. Other assets are the vast amounts of potash, bromine, and other minerals found in the Dead Sea. The climate in summer is hot and dry; in winter it is mild with some rain. The south of the country is arid and barren. Most of the population live on the coastal plain bordering the Mediterranean where Tel Aviv is the country's main commercial centre, as well as the site of most foreign embassies, since many countries do not recognize Jerusalem as the capital. The country is virtually self-sufficient in foodstuffs and a major exporter of its produce. A wide range of products is processed or finished in the country, and main exports include finished diamonds, textiles, fruit, vegetables, chemicals, machinery, and fertilizers. Tourism and foreign aid also makes an important contribution to the economy. Israel has had an uneasy relationship, which often flares into open conflict, with Palestinian nationals in the West Bank and Gaza Strip territories.

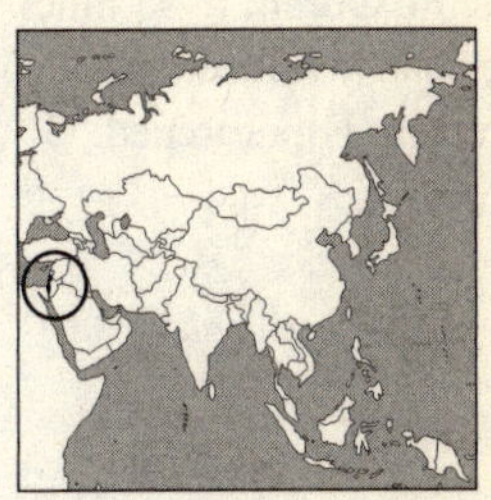

Area: 8,130 sq miles/21,056 sq km
Population: 6,100,000
Capital: Jerusalem
Other major cities: Tel Aviv, Haifa
Form of government: Republic
Religions: Judaism, Sunni Islam, Christianity
Currency: New Israeli Shekel

Issyk-Kul' a lake in southern central Kazakhstan, set in the high mountains that line the border with China. (2,424 sq miles/6,280 sq km)

Italy a republic in southern Europe that comprises a large peninsula and the two main islands of Sicily and Sardinia. The Alps form a natural boundary with its northern and western European neighbours, and the Adriatic Sea to the east separates it from the countries of former Yugoslavia. The Apennine Mountains form the backbone of Italy and extend the full length of the peninsula. Between the Alps and the Apennines lies the Po Valley, a great fertile lowland. Sicily and Sardinia are largely mountainous. Much of Italy is geologically unstable, and it has a number of active volcanoes, the best known of which are Etna, Vesuvius and Stromboli. Italy enjoys warm dry summers and mild winters. In the south, farms are small and traditional. Industries in the north include motor vehicles, textiles, clothing, leather goods, glass, and ceramics. Although there is a lack of natural resources, almost 60 per cent of the land is under crops and pasture, and there is an abundance of building stone, particularly marble. The coastal waters are rich in marine life, with anchovy, sardine and tuna being of commercial importance. Tourism is an important source of foreign currency.

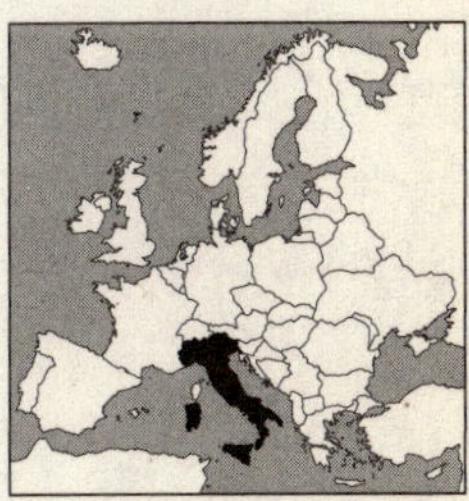

Area: 16,320 sq miles/301,268 sq km
Population: 58,082,000
Capital: Rome (Roma)
Other major cities: Milan, Naples, Turin, Genoa, Palermo
Form of government: Republic
Religion: RC
Currency: Euro

Ivory Coast *see* Côte d'Ivoire.

Iwo Jima the largest in the group of islands called the Volcano Islands belonging to Japan, which lie some 745 miles (1,200 kilometres) south of Tokyo in the Pacific Ocean. (8 sq miles/21 sq km)

Ixtacihuatl a volcanic peak south of Mexico City, which is twinned with neighbouring Popocatépetl. (17,342 ft/5,286 m)

J

Jamaica an island state in the Caribbean Sea about 93 miles (150 kilometres) south of Cuba. The centre of the island comprises a limestone plateau, and this is surrounded by narrow coastal flatlands and palm-fringed beaches. The highest mountains, the Blue Mountains, are in the east of the island. The climate is tropical, with high temperatures at the coast and slightly cooler and less humid conditions in the highlands. Jamaica suffers from severe earthquakes, and thermal springs can be found in areas of the country. The island lies right in the middle of the hurricane zone. The traditional crops grown are sugar cane, bananas, peppers, ginger, cocoa and coffee, and new crops such as winter vegetables, fruit, and honey are being developed for export. The mining of bauxite and alumina plays a very important part in Jamaica's economy and accounts for around 60 per cent of its total yearly exports. Industrialization has been encouraged, and clothing, footwear, cement, and agricultural machinery are now produced. Tourism is a particularly important industry, with over one million visitors annually.

Area: 4,243 sq miles/10,990 sq km
Population: 2,491,000
Capital: Kingston
Other city: Montego Bay
Form of government: Constitutional Monarchy
religions: RC, Protestantism, Anglicanism
Currency: Jamaican Dollar

James Bay the southern arm of the Hudson Bay, Canada, which extends 273 miles (440 kilometres) into Ontario and Québec.

Jammu and Kashmir the official name for the part of Kashmir presently under Indian control. Since 1947, Kashmir has been a disputed territory between India, Pakistan and China. A large area in northwest Kashmir is presently held by Pakistan and is known as Azad (Free) Kashmir, a smaller area in the east is held by China and the remaining area has been incorporated into India as the state of Jammu and Kashmir. (85,783 sq miles/222,236 sq km; pop. 10,267,000)

Jamuna the name given to the river formed by the Brahmaputra and the Tista Rivers, as it flows through Bangladesh to join the Ganges River.

Japan located on the eastern margin of Asia and consisting of four major islands, Honshu, Hokkaido, Kyushu, and Shikoku, and many small islands, Japan is separated from the mainland of Asia by the Sea of Japan. The country is made up of six chains of steep serrated mountains, which contain about 60 active volcanoes. Earthquakes are frequent and widespread and often accompanied by giant waves (tsunami). A devastating earthquake occurred in 1995 when more than 5,000 people died and over 300,000 were left homeless. Summers are warm and humid and winters mild, except on Hokkaido, which is covered in snow in winter. Japan's agriculture is highly advanced, with extensive use made of fertilizers and miniature machinery for the small fields. Fishing is very important, both for domestic consumption and export. Heavy industries, such as iron and steel, shipbuilding, chemicals and petrochemicals, used to account for almost three-quarters of Japan's export revenue, but now it relies on the success of its manufacturing industry which produces automobiles, televisions, videos, electronic equipment, cameras, watches, clocks, robots, and textiles. Japan's financial markets have experienced some problems in recent years, which has introduced some uncertainty into what was a very secure economy.

Area: 145,870 sq miles/377,801 sq km
Population: 125,761,000
Capital: Tokyo
Other major cities: Osaka, Nagoya, Sapporo, Kobe, Kyoto, Yokohama
Form of government: Constitutional Monarchy
Religions: Shintoism, Buddhism, Christianity
Currency: Yen

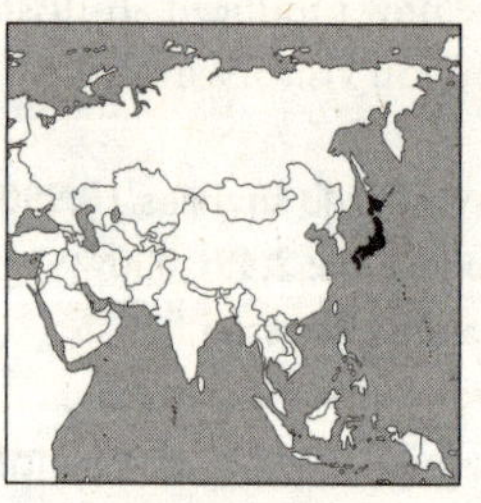

Japan, Sea of a part of the Pacific Ocean between Japan and Korea.

Java (Jawa) the central island in the southern chain of the islands of Indonesia. The capital is Jakarta. (50,574 sq miles/130,987 sq km; pop. 116,531,000)

Java Sea an arm of the Pacific Ocean that separates Java and Borneo.

Jersey the largest of the British Channel Islands. The capital is St Helier. (45 sq miles/117 sq km; pop. 89,000)

Jiangsu a heavily populated but highly productive province on the central east coast of China. The capital is Nanjing. (38,600 sq miles/100,000 sq km; pop. 76,815,000)

Jiangxi an inland province of southeastern China. Its capital is Nanchang. (64,300 sq miles/164,800 sq km; pop. 44,732,000)

Jilin (Kirin) a province of central Dongbei (Manchuria) in northern China. The capital is Changchun. (69,500 sq miles/180,000 sq km; pop. 27,991,000)

Jordan almost landlocked except for a short coastline on the Gulf of Aqaba, Jordan is bounded by Saudi Arabia, Syria, Iraq, and Israel. Almost 80 per cent of the country is desert and the rest comprises the East Bank Uplands and Jordan Valley, part of the Great Rift Valley. In general, summers are hot and dry and winters cool and wet, with variations related to altitude. The east has a desert climate. Since under 5 per cent of the land is arable, and only part of this is irrigated, production of grain is insufficient for the country's needs although some fruits and vegetables are grown for export. The capital, Amman, is the main industrial centre of the country, and industries include phosphates, petroleum products, cement, iron, and fertilizers. The rich Arab states, such as Saudi Arabia, give Jordan substantial economic aid and the country has a modern network of roads that link the cities. In 1994, a historical peace agreement was signed with Israel that ended 46 years of hostilities.

Area: 37,738 sq miles/97,740 sq km
Population: 5,581,000
Capital: Amman
Other cities: Irbid, Zarga
Form of government: Constitutional Monarchy
Religion: Sunni Islam
Currency: Jordanian Dinar

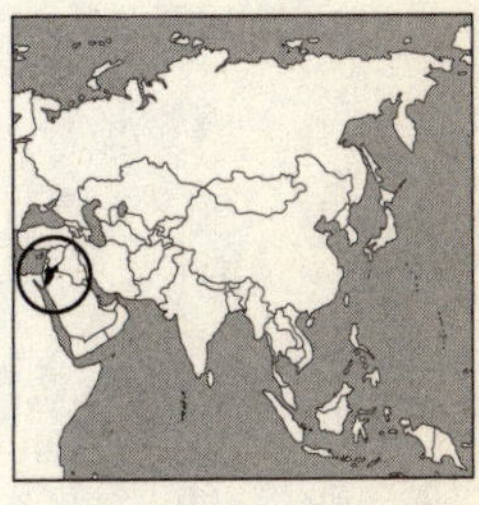

Jordan a river flowing southwards from Mount Hermon in southern Lebanon, through northern Israel to Lake Tiberias (Sea of Galilee) and then through Jordan to the Dead Sea, where it evaporates. The West Bank to the north of the Dead Sea is a disputed territory which was occupied by Israel during the Six Day War in 1967 but returned to the limited control of the Palestinian National Authority in 1994. (Length 159 miles/ 256 km)

Juan de Fuca Strait the channel to the south of Vancouver Island on the border between Canada and the USA, through which ships from Victoria, Vancouver and Seattle can pass to reach the Pacific Ocean.

Juan Fernández Islands a group of three remote islands in the Pacific Ocean belonging to Chile, some 400 miles (650 kilometres) due west of Santiago. (62 sq miles/181 sq km; pop. 280)

Jura (1) a large upland band of limestone in eastern central France which lines the border with Switzerland, giving its name to a department in France and a canton in Switzerland. A further extension continues across southern Germany as far as Nuremberg (the Swabian and Franconian Jura). (2) an island off the west coast of Scotland in the Inner Hebrides. (147 sq miles/381 sq km; pop. 250)

Jutland (Jylland) a large peninsula stretching some 250 miles (400 kilometres) northwards from Germany to separate the North Sea from the Baltic Sea. Most of it is occupied by the mainland part of Denmark, while the southern part belongs to the German state of Schleswig-Holstein.

K

K2 (Godwin Austen) the second highest mountain in the world after Mount Everest, situated in the Karakoram mountain range on the disputed border between Pakistan and China. (28,250 ft/8,611 m)

Kalahari a region of semi-desert occupying much of southern Botswana and straddling the border with South Africa and Namibia.

Kalimantan the greater part of Borneo, which is governed by Indonesia. (208,000 sq miles/538,718 sq km; pop. 12,339,000)

Kalmyk (Kalmuck) Republic an autonomous republic of the Russian Federation, lying to the northwest of the Caspian Sea. (29,300 sq miles/75,900 sq km; pop. 310,000)

Kamchatka a peninsula, some 750 miles (1,200 kilometres) long, which drops south from eastern Siberia into the north Pacific Ocean. (Pop. 356,000)

Kangchenjunga the world's third highest mountain (after Mount Everest and K2), situated in the eastern Himalayas, on the borders between Nepal, China and the Indian state of Sikkim. (28,165 ft/8,585 m)

KaNgwane one of ten former South African Homelands, the area is now part of the province of Mpumalanga in northeast South Africa.

Kansas a state in the Great Plains of the USA. The state capital is Topeka. (82,264 sq miles/213,064 sq km; pop. 2,701,000)

Karakoram a range of mountains at the western end of the Himalayas on the borders between Pakistan, China and India.

Kara Kum (Garagum, Karakumy) a sand desert in southern Turkmenistan, to the east of the Caspian Sea, and on the borders with Iran and Afghanistan.

Kara Sea a branch of the Arctic Ocean off the central northern coast of the Russian Federation.

Karelia a region which straddles the Finnish-Russian border.

Kariba Dam the hydroelectric dam on the River Zambezi on the border between Zambia and Zimbabwe which has created Lake Kariba. (Length 175 miles/282 kilometres)

Karnataka a state in southwest India. The capital is Bangalore. (74,031 sq miles/191,791 sq km; pop. 53,764,000)

Karoo (Karroo) an area of high semi-desert plateaux, including the Great Karoo and the Little Karoo, lying between the mountain ranges of southern South Africa.

Kasai (Cassai) a major river of the Democratic Republic of Congo. (Length 1,350 miles/2,150 km)

Kashmir a mountainous region of southwest central Asia. Since 1947, this region has been a disputed territory between India, Pakistan and China. A large area in the northwest of the region is held by Pakistan and is known as Azad (Free) Kashmir, a smaller area in the east is held by China and the remaining area has been incorporated into India as the state of Jammu and Kashmir.

Kattegat (Cattegat) the strait, 21 miles (34 kilometres) at its narrowest, at the entrance to the Baltic Sea which separates Sweden from Jutland.

Kavango (Cubango) a river, known formerly as the Okavango, which flows southeast from central Angola to form the border with Namibia before petering out in the swampy inland Okavango Delta in northern Botswana. (Length 1,000 miles/1,600 km)

Kaveri (Caveri, Cauvery) a holy river of southern India, flowing southeast from the Deccan plateau to the coast on the Bay of Bengal. (Length 497 miles/800 km)

Kazakhstan the second largest republic of the former USSR, which extends from the coast of the Caspian Sea to the northwest corner of Mongolia. The west of the country is low-lying, the east hilly, and in the southeast mountainous areas include parts of the Tian Shan and Altai ranges. The climate is continental and very dry, with great extremes of temperature. Much of the country is desert and semi-desert, with wastelands of stone, sand, and salt. Crops can be grown only in the wetter northwest regions or on land irrigated by the Syrdar'ya River. Extensive pastoral farming is carried out, and cattle, sheep, and goats are the main livestock reared. The country is rich in minerals, particularly copper, lead, zinc, coal, tungsten, iron ore, oil, and gas. Kazakhstan declared itself independent in 1991, since when economic prospects have remained positive, although environmental problems have been left as a legacy of past Soviet exploitation and have still to be tackled (e.g. the overdraining of the Aral Sea). Parts of the country, particularly the mountainous regions, are subject to earthquakes and the former capital, Almaty, has been largely rebuilt following extensive damage. In 1997, the capital was moved to Astana, a city located in a more stable geological region.

Area: 1,049,156 sq miles/2,717,300 sq km
Population: 15,671,000
Capital: Astana
Other major city: Almaty
Form of government: Republic
Religion: Sunni Islam
Currency: Tenge

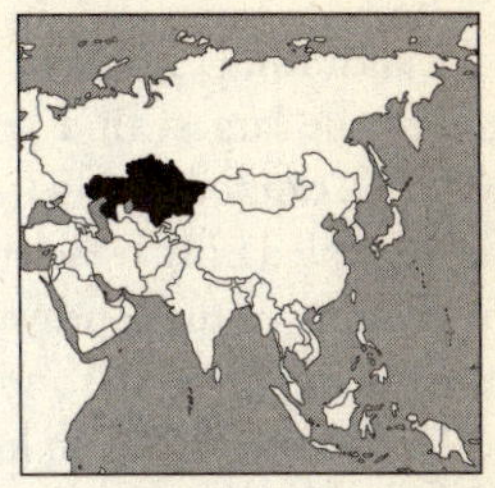

Kent a county in the extreme southeast of England, with its administrative centre in Maidstone. (1,441 sq miles/3,732 sq km; pop. 1,546,000)

Kentucky a state in east central USA. The state capital is Frankfort. (40,395 sq miles/104,623 sq km; pop. 4,090,000)

Kenya located in East Africa, Kenya straddles the Equator and extends from Lake Victoria in the southwest to the Indian Ocean in the southeast. Highlands run north to south through central Kenya and are divided by the steep-sided Great Rift Valley. The coastal lowlands have a hot humid climate but in the highlands it is cooler and rainfall heavier. In the east, it is very arid. The southwestern region is well watered, with huge areas of fertile soil, and this accounts for the bulk of the population and almost all its economic production. A wide variety of crops are grown for domestic consumption, such as wheat, maize, and cassava. Tea, coffee, sisal, sugar cane, and cotton are grown for export. Oil refining at Mombasa is the country's largest single industry, and other industry includes food processing and textiles. Mining is carried out on a small scale for soda ash, gold, and limestone, but large quantities of silver and lead exist near Mombasa. Tourism is an important source of foreign revenue, with the many wildlife and game reserves being a major attraction.

Area: 224,081 sq miles/580,367 sq km
Population: 31,806,000
Capital: Nairobi
Other cities: Mombasa, Kisumu
Form of government: Republic
Religions: RC, Protestantism, other Christianity, traditional African religions
Currency: Kenyan Shilling

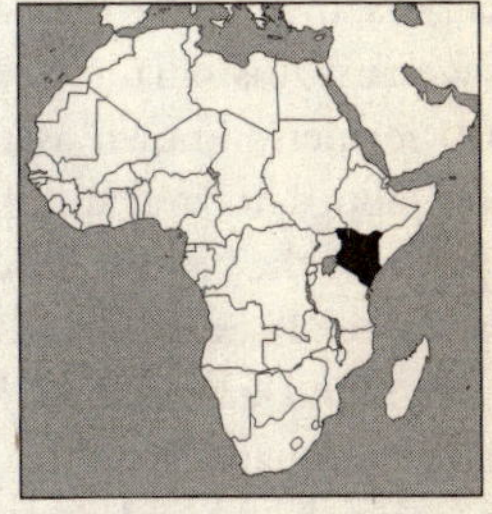

Kenya, Mount a towering extinct volcano in central Kenya, the second highest mountain in Africa after Mount Kilimanjaro. (17,058 ft/5,200 m)

Kerala a state occupying the western coast of the southern tip of India. The capital is Trivandrum. (15,005 sq miles/38,863 sq km; pop. 32,460,000)

Kerguelen the largest in a remote group of some 300 islands in the southern Indian Ocean forming part of the French Southern and Antarctic Territories, now occupied only by scientists. (1,318 sq miles/3,414 sq km)

Kerry a county in the southwest of the Republic of Ireland, noted for the rugged beauty of its peninsulas and its green dairy pastures. The county town is Tralee. (1,815 sq miles/4,701 sq km; pop. 132,000)

Kharg Island a small island in the northern Gulf where Iran has constructed a major oil terminal.

Khone Falls a massive set of waterfalls on the Mekong River in southern Laos. With a maximum width of 6.7 miles (10.8 kilometres), these are the widest falls in the world.

Khorasan the northeastern province of Iran, bordering Afghanistan and Turkmenistan. The capital is Mashhad. (Pop. 6,085,000)

Khuzestan (Khuzistan) a province in southwestern Iran, and the country's main oil-producing area. The capital is Ahvaz. (Pop. 4,537,000)

Khyber Pass a strategic route at a height of 3,518 feet (1,072 metres) over the Safed Koh Mountains connecting Peshawar in Pakistan with Kabul in Afghanistan.

Kigali the capital of Rwanda. (Pop. 291,000)

Kildare a county in the southeast of the Republic of Ireland, famous for its racehorses and the racecourse, the Curragh. The county town is Naas. (654 sq miles/ 1,694 sq km; pop. 141,000)

Kilimanjaro, Mount Africa's highest mountain, in northeastern Tanzania. (19,340 ft/ 5,895 m)

Kilkenny a county and county town in the southeast of the Republic of Ireland. (769 sq miles/2,062 sq km; pop. county 78,000/town 20,000)

Kimberleys, the (Kimberley Plateau) a vast plateau of hills and gorges in the north of Western Australia. (162,000 sq miles/420,000 sq km)

Kiribati formerly known as the Gilbert and Ellice Islands, Kiribati comprises three groups of coral atolls and one isolated volcanic island spread over a large expanse of the central Pacific Ocean. The group includes the former Gilbert Islands, the Phoenix Islands (now Rawaki), and the southern Line Islands. The largest island is Kiritimati, formerly known as Christmas Island. The climate is maritime equatorial, with a rainy season from October to March. Most islanders are involved in subsistence agriculture. Coconut, palm and breadfruit trees, bananas and papaws are grown, with coconuts and palm products being the main cash crops. Tuna fishing is an important industry. Ocean Island (Banaba) was a rich source of phosphate deposits (guano) but these are now exhausted and the mining has left severe environmental damage, causing most Banabans to resettle elsewhere. Tourism is becoming increasingly important but the country is still heavily dependent on overseas aid.

Area: 280 sq miles/726 sq km
Population: 80,000
Capital: Tarawa
Form of government: Republic
Religions: RC, Protestantism
Currency: Australian Dollar

Kiritimati the Pacific Ocean's largest coral atoll, situated at the northeastern end of the Kiribati group. (167 sq miles/432 sq km; pop. 5,000)

Kivu, Lake a lake in the Great Rift Valley on the border between Rwanda and the Democratic Republic of Congo. (1,100 sq miles/2,850 sq km)

Kizil Irmak the longest river in Turkey, flowing westwards from the centre, before curling north to the Black Sea. (Length 700 miles/1,130 km)

Knossos the site of an excavated royal palace of the Minoan civilization, 3 miles (5 kilometres) southeast of Iráklion, once the capital of Crete. The palace was built in about 1950 BC and destroyed in 1380 BC.

Kola Peninsula a bulging peninsula in the Barents Sea in the extreme northwest of the Russian Federation, to the east of Murmansk.

Kolyma a river in northeastern Siberia, flowing north from the gold-rich Kolyma Mountains into the East Siberian Sea. (Length 1,600 miles/2,600 km)

Komi Republic an autonomous republic of the Russian Federation, which produces timber, coal, oil and natural gas. (160,600 sq miles/415,900 sq km; pop. 1,085,000)

Komodo a small island of Indonesia in the Lesser Sunda group, between Sumbawa and Flores, noted above all as the home of the giant monitor lizard, the Komodo Dragon. (200 sq miles /520 sq km)

Korea, Democratic People's Republic of (North Korea) a country occupying the northern half of the Korean Peninsula in east Asia, still widely known as North Korea. The Yala and Tumen Rivers form its northern border with China and the Russian Federation. Its southern border with the Republic of Korea is just north of the 38th parallel. It is a mountainous country, three-quarters of which is forested highland or scrubland, with Paektu-San the highest peak at 9,003 feet (2,737 metres). The climate is warm temperate, although winters can be cold in the north. Most rain falls during the summer. Nearly 90 per cent of its arable land is farmed by cooperatives that employ over 40 per cent of the labour force, and rice is the main crop grown. North Korea is quite well endowed with fuel and minerals such as magnesite, zinc, copper, lead, tungsten, gold, and silver. Deposits of coal and hydroelectric power generate electricity, and substantial deposits of iron ore are found near Pyongyang and Musan. Sixty per cent of the labour force is employed in industry, the most important of which are metallurgical, building, cement, and chemicals. Fishing is carried on, with the main catches being tuna, anchovy, and seaweeds.

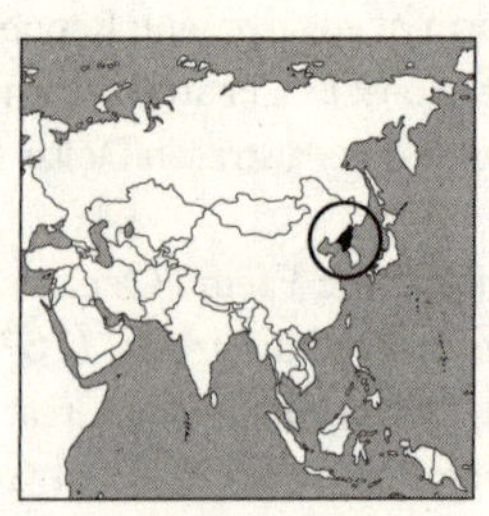

Area: 46,540 sq miles/120,538 sq km
Population: 22,466,000
Capital: Pyongyang
Other major cities: Hamhung, Chongjin
Form of government: Socialist Republic
Religions: Chondoism, Buddhism
Currency: Won

Korea, Republic of (South Korea) the Republic of Korea (still widely known as South Korea) occupies the southern half of the Korean Peninsula in eastern Asia. It is bordered in the north by a demilitarized zone which acts as a buffer between it and the Democratic People's Republic of Korea. Most of the country is hilly or mountainous, with the highest ranges running north to south along the east coast. The west is lowland and extremely densely populated. The extreme south has a humid warm temperate climate while farther north it is more continental. Most rain falls in summer. Cultivated land represents only 23 per cent of the country's total area, and the main crops are rice, onions, potatoes, barley, and maize. An increasing amount of fruit, such as melons, apples, and peaches, is now produced. The country has few natural resources but does produce coal, graphite, and iron ore. It has a flourishing manufacturing industry and is the world's leading supplier of ships and footwear. Other important industries are electronic equipment, electrical goods, steel, petrochemicals, motor vehicles, and toys.

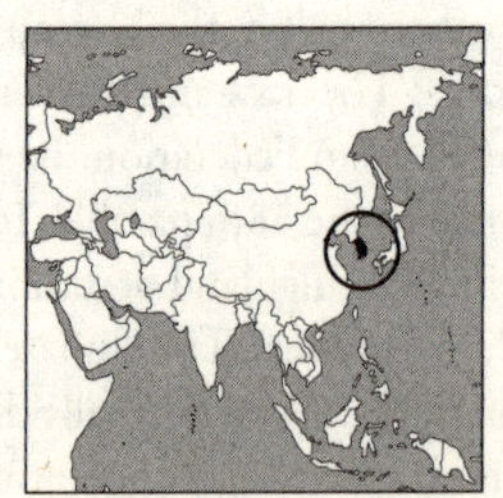

Area: 38,368 sq miles/99,373 sq km
Population: 46,430,000
Capital: Seoul (Soul)
Other major cities: Pusan, Taegu, Inch'on
Form of government: Republic
Religions: Buddhism, Christianity
Currency: Won

Korea Strait the stretch of water, 40 miles (64 kilometres) at its narrowest, which separates the southern tip of South Korea from Japan. It is also sometimes known as the Tsushima Strait, after the island of that name.

Kos (Cos) one of the Dodecanese Islands, belonging to Greece, in the Aegean Sea. (112 sq miles/290 sq km; pop. 20,300)

Kosciusko, Mount the highest mountain in Australia, a peak in the Snowy Mountains range in southern New South Wales. (7,316 ft/2,230 m)

Kosovo an autonomous province in the southwest of Serbia, in the former Yugoslavia. About 75 per cent of the population are ethnic Albanians. The capital is Pristina. The country was the scene of a wave of repression by the Serbian government after an ethnic Albanian independence campaign that turned into open warfare. After the NATO bombing of Serbia in 1999, Kosovo became an international protectorate. (4,202 sq miles/10,887 sq km; pop. 1,954,000)

Kra, Isthmus of the narrow neck of land, only some 30 miles (50 kilometres) wide and shared by Myanmar and Thailand, which joins the Malay Peninsula to the mainland of Southeast Asia.

Krakatau (Krakatoa) a volcano which erupted out of the sea between Java and Sumatra in Indonesia in 1883 in an explosion that was heard 3,100 miles (5,000 kilometres) away, and which killed 36,000 people. Today the site is marked by a more recent volcano called Anak Krakatau (Son of Krakatau).

Krishna (Kistna) a river that flows through southern India from its source in the Western Ghats to the Bay of Bengal. (Length 871 miles/1,401 km)

Krk (Veglia) a richly fertile island belonging to Croatia, in the northern Adriatic Sea. (158 sq miles/408 sq km; pop. 1,500)

Kurdistan a region of the Middle East occupied by the Kurdish people, spanning the borders of Iraq, Iran and Turkey.

Kuril (Kurile) Islands a long chain of some 56 volcanic islands stretching between the southern coast of the Kamchatka Peninsula in eastern Russian Federation and Hokkaido Island, northern Japan. The archipelago was taken from Japan by the former USSR in 1945; this remains an issue of contention between the Russian Federation and Japan. (6,020 sq miles/15,600 sq km)

Kutch (Kuchchh), Rann of an inhospitable coastal region on the border between Pakistan and India, which floods in the monsoon season and then dries out into a baking, salty desert. (17,060 sq miles/44,185 sq km)

Kuwait a tiny Arab state on The Gulf, comprising the city of Kuwait at the southern entrance of Kuwait Bay, a small undulating desert wedged between Iraq and Saudi Arabia, and nine small offshore islands. It has a dry desert climate, cool in winter but very hot and humid in summer. There is little agriculture because of lack of water. The major crops produced are melons, tomatoes, onions, and dates. The country's water comes from the desalination of seawater. Shrimp fishing is becoming an important industry. Large reserves of petroleum and natural gas are the mainstay of the economy although this wealth is limited. It has about 950 oil wells, but 600 were fired during the Iraqi occupation in 1991. Apart from oil, industries includes boat building, plastics, petrochemicals, gases, cement, and building materials. Although there are no railways, there are over 2,000 miles (3,220 kilometres) of roads and an international airport near the capital.

Area: 6,880 sq miles/17,818 sq km
Population: 1,866,000
Capital: Kuwait City (Al Kuwayt)
Form of government: Constitutional Monarchy
Religions: Sunni Islam, Shia Islam
Currency: Kuwaiti Dinar

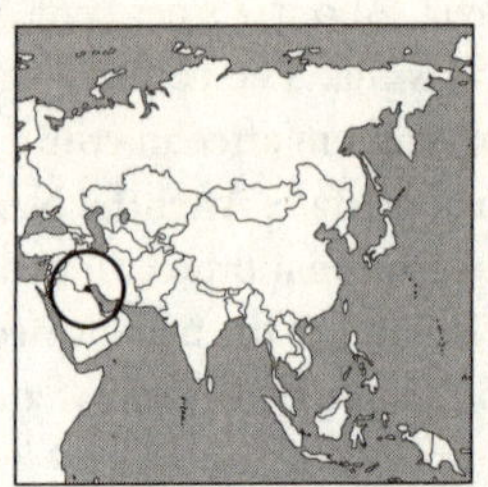

Kwai two tributaries of the Mae Khlong River in western Thailand, the Kwai Yai (Big Kwai) and the Kwai Noi (Little Kwai).

Kwajalein one of the largest atolls in the world, with a lagoon covering some 1,100 square miles (2,800 square kilometres). The island forms part of the Marshall Islands in the Pacific Ocean, and is leased to the USA as a missile target.

KwaNdebele one of ten former South African Homelands, the area is now part of the province of Mpumalanga in northeastern South Africa.

Kwango (Cuango) a river which rises in northern Angola and flows northwards to join the River Kasai in Democratic Republic of Congo. (Length 68 miles/110 km)

KwaZulu-Natal one of South Africa's nine provinces, in northeastern South Africa, with its administrative centre in Durban. (35,591 sq miles/92,100 sq km; pop. 9,360,000)

Kyrgyzstan a central Asian republic of the former USSR, independent since 1991. It is located on the border with northwest China. Much of the country is occupied by the Tian Shan Mountains, which rise to spectacular peaks. The highest is Pik Pobedy at 24,406 feet (7,439 metres) on the border with China. In the northeast of the country is Issyk Kul, a large lake heated by volcanic action, so it never freezes in winter. Most of the country is semi-arid or desert, but the climate is greatly influenced by altitude. Soils are badly leached except in the valleys, where some grains are grown. Grazing of sheep, horses, and cattle is extensive. Industries include non-ferrous metallurgy, machine building, coal mining, tobacco, food processing, textiles, gold mining, and hydroelectricity. The country has large mineral deposits of gold, coal, and uranium, while deposits of natural gas and oil have not, as yet, been developed. Parts of Kyrgyzstan are threatened by environmental pollution caused by storage of toxic waste and radioactive material which are the by-products of mining, former nuclear tests and the overuse of chemicals, especially fertilizers. The government is making efforts to address this problem, and to encourage foreign visitors.

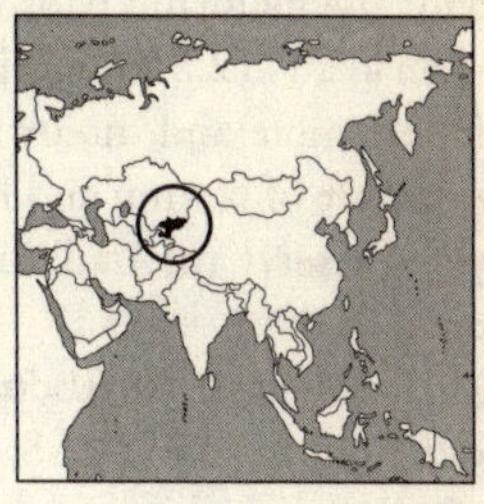

Area: 76,641 sq miles/198,500 sq km
Population: 4,575,000
Capital: Bishkek (formerly Frunze)
Form of government: Republic
Religion: Sunni Islam
Currency: Som

Kyushu the most southerly of Japan's main islands, and the third largest after Honshu and Hokkaido. (16,627 sq miles/43,065 sq km; pop. 13,276,000)

L

Labrador the mainland part of the province of Newfoundland, on the east coast of Canada. (112,826 sq miles/295,800 sq km)

Ladakh a remote and mountainous district in the northeastern part of the disputed state of Jammu and Kashmir, India, noted for its numerous monasteries which preserve the traditions of Tibetan-style Buddhism. The capital is Leh. (Pop. 118,000)

Ladoga (Laatokka), Lake (Ladozshkoye Ozero) Europe's largest lake, in the Russian Federation, northeast of St Petersburg. (7,100 sq miles/18,390 sq km)

Lake District a region of lakes and mountains in the county of Cumbria, in northwest England famed for their beauty. It includes England's highest peak, Scafell Pike (3,208 ft/978 m).

Lake of the Woods a lake spattered with some 17,000 islands in southwestern Ontario, Canada, on the USA border. (1,695 sq miles/4,390 sq km)

Lakshadweep a territory of India consisting of 27 small islands (the Amindivi Islands, Laccadive Islands and Minicoy Islands) lying 186 miles (300 kilometres) off the southwest coast of mainland India. (12 sq miles/32 sq km; pop. 62,000)

La Mancha a high, arid plateau in central Spain, some 100 miles (160 kilometres) south of Madrid, the setting for *Don Quixote*, a 17th-century novel by Miguel de Cervantes.

Lancashire a county in northwest England, once the heart of industrial Britain, with its administrative centre in Preston. (1,182 sq miles/3,063 sq km; pop. 1,424,000)

Landes a department of the Aquitaine region on the coast of southwest France. (Pop. 341,000)

Land's End the tip of the peninsula formed by Cornwall in southwest England, and the most westerly point of mainland England.

Languedoc-Rousillon a region of France which lines the Mediterranean coast from the River Rhône to the border with Spain. (10,567 sq miles/27,376 sq km; pop. 2,363,000)

Lantau the largest of the islands which form part of the New Territories of Hong Kong. (58 sq miles/150 sq km; pop. 17,000)

Laois a county in the centre of the Republic of Ireland. The county town is Portlaoise. (664 sq miles/1,718 sq km; pop. 55,000)

Laos a landlocked country in southeast Asia that is ruggedly mountainous, apart from the Mekong River plains along its border with Thailand. The Annam Mountains, which reach 8,203 feet (2,500 metres), form a natural border with Vietnam. It has a tropical monsoon climate, with high temperatures throughout the year and heavy rains in summer. Laos is one of the poorest countries in the world and its development has been retarded by war, drought, and floods. It is primarily an agricultural country, with rice, the principal crop, being grown on small peasant plots. The mighty Mekong River provides the main means of transport as well as irrigation for the rice paddies upon which the people's subsistence depends. Corn, potatoes, and cassava are also grown. There is some export of lumber, coffee, tin, and electricity. All manufactured goods (mainly food, machinery, petroleum products, and electrical equipment) must be imported. The capital and largest city, Vientiane, is the country's main trade outlet via Thailand.

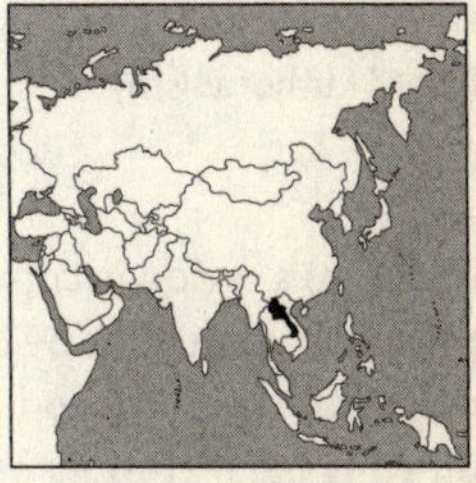

Area: 91,429 sq miles/236,800 sq km
Population: 5,035,000
Capital: Vientiane
Form of government: People's Republic
Religion: Buddhism
Currency: New Kip

Lappland (Lapland) the region of northern Scandinavia and the adjoining territory of the Russian Federation, traditionally inhabited by the nomadic Lapp people; also called 'Land of the Midnight Sun'.

Laptev Sea part of the Arctic Ocean bordering central northern Siberia.

Larne a district council area in Co. Antrim, northeast Northern Ireland. (130 sq miles/336 sq km; pop. 29,000)

Lascaux a set of caves in the Dordogne department of southwest France with Paleolithic wall paintings dating back to about 15000 BC.

Las Palmas de Gran Canaria the main port and largest city of the Canary Islands, on the island of Gran Canaria. (Pop. 366,000)

Latvia a Baltic state that regained its independence in 1991 with the break-up of the former Soviet Union. It is located in northeast Europe on the Baltic Sea and is sandwiched between Estonia and Lithuania. It has cool, wet summers, and long, cold winters. Traditionally, Latvians lived by forestry, fishing, and livestock rearing. Latvia's population is now over 70 per cent urban and agriculture is no longer the mainstay of the economy. The chief agricultural occupations are cattle and dairy farming, and the main crops grown are oats, barley, rye, potatoes, and flax. Latvia has a well-developed industrial base and produces electric railway carriages, electronic and electrical equipment (radios and refrigerators), paper, cement, chemicals, textiles, woollen goods, furniture, and foodstuffs. Latvia has abundant deposits of peat and gypsum but lacks other fossil fuels and minerals, which has made it heavily dependent on imported oil, gas, and electricity. Hydroelectric plants on the Daugava River supply over half of the domestic production of electricity. Economic development was difficult in the years following independence but the situation is gradually improving and Latvia is seeking full membership of the European Union.

Area: 24,942 sq miles/64,600 sq km
Population: 2,491,000
Capital: Riga
Other cities: Daugavpils, Liepaja
Form of government: Republic
Religion: Lutheranism
Currency: Lat

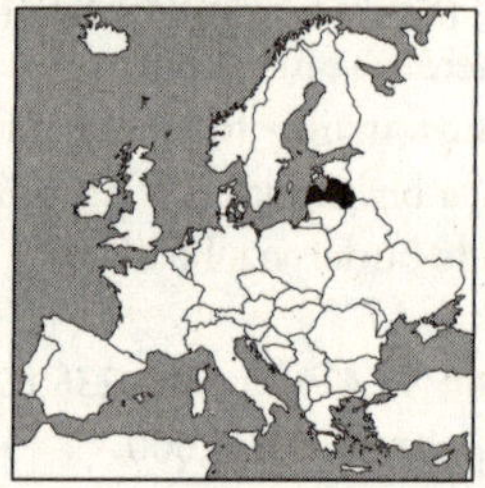

Lazio (Latium) a region occupying the central western coast of Italy around Rome, the regional capital. (6,642 sq miles/17,203 sq km; pop. 5,315,000)

Lebanon a mountainous country in the eastern Mediterranean. A narrow coastal plain runs parallel to its 149-mile (240-kilometre) Mediterranean coast and gradually rises to the spectacular Lebanon Mountains, which are snow-covered in winter. The Anti-Lebanon Mountains form the border with Syria, and between the two ranges lies the Beqa'a Valley. The climate is Mediterranean, with short warm winters and long hot and rainless summers. Rainfall can be torrential in winter and snow falls on high ground. Lebanon is an agricultural country, the main regions of production being the Beqa'a Valley and the coastal plain, although erosion is a common problem in the uplands. Main products include olives, grapes, bananas, citrus fruits, apples, cotton, tobacco, and sugar beet. Industry is small scale and manufactured goods include cement, fertilizers, and jewellery. There are oil refineries at Tripoli and Sidon. Lebanon's main economy is based on commercial services such as banking, but civil war, invasion by Israel, and factional fighting in the more recent past have created severe problems for the economy, causing high inflation and unemployment.

Area: 4,015 sq miles/10,400 sq km
Population: 3,084,000
Capital: Beirut (Beyrouth)
Other cities: Tripoli, Sidon
Form of government: Republic
Religions: Shia Islam, Sunni Islam, Christianity
Currency: Lebanese Pound

Lebowa one of ten former South African Homelands, the area is now part of the province of Limpopo in north South Africa.

Leeward and Windward Islands (1) the Lesser Antilles in the southern Caribbean are divided into two groups: the northern islands in the chain, from the Virgin Islands to Guadeloupe are the Leeward Islands; the islands further south, from Dominica to Grenada, form the Windward Islands. (2) the Society Islands of French Polynesia are also divided into Leeward and Windward Islands.

Leicestershire a county in central England, with its administrative centre in Leicester. (834 sq miles/2,553 sq km; pop. 593,000)

Leitrim a county in the northwest of the Republic of Ireland, with a small strip of coast and a border with Northern Ireland. The county town is Carrick-on-Shannon. (589 sq miles/1,525 sq km; pop. 26,000)

Léman, Lake another name for Lake Geneva.

Lena a river which flows north across eastern Siberia, from its source close to Lake Baikal to the Laptev Sea. (Length 2,650 miles/4,270 km)

Lesbos a large, fertile island in the Aegean, belonging to Greece, but only 6 miles (10 kilometres) from Turkey. (630 sq miles/1,630 sq km; pop. 106,000)

Lesotho a small, landlocked kingdom entirely surrounded by the Republic of South Africa. Snow-capped mountains and treeless uplands, cut by spectacular gorges, cover two-thirds of the country. The climate is pleasant with variable rainfall. Winters are generally dry with heavy frosts in lowland areas and frequent snow in the highlands. Because of the mountainous terrain, only one-eighth of the land can be cultivated and the main crop is maize. Yields are low because of soil erosion on the steep slopes and overgrazing by herds of sheep and cattle. Wool and mohair are exported but most foreign exchange comes from money sent home by Lesotho workers in South Africa. Tourism is beginning to flourish.

Area: 11,720 sq miles/30,355 sq km
Population: 2,078,000
Capital: Maseru
Form of government: Constitutional Monarchy
Religions: RC, other Christianity
Currency: Loti

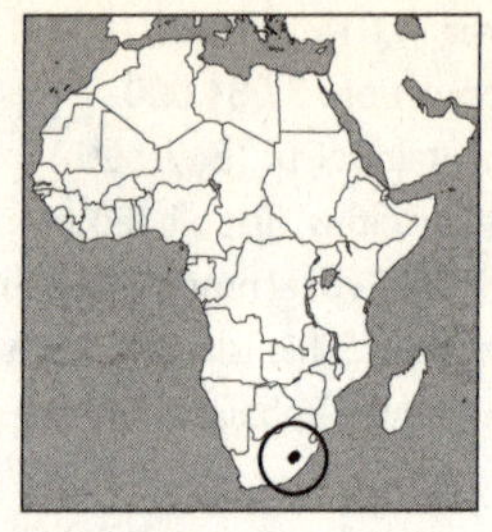

Lesser Sunda Islands (Nusa Tenggara) a chain of islands in the Malay Archipelago, to the east of Java and stretching from Bali to Timor.

Leyte an island in the central Philippines, one of the Visayan Islands group. The main town is Tacloban. (2,785 sq miles/7,213 sq km; pop. 1,480,000)

Liaoning a coastal province of Dongbei (Manchuria), northeast China, bordering North Korea. The capital is Shenyang. (54,000 sq miles/140,000 sq km; pop. 44,640,000)

Liberia located in West Africa, Liberia has a 348-mile (560-kilometre) coast stretching from Sierra Leone to Côte d'Ivoire. It is the only African country never to be ruled by a foreign power. It has a treacherous coast, with rocky cliffs and lagoons enclosed by sand bars. Inland the land rises to a densely forested plateau dissected by deep, narrow valleys. Farther inland still, there are beautiful waterfalls and the Nimba Mountains rise to a maximum height of 5,748 feet (1,752 metres). Agriculture employs three-quarters of the labour force, producing cassava and rice as subsistence crops, and rubber, coffee, and cocoa for export. The Nimba Mountains are rich in iron ore, which accounts for 70 per cent of export earnings, and wood, rubber, diamonds, and coffee are also exported. Liberia has a very large delivery tanker fleet, most of which have foreign owners. In the early 1990s, the economy suffered greatly because of civil war, leading to food shortages and the drying up of foreign investment. The situation remains uncertain, leaving Liberia with considerable problems to overcome.

Area: 43,000 sq miles/111,369 sq km
Population: 2,440,000
Capital: Monrovia
Form of government: Republic
Religions: traditional African religions, Sunni Islam, Christianity
Currency: Liberian Dollar

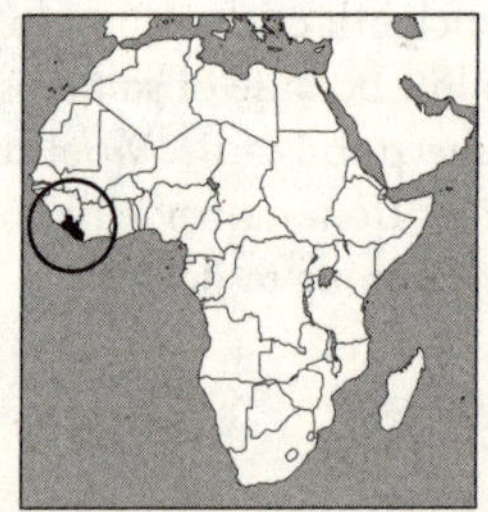

Libya a large North African country that stretches from the south coast of the Mediterranean to, and in some parts beyond, the Tropic of Cancer. The Sahara covers much of the country, extending right to the Mediterranean coast at the Gulf of Sirte. The only green areas are the scrublands found in the northwest and the forested hills near Benghazi. The coastal area has mild, wet winters and hot, dry summers, while the interior has had some of the highest recorded temperatures of anywhere in the world. Around 18 per cent of the people work on the land, the main agricultural region being in the northwest, near Tripoli, but this is dependent on rainfall. The main crops produced are wheat, tomatoes, fruits, and barley. Many sheep, goats, and cattle are reared, and there is an export trade in skins, hides, and hairs. Libya is one of the world's largest producers of oil and natural gas and also produces potash and marine salt. Other industries include food processing, textiles, cement, and handicrafts. The majority of consumer products are imported.

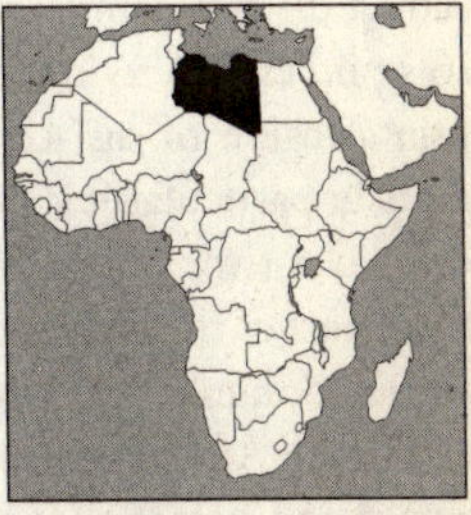

Area: 679,362 sq miles/1,759,540 sq km
Population: 4,389,000
Capital: Tripoli (Tarabulus)
Other cities: Benghazi, Misrātah
Form of government: Socialist People's Republic
Religion: Sunni Islam
Currency: Libyan Dinar

Liechtenstein the principality of Liechtenstein is a tiny central European state situated on the east bank of the River Rhine, bounded by Austria to the east and Switzerland to the west. To the east and south lie the foothills of the Austrian Alps. The highest peak, on the border with Switzerland, is Grauspitz at 8,527 feet (2,599 metres). The climate is mild alpine. Approximately one-third of the country is covered by forests. Once an agricultural country, Liechtenstein has rapidly moved into industry with a variety of light industries such as textiles, high-quality metal goods, precision instruments, ceramics, and pharmaceuticals. It is a popular location for the headquarters of foreign companies in order that they can benefit from the favourable tax laws. Other income is derived from tourism, international banking and financial services, and the sale of postage stamps.

Area: 62 sq miles/160 sq km
Population: 31,320
Capital: Vaduz
Form of government: Constitutional Monarchy
Religion: RC
Currency: Swiss Franc

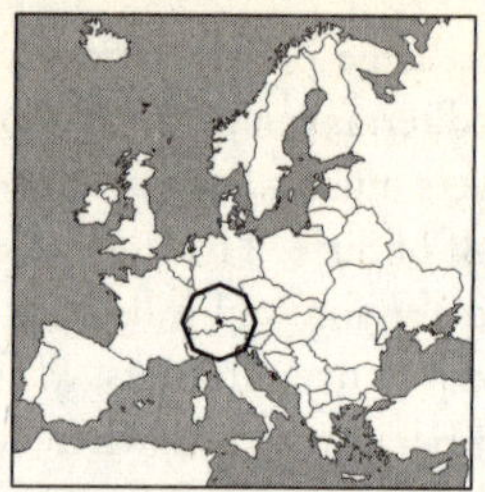

Liffey the river upon which Dublin, the capital of the Republic of Ireland, is set. (Length 49 miles/80 km)

Liguria the region of northwestern Italy which fronts the Gulf of Genoa; it has a border with France. (2,091 sq miles/5,415 sq km; pop. 1,603,000)

Ligurian Sea the northern arm of the Mediterranean Sea to the west of Italy, which includes the Gulf of Genoa.

Limavady a district council area in Co. Londonderry, north Northern Ireland. (226 sq miles/586 sq km; pop. 30,000)

Limousin a region of east-central France in the foothills of the Massif Central, famous in particular for its Limousin cattle.

Limpopo (1) a river in east South Africa which flows northwards and eastwards to form part of the border between South Africa and Botswana before crossing southern Mozambique to the Indian Ocean. (Length 1,000 miles/1,610 km) (2) one of South Africa's nine provinces, in north South Africa, formerly Northern Province and before that part of Northern Transvaal, with its administrative centre in Pietersburg. (47,829 sq miles/123,910 sq km; pop. 4,929,368)

Lincolnshire a county on the east coast of central England, with its administrative centre in Lincoln. (2,936 sq miles/7,604 sq km; pop. 922,000)

Lion, Golfe du (Lions, Gulf of) the arm of the Mediterranean Sea which forms a deep indent in the southern coast of France.

Lisburn (1) a town in Northern Ireland in the Lisburn district council area of Co. Antrim, noted for its linen industry. (Pop. 42,000) (2) a district council area in Co. Antrim, south Northern Ireland. (172 sq miles/446 sq km; pop. 100,000)

Lithuania a country that lies to the northwest of the Russian Federation and Belarus and is bounded to the north by Latvia and west by Poland. Lithuania is the largest of the three former Soviet Baltic republics. Before 1940, Lithuania was a mainly agricultural country but it has since been considerably industrialized, with shipbuilding, food processing, and electrical machinery production being the most significant industries. Most of the land is lowland, covered by forest and swamp, and the main products are rye, barley, sugar beet, flax, meat, milk, and potatoes. About 20 per cent of the population is engaged in agriculture, principally dairy farming and livestock production. Oil production has started from a small field at Kretinga in the west of the country, 10 miles (16 kilometres) north of Klaipeda. Amber is found along the Baltic coast and used by Lithuanian craftsmen for making jewellery. Financial scandals involving government members and banking institutions troubled the economy during the 1990s.

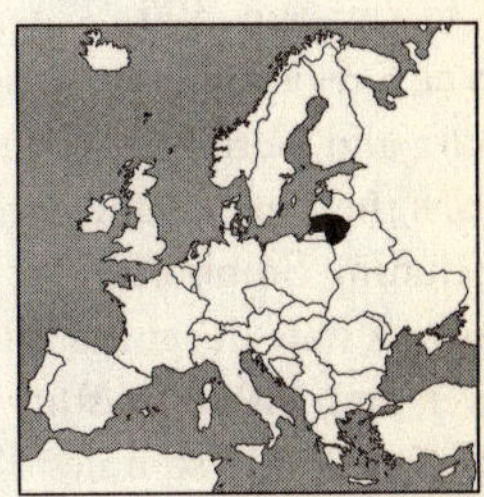

Area: 25,174 sq miles/65,200 sq km
Population: 3,701,000
Capital: Vilnius
Other cities: Kaunas, Klaipeda, Siauliai
Form of government: Republic
Religion: RC
Currency: Litas

Logan, Mount the highest mountain in Canada, and the second highest in North America after Mount McKinley. It is situated in southwest Yukon, on the border with Alaska. (19,524 ft/5,951 m)

Loire the longest river in France, flowing northwards from the southeastern Massif Central and then to the west to meet the Atlantic Ocean near Nantes. Its middle reaches are famous for their spectacular châteaux. (Length 635 miles/ 1,020 km)

Lombardy (Lombardia) the central northern region of Italy, which drops down from the Alps to the plain of the River Po, one of the country's most productive areas in both agriculture and industry. Milan is the regional capital. (9,210 sq miles/ 23,854 sq km; pop. 9,053,000)

Lombok an island of the Lesser Sunda group, east of Bali. (2,098 sq miles/ 5,435 sq km; pop. 1,300,200)

London (1) the capital city of England and the United Kingdom, which straddles both banks of the River Thames near its estuary. (2) **Greater** the administrative area of London, consisting of the city of London and 32 boroughs. (610 sq mil es;1,579 sq km; pop. 6,964,000) (3) an industrial city in southeastern Ontario, Canada. (Pop. 351,000)

Londonderry (Derry) (1) a historical county in northwest Northern Ireland. (814 sq miles/2,108 sq km) (2) a port and the second largest city in Northern Ireland after Belfast. (Pop. 72,000) *See also* **Derry**.

Longford a county in the centre of the Republic of Ireland, with a county town of the same name. (403 sq miles/1,044 sq km; pop. 32,000)

Long Island an island off the coast of New York State, USA, stretching some 118 miles (190 kilometres) to the northeast away from the city of New York.

Its western end forms part of the city of New York (the boroughs of Brooklyn and Queens) but the rest is a mixture of residential suburbs, farmland and resort beaches. (1,423 sq miles/3,685 sq km)

Lord Howe Island a small island lying some 375 miles (600 kilometres) to the east of the coast of New South Wales, Australia, now a popular resort. (6 sq miles/ 16 sq km; pop. 300)

Lorraine a region of northeast France, with a border shared by Belgium, Luxembourg and Germany. The regional capital is Metz.

Lothians the three council areas of East Lothian, West Lothian and Midlothian (including Edinburgh).

Louisiana a state in central southern USA, on the lower reaches of the Mississippi River, and with a coastline on the Gulf of Mexico. The state capital is Baton Rouge. (48,523 sq miles/125,675 sq km; pop. 4,463,000)

Louth a county on the northeast coast of the Republic of Ireland. The county town is Dundalk. (318 sq miles/823 sq km; pop. 96,000)

Lualaba a river that flows northwards across the eastern part of the Democratic Republic of Congo from the border with Zambia before joining the River Lomami to form the Congo River. (Length 1,120 miles/1,800 km)

Luxembourg the Grand Duchy of Luxembourg is a small landlocked country bounded by Belgium on the west, France on the south, and Germany on the east. In the north of the duchy, a wooded plateau, the Oesling, rises to 1,804 feet (550 metres) while in the south there is a lowland area of valleys and ridges, known as the Gutland. Northern winters are cold and raw, with snow covering the ground for almost a month, but southern winters are mild and summers cool. In the south, the land is fertile, and crops grown include maize, roots, tubers, and potatoes, with livestock also being raised. In the east, Luxembourg is bordered by the Moselle River in whose valley grapes are produced for wine. Beds of iron ore (declining) are found in the south, and these form the basis of the country's iron and steel industry. The country is very industrialized, with the tourism and the financial sector playing increasingly important parts in the country's economy. The capital, Luxembourg City, is the seat of the European Court of Justice.

Area: 998 sq miles/2586 sq km
Population: 412,000
Capital: Luxembourg City
Form of government: Constitutional Monarchy (Duchy)
Religion: RC
Currency: Euro

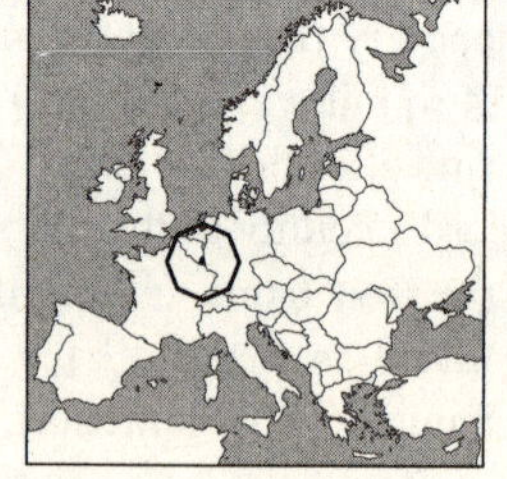

Luzon the largest island of the Philippines, in the north of the group, with the nation's capital, Manila, at its centre. (40,420 sq miles/104,688 sq km; pop. 32,211,000)

M

Macáu (Macao) a special administrative region on the south coast of China. Formerly a Portuguese province, Macao was handed back to China in 1999. (7 sq miles/18 sq km; pop. 440,000; cur. Pataca)

Macdonnell Ranges the parallel ranges of mountains of central Australia, in the southern part of the Northern Territory, near Alice Springs. The highest peak is Mount Ziel (4,954 ft/1,510 m).

Macedonia the largest region of Greece, occupying most of the northern mainland area, and bordering Albania, former Yugoslavia and Bulgaria. (Pop. 2,122,000)

Macedonia (FYROM) the Former Yugoslav Republic of Macedonia (FYROM) declared its independence from Yugoslavia under the name of Macedonia in November 1991. Greece, however, angered at the use of 'Macedonia' (also the name of the neighbouring Greek province) imposed a trade embargo and convinced the United Nations not to recognize the nation's independence. In 1993, Macedonia was admitted to the UN after changing its official name to the Former Yugoslav Republic of Macedonia. In 1995, an agreement was reached with Greece whereby both countries would respect the territory, sovereignty and independence of the other, with Macedonia agreeing to adopt a new flag. A landlocked country, Macedonia shares its borders with Albania, Bulgaria, Greece, and Yugoslavia. Its terrain is mountainous, covered by deep valleys, with several large lakes. The country's longest river, the Vardar, divides the country before it flows into Greece and eventually empties into the Aegean Sea. The climate consists of hot, dry summers and cold winters with considerable snow. It is the poorest of the six former Yugoslav republics but sustains itself through agriculture and its coal industries. Some of its natural resources include chromium, lead, zinc, nickel, iron ore, and lumber. Tourism is now starting to revive, having been badly affected by fighting in the region in the early 1990s.

Area: 9,928 sq miles/25,713 sq km
Population: 2,174,000
Capital: Skopje
Other cities: Kumanovo, Ohrid
Form of government: Republic
Religions: Eastern Orthodox, Sunni Islam
Currency: Denar

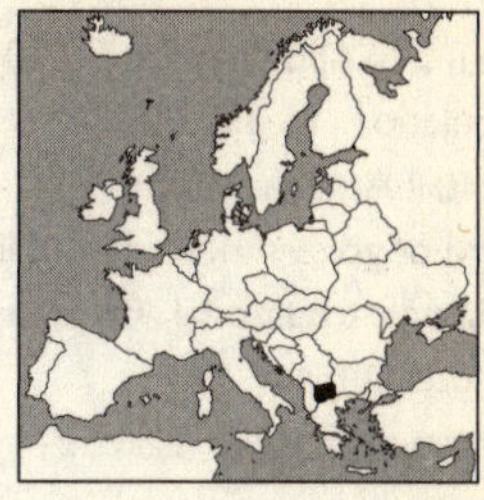

Macgillicuddy's Reeks a range of mountains in the southwest of the Republic of Ireland which includes the country's highest peak, Carrauntoohil (3,414 ft/1,040 m).

Mackenzie a river flowing northwards through the western part of the Northwest Territories of Canada from the Great Slave Lake to the Arctic Ocean. (Length 2,640 miles/4,250 km)

McKinley, Mount the highest mountain in North America, located in the Denali National Park in southern Alaska, USA. (20,322 ft/6,194 m)

MacMurdo Sound an arm of the Ross Sea, off Antarctica.

Madagascar an island state situated off the southeast coast of Africa, separated from the mainland by the Mozambique Channel. Madagascar is the fourth largest island in the world and its centre is made up of high savannah-covered plateaux. In the east, forested mountains fall steeply to the coast while in the southwest the land falls gradually through dry grassland and scrub. The staple food crop is rice, and although only 5 per cent of the land is cultivated, 80 per cent of the population grow enough to feed themselves. Cassava, potatoes, maize, beans, and bananas are also grown, but some 58 per cent of the land is pasture and there are more cattle than people. The main export earners are coffee, vanilla, cloves, and sugar cane. There is mining for chromite, graphite, mica, and salt, and an oil refinery at Toamasina on the east coast. Upon independence in 1960, Madagascar became known as the Malagasy Republic, but this was changed back to Madagascar by referendum in 1975. Madagascar's isolation from mainland Africa means that there are several species of plants and animals that are quite different from mainland species. As a result, many tourists come to Madagascar to explore this aspect of the country's fauna and flora.

Area: 226,658 sq miles/587,041 sq km
Population: 15,353,000
Capital: Antananarivo
Form of government: Republic
Religions: traditional African religions, RC, Protestantism
Currency: Franc Malgache

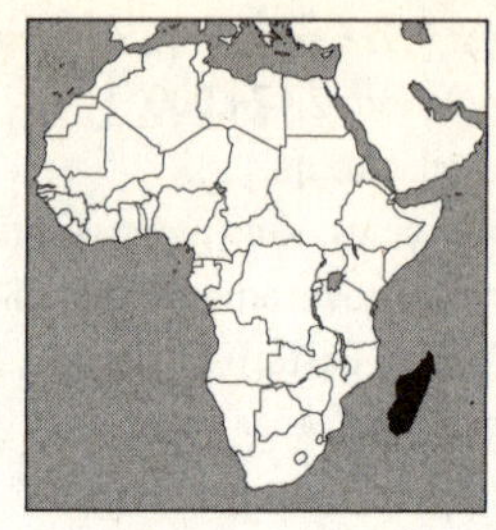

Madeira the main island in a small group in the eastern Atlantic Ocean which have belonged to Portugal since the 16th century, lying some 620 miles (1,000 kilometres) due west of Casablanca in Morocco. The capital is Funchal. (286 sq miles/740 sq km; pop. 243,000)

Madhya Pradesh the largest state in India, in the centre of the country. The capital is Bhopal. (171,170 sq miles/443,446 sq km; pop. 61,564,000)

Madura an island off the northeastern coast of Java. (2,042 sq miles/5,290 sq km; pop. 1,860,000)

Magdalena a river which flows northwards through western Colombia and into the Caribbean at Barranquila. (Length 965 miles/1,550 km)

Magellan, Strait of (Estrecho de Magallanes) the waterway, 2 miles (3 kilometres) wide at its narrowest point and 370 miles (600 kilometres) long, which separates the island of Tierra Del Fuego from the southern tip of mainland South America. It was discovered in 1521 by the Portuguese navigator, Ferdinand Magellan (*c.*1480–1521).

Magherafelt a district council area in Co. Londonderry, north Northern Ireland. (221 sq miles/572 sq km; pop. 36,000)

Maghreb (Maghrib) the name by which the countries of northwest Africa, Morocco, Algeria and Tunisia are often collectively known.

Maharashtra a state in the centre of the west coast of India, with Bombay as its capital. (118,768 sq miles/307,690 sq km; pop. 98,642,000)

Main a river that snakes its way westwards from its source near Bayreuth in central Germany, passing through Frankfurt am Main before joining the River Rhine at Mainz. (Length 325 miles/524 km)

Maine a state in the northeastern corner of the USA, bordering Canada. The state capital is Augusta. (33,215 sq miles/86,027 sq km; pop. 1,298,000)

Majorca (Mallorca) the largest of the Balearic Islands, in the western Mediterranean. The capital is Palma. (1,405 sq miles/3,639 sq km; pop. 460,000; cur. Euro)

Majuro an atoll of three islands (Dalap, Uliga and Darrit) which together form the capital of the Marshall Islands. (Pop. 32,000)

Makassar Strait the broad stretch of water, 81 miles (130 kilometres) across at its narrowest, which separates Borneo and Sulawesi in Indonesia.

Malabar Coast the name given to the coastal region of the state of Kerala in southwestern India.

Malacca, Strait of the busy waterway, just 31 miles (50 kilometres) wide at its narrowest point, which separates the island of Sumatra in Indonesia from the southern tip of Malaysia, with Singapore at its eastern end.

Malawi a country that lies along the southern and western shores of the third largest lake in Africa, Lake Malawi. To the south of the lake, the Shire River flows through a valley overlooked by wooded, towering mountains. The tropical climate has a dry season from May to October and a wet season for the remaining months. Agriculture is the predominant occupation and many Malawians live off their own crops. Exports include tea grown on the terraced hillsides in the south and tobacco on the central plateau plus peanuts and sugar, with maize also being an important crop. Malawi has bauxite and coal deposits but because of the inaccessibility of their locations, mining is limited. Hydroelectricity is now being used for manufacturing but imports of manufactured goods remain high and the country remains one of the poorest in the world. Malawi was formerly the British colony of Nyasaland, a name meaning 'Land of the Lake', which was given to it by the 19th-century explorer, David Livingstone.

Area: 45,747 sq miles/118,484 sq km
Population: 10,114,000
Capital: Lilongwe
Other cities: Blantyre, Mzuzu, Zomba
Form of government: Republic
Religions: traditional African religions, RC, Presbyterianism
Currency: Kwacha

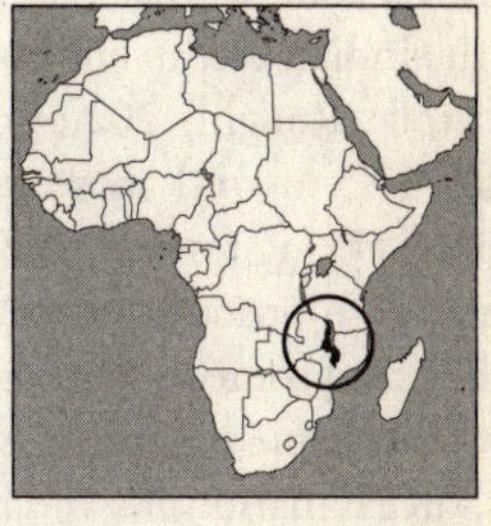

Malawi (Nyasa), Lake a long, narrow lake which runs down most of the eastern side of Malawi and forms Malawi's border with Tanzania and Mozambique. (9,000 sq miles/23,300 sq km)

Malaysia the Federation of Malaysia lies in the South China Sea in southeast Asia. It comprises peninsular Malaysia on the Malay Peninsula and the states of Sabah and Sarawak on the island of Borneo. Malaysia is affected by the monsoon climate. The northeast monsoon brings rain to the east coast of peninsular Malaysia in winter, and the southwest monsoon brings rain to the west coast in summer. Throughout the country, the climate is generally tropical and temperatures are uniformly hot throughout the year. Peninsular Malaysia has always had thriving rubber-growing and tin-dredging industries, and now oil palm growing is also important on the east coast. Sabah and Sarawak have grown rich by exploiting their natural resources, the forests. There is also some offshore oil, and around the capital, Kuala Lumpur, new industries, such as electronics, are expanding. In recent years, tourism has become an important industry. There are plans for a new international airport and a large dam for hydroelectric production. Malaysia was hit by economic recession in 1997, and it implemented a series of measures designed to restore confidence in its economy.

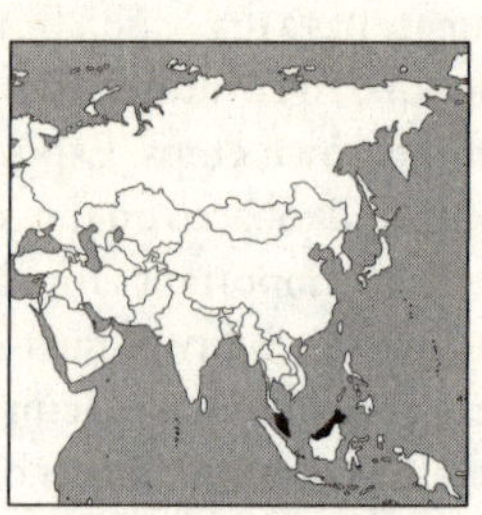

Area: 127,320 sq miles/329,749 sq km
Population: 20,581,000
Capital: Kuala Lumpur
Other cities: Ipoh, George Town, Johor Baharu
Form of government: Federal Constitutional Monarchy
Religion: Sunni Islam
Currency: Ringgi

Maldives a country that lies 398 miles (640 kilometres) southwest of Sri Lanka in the Indian Ocean and comprises 1,200 low-lying coral islands grouped into 12 atolls. Roughly 202 of the islands are inhabited. The highest point is only 5 feet (1.5 metres) above sea level. Independence was gained in 1965, with a republic being formed three years later. The climate is hot and humid and affected by monsoons from May to August. The islands are covered by coconut palms, and some millet, cassava, yams, and tropical fruit are grown. However, rice, the staple diet of its islanders, is imported. The most important natural resource is marine life, and fishing is an important occupation. The chief export is now canned or frozen tuna. Tourism is developing fast and has taken over from fishing as the major foreign currency earner.

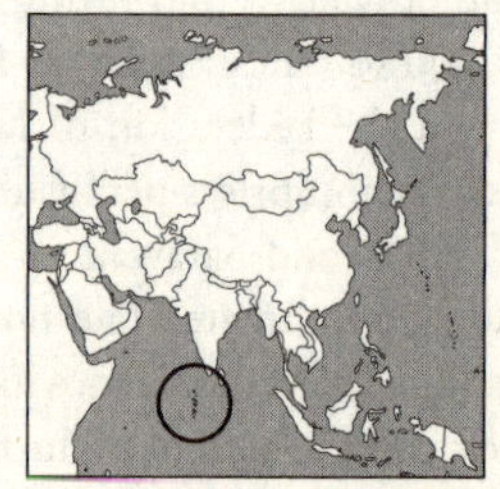

Area: 115 sq miles/298 sq km
Population: 263,000
Capital: Malé
Form of government: Republic
Religion: Sunni Islam
Currency: Rufiyaa

Malé the main atoll of the Maldives, and the town which is the country's capital. (2.6 sq km/1 sq mile; pop. 79,000)

Mali a landlocked state in West Africa. The country mainly comprises vast and monotonous plains and plateaus. It rises to 3,790 feet (1,155 metres) in the Adrar des Iforas range in the northeast. The Sahara in the north of the country is encroaching southwards. In the south, there is some rain and plains are covered by grassy savannah and a few scattered trees. The River Niger runs through the south of the country and small steamboats use it for shipping between Koulikoro and Gao. Fish are plentiful in the river and its water is used to irrigate the land. Only a fifth of the land can be cultivated. Rice, cassava, and millet are grown for domestic consumption and cotton for export. The country's main exports include cotton, gold, foodstuffs, livestock, and mangoes. Iron ore and bauxite have been discovered but have yet to be exploited. Mali is one of the poorest countries in the world. Droughts in the 1970s and mid-1980s resulted in thousands of cattle dying and in crop failure, with famine or disease killing many of the population.

Area: 478,841 sq miles/1,240,192 sq km
Population: 11,134,000
Capital: Bamako
Other cities: Ségou, Mopti
Form of government: Republic
Religions: Sunni Islam, traditional African religions
Currency: CFA Franc

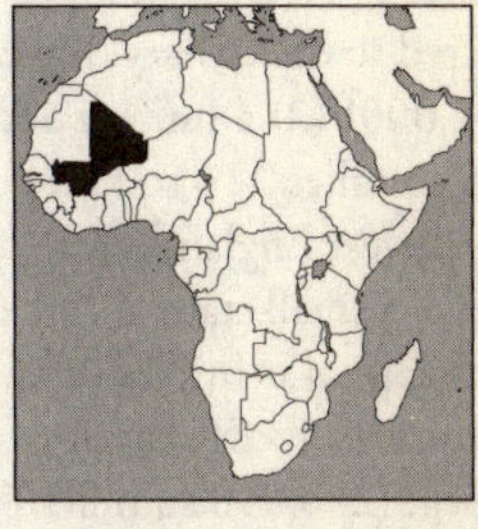

Malta a small republic in the middle of the Mediterranean Sea, lying just south of the island of Sicily. It comprises three islands, Malta, Gozo, and Comino, which are made up of low limestone plateaus with little surface water. The climate is Mediterranean, with hot, dry sunny summers and little rain. Lack of water has led to the production of desalination plants that produce up to 70 per cent of the country's needs. Winters are cooler and wetter. Malta is virtually self-sufficient in agricultural products and exports potatoes, vegetables, wine and cut flowers. The British military base on Malta was once the mainstay of the economy but after the British withdrew in the late 1970s, the naval dockyard was converted for commercial shipbuilding and repairs. Tourism is important to the economy and the island has become popular for retirement in the sunshine with low taxes.

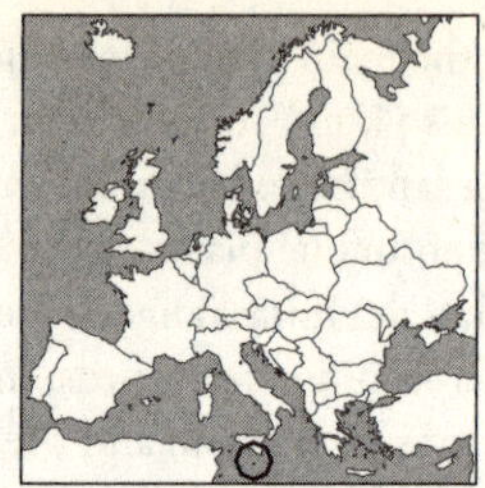

Area: 122 sq miles/316 sq km
Population: 376,000
Capital: Valletta
Form of government: Republic
Religion: RC
Currency: Maltese Pound

Maluku (Moluccas) a group of some 1,000 islands in eastern Indonesia, known as the Spice Islands because they were once the only source of cloves and nutmegs. The principal islands are Halmahera, Seram and Buru. The capital is Ambon. (28,766 sq miles/74,505 sq km; pop. 2,353,000)

Man, Isle of an island of the British Isles, in the Irish Sea, halfway between England and Ireland. It is a British crown possession, not a part of the UK, and has its own parliament, the Court of Tynwald. The capital is Douglas. (226 sq miles/585 sq km; pop. 77,000)

Manchester (1) a major industrial and commercial city in northwest England, connected to the estuary of the River Mersey by the Manchester Ship Canal. (Pop. 402,000) (2) a unitary authority in Greater Manchester, northwest England. (45 sq miles/116 sq km; pop. 433,000) (3) **Greater** a metropolitan county of northwest England. (496 sq miles/1,286 sq km)

Manipur a small state of India in the far northeast, on the border with Myanmar. The capital is Imphal. (8,618 sq miles/22,327 sq km; pop. 2,435,000)

Manitoba the most easterly of the prairie provinces of Canada. The capital is Winnipeg. (250,998 sq miles/650,087 sq km; pop. 1,163,000)

Maracaibo, Lake a shallow lake in northwest Venezuela, containing one of the richest oil fields in the world. (5,127 sq miles/13,280 sq km)

Marche (Marches) a region of central eastern Italy, lining the Adriatic coast. The capital is Ancona. (3,743 sq miles/9,694 sq km; pop. 1,463,000)

Marmara, Sea of a small sea lying between the Dardanelles and the Bosphorus, providing a vital link in the route between the Mediterranean Sea and the Black Sea. The surrounding coasts all belong to Turkey.

Marquesas Islands a group of a dozen or so fertile, volcanic islands in the northeastern sector of French Polynesia, lying about 875 miles (1,400 kilometres) northeast of Tahiti. (459 sq miles/1,189 sq km; pop. 9,000)

Marshall Islands formerly part of the United States-administered United Nations Trust Territory, this self-governing republic comprises a scattering of over 1,000 coral atolls and islets, arranged in two parallel chains, Ratak and Ralik, located in eastern Micronesia in the western Pacific Ocean and lying to the northwest of Kiribati. The climate is tropical maritime, with little variation in temperature, and rainfall that is heaviest from July to October. The republic remains in free association with the USA and the economy has been almost totally dependent on US-related payments for use of the islands as bases. The Bikini Atoll was used as a nuclear testing area in 1946. Attempts have been made to diversify the economy, but the main occupations remain fishing and agriculture, with the chief export being copra.

Area: 70 sq miles/181 sq km
Population: 58,000
Capital: Dalag-Uliga-Darrit [on Majuro atoll]
Form of government: Republic in free association with the USA
Religion: Protestantism
Currency: US Dollar

Martinique one of the larger of the islands in the Windward Islands group in the southern Caribbean, lying between Dominica and St Lucia. It is administered as a department of France. The centre of the island is mountainous, while the quality of its beaches has played a role in its development as a tourist resort. It has a volcano, Mont Pelée (4,583 ft/1,397 m), that erupted in 1902, wiping out the town of St Pierre and killing all but one of its inhabitants. Martinique is periodically subjected to hurricanes that can cause considerable damage. The island's economy relies mainly on tourism with sugar, bananas, pineapples, citrus fruits, nutmeg, and spices being grown in some parts of the island.

Area: 425 sq miles/1,102 sq km
Population: 384,000
Capital: Fort-de-France
Form of government: Overseas Department of France
Religion: RC
Currency: Euro

Maryland a state on the central east coast of the USA, virtually divided in two by Chesapeake Bay. The state capital is Annapolis. (10,577 sq miles/27,394 sq km; pop. 5,455,000)

Maseru the capital of Lesotho. (Pop. 169,000)

Massachusetts one of the New England states on the northeastern coast of the

USA. The capital is Boston. (8257 sq miles/21,386 sq km; pop. 6,410,000)

Massif Central the rugged upland region which occupies much of southern central France to the west of the River Rhône. The highest point is at Puy de Sancy (6,184 ft/1,885 m).

Matterhorn (Monte Cervino) a distinctive, pyramid-shaped peak on the border between Italy and Switzerland, 3 miles (5 kilometres) south of Zermatt. (14,688 ft/4,477 m)

Maui the second largest island of Hawaii, USA. (727 sq miles/1,885 sq km)

Mauna Kea a dormant volcano in the north of the island of Hawaii, USA. (13,796 ft/4,205 m)

Mauna Loa an active volcano in the centre of the island of Hawaii, USA. (13,677 ft/4,169 m)

Mauritania a country nearly twice the size of France, the Islamic Arab and African Republic of Mauritania is located on the west coast of Africa. About 47 per cent of the country is desert, the Sahara covering much of the north. The only settlements found in this area are around oases, where a little millet, dates, and vegetables can be grown. The main agricultural regions are in the Senegal River valley in the south. The rest of the country is made up of the drought-stricken Sahel grasslands. The majority of the people are traditionally nomadic herdsmen, but severe droughts since the late 1960s have killed about 70 per cent of the nation's animals, forcing the population to settle along the Senegal River. As a result, vast shanty towns have sprung up around all of the country's towns. The country's economy is very reliant on foreign aid. The production of iron ore and other deposits provide the country's main exports, and development of these and the fishing industry on the coast form the only hope for a brighter future. Mauritania has also experienced some internal political unrest and been involved in disputes with its neighbours. Conditions appear to have become more settled in recent years with a new constitution adopted in 1991.

Area: 395,956 sq miles/1,025,520 sq km
Population: 2,351,000
Capital: Nouakchott
Form of government: Republic
Religion: Sunni Islam
Currency: Ouguiya

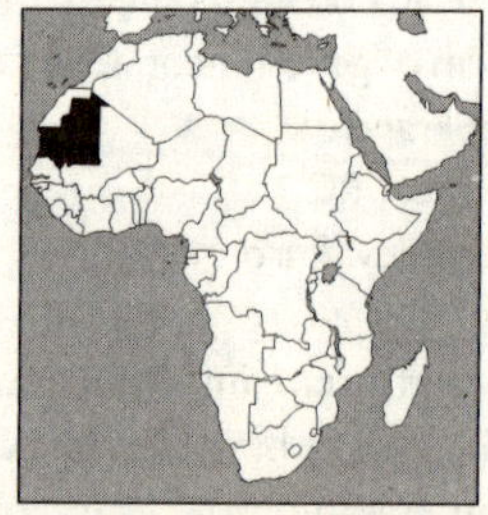

Mauritius a beautiful island with tropical beaches, lying about 20 degrees south in the Indian Ocean and 497 miles (800 kilometres) east of Madagascar, which gained independence in 1968. The islands of Rodrigues and Agalega are also part of Mauritius. Mauritius is a volcanic island with many craters surrounded by lava flows. The central plateau rises to over 2,625 feet (800 metres), then drops sharply to the south and west coasts. The climate is hot and humid with southwesterly winds bringing heavy rain in the uplands. There is the possibility of cyclones from December to April. The island has well-watered fertile soil, ideal for the sugar plantations that cover 45 per cent of the island. Although the export of molasses and sugar still dominates the economy, diversification is being encouraged. Other crops such as tea, tobacco, peanuts, and vegetables are grown. The clothing and electronic equipment industries are becoming increasingly important and tourism is now the third largest source of foreign currency.

Area: 788 sq miles/2,040 sq km
Population: 1,160,000
Capital: Port Louis
Form of government: Republic
Religions: Hinduism, RC, Sunni Islam
Currency: Mauritian Rupee

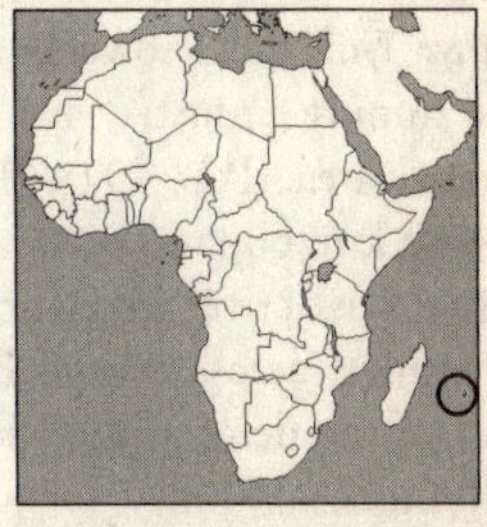

Mayo a county on the west coast of the Republic of Ireland. The county town is Castlebar. (1,865 sq miles/4,831 sq km; pop. 116,000)

Mayotte (Mahore) one of the Comoros Islands, lying between Madagascar and the mainland of Africa. Unlike the other three islands in the group, Mayotte voted to remain under the administration of France when the Comoros Islands became independent in 1974. (144 sq miles/373 sq km; pop. 174,000)

Meath a county on the east coast of the Republic of Ireland, north of Dublin. The county town is Navan. (902 sq miles/2,336 sq km; pop. 114,000)

Mediterranean Sea a large sea bounded by southern Europe, North Africa and southwest Asia. It is connected to the Atlantic Ocean by the Strait of Gibraltar. (970,000 sq miles/2,512,000 sq km)

Médoc one of the prime wine-producing regions of France, a flat, triangular-shaped piece of land situated between the Gironde estuary and the Atlantic Ocean.

Meghalaya a predominantly rural state in the hills of northeastern India, with Bangladesh to the south. (8,658 sq miles/22,429 sq km; pop. 2,351,000)

Mekong the great river of Southeast Asia, flowing from Tibet, through southern China, Laos and Cambodia before forming a massive and highly fertile delta in southern Vietnam and flowing into the South China Sea. (Length 2,562 miles/4,184 km)

Melanesia the central and southern group of islands in the South Pacific Ocean, including the Solomon Islands, Vanuatu, Fiji and New Caledonia.

Menai Strait the narrow strait, 590 feet (180 metres) across at its narrowest, separating mainland Wales from the island of Anglesey, spanned by road and rail bridges.

Mersey a river in northwest England. It forms an estuary to the south of Liverpool which is deep and wide enough to permit access for ocean-going ships to Liverpool and Manchester (via the Manchester Ship Canal). (Length 70 miles/110 km)

Merseyside a metropolitan county, centring on the River Mersey, in northwest England. (252 sq miles/652 sq km; pop. 1,409,000)

Merthyr Tydfil (1) a town in southeast Wales, formerly an important centre for the mining industry, and the administrative centre for the Merthyr Tydfil council area. (Pop. 40,000) (2) a council area in southeast Wales. (43 sq miles/111 sq km; pop. 60,000)

Meuse (Maas) a river which flows northwest from its source in the Lorraine region of France, across central Belgium and into the Netherlands, where it joins part of the delta of the River Rhine before entering the North Sea. (Length 580 miles/935 km)

Mexico the most southerly country in North America. It has its longest border with the United States to the north, a long coast on the Pacific Ocean and a smaller coast in the west of the Gulf of Mexico. It is a land of volcanic mountain ranges and high plateaux. The highest peak is Citlaltépetl at 18,697 feet (5,699 metres), which is permanently snow-capped. Coastal lowlands are found in the west and east. Its wide range of latitude and relief produce a variety of climates. In the north, there are arid and semi-arid conditions while in the south there is a humid tropical climate. Thirty per cent of the labour force is involved in agriculture, growing maize, wheat, kidney beans, and rice for subsistence, and coffee, cotton, fruit, and vegetables for export, although some irrigation is needed. Mexico has substantial and varied mineral deposits, such as silver, coal, phosphates, gold, and uranium, as well as large reserves of oil and natural gas. Forests cover around a quarter of the country with trees such as ebony, mahogany, and walnut. Developing industries are petrochemicals, textiles, motor vehicles, and food processing. Tourism also makes an important contribution to the country's economy.

Area: 756,066 sq miles/1,958,201 sq km
Population: 96,578,000
Capital: Mexico City (México)
Other cities: Guadalajara, Monterrey, Puebla
Form of government: Federal Republic
Religion: RC
Currency: Mexican Peso

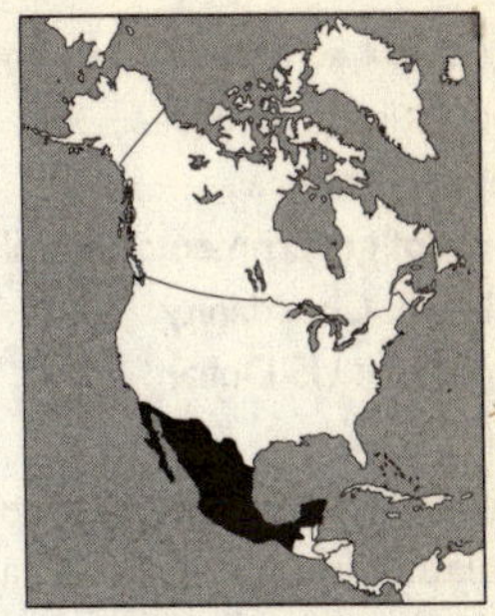

Mexico, Gulf of an arm of the Atlantic Ocean, bounded by the Florida Peninsula in southeast USA and the Yucatan Peninsula in Mexico, with the island of Cuba placed in the middle of its entrance.

Michigan a state in north central USA, formed out of two peninsulas between the Great Lakes, with Lake Michigan in the middle. The capital is Lansing. (58,216 sq miles/150,780 sq km; pop. 10,044,000)

Michigan, Lake one of the Great Lakes, and the only one to lie entirely within the USA. (22,300 sq miles/57,750 sq km)

Micronesia one of the three main groupings of islands of the Pacific Ocean, lying to the northwest of the other two main groupings, Melanesia and Polynesia, and stretching from Belau to Kiribati.

Micronesia, Federated States of formerly part of the United States-administered United Nations Trust Territory of the Pacific, known as the Caroline Islands, this self-governing republic became independent in 1990. It comprises an archipelago of over 600 islands, including Pohnpei (Ponape), the Truk (Churk) Islands, the Yap Islands, and Kosrae. Mostly uninhabited, they are located in the western Pacific Ocean, about 2,500 miles (4,025 kilometres) southwest of Hawaii. The climate is tropical maritime, with high temperatures and rainfall all year round but a pronounced precipitation peak between July and October. Micronesia is still closely linked to the USA, with a heavy reliance on aid. Attempts are being made to diversify the economy, the exports of which are mainly fishing and copra. There are significant phosphate deposits but the island's isolation restricts development. Tourism is a growing trade but the economy of the region remains fragile.

Area: 271 sq miles/702 sq km
Population: 109,000
Capital: Kolonia
Form of government: Republic
Religion: Christianity
Currency: US Dollar

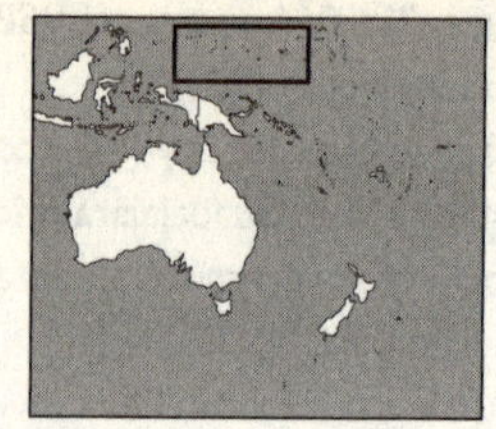

Middle East a non-specific term used to describe an area of southwest Asia, which is mainly Islamic and/or Arabic-speaking. Countries included are: Turkey, Iran, Iraq, Syria, Jordan, Israel, Saudi Arabia, Lebanon, Yemen, Oman, the United Arab Emirates, Qatar, Bahrain and Kuwait.

Midlands, the a term used to describe the central industrial counties of England: Derbyshire, Northamptonshire, Nottinghamshire, Staffordshire, Warwickshire, Leicestershire, and West Midlands.

Midlothian a council area in southeast central Scotland, with its administrative centre in the town of Dalkeith. (137 sq miles/356 sq km; pop. 80,000)

Midway Islands two atolls belonging to the USA, in the north Pacific Ocean, 1,242 miles (2,000 km) northwest of Hawaii. (2 sq miles/3 sq km; pop. 500)

Midwest (Middle West) a term used to describe the fertile north central part of the USA. States in the Midwest include Ohio, Michigan, Indiana, Illinois, Wisconsin, Minnesota, Iowa and Missouri, but others, such as Kansas, are also often included.

Minch, the a broad channel separating northwest Scotland from the Outer Hebrides.

Mindanao the second largest island of the Philippines. (36,537 sq miles/ 4,631 sq km; pop. 16,526,000)

Mindoro an island in west central Philippines. (3,759 sq miles/9,736 sq km)

Minorca (Menorca) the second largest of the Balearic Islands, after Majorca. The capital is Mahon. (271 sq miles/702 sq km; pop. 50,200; cur. Euro)

Mississippi (1) a state in central southern USA with a small coastline on the Gulf of Mexico. The state capital is Jackson. (47,716 sq miles/123,585 sq km; pop. 2,872,000) (2) the second longest river in the USA. It rises in Minnesota and runs south the length of the country to the Gulf of Mexico. (Length 2,348 miles/3,779 km)

Missouri (1) a state in the Midwest of the USA. The state capital is Jefferson City. (69,686 sq miles/180,487 sq km; pop. 5,664,000) (2) the main tributary of the Mississippi with which it is the longest river in North America. It rises in Montana, flows north, east and southeast to join the Mississippi at the port of St Louis. (Length 2,466 miles/3,969 km)

Mizoram a union territory of India, in the hilly northeast, on the border with Myanmar. The capital is Aijal. (8,137 sq miles/21,081 sq km; pop. 908,000)

Mojave (Mohave) Desert a desert in southern California, USA, stretching from Death Valley to Los Angeles. (15,000 sq miles/38,850 sq km)

Moldova (Moldavia) a Soviet socialist republic from 1940 until 1991 when it became independent of the former USSR. It is bounded to the west by Romania and to the north, east, and south by Ukraine. The republic consists of a hilly plain with an average height of around 500 feet (150 metres). Its main rivers are the Prut in the west and the Dnister in the north and east. Moldova's soils are fertile, and crops grown include wheat, corn, barley, tobacco, sugar beet, soybeans and sunflowers. There are also extensive fruit orchards, vineyards, and walnut groves. Beekeeping and silkworm breeding are widespread throughout the country. Food processing is the main industry, particularly sugar refining and winemaking. Other industries include metalworking, engineering, and the manufacture of electrical equipment. After independence, the economy declined, inflation soared, and assistance was gained from the International Monetary Fund and others.

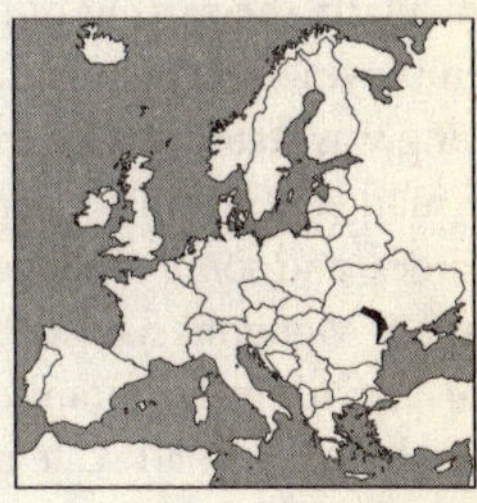

Area: 13,012 sq miles/33,700 sq km
Population: 4,327,000
Capital: Chisinau (Kishinev)
Other cities: Tiraspol, Bel'tsy
Form of government: Republic
Religion: Russian Orthodox
Currency: Leu

Molise a region of eastern Italy, on the Adriatic coast, between Abruzzi and Puglia. (1,714 sq miles/4,438 sq km; pop. 329,000)

Monaco a tiny principality on the Mediterranean Sea, surrounded landwards by the Alpes Maritimes department of France. It comprises a rocky peninsula and a narrow stretch of coast. It has mild moist winters and hot dry summers. The ancient fortified town of Monaco-Ville is situated on a rocky promontory and houses the royal palace and the cathedral. The Monte Carlo district has the world-famous casino, and La Condamine has thriving businesses, stores, banks, and attractive residential areas. Fontvieille is an area reclaimed from the sea where marinas and light industry are now located. The light industry includes chemicals, plastics, electronics, engineering, and paper, but it is tourism that is the main revenue earner. Tobacco, insurance, and banking industries, and the sale of stamps also contribute to the economy. Two well-known annual motoring events, the Monte Carlo Rally and Monaco Grand Prix, are held in the principality.

Area: 0.4 sq mile/1 sq km
Population: 32,000
Capital: Monaco
Form of government: Constitutional Monarchy
Religion: RC
Currency: Euro

Monaghan a county in the central north of the Republic of Ireland, with a county town of the same name. (498 sq miles/1,291 sq km; pop. 54,000)

Mongolia a landlocked country in northeast Asia that is bounded to the north by the Russian Federation and to the south, west, and east by China. Most of Mongolia is mountainous. In the northwest, there are the Hangayn Mountains and the Altai, rising to 14,312 feet (4,362 metres). In the south, there are grass-covered steppes and the desert wastes of the Gobi. The climate is very extreme and dry, with long, very cold winters and short, mild summers. Agriculture, particularly the rearing of livestock, is the main economic activity and source of employment in Mongolia. Under Communism, all cultivation and livestock rearing was state-controlled but Mongolia has now started to move towards a free market economy. Crops grown include cereals (wheat, barley, and oats), potatoes, and some other vegetables but cultivation is heavily dependent on irrigation. Mongolia has valuable reserves of iron ore, coal, copper, molybdenum, fluorspar, tungsten, uranium, gold, and silver. Manufacturing industries are generally on a small scale and include the processing of wool, hides, leather, furs, meat and dairy produce, textiles, wooden goods, agricultural equipment, and building products. The collapse of trade with the former Soviet Union has created severe economic problems for Mongolia and it is increasingly looking to Japan and China for trade and economic assistance.

Area: 604,829 sq miles/1,566,500 sq km
Population: 2,354,000
Capital: Ulan Bator (Ulaanbaatar)
Other cities: Darhan, Erdenet
Form of government: Republic
Religions: Buddhism, Shamanism, Sunni Islam
Currency: Tugrik

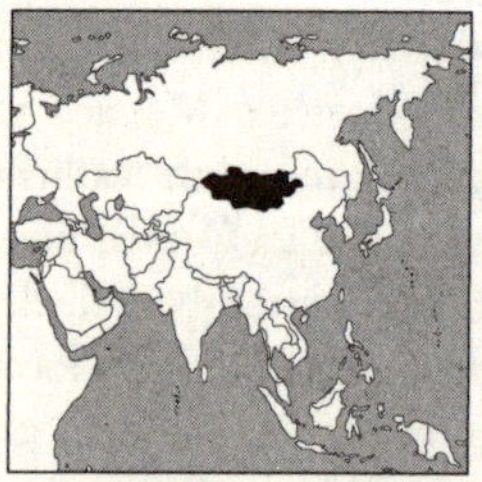

Monmouthshire a council area in east Wales, with its administrative centre in the town of Cwmbran. (329 sq miles/851 sq km; pop. 86,000)

Montana a state in northwest USA, on the border with Canada. The state capital is Helena. (147,138 sq miles/381,087 sq km; pop. 907,000)

Mont Blanc (Monte Bianco) the highest mountain in Western Europe, on the border between France and Italy. (15,770 ft/4,808 m)

Montserrat one of the Leeward Islands in the southeastern Caribbean, and a British Overseas Territory. Much of the island was left uninhabitable after the volcanic eruptions of 1997 but rebuilding of the island has begun, funded by the UK.

Area: 39 sq miles/100 sq km
Population: 7,000
Capital: Plymouth
Form of government: British Overseas Territory
Religions: Protestant, RC
Currency: East Caribbean Dollar

Moravia a historical region of the Czech Republic, east of Bohemia, west of Slovakia, with Poland to the north and Austria to the south.

Moray a council area in northeast Scotland, with its administrative centre in the town of Elgin. (874 sq miles/2,238 sq km; pop. 86,000)

Moray Firth an inlet of the North Sea cutting some 35 miles (56 kilometres) into the eastern coast of northeast Scotland, with Inverness at its head.

Mordvinian Republic (Mordovia) a republic of the Russian Federation, in west central Russia in the middle of the Volga basin. (10,110 sq miles/26,200 sq km; pop. 960,000)

Morocco a country in northwest Africa strategically placed at the western entrance to the Mediterranean Sea. It is a land of great contrasts, with high rugged mountains in the north, the arid Sahara in the south, and green Atlantic and Mediterranean coasts. The country is split from southwest to northeast by the Atlas Mountains. The north has a pleasant Mediterranean climate with hot, dry summers and mild, moist winters. Farther south winters are warmer and summers even hotter. Snow often falls in winter on the Atlas Mountains. Morocco is mainly a farming country, although agriculture accounts for less than 20 per cent of the land use. Wheat, barley, and maize are the main food crops, and it is one of the world's chief exporters of citrus fruit. Morocco's economy is very mixed. Its main wealth comes from phosphates, reserves of which are the largest in the world, while coal, lead, iron and manganese ores are also produced. It is self-sufficient in textiles, has automobile assembly plants, soap and cement factories, and a large sea fishing industry. Tourism is a major source of revenue, as are remittances sent home by Moroccans who work abroad.

Area: 172,414 sq miles/446,550 sq km
Population: 27,623,000
Capital: Rabat
Other cities: Casablanca, Fez, Marrakech
Form of government: Constitutional Monarchy
Religion: Sunni Islam
Currency: Dirham

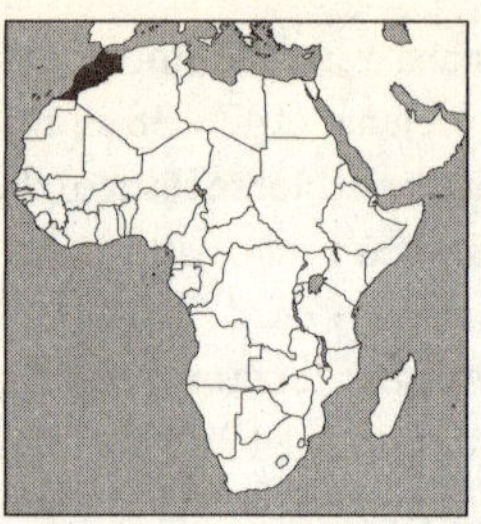

Moselle (Mosel) a river which flows northwards from the southeastern Lorraine region of eastern France to form part of the border between Luxembourg and Germany before flowing eastwards to meet the River Rhine at Koblenz. (Length 340 miles/550 km)

Mourne Mountains a mountain range of noted beauty in the south of Co. Down, Northern Ireland. The highest point is Slieve Donard (2,795 ft /852 m).

Moyle a district council area in Co. Antrim in northeast Northern Ireland. (191 sq miles/494 sq km; pop. 15,000)

Mozambique a republic located in southeast Africa and one of the world's poorest countries. A coastal plain covers most of the southern and central territory, giving way to the western highlands and north to a plateau including the Nyasa Highlands. The Zambezi River separates the high plateaux in the north from the lowlands in the south. The country has a humid tropical climate with highest temperatures and rainfall in the north. Normally conditions are reasonably good for agriculture but periods of drought and periods of severe flooding together with 16 years of civil war have taken their toll on the country's development. A lot of industry was abandoned when the Portuguese left the country and was not taken over by the local people because of lack of expertise. Forestry is mainly unexploited while fishing for lobster and shrimp is an important source of export revenue. The economy is now on the upturn but the country continues to rely heavily on aid.

Area: 309,496 sq miles/799,380 sq km
Population: 16,916,000
Capital: Maputo
Other cities: Beira, Nampula
Form of government: Republic
Religions: traditional African religions, RC, Sunni Islam
Currency: Metical

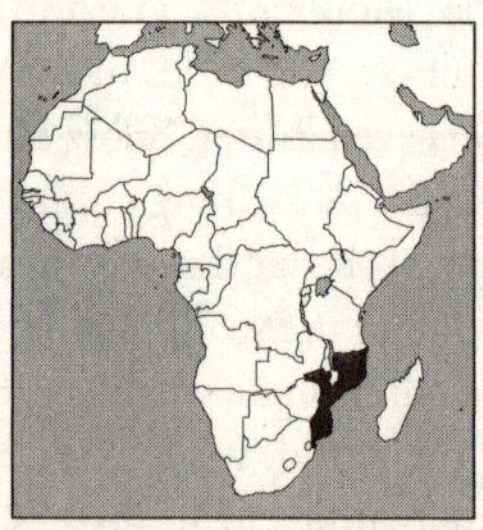

Mozambique Channel the broad strait, some 250 miles (400 kilometres) across at its narrowest point, which separates Madagascar from mainland east Africa.

Mpumalanga one of South Africa's nine provinces, in northeast South Africa, with its administrative centre in Nelspruit. (30,683 sq miles/79,490 sq km; pop. 2,801,000)

Mull an island off the central west coast of Scotland. (357 sq miles/925 sq km; pop. 2,600)

Munster one of the four historical provinces of Ireland, covering the southwest quarter of the country.

Murray a major river of southeast Australia, which flows westwards from the Snowy Mountains to form much of the boundary between New South Wales and Victoria. It is joined by the River Darling before flowing across the southeastern corner of South Australia and into the Antarctic Ocean. (Length 1,600 miles/2,570 km)

Mururoa an atoll in the southeastern sector of French Polynesia, used by France since 1966 as a testing ground for nuclear weapons.

Musandam a rocky, horn-shaped peninsula which juts out into the Persian Gulf to form the southern side of the Strait of Hormuz. It belongs to Oman, but is separated from it by part of the United Arab Emirates.

Mustique an island in the Grenadines, to the south of St Vincent, in the southeastern Caribbean. (Pop. 200)

Myanmar formerly Burma, the Union of Myanmar is the second largest country in Southeast Asia. The heartland of the country is the valley of the Irrawaddy River. The north and west of the country are mountainous and in the east the Shan Plateau runs along the border with Thailand. The climate is equatorial at the coast, changing to tropical monsoon over most of the interior. The Irrawaddy River flows into the Andaman Sea, forming a huge delta area that is ideal for rice cultivation. Rice is the country's staple food and accounts for half the country's export earnings. Tropical fruits, such as bananas, mangoes, citrus, and guavas, grow well in the fertile coastal regions. Myanmar is rich in lumber and mineral resources such as natural gas, petroleum, jade, and natural rubies, but poor communications, lack of development, and civil unrest mean that these resources have not been fully exploited, which has at least contributed to the preservation of the country's natural environment.

Area: 261,228 sq miles/676,578 sq km
Population: 45,992,000
Capital: Rangoon (Yangon)
Other cities: Mandalay, Moulmein, Pegu
Form of government: Republic
Religion: Buddhism
Currency: Kyat

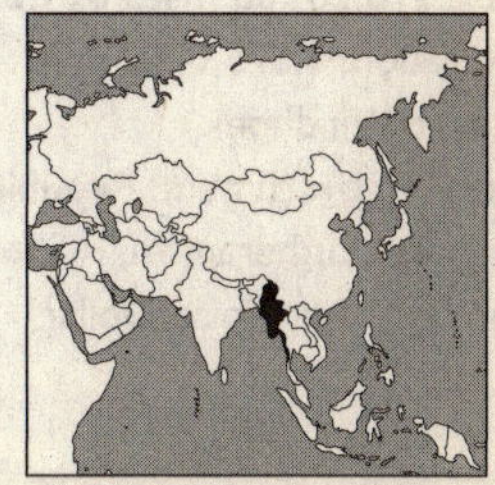

N

Nagaland a primarily agricultural state in the hilly far northeastern corner of India, bordering Myanmar. (6,399 sq miles/6,579 sq km; pop. 2,028,000)

Nagorny Karabakh Autonomous Region a disputed, autonomous enclave in Azerbaijan, which is claimed by Armenia. Three quarters of the population are Armenian. (1,700 sq miles/4,400 sq km; pop. 194,000)

Nakhichevan Autonomous Republic an enclave in Armenia, that belongs to Azerbaijan, which declared its secession from the former Soviet Union in 1990. The capital is Nakhichevan. (5500 sq km/2120 sq miles; pop. republic 366,000/capital 68,000)

Namib Desert a sand desert lining the coast of Namibia.

Namibia a country situated on the Atlantic coast of southwest Africa. There are three main regions in the country: running down the entire Atlantic coastline is the Namib Desert; east of which is the Central Plateau of mountains, rugged outcrops, sandy valleys, and poor grasslands; east again and north is the Kalahari Desert. Namibia is hot and dry and the little rain it does get falls mainly over Windhoek, the capital, and even here it only amounts to 8–10 inches (200–250 millimetres) per year. It is essentially a stock-rearing country (sheep, cattle, and goats) with subsistence agriculture to be found mainly in the north. Diamonds are mined just north of the River Orange, as are other minerals such as silver, lead, uranium, and copper. Namibia's output of diamonds amounts to almost a third of the world's total. One of Africa's richest fishing grounds lies off the coast of Namibia, and mackerel, anchovies, and pilchards are an important export although production has dropped in recent years because of overfishing.

Area: 318,261 sq miles/824,292 sq km
Population: 1,575,000
Capital: Windhoek
Form of government: Republic
Religions: Lutheranism, RC, other Christianity
Currency: Namibian Dollar

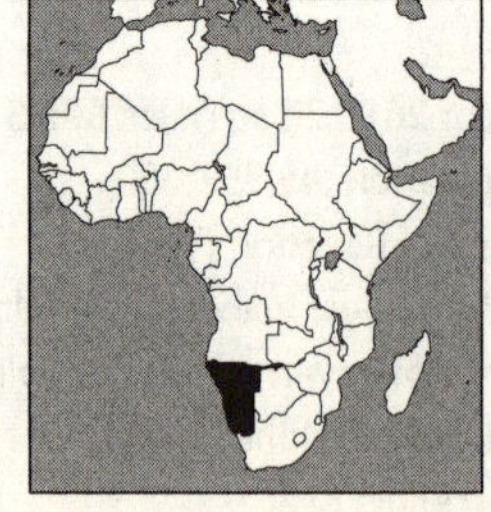

Nasser, Lake a massive artificial lake on the River Nile in southern Egypt, created when the Aswan High Dam was completed in 1971. (1,930 sq miles/ 5,000 sq km)

Nauru the world's smallest republic. Nauru is an island situated just 25 miles (40 kilometres) south of the Equator and halfway between Australia and Hawaii. It is an oval-shaped coral island only 12 miles (20 kilometres) in diameter and is surrounded by a reef. The centre of the island comprises a plateau that rises to 197 feet (60 metres) above sea level. Most of the population live along a narrow coastal belt of fertile land. The climate is tropical with a high and irregular rainfall. The country is rich, due entirely to the deposits of high-quality phosphate rock in the central plateau. This is sold for fertilizer to Australia, New Zealand, Japan, and Korea. Phosphate deposits are likely to be exhausted in the near future but the government is investing overseas and attempting to diversify to ensure the economic future of the country. Since around 80 per cent of the land will be uninhabitable once the mines are exhausted, considerable rehabilitation will be required.

Area: 8 sq miles/21 sq km
Population: 11,000
Capital: Yaren
Form of government: Republic
Religions: Protestantism, RC
Currency: Australian Dollar

Navarra (Navarre) a province in the mountainous northeastern part of Spain. The capital is Pamplona. (4023 sq miles/10,420 sq km; pop. 557,000)

Naxos a fertile Greek island in the southern Aegean Sea, the largest of the Cyclades Islands. (165 sq miles/428 sq km)

Neagh, Lough the largest freshwater lake in the British Isles, in the east of Northern Ireland. (147 sq miles/381 sq km)

Neath Port Talbot a council area in south Wales, with its administrative centre in the town of Port Talbot. (169 sq miles/439 sq km; pop. 106,000)

Nebraska a state in the Midwest of the USA. The capital is Lincoln. (77,227 sq miles/200,018 sq km; pop. 1,715,000)

Neckar a tributary of the River Rhine, rising in the Black Forest in the southwest of Germany. (227 miles/365 km)

Negev a semi-desert region in southern Israel, whose main town is Beersheba. (4,950 sq miles/12,820 sq km)

Negros the fourth largest island of the Philippines. (4,905 sq miles/12,704 sq km; pop. 2,750,000)

Nei Mongol Autonomous Region (Inner Mongolia, Nei Mongol Zizhiqu) a region of northeastern China, bordering Mongolia, whose capital is Hohhot. (460,000 sq miles/1,200,000 sq km; pop. 24,065,000)

Neisse a tributary of the River Oder, which flows north from its source in the Czech Republic to form part of the border between Germany and Poland. (Length 159 miles/256 km)

Nepal a long narrow rectangular country, landlocked between China and India on the flanks of the eastern Himalayas. Its northern border runs along the mountain tops. In this border area is Mount Everest, at 29,028 feet (8,848 metres) the highest mountain in the world, and Nepal also has the six other highest mountains within its borders. The climate is subtropical in the south and all regions are affected by the monsoon. Nepal is one of the world's poorest and least developed countries, with most of the population involved in subsistence farming. Some mineral deposits exist, such as copper, iron ore, mica, and ochre, but because of the country's inaccessible terrain they have not been completely charted. With Indian and Chinese aid, however, roads have been built from the north and south to Kathmandu. The construction of hydroelectric power schemes is underway, although at a high cost. Nepal's main exports are carpets, foodstuffs, clothing, and leather goods, with its principal sources of foreign revenue being tourism and the foreign earnings of its Gurkha soldiers. Nepal now attracts thousands of visitors each year, many of whom belong to trekking and climbing expeditions.

Area: 56,827 sq miles/147,181 sq km
Population: 21,127,000
Capital: Kathmandu (Katmandu)
Form of government: Constitutional Monarchy
Religions: Hinduism, Buddhism
Currency: Nepalese Rupee

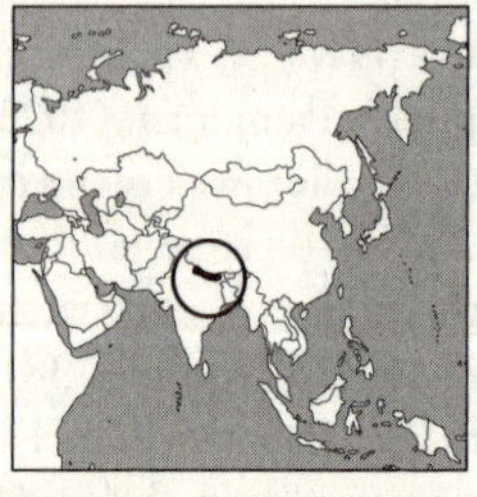

Netherlands, the situated in northwest Europe, the Netherlands (also known as Holland) is bounded to the north and west by the North Sea. Around half of the Netherlands is below sea level and the Dutch have tackled some huge reclamation schemes to add some land area to the country. One such scheme is the IJsselmeer, where four large reclaimed areas (polders) have added an extra 637 square miles (1,650 square kilometres) for cultivation and an overspill town for Amsterdam. The Netherlands has mild winters and cool summers. Agriculture and horticulture are highly mechanized, and the most notable feature is the sea of glass under which salad vegetables, fruit, and flowers are grown. Manufacturing industries include chemicals, machinery, petroleum, refining, metallurgy, and electrical engineering. Rotterdam, the main port of the Netherlands, is the largest port in the world.

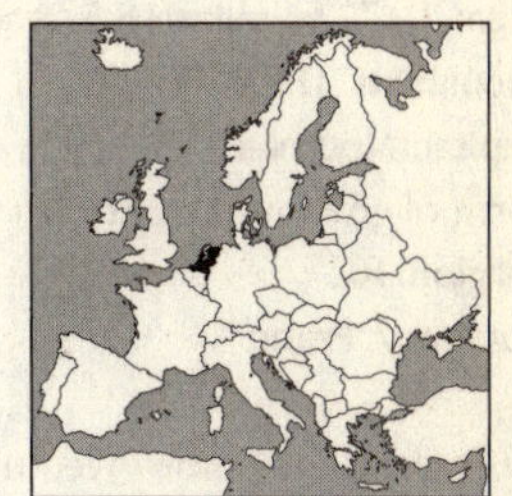

Area: 15,770 sq miles/40,844 sq km
Population: 15,517,000
Capital: Amsterdam
Seat of government: The Hague (Den Haag, 's-Gravenhage)
Other major cities: Eindhoven, Rotterdam
Form of government: Constitutional Monarchy
Religions: RC, Dutch reformed, Calvinism
Currency: Euro

Netherlands Antilles an Overseas Division of the Netherlands, consisting of two sets of islands spread over the southern Caribbean: the Southern Netherlands Antilles (Bonaire and Curaçao) and the Northern Netherlands Antilles (Saba, St Maarten and St Eustatius). Aruba was part of the group until 1986. The islands have a tropical climate. Oil refining and tourism are the most important economic activities. The capital is Willemstad. (309 sq miles/800 sq km; pop. 207,300; cur. Netherland Antilles Guilder)

Neva the river in northwest Russia which flows through St Petersburg. (Length 45 miles/74 km)

Nevada a state in the west of the USA, consisting mostly of desert. The state capital is Carson City. (110,540 sq miles/286,298 sq km; pop. 2,206,000)

New Britain the largest offshore island belonging to Papua New Guinea, in the Bismarck Archipelago. (14,100 sq miles/36,500 sq km; pop. 446,000)

New Brunswick a state on the coast in southeast Canada, bordering the USA. The state capital is Fredericton. (28,354 sq miles/73,436 sq km; pop. 763,000)

New Caledonia (Nouvelle Calédonie) the most southerly of the Melanesian countries in the Pacific Ocean. It is a French Overseas Territory but there has been ongoing unrest in the country between the indigenous Melanesians and the French settlers over the question of independence. The main island, Nouvelle Calédonie, is 248 miles (400 kilometres) long and rises to a height of 5,377 feet (1,639 metres) at Mount Panie. The island is divided into two natural regions by the mountain range that runs down its centre: a dry west coast covered with gum tree savannah and a tropical east coast. It has a Mediterranean-type climate with rainfall at its heaviest between December and March. The country is rich in mineral resources, particularly nickel, which accounts for 90 per cent of its exports. Other exports include coffee and copra. The main tourist resorts are on the east coast of Nouvelle Calédonie.

Area: 7,172 sq miles/18,575 sq km
Population: 189,000
Capital: Nouméa
Form of government: French Overseas Territory
Religion: RC
Currency: Franc

New England the name given to northeastern states of the USA: Maine, Vermont, New Hampshire, Connecticut, Massachusetts and Rhode Island.

Newfoundland a Canadian province in the extreme east of the country. The capital is St John's. (143,634 sq miles/372,000 sq km; pop. 531,000)

New Guinea one of the world's largest islands, divided into two parts: independent Papua New Guinea in the east and Irian Jaya, a state of Indonesia, in the west.

New Hampshire a state of New England, in the northeast of the USA. The state capital is Concord. (9,304 sq miles/24,097 sq km; pop. 1,283,000)

New Jersey a state on the Atlantic coast in the northeast of the USA. The state capital is Trenton. (7,836 sq miles/20,295 sq km; pop. 8,555,000)

New Mexico a state in the southwest of the USA, bordering Mexico. The state capital is Santa Fe. (121,666 sq miles/315,115 sq km; pop. 1,839,000)

Newport (1) a port and naval base in Rhode Island, USA. (Pop. 27,000) (2) a town and port in southeast Wales, the administrative centre for the Newport council area. (Pop. 130,000) (3) a council area in southeast Wales. (73 sq miles/190 sq km; pop. 133,000)

Newry and Mourne a district council area in Co. Down, southeast Northern Ireland. (351 sq miles/909 sq km; pop. 83,000)

New South Wales the most populous of the states of Australia, situated in the southeast of the country. The capital is Sydney. (309,433 sq miles/801,430 sq km; pop. 6,654,000)

Newtownabbey a district council area in Co. Antrim, east Northern Ireland. (58 sq miles/151 sq km; pop. 74,000)

New York (1) **City of** the most populous city in the USA, its most important port, and a major financial centre. It is sited in southeast New York State, on the mouth of the Hudson River, and comprises five boroughs: Manhattan, the Bronx, Queens, Brooklyn and Staten Island. (Pop. 8,039,000)

(2) **State of** a populous state in the northeast of the USA, on the Atlantic coast. The state capital is Albany (49,576 sq miles/128,402 sq km; pop. 19,048,000)

New Zealand (Aotearoa) a country that lies southeast of Australia in the South Pacific. It comprises two large islands (North Island and South Island), Stewart Island and the Chatham Islands, and many smaller islands. The vast majority of the population live on North Island. New Zealand enjoys very mild winters with regular rainfall and no extremes of heat or cold. North Island is hilly, with isolated mountains, active volcanoes, hot mineral springs, and geysers. Earthquakes occur, and in 1987 considerable damage was caused by one at Edgecumbe. On South Island, the Southern Alps run north to south, and the highest point is Mount Cook at 12,313 feet (3,753 metres). The Canterbury Plains lie to the east of the mountains. Two-thirds of New Zealand is suitable for agriculture and grazing. Meat, wool, and dairy goods are the main products. Forestry supports the pulp and paper industry, and a considerable source of hydroelectric power produces cheap electricity for the manufacturing industry, which now accounts for 30 per cent of New Zealand's exports. Mining is also an important industry, with petroleum, natural gas, limestone, gold, and iron ore being exploited.

Area: 104,454 sq miles/270,534 sq km
Population: 3,681,000
Capital: Wellington
Other major cities: Auckland, Christchurch, Dunedin, Hamilton
Form of government: Constitutional Monarchy
Religions: Anglicanism, RC, Presbyterianism
Currency: New Zealand Dollar

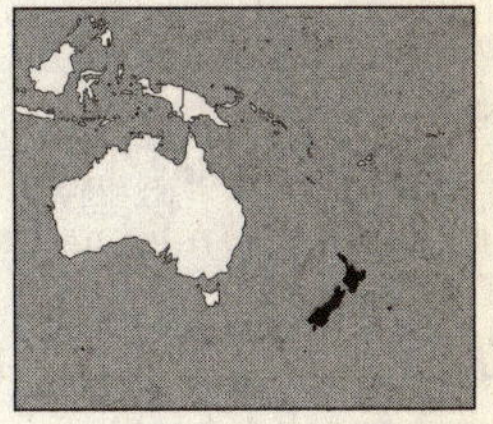

Niagara Falls spectacular waterfalls on the Niagara River, situated on the Canada-USA border between Lakes Erie and Ontario.

Nicaragua (1) a country that lies between the Pacific Ocean and the Caribbean Sea on the isthmus of Central America and is sandwiched between Honduras to the north and Costa Rica to the south. The east coast is the wettest part of the country. Behind this is a range of volcanic mountains, and the west coast is a belt of savannah lowland. The western region, which contains the two huge lakes, Nicaragua and Managua, is where most of the population live. The whole country is subject to devastating earthquakes. Nicaragua is primarily an agricultural country and 65 per cent of the labour force work on the land. The main export crops are coffee, bananas, cotton, meat, and gold. There are mineral deposits of gold, copper, and silver, with gold being of prime importance, but the country's economy is dependent on foreign aid. (2) **Lake** a large lake in the southwest of Nicaragua. (3,191 sq miles/8,264 sq km)

Area: 50,193 sq miles/130,660 sq km
Population: 4,663,000
Capital: Managua
Form of government: Republic
Religion: RC
Currency: Córdoba Oro

Niger a landlocked republic in West Africa, just south of the Tropic of Cancer. Over half the country is covered by the encroaching Sahara in the north, and the south lies in the drought-stricken Sahel grasslands. In the extreme southwest corner, the River Niger flows through the country, and in the extreme southeast lies Lake Chad, but the rest of the country is very short of water. Niger is an agricultural country, mainly of subsistence farmers, with the raising of livestock being the major activity. The people in the southwest fish and farm their own food, growing rice and vegetables on land flooded by the River Niger. Farther from the river, crops have failed as a result of successive droughts since 1968. Niger exports cotton and cowpea, but its main export is uranium mined in the Aïr Mountains. There has been unrest in the country involving the Tuareg people who wish for an independent state.

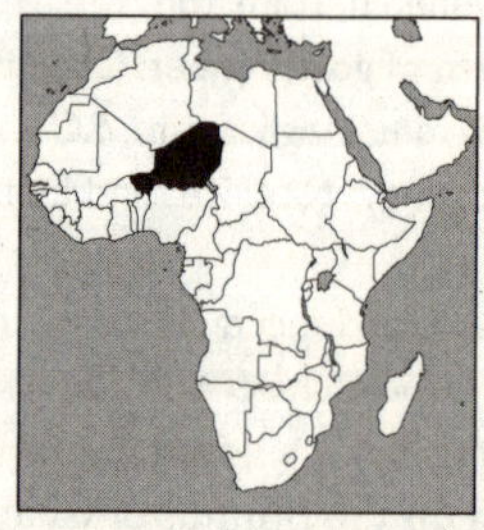

Area: 489,191sq miles/1,267,000 sq km
Population: 9,465,000
Capital: Niamey
Form of government: Republic
Religion: Sunni Islam
Currency: CFA Franc

Niger a river in West Africa flowing through Guinea, Mali, Niger and Nigeria to the Gulf of Guinea. (Length 2,590 miles/4,170 km)

Nigeria a large and populous country in West Africa. From the Gulf of Guinea it extends north to the border with Niger. It has a variable landscape, from the swampy coastal areas and tropical forest belts of the interior, to the mountains and savannah of the north. The two main rivers are the Niger and the Benue, and the Jos Plateau lies just north of their confluence. The climate is hot and humid, and rainfall is heavy at the coast, gradually decreasing inland. The dry far north is affected by the Harmattan, a hot, dry wind blowing from the Sahara. About three quarters of the land is suitable for agriculture and a wide variety of crops is raised by subsistence farmers. The main agricultural products are cocoa, rubber, groundnuts, and cotton, with only cocoa being exported. The country depends on revenue from its crude petroleum exports, which have a low sulphur content and therefore produce less air pollution, making them attractive to American and European countries. Full independence was achieved by Nigeria in 1960 but several factors, including the complex ethnic make-up of the country, mean that the country's progress has frequently been interrupted by strife and internal dissent.

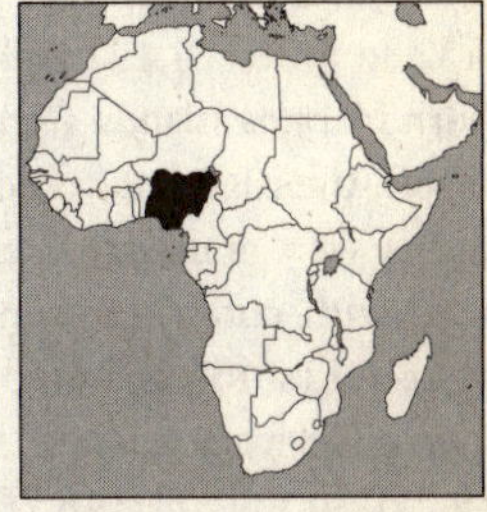

Area: 356,669 sq miles/923,768 sq km
Population: 118,700,000
Capital: Abuja
Other cities: Lagos, Ibadan, Kano, Ogbomosho
Form of government: Federal Republic
Religions: Sunni Islam, Christianity
Currency: Naira

Nile (An Nil) a major river of Africa and the longest river in the world. It rises in Burundi, flows into Lake Victoria and then flows northwards through Uganda, Sudan and Egypt to its delta on the Mediterranean. The river is called the White Nile (Bahr el Abiad) until it reaches Khartoum, in Sudan, where it is then joined by its main tributary, the Blue Nile (Bahr el Azraq), which rises in Ethiopia. (Length 4,160 miles/6,695 km)

Ningxia Hui Autonomous Region a region of central northern China, south of Inner Mongolia. The capital is Yinchuan. (23,000 sq miles/60,000 sq km; pop. 5,897,000)

Norfolk (1) a county in east England, with its administrative centre in the town of Norwich. (2,068 sq miles/5,355 sq km; pop. 790,000) (2) a port and naval base in southeast Virginia, USA. (Pop. 242,000)

Normandy (Normandie) an area of central northern France, now divided into two regions, Haute Normandie and Basse Normandie.

Northamptonshire a county in central England, with its administrative centre in the town of Northampton. (914 sq miles/2,367 sq km; pop. 616,000)

North Ayrshire a council area in west central Scotland, with its administrative centre in the town of Irvine. (341 sq miles/884 sq km; pop. 139,000)

North Cape (Nordkapp) one of Europe's most northerly points, 310 miles (500 kilometres) north of the Arctic Circle in Norway.

North Carolina a state on the southeastern coast of the USA. The state capital is Raleigh. (52,586 sq miles/136,198 sq km; pop. 8,325,000)

North Dakota a state in the west of the USA. The state capital is Bismarck. (70,665 sq miles/183,022 sq km; pop. 628,000)

North Down a district council area in Co. Down, east Northern Ireland. (32 sq miles/82 sq km; pop. 72,000)

Northern Cape one of South Africa's nine provinces, in southwest South Africa, formerly part of the Cape Province, with its administrative centre in Kimberley. (139,666 sq miles/361,830 sq km; pop. 840,000)

Northern Ireland a province of the UK, occupying most of the northern part of the island of Ireland. It is divided into six counties. The capital is Belfast. (5,452 sq miles/14,121 sq km; pop. 1,744,000)

Northern Mariana Islands a group of 14 islands in the northwest Pacific Ocean. In 1986, the islanders voted for commonwealth status in union with the USA and they were granted US citizenship. The country consists mainly of volcanic islands with coral limestone and lava shores. Tourism is the main industry. (179 sq miles/464 sq km; pop. 78,000; cur. US Dollar)

Northern Territory a state in northern Australia. The capital is Darwin. (519,770 sq miles/1,346,200 sq km; pop. 200,000)

North Lanarkshire a council area in central Scotland, with its administrative centre in the town of Motherwell. (684 sq miles/1,771 sq km; pop. 307,000)

North Pole the northernmost point on the earth's axis.

North Sea a comparatively shallow branch of the Atlantic Ocean that separates the British Isles from the European mainland.

Northumberland a county in northeastern England on the North Sea, with its administrative centre in the town of Morpeth. (1,943 sq miles/5,033 sq km; pop. 310,000)

North-West Province one of South Africa's nine provinces, in northwest South Africa, with its administrative centre in Mmabatho. (44,899 sq miles/ 116,320 sq km; pop. 3,354,825)

Northwest Territories a vast area of northern Canada, occupying almost a third of the country's whole land area. The capital is Yellowknife. (1,253,400 sq miles/ 3,246,000 sq km; pop. 44,000)

North Yorkshire a county in north England, with its administrative centre in Northallerton. (3,322 sq miles/8,603 sq km; pop. 1,016,000)

Norway a country that occupies the western half of the Scandinavian Peninsula in northern Europe and is surrounded to the north, west, and south by water.

It shares most of its eastern border with Sweden and almost one-third of the country is north of the Arctic Circle. It is a country of spectacular scenery with fjords, cliffs, rugged uplands, and forested valleys. It has some of the deepest fjords in the world and a huge number of glacial lakes. The climate is temperate as a result of the warming effect of the Gulf Stream. Summers are mild, and although the winters are long and cold, the waters off the west coast remain ice-free. The country's longest river is the Glåma. Agriculture is chiefly concerned with dairy farming and fodder crops. Fishing is an important industry, and the large reserves of forest, which cover just over a quarter of the country, provide lumber for export. Industry is now dominated by the petrochemicals industry based on the reserves of Norwegian oil in the North Sea. There are almost 60 airports in the country and transport by water is still of importance.

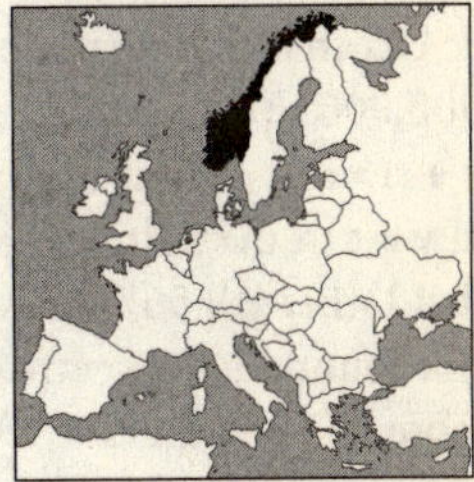

Area: 125,050 sq miles/323,877 sq km
Population: 4,445,000
Capital: Oslo
Other cities: Bergen, Trondheim, Stavanger
Form of government: Constitutional Monarchy
Religion: Lutheranism
Currency: Norwegian Krone

Norwegian Sea a sea lying between Norway, Greenland and Iceland; to the north it joins the Arctic Ocean, and to the south, the Atlantic.

Nottingham (1) a historical city situated on the River Trent in north central England associated with the legend of Robin Hood, also the administrative centre for Nottinghamshire. (Pop. 283,000) (2) a unitary authority in north central England.

Nottinghamshire a county in the Midlands of England, with its administrative centre in Nottingham. (836 sq miles/2,164 sq km; pop. 1,030,000)

Nova Scotia a province on the eastern coast of Canada. The capital is Halifax. (20,401 sq miles/52,841 sq km; pop. 958,000)

Nullarbor Plain a huge, dry and treeless (the name is from the Latin for 'no trees') plain which borders the Great Australian Bight, in Western and Southern Australia.

Nunavut a territory in northwest Canada created on 1 April, 1999, from part of the Northwest Territories of Canada as a semi-autonomous region for the Inuit. The capital is Iqaluit. (844,960 sq miles/2,201,400 sq km; pop. 29,000)

Nyasaland the former name of Malawi (until 1966).

O

Oahu the third largest of the islands of Hawaii, USA, where the state capital, Honolulu, and Pearl Harbour are located. (598 sq miles/1,549 sq km; pop. 797,400)

Ob' a river in the Russian Federation which rises near the border with Mongolia and flows northwards to the Kara Sea. (Length 3,460 miles/5,570 km)

Oceania a general term used to describe the central and southern islands of the Pacific Ocean including those of Australia and New Zealand. (3,400,000 sq miles/ 8,900,000 sq km; pop. 25,800,000)

Oder a river in central Europe rising in the Czech Republic and flowing north and west to the Baltic Sea; it forms part of the border between Germany and Poland. (Length 567 miles/912 km)

Offaly a county in the centre of the Republic of Ireland. The county town is Tullamore. (771 sq miles/1,998 sq km; pop. 62,000)

Ogaden a desert region of southeastern Ethiopia, claimed by Somalia.

Ohio a Midwest state of the USA, with a shoreline on Lake Erie. The capital is Columbus. (41,220 sq miles/106,765 sq km; pop. 11,395,00)

Ohio a river in the eastern USA, formed at the confluence of the Allegheny and Monongahela Rivers. It flows west and south and joins the Mississippi at Cairo, Illinois. (Length 980 miles/1,575 km)

Okhotsk, Sea of a part of the northwestern Pacific Ocean bounded by the Kamchatka Peninsula, the Kuril Islands, and the east coast of Siberia.

Oklahoma a state in the southwest of the USA. The state capital is Oklahoma City. (66,919 sq miles/173,320 sq km; pop. 3,470,000)

Olympus, Mount (Olimbos) a mountain in central mainland Greece, the home of the gods of ancient Greek myth. (9,570 ft/2,917 m)

Omagh (1) a market town in Northern Ireland. (Pop. 17,000) (2) a district council area in Co. Tyrone, west Northern Ireland. (436 sq miles/1,130 sq km; pop. 46,000)

Oman (Sultanate of Oman) situated in the southeast of the Arabian Peninsula, Oman is a small country in two parts: a small mountainous area overlooking the Strait of Hormuz, which controls the entrance to the Persian Gulf, and the main part of the country, which consists of barren hills rising sharply behind a narrow coastal plain. Inland the hills extend into the unexplored Rub al Khali (The Empty Quarter) in Saudi Arabia. Oman has a desert climate with exceptionally hot and humid conditions from April to October. As a result of the extremely arid environment, less than 1 per cent of the country is cultivated, the main produce being dates and limes, which are exported. The economy is almost entirely dependent on oil, which provides 90 per cent of its exports, although there are deposits of asbestos, copper, and marble, and a smelter at Sohar. Over 15 per cent of the resident population is made up by foreign workers. There are no political parties in Oman and the judicial system is centred on the law of Islam.

Area: 119,498 sq miles/309,500 sq km
Population: 2,302,000
Capital: Muscat (Masqat)
Form of government: Monarchy (Sultanate)
Religions: Ibadi Islam, Sunni Islam
Currency: Rial Omani

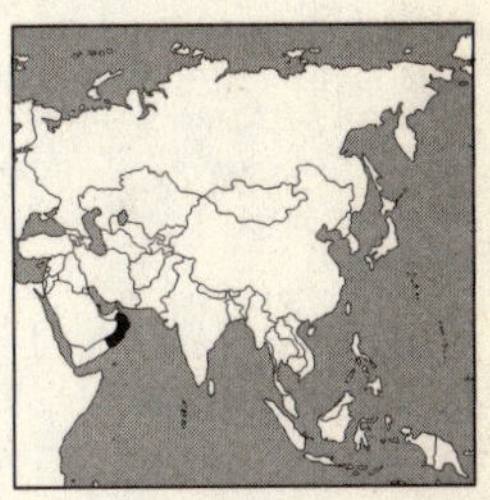

Oman, Gulf of a branch of the Arabian Sea leading to the Strait of Hormuz.

Ontario, Lake the smallest and most easterly of the Great Lakes; it drains into the St Lawrence River. (7,550 sq miles/19,550 sq km)

Orange the longest river in southern Africa, rising in Lesotho and flowing west to the Atlantic. (Length 1,299 miles/2,090 km)

Orange Free State the former name of South Africa's Free State Province.

Oregon a state in the northwest of the USA, on the Pacific. The state capital is Salem. (96,981 sq miles/251,180 sq km; pop. 3,525,000)

Orinoco a river in northern South America. It rises in southern Venezuela and flows west, then north and finally east to its delta on the Atlantic. It forms part of the border between Colombia and Venezuela. (Length 1,370 miles/2,200 km)

Orissa an eastern state of India. The capital is Bhubaneswar. (60,103 sq miles/155,707 sq km; pop. 37,424,000)

Orkney Islands a group of some 90 islands off the northeast coast of Scotland, which go to make up an island authority of Scotland, with its administrative centre in the town of Kirkwall. (377 sq miles/976 sq km; pop. 20,000)

Otranto, Strait of the waterway separating the heel of Italy from Albania.

Ottawa (1) the capital of Canada, in eastern Ontario, on the Ottawa River. (Pop. 348,000) (2) a river of central Canada which flows into the St Lawrence River at Montreal. (Length 790 miles/1,271 km)

Oxfordshire a inland county in southern central England, with its administrative centre in the city of Oxford. (1,008 sq miles/2,611 sq km; pop. 590,000)

P

Pacific Ocean the largest and deepest ocean on Earth, situated between Asia and Australia to the west and the Americas to the east. (63,838,000 sq miles/ 165,384,000 sq km)

Painted Desert a desert of colourful rocks in northern Arizona, USA. (7,500 sq miles/19,400 sq km)

Pakistan (Islamic Republic of Pakistan) a country that lies just north of the Tropic of Cancer and has the Arabian Sea as its southern border. The valley of the Indus River splits the country into a highland region in the west and a lowland region in the east. A weak form of tropical monsoon climate occurs over most of the country and conditions in the north and west are arid. Temperatures are high everywhere in summer but winters are cold in the mountains. Most agriculture is subsistence, with wheat and rice as the main crops. Cotton and rice are the main cash crops, but areas that can be cultivated are restricted because of waterlogging and saline soil. Pakistan's wide range of mineral resources has yet to be extensively developed and industry concentrates on food processing, textiles, consumer goods, and handicrafts. A lack of modern transport, due to its mountainous terrain, hinders the country's economic progress.

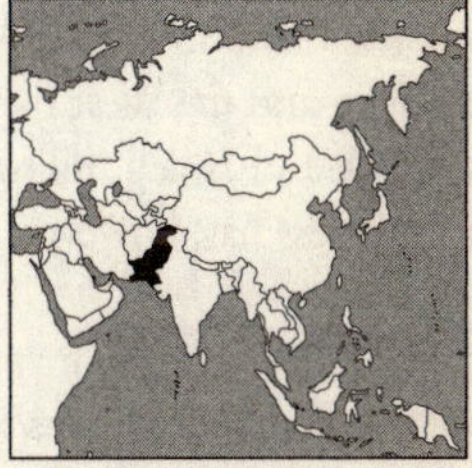

Area: 307,374 sq miles/796,095 sq km
Population: 134,146,000
Capital: Islamabad
Other cities: Faisalabad, Hyderabad, Karachi, Lahore
Form of government: Federal Islamic Republic
Religions: Sunni Islam, Shia Islam
Currency: Pakistan Rupee

Palau a republic consisting of a group of approximately 350 islands, lying in the western Pacific, 7 degrees north of the Equator and about 625 miles (900 kilometres) equidistant from New Guinea to the south and the Philippines to the west. A barrier reef to the west forms a large lagoon dotted with islands. Coral formations and marine life here are amongst the richest in the world.

Formerly known as Belau, the republic has an agreement of free association with the United States. Subsistence fishing and agriculture are the mainstays of the economy but there is also some tourism. In addition, natural resources include minerals (particularly gold and sea-bed deposits) and forests.

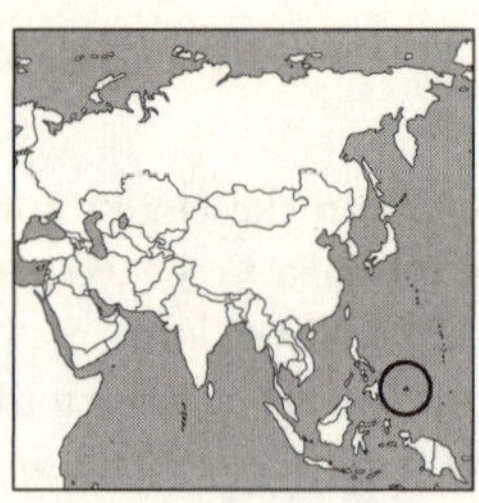

Area: 177 sq miles/459 sq km
Population: 17,000
Capital:Koror
Form of government: Free Associated Republic (USA)
Religions: RC, Modekngei
Currency: US Dollar

Palestinian Autonomous Regions Palestine was an ancient historical region on the eastern shore of the Mediterranean Sea, also known as 'The Holy Land' because of its symbolic importance for Christians, Jews, and Muslims. It was part of the Ottoman Empire from the early part of the 16th century until 1917, when it was captured by the British. The Balfour Declaration of 1917 increased Jewish hopes that they might be enabled to establish a Jewish state in Palestine. This was realized in 1948 with the United Nations' creation of the State of Israel, which partitioned Palestine between Jordan and Israel. This act created hostility among Israel's Arab neighbours and Palestinians indigenous to the area, many of whom left, particularly for neighbouring Jordan. Since that time, the territory has been disputed, leading to a series of wars between the Arabs and Israelis and to conflict between Israeli forces and the Palestine Liberation Organization. The disputed areas include the West Bank, the Gaza Strip, and parts of Jerusalem. In 1994, limited autonomy of the Gaza Strip and the West Bank was granted to the appointed Palestinian National Authority, and Israeli military forces began a withdrawal of the area. The whole peace process has, however, been compromised by ongoing violent conflict.

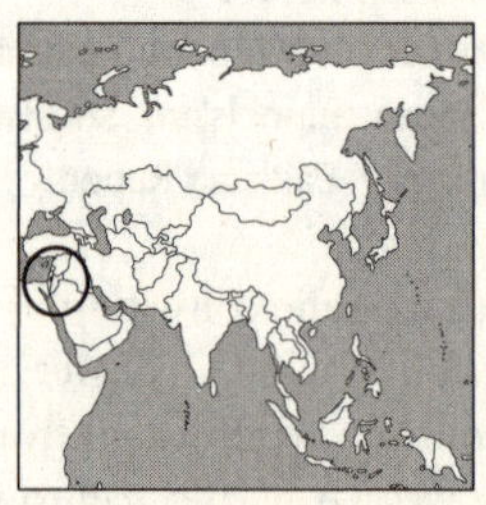

Area: Gaza Strip 146 sq miles/360 sq km, West Bank 2,269 sq miles/5,860 sq km
Population: Gaza Strip 924,200, West Bank 2,050,000
Form of government: Autonomous Regions (with limited powers)
Religions: Sunni Islam, Shia Islam, Eastern Catholicism
Currency: Israeli Shekel and Jordanian Dinar

Pamir a region of high plateaus in central Asia which straddles the borders of Tajikistan, Afghanistan and China.

Pampas the flat grasslands of central Argentina.

Panama a country located at the narrowest point in Central America. Only 36 miles (58 kilometres) separates the Caribbean Sea from the Pacific Ocean at Panama, and the Panama Canal, which divides the country, is the main route from the Caribbean and the Atlantic to the Pacific. The climate is tropical, with high temperatures throughout the year and only a short dry season from January to April. The country is heavily forested and very little is cultivated. Rice is the staple food. The economy is heavily dependent on the Canal and income from it is a major foreign currency earner. The country has extensive lumber resources, and mahogany is an important export. Other exports include petroleum products, coffee, shrimps, and raw sugar. In 1989, the country was briefly invaded by US military forces in order to depose the corrupt dictator General Noriega.

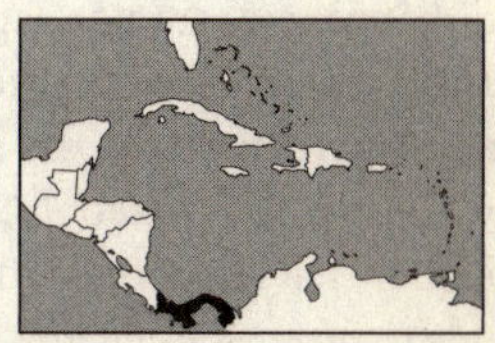

Area: 29,157 sq miles/75,517 sq km
Population: 2,674,000
Capital: Panamá
Other cities: San Miguelito, Colón
Form of government: Republic
Religion: RC
Currency: Balboa

Panama Canal a canal 40 miles (64 kilometres) long that runs through the centre of Panama, linking the Caribbean Sea to the Pacific Ocean. It was completed in 1914.

Papua New Guinea a country in the southwest Pacific, comprising the eastern half of the island of New Guinea together with hundreds of other islands including New Britain, the Bismarck Archipelago and New Ireland. There are active volcanoes on some of the islands and almost 100,000 people were evacuated in 1994 when two volcanoes erupted on New Britain. The country has a mountainous interior surrounded by broad swampy plains. The climate is tropical, with high temperatures and heavy rainfall. Subsistence farming is the main economic activity although some coffee, cocoa, and copra are grown for cash. Lumber is cut for export, and fishing and fish processing industries are developing. Minerals, such as copper, gold, silver, and oil, form the mainstay of the economy. The country still receives valuable aid from Australia, which governed it before independence was gained in 1975.

Area: 178,704 sq miles/462,840 sq km
Population: 4,400,000
Capital: Port Moresby
Form of government: Republic
Religions: Protestantism, RC
Currency: Kina

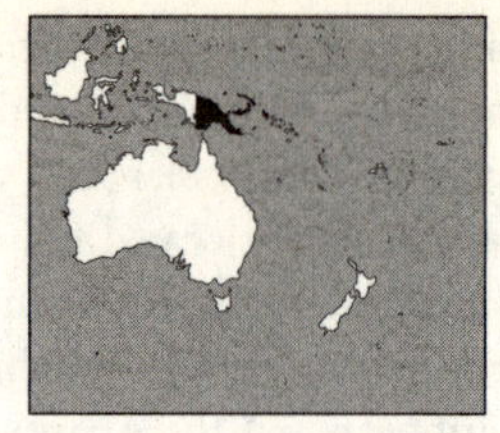

Paraguay a small landlocked country in central South America, bordered by Bolivia, Brazil, and Argentina. The climate is tropical, with abundant rain and a short dry season. The River Paraguay splits the country into the Chaco (a flat semi-arid plain on the west), and a partly forested undulating plateau on the east. Almost 95 per cent of the population live east of the river, where crops grown on the fertile plains include cassava, sugar cane, maize, cotton, and soya beans. Immediately west of the river, on the low Chaco, are huge cattle ranches that provide meat for export. Deposits of minerals, such as iron, petroleum, and manganese, are not exploited commercially. The lumber industry is important, however, with tannin and petitgrain oil also being produced. With three important rivers, the Paraguay, Paraná, and Pilcomayo, the country has many impressive waterfalls, such as the Guaira Falls. In cooperation with its neighbours, it has developed its potential for hydroelectric power to the full and is able to meet all its energy needs. Developed with Brazil and opened in 1991, the Itaipu Hydroelectric Dam on the (Alto) Paraná River is the largest dam in the world. Other hydroelectric schemes include the Yacyreta Dam, developed with Argentina and opened in 1994.

Area: 157,048 sq miles/406,752 sq km
Population: 4,955,000
Capital: Asunción
Other city: Ciudad del Este
Form of government: Republic
Religion: RC
Currency: Guaraní

Paraguay a major river of South America. It flows south from Brazil through into Paraguay to join the River Paraná. (Length 1,500 miles/2,400 km)

Paraná the second longest river in South America. It rises in Brazil and flows south to join the River Plate. (Length 1,800 miles/2,900 km)

Páros a Greek island in the Cyclades group. (75 sq miles/194 sq km; pop. 7,400)

Patagonia the most southerly region of South America in Argentina and Chile stretching from the Andes to the Atlantic.

Peace a river in western Canada, a tributary of the Slave/Mackenzie River, rising in British Columbia. (Length 1,065miles/1,715 km)

Pearl Harbour a harbour and naval base on Oahu, Hawaii; the Japanese attack on the US fleet based there in 1941 drew the USA into World War II.

Pelée, Mount an active volcano on Martinique, which destroyed the town of St Pierre in 1902. (4,583 ft /1,397 m)

Peloponnese, the a broad peninsula of southern Greece, joined to the northern part of the country by the Isthmus of Corinth.

Pembrokeshire a council area in southwest Wales, with its administrative centre in the town of Haverfordwest. (614 sq miles/1,589 sq km; pop. 113,000)

Penang a state of west Malaysia comprising Penang Island and the mainland province of Wellesley; the capital is George Town. (398 sq miles/1,031 sq km; pop. 1,142,000)

Pennines a range of hills that runs down the middle of northern England from the Scottish border to the Midlands, rising to 2,087 feet (894 metres) at Cross Fell.

Pennsylvania a state of the northeastern USA situated mainly in the Appalachian Mountains. The capital is Harrisburg. (45,333 sq miles/117,412 sq km; pop. 12,295,000)

Persian Gulf the huge inlet to the south of Iran which is connected to the Arabian Sea by the Strait of Hormuz. It is often referred to as the Gulf, or the Arabian Gulf.

Perth and Kinross a council area in north central Scotland, with its administrative centre in Perth. (2019 sq miles/5,321 sq km; pop. 133,000)

Peru a country located just south of the Equator, on the Pacific coast of South America. It has three distinct regions from west to east: the coast, the high sierra of the Andes, and the tropical jungle. The climate on the narrow coastal belt is mainly desert, while the Andes are wet, and east of the mountains is equatorial with tropical forests. Most large-scale agriculture is in the oases and fertile, irrigated river valleys that cut across the coastal desert. Sugar and cotton are the main exports. Sheep, llamas, vicunas, and alpacas are kept for wool. The fishing industry was once the largest in the world but recently the shoals have become depleted. Anchovies form the bulk of the catch and are used to make fish meal. Minerals such as iron ore, silver, copper, and lead, as well as natural gas and petroleum, are extracted in large quantities and are an important part of the economy. The economy in the late 1980s was damaged by the declining value of exports, inflation, drought, and guerrilla warfare, which made the government introduce an austerity program in the 1990s.

Area: 496,225 sq miles/1,285,216 sq km
Population: 25,015,000
Capital: Lima
Other cities: Arequipa, Callao, Cuzco, Trujillo
Form of government: Republic
Religion: RC
Currency: Nuevo Sol

Philippines a country comprising a group of 7,107 islands and islets in the western Pacific that are scattered over a great area. There are four main groups: Luzon and Mindoro to the north, the Visayan Islands in the centre, Mindanao and the Sulu Archipelago in the south, and Palawan in the southwest. Manila, the capital, is on Luzon. Most of the islands are mountainous and earthquakes are common. The climate is humid, with high temperatures and high rainfall. Typhoons can strike during the rainy season from July to October. Rice, cassava, sweet potatoes, and maize are the main subsistence crops, and coconuts, sugar cane, pineapples, and bananas are grown for export. Agriculture employs around 42 per cent of the workforce. Mining is an important industry, and its main products include gold, silver, nickel, copper, and salt. Fishing is also of major importance and there are sponge fisheries on some of the islands. Other prime industries include textiles, food processing, chemicals, and electrical engineering.

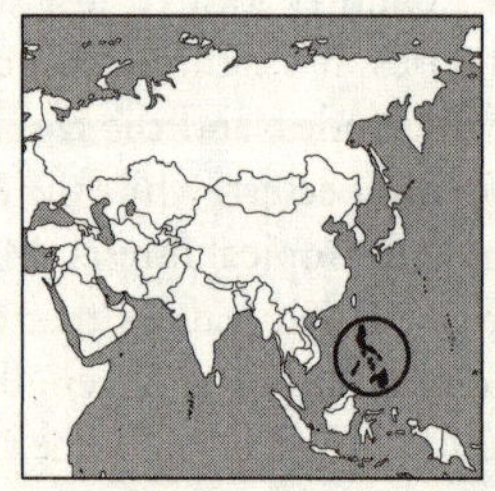

Area: 115,813 sq miles/300,000 sq km
Population: 71,899,000
Capital: Manila
Other cities: Cebu, Davao, Quezon City
Form of government: Republic
Religions: RC, Protestant, Sunni Islam
Currency: Philippines Peso

Piedmont (Piemonte) a region of northwest Italy. The main town is Turin. (Pop. 4, 269,000)

Pitcairn Islands an island group and a British Overseas Territory situated in the southeast Pacific Ocean. The islands are volcanic with high lava cliffs and rugged hills. The islanders are direct descendants of the HMS *Bounty* mutineers and their Tahitian wives. Subsistence agriculture produces a wide variety of tropical and subtropical crops but the sale of postage stamps is the country's main revenue earner.

Area: 17 sq miles/45 sq km
Population: 50
Form of government: British Overseas Territory
Religion: Protestant
Currency: New Zealand Dollar

Plate (Río de la Plata) the huge estuary of the Paraná and Uruguay Rivers on the southeast coast of South America. (Length 171 miles/275 km)

Plenty, Bay of the inlet on the north coast of the North Island, New Zealand.

Po the longest river in Italy, flowing eastwards from the Alps across a fertile plain to the Adriatic Sea. (Length 405 miles/642 km)

Pohnpei the island on which Kolonia, the capital of the Federated States of Micronesia, stands.

Poland a country situated on the North European Plain. It borders Germany to the west, the Czech Republic and Slovakia to the south, and Belarus and Ukraine to the east. Poland consists mainly of lowlands, and the climate is continental, marked by long, severe winters and short, warm summers. Over one-quarter of the labour force is involved in predominantly small-scale agriculture. The main crops are potatoes, wheat, barley, sugar beet, and fodder crops. The industrial sector of the economy is large-scale. Poland has large deposits of coal, and reserves of natural gas, copper and silver, and is one of the main producers of sulphur. Vast forests stretching inland from the coast supply the paper and furniture industries. Other industries include food processing, engineering, shipbuilding, textiles, and chemicals. The country has serious environmental problems, due to untreated sewage, industrial discharges, air pollution, and soil contamination, but some progress has been made to rectify matters. Tourism is on the increase, and the country's main tourist attractions include its Baltic resorts, mountains, and cultural and historical sites.

Area: 124, 808 sq miles/323,250 sq km
Population: 38,628,000
Capital: Warsaw (Warszawa)
Other cities: Gdansk, Cracow, Lódz, Wroclaw
Form of government: Republic
Religion: RC
Currency: Zloty

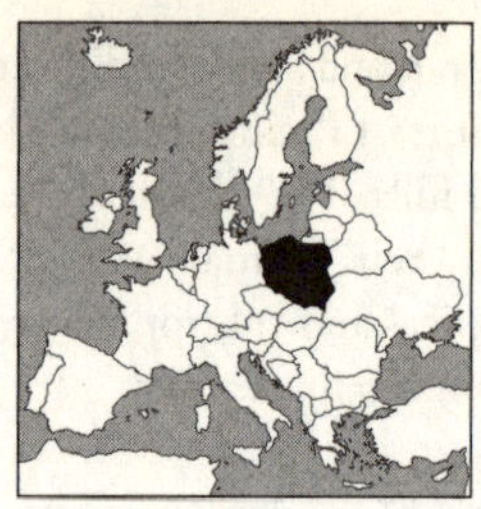

Polynesia the largest of the three island divisions of the Pacific, the others being Micronesia and Melanesia. The group includes Samoa, the Cook, Society, and Marquesas Islands, and Tonga.

Popocatépetl a volcano, twinned with Ixtacihuatl, 40 miles (65 kilometres) southeast of Mexico City. (17,887 ft/5,452 m)

Portugal a country in the southwest corner of Europe, Portugal makes up about 15 per cent of the Iberian Peninsula and is the least developed country in western Europe. The most mountainous areas of Portugal lie to the north of the River Tagus. In the northeast, are the steep-sided mountains of Tras-os-Montes, and to south of this the Douro valley runs from the Spanish border to Oporto on the Atlantic coast. South of the Tagus is the Alentejo, with wheat fields and cork plantations. The Alentejo continues to the hinterland of the Algarve where there are groves of almond, fig, and olive trees. Agriculture employs one-quarter of the labour force. Crops include wheat, maize, grapes, and tomatoes. Portugal's most important natural resources are minerals. These include coal, iron ore, tin, and copper. Port and Madeira wine are renowned, and the country is a main exporter of olive oil. Manufacturing industry includes textiles, clothing, footwear, food processing, and cork products. Tourism, particularly in the south, is the main foreign currency earner. A petrochemical plant and oil refinery is located near Lisbon and hydroelectric power has been developed in recent years. Portugal is also renowned for its high-quality craft products, especially lace, pottery, and tiles.

Area: 35,514 sq miles/91,982 sq km
Population: 10,300,000
Capital: Lisbon (Lisboa)
Other cities: Braga, Coimbra, Oporto, Setúbal
Form of government: Republic
Religion: RC
Currency: Euro

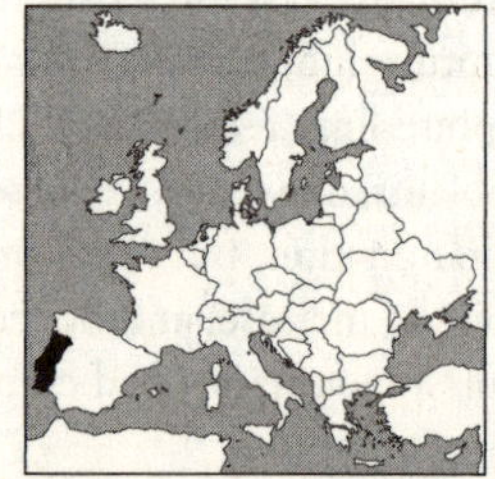

Powys a council area in mid-Wales, with its administrative centre in the town of

Llandrindod Wells. (1,960 sq miles/5,077 sq km; pop. 122,000)

Prince Edward Island the smallest of the provinces of Canada, an island in the Gulf of St Lawrence. The provincial capital is Charlottetown. (2,185 sq miles/ 5,660 sq km; pop. 141,000)

Provence a historical region of coastal southeast France.

Prussia a historical state of Germany, centred on its capital, Berlin.

Puerto Rico the most easterly of the Greater Antilles islands, lying in the Caribbean between the Dominican Republic and the Virgin Islands of the United States. It is a self-governing Commonwealth in association with the USA and includes the main island, Puerto Rico, the two small islands of Vieques and Culebra, and a fringe of smaller uninhabited islands. The climate is tropical, modified slightly by cooling sea breezes. The main mountains on Puerto Rico are the Cordillera Central, which reach 4,390 feet (1,338 metres) at the peak of Cerro de Punta. Dairy farming is the most important agricultural activity but the whole agricultural sector has been overtaken by industry in recent years. Tax relief and cheap labour encourage American businesses to be based in Puerto Rico. Products include textiles, clothing, electrical and electronic goods, plastics, pharmaceuticals, and petrochemicals. Tourism is another developing industry, and there is the potential for oil exploration both on and offshore. San Juan is one of the largest and best natural harbours in the Caribbean.

Area: 3,427 sq miles/8,875 sq km
Population: 3,736,000
Capital: San Juan
Form of government: Self-governing Commonwealth of the USA
Religions: RC, Protestantism;
Currency: US Dollar

Puglia (Apulia) a region of southeast Italy. The regional capital is Bari. (7,500 sq miles/19,250 sq km; pop. 4,170,000)

Punjab (1) a state in northwestern India. The capital is Chandigarh. (19,440 sq miles/ 50,362 sq km; pop. 24,764,000) (2) a fertile province in the north of Pakistan. The capital is Lahore. (79,283 sq miles/205,344 sq km; pop. 80,441,000)

Putumayo a river of northwest South America, rising in the Andes and flowing southeast to join the River Amazon. (Length 1,180 miles/1,900 km)

Pyrenees (Pyrénées, Pirineos) a range of mountains that runs from the Bay of Biscay to the Mediterranean, along the border between France and Spain. The highest point is Pico d'Aneto (11,170 ft/3,404 m).

Q

Qatar a little emirate that lies halfway along the coast of the Persian Gulf. It consists of a low barren peninsula and a few small islands. The climate is hot and uncomfortably humid in summer, and the winters are mild with rain in the north. Most fresh water comes from natural springs and wells or from desalination plants. Some vegetables and fruit are grown but the herding of sheep, goats, and some cattle is the main agricultural activity. The country is famous for its high-quality camels. The discovery and exploitation of oil has resulted in a high standard of living for the people of Qatar, with some of the revenue being used to build hospitals and a road system and to provide free education and medical care. The Dukhan oil field has an expected life of 40 years and the reserves of natural gas are enormous. In order to diversify the economy, new industries such as iron and steel, cement, fertilizers, and petrochemical plants, have been developed.

Area: 4,247 sq miles/11,000 sq km
Population: 558,000
Capital: Doha (Ad Dawhah)
Form of government: Absolute Monarchy (Emirate)
Religions: Wahhabi Sunni Islam
Currency: Qatari Riyal

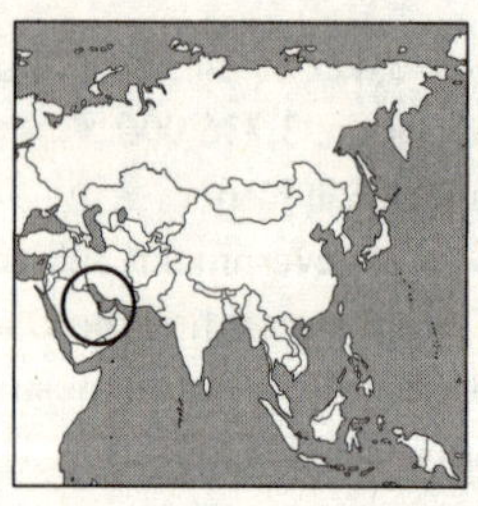

Qinghai a province of northwestern China. The capital is Xining. (280,000 sq miles/720,000 sq km; pop. 5,259,000)

Qiqihar a manufacturing city in Heilongjiang Province, China. (Pop. 770,000)

Québec the largest province of Canada, in the east of the country, and also the name of the capital of the province. The majority of the population are French-speaking. (524,300 sq miles/1,358,000 sq km; pop. province 7,471,000/city 171,000)

Queen Charlotte Islands a group of some 150 islands lying 100 miles (160 kilometres) off the west coast of Canada. (3,780 sq miles/9,790 sq km; pop. 5,620)

Queen Charlotte Strait a waterway, some 16 miles (26 kilometres) wide, between the northeastern coast of Vancouver Island and the mainland of Canada.

Queensland the northeastern state of Australia. The state capital is Brisbane. (491,200 sq miles/1,272,200 sq km; pop. 3,712,000)

Quercy a former province of southwestern France, around Cahors.

Qwaqwa one of ten former South African Homelands, the area is now part of the province of Free State, in central South Africa.

R

Rajasthan a state of northwest India. The state capital is Jaipur. (132,104 sq miles/342,239 sq km; pop. 57,576,000)

Rarotonga the largest of the Cook Islands, with the capital of the islands, Avarua, on its north coast. (26 sq miles/67 sq km; pop. 12,000)

Ras al Khaymah one of the United Arab Emirates, in the extreme northeast, on the Musandam Peninsula; also the name of its capital city. (653 sq miles/1,690 sq km; pop. emirate 188,000/city 101,000)

Recife a regional capital of eastern Brazil. (Pop. 1,461,000)

Red River (1) a river of the southern USA, rising in Texas and flowing east to join the Mississippi. (Length 1,018 miles/1,639 km) (2) (Song Hong, Yuan Jiang) a river that rises in southwest China and flows southeast across the north of Vietnam to the Gulf of Tongking, an inlet of the South China Sea. (Length 500 miles/800 km)

Red Sea a long, narrow sea lying between the Arabian Peninsula and the coast of northeast Africa.

Renfrewshire a council area in west central Scotland, with its administrative centre in the town of Paisley. (101 sq miles/261 sq km; pop. 179,000)

Réunion an island to the east of Madagascar, which is a French Overseas Department. The capital is Saint-Denis. (969 sq miles/2,510 sq km; pop. 530,000; cur. Euro)

Rhine (Rhein; Rhin, Rijn) one of the most important rivers of Europe. It rises in the Swiss Alps, flows north through Germany and then west through the Netherlands to the North Sea. (Length 825 miles/1,320 km)

Rhode Island the smallest state in the USA. The state capital is Providence. (1,214 sq miles/3,144 sq km; pop. 1,070,000)

Rhodes (Rodhos) the largest of the Dodecanese group of islands belonging to Greece; also the name of its capital. (540 sq miles/1,399 sq km; pop. city 49,000)

Rhondda Cynon Taff a council area in south Wales, with its administrative centre in the town of Tonypandy. (215 sq miles/558 sq km; pop. 232,000)

Rhône a major river of Europe, rising in the Swiss Alps and flowing west into France, and then south to its delta on the Golfe du Lion. (Length 505 miles/812 km)

Richmond the state capital of Virginia, USA. (Pop. 204,000)

Rio Grande (Río Bravo, Río Grande) a river of North America, rising in the state of Colorado, USA, and flowing southeast to the Gulf of Mexico. For much of its length it forms the border between the USA and Mexico. (Length 1,885 miles/3,078 km)

Rioja, La an autonomous area in the south of the Basque region of Spain, famous for its fine wine.

Roca, Cabo da a cape sticking out into the Atlantic in central Portugal, to the west of Lisbon, the westernmost point of mainland Europe.

Rockall a tiny, rocky, uninhabited island lying 250 miles (400 kilometres) west of Ireland, and claimed by the UK.

Rocky Mountains (Rockies) a huge mountain range in western North America, extending some 3,000 miles (4,800 kilometres) from British Columbia in Canada to New Mexico in the USA.

Romania apart from a small extension towards the Black Sea, Romania is almost a circular country. It is located in southeast Europe, bordered by Ukraine, Hungary, Serbia, and Bulgaria. The Carpathian Mountains run through the north, east, and centre of Romania, and these are enclosed by a ring of rich agricultural plains that are flat in the south and west but hilly in the east. The core of Romania is Transylvania within the Carpathian arc. Romania's main river is the Danube, which forms a delta in its lower course. The country has cold snowy winters and hot summers. Agriculture in Romania has been neglected in favour of industry, but major crops include maize, sugar beet, wheat, potatoes, and grapes for wine. Industry includes mining, metallurgy, mechanical engineering, and chemicals. Forests support the lumber and furniture industries in the Carpathians. There have been periods of severe food shortage, with high unemployment and a low standard of living. After the overthrow of the Communist regime in 1989, a new constitution was approved by referendum. The post-communist government has worked hard to bring about changes and improve the economy.

Area: 92,043 sq miles/238,391 sq km
Population: 23,000,000
Capital: Bucharest (Bucuresti)
Other cities: Brasov, Constanta, Timisoara
Form of government: Republic
Religions: Romanian Orthodox, RC
Currency: Leu

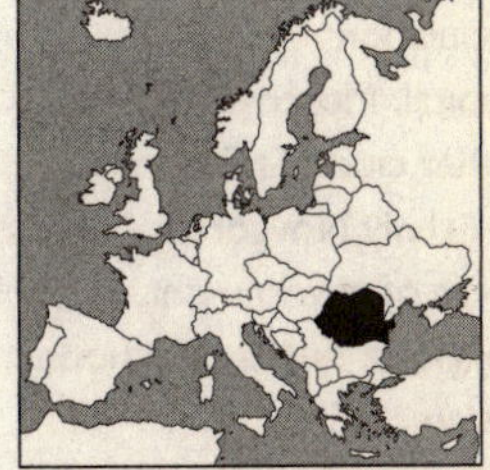

Roscommon a county in the northwest of the Republic of Ireland, with a county town of the same name. (950 sq miles/2,462 sq km; pop. 54,000)

Roseau the capital of the island republic of Dominica, in the east Caribbean. (Pop. 20,000)

Ross Sea a large branch of the Antarctic Ocean, south of New Zealand.

Rub al Khali the so-called 'Empty Quarter' – a vast area of sandy desert straddling the borders of Saudi Arabia, Oman and Yemen. (251,000 sq miles/650,000 sq km)

Ruhr the river in northwestern Germany whose valley forms the industrial heartland of western Germany. It joins the Rhine at Duisburg. (Length 146 miles/ 235 km)

Russia the old name for the Russian Empire, latterly used loosely to refer to the former USSR, and the present Russian Federation.

Russian Federation the largest country in the world, with over one-ninth of the world's land area. The Russian Federation extends from eastern Europe through the Ural Mountains east to the Pacific Ocean. The Caucasus Range forms its boundary with Georgia and Azerbaijan, and it is here that the highest peak in Europe, Mt Elbrus at 18,510 feet (5,642 metres), is located. In the east, Siberia is drained toward the Arctic Ocean by the great Rivers Ob, Yenisey, and Lena and their tributaries. Just to the south of the Central Siberian Plateau lies Lake Baikal, the world's deepest freshwater lake at 5,370 feet (1,637 metres). The Ural Mountains form the boundary between Asia and Europe and they contain a variety of mineral resources. The environment ranges from vast frozen wastes in the north to subtropical deserts in the south. Agriculture is organized into either state or collective farms that mainly produce sugar beet, cotton, potatoes, and vegetables. The country has extensive reserves of coal, oil, gas, iron ore, and manganese. Major industries include iron and steel, cement, transport equipment, engineering, armaments, electronic equipment, and chemicals. The Russian Federation is beset by many economic problems and recovery is likely to be a long and difficult process.

Area: 6,592,850 sq miles/17,075,400 sq km
Population: 146,100,000
Capital: Moscow (Moskva)
Other cities: St Petersburg (formerly Leningrad), Nizhniy Novgorod, Novosibirsk
Form of government: Republic
Religions: Russian Orthodox, Sunni Islam, Shia Islam, RC
Currency: Ruble

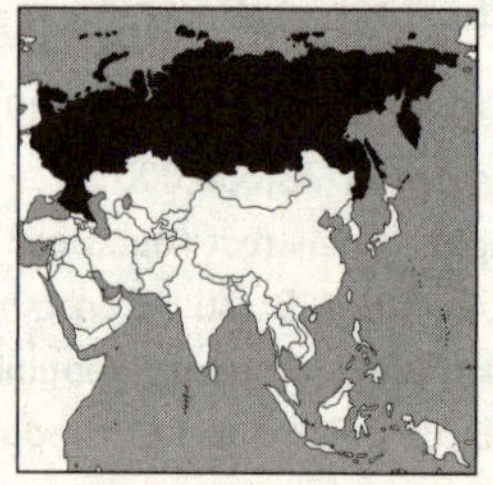

Rutland an inland county in central England, with its administrative centre in the town of Oakham. (152 sq miles/394 sq km; pop. 34,000)

Ruwenzori a mountain range on the border between the Democratic Republic of Congo and Uganda, also known as the 'Mountains of the Moon'. The highest peak is Mount Ngaliema (Mount Stanley) at 6,763 feet (5,109 metres).

Rwanda a small republic in the heart of central Africa that lies just 2 degrees south of the Equator. It is a mountainous country with a central spine of highlands from which streams flow west to the Congo River and east to the Nile. Active volcanoes are found in the north where the land rises to about 14,765 feet (4,500 metres). The climate is highland tropical, with temperatures decreasing with altitude. The soils are not fertile and subsistence agriculture dominates the economy. Staple food crops are sweet potatoes, cassava, dry beans, sorghum, and potatoes. Soil erosion, overgrazing, and droughts have led to famine, making the country very dependent on foreign aid. The main cash crops are arabica coffee, tea, and pyrethrum. There are major reserves of natural gas under Lake Kivu in the west, but these are largely unexploited. The country has faced massive upheaval and disruption of its economic life following the tragic tribal genocide wars in 1994, and there is ongoing ethnic division and rivalry between the Hutus and Tutsis.

Area: 10,169 sq miles/26,338 sq km
Population: 5,397,000
Capital: Kigali
Form of government: Republic
Religions: RC, traditional African religions
Currency: Rwandan Franc

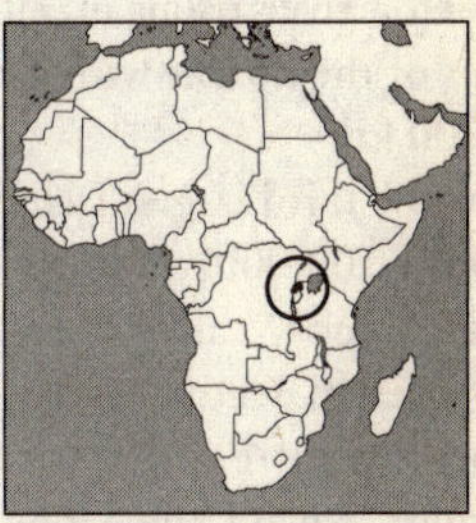

Ryukyu Islands (Nansei-shoto) a chain of islands belonging to Japan stretching 750 miles (1,200 kilometres) towards Taiwan. (Pop. 1,366,600)

S

Sabah the more easterly of the two states of Malaysia on northern coast of the island of Borneo. (28,450 sq miles/73,700 sq km; pop. 2,581,000)

Sahara Desert the world's largest desert, spanning much of northern Africa, from the Atlantic to the Red Sea, and from the Mediterranean to Mali, Niger, Chad and Sudan.

Sahel a semi-arid belt crossing Africa from Senegal to Sudan, separating the Sahara from tropical Africa to the south.

Saipan the largest and most heavily populated of the Northern Marianas group of islands in the west Pacific. The island group's capital, Susupe, is on the western side of Saipan. (47 sq miles/122 sq km; pop. 70,000)

Sakhalin a large island to the north of Japan, but belonging to the Russian Federation. (29,500 sq miles/76,400 sq km; pop. 570,000)

Salween a river rising in Tibet and flowing south through Myanmar, forming part of the border with Thailand, to the Andaman Sea. (Length 1,800 miles/ 2,900 km)

Samar the third largest island of the Philippines. (5,050 sq miles/13,080 sq km; pop. 1,100,000)

Samoa Samoa, called Western Samoa until 1997, is a state that lies in the Polynesian sector of the Pacific Ocean, about 447 miles (720 kilometres) northeast of Fiji. It consists of seven small islands and two larger volcanic islands, Savai'i and Upolu. Savai'i is largely covered by volcanic peaks and lava plateaux. Upolu is home to two-thirds of the population and the capital, Apia. The climate is tropical, with high temperatures and very heavy rainfall. The islands have been fought over by the Dutch, British, Germans, and Americans, but the islanders now enjoy a traditional Polynesian lifestyle. Subsistence agriculture is the main activity, and copra, cocoa, and coconuts are the main exports. There are some light manufacturing industries, and an automobile components factory, which is now the largest private employer and a major export industry. Many tourists visit the grave of the Scottish writer, Robert Louis Stevenson, who died here and whose home is now the official home of the king.

Area: 1,093 sq miles/2,831 sq km
Population: 166,000
Capital: Apia
Form of government: Constitutional Monarchy
Religion: Protestantism
Currency: Tala

Samoa, American an American territory, comprising a group of five islands, in the central South Pacific. The capital is Pago Pago. (77 sq miles/199 sq km; pop. 64,000)

Sámos a Greek island 1 mile (1.6 kilometres) off the coast of Turkey. (Pop. 43,000)

San Francisco Bay an inlet of the Pacific Ocean in western California, USA, joined to the ocean by the Golden Gate Strait.

San Marino a tiny landlocked state in central Italy, lying in the eastern foothills of the Apennines and one of the smallest republics in the world. Tradition has it that in AD 301, a Christian sought refuge from persecution on Mount Titano. The resulting community prospered and was recognized in 1291 by Pope Nicholas IV as being independent. San Marino has wooded mountains and pasture land clustered around Mount Titano's limestone peaks, which rise to 2,425 feet (739 metres). San Marino has a mild Mediterranean climate. Most of the population work on the land or in forestry. Wheat, barley, maize, olives, and vines are grown, and the main exports are wood machinery, chemicals, wine, textiles, tiles, varnishes, and ceramics, while dairy produce is the main agricultural product. Some 3.5 million tourists visit the country each year, and much of the country's revenue comes from the sale of stamps, postcards, souvenirs, and duty-free liquor. In 1992, San Marino became a member of the United Nations and it is a full member of the Council of Europe.

Area: 24 sq miles/1 sq km
Population: 25,000
Capital: San Marino
Form of government: Republic
Religion: RC
Currency: Euro

San Salvador (1) the capital and major city of El Salvador. (Pop. 496,000) (2) a small island in the centre of the Bahamas, the first place in the New World reached by Columbus (1492). (Pop. 480)

Santorini a volcanic island in the Cyclades group of Greek islands. (32 sq miles/ 84 sq km; pop. 7,100)

São Francisco a river of eastern Brazil, important for its hydroelectric dams. (Length 1,800 miles/2,900 km)

Saône a river of eastern France which merges with the River Rhône at Lyons. (Length 300 miles/480 km)

São Tomé e Principe a state comprising two volcanic islands that lie off the west coast of Africa. São Tomé is covered in extinct volcanic cones and its coastal areas are hot and humid. Príncipe is a craggy island lying to the northeast of São Tomé. The climate is tropical, with heavy rainfall from October to May. Seventy per cent of the workforce work on the land, mainly in state-owned cocoa plantations that were nationalized after independence in 1975. The other main agricultural products are coconuts, melons, copra, bananas, and melons. Since most of the crops grown are primarily for export, about 90 per cent of the country's food has to be imported. Small manufacturing industries include food processing and lumber products.

Area: 372 sq miles/964 sq km
Population: 135,000
Capital: São Tomé
Form of government: Republic
Religion: RC;
Currency: Dobra

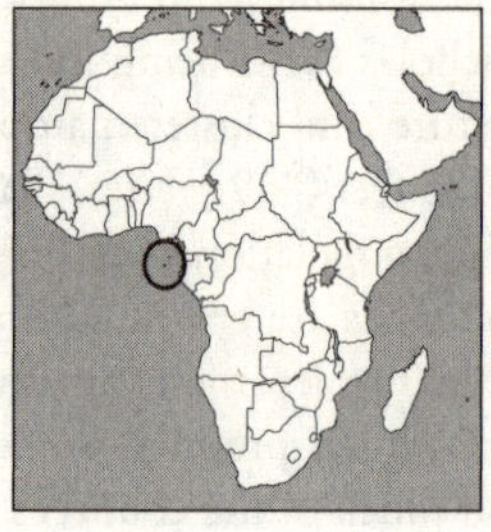

São Vincente, Cabo de (Cape St Vincent) the southwestern corner of Portugal.

Sarawak a state of Malaysia occupying much of the northwestern coast of Borneo. (48,342 sq miles/125,204 sq km; pop. 2,121,000)

Sardinia (Sardegna) the second largest island of the Mediterranean after Sicily, also belonging to Italy, lying just south of Corsica. The capital is Cagliari. (9,301 sq miles/24,089 sq km; pop. 1,669,000)

Saskatchewan (1) a province of western Canada, in the Great Plains. The capital is Regina. (251,000 sq miles/651,900 sq km; pop. 1,038,000) (2) a river of Canada, rising in the Rocky Mountains and flowing westwards into Lake Winnipeg. (Length 1,200 miles/1,930 km)

Saudi Arabia a state that occupies over 70 per cent of the Arabian Peninsula. Over 95 per cent of the country is desert, and the largest expanse of sand in the world, the Empty Quarter (Rub al Khali), is found in the southeast of the country. In the west, a narrow, humid coastal plain along the Red Sea is backed by steep mountains. The climate is hot, with very little rain, and some areas have no precipitation for years. The government has spent a considerable amount on reclamation of the desert for agriculture, and the main products are dates, tomatoes, watermelons, and wheat, which are grown in the fertile land around the oases. Saudi Arabia exports wheat and shrimps and is self-sufficient in some dairy products. However, the country's prosperity is based almost entirely on the exploitation of its vast reserves of oil and natural gas. Industries include petroleum refining, petrochemicals, and fertilizers. As a result of the Gulf War (1990–91), some 285 miles (460 kilometres) of the Saudi coastline were polluted by oil, threatening desalination plants and damaging the wildlife of salt marshes, mangrove forest, and mudflats.

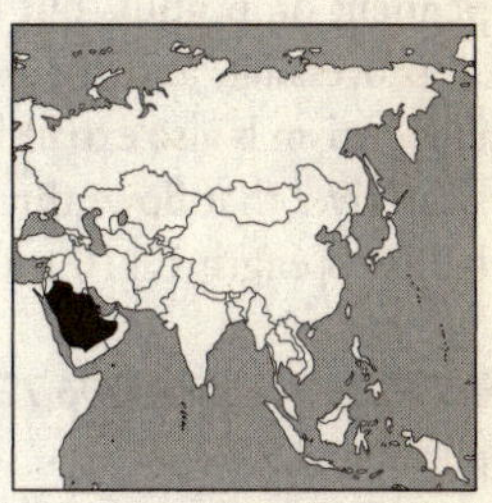

Area: 830,000 sq miles/2,149,690 sq km
Population: 18,836,000
Capital: Riyadh (Ar Riyād)
Other cities: Mecca, Jeddah, Medina, Ta'if
Form of government: Monarchy
Religions: Sunni Islam, Shia Islam
Currency: Riyal

Savoie (Savoy) a mountainous former duchy in southeast France, which has been a part of France since 1860 and is now divided into two departments, Savoie and Haute Savoie.

Scandinavia the countries on, or near, the Scandinavian Peninsula in northern Europe, usually taken to include Norway, Sweden, Denmark, Finland and Iceland.

Scapa Flow an anchorage surrounded by the Orkney Islands, famous as a wartime naval base.

Schelde a river rising in France and then flowing through Belgium and the Netherlands to the North Sea. (Length 270 miles/435 km)

Schleswig-Holstein the northernmost state of Germany. The capital is Kiel. (Pop. 2,807,000)

Scilly, Isles of a group of islands off the southwest tip of Cornwall, England. The main islands are St Mary's, St Martin, and Tresco. (Pop. 2,000)

Scotland a country of the United Kingdom, occupying the northern part of Great Britain. The capital is Edinburgh. (30,410 sq miles/78,762 sq km; pop. 5,056,000)

Scottish Borders a council area in southern Scotland, with its administrative centre in Newton St Boswells. (1,827 sq miles/4,734 sq km; pop. 106,000)

Seine a river of northern France, flowing through Paris to the English Channel. (Length 482 miles/775 km)

Senegal (1) a former French colony in West Africa that extends from Cape Verde, the most western point in Africa, to the border with Mali. Senegal is mostly low-lying and covered by savannah. The Fouta Djallon Mountains in the south rise to 4,971 feet (1,515 metres). The climate is tropical, with a dry season from October to Junc. The most densely populated region is in the southwest. Almost 80 per cent of the labour force work in agriculture, growing peanuts and cotton for export and millet, sugar cane, maize, rice, and sorghum as subsistence crops. Increased production of crops such as rice and tomatoes is encouraged in order to achieve self-sufficiency in food. The country's economy is largely dependent on peanuts but there is a growing manufacturing sector, including food processing, and the production of cement, chemicals, and tinned tuna, while tourism is also expanding. Senegal is dependent on foreign aid. (2) a West African river that flows through Guinea, Mali, Mauritania, and Senegal to the Atlantic. (Length 1,110 miles/1,790 km)

Area: 75,955 sq miles/196,722 sq km
Population: 8,572,000
Capital: Dakar
Other cities: Kaolack, Thiès, St Louis
Form of government: Republic
Religions: Sunni Islam, RC
Currency: CFA Franc

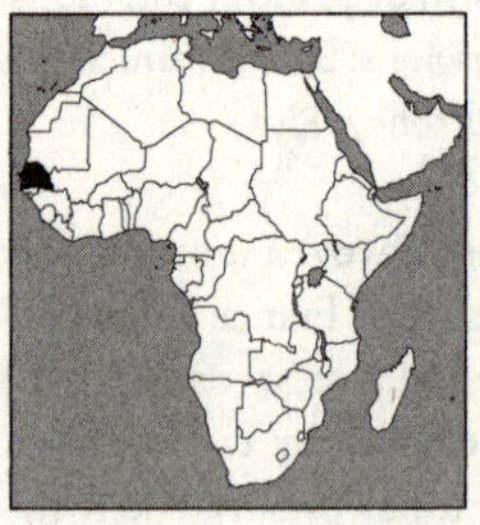

Seram (Ceram) an island in the Maluku group, Indonesia. (6,621 sq miles/ 17,148 sq km)

Serbia and Montenegro a recent (2003) union of states in southeastern Europe, bordering the Adriatic Sea between Albania and Bosnia-Herzegovina, that brings together the last of the former Yugoslavian republics of Serbia and Montenegro, and includes the nominally autonomous provinces of Kosovo and Vojvodina. Provision has been made for a a referendum to be held in each republic on full independence (2006). The capital city is Belgrade. (39,449 sq miles/102,173 sq km; pop.10,825,900)

Severn the longest river in the UK, flowing through Wales and the west of England. (Length 220 miles/350 km)

Seychelles a group of volcanic islands that lie in the western Indian Ocean, about 746 miles (1,200 kilometres) from the coast of East Africa. About 40 of the islands are mountainous and consist of granite, while just over 50 are coral islands. The climate is tropical maritime with heavy rain. The capital, Victoria, and about 90 per cent of the people can be found on the island of Mahé. The staple foods are coconut, imported rice, and fish, while some fruits are grown for home consumption. Tourism employs one-third of the labour force and accounts for about 90 per cent of the country's foreign exchange earnings. Export trade is based on petroleum (after importation), copra, cinnamon bark, and fish. The only mineral resource is guano. The Seychelles were a one-party socialist state until 1991, when a new constitution was introduced. The first free elections were held in 1993.

Area: 175 sq miles/455 sq km
Population: 76,000
Capital: Victoria
Form of government: Republic
Religion: RC
Currency: Seychelles Rupee

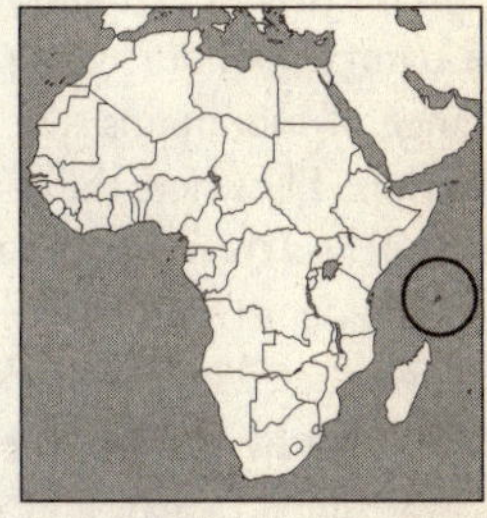

Shaanxi a province of northwestern China. The capital is Xi'an. (73,000 sq miles/ 190,000 sq km; pop. 37,736,000)

Shandong a province of northern China, with its capital at Jinan. (58,000 sq miles/ 150,000 sq km; pop. 95,077,000)

Shannon a river of the Republic of Ireland, and the longest river in the British Isles. It flows southwest into the Atlantic Ocean near Limerick. (Length 240 miles/386 km)

Shanxi a province of northern China, with its capital at Taiyuan. (58,000 sq miles/ 150,000 sq km; pop. 32,802,000)

Sharjah (Ash-Shariqah) the third largest of the United Arab Emirates. Its capital is also Sharjah. (1,000 sq miles/2,600 sq km; pop. emirate 522,000/city 417,000)

Shatt al Arab a waterway flowing into the Persian Gulf along the disputed border between Iran and Iraq, formed where the Rivers Euphrates and Tigris converge some 105 miles (170 kilometres) from the coast.

Shetland Islands a group of some 100 islands lying 100 miles (160 kilometres) northeast of mainland Scotland, which go to make up an island authority of Scotland, with an administrative centre in Lerwick. (550 sq miles/1,426 sq km; pop. 23,000)

Shikoku the smallest of the four main islands of Japan. (Pop. 4,139,000)

Shropshire a county of west central England, with its administrative centre in the town of Shrewsbury. (1,347 sq miles/3,490 sq km; pop. 416,000)

Siberia a huge tract of land, mostly in northern Russian Federation, that extends from the Ural Mountains to the Pacific coast. It is renowned for its inhospitable climate, but parts of it are fertile, and it is rich in minerals.

Sichuan (Szechwan) the most heavily populated of the provinces of China, in the southwest of the country. The capital is Chengdu. (220,000 sq miles/ 570,000 sq km; pop. 87,354,000)

Sicily (Sicilia) an island hanging from the toe of Italy, the largest island in the Mediterranean. The capital is Palermo. (9,926 sq miles/25,708 sq km; pop. 5,216,000)

Sierra Leone a country on the Atlantic coast of West Africa, bounded by Guinea to the north and east and by Liberia to the southeast. The country possesses a fine natural harbour where the capital and major port of Freetown is situated. A range of mountains, the Sierra Lyoa, rise above the capital on the Freetown Peninsula. Elsewhere the coastal plain is up to 70 miles (110 km) wide, rising to a plateau and then to mountains which are part of the Guinea Highlands Massif. The climate is tropical, with heavy rain during a rainy season lasting from May to November. The country's staple food is rice that is grown in the swamplands at the coast by the subsistence farmers. Other crops grown include sorghum, cassava, millet, sugar, and groundnuts. Civil War (1991–2002) and ongoing ethnic conflict resulted in the displacement of more than 2 million people. A UN peacekeeping force supported the country through national elections in 2002 but the gradual withdrawal of the force during 2004 and 2005 has challenged the country's long-term stability.

Area: 27,699 sq miles/71,740 sq km
Population: 4,297,000
Capital: Freetown
Form of government: Republic
Religion: traditional African religions, Sunni Islam, Christianity
Currency: Leone

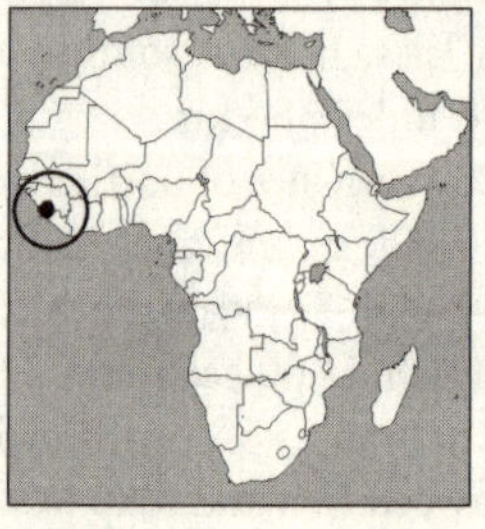

Sierra Madre Occidental the mountain range of western Mexico.

Sierra Madre Oriental the mountain range of eastern Mexico.

Sierra Nevada (1) a mountain range in southern Spain. (2) a mountain range in eastern California, USA.

Sikkim a state in northeastern India. The capital is Gangtok. (2,739 sq miles/ 7,096 sq km; pop. 551,000)

Silesia (Schlesien) a region straddling the borders of the Czech Republic, Germany and Poland.

Simpson Desert an arid, uninhabited region in the centre of Australia.

Sinai a mountainous peninsula in northeastern Egypt, bordering Israel, between the Gulf of Aqaba and the Gulf of Suez.

Sind a province of southeastern Pakistan. The capital is Karachi. (54,407 sq miles/ 140,914 sq km; pop. 33,237,000)

Singapore one of the world's smallest yet most successful countries. It comprises one main island and 58 islets that are located at the foot of the Malay Peninsula in southeast Asia. The main island of Singapore is very low-lying, and the climate is hot and wet throughout the year. Only 1.6 per cent of the land area is used for agriculture, most food being imported. The country has a flourishing manufacturing industry for which it relies heavily on imports. Products traded in Singapore include machinery and appliances, petroleum, food and beverages, chemicals, transport equipment, paper products and printing, and clothes. Shipbuilding is also an important industry. International banking and tourism are important sources of foreign revenue. Singapore's airport is one of the largest in Asia.

Area: 239 sq miles/618 sq km
Population: 3,044,000
Capital: Singapore
Form of government: Republic
Religions: Buddhism, Sunni Islam, Christianity, Hinduism
Currency: Singapore Dollar

Sirte, Gulf of a huge indent of the Mediterranean Sea on the coastline of Libya.

Skagerrak the channel, some 80 miles (130 kilometres) wide, separating Denmark and Norway. It links the North Sea to the Kattegat and Baltic Sea.

Skiathos the westernmost of the Greek Southern Sporades Islands which include the Dodecanese Islands. (Pop. 4,200)

Skye an island off the northwest coast of Scotland and the largest of the Inner Hebrides Islands. The main town is Portree. (547 sq miles/1,417 sq km; pop. 8,000)

Slavonia (Slavonija) a part of Croatia, southeast of Zagreb, mainly between the Drava and Slava Rivers.

Sligo a county on the northwest coast of the Republic of Ireland, with a county town of the same name. (693 sq miles/1,796 sq km; pop. 58,000)

Slovakia (or the **Slovak Republic**) is a country that was constituted on 1 January 1993 as a new independent nation, following the dissolution of the 74-year-old federal republic of Czechoslovakia. Landlocked in central Europe, its neighbours are the Czech Republic to the west, Poland to the north, Austria and Hungary to the south, and a short border with Ukraine in the east. The northern half of the republic is occupied by the Tatra Mountains, which form the northern arm of the Carpathian Mountains. This region has vast forests and pastures used for intensive sheep grazing, and is rich in high-grade minerals such as copper, iron, zinc, and lead. Farms, vineyards, orchards, and pastures for stock form the basis of southern Slovakia's economy. The inefficient industrialization of the old regime has left Slovakia with a legacy of economic and environmental problems. In the early 1990s, unemployment increased and inflation was high, resulting in a lowering in the standard of living. The tourism industry is beginning to contribute to the country's economy as visitors come to enjoy the country's ski resorts and historical cities.

Area: 18,928 sq miles/49,035 sq km
Population: 5,374,000
Capital: Bratislava
Other cities: Zilina, Trnava
Form of government: Republic
Religion: RC
Currency: Slovak Koruna

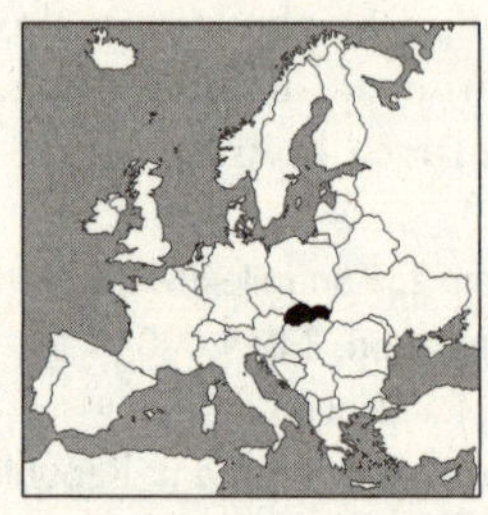

Slovenia a republic that made a unilateral declaration of independence from the former Yugoslavia on 25 June 1991 but whose sovereignty was not formally recognized by the European Community and the United Nations until early in 1992. Slovenia is bounded to the north by Austria, to the west by Italy, to the east by Hungary, and to the south by Croatia. Most of Slovenia is situated in the Karst Plateau and in the Julian Alps, where Mount Triglav (9,393 ft/ 2,863 m) is the country's highest peak. The Julian Alps are renowned for their scenery, and the Karst Plateau contains spectacular cave systems. The northeast of the republic is famous for its wine production, and tourism is also an important industry. Although farming and livestock raising are the chief occupations, Slovenia is very industrialized and urbanized. Iron, steel, and aluminium are produced, and resources include oil, coal, lead, uranium, mercury, natural gas and petroleum. Slovenia has also been successful in establishing many new light industries, and this has given the country a well-balanced economic base for the future, with unemployment lessening and industrial output increasing.

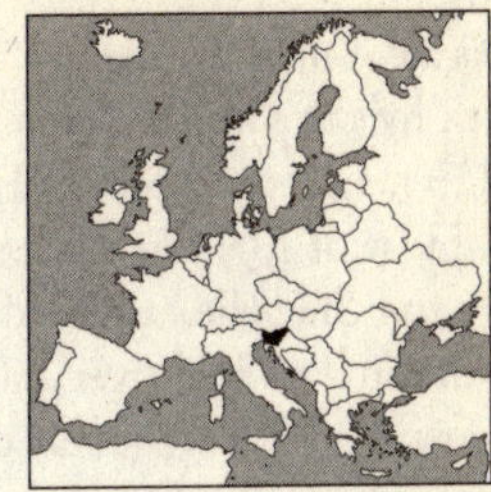

Area: 7,821 sq miles/20,256 sq km
Population: 1,998,912
Capital: Ljubljana
Other cities: Maribor, Celje
Form of government: Republic
Religion: RC
Currency: Slovene Tolar

Snake a river of the northwest USA, which flows into the Columbia River in the state of Washington. (Length 1,038 miles/1,670 km)

Snowdonia a mountainous region in the north of Wales. The highest peak is Mount Snowdon (3560 ft/1,085 m).

Snowy Mountains a range of mountains in southeastern Australia, where the River Snowy has been dammed to form the complex Snowy Mountains Hydroelectric Scheme. The highest peak is Mount Kosciusko (7,316 ft/2,230 m).

Society Islands a group of islands at the centre of French Polynesia. They are divided into the Windward Islands, which include Tahiti and Moorea, and the Leeward Islands, which include Raiatea and Bora-Bora. (Pop. 142,000)

Socotra an island in the northwestern Indian Ocean, belonging to Yemen.

Solent, the a strait in the English Channel that separates the Isle of Wight from mainland England.

Solomon Islands an island state in the Pacific Ocean in an area between 5 and 12 degrees south of the Equator, to the east of Papua New Guinea. The country consists of six large islands and innumerable smaller ones. The larger islands are mountainous and covered by forests, with rivers prone to flooding. Guadalcanal is the main island and the site of the capital, Honiara. The climate is hot and wet and typhoons are frequent. The main food crops grown are coconut, cassava, sweet potatoes, plantains, yams, rice, taros, and bananas. Other products include copra, processed fish, lumber, and trochus shells. Mineral resources such as phosphate rock and bauxite are found in large amounts and some alluvial gold is produced. Other industries include palm oil-milling, sawmilling, food, tobacco, and sodas.

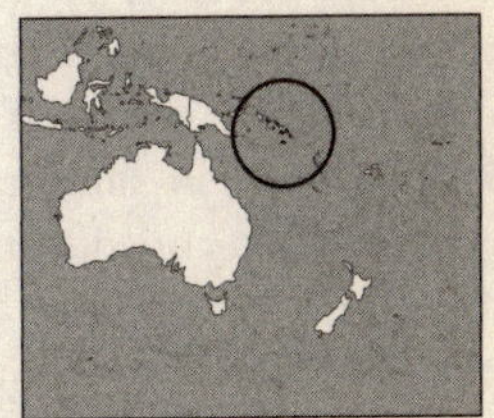

Area: 11,157 sq miles/28,896 sq km
Population: 391,000
Capital: Honiara
Form of government: Parliamentary democracy within the Commonwealth
Religions: Anglicanism, RC, other Christianity
Currency: Solomon Island Dollar

Somalia a country that lies on the horn of Africa's east coast. It is bounded on the north by the Gulf of Aden and on the south and east by the Indian Ocean, and its neighbours include Djibouti, Ethiopia, and Kenya. The country is arid, and most of it is low plateau with scrub vegetation. Its two main rivers, the Juba and Shebelle, are used to irrigate crops. Most of the population live in the mountains and river valleys, and there are a few towns on the coast. The country has little in the way of natural resourccs but there are deposits of copper, petroleum, iron, manganese, and marble, although not commercially exploited. Main exports are live animals, meat, hides, and skins. A few large-scale banana plantations are found by the rivers. Years of drought have left Somalia heavily dependent on foreign aid, and many of the younger people are emigrating to oil-rich Arab states. Civil war in the 1980s and early 1990s resulted in a huge loss of life and widespread famine. International UN peacekeeping forces were deployed and humanitarian aid given to try to avert a catastrophe but these withdrew in 1995. The situation remains unresolved although there has been some recovery in agriculture and food production.

Area: 246,201 sq miles/637,657 sq km
Population: 9,822,000
Capital: Mogadishu (Muqdisho)
Other cities: Hargeisa, Burco, Kismaayo
Form of government: Republic
Religion: Sunni Islam
Currency: Somali Shilling

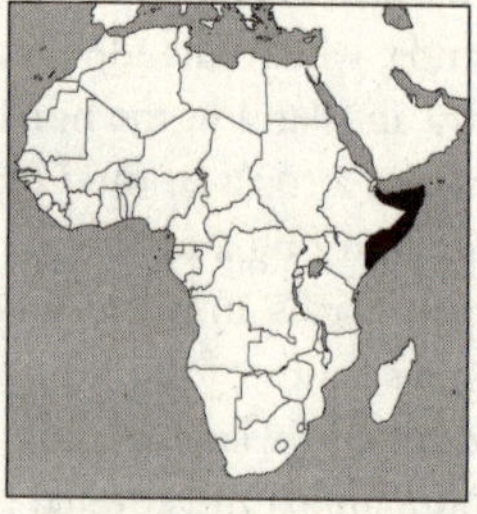

Somerset a county in the southwest of England, on the Bristol Channel, with its administrative centre in the town of Taunton. (1,620 sq miles/4,196 sq km; pop. 680,000)

Somme a river of northern France, the scene of a devastating battle during World War I. (Length 152 miles/245 km)

South Africa a republic that lies at the southern tip of the African continent and has a huge coastline on both the Atlantic and Indian Oceans. The country occupies a huge saucer-shaped plateau, surrounded by a belt of land that drops in steps to the sea. The rim of the saucer rises in the east to 11,424 feet (3,482 metres) in the Drakensberg Mountains. In general, the climate is healthy, with plenty of sunshine and relatively low rainfall. Of the total land area, 58 per cent is used as natural pasture although soil erosion is a problem. The main crops grown are maize, sorghum, wheat, groundnuts, and sugar cane. A drought-resistant variety of cotton is also now grown. South

Africa has extraordinary mineral wealth, including gold, coal, copper, iron ore, manganese, diamonds, and chrome ore. A system of apartheid existed in South Africa from 1948 until the early 1990s, denying black South Africans civil rights and promoting racial segregation. During this time, the country was subjected to international economic and political sanctions. In 1990, the ban on the outlawed African National Congress was lifted and its leader, Nelson Mandela, was released from prison. This heralded the dismantling of the apartheid regime and in the first multiracial elections held in 1994, the ANC triumphed, with Mandela voted in as the country's president. Since that time, South Africa has once again become an active and recognized member of the international community.

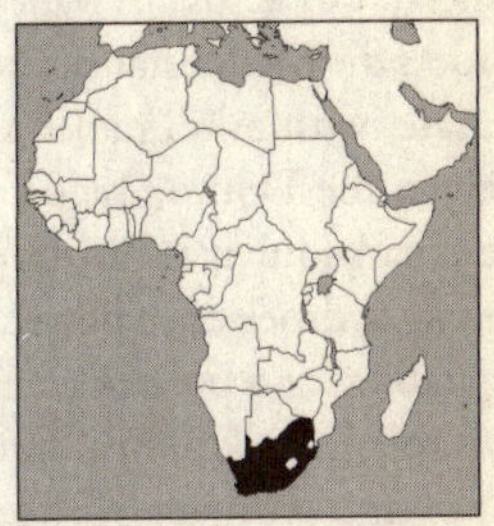

Area: 471,445 sq miles/1,221,037 sq km
Population: 40,584,000
Capital: Pretoria (administrative), Cape Town (legislative)
Other cities: Johannesburg, Durban, Port Elizabeth, Bloemfontein
Form of government: Republic
Religions: Christianity, Islam, Hinduism, traditional African religions
Currency: Rand

South Australia a state in central southern Australia, on the Great Australian Bight. Adelaide is the state capital. (380,069 sq miles/984,380 sq km; pop. 1,572,000)

South Ayrshire a council area in south Scotland, with its administrative centre in Ayr. (Pop. 114,000)

South Carolina a state in the southeast of the USA, with a coast on the Atlantic Ocean. The state capital is Columbia. (31,055 sq miles/80,432 sq km; pop. 4,114,000)

South China Sea an arm of the Pacific Ocean between southeast China, Malaysia and the Philippines.

South Dakota a state in western USA. The state capital is Pierre. (77,047 sq miles/199,552 sq km; pop. 758,000)

Southern Alps a range of mountains on the South Island of New Zealand.

South Georgia an island in the South Atlantic, and a dependency of the Falkland Islands. (1450 sq miles/3,755 sq km)

South Glamorgan a county in south Wales. The administrative centre is Cardiff. (161 sq miles/416 sq km; pop. 384,700)

South Lanarkshire a council area in south Scotland, with its administrative centre in Hamilton. (684 sq miles/1,771 sq km; pop. 307,000)

South Pole the most southerly point of the Earth's axis, in Antarctica.

South Sandwich Islands a group of islands in the South Atlantic which are dependencies of the Falkland Islands. (130 sq miles/340 sq km)

South Yorkshire a metropolitan county in northern England. (602 sq miles/ 1,560 sq km)

Spain a country located in southwest Europe and occupying the greater part of the Iberian Peninsula, which it shares with Portugal. It is a mountainous country, sealed off from the rest of Europe by the Pyrenees, which rise to over 11,155 feet (3,400 metres). Much of the country is a vast plateau, the Meseta Central, cut across by valleys and gorges. Its longest shoreline is the one that borders the Mediterranean Sea. Most of the country has a form of Mediterranean climate, with mild, moist winters and hot, dry summers. Spain's major rivers, such as the Douro, Tagus, and Guadiana, flow to the Atlantic Ocean while the Guadalquivir is the deepest. Although not generally navigable, they are of use for hydroelectric power. Spain's principal agricultural products are cereals, vegetables, and potatoes, and large areas are under vines for the wine industry. The soil is good, with almost one-third cultivable. Livestock production is important, particularly sheep and goats. Industry represents 72 per cent of the country's export value, and production includes textiles, paper, cement, steel, and chemicals. Tourism is a major revenue earner, especially from the resorts on the east coast.

Area: 195,365 sq miles/505,992 sq km
Population: 39,540,000
Capital: Madrid
Other cities: Barcelona, Seville, Zaragosa, Malaga, Bilbao
Form of government: Constitutional Monarchy
Religion: RC
Currency: Euro

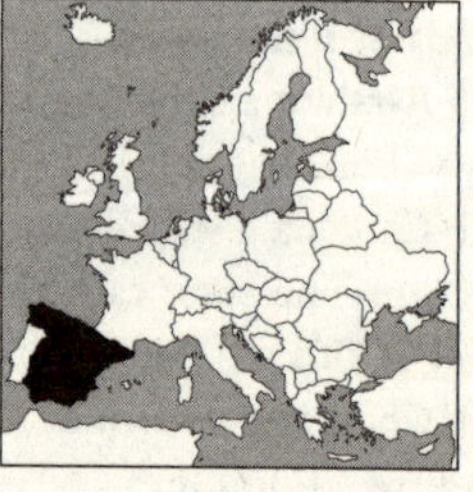

Spitsbergen a large island group in the Svalbard Archipelago, 360 miles (580 kilometres) to the north of Norway. (15,060 sq miles/39,000 sq km; pop. 2,000)

Spratly Islands a group of islands in the South China Sea between Vietnam and Borneo. Occupied by Japan during World War II, they are now claimed by almost all the surrounding countries.

Sri Lanka a teardrop-shaped island in the Indian Ocean, lying south of the Indian

Peninsula, from which it is separated by the Palk Strait. Its climate is equatorial, with a low annual temperature range, but it is affected by both the northeast and southwest monsoons. Agriculture engages 47 per cent of the workforce, and the main crops are rice, tea, rubber, and coconuts, although sugar, rice, and wheat have to be imported. Precious and semiprecious stones are among the chief minerals to be mined and exported. Graphite is also important. The main industries are food, beverages, tobacco, textiles, clothing, leather goods, chemicals, and plastics. Politically, Sri Lanka has been afflicted by ethnic divisions between the Sinhalese and Tamils. Attempts by the Tamil extremists to establish an independent homeland have at times brought the northeast of the country to the brink of civil war, and the situation remains volatile. The revenue from tourism is slowly increasing but the country was badly hit by the Asian tsunami of 2004 when much of its shoreline was damaged.

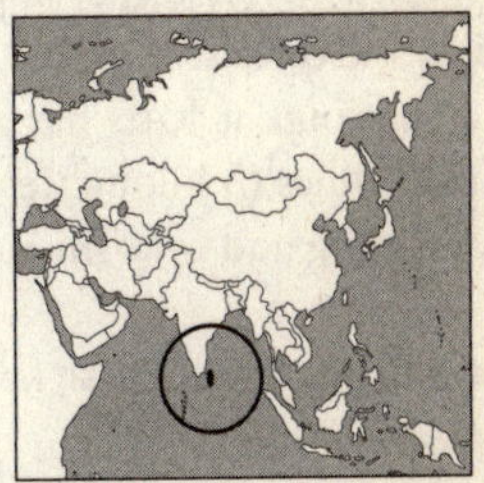

Area: 25,332 sq miles/65,610 sq km
Population: 18,354,000
Capital: Colombo
Other cities: Kandy, Moratuwa, Jaffna
Form of government: Republic
Religions: Buddhism, Hinduism, Christianity, Sunni Islam
Currency: Sri Lankan Rupee

Staffordshire a county in central England, with its administrative centre in the town of Stafford. (1,049 sq miles/2,716 sq km; pop. 1,054,000)

St Barthélémy a small island dependency of Guadeloupe in the east Caribbean. (Pop. 6,000)

St Croix the largest of the US Virgin Islands. The main town is Christiansted. (84 sq miles/218 sq km; pop. 71,000)

St Eustatius (Sint Eustatius, Statia) a Caribbean island, part of the Netherland Antilles. The capital is Oranjestad. (8 sq miles/21 sq km; pop. 2,000)

St Helena a volcanic island in the south Atlantic Ocean which is a British Overseas Territory and an administrative centre for the island of Tristan da Cunha to the south and Ascension Island to the north. Napoleon Bonaparte was exiled here by the British from 1815 until his death in 1821. The main exports are fish, lumber, and handicrafts. (47 sq miles/122 sq km; pop. 5,500; cur. St Helena Pound)

St Helena Dependencies the islands of Ascension and Tristan da Cunha are so-called dependencies of St Helena, a British Overseas Territory.

St Helens, Mount an active volcano in the Cascade Range of western Washington State, USA. It last erupted in 1980. (8,364 ft/2,549 m)

Stirling (1) a town in central Scotland, on the River Forth, and the administrative centre for the Stirling council area. (Pop. 30,000) (2) a council area in central Scotland. (839 sq miles/2,173 km; pop. 83,000)

St Kitts (St Christopher) and Nevis the islands of St Christopher (popularly known as St Kitts) and Nevis lie in the Leeward group in the eastern Caribbean and in 1983 became a sovereign democratic federation, with the British monarch as head of state. St Kitts consists of three extinct volcanoes linked by a sandy isthmus to other volcanic remains in the south. The highest point on St Kitts is Mount Liamuiga at 4,314 feet (1,315 metres). The islands have a tropical climate. Sugar cane is grown on the fertile soil covering the lower slopes and sugar is the chief export crop, but market gardening and livestock are being expanded on the steeper slopes above the cane fields. Some vegetables, coconuts, fruits, and cereals are grown. Industry includes sugar refining, brewing, distilling, and bottling. St Kitts has a major tourist development at Frigate Bay. Nevis, lying 2 miles (3 kilometres) south, is an extinct volcano. Agricultural activity is declining and tourism is now the main source of income.

Area: 101 sq miles/261 sq km
Population: 43,410
Capital: Basseterre
Form of government: Constitutional Monarchy
Religions: Anglicanism, Methodism
Currency: East Caribbean Dollar

St Lawrence (1) a commercially important river of southeast Canada, which flows northeast from Lake Ontario to the Gulf of St Lawrence, forming part of the border with the USA. (Length 744 miles/1,197 km) (2) **Gulf of** an arm of the Atlantic Ocean in northeastern Canada, into which the St Lawrence River flows. (3) **Seaway** a navigable waterway that links the Great Lakes, via the St Lawrence River, to the Atlantic Ocean.

St Lucia St Lucia is one of the Windward Islands in the eastern Caribbean. It lies to the south of Martinique and to the north of St Vincent. It was controlled alternately by the French and the British for some 200 years before becoming fully independent in 1979. St Lucia is an island of extinct volcanoes and the highest peak is 3,117 feet (950 metres). The climate is tropical, with a rainy season from May to August. The economy depends on the production of bananas and, to a lesser extent, coconuts and mangoes. Production, however, is often affected by hurricanes, drought, and disease. There are some manufacturing industries, which produce clothing, cardboard boxes, plastics, electrical parts, and drinks, and the country has two airports. Tourism is increasing in importance, and Castries, the capital, is a popular calling point for cruise liners.

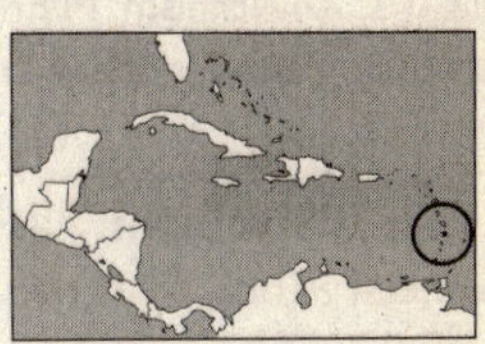

Area: 240 sq miles/622 sq km
Population: 146,600
Capital: Castries
Form of Government: Constitutional Monarchy
Religion: RC
Currency: East Caribbean Dollar

St Martin one of the Leeward Islands in the southeastern Caribbean. It is divided politically into two, one a part of Guadeloupe (France); the other (Sint Maarten) a part of the Netherlands Antilles. The capital of the French side is Marigot, and of the Dutch side, Philipsburg. (French 21 sq miles/54 sq km; pop. 29,000; Dutch 13 sq miles/33 sq km; pop. 37,000)

St Pierre and Miquelon two islands to the south of Newfoundland, Canada, which together are a French Overseas Territory. They are the last French possessions in North America, and have a substantial fishing industry. (93 sq miles/240 sq km; pop. 6,300; cur. Euro)

Strabane a district council area in Co. Tyrone, west Northern Ireland. (333 sq miles/862 sq km; pop. 36,000)

Strathclyde a former administrative region situated in western Scotland.

Stromboli an island with an active volcano in the Eolian Islands, to the north of Sicily. (Pop. 400)

St Vincent and the Grenadines St Vincent is an island of the Lesser Antilles, situated in the eastern Caribbean between St Lucia and Grenada. It is separated from Grenada by a chain of some 600 small islands known as the Grenadines, the northern islands of which form the other part of the country. The largest of these islands are Bequia, Mustique, Canouan, Mayreau, and Union. The climate is tropical, with very heavy rain in the mountains. St Vincent Island is mountainous and a chain of volcanoes runs up the middle of the island. The volcano Soufrière (4,049 feet/1,234 metres) is active. Farming is the main occupation on the island although tropical storms are always a threat to crops. Bananas are the main export, and it is the world's leading producer of arrowroot starch. There is little manufacturing and unemployment is high. The government is trying to promote tourism.

Area: 150 sq miles/388 sq km
Population: 113,000
Capital: Kingstown
Form of government: Constitutional Monarchy
Religions: Anglicanism, Methodism, RC
Currency: East Caribbean Dollar

Sudan the largest country in Africa, lying just south of the Tropic of Cancer in northeast Africa. The country covers much of the upper Nile basin, and in the north the river winds through the Nubian and Libyan deserts, forming a palm-fringed strip of habitable land. In 1994, the country was divided into 26 states, compared to the original 9 states. The climate is tropical and temperatures are high throughout the year. In winter, nights are very cold. Rainfall increases in amount from north to south, the northern areas being virtually desert. Sudan is an agricultural country. Subsistence farming accounts for 80 per cent of production, and livestock are also raised. Cotton is farmed commercially and accounts for about two-thirds of Sudan's exports. Sudan is the world's greatest source of gum arabic, used in medicines, perfumes, processed foods, and inks. Other forest products are tannin, beeswax, senna, and lumber. Because of the combination of years of civil war and drought, Sudan has a large foreign debt.

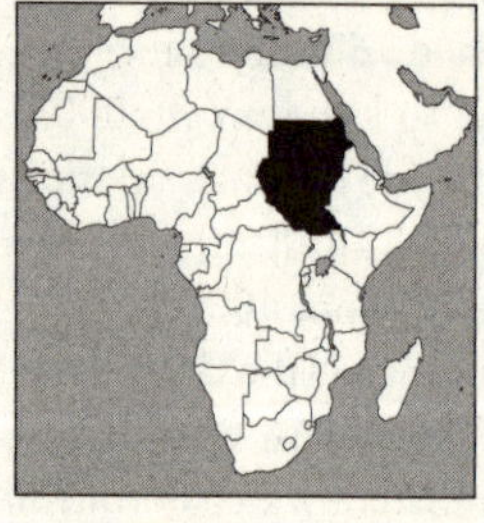

Area: 967,500 sq miles/2,505,813 sq km
Population: 27,291,000
Capital: Khartoum (El Khartum)
Other cities: Omdurman, Khartoum North, Port Sudan
Form of government: Republic
Religions: Sunni Islam, traditional African religions, Christianity
Currency: Sudanese Dinar

Sudety (Sudetenland) a mountainous region straddling the border between the Czech Republic and Poland.

Suez, Gulf of a northern arm of the Red Sea that leads to the Suez Canal.

Suez Canal a canal in northeast Egypt, linking the Mediterranean to the Red Sea. It was completed in 1869.

Suffolk a county in southeast England, with its administrative centre in the town of Ipswich. (1,467 sq miles/3,800 sq km; pop. 649,000)

Sulawesi (Celebes) a large, hook-shaped island in the centre of Indonesia.

(69,255 sq miles/179,370 sq km; pop. 15,328,000)

Sulu Archipelago a chain of over 400 islands off the southwest Philippines, stretching between the Philippines and Borneo.

Sulu Sea a part of the Pacific Ocean between the Philippines and Borneo.

Sumatra the main island of western Indonesia. (182,860 sq miles/473,607 sq km; pop. 44,703,000)

Sumba one of the Lesser Sunda Islands, Indonesia, to the south of Sumbawa and Flores. (4306 sq miles/11,153 sq km; pop. 251,100)

Sumbawa one of the Lesser Sunda Islands, Indonesia, between Lombok and Flores. (5,965 sq miles/15,448 sq km; pop. 195,000)

Sunda Strait the strait, 16 miles (26 kilometres) across at its narrowest point, which separates Java and Sumatra.

Superior, Lake the largest and most westerly of the Great Lakes. (31,800 sq miles/82,400 sq km)

Suriname a republic in northeast South America that was formerly known as Dutch Guiana. It is bordered to the west by Guyana, to the east by French Guiana, and to the south by Brazil. The country, formerly a Dutch colony, declared independence in 1975. Suriname comprises a swampy coastal plain, a forested central plateau, and southern mountains. The climate is tropical, with heavy rainfall from December to April. Agriculture remains fairly underdeveloped. Crops cultivated include rice, bananas, citrus fruits, sugar cane, coffee and cocoa. Molasses and rum are produced along with some manufactured goods and there is an important coastal shrimp fishery. Suriname's economy is based on the mining of bauxite, which accounts for 80 per cent of its exports. The country has important mineral reserves of iron ore, nickel, copper, platinum and gold. Suriname's natural resources also include oil and lumber, and forestry is an expanding industry. However, the country is politically unstable and in need of financial aid to develop its resources.

Area: 63,037 sq miles/163,265 sq km
Population: 423,000
Capital: Paramaribo
Form of government: Republic
Religions: Hinduism, RC, Sunni Islam
Currency: Suriname Guilder

Surrey a county in southeast England, with its administrative centre in the borough of Kingston upon Thames. (648 sq miles/1,679 sq km; pop. 1,041,000)

Svalbard an archipelago in the Arctic Ocean to the north of Norway, which has sovereignty. (23,958 sq miles/62,049 sq km; pop. 2,000)

Swansea (1) a port in south Wales, and the administrative centre for the Swansea council area. (Pop. 171,000) (2) a council area in south Wales. (146 sq miles/378 sq km; pop. 230,000)

Swaziland a landlocked hilly enclave almost entirely within the borders of the Republic of South Africa. The mountains in the west of the country rise to about 6,500 feet (almost 2,000 metres), then descend in steps of savannah towards hilly country in the east. The climate is subtropical, moderated by altitude. The land between 1,300–2,800 feet (approximately 400–850 metres) is planted with orange groves and pineapple fields, while on the lower land sugar cane flourishes in irrigated areas. Other important crops are citrus fruits, cotton, and pineapples. Forestry is an important industry, with production centring mainly on pine since it matures extremely quickly because of Swaziland's climate. Coal is mined and also asbestos, although in lessening amounts because of its associated health risks. Manufacturing includes fertilizers, textiles, leather, and tableware. Tourism is a growing industry, with the country's game reserves, mountain scenery, spas, and casinos proving to be popular destinations for visitors.

Area: 6,704 sq miles/17,364 sq km
Population: 938,000
Capital: Mbabane
Other towns: Big Bend, Manzini, Mhlume
Form of government: Monarchy
Religion: Christianity, traditional African religions
Currency: Lilangeni

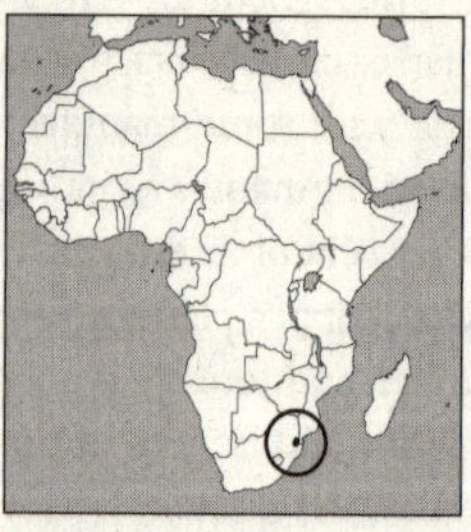

Sweden a large country in northern Europe that makes up half the Scandinavian Peninsula. It stretches from the Baltic Sea north to well within the Arctic Circle. The south is generally flat with many lakes, the north mountainous, and along the coast there are over 20,000 islands and islets. Summers are warm but short, while winters are long and cold. In the north snow may lie for four to seven months. Dairy farming is the predominant agricultural activity along with livestock production (cattle, pigs, and sheep). Only 7 per cent of Sweden is cultivated, with the emphasis on fodder crops, potatoes, rape seed, grain, and sugar beet. About 57 per cent of the country is covered by forest, and the sawmill, wood pulp, and paper industries are all of great importance to the country's economy. Sweden is one of the world's leading producers of iron ore, most of which is extracted from within the Arctic Circle. Other main industries are engineering and the production of electrical goods, motor vehicles, and furniture, as well as fine craftware, such as glassware, ceramics, silverware, and items made from stainless steel. In a referendum in 1994, Swedish voters approved membership of the European Union, and it became a member on 1 January 1995.

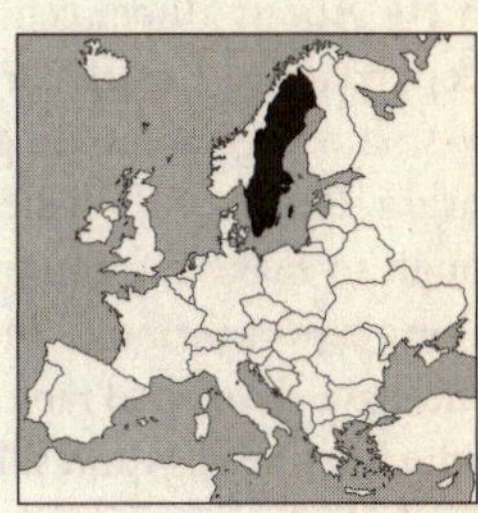

Area: 173,732 sq miles/ 449,964 sq km
Population: 8,500,000
Capital: Stockholm
Other major cities: Göteborg, Malmö, Uppsala, Örebro
Form of government: Constitutional Monarchy
Religion: Lutheranism
Currency: Krona

Switzerland a landlocked country in central Europe, sharing its borders with France, Italy, Austria, Liechtenstein, and Germany. The Alps occupy over 70 per cent of Switzerland's area, forming two main east-west chains divided by the Rivers Rhine and Rhône. The climate is either continental or mountain type. Summers are generally warm and winters cold, and both are affected by altitude. Northern Switzerland is the industrial part of the country and where its most important cities are located. Basle is famous for its pharmaceuticals, and Zürich for electrical engineering and machinery. Although the country has to import much of its raw materials, these become high-value exports such as clocks, watches, and other precision engineering products. It is also in this region that the famous cheeses and chocolates are produced. Hydroelectricity accounts for approximately 60 per cent of the country's power supplies, with most of the remainder coming from nuclear power plants. Switzerland has huge earnings from international finance and tourism.

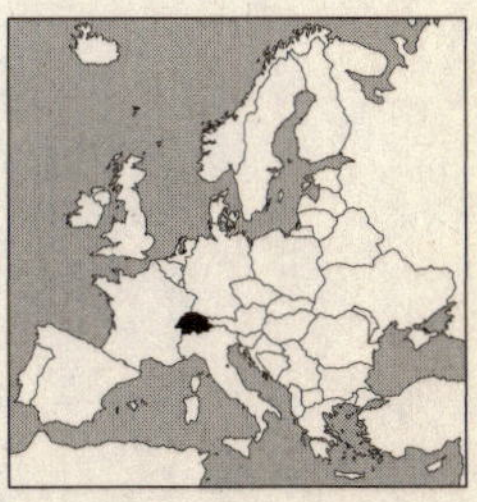

Area: 15,940 sq miles/41,284 sq km
Population: 7,076,000
Capital: Bern
Other major cities: Zürich, Basle, Geneva, Lausanne
Form of government: Federal Republic
Religions: RC, Protestantism
Currency: Swiss Franc

Syrdar'ya a river of central Asia, flowing through Kazakhstan to the Aral Sea. (Length 1,780 miles/2,860 km)

Syria a country in southwest Asia that borders on the Mediterranean Sea in the west. Much of the country is mountainous behind the narrow fertile coastal plain. The eastern region is desert or semi-desert, a stony, inhospitable land. The coast has a Mediterranean climate, with hot, dry summers and mild, wet winters. About 50 per cent of the workforce get their living from agriculture. Sheep, goats, and cattle are raised, and cotton, barley, wheat, tobacco, grapes, olives, and vegetables are grown. Some land is unused because of lack of irrigation. Reserves of oil are small compared to neighbouring Iraq, but there is enough to make the country self-sufficient and provide three-quarters of the nation's export earnings. Industries, such as textiles, leather, chemicals, and cement, have developed rapidly in the last 20 years, with the country's craftsmen producing fine rugs and silk brocades. Foreign revenue is gained from tourism and also from countries who pipe oil through Syria. The country is dependent on the main Arab oil-producing countries for aid.

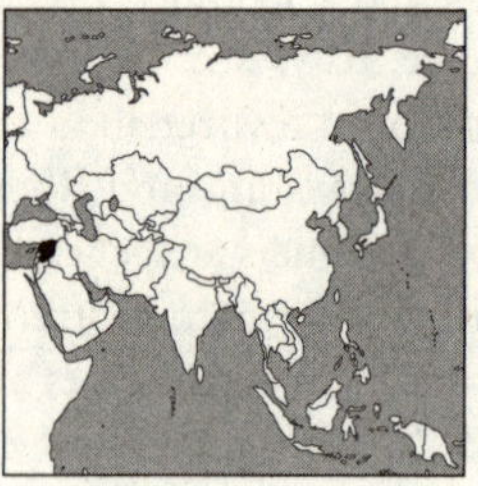

Area: 71,498 sq miles/185,180 sq km
Population: 14,619,000
Capital: Damascus (Dimashq)
Other cities: Aleppo (Halab), Latakia (Al Lãdhiqiyah)
Form of government: Republic
Religion: Sunni Islam
Currency: Syrian Pound

T

Table Mountain a flat-topped mountain overlooking Cape Town in southwest South Africa. (3,567 ft/1,087 m)

Tagus (Tajo, Tejo) a major river of southwest Europe, which rises in eastern Spain and flows west and southwest through Portugal to the Atlantic Ocean west of Lisbon. (Length 626 miles/1,007 km)

Tahiti the largest of the islands of French Polynesia in the South Pacific. The capital is Papeete. (388 sq miles/1,005 sq km; pop. 96,000)

T'aichung a major commercial and agricultural centre in western Taiwan. (Pop. 1,034,000)

Taiwan an island that straddles the Tropic of Cancer in East Asia. It lies about 100 miles (161 kilometres) off the southeast coast of mainland China. It is predominantly mountainous in the interior, with more than 60 peaks attaining heights of 10,000 feet (3,040 metres). The highest of all is the Jade Mountain (Yu Shan), which stands at 12,960 feet (3,940 metres). Taiwan's independence, resulting from the island's seizure by nationalists in 1949, is not fully accepted internationally and China lays claim to the territory. The climate is warm and humid for most of the year and winters are mild with summers rainy. The soils are fertile, and a wide range of crops, including tea, rice, sugar cane, and bananas, is grown. Natural resources include gas, marble, limestone, and small coal deposits. Taiwan is a major international trading nation with some of the most successful export-processing zones in the world, accommodating domestic and overseas companies. Exports include machinery, electronics, textiles, footwear, toys, and sporting goods.

Area: 13,800 sq miles/35,742 sq km
Population: 21,854,000
Capital: Taipei
Other major cities: Kaohsiung, Taichung, Tainan
Form of government: Republic
Religions: Taoism, Buddhism, Christianity
Currency: New Taiwan Dollar

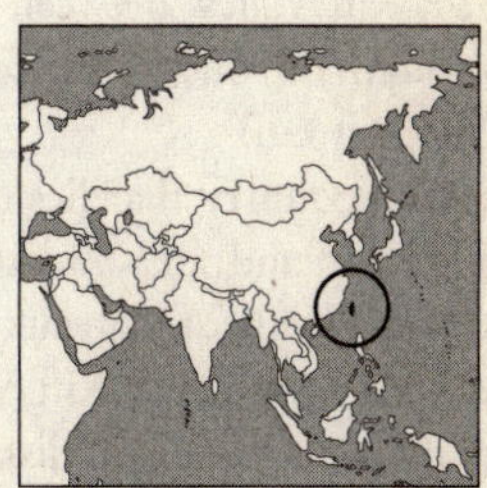

Taiwan Strait the stretch of water between Taiwan and China.

Tajikistan a republic of the southern central former USSR that declared itself independent in 1991. It borders on Afghanistan and China. The south is occupied by the Pamir mountain range, whose snow-capped peaks dominate the country. More than half the country lies over 9,840 feet (3,000 metres). Most of the country is desert or semi-desert, and the pastoral farming of cattle, sheep, horses, and goats is important. Some yaks are kept in the higher regions. The lowland areas in the Fergana and Amudar'ya valleys are irrigated so that cotton, mulberry trees, fruit, wheat, and vegetables can be grown. The Amudar'ya River is also used to produce hydroelectric power for industries such as cotton and silk processing. The republic is rich in deposits of coal, lead, zinc, oil, and uranium, which are being exploited. There has been an ongoing civil war in which tens of thousands of people have been killed or made homeless.

Area: 55,250 sq miles/143,100 sq km
Population: 5,919,000
Capital: Dushanbe
Form of government: Republic
Religion: Shia Islam
Currency: Tajik Ruble

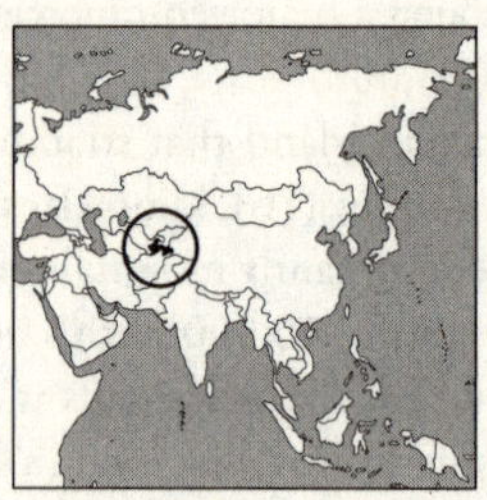

Taklimakan Desert the largest desert in China, consisting mainly of sand, in the west of the country.

Tamil Nadu a state in southeast India. The state capital is Madras. (50,839 sq miles/130,357 sq km; pop. 63,324,000)

Tana (Tsana), Lake a lake in the mountains of northwest Ethiopia, and the source of the Blue Nile. (1,418 sq miles/3,673 sq km)

Tanganyika, Lake the second largest lake in Africa after Lake Victoria, in the Great Rift Valley, between Tanzania and the Democratic Republic of Congo, although Burundi and Zambia also share the shoreline. (12,700 sq miles/32,893 sq km)

Tanzania a country that lies on the east coast of central Africa and comprises a large mainland area and the islands of Pemba and Zanzibar. The mainland consists mostly of plateaux broken by mountainous areas and the East African section of the Great Rift Valley. The climate is very varied and is controlled largely by altitude and distance from the sea. The coast is hot and humid, the central plateau drier, and the mountains semi-temperate. Eighty per cent of

Tanzanians make a living from the land, producing corn, cassava, millet, rice, plantains, and sorghum for home consumption. Cash crops include cotton, tobacco, tea, sisal, cashews, and coffee. The two islands produce the bulk of the world's cloves. Diamond mining is an important industry, and there are also sizable deposits of iron ore, coal, and tin. Fishing is also important with the bulk of the catch caught in inland waters. Although Tanzania is one of the poorest countries in the world, it has a wealth of natural wonders, such as the its wildlife, the Serengeti Plain, the Ngorongoro Crater, Mount Kilimanjaro, and the Olduvai Gorge, all of which attract large numbers of tourists, making a significant contribution to the country's economy.

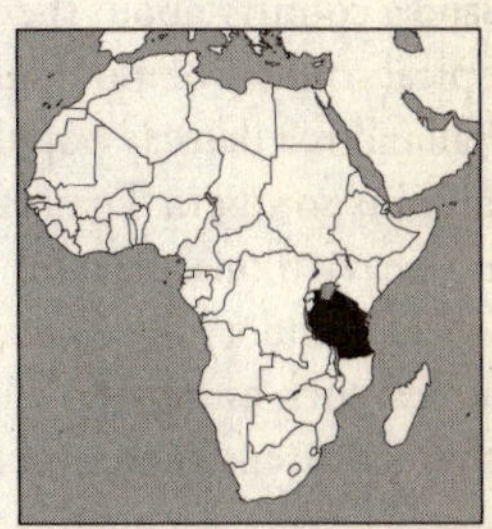

Area: 362,162 sq miles/938,000 sq km
Population: 32,102,000
Capital: Dodoma
Other towns: Dar es Salaam, Zanzibar, Mwanza, Tanga
Form of government: Republic
Religions: Sunni Islam, RC, Anglicanism, Hinduism
Currency: Tanzanian Shilling

Taranto, Gulf of (Taranto, Golfo di) an inlet of the Mediterranean Sea between the 'toe' and the 'heel' of Italy.

Tarawa the main atoll and capital of Kiribati in the west Pacific. (Pop. 29,000)

Tarsus an agricultural centre in southeast Turkey, the birthplace of St Paul. (Pop. 212,000)

Tashkent the capital of Uzbekistan, in the northeast. (Pop. 2,150,000)

Tasmania an island state to the south of Australia, separated from the mainland by the Bass Strait. The capital is Hobart. (26,383 sq miles/68,332 sq km; pop. 503,000)

Tasman Sea a branch of the Pacific Ocean that separates Australia and New Zealand.

Tatar Republic (Tatarstan) an autonomous republic of the Russian Federation, southwest of Moscow, around the River Volga. The capital is Kazan'. (26,250 sq miles/68,000 sq km; pop. 3,715,000)

Tatra Mountains a range of mountains that lines the border between Poland and Slovakia The highest peak is Gerlachovka (8,737 ft/2,663 m).

Tayside a former administrative region in east Scotland.

Tenerife the largest of the Canary Islands. The capital is Santa Cruz. (795 sq miles/2,058 sq km; pop. 558,000)

Tennessee a state in southern central USA. The state capital is Nashville. (42,244 sq miles/109,412 sq km; pop. 5,791,000)

Tennessee a river which flows southwest from the Appalachian Mountains of North Carolina and then through Alabama, Tennessee and Kentucky to join the Ohio River. (Length 652 miles/1,049 km)

Texas a state in the southwest of the USA, bordering Mexico. It is the nation's second largest state. The capital is Austin. (262,134 sq miles/678,927 sq km; pop. 21,806,000)

Thailand a country about the same size as France, located in southeast Asia. It is a tropical country of mountains and jungles, rainforests and green plains. Central Thailand is a densely populated, fertile plain and the mountainous Isthmus of Kra joins southern Thailand to Malaysia. Thailand has a subtropical climate, with heavy monsoon rains from June to October, a cool season from October to March and a hot season from March to June. It is rich in many natural resources, such as mineral deposits of gold, coal, lead, and precious stones, with rich soils, extensive areas of tropical forests, and natural gas offshore. The central plain of Thailand contains vast expanses of paddy fields that grow enough rice to rank Thailand as one of the world's leading producers. The narrow southern peninsula is very wet, and it is here that rubber is produced. Other crops grown are cassava, maize, pineapples, and sugar cane. Fishing is an increasingly important industry, with prawns being sold for export. Tourism also contributes to the country's economy.

Area: 198,115 sq miles/513,115 sq km
Population: 60,206,000
Capital: Bangkok (Krung Thep)
Other cities: Chiang-Mai, Khon Kaen, Nakhon Sawan
Form of government: Constitutional Monarchy
Religions: Buddhism, Sunni Islam
Currency: Baht

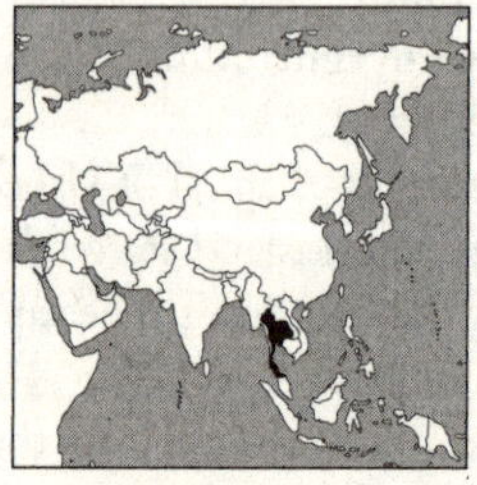

Thailand, Gulf of a branch of the South China Sea lying between the Malay Peninsula and the coasts of Thailand, Cambodia and Vietnam.

Thames a major river of southern England flowing eastwards from its source in the Cotswold Hills, past London to its estuary on the North Sea. (Length 210 miles/338 km)

Thar Desert (Indian Desert) a desert in northwest India, covering the border between the Indian state of Rajasthan and Pakistan.

Thousand Islands a group of over 1,000 islands scattered in the upper St Lawrence River, between the USA and Canada.

Tiber (Tevere) a river of central Italy, rising to the east of Florence and flowing south to Rome and into the Mediterranean. (Length 252 miles/405 km)

Tibet (Xizang Autonomous Region) a region of southwest China, consisting of a huge high plateau high beyond the Himalayas. Formerly a Buddhist kingdom led by its spiritual leader, the Dalai Lama, it was invaded by China in 1950 and has been gradually desecrated. (471,660 sq miles/1,221,600 sq km; pop. 2,729,000)

Tierra del Fuego the archipelago at the southern tip of South America, belonging to Argentina and Chile and separated from the mainland by the Strait of Magellan.

Tigray a province of northern Ethiopia, bordering Eritrea, whose people fought a separatist war against the central government from 1975 to 1991. The capital is Mekele. (Pop. 3,970,000)

Tigris a major river of the Middle East, rising in eastern Turkey, flowing through Syria and Iraq and joining the Euphrates to form a delta at the Shatt al Arab waterway as it enters the Persian Gulf. (Length 1,180 miles/1,900 km)

Timor an island at the eastern end of the Lesser Sunda Islands, divided into two parts: Indonesian West Timor and independent East Timor. (11,883 sq miles/ 30,775 sq km; pop. 3,085,000)

Timor Sea the arm of the Indian Ocean between the northwest coast of Australia and the island of Timor.

Tipperary a county in the south of the Republic of Ireland. It includes the town of Tipperary, but Clonmel is the county town. (1,643 sq miles/4,255 sq km; pop. 139,000)

Titicaca, Lake the largest lake in South America, in the Andes, on the border between Bolivia and Peru. (3,141 sq miles/8,135 sq km)

Tobago an island to the northeast of Trinidad, forming part of the republic of Trinidad and Tobago. (Pop. 56,000)

Togo Togo is a tiny West African country with a narrow coastal plain on the Gulf of Guinea and the heavily forested Togo Highlands inland. Over 80 per cent of the population are involved in agriculture, with yams and millet as the principal crops. Coffee, cocoa and cotton are grown for cash. Minerals, especially phosphates, are the main export.

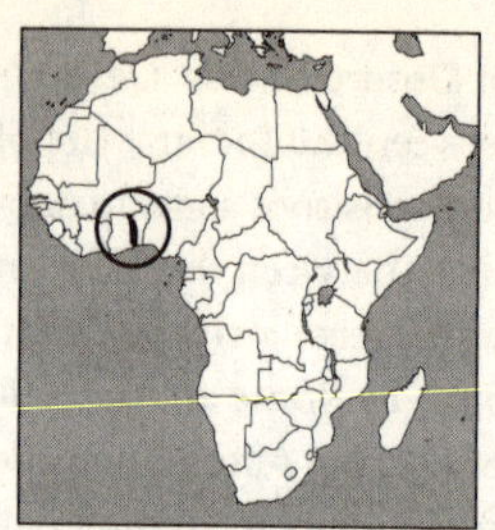

Area: 21,925 sq miles/56,785 sq km
Population: 4,201,000
Capital: Lomé
Form of government: Republic
Religions: traditional African religions, RC, Sunni Islam
Currency: CFA Franc

Tonga a country situated about 20 degrees south of the Equator and just west of the International Date Line in the Pacific Ocean. It comprises over 170 islands, only about 40 of which are inhabited, with a low limestone chain of islands in the east and a higher volcanic chain in the west. The climate is warm with heavy rainfall, and destructive cyclones are likely to occur every few years. The government owns all the land, and males can rent an allotment for growing food. Yams, cassava, and taro are grown as subsistence crops, and the islanders' diet is supplemented by fish from the sea. Pumpkins, bananas, vanilla, and coconuts are exported. The main industry is coconut processing. About 70 per cent of the workforce is occupied in either fishing or agriculture while many Tongans are employed overseas. Tourism, foreign aid, and money sent home by its workers overseas, all contribute to the country's economy.

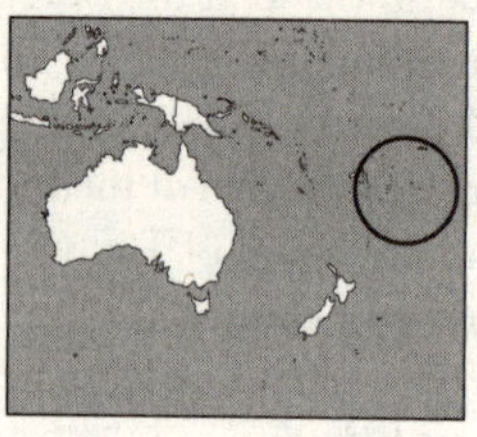

Area: 288 sq miles/747 sq km
Population: 99,000
Capital: Nuku'alofa
Form of government: Constitutional Monarchy
Religions: Methodism, RC
Currency: Pa'anga

Tonlé Sap a lake in central Cambodia which swells and quadruples in size when the Mekong River floods. (In flood 4,000 sq miles/10,400 sq km)

Torfaen a council area in southeast Wales, with its administrative centre in the town of Pontypool. (112 sq miles/290 sq km; pop. 90,000)

Torres Strait the stretch of water between the northeastern tip of Australia and New Guinea.

Tørshavn the capital of the Faeroe Islands. (Pop. 17,000)

Touraine a former province of northwest France, around Tours.

Trafalgar, Cape the southwestern tip of Spain.

Transkei one of ten former South African Homelands, the area is now part of the Eastern Cape Province, in southeast South Africa.

Transvaal a former province of north and central South Africa.

Transylvania a region of central and northwestern Romania.

Trent the main river of the Midlands of England, flowing northeast from Staffordshire to the Humber. (Length 170 miles/270 km)

Trinidad and Tobago the islands of Trinidad and Tobago constitute the third largest British Commonwealth country in the West Indies. They are situated off the Orinoco Delta in northeastern Venezuela. They are the most southerly of the Lesser Antilles Islands. Trinidad consists of the mountainous Northern Range in the north and undulating plains in the south. It has a huge, asphalt-producing lake, Pitch Lake, which is approximately 104 acres (42 hectares) in size. Tobago is actually a mountain that is about 1,800 feet (550 metres) above sea level at its peak. The climate is tropical with little variation in temperatures throughout the year and a rainy season from June to December. Trinidad is one of the oldest oil-producing countries in the world. Output is small but provides 90 per cent of the country's exports. Sugar cane, cocoa, citrus fruits, vegetables, and rubber trees are grown for export, while imported food now account for 10 per cent of total imports. Tobago depends mainly on tourism for revenue. A slump in the economy in the 1980s and early 1990s saw widespread unemployment but economic growth has improved in recent times.

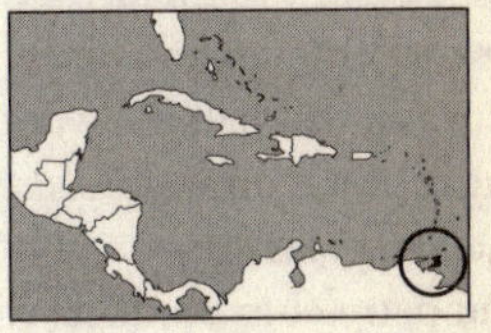

Area: 1,981 sq miles/5,130 sq km
Population: 1,297,000
Capital: Port of Spain
Form of government: Republic
Religions: RC, Hinduism, Anglicanism, Sunni Islam
Currency: Trinidad and Tobago Dollar

Tristan da Cunha a group of four remote, volcanic islands in the middle of the South Atlantic Ocean, which form part of the St Helena Dependencies. (40 sq miles/ 100 sq km; pop. 300)

Tunisia a North African country that lies on the south coast of the Mediterranean Sea. It is bounded by Algeria to the west and Libya to the south. Northern Tunisia consists of hills, plains, and valleys. Inland mountains separate the coastal zone from the central plains before the land drops down to an area of salt pans and the Sahara. The climate ranges from warm temperate in the north to desert in the south. Agriculture produces wheat, barley, olives, grapes, tomatoes, dates, vegetables, and citrus fruits, and the fishing industry is of growing importance, producing mainly pilchards, sardines, and tuna. Twenty-six per cent of the workforce is engaged in these two occupations, but overall there is a general lack of employment. The mainstays of Tunisia's modern economy are oil from the Sahara, phosphates, natural gas, and tourism on the Mediterranean coast.

Area: 62,592 sq miles/162,155 sq km
Population: 9,092,000
Capital: Tunis
Other cities: Sfax, Bizerte, Djerba
Form of government: Republic
Religion: Sunni Islam
Currency: Tunisian Dinar

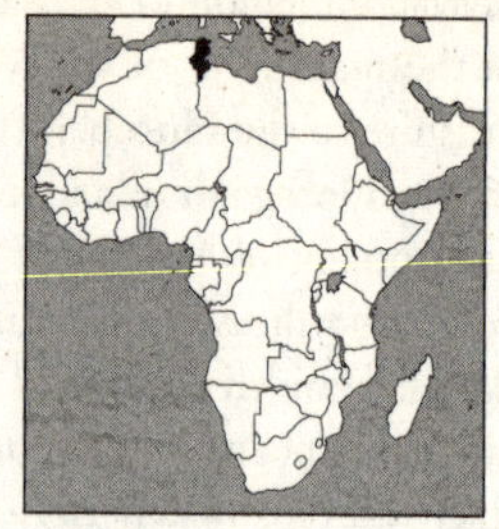

Turkey with land on the continents of Europe and Asia, Turkey forms a bridge between the two, and guards the sea passage between the Mediterranean and the Black Sea. It occupies an area in which seismic activity is a frequent occurrence and the country regularly experiences devastating earthquakes. Only 5 per cent of its area (Thrace) is in Europe and the much larger area (Anatolia) is in Asia. European Turkey is fertile agricultural land with a Mediterranean climate. Asiatic Turkey is bordered to the north by the Pontine Mountains and to the south by the Taurus Mountains. The climate ranges from Mediterranean on the coasts to hot summers and bitterly cold winters in the central plains. Agriculture employs almost half the workforce, and the major crops being grown are wheat, sugar beet, cotton, tobacco, barley, fruits, maize, and oil seeds. The country's main exports are iron and steel, textiles, dried fruits, tobacco, leather clothes, and petroleum products. The manufacturing industry includes iron and steel, textiles, motor vehicles, and Turkey's famous carpets. The main mineral resources are iron ore, coal, chromium, magnetite, zinc, and lead. Hydroelectric power is supplied by the Tigris and Euphrates Rivers. Tourism is a fast-developing industry and plays an increasingly important role in the economy.

Area: 299,158 sq miles/774,815 sq km
Population: 62,697,000
Capital: Ankara
Other cities: Istanbul, Izmir, Adana, Bursa
Form of government: Republic
Religion: Sunni Islam
Currency: Turkish Lira

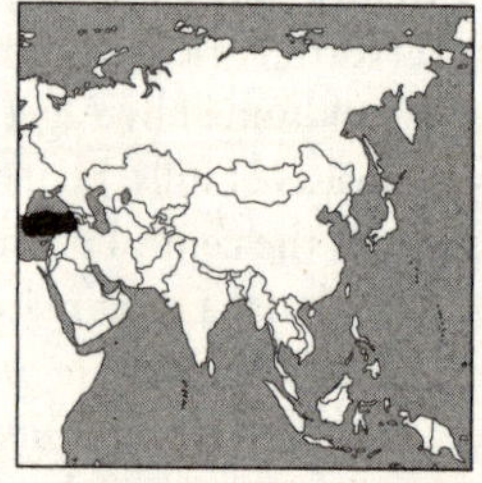

Turkmenistan a central Asian country of the former USSR that declared itself a republic in 1991. It lies to the east of the Caspian Sea and borders Iran and

Afghanistan to the south. Much of the west and central areas of Turkmenistan are covered by the sandy Karakum Desert. The east is a plateau that is bordered by the Amudar'ya River. The Amudar'ya has been diverted to form the important Kara Kum Canal which is one of the longest canals in the world and provides irrigation and drinking water for the southeastern parts of the country. The climate is extremely dry, and most of the population live in oasis settlements near the rivers and by the extensive network of canals. Agriculture is intensive around the settlements. Karakul sheep are reared and cotton, cereals, silk and fruit are produced. This occupies around 45 per cent of the workforce. There are rich mineral deposits, particularly natural gas, petroleum, sulphur, coal, salt, and copper, and manufacturing industries include textile manufacturing, food processing, and carpet weaving. Unlike what has happened in most of the other former Soviet republics, there has not been a wholesale emigration of ethnic minorities.

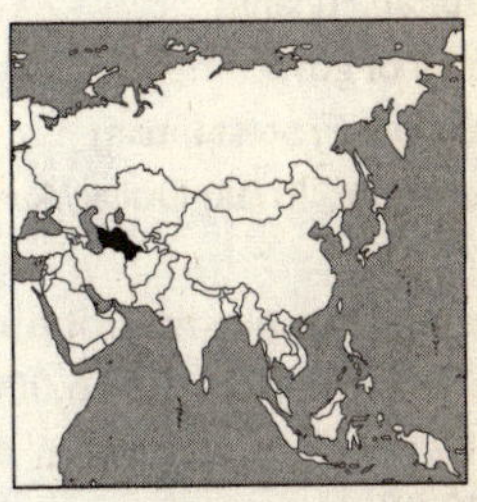

Area: 188,456 sq miles/488,100 sq km
Population: 4,569,000
Capital: Ashkhabad (Ashgabat)
Form of government: Republic
Religion: Sunni Islam
Currency: Manat

Turks and Caicos Islands two island groups which form the southeastern archipelago of the Bahamas in the Atlantic Ocean. Only six of the islands are inhabited. The climate is subtropical cooled by southeast trade winds which blow all the year round. A British Crown Colony, the country's economy relies mainly on tourism and the export of shellfish to the UK and the USA.

Area: 166 sq miles/430 sq km
Population: 23,000
Capital: Grand Turk
Form of government: British Crown Colony
Religion: Christianity
Currency: US Dollar

Tuscany (Toscana) a region of central western Italy, whose capital is Florence. (Pop. 3,505,000)

Tuvalu a country located just north of Fiji, in the South Pacific, consisting of nine coral atolls. The group was formerly known as the Ellice Islands, and the main island and capital is Funafuti. Tuvalu became independent in 1978. The climate is tropical, with an annual average rainfall of 120 inches (3,050 millimetres). Coconut palms are the main crop, and fruit and vegetables are grown for local consumption. Sea fishing is extremely good and largely unexploited, although licenses have been granted to Japan, Taiwan, and the Republic of Korea to fish the local waters. Revenue comes from copra, the country's only export product, foreign aid, the sale of elaborate postage stamps to philatelists, and income sent home from Tuvaluans who work abroad. There is an airport situated on Funafuti Atoll. Rising sea levels, possibly caused by global warming, are threatening to submerge Tuvalu, and preparations are being made for its evacuation.

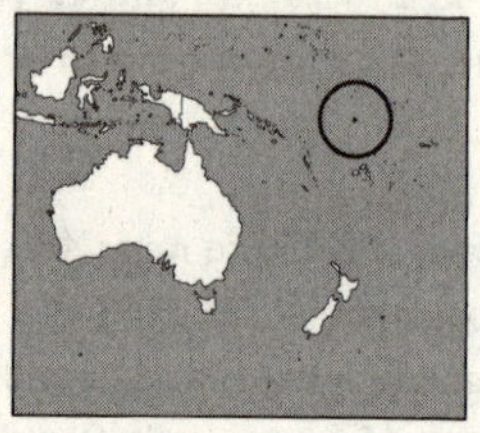

Area: 10 sq miles/24 sq km
Population: 10,000
Capital: Funafuti
Form of government: Constitutional Monarchy
Religion: Protestantism
Currency: Tuvalu Dollar/Australian Dollar

Tyne and Wear a metropolitan county in northeast England. (208 sq miles/ 540 sq km; pop. 1,116,000)

Tyrol a province of western Austria, in the Alps. The capital is Innsbruck. (Pop. 679,000)

Tyrone a historical county in the west of Northern Ireland, taking up a quarter of the total area of Northern Ireland.

Tyrrhenian Sea a part of the Mediterranean Sea between Sicily, Sardinia, and mainland Italy.

U

Uganda a landlocked country in east central Africa. The Equator runs through the south of the country, and for the most part it is a richly fertile land, well watered, with a kindly climate. In the west are the Ruwenzori Mountains, which reach heights of 16,762 feet (5,109 metres) and are snow-capped. The lowlands around Lake Victoria, once forested, have now for the most part been cleared for cultivation. Agriculture employs over 80 per cent of the labour force, and the main crops grown for subsistence are plantains, cassava, and sweet potatoes. Coffee is the main cash crop and accounts for over 90 per cent of the country's exports. Cotton and tea are also important to the economy, as is mahogany from the country's forests. Virtually all the country's power is produced by hydroelectricity, with the plant on the Victoria Nile being of major importance. Since the 1980s and following years of civil turmoil and unrest, Uganda has slowly been rebuilding its shattered economy and, in spite of some resurgence of earlier violence, attempts are being made to expand the tea plantations in the west, to develop a copper mine, and to introduce new industries to Kampala, the capital.

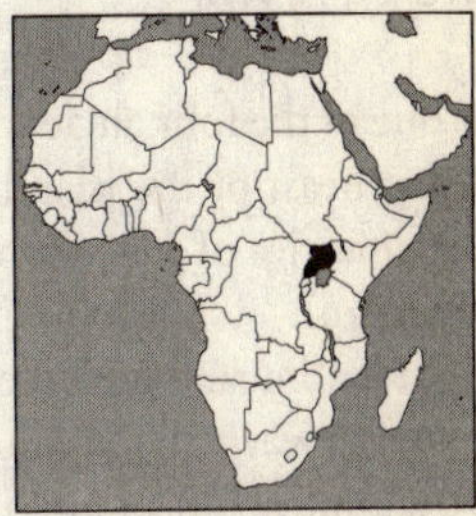

Area: 93,065 sq miles/241,038 sq km
Population: 19,848,000
Capital: Kampala
Other cities: Entebbe, Jinja, Masaka, Mbale
Form of government: Republic
Religions: RC, Protestantism, traditional African religions, Sunni Islam
Currency: Uganda Shilling

UK *see* **United Kingdom.**

Ukraine a former Soviet socialist republic that declared itself independent of the former USSR in 1991. Its neighbours to the west are Poland, Slovakia, Hungary, and Romania, and it is bounded to the south by the Black Sea. To the east lies the Russian Federation and to the north Belarus. Drained by the Dnieper, Dniester, Southern Bug, and Donets Rivers, Ukraine consists largely of fertile steppes. The climate is continental, although this is greatly modified by the proximity of the Black Sea. The Ukrainian steppe is one of the chief wheat-producing regions of Europe. Other major crops include corn, sugar beet, flax, tobacco, soya, hops, and potatoes, with agriculture accounting for around one quarter of all employment in Ukraine. There are rich reserves of coal and raw materials for industry, but the country is still reliant on the other former Soviet republics for supplies of natural gas and oil. The central and eastern regions form one of the world's densest industrial concentrations. Manufacturing industries include ferrous metallurgy, heavy machinery, chemicals, food processing, gas and oil refining. In 1986, a catastrophic accident at the country's Chernobyl nuclear power station occurred, which had far-reaching effects and caused widespread contamination. In 1996, a number of countries agreed to provide financial assistance to help the Ukraine to finally close the station.

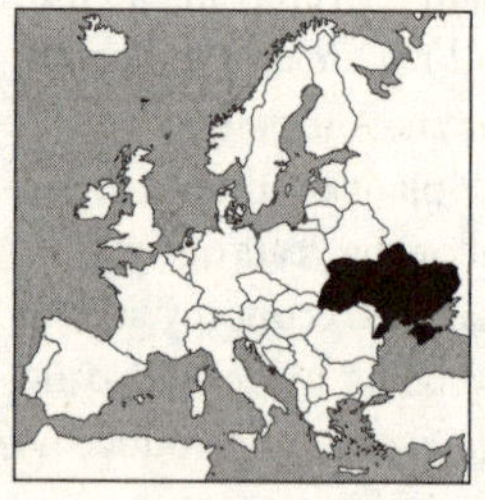

Area: 233,090 sq miles/603,700 sq km
Population: 51,094,000
Capital: Kiev (Kiyev)
Other cities: Dnepropetrovsk, Donetsk, Khar'kov, Odessa
Form of government: Republic
Religions: Russian Orthodox, RC
Currency: Hryvna

Ulster one of the four ancient provinces into which Ireland was divided, covering the northeast of the island. It is often used to refer to Northern Ireland, but three counties of Ulster are in the Republic of Ireland (Donegal, Monaghan and Cavan).

Umbria a landlocked region of central eastern Italy. (Pop. 845,000)

Umm al Qaywayn the second smallest emirate in the United Arab Emirates. (290 sq miles/750 sq km; pop. emirate 46,000/town 33,000)

United Arab Emirates (UAE) a federation of seven oil-rich sheikdoms located in the Persian Gulf, namely Abu Dhabi, Dubai, Sharjah, Ajman, Umm al Qaiwain, Ras el Khaimah, and Fujairah. As well as its main coast on the Gulf, the country has a short coast on the Gulf of Oman. The land is mainly flat sandy desert except to the north where the Hajar Mountains rise to 6,828 feet (2,081 metres). The summers are hot and humid with temperatures reaching 120°F (49°C), but from October to May the weather is warm and sunny with pleasant, cool evenings. The only fertile areas are the emirate of Ras al Khaimah, the coastal plain of Al Fujairah and the oases. Abu Dhabi and Dubai are the main industrial centres and, using their wealth from the oil industry, they are now diversifying by building aluminium smelters, cement factories, and steel-rolling mills. Prior to development of the oil industry, traditional occupations were pearl diving, growing dates, fishing, and camel breeding. Dubai is the richest state in the world.

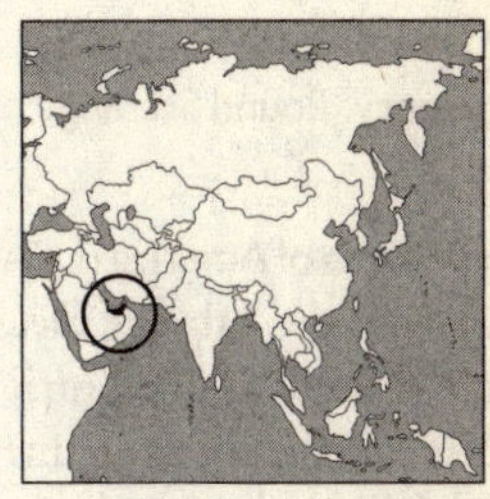

Area: 32,278 sq miles/83,600 sq km
Population: 2,260,000
Capital: Abu Dhabi (Abu Zabi)
Other major cities: Dubai, Sharjh, Ras al Khaymah
Form of government: Monarchy (Emirates)
Religion: Sunni Islam
Currency: Dirham

United Kingdom of Great Britain and Northern Ireland (UK) a country situated in northwest Europe, comprising the island of Great Britain and the six counties of Northern Ireland, plus many smaller islands, especially off the west coast of Scotland. The south and east of Britain is low-lying, and the Pennines form a backbone running through northern England. Scotland has the largest area of upland, and Wales is a highland block. The climate is cool temperate with mild conditions and an even annual rainfall. The UK is primarily a highly urbanized industrial and commercial country. Only 2 per cent of the workforce are employed in agriculture and, although production is high thanks to modern machinery and scientific methods, the UK still has to import one third of its food. Major crops include barley, potatoes, sugar beet, and wheat, while livestock includes sheep, cattle, pigs, and poultry. Fishing is also an important industry. The UK has to import most of the materials it needs for its industries as it lacks natural resources apart from coal, iron ore, oil, and natural gas. Many of the older industries, such as the coal, textiles and heavy engineering industries, have declined significantly in recent years while service industries play an increasingly large part in the UK's economy, as does tourism.

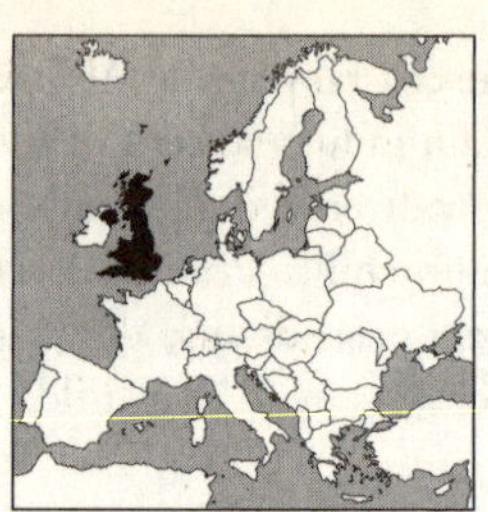

Area: 94,248 sq miles/244,101 sq km
Population: 58,784,000
Capital: London
Other major cities: Birmingham, Manchester, Glasgow, Liverpool, Belfast
Form of government: Constitutional Monarchy
Religion: Anglicanism, RC, Presbyterianism, Methodism
Currency: Pound Sterling

United States of America (USA) a country that stretches across central North America, from the Atlantic Ocean in the east to the Pacific Ocean in the west, and from Canada in the north to Mexico and the Gulf of Mexico in the south. It is the fourth largest country in the world and consists of fifty states, including outlying Alaska, northwest of Canada, and Hawaii in the Pacific Ocean. The climate varies a great deal in such a large country. In Alaska, there are polar conditions, while in the Gulf coast and in Florida conditions may be subtropical. The highest point is Mount McKinley at 20,322 feet (6,194 metres). Natural resources include vast mineral reserves, including oil and gas, coal, copper, lead, uranium gold, tungsten, and lumber. Although agricultural production is high, it employs only 1.5 per cent of the population primarily because of its advanced technology. The USA is a world leader in oil production. Its main industries are iron and steel, chemicals, motor vehicles, aircraft, telecommunications equipment, computers, electronics, and textiles. The USA is the richest and most powerful nation in the world.

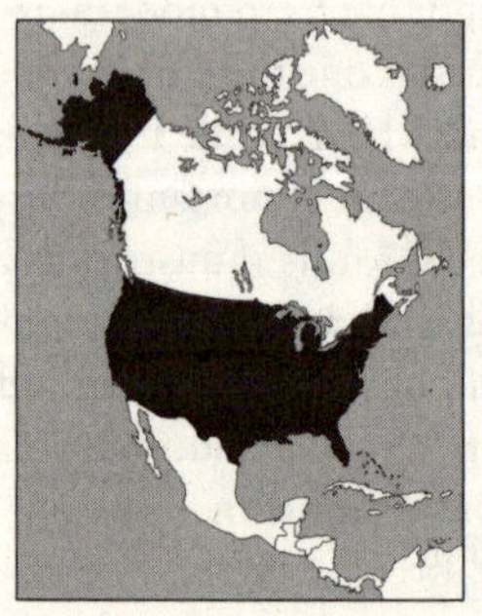

Area: 3,536,278 sq miles/9,158,960 sq km
Population: 249,630,000
Capital: Washington D.C.
Other major cities: New York, Chicago, Detroit, Houston, Los Angeles, Philadelphia, San Diego, San Francisco
Form of government: Federal Republic
Religion: Protestantism, RC, Judaism, Eastern Orthodox
Currency: US Dollar

Ural Mountains (Urals, Uralskiy Khrebet) a mountain range in western Russian Federation. Running north to south from the Arctic to the Aral Sea, the Urals form a dividing line between Europe and Asia. The highest point is Mount Narodnaya (6,214 ft/1,894 m).

Uruguay one of the smallest countries in South America. It lies on the east coast of the continent, to the south of Brazil, and is bordered by the Uruguay River to the west, Río de la Plata to the south, and the Atlantic Ocean to the east. The country consists of low plains and plateaux. The Negro River, which rises in Brazil, crosses the country from northeast to southwest, dividing Uruguay almost into two halves. The climate is temperate and rainfall plentiful, and the natural vegetation is prairie grassland. Some of the river valleys are wooded but Uruguay lacks dense forests. About 90 per cent of the land is suitable for agriculture but only about 8 per cent is cultivated, the remainder being used to graze the vast herds of cattle and sheep that provide over 35 per cent of Uruguay's exports in the form of wool, hides, and meat. The cultivated land is made up of vineyards, rice fields, and groves of olives and citrus fruits. The main crops grown are sugar beet and sugar cane, rice, wheat, potatoes, corn, and sorghum. The country has scarce mineral resources, and hydroelectric power supplies most of its energy needs. Important industries include textile manufacture, food processing, oil refining, steel, aluminium, electrical goods, and rubber.

Area: 68,500 sq miles/177,414 sq km
Population: 3,203,000
Capital: Montevideo
Form of government: Republic
Religions: RC, Protestantism
Currency: Peso Uruguayo

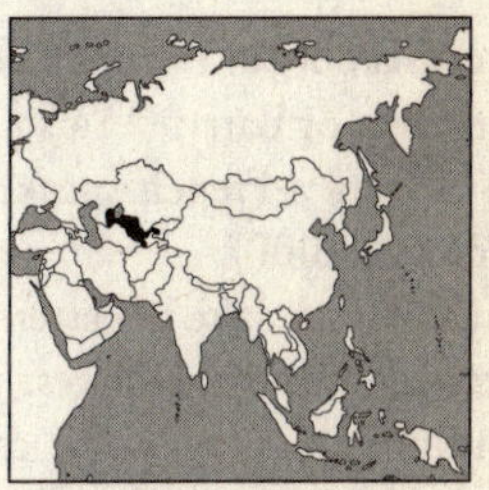

US/USA *see* **United States of America.**

Utah a state in the west of the USA. The state capital is Salt Lake City. (82,096 sq miles/212,628 sq km; pop. 2,307,000)

Uttar Pradesh the most populous state of India, in the north of the country. The capital is Lucknow. (113,654 sq miles/294,364 sq km; pop. 169,296,000)

Uzbekistan a central Asian republic of the former USSR that declared itself independent in 1991. It lies between Kazakhstan and Turkmenistan and encompasses the southern half of the Aral Sea. The republic has many contrasting regions. The Tian Shan region is mountainous, the Fergana region is irrigated and fertile, the Kyzlkum Desert (one of the world's largest) is rich in oil and gas, the lower Amudar'ya River region is irrigated and has oasis settlements, and the Usturt Plateau is a stony desert. Uzbekistan is one of the world's leading cotton producers, and Karakul lambs are reared for wool and meat. Its main industrial products are agricultural machinery, textiles, and chemicals. It also has significant reserves of natural gas. Economic growth has been checked by concerns about political instability and much of the economy remains based on the centralized state-owned model. There are serious pollution problems around the Aral Sea, which has greatly decreased in size from its use for irrigation and is contaminated with toxins, salts, and sands that poison the water supply of the surrounding population. Hydroelectric schemes supply much of the republic's electricity needs.

Area: 172,742 sq miles/447,400 sq km
Population: 24,000,000
Capital: Tashkent
Other cities: Samarkand, Urgench, Nukus, Bukhara
Form of government: Republic
Religion: Sunni Islam
Currency: Uzbekistan Sum

Vale of Glamorgan a council area in south Wales, with its administrative centre in the town of Barry. (114 sq miles/295 sq km; pop. 119,000)

Valle d'Aosta a French-speaking region of northwest Italy. The capital is Aosta. (Pop. 123,000)

Van, Lake a salt lake in eastern Turkey. (1,419 sq miles/3,675 sq km)

Vancouver Island the largest island off the Pacific coast of North America, in southwest Canada. The capital is Victoria. (12,408 sq miles/32,137 sq km; pop. 390,000)

Vanuatu a country, formerly known as the New Hebrides (so named by Captain Cook in 1774), located in the southwest Pacific Ocean, southeast of the Solomon Islands and about 1,087 miles (1,750 kilometres) east of Australia. It consists of some 12 islands and some 60 islets. Most of the islands are volcanic and densely forested, with raised coral beaches and fringed by coral reefs. The largest islands are Espíritu Santo, Malekula, and Efate, on which the capital, Vila, is sited. Vanuatu has a tropical climate that is moderated by the southeast trade winds from May to October. Cultivated land is generally restricted to the coastal plains and the main cash crops are copra, cocoa beans, and coffee. Meat and fish are also exported and light industries include food processing and handicrafts for an increasing tourist industry. The majority of the labour force are engaged in subsistence farming, growing taro, yams, and bananas. Tourism is an increasingly important industry. Vanuatu has international airports.

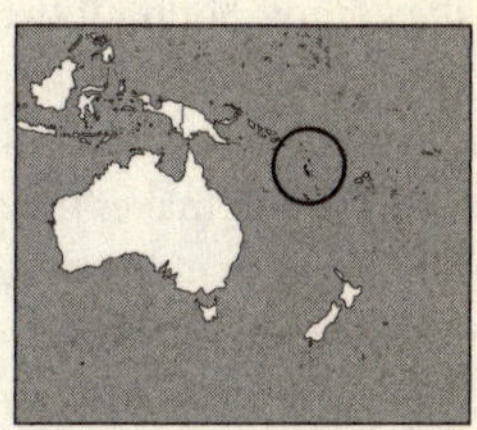

Area: 4,706 sq miles/12,189 sq km
Population: 169,000
Capital: Vila (Port-Vila)
Form of government: Republic
Religion: Protestantism, RC, traditional African religions
Currency: Vatu

Vatican City State a state, established in 1929, that lies in the heart of Rome on a low hill on the west bank of the River Tiber. It is the world's smallest independent state and headquarters of the Roman Catholic Church. It is a walled city with six gates, and is made up of the Vatican Palace, the Papal Gardens, St Peter's Square, and St Peter's Basilica. The state has its own police, newspaper, telephone and telegraph services, stamps, radio station, and train station. The radio station, Radio Vaticana, broadcasts a service in 34 languages from transmitters within the Vatican City. Its main tourist attractions are the frescoes of the Sistine Chapel, painted by Michelangelo Buonarroti. It also has outstanding museums, with collections of antiquities and works by Italian masters, and the Vatican Library's collection of ancient manuscripts is priceless. The Pope exercises sovereignty and has absolute legislative, executive, and judicial powers.

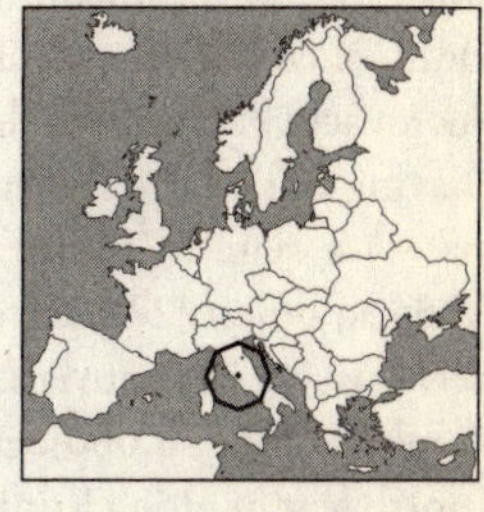

Area: 0.2 sq mile/0.44 sq km
Population: 1,000
Capital: Vatican City
Form of government: Papal Commission
Religion: RC
Currency: Euro

Venda one of ten former South African Homelands, the area is now part of the Limpopo Province in north South Africa.

Veneto a region of northeastern Italy, centring upon Venice. (Pop. 4,526,000)

Venezuela a country that forms the northernmost crest of South America. Its northern coast lies along the Caribbean Sea, and it is bounded to the west by Colombia, and to the southeast and south by Guyana and Brazil. In the north-west, a spur of the Andes Mountains runs southwest to northeast. Venezuela has one of the highest waterfalls in the world, the Angel Falls. The River Orinoco cuts the country in two, and north of the river run the undulating plains known as the Llanos. South of the river are the Guiana Highlands. The climate ranges from warm temperate to tropical. Temperatures vary little throughout the year and rainfall is plentiful. In the Llanos area, cattle are herded across the plains, and this region makes the country almost self-sufficient in meat. There are also rich fishing grounds around the coast and off Venezuela's 72 islands. Sugar cane and coffee are grown for export, but petroleum and gas account for around 80 per cent of export earnings. Venezuela's economy is built on its oilfields, located in the Maracaibo region, but it also has other important mineral reserves including bauxite, iron ore, coal, and precious metals and stones, such as gold, silver, platinum, and diamonds.

Area: 352,145 sq miles/912,050 sq km
Population: 21,710,000
Capital: Caracas
Other cities: Maracaibo, Valencia, Barquisimeto
Form of government: Federal Republic
Religion: RC
Currency: Bolívar

Vermont a state in the northeast of the USA, bordering Canada. The state capital is Montpelier. (9,609 sq miles/24,887 sq km; pop. 617,000)

Vesuvius an active volcano to the southeast of Naples, in southwest Italy, notorious for having buried the ancient city of Pompeii in AD 79. (4,203 ft/1,281 m)

Victoria (1) a state in southeastern Australia. The state capital is Melbourne. (87,884 sq miles/227,620 sq km; pop. 4,846,000) (2) a port on the southeastern coast of Vancouver Island, southwest Canada, and the capital of British Columbia. (Pop. 76,000) (3) a region in south China, part of Hong Kong, in the northwest of Hong Kong Island. (Pop. 1,026,900) (4) a port and the capital of the Seychelles, on the island of Mahé. (Pop. 23,000)

Victoria Falls one of the world's greatest waterfalls, where the River Zambezi tumbles some 355 feet (108 metres), on the Zambia-Zimbabwe border.

Victoria, Lake the largest lake in Africa, and the second largest freshwater lake in the world after Lake Superior. Its shoreline is shared by Uganda, Kenya, and Tanzania. (26,828 sq miles/69,485 sq km)

Vietnam a long narrow country in southeast Asia that runs down the coast of the South China Sea. It has a narrow central area that links broader plains centred on the Red (Hong) and Mekong Rivers. This narrow zone, now known as Mien Trung, is hilly and makes communications between north and south difficult. The climate is humid, with tropical conditions in the south and subtropical in the north. The far north can be very cold when polar air blows over Asia. Agriculture, fishing, and forestry employ around 74 per cent of the labour force. The main crop is rice but cassava, maize, and sweet potatoes are also grown for domestic consumption. Soya beans, tea, coffee, and rubber are grown for export. Major industries are food processing, textiles, cement, cotton and silk manufacture. Fishing is also an important export trade that is conducted mainly on the South China Sea, although there is some fish farming in flooded inland areas. Vietnam is still recovering from the ravages of many wars this century, and remains underdeveloped.

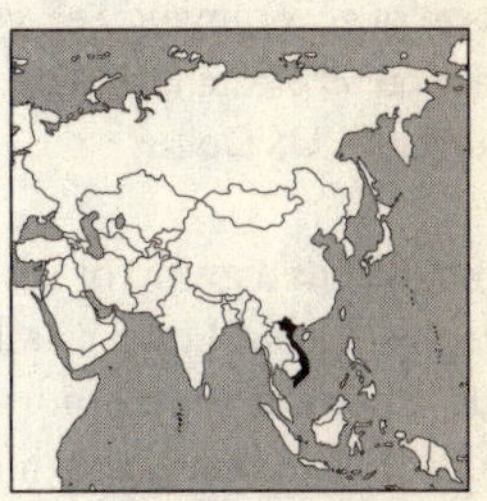

Area: 128,066 sq miles/331,689 sq km
Population: 75,181,000
Capital: Hanoi
Other cities: Ho Chi Minh City, Haiphong, Hué, Dà Nang
Form of government: Socialist Republic
Religion: Buddhism, Taoism, RC
Currency: New Dong

Virginia a state in the east of the USA, with a coast on the Atlantic Ocean. The state capital is Richmond. (39,780 sq miles/103,030 sq km; pop. 7,298,000)

Virgin Islands, British a British Overseas Territory lying at the northwestern end of the Lesser Antilles in the Caribbean Sea. It comprises 4 large islands and 36 islets and cays. Only 16 of the islands are inhabited. Most of the islands are hilly and wooded, and the climate is subtropical moderated by trade winds. Agriculture produces livestock, coconuts, sugar cane, fruit, and vegetables, but only a small percentage of the land available to agriculture is under cultivation. The main industries are construction, rum distilling and tourism, which is the mainstay of the economy.

Area: 58 sq miles/151 sq km
Population: 19,00
Capital: Road Town
Form of government: British Overseas Territory
Religion: Protestantism
Currency: US Dollar

Virgin Islands, US part of the Virgin Islands group in the northwest of the Lesser Antilles in the Caribbean Sea. A self-governing US territory, this group of 50 volcanic islands are rugged and mountainous with a subtropical climate. The main islands are St John (around two-thirds of which is a National Park), St Croix, and St Thomas. Agriculture is not well developed and most of the country's food has to be imported. There is a small manufacturing industry but tourism is the mainstay of the economy with many cruise ships calling at the island of St Thomas, in particular, because of its natural deep-water harbour.

Area: 134 sq miles/347 sq km
Population: 106,000
Capital: Charlotte Amalie
Form of government: Self-governing US Territory
Religion: Protestantism
Currency: US Dollar

Visayan Islands a group of islands in the centre of the Philippines, which includes Negros, Cebu, Leyte, Masbate, Bohol, Panay and Samar.

Vistula a river of central northern Poland, flowing through Cracow and Warsaw to the Baltic Sea. (Length 677 miles/1,090 km)

Vojvodina an autonomous province in the north of Serbia, in former Yugoslavia. The capital is Novi Sad. (8,301 sq miles/21,506 sq km; pop. 1,922,000)

Volga a largely navigable river of the western Russian Federation, flowing south from its source, to the northeast of Moscow, to the Caspian Sea. It is the longest river in Europe. (Length 2,293 miles/3,690 km)

Volta a river in Ghana, fed by the Black Volta and the White Volta, which flows south to the Bight of Benin. (Length 298 miles/480 km)

Volta, Lake a major artificial lake that occupies much of eastern Ghana, formed by the damming of the Volta River. (3,251 sq miles/8,480 sq km)

W

Wales a principality in the southwest of Great Britain, forming a part of the UK. Cardiff is the capital. (8,017 sq miles/20,768 sq km; pop. 2,935,000)

Wallis and Futuna Islands a French Overseas Territory that comprises two island groups lying 142 miles (230 kilometres) apart in the southern central Pacific Ocean. It is the smallest and poorest of France's overseas territories. The climate is warm and humid with a cyclone season between October and March. Subsistence farming and fishing are the main activities with copra the only important export.

Area: 77 sq miles/200 square km
Population: 15,000
Capital: Matā'Utu
Form of government: French Overseas Territory
Religion: RC
Currency: Pacific Franc

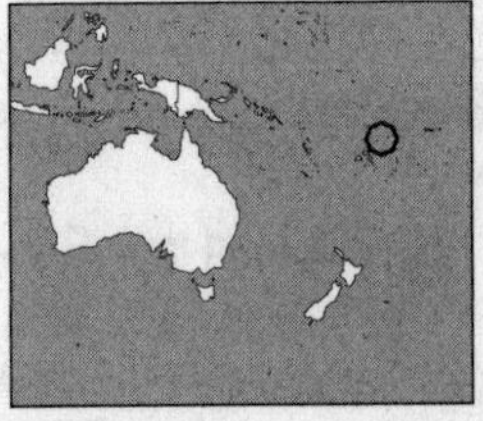

Warwickshire a county in central England, with its administrative centre in the town of Warwick. (765 sq miles/1,981 sq km; pop. 507,000)

Wash, the a shallow inlet formed by the North Sea in the coast of East Anglia, between the counties of Lincolnshire and Norfolk.

Washington a state in northwest USA, with a coast on the Pacific Ocean. The state capital is Olympia. (66,570 sq miles/172,416 sq km; pop. 6,083,000)

Waterford a county in the south of the Republic of Ireland. The county town is also called Waterford. (710 sq miles/1,838 sq km; pop. 99,000)

Weser a river in northwest Germany, flowing through Bremen and Bremerhaven to the North Sea. (Length 182 miles/292 km)

West Bank a piece of disputed territory to the west of the River Jordan, including a part of Jerusalem. It was taken by Israel from Jordan in the Arab-Israeli war of 1967 but given limited autonomy in 1994 under the auspices of the Palestinian National Authority. (2,262 sq miles/5,858 sq km; pop. 1,881,000)

West Bengal a state in eastern India, bordering Bangladesh. Calcutta is the capital. (34,258 sq miles/88,752 sq km; pop. 81,788,000)

Western Australia a state occupying much of the western half of Australia. The capital is Perth. (975,920 sq miles/2,527,636 sq km; pop. 1,964,000)

Western Cape one of South Africa's nine provinces, in south South Africa, formerly part of the old Cape Province, with its administrative centre in Cape Town. (49,937 sq miles/129,370 sq km; pop. 3,957,000)

Western Isles (Eilean Siar) an island council area in west Scotland, consisting of the Outer Hebrides, with its administrative centre in the town of Stornoway. (1,120 sq miles/2,900 sq km; pop. 31,000)

Western Sahara a disputed territory of western Africa, with a coastline on the Atlantic Ocean. Consisting mainly of desert, it is rich in phosphates. It was an overseas province of Spain until 1976, when it was partitioned between Morocco and Mauritania. Since 1979, the entire territory has been claimed and administered by Morocco, against the wishes of an active separatist movement, the Frente Polisario. Moroccan sovereignty is not universally recognized, and the United Nations has attempted to oversee a referendum to decide the struggle but without success so far. It is a poor country, with many of its people following a nomadic existence. The bulk of the country's food has to be imported. Phosphates comprise two-thirds of its meagre exports.

Area: 102,703 sq miles/266,000 sq km
Population: 266,000
Capital: Laâyoune (El Aaiún)
Form of government: Republic (de facto controlled by Morocco)
Religion: Sunni Islam
Currency: Moroccan Dirhama

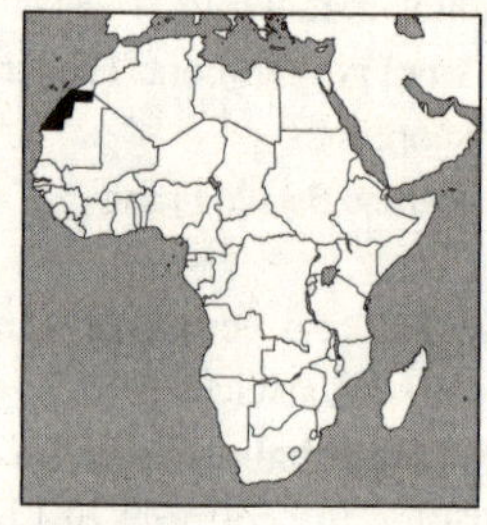

West Dunbartonshire a council area in west central Scotland, with its administrative centre in the town of Dumbarton. (63 sq miles/162 sq km; pop. 96,000)

West Glamorgan a former county in south Wales.

West Indies a general term for the islands of the Caribbean Sea.

West Lothian a council area in central Scotland, with its administrative centre in Livingston. (164 sq miles/425 sq km; pop. 151,000)

Westmeath a county in the central north of the Republic of Ireland. The county town is Mullingar. (681 sq miles/1,764 sq km; pop. 66,000)

West Midlands a metropolitan county in central England. (347 sq miles/899 sq km; pop. 2,628,000)

West Sussex a county in southeast England, with its administrative centre in the city of Chichester. (768 sq miles/1,989 sq km; pop. 752,000)

West Virginia a state of eastern USA. The capital is Charleston. (24,070 sq miles/ 62,341 sq km; pop. 1,796,000)

West Yorkshire a metropolitan county in northern England. (787 sq miles/ 2,039 sq km)

Wexford a county in the southeast of the Republic of Ireland. The county town is also called Wexford. (908 sq miles/2,352 sq km; pop. 109,000)

White Sea (Beloye More) an arm of the Barents Sea off the northwest of the Russian Federation, which is almost enclosed by the bulge of the Kola Peninsula.

Whitney, Mount a mountain in the Sequoia National Park in eastern California, with the highest peak in the USA outside of Alaska. (14,495 ft/4,418 m)

Wicklow a county in the southwest of the Republic of Ireland. The county town is also called Wicklow. (782 sq miles/2,025 sq km; pop. 107,000)

Wight, Isle of an island and county off the south coast of England, separated from the mainland by the Solent, with its administrative centre in Newport. (147 sq miles/380 sq km; pop. 125,000)

Wiltshire a county in central southern England, with its administrative centre in the town of Trowbridge. (1,344 sq miles/3,481 sq km; pop. 586,000)

Winnipeg, Lake a lake in the south of Manitoba, Canada, which drains into Hudson Bay via the Nelson River. (9,094 sq miles/23,553 sq km)

Wisconsin a state in north central USA, bordering Lake Superior and Lake Michigan. The state capital is Madison. (54,464 sq miles/141,061 sq km; pop. 5,440,000)

Witwatersrand (the Rand) a rocky ridge in northern South Africa containing the richest gold deposits in the world.

Worcestershire a county in west central England, with its administrative centre in the city of Worcester. (674 sq miles/1,742 sq km; pop. 528,000)

Wrexham (1) a town in north Wales, formerly known for its coal mining, the administrative centre for the Wrexham council area. (Pop. 41,000) (2) a council area in north Wales. (193 sq miles/500 sq km; pop. 123,000)

Wyoming a state in the west of the USA. The state capital is Cheyenne. (97,914 sq miles/253,597 sq km; pop. 495,000)

Xi Jiang (Si Kiang) the third longest river in China, flowing across the southwest of the country from Yunnan to its delta on the South China Sea near Guangzhou (Canton). (Length 1,437 miles/2,300 km)

Xinjiang (Sinkiang) Uygur Autonomous Region (Xinjiang Uygur Zizhiqu) a region of northwest China, bordering Mongolia, the Russian Federation, Afghanistan, Pakistan and India. It is also known as Dzungaria. The capital is Ürümqi. (635,829 sq miles/1,646,799 sq km; pop. 18,929,000)

Y

Yamuna (Jumna) a major river of north India, a tributary of the River Ganges. (Length 855 miles/1,376 km)

Yellow Sea a branch of the Pacific Ocean between the northeast coast of China and the peninsula of Korea. (180,000 sq miles/466,200 sq km)

Yemen a country bounded by Saudi Arabia in the north, Oman in the east, the Gulf of Aden in the south, and the Red Sea in the west. The country was formed after the unification of the previous Yemen Arab Republic (North)and the People's Democratic Republic of Yemen (South) in 1989. At that point, however, there was no active integration of the two countries and politically the country remained divided between North and South. In 1994, a civil war that lasted three months broke out between the former North and South Yemen, which resulted in a high rate of inflation, damage to the infrastructure, and devaluation of the currency. Most of the country comprises rugged mountains and trackless desert lands. The country is almost entirely dependent on agriculture even although only a very small percentage is fertile. The main crops are coffee, cotton, wheat, vegetables, millet, sorghum, and fruit. Fishing is an important industry, and there are some canning factories along the coast. Other industry is on a very small scale, consisting mainly of manufacturing industries which produce textiles, paints, matches, plastic, rubber, and aluminium goods. Attempts to modernize the country's industry are hampered by a lack of funds.

Area: 203,850 sq miles/527,978 sq km
Population: 15,919,000
Capital: Sana'a
Commercial capital: Aden
Form of government: Republic
Religion: Zaidism, Shia Islam, Sunni Islam
Currency: Yemeni Rial

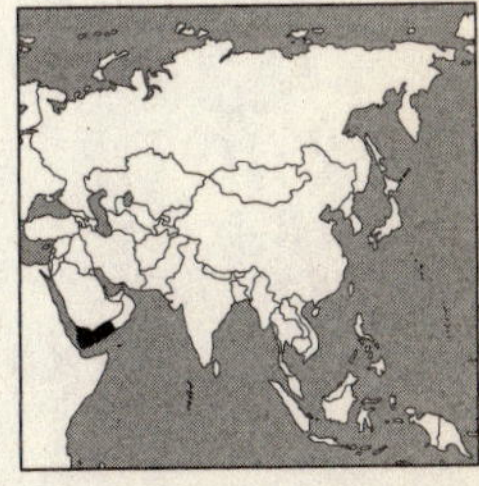

Yorkshire a former county of northeast England now divided into West Yorkshire, East Riding of Yorkshire, North Yorkshire and South Yorkshire.

Yucatan (Yucatán) a state of southeast Mexico on the broad Yucatan Peninsula. The capital is Mérida. (15,186 sq miles/39,340 sq km; pop. 1,556,000)

Yugoslavia the former Yugoslavia was a country created in 1918 which became a single federal republic of six after World War II under the leadership of Marshal Tito (1892–1980). Its six constituent republics were Serbia, Croatia, Slovenia, Bosnia-Herzegovina, Macedonia, and Montenegro. During the 1990s, the republics of Slovenia, Bosnia-Herzegovina, Macedonia, and Croatia all declared their independence from Yugoslavia. Slovenia and Macedonia managed to do this peacefully but declarations of independence in Bosnia and Croatia led to the worst violence seen in Europe since World War II. The last two republics, Serbia and Montenegro, recently agreed to the creation of a new union of two states to be known as Serbia and Montenegro. The creation of this new union brings about the final demise of the country known for so long as Yugoslavia.

Yukon Territory a mountainous territory in northwest Canada centring upon the River Yukon and including the River Klondike. (207,076 sq miles/536,372 sq km; pop. 29,000)

Yünnan a province in southwestern China. The capital is Kunming. (168,400 sq miles/436,200 sq km; pop. 43,178,000)

Z

Zagros Mountains (Kuhha-ye Zagros) a mountain range in southwest Iran, running parallel to the border with Iraq. The highest point is Zard Kuh (14,918 ft/ 4,548 m).

Zambezi a river of southern Africa. It rises in Zambia, then flows south to form the border with Zimbabwe, and then southeast across Mozambique to the Indian Ocean. (Length 1,700 miles/2,740 km)

Zambia a country made up of high plateaux in Central Africa. Bordering it to the south is the Zambezi River, and to the southwest, the Kalahari Desert. It has other large rivers, such as the Luangwa, and lakes, the largest of which is Lake Bangweulu. The climate is tropical, modified somewhat by altitude. The country has a wide range of wildlife, and there are large game parks on the Luangwa and Kafue Rivers. Agriculture is underdeveloped and vulnerable to weather variations. This has led to some food shortages, and as a result much of the country's food has to be imported. The principal subsistence crops grown are corn, sugar cane, and cassava, and the main livestock raised are cattle. Zambia's economy relies heavily on the mining of copper, lead, zinc, and cobalt. The poor market prospects for copper, and the fact that supplies will eventually be exhausted, make it imperative for Zambia to develop her vast agricultural potential. The majority of the country's power is provided by the Kariba Dam on the Zambezi River, and there is the potential for further hydroelectric development.

Area: 290,587 sq miles/752,618 sq km
Population: 8,500,000
Capital: Lusaka
Other cities: Kitwe, Ndola, Mufulira
Form of government: Republic
Religions: Christianity, traditional African religions
Currency: Kwacha

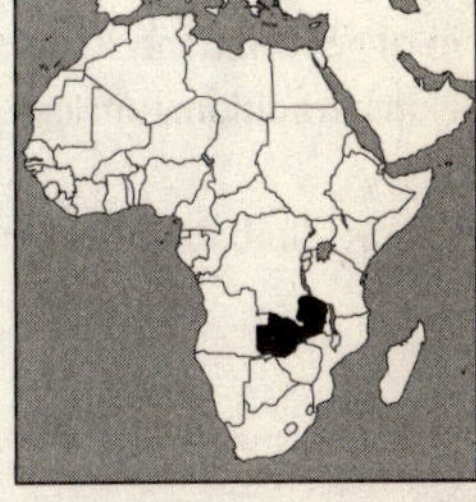

Zanzibar an island, now part of the United Republic of Tanzania, lying just off the east coast of Tanzania, in the Indian Ocean. The main town and port is also called Zanzibar. (950 sq miles/2,461 sq km; pop. 444,000)

Zealand (Sjaelland, Seeland) the largest island of Denmark, on which the capital, Copenhagen, is sited. (2,708 sq miles/7,014 sq km; pop. 2,224,000)

Zhejiang a province of eastern China, mountainous and densely populated with a coast on the East China Sea. The capital is Hangzhou. (39,780 sq miles/ 102,000 sq km; pop. 44,543,000)

Zimbabwe a landlocked country in southern Africa, Zimbabwe is a country with spectacular physical features, teeming with wildlife. It is bordered in the north by the Zambezi River, which flows over the mile-wide Victoria Falls before entering Lake Kariba. In the south, the River Limpopo marks its border with South Africa. A great plateau between 4,000–5,000 feet (about 1,200–1,500 metres) in height occupies the central area. Only one third of the population lives in its towns and cities, the largest of which is the capital, Harare. The climate is tropical in the lowlands and subtropical in the higher land. About 75 per cent of the workforce are employed in agriculture. Tobacco, sugar cane, cotton, wheat, and maize are grown and form the basis of processing industries. Zimbabwe is rich in mineral resources such as coal, chromium, nickel, gold, platinum, and precious metals, and mining accounts for around 30 per cent of foreign revenue. Tourism has the potential to be a major growth industry thanks to the country's many tourist attractions, including several wildlife parks, the Victoria Falls, and Great Zimbabwe. However, there has been ongoing conflict with the white farming community over the ownership of farms and the economy has declined rather than prospered, a situation further aggravated by political violence in recent years.

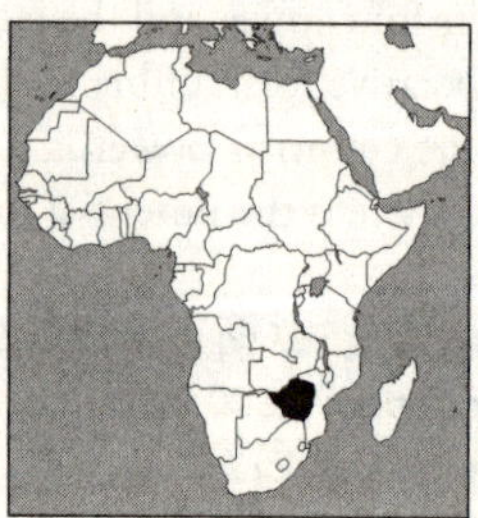

Area: 150,873 sq miles/390,580 sq km
Population: 11,908,000
Capital: Harare
Other cities: Bulawayo, Mutare, Gweru
Form of government: Republic
Religions: traditional African religions, Anglicanism, RC
Currency: Zimbabwe Dollar

Atlas

Index

A Coruña **33** A 1
Aachen **36** B 2
Aalen **36** C 3
Aare **36** B 3
Aasiaat **8** Aa 5
Aasleagh **31** B 2
Aba **56** D 4
Ābādeh **44** H 6
Abag Qi **49** J 2
Abagnar Qi **50** C 4
Abaiang **59** G 3
Abakaliki **56** D 4
Abakan **41** U 7
Abakanskiy Khrebet **41** T 7
Aban **41** V 6
Abariringa **59** H 4
Abashiri **54** D 2
Abay **45** M 3
Abaza **41** U 7
Abbeville (U.S.) **20** F 2
Abdulino **44** H 2
Abéché **56** F 3
Abel Tasman National Park **62** B 3
Abemama **59** G 3
Abengourou **56** C 4
Abeokuta **56** D 4
Aberdeen (South Dakota, U.S.) **16** D 2
Aberdeen (U.K.) **30** C 3
Aberdeen (Washington, U.S.) **18** B 2
Aberdeen Lake **8** R 6
Abert, Lake **18** B 3
Aberystwyth **28** B 3
Abganerovo **44** F 3
Abidjan **56** C 4
Abilene **16** D 5
Abisko **38** J 2
Åbo **38** K 3
Abruka Saar **38** K 4
Abū Kamāl **44** F 6
Abu Road **46** C 4
Abuja **56** D 4
Acadia National Park **14** F 2
Acámbaro **20** D 3
Acaponeta **20** C 3
Acapulco **20** E 4
Acarigua **22** J 6
Acatlán de Osorio **20** E 4
Acayucan **20** F 4
Accomac **14** D 3
Accra **56** C 4
Acebuches **20** D 2
Acheng **50** E 3
Achill Head **31** A 2
Achinsk **41** U 6
Acireale **34** D 3
Acklins Island **22** H 3
Acri **34** D 3
Actopan **20** E 3
Açude Araras **24** G 3
Adū Damar **56** G 3
Ad Damazīn **56** G 3
Aḑ Diffah **56** F 2
Ad Dīwānīyah **44** F 6
Ad Duwaym **56** G 3
Ada (U.S.) **16** D 5
Adair, Bahía de **18** D 5
Adair, Cape **8** W 4
Adak Island **43** U 6
Adamstown **59** M 6
Adana **35** F 6
Adapazarı **35** D 4
Addua Atoll **46** C 9
Adelaide **60** F 6
Adele Island **60** C 3
Adi **52** J 6
Adilabad **46** D 5
Adirondack Mountains **14** E 2
Ādīs Ābeba **56** G 4
Adıyaman **35** H 6
Adjud **35** B 1
Adler **35** H 3
Admiralty Island **10** Q 7
Admiralty Islands **59** D 4
Ādoni **46** D 5
Adra **33** B 2
Adrian **14** C 2
Adriatic Sea **34** D 2
Adycha **42** L 3
Adzhima **54** C 1
Aē Ēaūan **35** G 7
Aegean Sea **34** F 3
Āfar **56** G 3
Afghanistan **45** K 6
Afognak Island **43** Z 5
Afyon **35** D 5
Agadez **56** D 3
Agadir **56** C 1
Agalta, Sierra de **20** G 5
Agartala **47** G 4
Agata **41** U 4
Agattu Island **43** S 6
Agen **32** C 3
Agiabampo, Estero de **20** B 2
Agra **46** D 3
Ağrı **35** K 5
Ağrı Dağı **35** L 5
Agrigento **34** C 3
Agrihan **59** D 2
Agrinio **34** E 3
Agua Caliente de Chínipa **20** C 2
Agua Prieta **18** E 5
Aguascalientes (Mexico) **20** D 3
Aguascalientes (State, Mexico) **20** D 3
Águilas **33** B 2
Aguililla **20** D 4
Ahar **44** G 5
Ahe **59** L 5
Ahlat **44** F 5
Ahmadābād **46** C 4
Ahmadnagar **46** C 5
Ahmadpur East **46** C 3
Ahome **20** C 2
Ahunui **59** L 5
Ahvenanmaa **38** J 3
Aihun **50** E 2
Aiken **14** C 4
Aileron **60** E 4
Ailinglapalap **59** F 3
Ailuk **59** F 2
Aim **42** K 5
Aïn Beïda **34** B 3
Ainažl **38** K 4
Aïr **56** D 3
Air Force Island **8** W 5
Aitutaki Island **59** K 5
Aix-en-Provence **34** B 2
Āīzawl **47** G 4
Aizuwakamatsu **54** C 3
Ajaccio **34** B 2
Ajanta Range **46** D 4
Ajigasawa **54** D 2
Ajka **36** D 3
Ajmer **46** C 3
Ajo **18** D 5
Ākūakūi Beseka **56** G 4
Akaroa **62** B 3
Akashi **54** B 4
Akbaba Tepe **44** E 5
Akbulak **40** N 7

Akçadağ **35** G 5
Akçakale **35** H 6
Ak-Dovurak **41** U 7
Akelamo **52** H 5
Akhaltsūikhe **35** K 4
Akhisar **35** B 5
Akhtubinsk **44** G 3
Akimiski Island **8** U 8
Akita **54** D 3
Aklé Aouâna **56** C 3
Akola **46** D 4
Akpatok Island **8** X 6
Akron **14** C 2
Aksaray **35** E 5
Akşehir **35** D 5
Aksha **50** B 2
Aksu **48** C 2
Aktau **44** H 4
Aktobe **45** H 4
Akun Island **43** W 6
Akureyri **38** B 2
Akutan Island **43** W 6
Alū Amārah **44** G 6
Al Bādī **35** J 7
Al Başrah **44** G 6
Al Bayḑā (Beida) **56** F 1
Al Fallūjah **44** F 6
Al Fāshir (El Fasher) **56** F 3
Al Fashn **56** G 2
Al Fatḩah **35** K 7
Al Fayyūm **56** G 2
Al Hamādah al Hamrā **56** E 2
Al Hanīyah **44** G 7
Al Ḩaḑr **35** K 7
Al Ḩasakah **35** J 6
Al Ḩillah **44** F 6
Al Iskandarīyah (Alexandria) **56** F 1
Al Jahra **44** G 7
Al Jazāūir (Algiers) **56** C 1
Al Jazīrah **44** F 6
Al Jīzah (Giza) **56** F 2
Al Junaynah **56** F 3
Al Kāf **34** B 3
Al Khālis **44** F 6
Al Kharţūm (Khar Toum) **56** F 3
Al Kharţūm Bahrī **56** G 3
Al Khums **56** E 1
Al Kufrah **56** F 2
Al Kūt **44** G 6
Al Kuwayt **44** G 7
Al Lādhiqīyah **35** F 7
Al Marj **56** F 1
Al Mawşil **35** K 6
Al Minyā **56** G 2
Al Miqdādīyah **44** F 6
Al Musayyib **44** F 6
Al Qadārif **56** G 3
Al Qāmishlī **35** J 6
Al Qūşīyah **56** G 2
Al Ubayyid (El Obeid) **56** F 3
Alabama **14** B 4
Alabama River **14** B 4
Alacrán, Arrecife **20** G 3
Alagir **35** L 3
Alagoinhas **24** H 4
Alajuela **22** F 5
Alaköl **45** O 3
Alakurtti **40** H 4
Alamagan **59** D 2
Alamogordo **18** E 5
Alamos **20** C 2
Alamos, Sierra **20** D 2
Alamosa **18** E 4
Åland **38** J 3
Ålands hav **38** K 4
Alanya **35** D 6
Alapaha River **14** C 4
Alapayevsk **40** O 6
Alaşehir **35** C 5
Alaska **10** K 5
Alaska Peninsula **43** X 5
Alaska Range **10** M 6
Alaska, Gulf of **10** N 7
Alatyrū **44** G 2
Alava, Cape **18** A 2
Alazeya **43** O 3
Alazeyskoye Ploskogorūye **42** N 3
Alb **8** U 8
Alba **34** B 2
Albacete **33** B 2
Alba-Iulia **36** E 3
Al-Balyanā **56** G 2
Albania **34** D 2
Albano Laziale **34** C 2
Albany (Aust.) **60** B 7
Albany (Georgia, U.S.) **14** C 4
Albany (New York, U.S.) **14** E 2
Albany (Oregon, U.S.) **18** B 3
Albany River **8** U 9
Albatross Bay **60** G 2
Albatross Point **62** B 2
Albemarle Sound **14** D 3
Albert Lea **16** E 3
Alberta **10** T 7
Albi **32** C 3
Ålborg **38** G 4
Albufeira Cahora Bassa **58** C 3
Albuquerque **18** E 4
Albuquerque, Cayos de **22** F 5
Albury **60** H 7
Alcalá de Guadaira **33** A 2
Alcalá de Henares **32** B 3
Alcamo **34** C 3
Alcázar de San Juan **33** B 2
Alchevsūk **44** E 3
Alcolea del Pinar **32** B 3
Alcoy **33** B 2
Aldabra Islands **58** D 2
Aldama **20** C 2
Aldan **42** J 5
Aldan (River) **42** K 4
Aldanskoye Nagorūye **42** J 5
Aldershot **28** D 4
Alegrete **24** F 6
Aleksandrov **40** J 6
Aleksandrov Gay **44** G 2
Aleksandrovsk-Sakhalinskiy **42** M 6
Alekseyevka **44** E 2
Alençon **32** C 2
Alenuihaha Channel **12** E 7
Aleppo **35** G 6
Aléria **34** B 2
Alert Point **8** T 2
Alès **32** C 3
Alessandria **34** B 2
Ålesund **38** G 3
Aleutian Islands **43** T 6
Aleutian Range **43** Y 5
Alexander Archipelago **10** P 7
Alexander Island **63** Y 5
Alexander, Kap **8** W 3
Alexandra **62** A 4
Alexandra Falls **10** T 6
Alexandria (Louisiana, U.S.) **16** E 5
Alexandria (Romania) **34** F 2
Alexandria (Virginia, U.S.) **14** D 3
Alexandroupoli **34** F 2
Aleysk **41** S 7
Algarve **33** A 2
Algeciras **33** A 2
Algeria **56** C 2
Algha **45** J 3
Alghero **34** B 2
Algona **16** E 3
Algurd **35** L 6
Al-Hoceima **56** C 1
Äli-Bayramlı **44** G 5
Alicante **33** B 2
Alice **20** E 2
Alice Springs **60** E 4
Aligarh **46** D 3
Alīgūdarz **44** G 6
Alim Island **59** D 4
Alitak, Cape **10** L 7
Allahabad **46** E 3
Allakaket **10** M 5
Allanmyo **47** H 5
Allegheny Mountains **14** C 3
Allegheny Plateau **14** C 3
Allegheny River **14** C 2
Allende **20** D 2
Allentown **14** D 2
Alleppey **46** D 7
Alliance **16** C 3
Alloa **30** C 3
Alma **8** W 9
Alma-Ata **45** N 4
Almansa **33** B 2
Almaty **45** N 4
Almaznyy **41** Y 5
Almerūa **33** B 2
Alūmetūyevsk **44** H 2

Alofi, Île **59** H 5
Alor **52** G 7
Alor Setar **52** C 4
Alpena **8** U 9
Alphonse **58** E 2
Alpine **16** C 5
Alps, The **36** B 3
Alta **38** K 2
Altai Shan **48** D 1
Altamaha River **14** C 4
Altamira **24** F 3
Altamont **18** B 3
Altamura **34** D 2
Altanbulag **41** X 7
Altar **18** D 5
Altata **20** C 3
Altay **48** D 1
Altayskiy **41** T 7
Alton **16** E 4
Altoona **14** D 2
Altun Ha **20** G 4
Altun Shan **48** E 3
Alturas **18** B 3
Altus **16** D 5
Alushta **35** F 2
Alva **16** D 4
Alvarado **20** E 4
Älvdalen **38** H 3
Alvord Valley **18** C 3
Alwar **46** D 3
Alxa Zuoqi **49** H 3
Alyaskitovyy **42** M 4
Alytus **36** E 2
Alzamay **41** V 6
Alzira **33** B 2
Amadeus, Lake **60** E 5
Amadjuak Lake **8** W 6
Amahai **52** H 6
Amami-ō-shima **50** E 7
Amanu **59** L 5
Amanu-Runga **59** L 6
Amanzimtoti **58** C 5
Amapu-Raro **59** L 6
Āmara **56** G 3
Amarillo **16** C 4
Amasya **35** F 4
Amatique, Bahía de **20** G 4
Ambala **46** D 2
Ambarawa **52** E 7
Ambarchik **43** Q 3
Ambardakh **42** L 2
Ambato **24** D 3
Ambatondrazaka **58** D 3
Amberg **36** C 3
Ambikapur **46** E 4
Ambilobe **58** D 3
Ambon **52** H 6
Ambon (Island) **52** H 6
Ambositra **58** D 4
Ambovombe **58** D 4
Ambrym **59** F 5
Amderma **40** O 4
Amdo **48** E 4
Ameca **20** D 3
American Falls Reservoir **18** D 3
American Samoa **59** J 5
Americus **14** C 4
Ames **16** E 3
Amga **42** K 4
Amgu **54** C 1
Amgunū **42** L 6
Amherst Island **14** D 2
Amiens **32** C 2
Amīndīvi Islands **46** C 6
Amirante Islands **58** E 2
Amlia Island **43** V 6
Ammassalik **8** Dd 5
Ammochostos **35** E 7
Āmol **44** H 5
Amorgos **34** F 3
Amos **8** V 9
Åmot **38** G 4
Amoy **49** K 6
Ampanihy **58** D 4
Amravati **46** D 4
Amritsar **46** C 2
Amund Ringnes Island **8** R 3
Amundsen Gulf **10** R 4
Amur **42** J 6
An Nahūd **56** F 3
An Najaf **44** F 6
An Nāsirīyah **44** G 6
An Nuūmānīyah **44** G 6
Anaa **59** L 5
Anabar **41** Y 3
Anabarskiy Zaliv **41** Y 3
Anabarskoye Ploskogorūye **41** X 3
Anaco **22** K 6
Anaconda **18** D 2
Anadoli (Anatolia) **35** D 5
Anadyrū **43** T 4
Anadyrskaya Nizmennostū **43** T 3
Anadyrskiy Liman **43** T 4
Anadyrskiy Zaliv **43** U 3
Anadyrskoye Ploskogorūye **43** R 3
Anafi **34** F 3
Anáhuac **20** D 2
Anakapalle **46** E 5
Analalava **58** D 3
Anambas, Kepulauan **52** D 5
Anamur **35** E 6
Anamur Burnu **44** D 5
Anantapur **46** D 6
Ananūyiv **36** F 3
Anapa **35** G 2
Anápolis **24** F 4
Anatahan **59** D 2
Anatòm **59** F 6
Anby n **50** E 5
Anbyŏn **54** A 3
Anchorage **10** N 6
Anchorage Island **59** J 5
Ancona **34** C 2
Anda **50** E 3
Åndalsnes **38** G 3
Andalucūa **33** A 2
Andaman Islands **47** G 6
Andaman Sea **47** G 6
Andenes **38** J 2
Anderson (Indiana, U.S.) **14** B 2
Anderson (South Carolina, U.S.) **14** C 4
Andhra Pradesh **46** E 6
Andijon **45** M 4
Andīmeshk **44** G 6
Andirlangar **48** C 3
Andkhui **45** L 5
Andong **50** D 4
Andong (South Korea) **54** A 3
Andorra **32** C 3
Andorra la Vella **32** C 3
Andøya **38** J 2
Andreanof Islands **43** U 6
Andreasen, Cape **10** T 3
Andrée Land **8** Ff 4
Andrews **16** C 5
Andringitra **58** D 4
Andros **34** E 3
Andros Island **14** D 5
Androth **46** C 6
Aneto, Pico de **32** C 3
Angūangxi **50** D 3
Angara **41** U 6
Angarsk **41** W 7
Angaul **41** W 7
Angaur **59** C 3
Angel de la Guarda, Isla **20** B 2
Angel Falls **22** K 6
Angeles **52** G 2
Ångermanälven **38** J 3
Ångermanland **38** J 3
Angers **32** B 2
Angijak Island **8** Y 5
Angikuni Lake **8** R 6
Angkor Wat **47** J 6
Anglesey **28** B 3
Anglet **32** B 3
Angola **58** A 3
Angostura **20** C 2
Angoulême **32** C 2
Angūren **45** M 4
Anguilla **22** K 4
Anguo **49** K 3
Anhua **49** J 5
Anhui **49** K 4
Anikovo **40** K 6
Animas Peak **18** E 5
Anina **36** E 3
Aniva **54** D 1
Aniva, Mys **50** H 3
Aniva, Zaliv **50** H 3
Aniwa **59** F 5
Anju **50** E 5

Ankang **49** H 4
Ankara **35** E 5
Ankleshwar **46** C 4
Anlak **43** Y 4
Anlong **49** H 5
Anlu **49** J 4
Ann Arbor **14** C 2
Anna **44** F 2
Anna (U.S.) **14** B 3
Annaba **56** D 1
Annapolis **14** D 3
Annapurna **46** E 3
Anniston **14** B 4
Anoka **16** E 2
Anqing **49** K 4
Anshan **50** D 4
Anshun **49** H 5
Ansley **16** D 3
Antakya **35** G 6
Antalaha **58** D 3
Antalya **35** D 6
Antalya Körfezi **35** D 6
Antananarivo **58** D 3
Anthony **18** E 5
Antibes **34** B 2
Anticosti, Île dū **8** Y 9
Antigua **22** K 4
Antigua (Guatemala) **20** F 5
Antigua and Barbuda **22** K 4
Antillas Mayores **22** H 4
Antillas Menores **22** K 4
Antioch **35** G 6
Antiope Reef **59** J 5
Antofagasta **24** D 5
Antrim **31** C 1
Antsirabe **58** D 4
Antsirañana **58** D 3
Antsohihy **58** D 3
Antu **54** A 2
Antunū **54** C 1
Anugul **46** F 4
Anuradhapura **46** E 7
Anuta **59** F 5
Anvik **43** X 4
Anxiang **49** J 5
Anxious Bay **60** E 6
Anyang **49** J 3
Aūnyemaqen Shan **48** F 3
Anūyudin **40** N 5
Anyue **49** H 4
Anyuysk **43** Q 3
Anyuyskiy Khrebet **43** R 3
Anzhero-Sudzhensk **41** T 6
Anzio **34** C 2
Aoga-shima **54** C 4
Aoji **54** B 2
Aomori **54** D 2
Aosta **36** B 3
Apalachee Bay **14** C 5
Apalachicola **20** G 2
Apan **20** E 4
Aparri **52** G 2
Apataki **59** L 5
Apatzingán **20** D 4
Apeldoorn **36** B 2
Apennines **34** C 2
Apia **59** H 5
Apizaco **20** E 4
Apostolove **44** D 3
Appalachian Mountains **14** C 3
Appennino **34** C 2
Appennino Calabro **34** D 3
Appleton **14** B 2
Apsheronsk **44** E 4
Aqköl **45** M 2
Aqsay **44** H 2
Aqsū (Kazakhstan) **45** N 2
Aqtaū **45** M 2
Aqtöbe **40** N 7
Aqtoghay **45** N 3
Ar Ramādī **44** F 6
Ar Raqqah **35** H 7
Arabian Sea **46** B 5
Aracaju **24** H 4
Araçatuba **24** F 5
Arad **36** E 3
Arafura Sea **53** J 8
Arafura, Laut **52** J 7
Aragats Lerr **35** L 4
Aragón **32** B 3
Arāk **44** G 6
Arakan Yoma **47** G 4
Aral **45** K 3
Aral Sea **45** J 4
Aralūskoye More **45** J 4
Aran Island **31** B 1
Aran Islands **31** B 2
Aranda de Duero **32** B 3
Arani **46** D 6
Aranjuez **32** B 3
Aranuka **59** G 4
Ararat **60** G 7
Aras Nehri **44** F 5
Aratika **59** L 5
Arbīl **35** L 6
Arbroath **30** C 3
Arcachon **32** B 3
Arcas, Cayos **20** F 3
Arcata **18** B 3
Arcelia **20** D 4
Archipiélago Juan Fernández (Chile) **24** C 6
Arco **18** D 3
Arctic Bay **8** U 4
Arctic Circle **8** Bb 5
Arctic Ocean **8** V 2
Arctic Village **10** N 5
Ardabīl **44** G 5
Ardakān **45** H 6
Ardmore **16** D 5
Arena Island **52** G 4
Arenas, Cayo **20** F 3
Arendal **38** G 4
Arequipa **24** D 4
Arezzo **34** C 2
Arga-Sala **41** Y 4
Argentina **24** E 6
Argos **34** E 3
Argun **50** C 2
Argyle, Lake **60** D 3
Argyll **30** B 3
Arholma **38** J 3
Århus **38** H 4
Ari Atoll **46** C 8
Arica **24** D 4
Arid, Cape **60** C 6
Ariquemes **24** E 3
Arismendi **22** J 6
Arizgoit **32** B 3
Arizona (U.S.) **18** D 5
Arjeplog **38** J 2
Arjona **22** G 5
Arkadak **44** F 2
Arkadelphia **16** E 5
Arkansas **16** E 4
Arkansas City **16** D 4
Arkansas River **16** E 5
Arkhangelūsk **40** K 5
Arkhara **54** B 1
Arklow **31** C 2
Arkticheskogo Instituta, Ostrova **41** S 2
Arles **32** C 3
Arlington **18** B 2
Arlington (Texas, U.S.) **16** D 5
Arlington (Virginia, U.S.) **14** D 3
Armadale **60** B 6
Armagh **31** C 1
Armagnac **32** C 3
Armant **56** G 2
Armavir **35** J 2
Armenia **44** F 4
Armenia (Colombia) **22** G 7
Armenia (Country) **35** L 4
Armeria **20** D 4
Armidale **60** J 6
Armstrong **8** T 8
Arnhem **36** B 2
Arnhem Land **60** E 2
Arno **59** G 3
Arnøy **38** K 1
Arnstadt **36** C 2
Arod **48** F 2
Arorae **59** G 4
Arqalyq **45** L 2
Arrah **46** E 3
Arran **28** B 2
Arrecife **56** B 2
Arriaga **20** F 4
Arsenūyev **54** B 2
Artá **33** C 2
Arta **34** E 3
Arteaga **20** D 4
Artem **54** B 2
Artemisa **20** H 3
Artemivsūk **44** E 3

Artemovsk **41** U 7
Artemovskiy **40** O 6
Artesia **16** C 5
Artillery Lake **10** V 6
Aru, Kepulauan **53** K 7
Arua **58** C 1
Aruba **22** J 5
Arun Qi **50** D 3
Arunāchal Pradesh **47** G 3
Arusha **58** C 2
Arvada **18** E 4
Arviat **8** S 6
Arvidsjaur **38** J 2
Arxan **50** C 3
Ary **42** H 2
Arys **45** L 4
Arzamas **40** K 6
Aş Sahrāū al Gharbīyah **56** F 2
Aş Sahrāū al Janūbīyah **56** F 2
As Samāwah **44** G 6
As Sulaymānīyah **44** G 5
As Suwaydāh **44** E 6
As Suways (Suez) **56** G 2
Asahikawa **54** D 2
Āsānsol **46** F 4
Asbest **40** O 6
Ascoli Piceno **34** C 2
Āsela **56** G 4
Åsele **38** J 3
Aşgabat **45** J 5
Ash Shallāl al Khāmis **56** G 3
Asha **40** N 7
Ashburton **62** B 3
Asheville **14** C 3
Ashkhabad **45** J 5
Ashland (Kentucky, U.S.) **14** C 3
Ashland (Oregon, U.S.) **18** B 3
Ashland (Wisconsin, U.S.) **16** E 2
Ashmore Reef **60** C 2
Ashtabula **14** C 2
Ashton **18** D 3
Asino **41** T 6
Asipovichy **36** F 2
Aşkale **35** J 5
Askim **38** H 4
Askiz **41** U 7
Asmara **56** G 3
Aspen **18** E 4
Assab **56** H 3
Assam **47** G 3
Assen **36** B 2
Assiniboia **18** E 2
Assiniboine River **16** D 2
Astana **45** M 2
Asti **34** B 2
Astorga **33** A 1
Astoria **18** B 2
Astrakhanū **44** G 3
Astrolabe, Récifs de **59** F 5
Astypalaia **34** F 3
Asunción **24** F 5
Asuncion Island **59** D 2
Aswān **56** G 2
Asyūt **56** G 2
Atafu **59** H 4
Atascadero **18** B 4
Atasu **45** M 3
Atauro **52** H 7
Atbara **56** G 3
Atbasar **45** L 2
Atchafalaya Bay **20** F 2
Atchison **16** D 4
Athabasca **10** U 8
Athabasca, Lake **10** V 7
Athens (Georgia, U.S.) **14** C 4
Athens (Greece) **34** E 3
Athens (Ohio, U.S.) **14** C 3
Athina **34** E 3
Athlone **31** C 2
Atikoķan **16** E 2
Atka **43** V 6
Atka Island **43** U 6
Atkarsk **44** F 2
Atlanta **14** C 4
Atlantic **16** D 3
Atlantic City **14** E 3
Atlantic Ocean **24** G 6
Atlasova, Ostrov **43** P 6
Atlin Lake **10** Q 7
Atmore **14** B 4
Atoka **16** D 5
Atoyac de Alvarez **20** D 4
Atqasuk **10** L 4
Attapu **47** K 6
Attersee **36** C 3
Attu Island **43** S 6
Atyraū **44** H 3
Aubagne **34** B 2
Aubry Lake **10** R 5
Auburn (California, U.S.) **18** B 4
Auburn (Maine, U.S.) **14** E 2
Auburn (Nebraska, U.S.) **16** D 3
Auckland **62** B 2
Augsburg **36** C 3
Augusta (Arkansas, U.S.) **16** E 4
Augusta (Australia) **60** B 6
Augusta (Georgia, U.S.) **14** C 4
Augusta (Maine, U.S.) **14** F 2
Augusta (Maine, U.S.A.) **8** X 10
Augustów **36** E 2
Auld, Lake **60** C 4
Aur **59** G 3
Aurangabad **46** D 5
Aurangābād **46** E 4
Aurich **36** B 2
Aurillac **32** C 3
Aurora (U.S.) **16** C 4
Aust-Agder **38** G 4
Austin (Minnesota, U.S.) **16** E 3
Austin (Nevada, U.S.) **18** C 4
Austin (Texas, U.S.) **16** D 5
Austin, Lake **60** B 5
Australia **60** D 4
Australian Alps **60** H 7
Australian Capital Territory **60** H 7
Austria **36** C 3
Austvågøy **38** H 2
Autlán **20** D 4
Auxerre **32** C 2
Auyuittuq National Park **8** X 5
Avallon **32** C 2
Avan **45** K 3
Avarua **59** K 6
Aveiro **33** A 1
Avellino **34** C 2
Averøya **38** G 3
Avesta **38** J 3
Avezzano **34** C 2
Avignon **32** C 3
Ávila **32** B 3
Avilés **33** A 1
Avola **34** D 3
Avon Park **14** C 5
Awakino **62** B 2
Awanui **62** B 2
Awka **56** D 4
Axel Heiberg Island **8** S 3
Ayacucho **24** D 4
Ayagoz **45** O 3
Ayamonte **33** A 2
Ayan **42** L 5
Aydın **35** B 6
Ayers Rock-Mount Olga National Park **60** E 5
Aylesbury **28** D 4
Aylmer Lake **10** V 6
Ayon, Ostrov **43** R 3
Ayr (U.K.) **28** B 2
Ayteke Bi **45** K 3
Ayutla **20** E 4
Ayya, Mys **35** E 2
Az Zubayr **44** G 6
Azamgarh **46** E 3
Azare **56** E 3
A'zāz **35** G 6
Azerbaijan **44** G 5
Azoum **56** E 3
Azov **44** E 3
Azov, Sea of **44** E 3
Azovskoye More **44** E 3
Azovskoye More (Sea of Azov) **35** G 2
Azul **24** F 6
Baba Burun **34** F 3
Babaeski **35** B 4
Babar, Kepulauan **52** H 7
Babayevo **40** J 6
Babi **52** B 5
Babine Lake **10** R 8
Bābol **44** H 5
Baborigame **20** C 2
Babruysk **36** F 2
Babuyan **49** L 7
Bac Can **47** K 4
Bac Ninh **47** K 4

Bacabal **24** G 3
Bacan **52** H 6
Bacău **36** F 3
Bachu **48** B 3
Bacolod **52** G 3
Bad Hersfeld **36** B 2
Badagara **46** D 6
Badajoz **33** A 2
Baden-Baden **36** B 3
Badin **46** B 4
Badiraguato **20** C 2
Badjawa **52** G 7
Badland **16** C 2
Badulla **46** E 7
Badzhalūskiy Khrebet **54** B 1
Baffin Bay **8** W 4
Baffin Island **8** U 4
Bafoussam **56** E 4
Bafra **35** F 4
Bafra Burnu **35** F 4
Baga Bogd Uul **49** G 2
Bagalkot **46** D 5
Baganga **52** H 4
Bagansiapiapi **52** C 5
Baghdād **44** F 6
Bagheria **34** C 3
Baghlan **45** L 5
Bagley **16** D 2
Bagulo **52** G 2
Bahamas, The **14** E 5
Bahawalpur **46** C 3
Bahía Blanca **24** E 6
Bahía Kino **20** B 2
Bahía, Islas de la **20** G 4
Bahir Dar **56** G 3
Baḩral Abyaḑ (White Nile) **56** F 4
Baḩral Azraq (Blue Nile) **56** G 3
Baía de Sofala **58** C 4
Baia Mare **36** E 3
Baicheng **50** D 3
Baie-Comeau **8** X 9
Baile Átha Cliath **31** C 2
Bailieborough **31** C 2
Bainbridge **14** C 4
Baiquan **50** E 3
Bairiki **59** G 3
Bairin Zuoqi **50** C 4
Bairnsdale **60** H 7
Baja **36** D 3
Baja California **20** B 2
Baja California Norte **18** C 6
Baja California Sur **20** B 2
Bājah **34** B 3
Bajandelger **50** A 3
Bajan-Öndör **48** F 2
Bakal **40** N 7
Bakchar **41** S 6
Bake **52** C 6
Baker (California, U.S.) **18** C 4
Baker (Montana, U.S.) **16** C 2
Baker (Oregon, U.S.) **18** C 3
Baker Lake (Australia) **60** D 5
Baker Lake (Canada) **8** R 6
Bakersfield **18** C 4
Bakhmach **36** G 2
Bakı **44** G 4
Bala Murghab **45** K 5
Balabac Island **52** F 4
Balad **44** F 6
Balagannoye **43** N 5
Balaghat **46** E 4
Bālāghat Range **46** D 5
Balakhna **40** K 6
Balakhta **41** U 6
Balakliya **44** E 3
Balakovo **44** G 2
Balangan Islands **52** F 6
Balangan, Kepulauan **52** F 6
Bālangīr **46** E 4
Balashov **44** F 2
Balchik **34** F 2
Balclutha **62** A 4
Baldy Peak **18** E 5
Baleares, Islas **33** C 2
Balearic Islands **33** C 2
Baler **52** G 2
Bāleshwar **46** F 4
Baley **42** G 6
Balezino **40** M 6
Bali **52** F 7
Balıkesir **35** B 5
Balikpapan **52** F 6
Balintang Channel **49** L 7
Balkanabad **44** H 5
Balladonia **60** C 6
Ballarat **60** G 7
Ballard, Lake **60** C 5
Ballenas, Bahía **20** B 2
Ballia **46** E 3
Ballina (Ireland) **31** B 1
Ballinger **16** D 5
Ballinrobe **31** B 2
Ballygawley **31** C 1
Ballymena **31** C 1
Balotra **46** C 3
Balqash **45** M 3
Balqash Köli **45** N 3
Balrampur **46** E 3
Balsas **20** D 4
Balsas, Deprésion del **20** D 4
Balsas, Río **20** D 4
Balta **36** F 3
Bălţi **36** F 3
Baltic Sea **38** J 4
Baltimore (U.S.) **14** D 3
Baltiysk **36** D 2
Balurghat **47** F 3
Balykchy **45** N 4
Bamaga **60** G 2
Bamako **56** C 3
Bambari **56** F 4
Bamberg **36** C 3
Ban Ban **47** J 5
Ban Na Shan **47** H 7
Banbury **28** D 3
Bancoran **52** F 4
Bancroft **14** D 1
Banda **46** E 3
Banda Aceh **52** B 4
Banda Sea **52** H 7
Banda, Kepulauan **52** H 6
Banda, Laut **52** H 7
Bandao **49** L 3
Bandar Seri Begawan **52** E 5
Bandar-e Anzalī **44** G 5
Bandar-e Māhshar **44** G 6
Bandar-e Torkaman **44** H 5
Bandarlampung **52** D 7
Bandırma **35** B 4
Bandon **31** B 3
Bandundu **58** A 2
Bandung **52** D 7
Banes **22** G 3
Banff National Park **10** T 8
Bangalore **46** D 6
Bangar **52** F 5
Banggai, Kepulauan **52** G 6
Banggi **52** F 4
Banghāzī **56** F 1
Bangka **52** D 6
Bangkinang **52** C 5
Bangko **52** C 6
Bangkok **47** J 6
Bangladesh **47** F 4
Bangor (Northern Ireland, U.K.) **28** B 2
Bangor (U.S.) **14** F 2
Bangor (Wales, U.K.) **28** B 3
Bangor Erris **31** B 1
Bangui **56** E 4
Banī Suwayf **56** G 2
Banihāl Pass **45** N 6
Banja Luka **34** D 2
Banjarmasin **52** E 6
Banjul **56** B 3
Banks Island (British Columbia, Canada) **10** Q 8
Banks Island (Northwest Territories, Canada) **10** S 4
Banks Peninsula **62** B 3
Banks, Îles **59** F 5
Bannu **45** M 6
Banská Bystrica **36** D 3
Bantaeng **52** F 7
Bantry **31** B 3
Bantry Bay **31** A 3
Banyuwangi **52** E 7
Bao Ha **47** J 4
Bao Loc **47** K 6
Baoding **49** K 3
Baoji **49** H 4
Baoqing **54** B 1
Baoshan **48** F 5
Baoting **47** K 5
Baotou **49** H 2
Baoying **49** K 4

Baqanas **45** N 4
Bar Harbor **14** F 2
Barabinsk **41** R 6
Barabinskaya Stepū **41** R 7
Baragarh **46** E 4
Barahona **22** H 4
Barakaldo **32** B 3
Baranagar **46** F 4
Baranavichy **36** F 2
Baranof Island **10** P 7
Barbados **22** L 5
Barbaria, Cap de **33** C 2
Barbuda **22** K 4
Barca **20** D 3
Barcaldine **60** H 4
Barcelona (Venezuela) **22** K 5
Bardeskan **45** J 5
Bareilly **46** D 3
Barents Sea **40** J 3
Barentsevo More **40** J 3
Barguzinskiy Khrebet **41** X 6
Bari **34** D 2
Barinas **22** H 6
Barisal **47** G 4
Barisan, Pegunungan **52** C 6
Barkly Tableland **60** F 3
Bârlad **36** F 3
Bârlad (Romania) **35** B 1
Barlee Range **60** B 4
Barlee, Lake **60** C 5
Barletta **34** D 2
Barmer **46** C 3
Barmouth **28** B 3
Barnaul **41** S 7
Barnes Icecap **8** W 4
Barnstaple **28** B 4
Barquisimeto **22** J 5
Barra (U.K.) **30** A 3
Barra Patuca **20** H 4
Barragem de Sobradinho **24** G 4
Barrancabermeja **22** H 6
Barranquilla **22** H 5
Barraute **14** D 1
Barreiras **24** G 4
Barren Island, Cape **60** H 8
Barren Islands **43** Z 5
Barrie **14** D 2
Barro **31** C 2
Barrow **10** L 4
Barrow Island **60** B 4
Barrow Range **60** D 5
Barrow, Point **10** L 4
Barrow-in-Furness **28** C 2
Barry **28** C 4
Barsak, Poluo **45** J 3
Barshyn **45** L 3
Bārsi **46** D 5
Barstow **18** C 5
Bartın **35** E 4
Bartlesville **16** D 4
Baruun Urt **50** B 3
Barysaw **36** F 2
Basel **36** B 3
Bashi Haixia **49** L 6
Basilan **52** G 4
Basilan City **52** G 4
Basildon **28** E 4
Basingstoke **28** D 4
Başkale **35** L 5
Baskatong, Réservoir **14** D 1
Basmat **46** D 5
Baso **52** C 6
Basra **44** G 6
Bass Strait **60** G 8
Bass, Îlots de **59** L 6
Bassein **47** G 5
Basse-Terre (Guadeloupe) **22** K 4
Basseterre (St. Kitts and Nevis) **22** K 4
Bastia **34** B 2
Bastrop **16** E 5
Basuo **47** K 5
Batabanó, Golfo del **20** H 3
Batac **52** G 2
Bataklik Gölü **44** D 5
Batam **52** C 5
Batang **52** D 7
Batangas **52** G 3
Batchawana Mountain **14** C 1
Bătdâmbăng **47** J 6
Bath (U.K.) **28** C 4
Bath (U.S.) **14** F 2
Batha **56** E 3
Bathurst (Australia) **60** H 6
Bathurst (Canada) **8** X 9
Bathurst Inlet **10** V 5
Bathurst Island (Australia) **60** E 2
Bathurst Island (Canada) **8** R 3
Bathurst, Cape **10** R 4
Batman **44** F 5
Batna **56** D 1
Baton Rouge **16** E 5
Batopilas **20** C 2
Batti Malv **47** G 7
Batticaloa **46** E 7
Battle Creek **14** B 2
Battle Harbour **8** Z 8
Battle Mountain **18** C 3
Batu Pahat **52** C 5
Batulicin **52** F 6
Batūumi **35** J 4
Baturaja **52** C 6
Baubau **52** G 7
Bauchi **56** D 3
Bauld, Cape **8** Z 8
Bauru **24** F 5
Bavispe **18** E 5
Bawean **52** E 7
Bay Bulls **8** Aa 9
Bay City (Michigan, U.S.) **14** C 2
Bay City (Texas, U.S.) **20** E 2
Bay Springs **14** B 4
Bayamo **22** G 3
Bayan **50** E 3
Bayan Har Shan **48** F 4
Bayan Har Shankou **48** F 4
Bayan Mod **49** G 2
Bayan Obo **49** H 2
Bayanaūyl **45** N 2
Bayburt **35** J 4
Baydhabo **58** D 1
Bayerischer Wald **36** C 3
Baykal **41** W 7
Baykal, Ozero **41** X 7
Baykalūskiy Khrebet **41** X 7
Baykit **41** V 5
Baymak **40** N 7
Bayo Nuevo **22** G 4
Bayombong **52** G 2
Bayonne **32** B 3
Bayramali **45** K 5
Bayreuth **36** C 3
Baysa **42** F 6
Baytik Shan **48** E 1
Baytown **20** F 2
Baza **33** B 2
Bazhi **45** P 2
Bazhong **49** H 4
Beach **16** C 2
Beacon **60** B 6
Beal Range **60** G 5
Bear Lake **18** D 3
Bear Lodge Mountains **18** E 3
Bears Paw Mountain **18** E 2
Bearskin Lake **10** Y 8
Beata, Cabo **22** H 4
Beatrice **16** D 3
Beatrice, Cape **60** F 2
Beatton River **10** S 7
Beatty **18** C 4
Beaufort (U.S.) **14** C 4
Beaufort Sea **10** N 4
Beaumont **16** E 5
Beaune **32** C 2
Beaupré **8** W 9
Beausejour **16** D 1
Beauvais **32** C 2
Beaver (Utah, U.S.) **18** D 4
Beaver Dam **14** B 2
Beaver Island **8** T 9
Beaverton **18** B 2
Beawar **46** C 3
Becan **20** F 4
Bečej **36** E 3
Béchar **56** C 1
Becharof Lake **10** L 7
Beckley **14** C 3
Bedford (Indiana, U.S.) **14** B 3
Bedford (Pennsylvania, U.S.) **14** D 2
Bedford (U.K.) **28** D 3
Beech Grove **14** B 3
Beeville **20** E 2
Beger **48** F 1
Bégles **32** B 3

Behbehān **44** H 6
Behshahr **44** H 5
Bei Hulsan Hu **48** E 3
Bei Shan **48** F 2
Beian **50** E 3
Beibu Wan **47** K 4
Beihai **49** H 6
Beijing **49** K 3
Beiliu **49** J 6
Bein Hoa **47** K 6
Beipiao **50** D 4
Beira **58** C 3
Beirut **44** E 6
Beishan **48** F 2
Beizhen **50** D 4
Beja **33** A 2
Béjah **56** D 1
Bejaïa **56** D 1
Bekasi **52** D 7
Békéscsaba **36** E 3
Bekobod **45** L 4
Bela **46** B 3
Belaga **52** E 5
Belarus **36** E 2
Belaya **40** N 6
Belaya Glina **44** F 3
Belaya Kalitva **44** F 3
Belaya Kholunitsa **40** M 6
Bełchatów **36** D 2
Belcher Islands **8** U 7
Belcheragh **45** L 5
Belebey **44** H 2
Beledweyne **56** H 4
Belém **24** G 3
Belen **18** E 5
Belfast **28** B 2
Belfield **16** C 2
Belfort **36** B 3
Belgaum **46** C 5
Belgorod **44** E 2
Belgrade **34** E 2
Belinyu **52** D 6
Belitung **52** D 6
Belize **20** G 4
Belize (Country) **20** G 4
Belize (River, Belize) **20** G 4
Bella Coola **10** R 8
Bellary **46** D 5
Belle Fourche River **16** C 3
Belle Glade **14** C 5
Belle Isle **8** Z 8
Belle-Île **32** B 2
Belleville (Canada) **14** D 2
Belleville (Kansas, U.S.) **16** D 4
Bellevue (Nebraska, U.S.) **16** D 3
Bellevue (Washington, U.S.) **18** B 2
Bellingham **18** B 2
Bello **22** G 6
Bellona Island **61** K 2
Belluno **36** C 3
Belmopan **20** G 4
Belmullet **31** B 1
Belo Horizonte **24** G 5
Belo Tsiribihina **58** D 3
Belogorsk **50** E 2
Beloit **14** B 2
Belomorsk **40** H 5
Belorechensk **44** E 4
Belot, Lac **10** R 5
Belovo **41** T 7
Beloye More **40** J 4
Beloye, Ozero **40** J 5
Belozersk **40** J 5
Belsham **48** F 2
Belukha **45** P 2
Belushūya Guba **40** M 3
Belyy Yar **41** T 6
Belyy, Ostrov **40** Q 3
Bemidji **16** D 2
Bemidji, Lake **16** E 2
Ben Tre **47** K 6
Benares **46** E 3
Benavente **33** A 1
Bend **18** B 3
Bendigo **60** G 7
Benevento **34** C 2
Bengal, Bay of **47** F 5
Bengbu **49** K 4
Bengkulu **52** C 6
Benguela **58** A 3
Beni Mellal **56** C 1
Benidorm **33** C 2
Benin **56** D 3
Benin City **56** D 4
Benito Juarez **20** F 4
Benkelman **16** C 3
Benson **18** D 5
Bentinck Island **60** F 3
Benton **16** E 5
Bentong **52** C 5
Benue **56** E 4
Benxi **50** D 4
Beograd **34** E 2
Beppu **54** B 4
Berat **34** D 2
Berbera **56** H 3
Berbérati **56** E 4
Berchtesgaden **36** C 3
Berdigestyakh **42** J 4
Berdsk **41** S 7
Berdyansūk **35** G 1
Berdychiv **36** F 3
Berehove **36** E 3
Berens River **10** X 8
Berezevo **40** P 5
Berezivka **44** D 3
Berezniki **40** N 6
Berezovo **40** O 5
Berezovskiy **41** T 6
Berg **38** J 2
Berga **32** C 3
Bergamo **35** B 5
Bergamo **36** B 3
Bergen **38** G 3
Bergerac **32** C 3
Bergö **38** K 3
Bergslagen **38** H 3
Berhampore **46** F 4
Berhampur **46** E 5
Bering Glacier **10** O 6
Bering Land Bridge National Reserve **43** X 3
Bering Sea **43** T 5
Beringa, Ostrov **43** R 5
Beringovskiy **43** T 4
Berkeley **18** B 4
Berkner Island **63** N 4
Berlin (Germany) **36** C 2
Berlin (U.S.) **14** E 2
Bern **36** B 3
Bernalillo **18** E 4
Berner Alpen **36** B 3
Berry Islands **14** D 5
Berwick-upon-Tweed **28** C 2
Besançon **36** B 3
Beskidy Zachodnie **36** D 3
Beslan **35** L 3
Besni **35** G 6
Bessemer **14** B 4
Bestöbe **45** M 2
Bethany **16** D 4
Bethlehem **58** B 4
Béticos, Sistemas **33** B 2
Betong **47** J 7
Betpak-Dala **45** M 3
Betroka **58** D 4
Bettiah **46** E 3
Bettles **10** M 5
Betul **46** D 4
Beveridge Reef **59** J 5
Beverley **28** D 3
Bexhill **28** E 4
Beyoneisu-retsugan **54** D 4
Beypazarı **35** D 4
Beyşehir **35** D 6
Bezhetsk **40** J 6
Béziers **32** C 3
Bhadrakh **46** F 4
Bhadravāti **46** D 6
Bhagalpur **46** F 3
Bhairab Bāzār **47** G 4
Bhakkar **46** C 2
Bhaktapur **46** F 3
Bharatpur **46** D 3
Bharuch **46** C 4
Bhātpāra **46** F 4
Bhawanipatna **46** E 5
Bhilwara **46** C 3
Bhiwani **46** D 3
Bhongir **46** D 5
Bhopal **46** D 4
Bhubaneshwar **46** F 4
Bhuj **46** B 4
Bhusawal **46** D 4
Bhutan **47** F 3

Biak **59** C 4
Biała Podlaska **36** E 2
Białogard **36** D 2
Białystok **36** E 2
Biaora **46** D 4
Biaro **52** H 5
Biarritz **32** B 3
Bickerton Island **60** F 2
Bīd **46** D 5
Bīdar **46** D 5
Biddeford **14** E 2
Bideford **28** B 4
Bidzhan **50** F 3
Biel **36** B 3
Bielefeld **36** B 2
Bielsk Podlaski **36** E 2
Bielsko-Biała **36** D 3
Bienville, Lac **8** W 7
Big Belt Mountains **18** D 2
Big Bend National Park **20** D 2
Big Cypress National Reserve **14** C 5
Big Horn Lake **18** E 2
Big Horn Mountains **18** E 3
Big Horn River **18** E 2
Big Island **8** W 6
Big Rapids **14** B 2
Big Sioux River **16** D 3
Big Smoky Valley **18** C 4
Big Snowy Mountains **18** E 2
Big Spring **16** C 5
Big Trout Lake **8** T 8
Bighorn Basin **18** E 3
Bight of Benin **56** D 4
Bihać **34** D 2
Bihār **46** F 3
Bihār (State) **46** F 3
Bijapur **46** D 5
Bijeljina **34** D 2
Bijelo Polje **34** D 2
Bijie **49** H 5
Bijoutier **58** E 2
Bikaner **46** C 3
Bikar **59** G 2
Bikin **50** F 3
Bikini **59** F 2
Bila Tserkva **44** D 3
Bilaspur **46** E 4
Bilauktaung Range **47** H 6
Bilbao **32** B 3
Bilecik **35** C 4
Bilhorod-Dnistrovsūkyy **35** D 1
Billings **18** E 2
Bilopillya **36** G 2
Biloxi **14** B 4
Bimini Islands **14** D 5
Bin Xian **50** E 3
Bin Xian (Heilongjiang, China) **54** A 1
Bina-Etāwa **46** D 4
Binaiya, Gunung **52** H 6
Binghampton **14** D 2
Bingöl **35** J 5
Binhai **49** K 4
Binjai (Indonesia) **52** B 5
Binjai (Indonesia) **52** D 5
Binongko **52** G 7
Bintan **52** C 5
Bintuhan **52** C 6
Bintulu **52** E 5
Binyang **49** H 6
Bioko **56** D 4
Bira **50** G 3
Bira (Russia) **54** B 1
Bira (Russia) **50** G 3
Birakan **54** B 1
Biratnagar **46** F 3
Bird **8** S 7
Birdsville **60** F 5
Birikchulū **41** T 7
Birkenhead **28** C 3
Birksgate Range **60** D 5
Birmingham (U.K.) **28** D 3
Birmingham (U.S.) **14** B 4
Birmitrapur **46** E 4
Birnie Island **59** H 4
Birnin-Kebbi **56** D 3
Birobidzhan **50** F 3
Birsk **40** N 6
Biryusa **41** V 7
Bisbee **18** E 5
Biscay, Bay of **32** B 2
Bishkek **45** M 4
Bishop **18** C 4
Bishop Rock **28** A 5
Biskra **56** D 1
Bislig **52** H 4
Bismarck **16** C 2
Bismarck Archipelago **59** D 4
Bismarck Range **59** D 4
Bismarck Sea **59** D 4
Bismarck, Kap **8** Hh 3
Bison **16** C 2
Bissau **56** B 3
Bissett **16** D 1
Bistriţa **36** E 3
Bitlis **35** K 5
Bitola **34** E 2
Bitterroot Range **18** C 2
Biu **56** E 3
Biwa-ko **54** C 3
Biya **41** T 7
Biysk **41** T 7
Björkön **38** K 3
Björneborg **38** K 3
Black Hills **16** C 3
Black Mountain **14** C 3
Black Mountains **28** C 3
Black Range **18** E 5
Black River Falls **16** E 3
Black Rock Desert **18** C 3
Black Sea **35** E 3
Blackall **60** H 4
Blackburn **28** C 3
Blackfoot **18** D 3
Blackpool **28** C 3
Blackwater (U.K.) **31** B 2
Blackwell **16** D 4
Blagodatnyy **50** G 3
Blagoevgrad **34** E 2
Blagoveshchensk (Russia) **40** N 6
Blagoveshchensk (Russia) **42** J 6
Blaine **16** E 2
Blair **16** D 3
Blanche, Lake **60** F 5
Blanco, Cape **18** B 3
Blanc-Sablon **8** Z 8
Blantyre **58** C 3
Būldudalur **38** A 2
Blekinge **38** J 4
Blenheim **62** B 3
Blida **56** D 1
Blind River **14** C 1
Blitar **52** E 7
Bloemfontein **58** B 4
Blois **32** C 2
Bloody Foreland **31** B 1
Bloomington (Illinois, U.S.) **14** B 2
Bloomington (Indiana, U.S.) **14** B 3
Bloomington (Minnesota, U.S.) **16** E 3
Blora **52** E 7
Blosseville Kyst **8** Ff 5
Blossom, Mys **43** T 2
Blue Mountain Lake **14** E 2
Blue Mountains **60** H 6
Blue Ridge **14** C 3
Bluefield **14** C 3
Bluenose Lake **10** S 5
Bluff **62** A 4
Blumenau **24** G 5
Blyth **28** D 2
Blythe **18** D 5
Blytheville **14** B 3
Bo **56** B 4
Bo Hai **49** K 3
Bo Xian **49** K 4
Boa Vista **56** A 3
Boa Vista (Brazil) **22** K 7
Boac **52** G 3
Boano **52** H 6
Bobai **49** H 6
Bobbili **46** E 5
Bobo Dioulasso **56** C 3
Bobrov **44** F 2
Bobrynetsū **44** D 3
Boca Grande **22** K 6
Boca Raton **14** C 5
Bochum **36** B 2
Bocşa **36** E 3
Bodaybo **42** F 5
Bodélé **56** E 3

Bodhan **46** D 5
Bodjonegoro **52** E 7
Bodmin Moor **28** B 4
Bodø **38** H 2
Bodrum **35** B 6
Boeng Tonle Chhma **47** J 6
Bogale **47** H 5
Bogalusa **14** B 4
Boghra Dam **45** K 6
Bognor Regis **28** D 4
Bogo **52** G 3
Bogor **52** D 7
Bogoroditsk **44** E 2
Bogotá **22** H 7
Bogotol **41** T 6
Bogra **47** F 4
Boguchany **41** V 6
Bohai Haixia **49** L 3
Böhmerwald **36** C 3
Bohodukhiv **44** E 2
Bohol **52** G 4
Bohuslän **38** H 4
Bois, Lac des **10** R 5
Boise **18** C 3
Boise City **16** C 4
Boise River **18** C 3
Boissevain **16** C 2
Bojnūrd **45** J 5
Bolan Pass **46** B 3
Bole (China) **48** C 2
Bolesławiec **36** D 2
Bolgatanga **56** C 3
Boli **50** F 3
Bolivia **24** E 4
Bolkhov **44** E 2
Bollnäs **38** J 3
Bologna **34** C 2
Bologoye **40** H 6
Bolonū **50** G 3
Bolotnoye **41** S 6
Bolūshaya Chernigovka **44** H 2
Bolūshaya Glushitsa **44** H 2
Bolūshaya Kuonamka **41** X 4
Bolūsheretsk **43** P 6
Bolūshevik, Ostrov **41** W 2
Bolūshezemelūskaya Tundra **40** N 4
Bolūshoy Begichev, Ostrov **41** Y 3
Bolūshoy Kamenū **54** B 2
Bolūshoy Kavkaz **35** J 3
Bolūshoy Lyakhovskiy, Ostrov **42** M 2
Bolūshoy Porog **41** U 4
Bolūshoy Shantar **42** L 6
Bolton **28** C 3
Bolu **35** D 4
Bolvadin **35** D 5
Bolzano **36** C 3
Boma **58** A 2
Bombala **60** H 7
Bombay **46** C 5
Bømlo **38** F 4
Bon, Cap **34** C 3
Bona, Mount **10** O 6
Bonaire **22** J 5
Bonampak **20** F 4
Bonanza **20** H 5
Bonaparte Archipelago **60** C 2
Bondowoso **52** E 7
Bongka **52** G 6
Bongor **56** E 3
Bonifacio, Strait of **34** B 2
Bonito, Pico **20** G 4
Bonn **36** B 2
Bonners Ferry **18** C 2
Bonneville Saltflats **18** D 3
Boon **14** C 1
Böön Tsagaan Nuur **48** F 1
Boone **16** E 3
Booneville **16** E 4
Boosaaso **56** H 3
Boothia, Gulf of **8** S 4
Boquillas del Carmen **20** D 2
Bor (Russia) **40** K 6
Bor (Turkey) **35** F 6
Bor (Yugoslavia) **34** E 2
Bora-Bora **59** K 5
Borås **38** H 4
Borçka **44** F 4
Bordeaux **32** B 3
Borden Island **10** U 3
Borden Peninsula **8** U 4
Bordertown **60** G 7
Borgholm **38** J 4
Borisoglebsk **44** F 2
Borlänge **38** J 3
Borneo **52** E 6
Bornholm **36** D 2
Borogontsy **42** K 4
Borohoro Shan **48** C 2
Boroko **52** G 5
Borovichi **40** H 6
Borovskoye **40** O 7
Borroloola **60** F 3
Borşa **36** E 3
Boryslav **36** E 3
Boryspilū **36** G 2
Borzya **42** G 6
Bose **49** H 6
Boshan **49** K 3
Boshnyakovo **54** D 1
Bosnia-Herzegovina **34** D 2
Bosnian-Croat Federation **34** D 2
Bosporus **35** C 4
Bossier City **16** E 5
Bosten Hu **48** D 2
Boston (U.K.) **28** D 3
Boston (U.S.) **14** E 2
Boston Mountains **16** E 4
Bothnia, Gulf of **38** J 3
Botoşani **36** F 3
Botswana **58** B 4
Bou Saâda **56** D 1
Bouaké **56** C 4
Bouar **56** E 4
Boufarik **33** C 2
Bougainville Island **59** E 4
Bougainville Reef **59** E 5
Bougainville Strait **59** E 4
Bouïra **33** C 2
Boulder (U.S.) **18** E 3
Boulia **60** F 4
Boulogne-sur-Mer **28** E 4
Bountiful **18** D 3
Bourg-en-Bresse **36** B 3
Bourges **32** C 2
Bourgogne **32** C 2
Bourke **60** H 6
Bournemouth **28** D 4
Bow River **18** D 1
Bowen **60** H 3
Bowling Green **14** B 3
Bowling Green, Cape **60** H 3
Bowman **16** C 2
Boxing **49** K 3
Boyabat **35** F 4
Boyang **49** K 5
Boyarka **41** V 3
Boyle **31** B 2
Bozashchy Tūbegi **44** H 3
Bozema **18** D 2
Brač **34** D 2
Bräcke **38** J 3
Bradenton **14** C 5
Bradford (U.K.) **28** D 3
Bradford (U.S.) **14** D 2
Brady **16** D 5
Braemar **30** C 3
Braga **33** A 1
Bragança (Portugal) **33** A 1
Brahmapur **46** E 5
Brahmaputra **48** E 5
Braich y Pwll **28** B 3
Brăila **35** B 2
Brainerd **16** E 2
Brakna **56** B 3
Brampton **14** D 2
Brandenburg **36** C 2
Brandon **16** D 2
Braniewo **36** D 2
Brantford **14** C 2
Bras dūOr, Lake **8** Y 9
Brasília **24** G 4
Braşov **35** A 2
Bratislava **36** D 3
Bratsk **41** W 6
Bratskoye Vodokhranilishche **41** W 6
Brattleboro **14** E 2
Braunschweig **36** C 2
Brava **56** A 3
Bravo del Norte, Río **18** E 5
Brawley **18** C 5
Bray Island **8** V 5
Brazas River **16** D 5

Brazil **24** F 3
Brazilian Highlands **24** G 5
Brazzaville **58** A 2
Brčko **34** D 2
Brebes **52** D 7
Breckenridge **16** D 5
Břeclav **36** D 3
Brecon **28** C 4
Bredbyn **38** J 3
Bredy **45** K 2
Breiðafjörður **38** A 2
Breiðdalur **38** C 3
Bremen **36** B 2
Bremer Bay **60** B 6
Bremerhaven **36** B 2
Bremerton **18** B 2
Brenner Pass **36** C 3
Brescia **36** C 3
Bressay **30** D 1
Bressuire **32** B 2
Brest (Belarus) **36** E 2
Brest (France) **32** B 2
Bretagne **32** B 2
Brett, Cape **62** B 2
Breueh **47** G 7
Brevoort Island **8** Y 6
Brewster, Kap **8** Gg 4
Brewton **14** B 4
Bridgeport (California, U.S.) **18** C 4
Bridgeport (Connecticut, U.S.) **14** E 2
Bridger Peak **18** E 3
Bridgetown **22** L 5
Bridgwater **28** C 4
Bridlington **28** D 2
Bridlington Bay **28** D 3
Brigham City **18** D 3
Brighton **28** D 4
Brindisi **34** D 2
Brisbane **60** J 5
Bristol (U.K.) **28** C 4
Bristol (U.S.) **14** C 3
Bristol Bay **43** X 5
Bristol Channel **28** B 4
British Columbia **10** R 7
British Virgin Islands **22** K 4
Brive-la-Gaillarde **32** C 2
Brno **36** D 3
Broadford **30** B 3
Broadus **18** E 2
Broadview **16** C 1
Brochet, Lac **10** W 7
Brock Island **10** U 3
Brockville **14** D 2
Brodeur Peninsula **8** T 4
Brodnica **36** D 2
Brody **36** F 2
Broken Hill **60** G 6
Brønnøysund **38** H 2
Brookfield **16** E 4
Brookhaven **16** E 5
Brookings (Oregon, U.S.) **18** B 3
Brookings (South Dakota, U.S.) **16** D 3
Brooks **18** D 1
Brooks Range **10** L 5
Broome **60** C 3
Brora **30** C 2
Broutona, Ostrov **50** J 3
Browne Range Nature Reserve **60** C 4
Brownfield **16** C 5
Browning **18** D 2
Brownsville **20** E 2
Brownwood **16** D 5
Bruce Peninsula **14** C 1
Bruneau **18** C 3
Brunei **52** E 4
Brunswick **14** C 4
Bryan **16** D 5
Bryansk **36** G 2
Brzeg **36** D 2
Bucak **35** D 6
Bucaramanga **22** H 6
Buccaneer Archipelago **60** C 3
Buchanan, Lake (Australia) **60** C 5
Buchanan, Lake (U.S.) **16** D 5
Bucharest **34** F 2
București **35** B 2
Bucyrus **14** C 2
Budapest **36** D 3
Budaun **46** D 3
Bude **28** B 4
Bude Bay **28** B 4
Budennovsk **35** L 2
Buēagra **35** J 7
Buenaventura **22** G 7
Buenaventura (Mexico) **20** C 2
Buenos Aires **24** E 6
Buffalo (New York, U.S.) **14** D 2
Buffalo (South Dakota, U.S.) **16** C 2
Buffalo (Wyoming, U.S.) **18** E 3
Buffalo Lake **10** T 6
Buftea **35** A 2
Buga **22** G 7
Bugrino **40** L 4
Bugsuk Island **52** F 4
Bugt **50** D 3
Bugulūma **44** H 2
Buguruslan **44** H 2
Builth Wells **28** C 3
Buinsk **44** G 2
Bujumbura **58** B 2
Buka Island **59** E 4
Bukachacha **42** G 6
Bukavu **58** B 2
Bukhta Tikhaya **40** M 1
Bukit Gandadiwata **52** F 6
Bukittinggi **52** C 6
Bula **52** J 6
Būlaevo **40** Q 7
Bulan **52** G 3
Bulandshahr **46** D 3
Bulawayo **58** B 4
Buldan **35** C 5
Buldir Island **43** T 6
Bulgaria **34** F 2
Bull Shoals Lake **16** E 4
Buller **62** B 3
Bullfinch **60** B 6
Bulukumba **52** G 7
Bulun **42** J 2
Bumba **58** B 1
Bunbury **60** B 6
Buncrana **31** C 1
Bundaberg **60** J 4
Bungo-suido **54** B 4
Bunia **58** B 1
Bunkie **16** E 5
Buntok **52** E 6
Bünyan **35** F 5
Buolkalakh **42** G 2
Buon Me Thuot **47** K 6
Buorkhaya, Mys **42** K 2
Būr Saūīd (Port Said) **56** G 1
Būr Sūdān (Port Sudan) **56** G 2
Burco **56** H 4
Burdur **35** D 6
Burdur Gölü **44** C 5
Burdwan **46** F 4
Bureiskiy, Khrebet **42** K 6
Burgas **35** B 3
Burgaski Zahiv **35** C 3
Burgos **32** B 3
Burgos (Mexico) **20** E 3
Burgsvik **38** J 4
Burhanpur **46** D 4
Buri Ram **47** J 5
Burias **52** G 3
Burica, Punta **22** F 6
Burketown **60** F 3
Burkina Faso **56** C 3
Burley **18** D 3
Burlington (Colorado, U.S.) **16** C 4
Burlington (Iowa, U.S.) **16** E 3
Burlington (Vermont, U.S.) **14** E 2
Burma **47** G 4
Burney **18** B 3
Burnie **60** H 8
Burns **18** C 3
Burns Lake **10** R 8
Burra **60** F 6
Bursa **35** C 4
Burtha Qi **50** D 3
Buru **52** H 6
Burundi **58** B 2
Bury St Edmunds **28** E 3
Burylbaytal **45** M 3
Buskerud **38** G 3
Buskul **45** K 2
Busselton **60** B 6

Bussolū, Proliv **50** K 3
Busuanga **52** F 3
Butembo **58** B 2
Buton **52** G 6
Butt of Lewis **30** A 2
Butte **18** D 2
Butterworth **52** C 4
Button Islands **8** X 6
Butuan **52** H 4
Buturlinovka **44** F 2
Buxoro **45** K 5
Buy **40** K 6
Buynaksk **44** G 4
Buzău **36** F 3
Buzluk Dağ **35** F 4
Buzuluk **44** H 2
Byahomlū **36** F 2
Byam Martin Island **10** W 3
Byam Martin, Cape **8** V 4
Bydgoszcz **36** D 2
Bykhaw **36** G 2
Bykov **54** D 1
Bykovo **40** L 5
Bylot Island **8** V 4
Byrranga, Gory **41** V 3
Bytom **36** D 2
Ca Mau **47** K 7
Cabadbaran **52** H 4
Caballo Reservoir **18** E 5
Cabanatuan **52** G 2
Cabimas **22** H 5
Cabinda (Angola) **58** A 2
Cabinet Mountains **18** C 2
Cabo De Santa Marta **58** A 3
Cabo Frio **24** G 5
Cabonga, Réservoir **14** D 1
Caborca **18** D 5
Cabrera, Isla de **33** C 2
Čačak **34** E 2
Caçapava do Sul **24** F 6
Caccia, Capo **34** B 2
Cáceres (Spain) **33** A 2
Cachoeira Aquibi **24** F 4
Cachoeira das Ilhas **24** F 3
Cachoeira do Chacorão **24** F 3
Cachoeira dos Patos **24** E 3
Cachoeira Nova Vida **24** E 3
Cachoeira Pereira **24** F 3
Cachoeira Santana **24** G 4
Cadillac **14** B 2
Cádiz **33** A 2
Cadiz **52** G 3
Cádiz, Golfo de **33** A 2
Caen **32** B 2
Caernarfon **28** B 3
Caernarfon Bay **28** B 3
Cagayan de Oro **52** G 4
Cagayan Islands **52** F 4
Cagliari **34** B 3
Cagnes **34** B 2
Caguas **22** J 4
Caha Mountains **31** B 3
Cahersiveen **31** A 3
Cahir **31** C 2
Cahore Point **31** C 2
Cahors **32** C 3
Caibarién **22** G 3
Caicos Islands **22** H 3
Cairngorm Mountains **30** C 3
Cairns **60** H 3
Caithness **30** C 2
Cajamarca **24** D 3
Calabozo **22** J 6
Calafat **34** E 2
Calagua Islands **52** G 3
Calahorra **32** B 3
Ćalāūib **56** G 2
Calais **28** E 4
Calais, Pas de **28** E 4
Calakmul **20** G 4
Calamian Group **52** F 3
Calapan **52** G 3
Calatayud **32** B 3
Calayan **49** L 7
Calbayog **52** G 3
Calcutta **46** F 4
Caldas da Rainha **33** A 2
Caldwell **18** C 3
Calgary **10** U 8
Cali **22** G 7
Calicut **46** D 6
Caliente **18** D 4
California **18** B 4
California, Golfo de **20** B 2
Callao **24** D 4
Caltanissetta **34** C 3
Calvi **34** B 2
Cam Ranh **47** K 6
Camagüey **22** G 3
Camarat, Cap **34** B 2
Camarón, Cabo **20** G 4
Cambodia **47** J 6
Cambrian Mountains **28** B 4
Cambridge (Idaho, U.S.) **18** C 3
Cambridge (Maryland, U.S.) **14** D 3
Cambridge (Massachusetts, U.S.) **14** E 2
Cambridge (U.K.) **28** E 3
Cambridge Bay **10** V 5
Camden **16** E 5
Cameron **16** E 2
Cameroon **56** D 4
Camiguin **52** G 2
Camooweal **60** F 3
Camorta **47** G 7
Camp Verde **18** D 5
Campbell River **10** R 8
Campbell, Cape **62** B 3
Campbelltown **60** J 6
Campbeltown **28** B 2
Campeche (Mexico) **20** F 4
Campeche (State, Mexico) **20** F 4
Campeche, Bahía de **20** F 4
Campina Grande **24** H 3
Campinas **24** G 5
Campo Grande **24** F 5
Campobasso **34** C 2
Campos **24** G 4
Campos **24** G 5
Camrose **10** U 8
Can Tho **47** K 6
Canada **10** V 7
Canadian **16** C 4
Canadian River **16** C 4
Çanakkale (Turkey) **35** B 4
Çanakkale Boğazi **34** F 3
Cananea **18** D 5
Canarreos, Archipiélago de los **22** F 3
Canary Islands (Spain) **56** B 2
Canaveral, Cape **14** C 5
Canberra **60** H 7
Cancún **20** G 3
Candelaria **20** F 4
Cando **16** D 2
Cangzhou **49** K 3
Çankırı **35** E 4
Cannanore **46** D 6
Cannes **34** B 2
Canoas **24** F 5
Canon City **18** E 4
Canora **10** W 8
Cantábrica, Cordillera **33** A 1
Canterbury **28** E 4
Canterbury Bight **62** B 3
Canterbury Plains **62** B 3
Canton (China) **49** J 6
Canton (Mississippi, U.S.) **16** E 5
Canton (Ohio, U.S.) **14** C 2
Canyon **16** C 5
Cao Bang **47** K 4
Cao Xian **49** K 4
Cap Blanc **56** B 2
Cap de Formentor **33** C 2
Cap Rhir **56** B 1
Cap Vert **56** B 3
Cap-de-la-Madeleine **14** E 1
Cape Arid National Park **60** C 6
Cape Breton Highlands National Park **8** Y 9
Cape Breton Island **8** Y 9
Cape Charles **14** D 3
Cape Coast **56** C 4
Cape Cod Bay **14** E 2
Cape Columbine **58** A 5
Cape Coral **14** C 5
Cape Dorset **8** V 6
Cape Girardeau **14** B 3
Cape Horn **24** E 8
Cape Krusenstern National Monument **10** K 5
Cape May **14** E 3
Cape of Good Hope **58** A 5
Cape Smith **8** V 6

Cape Town **58** A 5
Cape Verde **56** A 3
Cape Yakataga **10** O 6
Cape York Peninsula **60** G 2
Cap-Haïtien **22** H 4
Capreol **14** C 1
Capricorn Channel **60** J 4
Capricorn Group **60** J 4
Car Nicobar **47** G 7
Caracal **34** E 2
Caracas **22** J 5
Caratasca, Laguna de **20** H 4
Carbonara, Capo **34** B 3
Carbonia **34** B 3
Carcassonne **32** C 3
Carcross **10** Q 6
Cárdenas **22** F 3
Cárdenas (Mexico) **20** E 3
Cardiff **28** C 4
Cardigan **28** B 3
Cardigan Bay **28** B 3
Cardston **18** D 2
Carei **36** E 3
Carey Øer **8** W 3
Carey, Lake **60** C 5
Caribbean Sea **22** G 5
Caribou **14** F 1
Carleton Place **14** D 1
Carletonville **58** B 4
Carlisle **28** C 2
Carlow **31** C 2
Carloway **30** A 2
Carlsbad (California, U.S.) **18** C 5
Carlsbad (New Mexico, U.S.) **16** C 5
Carlyle **16** C 2
Carmacks **10** P 6
Carmarthen **28** B 4
Carmel **18** B 4
Carmel Head **28** B 3
Carmen, Isla **20** B 2
Carmi **14** B 3
Carmichael **18** B 4
Carnarvon (Australia) **60** A 4
Carndonagh **31** C 1
Carnegie, Lake **60** C 5
Carnsore Point **31** C 2
Carolina **24** G 3
Carolina Beach **14** D 4
Caroline Islands **59** D 3
Carondelet **59** H 4
Carora **22** H 5
Carozal **22** G 6
Carpathian Mountains **36** E 3
Carpaţii Meridionali **36** E 3
Carpentaria, Gulf of **60** F 2
Carrara **34** C 2
Carrick-on-Shannon **31** B 2
Carrillo **20** D 2
Carrizal **18** E 5
Carrizo Springs **20** E 2
Carrizozo **18** E 5
Carroll **16** E 3
Carrollton **14** B 4
Çarsamba **35** G 4
Carson **18** B 2
Carson City **18** C 4
Cartagena (Colombia) **22** G 5
Cartagena (Spain) **33** B 2
Carthage **16** E 4
Caruaru **24** H 3
Carupano **22** K 5
Carutapera **24** G 3
Casa Grande **18** D 5
Casablanca **56** C 1
Cascade Range **18** B 3
Cascavel **24** F 5
Caserta **34** C 2
Casino **60** J 5
Casper **18** E 3
Caspian Sea **44** H 4
Cassiar **10** R 7
Castelló de la Plana **33** B 1
Castelo Branco **33** A 2
Castelvetrano **34** C 3
Castilla La Mancha **32** B 3
Castilla y León **33** B 1
Castle Douglas **28** C 2
Castlebar **31** B 2
Castlegar **18** C 2
Castlepoint **62** C 3
Castletown **28** B 2
Castres **32** C 3
Castries **22** K 5
Cat Island **22** G 3
Cataluña **32** C 3
Catanduanes **52** G 3
Catania **34** D 3
Catanzaro **34** D 3
Catastrophe, Cape **60** F 6
Catbalogan **52** G 3
Catoche, Cabo **20** G 3
Catwick Islands **47** K 6
Caucasus **35** J 3
Cavan **31** C 1
Cavell **16** F 1
Cavili **52** F 4
Caxais do Sul **24** F 5
Çay **35** D 5
Çaycuma **35** E 4
Cayenne **24** F 2
Cayman Brac **22** G 4
Cayman Islands **22** F 4
Cebaco, Isla **22** F 6
Ceballos **20** D 2
Ceboruco,Volcán **20** D 3
Cebu **52** G 3
Cedar City **18** D 4
Cedar Creek Reservoir **16** D 5
Cedar Falls **16** E 3
Cedar Rapids **16** E 3
Cedar River **16** E 3
Cedros, Isla **18** C 6
Ceduna **60** E 6
Cefalù **34** C 3
Celaya **20** D 3
Celebes **52** F 6
Celebes Sea **52** G 5
Celestún **20** F 3
Celje **36** D 3
Celle **36** C 2
Celtic Sea **31** C 3
Cendrawasih, Teluk **59** C 4
Centerville **16** E 3
Central African Republic **56** E 4
Central Brahui Range **46** B 3
Central Makrān Range **46** A 3
Central Range **59** D 4
Central, Cordillera (Philippines) **52** G 2
Centralia **18** B 2
Cepu **52** E 7
Ceram **52** H 6
Cereal **10** U 8
Cereté **22** G 6
Cerf **58** E 2
Cerralvo, Isla **20** C 3
Cerritos **20** D 3
Cerro de Pasco **24** D 4
České Budějovice **36** C 3
Çeşme **34** F 3
Cessnock **60** J 6
Ceuta **33** A 2
Cevennes **32** C 3
Ceylânpinar **35** J 6
Cha-Am **47** H 6
Chachoengsao **47** J 6
Chaco Austral **24** E 5
Chaco Boreal **24** E 5
Chaco Central **24** E 5
Chad **56** E 3
Chadron **16** C 3
Chāgai Hills **45** K 7
Chagda **42** K 5
Chagyl **45** J 4
Chai Nat **47** J 5
Chāībāsa **46** F 4
Chakwal **46** C 2
Chalkida **34** E 3
Challenger Deep **59** D 2
Challis **18** D 3
Châlons-en-Champagne **32** C 2
Chalon-sur-Saône **32** C 2
Chaman **45** L 6
Chambéry **36** B 3
Chamela **20** C 4
Champagne **32** C 2
Champasak **47** K 6
Champlain, Lake **14** E 2
Champotón **20** F 4
Chanbogd **49** H 2
Chandalar **10** N 5
Chandeleur Islands **20** G 2
Chandigarh **46** D 2
Chandrapur **46** D 5

Chang Cheng **50** C 4
Chang Rai **47** H 5
Changbai Shan **50** E 4
Changchun **50** E 4
Changde **49** J 5
Chang-hua **49** L 6
Changji **48** D 2
Changjiang **47** K 5
Changjiang (River) **49** H 4
Changli **49** K 3
Changling **50** D 4
Changsha **49** J 5
Changshu **49** L 4
Changting **49** K 5
Changwu **49** H 3
Changzhi **49** J 3
Changzhou **49** K 4
Chania **34** E 3
Channapatna **46** D 6
Channel Islands **32** B 2
Channel Islands (U.S.) **18** C 5
Channel Tunnel **28** E 4
Chanthaburi **47** J 6
Chany, Ozero **45** N 1
Chao Hu **49** K 4
Chaoūan **49** K 6
Chaoyang **50** D 4
Chapaev **44** H 2
Chapala **20** D 3
Chapala, Laguna de **20** D 3
Chapayevsk **44** G 2
Chapleau **8** U 9
Chaplygin **44** E 2
Chara **42** G 4
Charcas **20** D 3
Chari **56** E 3
Charles City **16** E 3
Charles Island **8** W 6
Charles Louis, Pegunungan **59** C 4
Charles Point **60** E 2
Charlesbourg **8** W 9
Charleston (South Carolina, U.S.) **14** D 4
Charleston (West Virginia, U.S.) **14** C 3
Charleville **60** H 5
Charlotte **14** C 3
Charlotte Harbor **14** C 5
Charlottesville **14** D 3
Charlottetown **8** Y 9
Charlton Island **8** U 8
Charsadda **45** M 6
Charters Towers **60** H 4
Chartres **32** C 2
Chasma Barrage **46** C 2
Chasŏng **54** A 2
Châteauroux **32** C 2
Châtellerault **32** C 2
Chatham (Ontario, Canada) **14** C 2
Chatham (U.K.) **28** E 4
Chatham Islands **59** E 5
Chattahoochee **14** C 4
Chattahoochee River **14** C 4
Chattanooga **14** B 3
Chau Phu **47** K 6
Chauk **47** G 4
Chaumont **36** B 3
Chaves **33** A 1
Chaykovskiy **40** M 6
Chazhegovo **40** M 5
Cheb **36** C 2
Cheboksary **40** L 6
Chechūon **50** E 5
Cheduba Island **47** G 5
Chegdomyn **42** K 6
Cheju **50** E 6
Cheju-do **50** E 6
Cheju-haehyŏb **50** E 6
Chekanovskiy **41** W 6
Chekhov **54** D 1
Chełm **36** E 2
Chelmsford **28** E 4
Cheltenham **28** C 4
Chelyabinsk **40** O 6
Chelyuskin, Mys **63** E 1
Chemnitz **36** C 2
Chemult **18** B 3
Chencoyi **20** F 4
Chengūan **49** J 3
Chengde **50** C 4
Chengdu **49** G 4
Chengmai **47** L 5
Chennai **46** E 6
Chenxi **49** J 5
Chenzhou **49** J 5
Chūeŏnan **50** E 5
Cherbaniani Reef **46** C 6
Cherbourg **32** B 2
Cheremkhovo **41** W 7
Cherepanovo **41** S 7
Cherepovets **40** J 6
Cherkasy **44** D 3
Cherkessk **35** K 2
Chermoz **40** N 6
Chernigovka **54** B 2
Chernihiv **36** G 2
Chernivtsi **36** F 3
Chernogorsk **41** U 7
Chernyakhiv **36** F 2
Chernyakhovsk **36** E 2
Chernyy Yar **44** G 3
Chernyye Zemli **44** F 3
Cherokee **16** D 3
Cherokees, Lake oū the **16** E 4
Cherskiy **43** Q 3
Cherskogo, Khrebet **42** F 6
Chervonohrad **36** E 2
Chervyanka **41** V 6
Chervyenū **36** F 2
Chesapeake Bay **14** D 3
Chesapeake Bay Bridge-Tunnel **14** D 3
Cheshkaya Guba **40** L 4
Chester **28** C 3
Chesterfield **28** D 3
Chesterfield Inlet **8** S 6
Chesuncook Lake **14** E 1
Chetlat **46** C 6
Chetumal **20** G 4
Chetumal, Bahía de **20** G 4
Cheviot (New Zealand) **62** B 3
Cheviot Hills **28** C 2
Cheyenne **16** C 3
Cheyenne River **16** C 3
Cheyenne Wells **16** C 4
Cheyne Bay **60** B 6
Chhatarpur **46** D 4
Chhattīsgarh **46** E 4
Chhindwara **46** D 4
Chiai **49** L 6
Chiang Mai **47** H 5
Chiapas **20** F 4
Chiavari **34** B 2
Chiba **54** D 3
Chibougamau **8** W 9
Chicago **14** B 2
Chichagof Island **10** P 7
Chichén Itzá **20** G 3
Chichester Range National Park **60** B 4
Chickasha **16** D 4
Chiclayo **24** C 3
Chico **18** B 4
Chicoutimi **8** W 9
Chidambaram **46** D 6
Chieti **34** C 2
Chifeng **50** C 4
Chihli, Gulf of **49** K 3
Chūihshang **49** L 6
Chihuahua (Mexico) **20** C 2
Chihuahua (State, Mexico) **20** C 2
Chikhacheva **42** N 2
Chilapa de Alvarez **20** E 4
Chilaw **46** D 7
Childress **16** C 5
Chile **24** D 6
Chilecito **24** E 5
Chilik **44** H 2
Chililabombwe **58** B 3
Chilka Lake **46** F 5
Chillán **24** D 6
Chillicothe (Iowa, U.S.) **16** E 4
Chillicothe (Ohio, U.S.) **14** C 3
Chiloquin **18** B 3
Chilpancingo **20** E 4
Chilung **49** L 5
Chimaltenango **20** F 5
Chimbote **24** C 3
Chimoio **58** C 3
Chin Hills **47** G 4
China **49** E 4
Chinandega **22** E 5
Chinchilla **60** J 5

Chinchorro, Banco **20** G 4
Chin-do **50** E 6
Chindwin **47** G 4
Chingola **58** B 3
Chinju **50** E 5
Chioggia **36** C 3
Chios **34** F 3
Chios (Greece) **35** B 5
Chios (Island) **34** F 3
Chippewa Falls **16** E 3
Chippewa, Lake **16** E 2
Chirala **46** E 5
Chirchiq **45** L 4
Chirikof Island **43** Y 5
Chirinda **41** W 4
Chiriqui, Golfo de **22** F 6
Chirpan **35** A 3
Chisasibi **8** V 8
Chişinău **36** F 3
Chistoozernoye **41** R 7
Chistopolū **40** M 6
Chita **42** F 6
Chitose **54** D 2
Chitradurga **46** D 6
Chittagong **47** G 4
Chittaurgarh **46** C 4
Chittoor **46** D 6
Choiseul Island **59** E 4
Choix **20** C 2
Chojnice **36** D 2
Cholet **32** B 2
Choluteca **20** G 5
Chomutov **36** C 2
Chon Buri **47** J 6
Chŏnan **54** A 3
Chongūan **49** K 5
Chŏngjin **54** A 2
Chŏngju **54** A 3
Chongqing **49** H 5
Chŏnju **54** A 3
Chornobylū **36** G 2
Chorog **45** M 5
Chŏrwŏn **54** A 3
Chotanagpur Plateau **46** E 4
Chott ech Chergui **56** D 1
Chott Melrhir **34** B 4
Choybalsan **50** B 3
Christchurch **62** B 3
Christian IV Gletscher **8** Ff 5
Christianshåb **8** Aa 5
Christmas Island (Australia) **52** D 8
Christmas Island (Kiribati) **59** K 3
Chudskoye Ozero **38** L 4
Chuginadak Island **43** V 6
Chuhuichupa **20** C 2
Chukai **52** C 5
Chukchi Sea **43** U 3
Chukotskiy Poluostrov **43** U 3
Chula Vista **18** C 5
Chulym **41** S 6
Chum **40** O 4
Chumikan **42** L 6
Chumphon **47** H 6
Chuna **41** V 6
Chūunchūŏn **50** E 5
Chūungju **54** A 3
Chunya (Russia) **41** V 5
Chuor Phnum Dangrek **47** J 6
Chur **36** B 3
Churapcha **42** K 4
Churchill **8** S 7
Churchill Falls **8** Y 8
Churchill Lake **10** V 7
Chureg **45** Q 2
Chureg-Tag, Gora **41** U 7
Churu **46** C 3
Chusovoy **40** N 6
Chust **45** M 4
Chutes Boyoma (Stanley Falls) **58** B 1
Chutes De La Lufira (Lufira Falls) **58** B 2
Chutes Tembo (Tembo Falls) **58** A 2
Chuuk Islands **59** E 3
Chuxian **49** K 4
Chuxiong **49** G 5
Chybalsan **50** B 3
Cianjur **52** D 7
Cibuta, Cerro **18** D 5
Ciénaga **22** H 5
Cienfuegos **22** F 3
Cieza **33** B 2
Cihanbeyli **35** E 5
Cihanbeyli Platosu **35** E 5
Cikobia **59** H 5
Cilacap **52** D 7
Cimaltepec, Sierra **20** E 4
Cincinnati **14** C 3
Cintalapa de Figueroa **20** F 4
Circle (Alaska, U.S.) **10** O 5
Circle (Montana, U.S.) **18** E 2
Cirebon **52** D 7
Cisco **16** D 5
Ciudad Acuña **20** D 2
Ciudad Altamirano **20** D 4
Ciudad Bolūvar **22** K 6
Ciudad Camargo **20** C 2
Ciudad Cuauhtémoc **20** F 4
Ciudad de Río Grande **20** D 3
Ciudad del Carmen **20** F 4
Ciudad del Maíz **20** E 3
Ciudad Guayana **22** K 6
Ciudad Guzman **20** D 4
Ciudad Hidalgo **20** F 5
Ciudad Juárez **18** E 5
Ciudad Lerdo **20** D 2
Ciudad Madero **20** E 3
Ciudad Mante **20** E 3
Ciudad Mendoza **20** E 4
Ciudad Obregón **20** C 2
Ciudad Ojeda **22** H 5
Ciudad Real **33** B 2
Ciudad Rodrigo **33** A 1
Ciudad Valles **20** E 3
Ciudad Victoria **20** E 3
Civa Burnu **35** G 4
Civitanova Marche **34** C 2
Civitavecchia **34** C 2
Çivril **35** C 5
Cizre **35** K 6
Clacton-on-Sea **28** E 4
Claire Eagle Lake **18** B 3
Claire, Lake **10** U 7
Claremorris **31** B 2
Clarendon **16** C 5
Claresholm **18** D 1
Clarinda **16** D 3
Clark Fork **18** C 2
Clark Hill Lake **14** C 4
Clarke Island **60** H 8
Clarke Range **60** H 4
Clarksburg **14** C 3
Clarksdale **16** E 5
Clarkston **18** C 2
Clarksville **14** B 3
Claveria **52** G 2
Clavering Ø **8** Gg 4
Clear Island **31** B 3
Clear Lake **18** B 4
Clear Lake Reservoir **18** B 3
Clearfield **18** D 3
Clearwater **14** C 5
Clearwater Mountains **18** C 2
Clermont **60** H 4
Clermont-Ferrand **32** C 2
Cleveland (Mississippi, U.S.) **16** E 5
Cleveland (Ohio, U.S.) **14** C 2
Cleveland (Tennessee U.S.) **14** C 3
Clew Bay **31** B 2
Clifden **31** A 2
Clifton **14** C 3
Clinton (Iowa, U.S.) **16** E 3
Clinton (Oklahoma, U.S.) **16** D 4
Cloncurry **60** G 4
Clonmel **31** C 2
Cloquet **16** E 2
Clovis **16** C 5
Cluj-Napoca **36** E 3
Clutha **62** A 4
Clyde Inlet **8** X 4
Clyde River **8** X 4
Clyde, Firth of **28** B 2
Coahuila **20** D 2
Coalcoman, Sierra de **20** D 4
Coalinga **18** B 4
Coast Mountains **10** Q 7
Coast Range **60** J 5
Coast Range (U.S.) **18** B 3
Coatepec **20** E 4
Coats Island **8** U 6
Coatzacoalcos **20** F 4
Coatzacoalcos, Bahía **20** F 4

Coba **20** G 3
Cobán **20** F 4
Cobar **60** H 6
Cobourg Peninsula **60** E 2
Coburg **36** C 2
Coburg Island **8** V 3
Cochabamba **24** E 4
Cochin **46** D 6
Cochrane **8** U 9
Coco Islands **47** G 6
Coco, Isla del **22** E 6
Coco, Río **20** G 5
Cocoa **14** C 5
Cocula **20** D 3
Cod, Cape **14** F 2
Cody **18** E 3
Coesfeld **36** B 2
Coëtivy **58** E 2
Coeur dūAlene **18** C 2
Coffeyville **16** D 4
Coffs Harbour **60** J 6
Cogt-Ovoo **49** H 2
Coiba, Isla de **22** F 6
Coihaique **24** D 7
Coimbatore **46** D 6
Coimbra **33** A 1
Cojutepeque **20** G 5
Colchester **28** E 4
Coleman **16** D 5
Coleraine **31** C 1
Colfax **18** C 2
Colima (Mexico) **20** D 4
Colima (State, Mexico) **20** D 4
Colima, Nevado de **20** D 4
Coll **30** A 3
College Station **16** D 5
Collier Ranges National Park **60** B 4
Collingwood (New Zealand) **62** B 3
Collingwood (U.S.) **14** C 2
Collooney **31** B 1
Colmar **36** B 3
Colombia **22** H 7
Colombo (Sri Lanka) **46** D 7
Colón (Cuba) **22** F 3
Colón (Panama) **22** G 6
Colonet **18** C 5
Colonia Morelos **18** E 5
Colonna, Capo **34** D 3
Colonsay **30** A 3
Colorado **18** E 4
Colorado Plateau **18** D 4
Colorado River (Texas, U.S.) **16** D 5
Colorado River (Utah, U.S.) **18** D 4
Colorado Springs **16** C 4
Colorado, Cerro (Mexico) **18** C 5
Colotlán **20** D 3
Columbia (Missouri, U.S.) **16** E 4
Columbia (South Carolina, U.S.) **14** C 4
Columbia (Tennessee, U.S.) **14** B 3
Columbia Falls **18** D 2
Columbia Plateau **18** C 3
Columbia River **10** T 8
Columbus (Georgia, U.S.) **14** C 4
Columbus (Indiana, U.S.) **14** B 3
Columbus (Mississippi, U.S.) **14** B 4
Columbus (Nebraska, U.S.) **16** D 3
Columbus (Ohio, U.S.) **14** C 2
Colville Channel **62** C 2
Colville Lake **10** R 5
Colville Lake (Lake) **10** R 5
Colwyn Bay **28** C 3
Comalcalco **20** F 4
Comayagua **20** G 5
Comelio **20** B 2
Comino, Capo **34** B 2
Comitán **20** F 4
Como **36** B 3
Comodoro Rivadavia **24** E 7
Comondú **20** B 2
Comorin, Cape **46** D 7
Compiégne **32** C 2
Comrat **36** F 3
Con Son **47** K 7
Conakry **56** B 4
Concepción **24** D 6
Concepcíon del Oro **20** D 3
Conception Bay **58** A 4
Conception, Point **18** B 5
Conchos, Río **20** C 2
Concord **14** E 2
Concordia (Mexico) **20** C 3
Condobolin **60** H 6
Condon **18** B 2
Conecuh River **14** B 4
Conghua **49** J 6
Congo (Country) **58** A 1
Congo (River) **58** A 2
Conn, Lough **31** B 1
Connaught **31** B 2
Connecticut **14** E 2
Connellsville **14** D 2
Conrad **18** D 2
Conroe **16** D 5
Constanta **35** C 2
Constantine **56** D 1
Constantine, Cape **43** Y 5
Contwoyto Lake **10** U 5
Conway (Arkansas, U.S.) **16** E 4
Conway (South Carolina, U.S.) **14** D 4
Coober Pedy **60** E 5
Cooch Behār **47** F 3
Cook Inlet **10** M 6
Cook Islands **59** J 5
Cook Strait **62** B 3
Cookes Peak **18** E 5
Cookstown **31** C 1
Cooktown **60** H 3
Coolgardie **60** C 6
Coolidge **18** D 5
Cooma **60** H 7
Coonoor **46** D 6
Cooper Creek **61** F 5
Cooray **60** J 5
Coos Bay **18** B 3
Cootamundra **60** H 6
Copán **20** G 5
Copenhagen **38** H 4
Copiapó **24** D 5
Copper Cliff **8** U 9
Copper Harbor **8** T 9
Coral Harbour **8** U 6
Coral Sea **60** J 2
Coral Sea Islands Territory **60** J 3
Corato **34** D 2
Corbeil-Essonnes **32** C 2
Corbett National Park **46** D 3
Corcaigh **31** B 3
Cordele **14** C 4
Córdoba **24** E 6
Córdoba (Mexico) **20** E 4
Córdoba (Spain) **33** B 2
Cordova **10** N 6
Corigliano Calabro **34** D 3
Corinth **14** B 4
Cork **31** B 3
Çorlu **35** B 4
Corner Brook **8** Z 9
Cornwall Island **8** R 3
Cornwallis Island **8** R 3
Coro **22** J 5
Coromandel Coast **46** E 6
Coronation Gulf **10** U 5
Corozal (Belize) **20** G 4
Corpus Christi **20** E 2
Corquin **20** G 5
Corrib, Lough **31** B 2
Corrientes **24** F 5
Corrientes, Cabo **22** G 6
Corrigin **60** B 6
Corse **34** B 2
Corse, Cap **34** B 2
Corsica **34** B 2
Corsicana **16** D 5
Cortegana **33** A 2
Cortez **18** E 4
Çorum **35** F 4
Corumbá **24** F 4
Corvallis **18** B 3
Cosamaloapan **20** E 4
Cosenza **34** D 3
Coshocton **14** C 2
Costa Blanca **33** B 2
Costa Brava **32** C 3
Costa de Mosquites **22** F 5
Costa de Mosquitos **20** H 5
Costa del Azahar **33** C 2
Costa del Sol **33** B 2

Costa Rica **22** E 5
Costa, Cordillera de la **22** J 6
Cotabato **52** G 4
Côte dūArgent **32** B 3
Côte dūAzur **34** B 2
Côte dūIvoire **56** B 4
Cotswold Hills **28** C 4
Cottbus **36** C 2
Cotulla **20** E 2
Coubre, Pointe de la **32** B 2
Council Bluffs **16** D 3
Courtenay **18** A 2
Coventry **28** D 3
Covington (Georgia, U.S.) **14** C 4
Covington (Kentucky, U.S.) **14** C 3
Covington (Tennessee, U.S.) **14** B 3
Covington (Virginia, U.S.) **14** D 3
Cowan, Lake **60** C 6
Cowell **60** F 6
Coxūs Bazar **47** G 4
Coyame **20** C 2
Coyotitán **20** C 3
Cozumel, Isla de **20** G 3
Cradock **58** B 5
Craig (Colorado, U.S.) **18** E 3
Craiova **34** E 2
Cranbrook (Canada) **18** C 2
Crater Lake **18** B 3
Crawfordsville **14** B 2
Crawley **28** D 4
Crazy Peak **18** D 2
Cree Lake **10** V 7
Creel **20** C 2
Creil **32** C 2
Cremona **36** C 3
Crescent City **18** B 3
Creston **16** E 3
Crestview **14** B 4
Crete **34** E 3
Creus, Cap de **32** C 3
Crewe **28** C 3
Croatia **36** D 3
Crockett **16** D 5
Croker Island **60** E 2
Croker, Cape **60** E 2
Cromer (England, U.K.) **28** E 3
Cromer (Scotland, U.K.) **30** A 2
Crooked Creek **43** Y 4
Crooked Island **22** H 3
Crooked Island Passage **22** G 3
Crookston **16** D 2
Crosby **16** C 2
Cross City **14** C 5
Crossett **16** E 5
Crotone **34** D 3
Crow Agency **18** E 2
Crow Lake **16** E 2
Crowley **16** E 5
Crown Prince Frederiklsland **8** T 5
Crowsnest Pass **18** D 2
Croydon **60** G 3
Cruz Grande **20** E 4
Cruz, Cabo **22** G 3
Cruzeiro do Sul **24** D 3
Cu Lao Cham **47** K 5
Cu Lao Re **52** D 2
Cuahtémoc **20** C 2
Cuando Cubango **58** A 3
Cuango **58** A 2
Cuanza **58** A 2
Cuba **20** H 3
Cubango **58** A 3
Cucurpe **18** D 5
Cúcuta **22** H 6
Cuddalore **46** D 6
Cuddapah **46** D 6
Cue **60** B 5
Cuéllar **33** B 1
Cuenca **24** D 3
Cuenca (Spain) **32** B 3
Cuencamé de Ceniceros **20** D 3
Cuernavaca **20** E 4
Cuero **20** E 2
Cuiabá **24** F 4
Cuilapa **20** F 5
Culiacán **20** C 3
Cullman **14** B 4
Cumaná **22** K 5
Cumberland **14** D 3
Cumberland Lake **10** W 8
Cumberland Plateau **14** B 3
Cumberland Sound **8** X 5
Cumberland, Lake **14** C 3
Çumra **35** E 6
Cunene **58** A 3
Cuneo **34** B 2
Cunnamulla **60** H 5
Curaçao **22** J 5
Curitaba **24** F 5
Curtis Island **60** J 4
Curupira, Sierra de **22** K 7
Cusco **24** D 4
Cushing **16** D 4
Cuttack **46** F 4
Cuxhaven **36** B 2
Cyclades **34** E 3
Cypress Hills **18** D 2
Cyprus **35** E 7
Czech Republic **36** C 3
Częstochowa **36** D 2
Człuchów **36** D 2
Da Lat **47** K 6
Da Nang **47** K 5
Da Yunhe **49** K 3
Daba Shan **49** H 4
Dabhoi **46** C 4
Dacca **47** G 4
Dadiangas **52** H 4
Dadu **46** B 3
Daet **52** G 3
Dafang **49** H 5
Dafeng **49** L 4
Dafni **34** E 3
Dagu **49** K 3
Dagupan **52** G 2
Daheiding Shan **54** A 1
Dahlonega **14** C 4
Dahongliutan **48** B 3
Dahūk **35** K 6
Daintree River National Park **60** H 3
Dajarra **60** F 4
Dakar **56** B 3
Dákura **20** H 5
Dalū **49** H 4
Dalälven **38** J 3
Dalandzadgad **49** G 2
Dalanjagalan **50** A 3
Dalarna **38** H 3
Dalbandin **46** A 3
Dalby **60** J 5
Dale Hollow Lake **14** B 3
Daley **60** E 2
Dalhart **16** C 4
Dali **48** G 5
Dalian **49** L 3
Dall **10** Q 8
Dallas **16** D 5
Dalles, The **18** B 2
Dalūnegorsk **54** C 2
Dalūnerechensk **50** F 3
Dalūnyaya **50** H 3
Dalou Shan **49** H 5
Dalton **14** C 4
Dāltonganj **46** E 4
Dalupiri **52** G 2
Daly Waters **60** E 3
Damān **46** C 4
Damān and Diu **46** C 4
Damar (Indonesia) **52** H 6
Damaraland **58** A 4
Damascus **44** E 6
Damavand, Qolleh-ye **44** H 5
Dāmghān **45** H 5
Damoh **46** D 4
Dampier **60** B 4
Dampier Land **60** C 3
Danau Toba **52** B 5
Danba **49** G 4
Dandeli **46** C 5
Danforth **14** F 1
Dangara **45** L 5
Danghe Nanshan **48** F 3
Dangriga **20** G 4
Dangshan **49** K 4
Danilov **40** K 6
Danilovka **44** F 2
Danli **20** G 5
Danmarkshavn **8** Hh 3
Dannevirke **62** C 3
Danube **35** B 2
Danube **36** D 3
Danville (Illinois, U.S.) **14** B 2

Danville (Kentucky, U.S.) **14** C 3
Danville (Virginia, U.S.) **14** D 3
Danxian **47** K 5
Danzig, Gulf of **36** D 2
Dao Phu Quoc **47** J 6
Daocheng **48** G 5
Daotiandi **54** B 1
Daoxian **49** J 5
Daqing **50** D 3
Dar Es Salaam **58** C 2
Darūa **44** E 6
Darbhanga **46** F 3
Darbod **50** D 3
Dardanelle Lake **16** E 4
Dardanelles **34** F 3
Darganata **45** K 4
Dargaville **62** B 2
Darhan **41** X 8
Darien, Serranía del **22** G 6
Darīya **45** M 3
Darjeeling **46** F 3
Darlag **48** F 4
Darling **60** G 6
Darling Downs **60** J 5
Darling Range **60** B 6
Darlington **28** D 2
Darlot, Lake **60** C 5
Darmstadt **36** B 3
Darnah **56** F 1
Darreh Gaz **45** J 5
Dartmoor **28** C 4
Dartmouth **8** Y 10
Darwin **60** E 2
Daryācheh-ye Orūmīyeh **44** F 5
Daryā-ye Māzandarān **44** H 5
Daşhowuz **45** J 4
Dasht-e Kavīr **45** H 5
Date **54** D 2
Datia **46** D 3
Datong **49** J 2
Datong (Qinghai, China) **49** G 3
Datong Shan **48** F 3
Datta **54** D 1
Daugaard-Jensen Land **8** Y 2
Daugava **38** L 4
Daugavpils **38** L 4
Daung Kyun **47** H 6
Dauphin **16** C 1
Dāvangere **46** D 6
Davao **52** H 4
Davenport **16** E 3
David **22** F 6
Davis Inlet **8** Y 7
Davis Strait **8** Z 5
Dawei **47** H 6
Dawson **10** P 6
Dawson Creek **10** S 7
Dax **32** B 3
Daxian **49** H 4
Daxing **49** K 3
Dayangshu **50** D 3
Dayao **49** G 5
Dayong **49** J 5
Dayr az Zawr **44** F 5
Dayton **14** C 3
Daytona Beach **14** C 5
Dayu **49** J 5
Dazhu **49** H 4
De Aar **58** B 5
De Kastri **42** M 6
De Land **14** C 5
De Pere **14** B 2
De Ridder **16** E 5
Deadhorse **10** N 4
Dease Lake **10** Q 7
Death Valley **18** C 4
Death Valley National Monument **18** C 4
Dęblin **36** E 2
Deborah East, Lake **60** B 6
Deborah West, Lake **60** B 6
Debre Markūos **56** G 3
Debrecen **36** E 3
Decatur (Alabama, U.S.) **14** B 4
Decatur (Illinois, U.S.) **14** B 3
Deccan **46** D 6
Decelles, Réservoir **14** D 1
Decheng **49** G 5
Děčín **36** C 2
Deda **36** E 3
Dee **30** C 3
Deer Lodge **18** D 2
Dêgê **48** F 4
Dehiwala-Mount Lavinia **46** D 7
Dehra Dun **46** D 2
Dehui **50** E 4
Dej **36** E 3
Del City **16** D 4
Del Norte **18** E 4
Del Rio **20** D 2
Del Verme Falls **56** H 4
Delaram **45** K 6
Delaware **14** D 3
Delaware Bay **14** D 3
Delfoi **34** E 3
Delhi **46** D 3
Delicias **20** C 2
Déline **10** S 5
Delmenhorst **36** B 2
Delta (Colorado, U.S.) **18** E 4
Delta (Utah, U.S.) **18** D 4
Delta Junction **10** N 6
Deming **18** E 5
Demirci **35** C 5
Democratic Republic of the Congo **58** B 2
Demopolis **14** B 4
Demūyanka **40** Q 6
Demūyanskoye **40** P 6
Denakil **56** G 3
Denali **10** N 6
Denali National Park **10** M 6
Dengkou **49** H 2
Dengxian **49** J 4
Denia **33** C 2
Deniliquin **60** G 7
Denison (Iowa, U.S.) **16** D 3
Denison (Texas, U.S.) **16** D 5
Denizli **35** C 6
Denmark **38** G 4
Denmark (Australia) **60** B 6
Denov **45** L 5
Denpasar **52** F 7
Denton **16** D 5
DūEntrecasteaux Islands **59** E 4
Denver **18** E 4
Deoghar **46** F 4
Deolāli **46** C 5
Depoe Bay **18** B 3
Dépression du Mourdi **56** F 3
Dêqên **48** F 5
Deqing **49** J 6
Dequeen **16** E 5
Dera Ghāzi Khān **46** C 2
Dera Ismāīl Khān **46** C 2
Derbent **44** G 4
Derby (Australia) **60** C 3
Derby (U.K.) **28** D 3
Derdap **34** E 2
Derg, Lough **31** B 2
Dergachi **44** G 2
Derweza **45** J 4
Derzhavīnsk **45** L 2
Des Moines **16** E 3
Des Moines River **16** E 3
Désappointement, Îles du **59** L 5
Deschambault Lake **10** W 8
Desē **56** G 3
Desierto de Sechura **24** C 3
Desierto do Atacama (Atacama Desert) **24** E 5
Dessau **36** C 2
Destruction Bay **10** P 6
Detmold **36** B 2
Detroit **14** C 2
Detroit Lakes **16** D 2
Deva **36** E 3
Devils Lake **16** D 2
Devon Island **8** S 3
Devonport **60** H 8
Deyang **49** G 4
Dey-Dey, Lake **60** E 5
Dezfūl **44** G 6
Dezhou **49** K 3
Dhaka **47** G 4
Dhamtari **46** E 4
Dhanbad **46** F 4
Dharān **46** F 3
Dharmapuri **46** D 6
Dharwar **46** D 5
Dhawalāgiri **46** E 3
Dhenkanal **46** F 4
Dholpur **46** D 3
Dhorāji **46** C 4
Dhule **46** C 4
Diablo Range **18** B 4

Diamante, Punta del **20** D 4
Diamond Peak **18** C 4
Dianbai **49** J 6
Diane Bank **60** J 3
Dianjiang **49** H 4
Dibrugrh **47** G 3
Dickinson **16** C 2
Dicle Nehri **35** J 6
Didao **50** F 3
Dieppe **32** C 2
Digboi **47** H 3
Digby **14** F 2
Digne-les-Bains **34** B 2
Digos **52** H 4
Dijon **36** B 3
Dikson **41** S 3
Dili **52** H 7
Dillingham **43** Y 5
Dillon **18** D 2
Dimāpur **47** G 3
Dimashq **44** E 6
Dimbokro **56** C 4
Dimitrovgrad (Bulgaria) **34** F 2
Dimitrovgrad (Russia) **44** G 2
Dinagat **52** H 3
Dinājpur **46** F 3
Dınar **35** D 5
Dindigul **46** D 6
Dinghai **49** L 4
Dingle Bay **31** A 3
Dingwall **30** B 3
Dingxi **49** G 3
Dingxing **49** K 3
Diomede Islands **10** H 5
Dipolog **52** G 4
Dirē Dawa **56** H 3
Dirranbandi **60** H 5
Disappointment, Lake **60** C 4
Disko **8** Aa 5
Dispur **47** G 3
Diu **46** C 4
Divinópolis **24** G 5
Divnoye **44** F 3
Divriği **35** H 5
Dixon **14** B 2
Diyarbakır **35** J 6
Djabung, Tanjung **52** C 6
Djelfa **56** D 1
Djember **52** E 7
Djibouti **56** H 3
Dlinnyy, Ostrov **41** U 2
Dnipropetrovsūk **44** E 3
Dnyapro **36** G 2
Do Gonbadān **44** H 6
Doba **56** E 4
Doboj **34** D 2
Dobrich **35** B 3
Doctor Arroyo **20** D 3
Dodge City **16** C 4
Dodoma **58** C 2
Doero, Rio **32** B 3
Dogai Coring **48** D 4
Dōgo **54** B 3
Doğu Karadeniz Dağları **35** H 4
Doi Inthanon **47** H 5
Doilungdêqên **48** E 5
Dolak, Pulau **59** C 4
Dole **36** B 3
Dolgiy, Ostrov **40** N 4
Dolinsk **50** H 3
Dolores Hidalgo **20** D 3
Dolynsūka **44** D 3
Doma Peaks **59** D 4
Dombarovskiy **40** N 7
Dombas **38** G 3
Dominica **22** K 4
Dominican Republic **22** J 3
Don **44** F 3
Don Benito **33** A 2
Donau **36** C 3
Donegal **31** B 1
Donegal Bay **31** B 1
Donetsūk **44** E 3
Dong Hai **49** L 5
Dong Hoi **47** K 5
Dong Taijnar Hu **48** E 3
Dongan **50** F 3
Dongūan (Heilongjiang, China) **54** B 1
Dongara **60** A 5
Dongchuan **49** G 5
Dongfang **47** K 5
Dongfeng **50** E 4
Donggou **49** L 3
Donghai Dao **49** J 6
Dongning **54** B 2
Dongping **49** K 3
Dongshan Dao **49** K 6
Dongsheng **49** H 3
Dongtai **49** L 4
Dongting Hu **49** J 5
Dongxiang **49** K 5
Dønna **38** H 2
Donostia-San Sebastian **32** B 3
Door Peninsula **14** B 2
Dooxo Nugaaleed **56** H 4
Dora, Lake **60** C 4
Dorchester **28** C 4
Dorda Head **46** E 7
Dordogne **32** C 3
Dornoch **30** C 3
Dornod **50** B 3
Doro **56** C 3
Doro (Indonesia) **52** H 5
Dorohoi **36** F 3
Döröö Nuur **48** E 1
Dorotea **38** J 3
Dortmund **36** B 2
Dos Hermanas **33** A 2
Doshi **45** L 5
Dostyq **45** O 3
Dothan **14** B 4
Douala **56** D 4
Double Island Point **60** J 5
Doubtful Sound **62** A 4
Douglas (Arizona, U.S.) **18** E 5
Douglas (U.K.) **28** B 2
Douglas (Wyoming, U.S.) **18** E 3
Douro, Rio **33** A 1
Dover (U.K.) **28** E 4
Dover (U.S.) **14** D 3
Dover, Strait of **28** E 4
Dow Rūd **44** G 6
Downpatrick **28** B 2
Downpatrick Head **31** B 1
Dozois, Réservoir **14** D 1
Drain **18** B 3
Drama **34** E 2
Drammen **38** H 4
Drava **36** D 3
Dresden **36** C 2
Dreux **32** C 2
Drobeta-Turnu Severin **34** E 2
Drogheda **31** C 2
Drohobych **36** E 3
Droichead Átha **31** C 2
Dronning Louise Land **8** Ff 3
Dronning Maud Land **63** P 4
Drummond **18** D 2
Drummond Range **60** H 4
Drummondville **8** W 9
Dry Tortugas **22** F 3
Dryden **16** E 2
Drysdale River National Park **60** D 3
Du Bois **14** D 2
Duarte **22** H 4
Dubăsari **36** F 3
Dubawnt Lake **10** W 6
Dubbo **60** H 6
Dublin (Ireland) **31** C 2
Dublin (U.S.) **14** C 4
Dubna **40** J 6
Dubno **36** F 2
Dubovka **44** F 3
Dubovskoye **44** F 3
Dubrovnik **34** D 2
Dubrovytsya **36** F 2
Dubuque **16** E 3
Duc de Gloucester, Îles du **59** L 5
Duchesne **18** D 3
Ducie Island **59** N 6
Dudinka **41** T 4
Dudley **28** C 3
Dudwa National Park **46** E 3
Dudypta **41** U 3
Duero, Rio **32** B 3
Duga-Zapadnaya, Mys **42** M 5
Duisburg **36** B 2
Duitama **22** H 6
Duki **42** L 6
Dukou **49** G 5
Dulan **48** F 3
Dulce, Bahía **20** E 4
Dulgalakh **42** K 3

Duluth **16** E 2
Dūmā **44** E 6
Dumaguete **52** G 4
Dumai **52** C 5
Dumaran Island **52** F 3
Dumaring **52** F 5
Dumbarton **28** B 2
Dumfries **28** C 2
Dumont dūUrville Sea **63** T 5
Dún Dealgan **31** C 1
Dún Laoghaire **31** C 2
Duna **36** D 3
Dunărea **36** F 3
Dunării, Delta **35** C 2
Dunaújváros **36** D 3
Dunav **34** F 2
Dunay, Ostrova **42** H 2
Dunayivtsi **36** F 3
Dunbar **60** G 3
Duncan **16** D 5
Duncansby Head **30** C 2
Dundalk **31** C 1
Dundalk Bay **31** C 2
Dundas Strait **60** E 2
Dundas, Lake **60** C 6
Dundee (U.K.) **30** C 3
Dundgovĭ **49** H 1
Dunedin **62** B 4
Dunfermline **30** C 3
Dungarvan **31** C 2
Dunhua **50** E 4
Dunkirk **14** D 2
Dunrankin **14** C 1
Dunsmuir **18** B 3
Duolun **50** C 4
Durack Ranges **60** D 3
Durand, Récifs **59** F 6
Durango (Mexico) **20** D 3
Durango (Spain) **32** B 3
Durango (State, Mexico) **20** C 3
Durango (U.S.) **18** E 4
Durant **16** D 5
Durban **58** C 4
Durg **46** E 4
Durgāpur **46** F 4
Durham (U.K.) **28** D 2
Durham (U.S.) **14** D 3
Durness **30** B 2
Durrow **31** C 2
Durrūs **34** D 2
Dursey Island **31** A 3
Durusu Gölü **35** C 4
DūUrville Island **62** B 3
Dushan **49** H 5
Dushanbe **45** L 5
Düsseldorf **36** B 2
Dutch Harbor **43** W 6
Duyun **49** H 5
Düzce **35** D 4
Dyatūkovo **36** G 2
Dyer, Cape **8** Y 5
Dyersburg **14** B 3
Dzerzhinsk **40** K 6
Dzhagdy, Khrebet **42** J 6
Dzhalinda **50** D 2
Dzhaltyr **45** L 2
Dzhankoy **35** F 2
Dzhugdzhur, Khrebet **42** L 5
Dzhungarian Gate **48** C 1
Dzibalchén **20** G 4
Dzyarzhynsk **36** F 2
Eagle **10** O 6
Eagle Lake (Canada) **16** E 2
Eagle Lake (U.S.) **18** B 3
Eagle Pass **20** D 2
Ear Falls **10** Y 8
East Cape **62** C 2
East China Sea **49** L 5
East Coast Bays **62** B 2
East Kilbride **28** B 2
East London **58** B 5
East Point **14** C 4
East Siberian Sea **43** Q 2
East Timor **52** H 7
Eastbourne **28** E 4
Eastend **18** E 2
Easter Ross **30** B 3
Eastern Ghāts **46** E 6
Eastleigh **28** D 4
Eastmain **8** V 8
Eastman **14** C 4
Easton **14** D 2
Eastport **14** F 2
Eatonville **18** B 2
Eau Claire **16** E 3
Eauripik **59** D 3
Ebano **20** E 3
Ebe **42** M 4
Eberswalde **36** C 2
Ebingen **36** B 3
Eboli **34** D 2
Ebro, Rio **32** B 3
Ecatepec **20** E 4
Echeng **49** J 4
Echmiadzin **44** F 4
Echo Bay **10** T 5
Echuca **60** G 7
Écija **33** A 2
Eckerö **38** J 3
Ecuador **24** C 3
Ede **56** D 4
Edenton **14** D 3
Edgar Range **60** C 3
Edgell Island **8** Y 6
Edgemont **16** C 3
Edina **16** E 3
Edinburgh **28** C 2
Edineţ **36** F 3
Edirne **35** B 4
Edmonds **18** B 2
Edmonton **10** U 8
Edmundston **8** X 9
Edremit **35** B 5
Edwards Plateau **16** C 5
Eek **43** X 4
Éfaté **59** F 5
Effingham **14** B 3
Egedesminde **8** Aa 5
Egegik **43** Y 5
Egersund **38** G 4
Eglinton Island **10** T 3
Egmont, Cape **62** B 2
Eğrıdir **35** D 6
Egvekinot **43** U 3
Egypt **56** F 2
Eiao **59** L 4
Eifel **36** B 2
Eigg **30** A 3
Eight Degree Channel **46** C 7
Eighty Mile Beach **60** B 3
Eiler Rasmussen, Kap **8** Gg 2
Eindhoven **36** B 2
Eire **31** B 2
Eisenach **36** C 2
Eisenhüttenstadt **36** C 2
Eisleben **36** C 2
Eivissa **33** C 2
Ekarma, Ostrov **50** K 3
Ekibastuz **45** N 2
Ekimchan **42** K 6
Ekonda **41** X 4
El Aaiún **56** B 2
El Alamo **18** C 5
El Cajon **18** C 5
El Canelo **20** D 3
El Casco **20** D 2
El Centro **18** C 5
El Descanso **18** C 5
El Dorado (Arkansas, U.S.) **16** E 5
El Dorado (Kansas, U.S.) **16** D 4
El Dorado (Mexico) **20** C 3
El Espinal **22** H 7
El Eulma **34** B 3
El Ferrol **33** A 1
El Goléa **56** D 1
El Kef **56** D 1
El Mirador **20** F 4
El Paso **18** E 5
El Pital, Cerro **20** G 5
El Potosi **20** D 3
El Progreso **20** G 4
El Reno **16** D 4
El Salto **20** C 3
El Salvador **22** D 5
El Sáuz **20** C 2
El Sueco **18** E 5
El Tajin **20** E 3
El Tigre **22** K 6
El Triumfo **20** B 3
El Tuito **20** C 3
Elâziğ **35** H 5
Elba **34** C 2
Elbasan **34** E 2
Elbe **36** C 2
Elbistan **35** G 5

Elbląg **36** D 2
Elbow **18** E 1
Elūbrus, gora **44** F 4
Elche **33** B 2
Elcho Island **60** F 2
Elda **33** B 2
Elūdikan **42** L 4
Eldoret **58** C 1
Elektrostalū **40** J 6
Elephant Butte Reservoir **18** E 5
Eleuthera Island **14** D 5
Elgin **30** C 3
Elūginskoye Ploskogorūye **42** L 3
Elim **43** X 4
Elista **35** L 1
Elizabeth **60** F 6
Elizabeth City **14** D 3
Elizabeth Falls **10** V 7
Elizabethtown **14** B 3
Elizavety, Mys **42** M 6
Ełk **36** E 2
Elk City **16** D 4
Elkhart **14** B 2
Elkhovo **34** F 2
Elkins **14** D 3
Elko **18** C 3
Ellef Ringnes Island **10** W 3
Ellendale **16** D 2
Ellensburg **18** B 2
Ellesmere Island **8** U 3
Ellesmere Port **28** C 3
Ellice Islands **59** G 4
Ellisburg **14** D 2
Elliston **60** E 6
Elmadağ **35** E 5
Elmalı **35** C 6
Elmira **14** D 2
Elmshorn **36** B 2
Eloy **18** D 5
Eltham **62** B 2
Elūru **46** E 5
Elvas **33** A 2
Ely (U.K.) **28** E 3
Ely (U.S.) **18** D 4
Embalse Ezequiel Ramos Mexia **24** E 6
Embi **45** J 3
Emden **36** B 2
Emei **49** G 5
Emerald **60** H 4
Emerald Isle **10** U 3
Emiliano Zapata **20** F 4
Eminska Planina **35** B 3
Emirdağ **35** D 5
Emmen **36** B 2
Emmett **18** C 3
Empalme **20** B 2
Emporia (Kansas, U.S.) **16** D 4
Emporia (Virginia, U.S.) **14** D 3
Enarotali **59** C 4
Encinal **20** E 2
Endeh **52** G 7
Enderbury Island **59** H 4
Endwell **14** D 2
Engelūs **44** G 2
Enggano **52** C 7
England **28** D 3
Englee **8** Z 8
English Channel **32** B 2
Enid **16** D 4
Eniwa **54** D 2
Eniwetok **59** F 2
Enköping **38** J 4
Enna **34** C 3
Ennadai **10** W 6
Ennadai Lake **10** W 6
Ennis **31** B 2
Enniscorthy **31** C 2
Enniskillen **31** C 1
Ennistimon **31** B 2
Enschede **36** B 2
Ensenada **18** C 5
Enshi **49** H 4
Enterprise (Canada) **10** T 6
Enterprise (U.S.) **18** C 2
Entroncamento **33** A 2
Enugu **56** D 4
Enugu Gboko **56** D 4
Envigado **22** G 6
Épernay **32** C 2
Épi **59** F 5
Épinal **36** B 3
Eqlīd **44** H 6
Équateur **58** A 1
Equatorial Guinea **56** D 4
Érd **36** D 3
Erdemlı **35** F 6
Erdenet **49** J 2
Ereğli (Turkey) **35** D 4
Ereğli (Turkey) **35** F 6
Erenhot **49** J 2
Ereymentaū **45** M 2
Erfoud **56** C 1
Erfurt **36** C 2
Ergani **35** H 5
Ergun Zuoqi **50** D 2
Erichsen Lake **8** U 4
Erie **14** C 2
Erie Canal **14** D 2
Erie, Lake **14** C 2
Erikub **59** F 3
Erimo-misaki **54** D 2
Eritrea **56** G 3
Erlangen **36** C 3
Ermenek **35** E 6
Ernest Legouve Reef **59** K 7
Erode **46** D 6
Erris Head **31** A 1
Erromango **59** F 5
Ertilū **44** F 2
Ertis **45** N 2
Ertis (River) **45** N 2
Erzgebirge **36** C 2
Erzincan **35** H 5
Erzurum **35** J 5
Esbjerg **38** G 4
Esbo **38** K 3
Escalante **18** D 4
Escalón **20** D 2
Escanaba **8** T 9
Esch-sur-Alzette **36** B 3
Escondido **18** C 5
Escuinapa de Hidalgo **20** C 3
Escuintla **20** F 5
Eşfahān **44** H 6
Esik **45** N 4
Esil **45** L 2
Esil (River) **45** L 2
Esil Zhazyghy **40** P 7
Eskilstuna **38** J 4
Eskişehir **35** D 5
Eslāmābād-e Gharb **44** G 6
Eşme **35** C 5
Esmeraldas **22** G 7
Espanola **18** E 4
Esperance **60** C 6
Esperanza (Mexico) **20** C 2
Espoo **38** K 3
Espūritu Santo **59** F 5
Esquel **24** D 7
Essaouira **56** C 1
Essen **36** B 2
Esso **43** P 5
Est, Pointe de lū **8** Y 9
Estaca de Bares, Punta da **33** A 1
Estacado, Llano **16** C 5
Estats, Pic dū **32** C 3
Estelū **22** E 5
Estelí **20** G 5
Estevan **16** C 2
Estherville **16** E 3
Estonia **38** K 4
Esztergom **36** D 3
Etah **8** W 3
Étampes **32** C 2
Etawah **46** D 3
Ethiopia **56** G 4
Etolin Island **10** Q 7
Etzná Tixmucuy **20** F 4
ŪEua **59** H 6
Eucla Motel **60** D 6
Eufaula **14** B 4
Eufaula Lake **16** D 4
Eugene **18** B 3
Eugenia, Punta **18** C 6
Eugmo **38** K 3
Euphrates **44** F 6
Euphrates, River **35** M 7
Eureka (California, U.S.) **18** B 3
Eureka (Canada) **8** T 2
Eureka (Nevada, U.S.) **18** C 4
Evanston (Illinois, U.S.) **14** B 2
Evanston (Wyoming, U.S.) **18** D 3
Evansville **14** B 3

Everard Range **60** 5
Everard, Lake **60** E 6
Everett **18** B 2
Everglades City **14** C 5
Everglades National Park **14** C 5
Everglades, The **14** C 5
Evergreen **14** B 4
Evje **38** G 4
Évora **33** A 2
Évreux **32** C 2
Evvoia **34** E 3
Excelsior Springs **16** E 4
Exeter **28** C 4
Exmoor **28** C 4
Expedition Range **60** H 4
Extremadura **33** A 2
Exuma Cays **22** G 3
Eyre Peninsula **60** F 6
Eyre, Lake (North) **60** F 5
Eyre, Lake (South) **60** F 5
Eysturoy **38** D 3
Ezine **35** B 5
Fabens **18** E 5
Faber Lake **10** T 6
Faddeyevskiy, Ostrov **42** M 1
Faenza **34** C 2
Făgăras **35** A 2
Fagataufa **59** M 6
Fagatogo **59** J 5
Fair Bluff **14** D 4
Fair Isle **30** D 2
Fairbanks **10** N 6
Fairborn **14** C 3
Fairfield **18** B 4
Fairmont **16** E 3
Faisalabad **46** C 2
Faith **16** C 2
Faizabad (Afghanistan) **45** M 5
Faizabad India) **46** E 3
Fakaofo **59** H 4
Fakarava **59** L 5
Faku **50** D 4
Falam **47** G 4
Falcon Lake **20** E 2
Falfurrias **20** E 2
Falkenberg **38** H 4
Falkland Islands (Islas Malvinas, U.K.) **24** E 8
Fall River **14** E 2
Fallon **18** C 4
Falls City **16** D 3
Falmouth **28** B 4
False Pass **43** X 6
Falster **36** C 2
Fălticeni **36** F 3
Falun **38** J 3
Famagusta **35** E 7
Fan si Pan **47** J 4
Fanchang **49** K 4
Fang Xian **49** J 4
Fangatau **59** M 5
Fangcheng **49** H 6
Fangzheng **54** A 1
Fano **34** C 2
Fanø **38** G 4
Farafangana **58** D 4
Farāh **45** K 6
Farallon de Medinilla **59** D 2
Farallon de Pajaros **59** D 1
Farewell, Cape **62** B 3
Fargo **16** D 2
Fargūona **45** M 4
Faridpur **47** F 4
Farmington **18** E 4
Fårö **38** J 4
Faro (Canada) **10** Q 6
Faro (Portugal) **33** A 2
Faroe Islands **38** D 3
Fårösund **38** J 4
Farquhar Islands **58** E 2
Farvel, Kap **8** Cc 7
Fasano **34** D 2
Fastiv **36** F 2
Fatehabad **46** D 3
Fatsa **35** G 4
Fatu Hiva **59** M 5
Făurei **36** F 3
Faxaflói **38** A 3
Fayetteville (Arkansas, U.S.) **16** E 4
Fayetteville (North Carolina, U.S.) **14** D 3
Fayu **59** D 3
Fear, Cape **14** D 4
Fécamp **32** C 2
Feira de Santana **24** H 4
Feklistova, Ostrova **42** L 5
Felipe Carrillo Puerto **20** G 4
Felixstowe **28** E 4
Fener Burnu **35** H 4
Fengcheng **50** D 4
Fengdu **49** H 5
Fenghuang **49** H 5
Fengqing **48** F 6
Fengzhen **49** J 2
Feni **47** G 4
Fenyang **49** J 3
Feodosiya **35** F 2
Fergus Falls **16** D 2
Ferguson Lake **10** V 5
Ferlo **56** B 3
Ferrara **34** C 2
Ferriday **16** E 5
Fès **56** C 1
Festus **16** E 4
Fetești **34** F 2
Fethiye **35** C 6
Fetlar **30** D 1
Fezzan **56** E 2
Fianarantsoa **58** D 4
Fichē **56** G 3
Fier **34** D 2
Fife Ness **30** C 3
Figueres **32** C 3
Figuig **56** C 1
Fiji Islands **59** G 5
Filchner Ice Shelf **63** N 4
Filiași **34** E 2
Findlay **14** C 2
Finke **60** E 5
Finke Gorge NationalPark **60** E 4
Finland **38** L 3
Finland, Gulf of **38** K 4
Finlay Forks **10** S 7
Finlay River **10** R 7
Finnmark **38** K 1
Finnmarksvidda **38** K 2
Fiordland National Park **62** A 4
Firenze **34** C 2
Firozabad **46** D 3
Firūzābād **44** H 7
Fishguard **28** B 3
Fisterra, Cabo **33** A 1
Fitzgerald River National Park **60** B 6
Fitzroy (River) **60** C 3
Fitzroy (River) **60** J 4
Fitzroy Crossing **60** D 3
Flade Isblink **8** Hh 2
Flagler Beach **14** C 5
Flagstaff **18** D 4
Flåm **38** G 3
Flaming Gorge Reservoir **18** E 3
Flannan Isles **30** A 2
Flasher **16** C 2
Flat Island **52** F 3
Flathead Lake **18** C 2
Flattery, Cape (Australia) **60** H 2
Flattery, Cape (U.S.) **18** A 2
Fleetwood **28** C 3
Flekkefjord **38** G 4
Flensburg **36** B 2
Flers **32** B 2
Flin Flon **10** W 8
Flinders **60** G 3
Flinders Chase National Park **60** F 7
Flinders Island **60** H 7
Flinders Range **60** F 6
Flinders Ranges National Park **60** F 6
Flinders Reefs **60** H 3
Flint (Kiribati) **59** K 5
Flint (U.S.) **14** C 2
Flint Hills **16** D 4
Flint River **14** C 4
Flisa **38** H 3
Florence **34** C 2
Florence (Alabama, U.S.) **14** B 4
Florence (Oregon, U.S.) **18** B 3
Florence (South Carolina, U.S.) **14** D 4
Florencia **22** G 7
Flores (Guatemala) **20** G 4
Flores (Indonesia) **52** G 7
Flores Sea **52** F 7

Flores, Laut **52** F 7
Florianópolis **24** G 5
Florida (Cuba) **22** G 3
Florida (U.S.) **14** C 5
Florida Keys **14** C 6
Florida, Straits of **22** F 3
Floridablanca **22** H 6
Florina **34** E 2
Florø **38** F 3
Flowers Cove **8** Z 8
Fluk **52** H 6
Focşani **36** F 3
Foggia **34** D 2
Fogo **56** A 3
Fogo Island **8** Aa 9
Foley Island **8** V 5
Foleyer **8** U 9
Folkestone **28** E 4
Folkston **14** C 4
Fond du Lac **10** V 7
Fond du Lac (U.S.) **14** B 2
Fonseca, Golfo de **20** G 5
Fontas **10** S 7
Fontur **38** C 2
Fonualei **59** H 6
Forest **14** B 4
Forfar **30** C 3
Forlì **34** C 2
Formentera **33** C 2
Formentor, Cap de **32** C 3
Formia **34** C 2
Formosa **24** F 5
Formosa **49** L 6
Formosa Strait **49** L 6
Forrest **60** D 6
Forrest City **16** E 4
Forsayth **60** G 3
Forst **36** C 2
Fort Albany **8** U 8
Fort Augustus **30** B 3
Fort Beaufort **58** B 5
Fort Benton **18** D 2
Fort Black **10** V 7
Fort Bragg **18** B 4
Fort Bridger **18** D 3
Fort Chimo **8** X 7
Fort Chipewyan **10** U 7
Fort Collins **18** E 3
Fort Collinson **10** T 4
Fort Dodge **16** E 3
Fort Edward **14** E 2
Fort Frances **16** E 2
Fort Good Hope **10** R 5
Fort Kent **14** F 1
Fort Knox **14** B 3
Fort Lauderdale **14** C 5
Fort Liard **10** S 6
Fort Mackay **10** U 7
Fort Macleod **18** D 2
Fort Madison **16** E 3
Fort McMurray **10** U 7
Fort McPherson **10** Q 5
Fort Morgan **16** C 3
Fort Myers **14** C 5
Fort Nelson **10** S 7
Fort Peck **18** E 2
Fort Peck Dam **18** E 2
Fort Peck Lake **18** E 2
Fort Pierce **14** C 5
Fort Providence **10** T 6
Fort QuūAppelle **16** C 1
Fort Saint James **10** S 8
Fort Saint John **10** S 7
Fort Saskatchewan **10** U 8
Fort Scott **16** E 4
Fort Severn **8** T 7
Fort Simpson **10** S 6
Fort Smith (Canada) **10** U 6
Fort Smith (U.S.) **16** E 4
Fort Stockton **16** C 5
Fort Summer **16** C 5
Fort Vermillion **10** T 7
Fort Walton Beach **14** B 4
Fort Wayne **14** B 2
Fort William **30** B 3
Fort Worth **16** D 5
Fort Yukon **10** O 5
Fortaleza **24** H 3
Fort-de-France **22** 5
Forth, Firth of **30** C 3
Foshan **49** J 6
Fosna **38** H 3
Fou-ling **49** H 5
Foumban **56** E 4
Foveaux Strait **62** A 4
Fox Islands **43** W 6
Foxe Basin **8** V 5
Foxe Channel **8** U 5
Foxford **31** B 2
Foyle, Lough **31** C 1
Franca **24** G 5
France **32** B 2
France, Île de **8** Hh 3
Francia, Cabo **20** H 3
Francis Case, Lake **16** D 3
Francisco Escárcega **20** F 4
Francistown **58** B 4
Francs Peak **18** E 3
Frankfort **14** C 3
Frankfurt am Main **36** B 2
Frankfurt an der Oder **36** C 2
Franklin Lake **8** R 5
Franz Josef Land **40** L 2
Franzz **8** U 9
Fraser Island **60** J 5
Fraser Plateau **10** S 8
Fraser River **10** S 8
Fraserburgh **30** C 3
Frederick Hills **60** E 2
Frederick Reefs **61** K 4
Fredericksburg **14** D 3
Fredericton **8** X 9
Frederikshåb **8** Bb 6
Frederikshåb Isblink **8** Aa 6
Frederikshavn **38** H 44
Fredrikstad **38** H 4
Freeport (Bahamas) **14** D 5
Freeport (Illinois, U.S.) **14** B 2
Freeport (Texas, U.S.) **20** E 2
Freetown **56** B 4
Freiberg **36** C 2
Freiburg **36** B 3
Freising **36** C 3
Fréjus **34** B 2
Fremantle **60** B 6
French Guiana (France) **24** F 2
French Polynesia **59** L 6
Frenchman River **18** E 2
Fresnillo **20** D 3
Fresno **18** C 4
Freuchen Land **8** Cc 2
Freycinet Peninsula **60** H 8
Frisian Islands **36** B 2
Friza, Proliv **54** E 1
Frolovo **44** F 3
Front Range **18** E 3
Frontera **20** F 4
Fronteras **18** E 5
Frosione **34** C 2
Frøya **38** G 3
Frýdek-Mūstek **36** D 3
Fuūan **49** K 5
Fuding **49** L 5
Fuga **52** G 2
Fugloy **38** D 3
Fuji **54** C 3
Fujian **49** K 5
Fujin **50** F 3
Fuji-san **54** C 3
Fukue **54** A 4
Fukue-Jima **54** A 4
Fukui **54** C 3
Fukuoka **54** B 4
Fukushima (Hokkaidō, Japan) **54** D 2
Fukushima (Honshū, Japan) **54** D 3
Fukuyama **54** B 4
Fulaga **59** H 5
Fulda **36** B 2
Funabashi **54** C 3
Funchal **56** B 1
Fundy, Bay of **14** F 2
Funing **49** K 4
Fuqing **49** K 5
Furano **54** D 2
Furmanov **40** K 6
Furneaux Group **60** H 8
Fürstenwalde **36** C 2
Fürth **36** C 3
Furukawa **54** D 3
Fushun **50** D 4
Fusong **50** E 4
Futuna, Île **59** H 5
Fuxian **49** L 3
Fuxin **50** D 4

Fuyang **49** K 4
Fuyu **50** D 3
Fuyuan **49** G 5
Fuyuan (Heilongjiang, China) **54** B 1
Fuyun **48** D 1
Fuzhou (Fujian, China) **49** K 5
Fuzhou (Jiangxi, China) **49** K 5
Fyn **38** H 4
Fyne, Loch **30** B 3
Gabbs **18** C 4
Gabon **56** D 5
Gaborone **58** B 4
Gäddede **38** H 3
Gadsden **14** B 4
Gadwāl **46** D 5
Gaffney **14** C 3
Gag **52** H 6
Gagarin **40** H 6
Gagnon **8** X 8
Gagra **35** J 3
Gaillimh **31** B 2
Gainesville (Florida, U.S.) **14** C 5
Gainesville (Texas, U.S.) **16** D 5
Gainsville **14** C 4
Gairdner, Lake **60** F 6
Gaixian **50** D 4
Gakona **10** N 6
Galapagos Islands (Ecuador) **24** B 2
Galashiels **28** C 2
Galaţi **35** C 2
Galatina **34** D 2
Galeana **18** E 5
Galela **52** H 5
Galena **43** Y 4
Galesburg **16** E 3
Gali **35** J 3
Galich **40** K 6
Galicia **33** A 1
Galicia **36** E 3
Galle **46** E 7
Gallinas, Punta **22** H 5
Gällivare **38** K 2
Gallo Mountains **18** E 5
Gallup **18** E 4
Galnesvelle **14** C 4
Galveston **20** F 2
Galveston Bay **20** F 2
Galway **31** B 2
Galway Bay **31** B 2
Gambia **56** B 3
Gambier, Îles **59** M 6
Ganāveh **44** H 7
Gäncä **44** G 4
Gandūa **33** B 2
Gandajika **58** B 2
Gāndhi Sāgar **46** D 4
Gándhinagar **46** C 4
Ganga **46** F 3
Gangānagar **46** C 3
Gangapur **46** C 3
Gangaw **47** G 4
Gangawati **46** D 5
Gangdisê Shan **48** C 4
Ganges **46** F 3
Ganges, Mouths of the **47** F 4
Gangtok **46** F 3
Gangu **49** H 4
Gannan **50** D 3
Gannett Peak **18** E 3
Ganquan **49** H 3
Gansu **49** G 3
Ganzhou **49** J 5
Gao **56** D 3
Gaoūan **49** K 5
Gaoping **49** J 3
Gaotang **49** K 3
Gaoxian **49** G 5
Gaoyou **49** K 4
Gaozhou **49** J 6
Gap **34** B 2
Gapan **52** G 2
Garabogazköl Aylagy **44** H 4
Garagum Kanaly **45** K 5
Garanhuns **24** H 3
Garberville **18** B 3
Gardaneh-ye Āvej **44** G 5
Garden City **16** C 4
Garden Reach **46** F 4
Gardez **45** L 6
Gardiner **18** D 2
Gariep Dam **58** B 5
Garmisch-Partenkirchen **36** C 3
Garnett **16** D 4
Garonne **32** B 3
Garoua **56** E 4
Garrison Dam **16** C 2
Garry Lake **10** W 5
Garut **52** D 7
Gary **14** B 2
Garyarsa **48** C 4
Garzê **48** F 4
Gascogne **32** B 3
Gascoyne Junction **60** B 5
Gashua **56** E 3
Gaspé **8** Y 9
Gaspé, Cap de **8** Y 9
Gastonia **14** C 3
Gästrikland **38** J 3
Gata, Cabo de **33** B 2
Gatchina **40** H 6
Gatehouse of Fleet **28** B 2
Gates of the Arctic National Park **10** M 5
Gateshead Island **8** R 4
Gatineau, Parc de la **8** V 9
Gaua **59** F 5
Gauhati **47** G 3
Gāuwān **46** E 4
Gävle **38** J 3
Gawler Ranges **60** F 6
Gaya (India) **46** E 4
Gaylord **14** C 1
Gayndah **60** J 5
Gaza **44** D 6
Gaziantep **35** G 6
Gdańsk **36** D 2
Gdynia **36** D 2
Gearhart Mountain **18** B 3
Gebe **52** H 6
Gebze **35** C 4
Gediz (Turkey) **35** C 5
Gedser **36** C 2
Geelong **60** G 7
Geelvink Channel **60** A 5
Geesthacht **36** C 2
Gejiu **49** G 6
Gela **34** C 3
Gelendzhik **44** E 4
Gelibolu **35** B 4
Gemena **58** A 1
General Bravo **20** E 2
General Santos **52** H 4
General Treviño **20** E 2
General Trías **20** C 2
Geneva **14** D 2
Geneva, Lake **36** B 3
Genève **36** B 3
Gengma **48** F 6
Genova **34** B 2
Geographical Society Ø **8** Gg 4
George Town (Cayman Islands) **22** F 4
George Town (Malaysia) **52** C 4
George V Land **63** U 5
George, Lake **60** C 4
George, Lake (Florida, U.S.) **14** C 5
George, Lake (New York, U.S.) **14** E 2
Georgetown **14** D 6
Georgetown **24** F 2
Georgetown (South Carolina, U.S.) **14** D 4
Georgetown (Texas, U.S.) **16** D 5
Georgia **44** E 4
Georgia (U.S.) **14** C 4
Georgian Bay **8** U 9
Georgīevka **45** O 3
Georgiyevsk **35** K 2
Gera **36** C 2
Geraldton **60** A 5
Geraldton (Canada) **14** B 1
Gerba **43** O 4
Gerede **35** E 4
Gereshk **45** K 6
Gering **16** C 3
Germania Land **8** Gg 3
Germany **36** B 2
Getafe **32** B 3
Gettysburg **16** D 2
Geysir **38** A 3
Geyve **35** D 4
Ghana **56** C 4

Gharb Dārfūr **56** F 3
Ghardaïa **56** D 1
Ghazni **45** L 6
Gheorghieni **36** F 3
Ghurian **45** K 6
Giannitsa **34** E 2
Gibraltar **33** A 2
Gibraltar, Estrecho de **33** A 2
Gibraltar, Strait of **33** A 2
Gibson Desert **60** C 4
Gichgeniyn Nuruu **48** E 1
Gideälven **38** J 3
Gidgi, Lake **60** D 5
Gifu **54** C 3
Gijón **33** A 1
Gila Bend **18** D 5
Gila River **18** D 5
Gilbert Islands **59** G 3
Gilgit **45** M 5
Gillen, Lake **60** D 5
Gillette **18** E 3
Gilroy **18** B 4
Gimli **16** D 1
Gingoog **52** H 4
Gir National Park **46** C 4
Gīr Range **46** C 4
Girardot **22** H 7
Giresun **35** H 4
Giridih **46** F 4
Girona **32** C 3
Girvan **28** B 2
Gisborne **62** C 2
Giurgiu **34** F 2
Gizjiga **43** Q 4
Giżycko **36** E 2
Gjirokastër **34** E 2
Gjoa Haven **8** R 5
Gjøvik **38** H 3
Glacier Bay National Park and Reserve **10** P 7
Glacier National Park **18** D 2
Gladstone **60** J 4
Glasgow (Kentucky, U.S.) **14** B 3
Glasgow (Montana, U.S.) **18** E 2
Glasgow (U.K.) **28** B 2
Glazov **40** M 6
Glen Canyon National Recreation Area **18** D 4
Glen Innes **60** J 5
Glen Mòr **30** B 3
Glendale **18** D 5
Glendive **16** C 2
Glennallen **10** N 6
Glenrock **18** E 3
Glenrothes **30** C 3
Glens Falls **14** E 2
Glenwood Springs **18** E 4
Gliwice **36** D 2
Globe **18** D 5
Głogów **36** D 2
Glomfjord **38** H 2
Glomma **38** H 4
Glommersträsk **38** J 2
Gloucester (U.K.) **28** C 4
Gloucester (U.S.) **14** E 2
Glūbokoe **45** O 2
Gniezno **36** D 2
Goa **46** C 5
Gobi Desert **49** G 2
Godavari **46** E 5
Godavari, Mouths of the **46** E 5
Godby **38** J 3
Godhavn **8** Aa 5
Godhra **46** C 4
Gödöllő **36** D 3
Gods Lake **10** Y 8
Godthåb **8** Aa 6
Gogebic Range **16** E 2
Gogland, Ostrov **38** L 4
Goiânia **24** F 4
Gojra **46** C 2
Gökçeada **34** F 2
Gökırmak **35** F 4
Göksun **35** G 5
Gol **38** G 3
Golūchikha **41** S 3
Golconda **18** C 3
Gold Rock **16** E 2
Golden **10** T 8
Golden Hinde **18** A 2
Goldfield **18** C 4
Goldsboro **14** D 3
Golfo de Cintra **56** B 2
Golfo de San Jorge **24** E 7
Golfo San Matías **24** E 7
Gölköy **35** G 4
Golmud **48** E 3
Golpāyegān **44** H 6
Gombe **56** E 3
Gomera **56** B 2
Gómez Palacio **20** D 2
Gomo Co **48** D 4
Gonaïves **22** H 4
Gonáve, Île de la **22** H 4
Gonbad-e Qābūs **45** J 5
Gondal **46** C 4
Gonder **56** G 3
Gondia **46** E 4
Gönen **35** B 4
Gongan **49** J 4
Gongcheng **49** J 6
Gongga Shan **49** G 5
Gonghe **48** G 3
Gongliu **48** C 2
Gonzalés **20** E 3
Gooding **18** D 3
Goodland **16** C 4
Goodnews Bay **43** X 5
Goondiwindi **60** J 5
Goose Lake **18** B 3
Gorakhpur **46** E 3
Goražde **34** D 2
Gore **62** A 4
Görele **35** H 4
Gorey **31** C 2
Gorgan **45** H 5
Gorgona, Isla **22** G 7
Gori **35** L 4
Gorizia **36** C 3
Gorkiy **40** K 6
Gorna Oryakhovitsa **34** F 2
Gorno-Altaysk **41** T 7
Gornozavodsk **50** H 3
Gornozavodsk (Russia) **54** D 1
Gornyak **45** O 2
Gorodets **40** K 6
Goroka **59** D 4
Gorong **52** J 6
Gorontalo **52** G 5
Gorzów Wielkopolski **36** D 2
Goshogahara **54** D 2
Gosnells **60** B 6
Götaland **38** H 4
Göteborg **38** H 4
Gotha **36** C 2
Gothenburg (U.S.) **16** C 3
Gotland **38** J 4
Gotō-rettō **54** A 4
Gotse Delchev **34** E 2
Gotska Sandön **38** J 4
Gōtsu **54** B 4
Göttingen **36** B 2
Goulburn **60** H 6
Goulburn Island **60** E 2
Governador Valadares **24** G 4
Governorūs Harbour **14** D 5
Govind Ballabah Pant Sagar **46** E 4
Gozho Co **48** C 3
Graaff Reinet **58** B 5
Grace, Lake **60** B 6
Gracias a Dios, Cabo de **22** E 5
Grafton **60** J 5
Grafton (U.S.) **16** D 2
Graham **16** E 2
Graham Island (British Columbia, Canada) **10** Q 8
Graham Island (Nunavut, Canada) **8** S 3
Grahamstown **58** B 5
Grain Coast **56** B 4
Grajewo **36** E 2
Grampian Mountains **30** B 3
Gran Altiplanicie Central **24** D 7
Gran Canaria **56** B 2
Gran Chaco **24** E 5
Granada (Nicaragua) **22** E 5
Granada (Spain) **33** B 2
Granby **8** W 9
Grand Bahama Island **14** D 5
Grand Canal **31** C 2
Grand Canal **49** K 3
Grand Canyon **18** D 4
Grand Canyon National Park **18** D 4
Grand Cayman **22** F 4

Grand Coulee **18** C 2
Grand Coulee Dam **18** C 2
Grand Forks **16** D 2
Grand Island **16** D 3
Grand Junction **18** E 4
Grand Manan Island **8** X 10
Grand Marais (Michigan, U.S.) **14** B 1
Grand Marais (Minnesota, U.S.) **16** E 2
Grand Portage **14** B 1
Grand Rapids (Michigan, U.S.) **14** B 2
Grand Rapids (Minnesota, U.S.) **16** E 2
Grand River **14** B 2
Grand Teton **18** D 3
Grand Traverse Bay **14** B 1
Grand-Bassam **56** C 4
Grande de Matagalpa, Rio **20** G 5
Grande de Santiago, Río **20** D 3
Grande Prairie **10** T 7
Grande Ronde River **18** C 2
Grande, Cerro **20** D 3
Grandin, Lac **10** T 6
Grane **38** H 2
Grangeville **18** C 2
Granite City **16** E 4
Granite Dam **8** Z 9
Granollers **32** C 3
Grantham **28** D 3
Grants **18** E 4
Grants Pass **18** B 3
Granville **32** B 2
Gras, Lac de **10** U 6
Gravelbourg **18** E 2
Grayling **14** C 2
Grays Harbor **18** A 2
Graz **36** D 3
Great Abaco Island **14** D 5
Great Artesian Basin **60** G 4
Great Australian Bight **60** D 6
Great Barrier Island **62** C 2
Great Barrier Reef **60** G 2
Great Basin **18** C 3
Great Bear Lake **10** S 5
Great Bear River **10** R 5
Great Bend **16** D 4
Great Dividing Range **60** G 3
Great Exuma Island **22** G 3
Great Falls **18** D 2
Great Himalaya Range **46** D 2
Great Inagua Island **22** H 3
Great Indian Desert **46** B 3
Great Malvern **28** C 3
Great Namaqualand **58** A 4
Great Nicobar Island **47** G 7
Great Ouse **28** E 3
Great Pee Dee River **14** D 4
Great Plain of the Koukdjuak **8** W 5
Great Plains **16** C 3
Great Plains (Canada) **10** T 7
Great Salt Lake **18** D 3
Great Salt Lake Desert **18** D 4
Great Sandy Desert **60** C 4
Great Sitkin Island **43** U 6
Great Slave Lake **10** T 6
Great Victoria Desert **60** D 5
Great Victoria Desert Nature Reserve **60** D 5
Great Yarmouth **28** E 3
Greater Antilles **22** H 4
Gredos, Sierra de **33** A 2
Greece **34** E 3
Greeley (Colorado, U.S.) **16** C 3
Greeley (Nebraska, U.S.) **16** D 3
Greemville **16** D 5
Green Bay (Michigan, U.S.) **14** B 1
Green Bay (Wisconsin, U.S.) **14** B 2
Green Islands **59** E 4
Green River (Kentucky, U.S.) **14** B 3
Green River (River, Utah, U.S.) **18** D 4
Green River (Utah, U.S.) **18** D 4
Green River (Wyoming, U.S.) **18** E 3
Greenland **8** Aa 3
Greenland Sea **38** B 2
Greenock **28** B 2
Greensboro (Georgia, U.S.) **14** C 4
Greensboro (North Carolina, U.S.) **14** D 3
Greenville (Alabama, U.S.) **14** B 4
Greenville (Maine, U.S.) **14** F 1
Greenville (Mississippi, U.S.) **16** E 5
Greenville (North Carolina, U.S.) **14** D 3
Greenville (South Carolina, U.S.) **14** C 4
Greenwood **14** C 4
Gregory Range **60** G 3
Gregory, Lake (South Australia) **60** F 5
Gregory, Lake (Western Australia) **60** B 5
Gregory, Lake (Western Australia) **60** D 4
Greifswald **36** C 2
Grenå **38** H 4
Grenada **22** K 5
Grenada (U.S.) **14** B 4
Grenadine Islands **22** K 5
Grenoble **36** B 3
Grenville, Cape **60** G 2
Gresik **52** E 7
Gretna (Louisiana, U.S.) **20** G 2
Grey Islands **8** Z 8
Grey Range **60** G 5
Greymouth **62** B 3
Griffin **14** C 4
Griffith **60** H 6
Grimsby **28** D 3
Grimshaw **10** T 7
Grinnell **16** E 3
Grise Fjord **8** U 3
Gris-Nez, Cap **28** E 4
Grodekovo **54** B 2
Groix, Île de **32** B 2
Grong **38** H 3
Groningen **36** B 2
Groote Eylandt **60** F 2
Grosseto **34** C 2
Grotte de Lascaux **32** C 2
Groundhog River **14** C 1
Groznyy **35** L 3
Grudziądz **36** D 2
Grundy **14** C 3
Gryada Chernysheva **40** N 4
Gryazi **44** E 2
Gryłice **36** D 2
Guadalajara (Spain) **32** B 3
Guadalajara Tepatitlán **20** D 3
Guadaloupe Mountains **16** C 5
Guadalquivir, Río **33** A 2
Guadalupe (Island, Mexico) **20** B 3
Guadalupe (Mexico) **20** D 2
Guadeloupe **22** K 4
Guadiana, Río **33** A 2
Guadix **33** B 2
Guaini, Rio **22** H 7
Guam **59** D 2
Guamúchil **20** C 2
Guan Xian **49** G 4
Guanajuato (Mexico) **20** D 3
Guanajuato (State, Mexico) **20** D 3
Guanare **22** J 6
Guane **20** H 3
Guangdong **49** J 6
Guanghua **49** J 4
Guangji **49** K 5
Guangxi Zhuangzu Zizhiqu **49** H 6
Guangyaun **49** H 4
Guangzhou **49** J 6
Guantanamo **22** G 3
Guanyun **49** K 4
Guarda **33** A 1
Guárico, Embalse del **22** J 5
Guasave **20** C 2
Guatemala **22** D 5
Guatemala (Country) **20** F 4
Guatemala (Guatemala) **20** F 5
Guayaquil **24** C 3
Guaymas **20** B 2
Gubakha **40** N 6
Guben **36** C 2

Gubkin **44** E 2
Gudbrandsdalen **38** G 3
Gudermes **35** M 3
Gudivāda **46** E 5
Gudur **46** D 6
Guelma **34** B 3
Guelph **14** C 2
Guéra Baguirmi **56** E 3
Guernsey **32** B 2
Guerrero (Mexico) **20** E 2
Guerrero (State, Mexico) **20** D 4
Guguan (Mariana Islands, U.S.A.) **59** D 2
Guguan (Micronesia) **59** F 3
Guiana Highlands **22** K 7
Guichi **49** K 4
Guiding **49** H 5
Guildford **28** D 4
Guilin **49** J 5
Guimaras Island **52** G 3
Guinea **56** B 3
Guinea-Bissau **56** B 3
Güines **22** F 3
Guisikha **41** X 3
Guixi **49** K 5
Guixian **49** H 6
Guiyang **49** H 5
Guizhou **49** H 5
Gujar Khan **45** M 6
Gujarat **46** B 4
Gujrānwāla **46** C 2
Gujrat **46** C 2
Gulbarga **46** D 5
Gulf of Aden **56** H 3
Gulf of Guinea **56** D 4
Gulfport **14** B 4
Gulian **50** D 2
Gull Lake **10** V 8
Gullfoss **38** B 3
Gulu **58** C 1
Gumdag **45** H 5
Guna **46** D 4
Güneydoğu Toroslar **35** H 5
Gunnarn **38** J 3
Gunnbjorn Fjeld **8** Ff 5
Gunnison **18** E 4
Guntakal **46** D 5
Guntersville Lake **14** B 4
Guntūr **46** E 5
Gunungsitoli **52** B 5
Guoyang **49** K 4
Gurbantünggüt Shamo **48** D 1
Guri, Embalse de **22** K 6
Gurskøy **38** F 3
Gurskoye **42** L 6
Gürun **35** G 5
Gurvan Sayhan Uul **49** G 2
Guryevsk **41** T 7
Gusau **56** D 3
Guşgy **45** K 5
Gushi **49** K 4
Gusicha **41** X 3
Gusinoozersk **41** X 7
Gusū-Khrustalūnyy **40** K 6
Gusmp, Ostrov **43** Q 3
Gustav Holm, Kap **8** Ee 5
Gustavus **10** P 7
Guthrie (Oklahoma, U.S.) **16** D 4
Guthrie (Texas, U.S.) **16** C 5
Guyana **24** E 2
Gwalior **46** D 3
Gweru **58** C 3
Gya La **48** C 5
Gydanskiy, Poluostrov **41** R 3
Gympie **60** J 5
Gyöngyös **36** D 3
Győr **36** D 3
Gyula **36** E 3
Gyumri **35** K 4
Gyżylarbat **45** J 5
Ha Dong **47** K 4
Ha Giang **47** J 4
Ha Nôi **47** K 4
Ha Tinh **47** K 5
Haūapai Group **59** H 6
Haapsalu **38** K 4
Haast **62** A 3
Habay **10** T 7
Hachijō-jima **54** C 4
Hachinohe **54** D 2
Hadejia **56** D 3
Hadım **35** E 6
Hadrianūs Wall **28** C 2
Haeju **50** E 5
Hafnarfjörður **38** A 3
Hagemeister Island **43** X 5
Hagerstown **14** D 3
Hagfors **38** H 4
Häggenäs **38** H 3
Hagi **54** B 4
Hags Head **31** B 2
Hague, Cap de la **32** B 2
Haiūan **49** L 4
Haikang **49** J 6
Haikou **47** L 5
Hailar **50** C 3
Hailin **50** E 4
Hailong **54** A 2
Hailun **50** E 3
Hailuoto **38** K 2
Haimen (Guangdong, China) **49** K 6
Haimen (Zhejiang, China) **49** L 5
Hainan **47** K 5
Hainan Dao **52** E 2
Haines **10** P 7
Haines Junction **10** P 6
Haining **49** L 4
Haiphong **47** K 4
Haiti **22** H 4
Haizhou Wan **49** K 4
Hakkâri **35** K 6
Hakodate **54** D 2
Haku-san **54** C 3
Halab **35** G 6
Halbei **50** E 3
Halberstadt **36** C 2
Halden **38** H 4
Halifax (Canada) **8** Y 10
Halifax (U.K.) **28** C 3
Halkett, Cape **10** M 4
Hall Beach **8** U 5
Hall Islands **59** E 3
Hall Land **8** Y 2
Halland **38** H 4
Halla-san **54** A 4
Halle **36** C 2
Halle-san **50** E 6
Hällnäs **38** J 3
Halls Creek **60** D 3
Halmahera **52** H 5
Halmstad **38** H 4
Hälsingland **38** J 3
Hamada **54** B 4
Hamadān **44** G 6
Hamāh **44** E 5
Hamamatsu **54** C 4
Hamanaka **54** E 2
Hamar **38** H 3
Hambantota **46** E 7
Hamburg **36** B 2
Häme **38** K 3
Hämeenlinna **38** K 3
Hameln **36** B 2
Hamersley Range **60** B 4
Hamersley Range National Park **60** B 4
Hamgyŏng-sanmaek **54** A 2
Hamhŭng **50** E 5
Hami **48** E 2
Hamilton (Australia) **60** G 7
Hamilton (Canada) **14** D 2
Hamilton (New Zealand) **62** C 2
Hamilton (U.S.) **18** D 2
Hammamet, Golfe de **34** C 3
Hammerdal **38** J 3
Hammerfest **38** K 1
Hammond **16** E 5
Hampden **62** B 4
Hampton Tableland **60** D 6
Hāmūn-i-Lora **45** K 7
Hanahan **14** C 4
Hanamaki **54** D 3
Hâncești **36** F 3
Hanceville **10** S 8
Hancheng **49** J 3
Hanchuan **49** J 4
Handan **49** J 3
Hangayn Nuruu **41** V 8
Hanggin Houqi **49** H 2
Hangö **38** K 4
Hangu **49** K 3
Hangzhou **49** L 4
Hanko **38** K 4
Hanksville **18** D 4
Hanna **10** U 8

Hannibal **16** E 4
Hannover **36** B 2
Hanöbukten **38** H 4
Hanstholm **38** G 4
Hanumangarh **46** C 3
Hanzhong **49** H 4
Hao **59** L 5
Haora **46** F 4
Haparanda **38** K 2
Hapo **52** H 5
Happy Valley-Goose Bay **8** Y 8
Har Us Nuur **41** U 8
Haraiki **59** L 5
Harare **58** C 3
Har-Ayrag **50** A 3
Harbin **50** E 3
Harbor Beach **14** C 2
Harda Khas **46** D 4
Hardin **18** E 2
Hārer **56** H 4
Hargeysa **56** H 4
Haridwār **46** D 3
Harihari **62** B 3
Harlingen **20** E 2
Harlow **28** E 4
Harney Basin **18** B 3
Harney Peak **16** C 3
Härnön **38** J 3
Härnösand **38** J 3
Harrington Harbour **8** Z 8
Harris, Sound of **30** A 3
Harrisburg **14** D 2
Harrison **16** E 4
Harrisonburg **14** D 3
Harrogate **28** D 3
Harry S. Truman Reservoir **16** E 4
Hartford **14** E 2
Hartland Point **28** B 4
Hartlepool **28** D 2
Hartwell Lake **14** C 4
Hartz Mountains National Park **60** H 8
Harve-Saint-Pierre **8** Y 8
Harvey (U.S.) **16** D 2
Harwich **28** E 4
Haryāna **46** D 3
Hastings (Minnesota, U.S.) **16** E 3
Hastings (Nebraska, U.S.) **16** D 3
Hastings (New Zealand) **62** C 2
Hastings (U.K.) **28** E 4
Hat Yai **47** J 7
Hattiesburg **14** B 4
Hatutu **59** L 4
Haukeligrend **38** G 4
Hauraki Gulf **62** B 2
Haut Atlas **56** C 1
Havana **20** H 3
Havelock Island **47** G 6
Haverhill **14** E 2
Havlićkuv Brod **36** D 3
Havre **18** E 2
Havsa **34** F 2
Havza **35** F 4
Hawaii **12** D 8
Hawaiian Islands **12** E 7
Hawera **62** B 2
Hawick **28** C 2
Hawke Bay **62** C 2
Hawthorne **18** C 4
Hay **60** G 6
Hay River **10** T 6
Hayes, Mount **10** N 6
Hays **16** D 4
Haysyn **36** F 3
Hayward **18** B 4
Hazaradjat **45** K 6
Hazard **14** C 3
Hazaribagh **46** F 4
Hazelton **10** R 7
Hazen Strait **10** U 3
Hazen, Lake **8** W 2
Hazlehurst **14** C 4
Hazleton **14** D 2
Hazlett, Lake **60** D 4
Hearne **16** D 5
Hearst **8** U 9
Hebei **49** J 3
Hebi **49** J 3
Hebrides, Sea of the **30** A 3
Hebron **8** Y 7
Hechi **49** H 6
Hechuan **49** H 4
Hecla, Cape **8** Y 2
Hede **38** H 3
Hedmark **38** H 3
Hefei **49** K 4
Hegang **50** F 3
Heidelberg **36** B 3
Heidenheim **36** C 3
Heilbronn **36** B 3
Heilongjiang **50** E 3
Heilprin Land **8** 2
Heilprin Ø **8** Y 3
Heimaey **38** A 3
Heishan **50** D 4
Hejiang **49** H 5
Hejlong-Jiang **50** D 2
Hekimhan **35** G 5
Helena (Arkansas, U.S.) **16** E 5
Helena (Montana, U.S.) **18** D 2
Helensville **62** B 2
Helgoländer Bucht **36** B 2
Helgøy **38** J 1
Heli **50** F 3
Hellūn **33** B 2
Helmsdale **30** C 2
Helodrano Antongila **58** D 3
Helong **54** A 2
Helsingborg **38** H 4
Helsingfors **38** K 3
Helsinki **38** K 3
Helston **28** B 4
Hemsön **38** J 3
Henan **49** J 4
Henderson (Nevada, U.S.) **18** D 4
Henderson (North Carolina, U.S.) **14** D 3
Henderson (Texas, U.S.) **16** E 5
Henderson Island **59** N 6
Hendersonville (North Carolina, U.S.) **14** C 3
Hendersonville (Tennessee, U.S.) **14** B 3
Hengdnan Shan **48** F 5
Hengshan **49** J 5
Hengshui **49** K 3
Hengxian **49** H 6
Hengyang **49** J 5
Henichesūk **35** F 1
Henrietta Maria, Cape **8** U 7
Henryetta **16** D 4
Henzada **47** H 5
Hepu **49** H 6
Herat **45** K 6
Herbert **18** E 1
Hereford (U.K.) **28** C 3
Hereford (U.S.) **16** C 5
Herlen Gol **50** B 3
Hermanas **20** D 2
Hermiston **18** C 2
Hermit Islands **59** D 4
Hermosillo **20** B 2
Herning **38** G 4
Heroica Zitácuaro **20** D 4
Herrero, Punta **20** G 4
Herschel Island **10** P 5
Hertungen af Orléans Land **8** Gg 3
Hexian **49** J 6
Heyuan **49** J 6
Heze **49** K 3
Hialeah **14** C 5
Hibbing **16** E 2
Hibernia Reef **60** C 2
Hidaka-Sammyaku **54** D 2
Hidalgo **20** E 3
Hidalgo del Parral **20** C 2
High Level **10** T 7
High Point **14** D 3
High Prairie **10** T 7
High River **18** D 1
High Wycombe **28** D 4
Highrock Lake **10** W 7
Hiiumaa **38** K 4
Hikueru **59** L 5
Hildesheim **36** B 2
Hill Bank **20** G 4
Hillsboro **16** D 5
Hilo **59** K 2
Hilo Bay **20** G 4
Hilton Head Island **14** C 4
Himachal **46** D 2

Himalayas **46** D 2
Himi **54** C 3
Hims **44** E 6
Hinchinbrook Island (Australia) **60** H 3
Hinchinbrook Island (U.S.) **10** N 6
Hindukush **45** L 6
Hindupur **46** D 6
Hinganghat **46** D 4
Hinnøya **38** J 2
Hinton **10** T 8
Hirado **54** A 4
Hiriyūr **46** D 6
Hirosaki **54** D 2
Hiroshima **54** B 4
Hirtshals **38** G 4
Hisār **46** D 3
Hispaniola **22** H 4
Hita **54** B 4
Hitachi **54** D 3
Hiti **59** L 5
Hitra **38** G 3
Hlukhiv **36** G 2
Ho Chi Minh **47** K 6
Hoa Binh **47** K 4
Hobart **60** H 8
Hobart (U.S.) **16** D 4
Hobbs **16** C 5
Hoburgen **38** J 4
Hochstetter Forland **8** Gg 3
Hodh **56** C 3
Hódmezővásárhely **36** E 3
Hodonin **36** D 3
Hofsjökull **38** B 3
Hōfu **54** B 4
Hogback Mountain **18** D 3
Hoggar **56** D 2
Hoh Sai Hu **48** E 3
Hoh Xil Hu **48** E 3
Hoh Xil Shan **48** D 3
Hoi An **47** K 5
Hokitika **62** B 3
Hokkaidō **54** D 2
Hoktemberyan **35** L 4
Hol **38** G 3
Hola Prystan **44** D 3
Holbox, Isla **20** G 3
Holbrook **18** D 5
Holdenville **16** D 4
Holdrege **16** D 3
Holguín **22** G 3
Holland **14** B 2
Holly Springs **14** B 4
Hollywood **14** C 5
Holm Land **8** Hh 2
Holm Ø **8** Z 4
Holman **10** T 4
Holmes Reefs **59** E 5
Holmön **38** K 3
Holovanivsūk **44** D 3
Holstebro **38** G 4
Holsteinsborg **8** Aa 5
Holycross **43** Y 4
Holyhead **28** B 3
Homer **43** Z 5
Homestead (U.S.) **14** C 5
Homewood **14** B 4
Homs **44** E 6
Homyelū **36** G 2
Hon Gai **47** K 4
Hon Khoci **47** J 7
Hon Tho Chau **47** J 7
Honāvar **46** C 6
Honda **22** H 6
Honduras **22** E 5
Honduras, Golfo de **20** G 4
Hönefoss **38** H 3
Hong Kong **49** J 6
Hongjiang **49** H 5
Hongor **50** B 3
Hongshui He **49** H 6
Hongwon **50** E 4
Hongyuan **49** G 4
Hongze **49** K 4
Hongze Hu **49** K 4
Honiara **59** E 4
Honningsvåg **38** L 1
Honolulu **12** E 7
Honshū **54** D 3
Hood Point **60** B 6
Hood River **18** B 2
Hoogeveen **36** B 2
Hoorn **36** B 2
Hoover Dam **18** D 4
Hope **16** E 5
Hopedale **8** Y 7
Hopes Advance, Cap **8** X 6
Hopewell, Isles **8** V 7
Hopkinsville **14** B 3
Hoquiam **18** B 2
Hordaland **38** G 3
Horlivka **44** E 3
Horn **38** A 2
Horn Plateau **10** S 6
Hornavan **38** J 2
Hornell **14** D 2
Horodenka **36** F 3
Horqin Youyi Qiahqi **50** D 3
Horqin Zuoyi Zhongqi **50** D 4
Horsens **38** G 4
Horsham **60** G 7
Horten **38** H 4
Hose Mountains **52** E 5
Hot Springs (Arkansas, U.S.) **16** E 5
Hot Springs (New Mexico, U.S.) **18** E 5
Hot Springs (South Dakota, U.S.) **16** C 3
Hotan **48** B 3
Hoting **38** J 3
Hottah Lake **10** T 5
Houghton **14** B 1
Houghton Lake **14** 2
Houlton **14** F 1
Houma (China) **49** J 3
Houma (U.S.) **20** F 2
Houston **20** E 2
Houterive **8** X 9
Houtman Abrolhos **60** A 5
Hovd **48** E 1
Hovgaard Ø **8** Hh 2
Hövsgõi **49** H 2
Hövsgöl Nuur **41** V 7
Howe, Cape **60** H 7
Howland **14** F 1
Howrah **46** F 4
Hoy **30** C 2
Hradec Králové **36** D 2
Hrebinka **36** G 2
Hrodna **36** E 2
Hsilo **49** L 6
Hsinchu **49** L 6
Hu Men **49** J 6
Hua Hin **47** H 6
Huadian **50** E 4
Huahine **59** K 5
Huaiūan **49** J 2
Huaide **50** D 4
Huaiji **49** J 6
Huailai **50** C 4
Huainan **49** K 4
Huairen **49** J 3
Huajuapan de Léon **20** E 4
Hua-lien **49** L 6
Huambo **58** A 3
Huanan **50** F 3
Huancayo **24** D 4
Huang Hai **49** L 3
Huang He **49** J 3
Huangchuan **49** K 4
Huangliu **47** K 5
Huangshi **49** K 4
Huangxian **49** L 3
Huangyan **49** L 5
Huangzhong **49** G 3
Huanren **54** A 2
Huarmey **24** D 4
Huatabampo **20** C 2
Huauchinanco **20** E 3
Huautla **20** E 3
Huazhou **49** J 6
Hubei **49** J 4
Huddersfield **28** D 3
Huder **50** D 2
Hudiksvall **38** J 3
Hudson Bay **8** T 7
Hudson Land **8** Gg 4
Hudson Strait **8** V 6
Hue **47** K 5
Huehuetenango **20** F 4
Huelva **33** A 2
Huesca **32** B 3
Hugh Town **28** A 5
Hughenden **60** G 4

Hugli **46** F 4
Hugo **16** D 5
Huhhot **49** J 2
Huiūan **49** K 5
Huiarau Range **62** C 2
Hŭichŭŏn **50** E 4
Huilai **49** K 6
Huili **49** G 5
Huimin **49** K 3
Huinan **54** A 2
Huiten Nur **48** E 3
Huixtla **20** F 4
Huize **49** G 5
Hŭksan-chedo **50** E 6
Hulan **54** A 1
Hulan Ergi **50** D 3
Hulin **50** F 3
Hull **8** V 9
Hulun Buir Meng **50** C 3
Hulun Nur **50** C 3
Humaitá **24** E 3
Humber **28** E 3
Humboldt (U.S.) **14** B 3
Humboldt Gletscher **8** Y 3
Humboldt River **18** C 4
Hunan **49** J 5
Hunchun **50** F 4
Hunedoara **36** E 3
Hungary **36** D 3
Hŭngnam **50** E 5
Hunjiang **50** E 4
Hunter Island **60** G 8
Hunterville **62** C 2
Huntington **14** C 3
Huntsville (Alabama, U.S.) **14** B 4
Huntsville (Canada) **14** D 1
Huntsville (Texas, U.S.) **16** D 5
Hunyuan **49** J 3
Huon Peninsula **59** D 4
Huoshan **49** K 4
Huoxian **49** J 3
Huron **16** D 3
Huron Mountains **14** B 1
Huron, Lake **14** C 2
Hurricane **18** D 4
Hurst **16** D 5
Hūsavik **38** B 2
Huskvarna **38** H 4
Huslia **10** L 5
Hutchinson (Kansas, U.S.) **16** D 4
Hutchinson (Minnesota, U.S.) **16** E 3
Hutou **54** B 1
Huzhou **49** L 4
Hvar **34** D 2
Hwange **58** B 3
Hyannis **14** E 2
Hyargas Nuur **41** 8
Hyderabad (India) **46** D 5
Hyderabad (Pakistan) **46** B 3
Hyères **34** B 2
Hyesan **50** E 4
Hysham **18** E 2
Hyūga **54** B 4
Hyvinge **38** K 3
Hyvinkää **38** K 3
Iaşi **36** F 3
Ibadan **56** D 4
Ibagué **22** G 7
Ibérico, Sistema **32** B 3
Ibonma **53** J 6
Ica **24** D 4
İçel (Turkey) **35** F 6
Iceland **38** A 3
Ichalkaranji **46** C 5
Ichchapuram **46** E 5
Ichinskaya Sopka **43** P 5
Ichnya **36** G 2
Ichuan **49** G 4
Idabel **16** E 5
Idah **56** D 4
Idaho **18** C 3
Idaho Falls **18** D 3
Idhān Awbārī **56** E 2
Idlib **44** E 5
Idre **38** H 3
Ife **56** D 4
Igarka **41** T 4
Igatpuri **46** C 5
İğdır **35** L 5
Iglesias **34** B 3
Igloolik **8** U 5
Ignace **16** E 2
İğneada **35** B 4
Igoumenitsa **34** E 3
Iguala **20** E 4
Igualada **32** C 3
Iguatu **24** H 3
Iguigik **43** Y 5
Ihosy **58** D 4
Iida **54** C 3
Ilhéus **24** H 4
Iisalmi **38** L 3
IJsselmeer **36** B 2
Ikaria **44** C 5
Ikatskiy Khrebet **41** X 7
Ikeda **54** D 2
Ila **56** D 4
Ilagan **53** G 2
Ilan **49** L 6
Ilanskiy **41** V 6
Iława **36** D 2
Île Des Noefs **58** E 2
Ilebo **58** B 2
Îlede **32** C 2
Îles de Los **56** B 4
Ilford **10** Y 8
Ilgın **35** D 5
Ilha de Marajó **24** F 3
Ilha do Bananal **24** F 4
Ilhas Selvagens (Portugal) **56** B 1
Iliamna Lake **43** Y 5
Iligan **53** G 4
Ilimananngip Nunaa **8** Ff 4
Ilimsk **41** W 6
Ilinskiy **50** H 3
Ilūinskiy (Russia) **54** D 1
Illichivsūk **35** D 1
Illinois **14** B 2
Illinois River **16** E 4
Illoqqortoormiut **8** 4
Iloilo **53** G 3
Ilorin **56** D 4
Ilūpi **43** S 4
Ilulissat **8** Aa 5
Ilych **40** N 5
Imabari **54** B 4
Imandra, Ozero **40** H 4
Imatra **38** L 3
Imeni Ismail Samani, Pik **45** M 5
Imeni Mariny **42** N 4
Imperatriz **24** G 3
Imperia **34** B 2
Imphal **47** G 4
Inanwatan **53** J 6
Inari **38** L 2
Inarigda **41** X 5
Inarijärvi **38** L 2
İnce Burnu **35** F 3
İncekum Burnu **44** D 5
Inchūŏn **50** E 5
Independence (Kansas, U.S.) **16** D 4
Independence (Missouri, U.S.) **16** E 4
India **46** D 5
Indian Harbour **8** Z 8
Indian Ocean **46** E 6
Indian Springs **18** 4
Indiana **14** B 2
Indianapolis **14** B 3
Indias Occidentales **22** J 3
Indiga **40** L 4
Indigirka **42** M 4
Indonesia **52** D 6
Indore **46** D 4
Indramayu **52** D 7
Indus **46** B 4
Inebolu **44** D 4
İnecik **35** B 4
İnegöl **35** C 4
Ingham **60** H 3
Inglefield Land **8** W 3
Ing-Ifshöfði **38** B 3
Ingolstadt **36** C 3
Inhuletsū **44** D 3
Innamincka **60** G 5
Inner Hebrides **30** A 4
Inner Islands **58** E 2
Innisfail **60** H 3
Innokentūyevka **54** C 1
Innsbruck **36** C 3
Inobonto **53** G 5

Inowrocław **36** D 2
Insan-ni **54** A 2
Inta **40** O 4
Interview Island **47** G 6
Inukjuak **8** V 7
Inuvik **10** Q 5
Inveraray **30** B 3
Invercargill **62** A 4
Inverness **30** B 3
Inya **42** M 4
Inza **44** G 2
Ioannina **34** E 3
Iokanga **40** J 4
Iona (U.K.) **30** A 3
Ionian Sea **34** D 3
Ionioi Nisoi **34** D 3
Iony, Ostrov **42** M 5
Ios **34** F 3
Iossar **40** M 5
Iowa **16** D 3
Iowa City **16** E 3
Ipatinga **24** G 4
Ipatovo **44** F 3
Ipeiros **34** E 3
Ipiales **22** G 7
Ipoh **52** C 5
İpsala **35** B 4
Ipswich (Australia) **60** J 5
Ipswich (U.K.) **28** E 3
Iqaluit **8** X 6
Iquique **24** D 5
Iquitos **24** D 3
Irakleio **34** F 3
Iran **44** H 6
Iran Gate **34** E 2
Iran, Pegunungan **52** E 5
Irapuato **20** D 3
Irbit **40** O 6
Ireland **31** B 2
Iringa **58** C 2
Iriomote-jima **49** L 6
Iriona **20** G 4
Irish Sea **28** B 3
Irkutsk **41** W 7
Iron Mountain **14** B 1
Ironwood **8** T 9
Irrawaddy **47** H 4
Irrawaddy, Mouths of the **47** G 5
Irtysh **40** Q 6
Irún **32** B 3
Irving **16** D 5
Isabel **16** C 2
Isabella, Cordillera **20** G 5
Isachenka, Ostrov **41** T 2
Isachsen **10** W 3
Isachsen, Cape **10** V 3
Ísafjörður **38** A 2
Isa-haya **54** B 4
Isaly **30** A 4
Ise **54** C 4
Isernia **34** C 2
Ise-wan **54** C 4
Isfara **45** M 4
Ishikari-wan **54** C 2
Ishikawa **50** E 7
Ishim **40** P 6
Ishim (River) **40** Q 6
Ishimbay **40** N 7
Ishinomaki **54** D 3
Isilūkulū **40** Q 7
Isiro **58** B 1
Isjichly **44** G 5
İskenderun **35** G 6
İskenderun Körfezi **35** F 6
Iskitim **41** S 7
Isla de Chiloé **24** D 7
Isla Española **24** C 3
Isla Fernandina **24** B 3
Isla Grande de Tierra del Fuego **24** E 8
Isla Isabela **24** B 3
Isla Marchena **24** B 2
Isla Pinta **24** B 2
Isla San Cristóbal **24** C 3
Isla San Salvador **24** B 3
Isla Santa Cruz **24** B 3
Isla Santa María **24** B 3
Islamabad **45** M 6
Island Lake **10** X 8
Islas Galápagos (Ecuador) **24** B 2
Islas Revillagigedo (Mexico) **20** B 4
Îsles Tristao **56** B 3
İsparta **44** D 5
Israel **44** D 6
İstanbul **35** C 4
İstanbul Boğazı **35** C 4
Istra **36** C 3
Isua **8** Bb 6
Itaberaba **24** G 4
Itabuna **24** H 4
Itagüí **22** G 6
Itajaí **24** G 5
Italy **34** C 2
Itanagar **47** G 3
Itaquari **24** H 5
Itarsi **46** D 4
Ithaca **14** D 2
Ithaki **34** E 3
Itoigawa **54** C 3
Ittoqqortoormiit **8** Gg 4
Iturup, Ostrov **54** E 2
Itzehoe **36** B 2
Iulūtin **43** U 3
Ivakoany **58** D 4
Ivalo **38** L 2
Ivanava **36** F 2
Ivanhoe **60** G 6
Ivano-Frankivsūk **36** E 3
Ivanovka **44** H 2
Ivanovo **40** K 6
Ivao, Gora **54** E 1
Ivdelū **40** O 5
Ivittuut **8** Bb 6
Ivory Coast **56** C 4
Ivrea **36** B 3
Ivujivik **8** V 6
Iwaki **54** D 3
Iwakuni **54** B 4
Iwamisawa **54** D 2
Iwanai **54** D 2
Iwŏn **54** A 2
Izamal **20** G 3
Izhevsk **40** M 6
Izmayil **35** C 2
İzmir **35** B 5
İzmit **35** C 4
Izuhara **54** A 4
Izu-Shotō **54** C 4
Izvestiy Tsik, Ostrov **41** S 2
Izyum **44** E 3
Jabalpur **46** D 4
Jackpot **18** D 3
Jacksboro **16** D 5
Jackson (Michigan, U.S.) **14** C 2
Jackson (Mississippi, U.S.) **16** E 5
Jackson (Tennessee, U.S.) **14** B 3
Jackson Head **62** A 3
Jackson Lake **18** D 3
Jacksonville (Florida, U.S.) **14** C 4
Jacksonville (Illinois, U.S.) **16** E 4
Jacksonville (North Carolina, U.S.) **14** D 4
Jacksonville (Texas, U.S.) **16** D 5
Jacksonville Beach **14** C 4
Jäckvik **38** J 2
Jacobabad **46** B 3
Jacona **20** D 4
Jaén (Spain) **33** B 2
Jaffa, Cape **60** F 7
Jaffna **46** E 7
Jagdalpur **46** E 5
Jagdaqi **50** D 2
Jagodina **34** E 2
Jagtiāl **46** D 5
Jaipur **46** D 3
Jaisalmer **46** C 3
Jakarta **52** D 7
Jakobshavn **8** Aa 5
Jalalabad **45** M 6
Jalapa Enríquez **20** E 4
Jalgaon **46** D 4
Jalisco **20** C 3
Jalna **46** D 5
Jālor **46** C 3
Jalostotitlán **20** D 3
Jalpa **20** D 3
Jalpāiguri **47** F 3
Jamaica **22** G 4
Jamaica Channel **22** G 4
Jambi **52** C 6
Jambusar **46** C 4

James Bay **8** U 8
James River (North Dakota, U.S.) **16** D 2
James River (Virginia, U.S.) **14** D 3
Jameson Land **8** Gg 4
Jamestown (New York, U.S.) **14** D 2
Jamestown (North Dakota, U.S.) **16** D 2
Jamiltepec **20** E 4
Jammu **46** C 2
Jammu and Kashmir **45** N 6
Jamnagar **46** C 4
Jampur **46** C 3
Jamshedpur **46** F 4
Jämtland **38** H 3
Jamuna **47** F 3
Janchuan **48** F 5
Janesville **14** B 2
Janos **18** E 5
Jaora **46** D 4
Japan **54** C 4
Japan, Sea of **54** B 2
Jardines de la Reina, Archipiélago de los **22** F 3
Jarkant **48** B 3
Jarosław **36** E 2
Järpen **38** H 3
Jarud Qi **50** D 4
Järvenpää **38** L 3
Jarvis **59** J 4
Jasło **36** E 3
Jasper **10** T 8
Jasper (Alabama, U.S.) **14** B 4
Jasper (Texas, U.S.) **16** E 5
Jasper National Park **10** T 8
Jászberény **36** D 3
Jatni **46** F 4
Jaumave **20** E 3
Jaunpur **46** E 3
Java **52** D 7
Java Sea **52** D 7
Jawa **52** D 7
Jawa, Laut **52** D 7
Jayapura **59** D 4
Jaypur **46** E 5
Jedburgh **28** C 2
Jędrzejów **36** E 2
Jefferson City **16** E 4
Jefferson River **18** D 2
Jefferson, Mount (Nevada, U.S.) **18** C 4
Jega **56** D 3
Jēkabpils **38** L 4
Jelenia Góra **36** D 2
Jelgava **38** K 4
Jemaja **52** D 5
Jena **36** C 2
Jeneponto **53** F 7
Jengish Chokusu **45** O 4
Jenny Lind Island **10** W 5
Jens Munk Island **8** U 5
Jens Munk Ø **8** Cc 6
Jequié **24** H 4
Jerada **56** C 1
Jerez dé García Salinas **20** D 3
Jeréz de la Frontera **33** A 2
Jerome **18** D 3
Jersey **32** B 2
Jessore **47** F 4
Jesup **14** C 4
Jesus Carranza **20** E 4
Jhālāwār **46** D 4
Jhang Sadar **46** C 2
Jhansi **46** D 3
Jharkhand **46** E 4
Jhelum **46** C 2
Jiahe **49** J 5
Jiaji **52** E 2
Jiamusi **50** F 3
Jiūan **49** J 5
Jian **50** E 4
Jiūan (Jilin, China) **54** A 2
Jianchuan **48** F 5
Jianghua **49** J 5
Jiangjin **49** H 5
Jiangle **49** K 5
Jiangling **49** J 4
Jiangmen **49** J 6
Jiangsu **49** K 4
Jiangxi **49** J 5
Jiangyou **49** G 4
Jianli **49** J 5
Jianūou **49** K 5
Jianping **50** C 4
Jianshui **49** G 6
Jianyang **49** G 4
Jiaohe **50** E 4
Jiaozuo **49** J 3
Jiashan **49** K 4
Jiaxing **49** L 4
Jiayu **49** J 5
Jiayuguan **48** F 3
Jiexiu **49** J 3
Jieyang **49** K 6
Jihlava **36** D 3
Jilin **50** E 4
Jilin (China) **54** A 2
Jilin (State, China) **54** A 2
Jīma **56** G 4
Jiménez **20** D 2
Jimo **49** L 3
Jimsar **48** D 2
Jinan **49** K 3
Jingbian **49** H 3
Jingdezhen **49** K 5
Jinghai **49** K 3
Jinghe **48** C 2
Jingpo Hu **54** A 2
Jingxian **49** H 5
Jingyu **50** E 4
Jingyuan **49** G 5
Jinhua **49** K 5
Jining **49** J 2
Jining (Shandong, China) **49** K 3
Jinja **58** C 1
Jinotepe **20** G 5
Jinsha **49** H 5
Jinsha Jiang **49** G 5
Jinxi **50** D 4
Jinxian **49** L 3
Jinxiang **49** K 3
Jinzhai **49** K 4
Jinzhou **50** D 4
Jishou **49** H 5
Jisr ash-Shughūr **35** G 7
Jiujiang **49** K 5
Jiuquan **48** F 3
Jiutai **50** E 4
Jiwen **50** D 2
Jixi **54** B 1
Jizzax **45** L 4
João Pessoa **24** H 3
Jodhpur **46** C 3
Joensuu **38** L 3
Jōetsu **54** C 3
Johannesburg **58** B 4
John Day **18** C 3
John Day River **18** B 2
John oū Groats **30** C 2
Johnson **16** C 4
Johnson City (Tennessee, U.S.) **14** C 3
Johnson City (Texas, U.S.) **16** D 5
Johnsonburg **14** D 2
Johnsons Crossing **10** Q 6
Johnston Lakes, The **60** B 6
Johnstown **14** D 2
Johor Bharu **52** C 5
Joinville **24** G 5
Jokkmokk **38** J 2
Joliette **8** W 9
Jolo **52** G 4
Jolo (Island) **52** G 4
Jonava **38** K 4
Jonesboro **16** E 4
Jönköping **38** H 4
Jonquière **8** W 9
Jonuta **20** F 4
Joplin **16** E 4
Jordan (U.S.) **18** E 2
Jordan Valley **18** C 3
Jorhāt **47** G 3
Jörn **38** K 2
Jos **56** D 3
Joseph Boanparte Gulf **60** D 2
Joshua Tree National Monument **18** C 5
Jostedalsbreen **38** G 3
Jotunheimen **38** G 3
Juan Aldama **20** D 3
Juan de Fuca, Strait of **18** A 2
Juan De Nova (France) **58** D 3
Juárez, Sierra de **18** C 5
Juàzeiro **24** G 3

Juàzeiro do Norte **24** G 3
Juba **56** G 4
Jubba **58** D 1
Jubbada **58** D 1
Júcar, Rio **33** B 2
Juchitlán de Zaragoza **20** E 4
Jucuapa **20** G 5
Juigalpa **20** G 5
Juiz de Fora **24** G 5
Julianehåb **8** Bb 6
Julimes **20** C 2
Jullundur **46** D 2
Junction **16** D 5
Junction City **16** D 4
Juneau **10** Q 7
Junín **24** E 6
Junlian **49** G 5
Junsele **38** J 3
Jura (France) **36** B 3
Jura (U.K.) **30** B 3
Jura, Sound of **30** A 4
Jurhen Ul Shan **48** E 4
Jūrmala **38** K 4
Jutiapa **20** G 5
Juticalpa **20** G 5
Juxian **49** K 3
Juzur Qarqannah **34** C 4
Jylland **38** G 4
Jyväskylä **38** L 3
K.J.V. Steenstrup Nordre Bræ **8** Dd 5
Ka Lae **12** E 8
Kabaena **53** G 7
Kabara **59** H 5
Kabinakagami Lake **14** B 1
Kabinda **58** B 2
Kābul **45** L 6
Kabwe **58** B 3
Kachikattsy **42** J 4
Kachug **41** X 7
Kadan Kyun **47** H 6
Kadıköy **35** B 4
Kadınhanı **35** E 5
Kadirli **44** E 5
Kadoka **16** C 3
Kadoma **58** B 3
Kāduglī **56** F 3
Kaduna **56** D 3
Kaechnay Darweyhān **45** K 6
Kaédi **56** B 3
Kaes ng **50** E 5
Kaesŏng **54** A 3
Kafiau **53** H 6
Kafue **58** B 3
Kagalaska Island **43** U 6
Kagayan de Sulu Island **52** F 4
Kagoshima **54** B 4
Kahoolawe **12** E 7
Kahramanmaraş **35** G 6
Kahuku Point **12** E 7
Kai Besar **53** J 7
Kai Xian **49** H 4
Kai, Kepulauan **52** J 7
Kaifeng **49** J 4
Kaikoura **62** B 3
Kaili **49** H 5
Kailu **50** D 4
Kainji Reservoir **56** D 3
Kaipara Harbour **62** B 2
Kairouan **56** E 1
Kaiserslautern **36** B 3
Kaitaia **62** B 2
Kaiyuan (Liaoning, China) **50** D 4
Kaiyuan (Yunnan, China) **49** G 6
Kajaani **38** L 3
Kajabbi **60** G 4
Kajakī Dam **45** L 6
Kakana **47** G 7
Kākināda **46** E 5
Kaktovik **10** O 4
Kalaallit Nunaat **8** Aa 4
Kalabahi **52** G 7
Kalabarri National Park **60** A 5
Kalach **44** F 2
Kalachinsk **40** Q 6
Kalach-na-Donu **44** F 3
Kalahari Desert **58** B 4
Kalaheo **12** E 7
Kalakan **42** G 5
Kalamata **34** E 3
Kalamazoo **14** B 2
Kalana **38** K 4
Kalao **53** G 7
Kalaotoa **52** G 7
Kalasin **47** J 5
Kalat **46** B 3
Kalegauk **47** H 5
Kalémié **58** B 2
Kalevala **40** H 4
Kalgoorlie **60** C 6
Kalibo **52** G 3
Kalima **58** B 2
Kalimantan **52** E 6
Kalinin **40** J 6
Kaliningrad **36** E 2
Kalinino **54** A 1
Kalinkavichy **36** F 2
Kalispell **18** D 2
Kalisz **36** D 2
Kalix **38** K 2
Kalixälven **38** K 2
Kalmar **38** J 4
Kalsong **53** G 4
Kaltag **43** Y 4
Kaltan **41** T 7
Kaluga **44** E 2
Kalukalukuang **52** F 7
Kalush **36** E 3
Kalutara **46** E 7
Kalyazin **40** J 6
Kalymnos **34** F 3
Kalymnos (Greece) **35** B 6
Kalymnos (Island, Greece) **35** B 6
Kama **40** M 6
Kamaishi **54** D 3
Kaman **35** E 5
Kamas **18** D 3
Kambarka **40** M 6
Kamchatka, Poluostrov **43** P 5
Kamchatskiy Poluostrov **43** Q 5
Kamenjak, Rt **34** C 2
Kamenka **44** F 2
Kamenū-na-Obi **41** S 7
Kamensk **41** X 7
Kamenskoye **43** R 4
Kamensk-Shakhtinskiy **44** F 3
Kamensk-Uralūskiy **40** O 6
Kamina **58** B 2
Kaminak Lake **8** R 6
Kạminuriak Lake **8** RS 6
Kamkaly **45** M 4
Kamloops **10** S 8
Kamo **35** L 4
Kampala **58** C 1
Kampar **52** C 5
Kampen **36** B 2
Kamphaeng Phet **52** B 2
Kâmpóng Cham **52** D 3
Kâmpóng Chhnăng **52** C 3
Kampuchea **52** C 3
Kāmthī **46** D 4
Kamūūyanetsū-Podilūsūkyy **36** F 3
Kamyshin **44** G 2
Kamyshlov **40** O 6
Kanab **18** D 4
Kanaga Island **43** U 6
Kananga **58** B 2
Kanangra Boyd National Park **60** J 6
Kanazawa **54** C 3
Kanchana-buri **52** B 3
Kanchenjunga **48** D 5
Kānchipuram **46** D 6
Kandahār **46** B 2
Kandalaksha **40** H 4
Kandavu Island **59** G 5
Kandhkot **46** B 3
Kandi, Tanjung **52** G 5
Kandukūr **46** D 5
Kandy **46** E 7
Kane Basin **8** X 3
Kanem **56** E 3
Kanevskaya **35** H 1
Kangaarsussuaq **8** W 3
Kangar **52** C 4
Kangaroo Island **60** F 7
Kangāvar **44** G 6
Kangbao **49** J 2
Kangding **49** G 4
Kangean **52** F 7
Kangerlussuaq **8** Aa 5
Kangersuatsiaq **8** Z 4
Kanggye **50** E 4
Kangikajik **8** Gg 4

Kangiqsualujjuaq **8** X 7
Kangirsuk **8** W 6
Kangnŭng **50** E 5
Kangping **50** D 4
Kangshan **49** L 6
Kangto **47** G 3
Kaniet Islands **59** D 4
Kanin Nos **40** K 4
Kanin Nos, Mys **40** K 4
Kankakee **14** B 2
Kankan **56** C 3
Kānker **46** E 4
Kankesanturai **46** E 7
Kanmaw Kyun **47** H 6
Kannapolis **14** C 3
Kano **56** D 3
Kanowit **52** E 5
Kanoya **54** B 4
Kanpur **46** E 3
Kansas **16** C 4
Kansas City **16** E 4
Kansk **41** V 6
Kansŏng **54** A 3
Kantang **52** B 4
Kanton **49** J 6
Kanye **58** B 4
Kaohsiung **49** L 6
Kaolack **56** B 3
Kapfenberg **36** D 3
Kaposvár **36** D 3
Kapuskasing **8** U 9
Kara Sea **40** Q 3
Karabalta **45** M 4
Karabash **40** O 6
Karabük **35** E 4
Karabula **41** V 6
Karacabey **34** F 2
Karachev **36** G 2
Karachi **46** B 4
Karad **46** C 5
Karaginskiy, Ostrov **43** Q 5
Karaikkudi **46** D 6
Karakelong **53** H 5
Karakol **45** N 4
Karakoram Range **45** N 5
Karaman **35** E 6
Karamea Bight **62** B 3
Karapınar **35** E 6
Karaqoyyn Köli **45** L 3
Karasjok **38** L 2
Karasu **44** F 5
Karasu (Turkey) **35** D 4
Karasu-Aras Dağları **35** J 5
Karasuk **41** R 7
Karaul **41** S 3
Karawang **52** D 7
Karbalāū **44** F 6
Karditsa **34** E 3
Karen **47** G 6
Karesuando **38** K 2
Kargasok **41** S 6
Kargopolū **40** J 5
Karigasniemi **38** L 2
Karik Shan **48** E 2
Karimata **52** D 6
Karimata, Selat **52** D 6
Karimganj **47** G 4
Karkar Island **59** D 4
Karkinitsūka Zatoka **35** E 2
Karleby **38** K 3
Karlovac **36** D 3
Karlovy Vary **36** C 2
Karlshamn **38** J 4
Karlskoga **38** H 4
Karlskrona **38** J 4
Karlsruhe **36** B 3
Karlstad **38** H 4
Karluk **43** Z 5
Karmøy **38** F 4
Karnātaka **46** D 6
Karnobat **34** F 2
Karossa, Tanjung **52** F 7
Karpathos **34** F 3
Karpinsk **40** N 6
Kars **35** K 4
Kārsava **38** L 4
Karskiye Vorota, Proliv **40** N 3
Karskoye More **40** P 2
Kartaly **45** K 2
Karūr **46** D 6
Karviná **36** D 3
Kārwār **46** C 6
Karymskoye **42** F 6
Kasaï-Occidental **58** B 2
Kasaï-Oriental **58** B 2
Kasaragod **46** D 6
Kasba Lake **10** W 6
Kāshān **44** H 6
Kashi **48** B 3
Kashin **40** J 6
Kashiwazaki **54** C 3
Kashmor **46** B 3
Kasimov **44** F 2
Kasiruta **53** H 6
Kaskinen **38** K 3
Kaskö **38** K 3
Kasongo **58** B 2
Kasos **34** F 3
Kaspiskoye More **44** G 4
Kaspīy Mangy Oypaty **44** G 3
Kaspiyskoye More **44** G 3
Kassalā **56** G 3
Kassel **36** B 2
Kastamonu **35** E 4
Kastoria **34** E 2
Kasungan **52** E 6
Katanga (Dem. Rep. of the Congo) **58** B 2
Katanga (River, Russia) **41** V 5
Katangli **42** M 6
Katanning **60** B 6
Katav-Ivanovsk **40** N 7
Katchall Island **47** G 7
Katerini **34** E 2
Katherine **60** E 2
Kathmandu **46** F 3
Katihar **46** F 3
Katiu **59** L 5
Katowice **36** D 2
Katsina **56** D 3
Kattaqoūrgūon **45** L 5
Kattegat **38** H 4
Kauai **12** E 7
Kauai Channel **12** E 7
Kaufbeuren **36** C 3
Kaukura **59** L 5
Kaunas **36** E 2
Kaura-Namoda **56** D 3
Kautokeino **38** K 2
Kavajū **34** D 2
Kavala **34** E 2
Kavali **46** D 6
Kavaratti **46** C 6
Kavīr-e Namak **45** J 6
Kawakawa **62** B 2
Kawalusu **53** H 5
Kawerau **62** C 2
Kawich Peak **18** C 4
Kawio, Kepulauan **53** H 5
Kawm Umbū **56** G 2
Kayak Island **10** O 7
Kayan **47** H 5
Kayangel Islands **53** J 4
Kayenta **18** D 4
Kayes **56** B 3
Kayseri **35** F 5
Kayuagung **52** C 6
Kazachinskoye **41** X 6
Kazachūye **42** L 2
Kazakhstan **45** J 3
Kazanū **40** L 6
Kazanka **44** D 3
Kazanlŭk **34** F 2
Kazantip, Mys **44** E 3
Kazbek **44** F 4
Kāzerūn **44** H 7
Kazincbarcika **36** E 3
Kazyatyn **36** F 3
Kazym **40** P 5
Kealakekua Bay **12** E 8
Keams Canyon **18** D 4
Kearney **16** D 3
Kebumen **52** D 7
Kecskemét **36** D 3
Kediri **52** E 7
Keewatin **16** E 2
Kefallonia **34** D 3
Kefamenanu **52** G 7
Keffi **56** D 4
Keflavūk **38** A 3
Kegulūta **44** F 3
Keitele **38** L 3
Keith (Scotland) **30** C 3
Kekaha **12** E 7
Kelaa Kebira **34** C 3
Kelang **52** C 5

Kelkit Cayı **35** G 4
Kellett, Cape **10** R 4
Kellogg **18** C 2
Kelloselkä **38** L 2
Kélo **56** E 4
Kelowna **18** C 2
Kelsey Bay **10** R 8
Kelso **18** B 2
Keluang **52** C 5
Kemū **40** H 5
Kemerovo **41** T 6
Kemi **38** K 2
Kemijärvi **38** L 2
Kemijoki **38** L 2
Kempendyayi **42** G 4
Kempt, Lac **14** E 1
Kempten **36** C 3
Kenai Fjords National Park **43** Aa 5
Kenal **10** M 6
Kendal **28** C 2
Kendallville **14** B 2
Kendari **53** G 6
Kendawangan **52** 6
Kenema **56** B 4
Keng Tung **47** H 4
Kenitra **56** C 1
Kenmare (Ireland) **31** B 3
Kenmare (U.S.) **16** C 2
Kennedy Channel **8** X 2
Kennedy Peak **47** G 4
Kennedy Range National Park **60** A 4
Kennett **16** E 4
Kennewick **18** C 2
Keno Hill **10** P 6
Kenora **16** E 2
Kentaū **45** L 4
Kentucky **14** B 3
Kentucky Lake **14** B 3
Kentucky River **14** C 3
Kenya **58** C 1
Keokuk **16** E 3
Keoladao National Park **46** D 3
Kep Kai **59** C 4
Kepi i Gjuhëzës **34** D 2
Kepulanan Aru **59** C 4
Kepulanan Tanimbar **59** C 4
Kerala **46** D 6
Kerama-rettō **50** E 7
Kerch **44** E 3
Kerempe Burnu **35** E 3
Keren **56** G 3
Kerinci, Gunung **52** C 6
Keriya Shankou **48** C 3
Kerki **45** L 5
Kerkyra **34** D 3
Kerkyra (Island) **34** D 3
Kermadec Islands **59** H 6
Kermān **45** J 6
Kermānshāh **44** G 6
Kermit **16** C 5
Kerrville **16** D 5
Kerry Head **31** A 2
Kertamulta **52** D 6
Kerteh **52** C 5
Kerulen **50** B 3
Keşan **35** B 4
Kesenūnuma **54** D 3
Keshan **50** E 3
Keskin **35** E 5
Ketū **41** S 6
Ketapang **52** D 6
Ketchikan **10** Q 7
Ketchum Mountain **16** C 5
Ket-Kap, Khrebet **42** K 5
Kettle River Range **18** C 2
Kewanee **14** B 2
Keweenaw Peninsula **14** B 1
Key Largo **14** C 5
Key West **14** C 6
Keyano **8** W 8
Kezhma **41** W 6
Khabarovsk **54** C 1
Khābūr, Nahr al **35** J 7
Khadki **46** C 5
Khairpur **46** B 3
Khalīj Surt (Gulf of Sidra) **56** E 1
Khalūmer-Yu **40** O 4
Khalturin **40** L 6
Khambhaliya **46** B 4
Khambhat **46** C 4
Khambhāt, Gulf of **46** C 4
Khammam **46** E 5
Khampa **42** H 4
Khamseh **44** G 5
Khanabad **45** L 5
Khandwa **46** D 4
Khandyga **42** L 4
Khanka, Ozero **50** F 4
Khānpur **46** C 3
Khantayskoye Vodokhranilishche **41** T 4
Khantayskoye, Ozero **41** T 4
Khanty-Mansiysk **40** P 5
Khapcheranga **42** F 7
Kharagpur **46** F 4
Kharal **41** V 7
Kharaulakhskiy Khrebet **42** J 2
Kharkiv **44** E 3
Kharmanli **35** A 4
Kharovsk **40** K 6
Khasavūyurt **44** G 4
Khashuri **35** K 4
Khaskovo **34** F 2
Khatanga **41** W 3
Khatangskiy Zaliv **41** X 3
Khatyrka **43** T 4
Khenchela **34** B 3
Kherson **44** D 3
Kheta **41** V 3
Khimki **40** J 6
Khmelūnytsūkyy **36** F 3
Khok Kloi **52** B 4
Kholm **40** H 6
Kholmogory **40** K 5
Kholmsk **50** H 3
Khomeynīshahr **44** H 6
Khon Khaen **47** J 5
Khor **50** F 3
Khorugh **45** M 5
Khowst **45** L 6
Khoyinki **36** F 2
Khromtaū **45** J 2
Khrustalūnyy **54** C 2
Khujand **45** L 4
Khulna **47** F 4
Khust **36** E 3
Khuzdār **46** B 3
Khvalynsk **44** G 2
Khvoy **44** F 5
Khyber Pass **45** M 6
Kiatassuag **8** Z 4
Kichiga **43** Q 5
Kicking Horse Pass **10** T 8
Kidnappers, Cape **62** C 2
Kiel **36** C 2
Kielce **36** E 2
Kiev **36** G 2
Kigali **58** B 2
Kigilyakh **42** L 2
Kihnu Saar **38** K 4
Kii-suidō **54** B 4
Kikaishima **50** F 7
Kikinda **36** E 3
Kikwit **58** A 2
Kilauea **12** E 7
Kilchu **50** E 4
Kildare **31** C 2
Kilūdin **40** J 3
Kili **59** F 3
Kilian Island **10** V 4
Kilindini **58** C 2
Kilis **35** G 6
Kiliya **36** F 3
Kilkee **31** B 2
Kilkenny **31** C 2
Kilkis **34** E 2
Killarney **31** B 2
Killeen **16** D 5
Killiniq Island **8** Y 6
Kilmarnock **28** B 2
Kilūmezū **40** M 6
Kilūmezū (River) **40** M 6
Kilpisjärvi **38** K 2
Kilttān Island **46** C 6
Kimball **16** D 3
Kimberley **18** C 2
Kimberley **58** B 4
Kimberley Plateau **60** D 3
Kimchūaek **54** A 2
Kimchūōn **54** A 3
Kimito Kemiö **38** K 3
Kimmirut **8** X 6
Kimovsk **44** E 2
Kimry **40** J 6

Kinchega National Park **60** G 6
Kinder **16** E 5
Kindu **58** B 2
Kineshma **40** K 6
King Christian Island **10** W 3
King City **18** B 4
King George Islands **8** V 7
King Island **60** G 7
King Leopold and Astrid Coast **63** R 5
King Leopold Ranges **60** C 3
King William Island **8** R 5
Kingisepp **38** L 4
Kingman **18** D 4
Kingūs Lynn **28** E 3
Kingsport **14** C 3
Kingston (Australia) **60** F 7
Kingston (Canada) **14** D 2
Kingston (Jamaica) **22** G 4
Kingston upon Hull **28** D 3
Kingstown **22** K 5
Kingsville **20** E 2
Kinnaird Head **30** D 3
Kinnegad **31** C 2
Kinsale **31** B 3
Kinshasa **58** A 2
Kinston **14** D 3
Kintyre **28** B 2
Kipawa, Lac **14** D 1
Kipnuk **43** X 5
Kipti **36** G 2
Kirandul **46** E 5
Kirensk **41** X 6
Kiribati **59** J 4
Kırıkkale **35** E 5
Kirishi **40** H 6
Kiritimati **59** K 3
Kiriwina Island **59** E 4
Kirkcaldy **30** C 3
Kirkenes **38** L 2
Kirkland Lake **14** C 1
Kırklareli **35** B 4
Kirksville **16** E 3
Kirkūk **44** F 5
Kirkwall **30** C 2
Kirkwood (U.S.) **16** E 4
Kirov (Russia) **36** G 2
Kirov (Russia) **40** L 6
Kirova, Ostrov **41** U 2
Kirovabad **44** G 4
Kirovo-Chepetsk **40** M 6
Kirovohrad **44** D 3
Kīrovskīy **45** N 4
Kirovskiy (Russia) **42** J 6
Kirovskiy (Russia) **43** P 6
Kirs **40** M 6
Kirsanov **44** F 2
Kirşehir **35** F 5
Kirthar National Park **46** B 3
Kirthar Range **46** B 3
Kiruna **38** K 2
Kisangani **58** B 1
Kisar **53** H 7
Kisaran **52** B 5
Kishangarh Bās **46** C 3
Kishoreganj **47** F 3
Kiska Island **43** T 6
Kiskunhalas **36** D 3
Kislovodsk **44** F 4
Kismaayo **58** D 2
Kisumu **58** C 2
Kita Kyūshū **54** B 4
Kitakyūshū **50** F 6
Kitale **58** C 1
Kitami **54** D 2
Kitami-sanchi **54** D 2
Kitchener **14** C 2
Kitigan Zibi **14** D 1
Kitimat **10** R 8
Kitsissut **8** W 3
Kittanning **14** D 2
Kitwe **58** B 3
Kivalina **10** K 5
Kiviõli **38** L 4
Kizel **40** N 6
Kizema **40** K 5
Kızılcahamam **35** E 4
Kızıltepe (Turkey) **35** J 6
Kizlyar **44** G 4
Kjöpsvik **38** J 2
Kladno **36** C 2
Klagenfurt **36** C 3
Klamath Falls **18** B 3
Klamath Mountains **18** B 3
Klamath River **18** B 3
Klarälven **38** H 3
Klerksdorp **58** B 4
Klimpfjäll **38** H 2
Klin **40** J 6
Klintsy **36** G 2
Klodzko **36** D 2
Klondike Plateau **10** O 6
Kluczbork **36** D 2
Klyuchevskaya Sopka **43** Q 5
Knezha **34** E 2
Knjaževac **34** E 2
Knoxville (Iowa, U.S.) **16** E 3
Knoxville (Tennessee, U.S.) **14** C 3
Knud Rasmussen Land **8** Z 2
Ko Khrot Kra **52** B 3
Ko Kut **52** C 3
Ko Phangan **52** C 4
Ko Phuket **52** B 4
Ko Samui **52** C 4
Ko Tao **52** B 3
Koba **52** D 6
Kōbe **54** C 4
København **38** H 4
Koblenz **36** B 2
Kobroor **52** J 7
Kobryn **36** E 2
Kobuk Valley National Park **10** L 5
Kocaeli **35** C 4
Koch Island **8** V 5
Kochenevo **41** S 7
Kochi **54** B 4
Koçhisar Ovası **35** E 5
Kodar, Khrebet **42** G 5
Kodiak **43** Z 5
Kodiak Island **43** Z 5
Koechechum **41** V 5
Koforidua **56** C 4
Kōfu **54** C 3
Kogon **45** K 5
Kohat **45** M 6
Kohīma **47** G 3
Koh-i-Mazar **45** L 6
Kohtla-Järve **38** L 4
Kohunlich **20** G 4
Koindu **56** B 4
Kokkola **38** K 3
Kokomo **14** B 2
Kökpekti **45** O 3
Kokshetaū **45** L 2
Kola **40** H 4
Kola Peninsula **40** J 4
Kolaka **52** G 6
Kolar **46** D 6
Kolari **38** K 2
Kolding **38** G 4
Kolguyev, Ostrov **40** M 4
Kolhapur **46** C 5
Kolhoa **47** G 7
Kolka **38** K 4
Kolkata **46** F 4
Kolky **36** F 2
Kollegal **46** D 6
Köln **36** B 2
Kołobrzeg **36** D 2
Kolombangara Island **59** E 4
Kolomna **40** J 6
Kolomyya **36** F 3
Kolpashevo **41** S 6
Kolpino **40** H 6
Kolūskiy Poluostrov **40** J 4
Kolwezi **58** B 3
Kolyma **43** O 3
Kolymskaya **43** P 3
Kolymskaya Nizmennostū **43** O 3
Kolymskiy, Khrebet **43** P 4
Komandorskiye Ostrova **43** R 5
Komárno **36** D 3
Komatsu **54** C 3
Komfane **53** J 7
Komló **36** D 3
Komotini **34** F 2
Komsomolets, Ostrov **41** U 1
Komsomolūsk-na-Amure **42** L 6
Komsomolūskoy Pravdy, Ostrova **41** X 2
Komusan **54** A 2
Kon Tum **47** K 6
Konakovo **40** J 6
Konarak **46** F 5

Kondagaon **46** E 5
Kondopoga **40** H 5
Kong Christian X Land **8** Ee 4
Kong Frederik IX Land **8** Aa 5
Kong Frederik VIIIūs Land **8** Ff 3
Kong Frederik VI-Kyst **8** Cc 6
Kong Wilhelm Land **8** Gg 3
Konginskiye Gory **43** P 3
Kongsvinger **38** H 3
Kongur Shan **48** B 3
Koni, Poluostrov **43** O 5
Konin **36** D 2
Konitsa **34** E 2
Konosha **40** K 5
Konotop **36** G 2
Konstanz **36** B 3
Konya **35** E 6
Konya Ovası **35** E 5
Koolivoo, Lake **60** F 4
Kootenay National Park **10** T 8
Kópavogur **38** A 3
Kopeysk **40** O 6
Köping **38** J 4
Koppang **38** H 3
Kopychyntsi **36** F 3
Korāput **46** E 5
Korba **46** E 4
Korçë **34** F 2
Korčula **34** D 2
Kordestan **44** G 5
Korea Strait **50** E 6
Korenovsk **44** E 3
Korf **43** R 4
Korhogo **56** C 4
Korinthos **34** E 3
Kōriyama **54** D 3
Korkodon **43** O 4
Korkuteli **35** D 6
Korla **48** D 2
Kornat **34** D 2
Koro **59** G 5
Koro Sea **59** G 5
Köroğlu Dağları **35** D 4
Koronadal **53** G 4
Koror **59** C 3
Korostenū **36** F 2
Korostyshiv **36** F 2
Korsakov **50** H 3
Koryakskaya Sopka **43** P 6
Koryakskiy Khrebet **43** R 4
Koryazhma **40** L 5
Kos **34** F 3
Kos (Greece) **35** B 6
Kos (Island, Greece) **35** B 6
Kos ng **50** E 5
Kosava **36** F 2
Kosciusko **14** B 4
Kosiče **36** E 3
Koslan **40** L 5
Kosŏng **54** A 3
Kosovo **34** E 2
Kosovska Mitrovica **34** E 2
Kostino **41** T 4
Kostopilū **36** F 2
Kostroma **40** K 6
Kostyantynivka **44** E 3
Koszalin **36** D 2
Kot Addu **46** C 2
Kota **46** D 3
Kota Bharu **52** C 4
Kota Kinabalu **52** F 4
Kotaagung **52** C 7
Kotabumi **52** C 6
Kotchevo **40** M 6
Kotelūnich **40** L 6
Kotelūnikovo **44** F 3
Kotelūnyy, Ostrov **42** L 1
Kotikovo **54** D 1
Kotka **38** L 3
Kotlas **40** L 5
Kotlik **43** X 4
Kotovsūk **36** F 3
Kotri **46** B 3
Kottayam **46** D 7
Kotuy **41** W 3
Kotzebue **10** K 5
Kotzebue Sound **10** K 5
Koukdjuak River **8** W 5
Koumbi Saleh **56** C 3
Koutiala **56** C 3
Kouvola **38** L 3
Kovelū **36** E 2
Kovrov **40** K 6
Kowloon **49** J 6
Koyuk **43** X 4
Koyukuk **43** Y 4
Kozan **35** F 6
Kozani **34** E 2
Kozelūsk **44** E 2
Kozlu **44** D 4
Kra, Isthmus of **47** H 6
Kragerø **38** G 4
Kragujevac **34** E 2
Kraków **36** D 2
Kraljevo **34** E 2
Kramatorsūk **44** E 3
Kramfors **38** J 3
Kranj **36** C 3
Kraśnik **36** E 2
Krasnoarmeysk **44** G 2
Krasnoarmeyskiy **44** F 3
Krasnodar **44** E 3
Krasnogorsk **50** H 3
Krasnohrad **44** E 3
Krasnokamensk **42** G 6
Krasnoperekopsūk **35** E 2
Krasnoselūkup **41** S 4
Krasnoslobodsk **44** F 3
Krasnoturūinsk **40** O 6
Krasnouralūsk **40** O 6
Krasnovishersk **40** N 5
Krasnoyarsk **41** U 6
Krasnoyarskoye Vodokhranilishche **41** U 7
Krasnozatonskiy **40** M 5
Krasnoznamenskoe **45** L 2
Krasnystaw **36** E 2
Krasnyy Kut **44** G 2
Krasnyy Luch **44** E 3
Krasnyy Yar (Russia) **44** F 2
Krasyliv **36** F 3
Kraulshavn **8** Z 4
Kremenchuk **44** D 3
Kremenetsū **36** F 2
Kremmling **18** E 3
Kretinga **38** K 4
Krishna, Mouths of the **46** E 5
Kristiansand **38** G 4
Kristianstad **38** H 4
Kristiansund **38** G 3
Kriti **34** E 3
Kriti (Crete) **35** B 7
Kronotskiy Poluostrov **43** Q 6
Kronprins Christian Land **8** Gg 2
Kronprinsesse Märtha Kyst **63** O 5
Kronshtadt **38** L 4
Kroonstad **58** B 4
Kropotkin **44** F 3
Kropotkin (Russia) **35** J 2
Krosno **36** E 3
Kruglikovo **54** C 1
Krui **52** C 7
Krung Thep **47** J 6
Kruševac **34** E 2
Kruzof Island **10** P 7
Krychaw **36** G 2
Krym **35** E 2
Krymsk **44** E 4
Krytiko Pelagos **34** F 3
Krytiko Pelagos (Sea of Crete) **35** B 6
Kuala Dungun **52** C 5
Kuala Kangsar **52** C 5
Kuala Kerai **52** C 4
Kuala Lipis **52** C 5
Kuala Lumpur **52** C 5
Kuala Selangor **52** C 5
Kuala Terengganu **52** C 4
Kualakapuas **52** E 6
Kualamanjual **52** E 6
Kuandian **50** D 4
Kuantan **52** C 5
Kubanū **44** F 3
Kuchaman **46** C 3
Kuching **52** E 5
Kuçovū **34** D 2
Kudat **53** F 4
Kudus **52** E 7
Kudymkar **40** M 6
Kugaaruk **8** T 5
Kugluktuk **10** T 5
Kuhn Ø **8** Gg 4
Kūhpāyeh **45** J 6
Kuiu Island **10** Q 7
Kuji **54** D 2

Kukan **54** B 1
Kukës **34** E 2
Kula, Kryazh **42** K 3
Kūlagīno **44** H 3
Kuldīga **38** K 4
Kulūdur **54** B 1
Kulgera **60** E 5
Kulob **45** L 5
Kultuk **41** W 7
Kulu (Turkey) **35** E 5
Kulunda **45** N 2
Kulundinskoye, Ozero **45** N 2
Kulusuk **8** Dd 5
Kumagaya **54** C 3
Kumai **52** E 6
Kumamoto **54** B 4
Kumanovo **34** E 2
Kumara **50** E 2
Kumasi **56** C 4
Kumbakonam **46** D 6
Kume-jima **50** E 7
Kumertau **40** N 7
Kumluca **35** D 6
Kumukahi, Cape **12** F 8
Kümüx **48** D 2
Kundāpura **46** C 6
Kunduz **45** L 5
Kungälv **38** H 4
Kunlun Shan **48** C 3
Kunming **49** G 5
Kunsan **50** E 5
Kununurra **60** D 3
Kuopio **38** L 3
Kuoqiang **48** D 3
Kupang **53** G 8
Kupino **41** R 7
Kupreanof Island **10** Q 7
Kupūūyansūk **44** E 3
Kuqa **48** C 2
Kurashiki **54** B 4
Kŭrdzhali **34** F 2
Kure **54** B 4
Küre Dağları **35** F 4
Kuressaare **38** K 4
Kurgan **40** P 6
Kuria **59** G 3
Kurilūsk **54** E 1
Kurilūskiye Ostrova **50** J 3
Kurkure Bazhi, Gora **41** T 7
Kurnool **46** D 5
Kuroiso **54** D 3
Kursk **44** E 2
Kurskaya **44** F 4
Kurskiy Zaliv **38** K 4
Kurtalan **35** J 6
Kurtamysh **40** O 7
Kurume **54** B 4
Kurunegala **46** E 7
Kushiro **54** D 2
Kuskokwim Bay **43** X 5
Kuskokwim Mountains **10** L 6
Kuskokwim River **43** X 4
Kussharo-Ko **54** D 2
Kūstī **56** G 3
Kütahya **35** C 5
Kūutūaisi **44** F 4
Kutan **44** G 4
Kutch Peninsula **46** B 4
Kutch, Gulf of **46** B 4
Kutno **36** D 2
Kuujjuaq **8** X 7
Kuummiut **8** Dd 5
Kuusamo **38** L 2
Kuwait **44** G 7
Kuya **40** K 4
Kuybyshev **44** H 2
Kuybysheva, Mys **41** U 1
Kuybyshevo **54** E 1
Kuybyshevskoye Vodokhranilishche **44** G 2
Kuytun, Gora **41** T 8
Kuznetsk **44** G 2
Kuznetsova **50** G 3
Kuznetsovo **54** C 1
Kvaløy **38** J 2
Kvikkjokk **38** J 2
Kwajalein **59** F 3
Kwangju **50** E 5
Kwanmo-Bong **50** E 4
Kwekwe **58** B 3
Kwidzyń **36** D 2
Kwoka, Gunung **52** J 6
Ky ngju **50** E 5
Kyaikto **47** H 5
Kyancutta **60** F 6
Kyaukse **47** H 4
Kyiv **36** G 2
Kyklades **34** E 3
Kyle of Lochalsh **30** B 3
Kymi **34** E 3
Kyŏngju **54** A 3
Kyōto **54** C 3
Kyparissiakos Kolpos **34** E 3
Kyrgyzstan **45** M 4
Kyshchevskya **35** H 1
Kyshtym **40** O 6
Kythira **34** E 3
Kythnos **34** E 3
Kyūshū **54** B 4
Kyustendil **34** E 2
Kyusyur **42** J 2
Kyzyl **41** U 7
Kyzyl-Dzhar **45** L 3
Kyzylkum **45** K 4
La Boquilla, Presa de **20** C 2
La Cadena **20** D 2
La Carolina **33** B 2
La Ceiba (Honduras) **20** G 4
La Chorrera **22** G 6
La Colorada **20** B 2
La Crosse **16** E 3
La Cruz (Mexico) **20** C 3
La Dorada **22** H 6
La Encantada, Cerro de **18** C 5
La Encantada, Sierra de **20** D 2
La Fuente de San Esteban **33** A 1
La Gatineau, Parc de **14** D 1
La Giganta, Sierra de **20** B 2
La Gran Sabana **22** K 6
La Grande **18** C 2
La Grande Riviére **8** W 8
La Grange **14** B 4
La Habana **20** H 3
La Huacan **20** D 4
La Junta (Mexico) **20** C 2
La Junta (U.S.) **16** C 4
La Juventud Isla de **20** H 3
La Libertad **20** G 5
La Loche **10** V 7
La Malbaie **8** W 9
La Mancha **33** B 2
La Marque **20** E 2
La Marsa **56** E 1
La Mauricie National Park **8** W 9
La Oroya **24** D 4
La Paz **24** E 4
La Paz (Mexico) **20** B 3
La Paz, Bahía **20** B 3
La Pesca **20** E 3
La Piedad **20** D 3
La Plata **24** F 6
La Rioja (Spain) **32** B 3
La Rochelle **32** B 2
La Roche-sur-Yon **32** B 2
La Roda **33** B 2
La Romana **22** J 4
La Ronge **10** V 7
La Salina **18** D 5
La Salle **14** B 2
La Serena **24** D 5
La Serena (Spain) **33** A 2
La Spezia **34** B 2
La Tasajera, Sierra de **20** C 2
La Tuque **8** W 9
La Union (El Salvador) **20** G 5
La Unión (Mexico) **20** D 4
La Vega **22** H 4
La Venta **20** F 4
La Ventura **20** D 3
La Zarca **20** D 2
Labé **56** B 3
Labelle **14** E 1
Labengke **53** G 6
Labinsk **35** J 2
Labis **52** C 5
Labrador **8** Cc 8
Labrador City **8** X 8
Labrador Sea **8** Z 7
Labrador, Coast of **8** Y 7
Labuhan **52** D 7
Labuhanbadjo **53** G 7
Labuhanbilik **52** C 5
Labytnangi **40** P 4
Lac Mai-Ndombe **58** A 2
Lac Moero **58** B 2

Laccadive Islands **46** C 6
Lacepede Bay **60** F 7
Lackawanna **14** D 2
Lac-Mégantic **14** E 1
Ladakh Range **45** N 6
Ladnūn **46** C 3
Ladozhskoye Ozero **40** H 5
Ladysmith **58** B 4
Lae (Marshall Islands) **59** F 3
Lae (Papua New Guinea) **59** D 4
Lafayette (Indiana, U.S.) **14** B 2
Lafayette (Louisiana, U.S.) **16** E 5
Laghouat **56** D 1
Lago do Erepecu **24** F 3
Lago Titicaca **24** D 4
Lagoa dos Patos **24** F 6
Lagoa Mirim **24** F 6
Lagos **56** D 4
Lagos (Portugal) **33** A 2
Lagos de Moreno **20** D 3
Laha **50** D 3
Lahad Datu **52** F 4
Lahat **52** C 6
Lāhījān **44** G 5
Lahore **46** C 2
Lahr **36** B 3
Lahti **38** L 3
Lai **56** E 4
Lais **52** C 6
Laiyang **49** L 3
Laizhou Wan **49** K 3
Lajes **24** F 5
Lake Bangweulu **58** B 3
Lake Chad **56** E 3
Lake Charles **16** E 5
Lake City (Florida, U.S.) **14** C 4
Lake City (South Carolina, U.S.) **14** D 4
Lake Clark National Park **10** M 6
Lake District **28** C 2
Lake Edward **58** B 2
Lake Eyasi **58** C 2
Lake Harbour **8** X 6
Lake Havasu City **18** D 5
Lake Jackson **20** E 2
Lake Kariba **58** B 3
Lake Kyoga **58** C 1
Lake Malawi **58** C 3
Lake Mead National Recreational Area **18** D 4
Lake Minchumina **10** M 6
Lake Nasser **56** G 2
Lake Placid **14** E 2
Lake River **8** U 8
Lake Rukwa **58** C 2
Lake Tanganyika **58** B 2
Lake Turkana **58** C 1
Lake Victoria **58** C 2
Lake Volta **56** C 4
Lake Worth **14** C 5
Lakeland **14** C 5
Lakeview **18** B 3
Lakewood **18** E 4
Lakselv **38** L 1
Lakshadweep **46** C 6
Lalitpur **46** D 4
Lama, Ozero **41** T 4
Lamar **16** C 4
Lambaréné **56** E 5
Lambert Land **8** Gg 3
Lambert, Cape **59** E 4
Lamesa **16** C 5
Lamezia Terme **34** D 3
Lamia **34** E 3
Lamington National Park **60** J 5
Lampang **47** H 5
Lampasas **16** D 5
Lampazos de Naranjo **20** D 2
Lamphun **47** H 5
Lanai **12** E 7
Lanbi Kyun **47** H 6
Lancang Jiang **48** G 6
Lancaster (U.K.) **28** C 2
Lancaster (U.S.) **18** C 5
Lancaster Sound **8** T 4
Lancun **49** L 3
Landegode **38** H 2
Lander **18** E 3
Landes **32** B 3
Landfall Island **47** G 6
Lands End (Canada) **10** S 3
Landūs End (U.K.) **28** B 4
Landshut **36** C 3
Lang Son **49** H 6
Langdon **16** D 2
Langjökull **38** A 3
Langkawi **52** B 4
Langlade **14** D 1
Langon **32** B 3
Langøya **38** H 2
Langres **36** B 3
Langsa **52** B 5
Languedoc **32** C 3
Langzhong **49** H 4
Länkäran **44** G 5
Lansing **14** C 2
Lanxi **49** K 5
Lanzhou **49** G 3
Lao Cai **47** J 4
Laoag **53** G 2
Laoang **53** H 3
Laon **32** C 2
Laos **47** J 5
Laoye Ling **54** B 2
Lapine **18** B 3
Lappeenranta **38** L 3
Lappland **38** J 2
Lâpseki **34** F 2
Laptevykh, More **42** H 1
Lapua **38** K 3
LūAquila **34** C 2
Lār Koh **45** K 6
Larache **56** C 1
Laramie **18** E 3
Laramie Mountains **18** E 3
Laramie River **18** E 3
Larantuka **53** G 7
Laredo (U.S.) **20** E 2
Larisa **34** E 3
Larkana **46** B 3
Larnaka **44** D 6
Larne **28** B 2
Larned **16** D 4
Larūyak **41** S 5
Las Ballenas, Canal de **20** B 2
Las Cruces **18** E 5
Las Mesas, Cerro de **20** E 4
Las Minas, Cerro **20** G 5
Las Minas, Sierra de **20** F 5
Las Palmas **56** B 2
Las Palomas **18** E 5
Las Tres Vírgenes,Volcán **20** B 2
Las Tunas, Sierra de **18** E 5
Las Vegas (Nevada, U.S.) **18** C 4
Las Vegas (New Mexico, U.S.) **18** E 4
Lasan **52** F 5
Lāsh-e Joveyn **45** K 6
Lashkar Gāh **45** K 6
Latakia **44** E 5
Latehar **46** E 4
Latina **34** C 2
Lātūr **46** D 5
Latvia **38** L 4
Lau Group **59** H 5
Launceston **60** H 8
Laurel (Mississippi, U.S.) **14** B 4
Laurel (Montana, U.S.) **18** E 2
Laurentian Scarp **8** V 9
Laurentides, Plateau **8** W 9
Lausanne **36** B 3
Laut (Indonesia) **52** D 5
Laut (Indonesia) **53** F 6
Lautoka **59** G 5
Laval (Canada) **8** W 9
Laval (France) **32** B 2
Laverton **60** C 5
Lavka Integralsoyuza **43** R 3
Lavrentiya **43** V 3
Lawrence **16** D 4
Lawrenceburg **14** B 3
Lawton **16** D 5
Layton **18** D 3
Lazarevac **34** E 2
Lazo (Russia) **54** B 2
Le Chaux de-Fonds **36** B 3
Le Creusot **32** C 2
Le Havre **32** C 2
Le Mans **32** C 2
Le Mars **16** D 3
Le Mont-Saint-Michel **32** B 2
Le Puy-en-Velay **32** C 2
Leadville **18** E 4
Leavenworth **16** D 4

Lebanon **44** D 6
Lebanon (U.S.) **16** E 4
Lebedyanū **44** E 2
Lebedyn **36** G 2
Lębork **36** D 2
Lebrija **33** A 2
Lecce **34** D 2
Lecco **36** B 3
Leduc **10** U 8
Leeds **28** D 3
Leeuwarden **36** B 2
Leeuwin, Cape **60** B 6
Leeward Islands (Caribbean Sea) **22** K 4
Leeward Islands (Polynesia) **59** K 5
Lefkada **34** E 3
Lefkosia **44** D 5
Lefroy, Lake **60** C 6
Leganés **32** B 3
Legaspi **53** G 3
Legnica **36** D 2
Lehi **18** D 3
Leiah **46** C 2
Leicester **28** D 3
Leinster **31** C 2
Leipzig **36** C 2
Leira **38** G 3
Leiria **33** A 2
Leiyang **49** J 5
Leizhou Wan **49** J 6
Leka **38** H 2
Lemesos **44** D 6
Lemieux Islands **8** Y 6
Lemmon **16** C 2
Lemtybozh **40** N 5
Len Malaäs **53** J 6
Lena **42** J 2
Lenger **45** L 4
Lenin Atyndagy Choku **45** M 5
Leninogorsk **44** H 2
Lenīnogorsk **45** O 2
Leninsk-Kuznetskiy **41** T 7
Lenīnskoe **44** G 3
Leninskoye **54** B 1
Leno Angarskoye Plato **41** W 7
Lensk **41** Y 5
Lentini **34** C 3
Leoben **36** D 3
Leominster **28** C 3
León (Mexico) **20** D 3
León (Nicaragua) **22** E 5
León (Spain) **33** A 1
Leonora **60** C 5
Leopold Mūclintock, Cape **10** T 3
Lepar **52** D 6
Leping **49** K 5
Lerwick **30** D 1
Leshan **49** G 5
Leskovac **34** E 2
Lesogorsk **50** H 3
Lesogorskiy **38** L 3
Lesosibirsk **41** U 6
Lesotho **58** B 4
Lesozavodsk **50** F 3
Lesser Antilles (Caribbean Sea) **22** K 4
Lesser Antilles (Netherlands) **22** J 5
Lesser Slave Lake **10** T 7
Lesser Sunda Islands **52** G 7
Lesvos **34** F 3
Leszno **36** D 2
Lethbridge **18** D 2
Leti, Kepulauan **53** H 7
Letnyaya Zolotitsa **40** J 5
Letsok-aw Kyun **47** H 6
Letterkenny **31** C 1
Leuser, Gunong **52** B 5
Levanger **38** H 3
Lévêque, Cape **60** C 3
Levice **36** D 3
Levin **62** C 3
Lévis **8** W 9
Levokumskoye **44** F 4
Lewis, Isle of **30** A 2
Lewiston (Maine, U.S.) **14** E 2
Lewiston (Montana, U.S.) **18** C 2
Lewistown (Montana, U.S.) **18** E 2
Lewistown (Pennsylvania, U.S.) **14** D 2
Lexington (Kentucky, U.S.) **14** C 3
Lexington (North Carolina, U.S.) **14** C 3
Leyte **53** H 3
Lūgov **44** E 2
Lhasa **48** E 5
Lhaze **48** D 5
Lhokseumawe **52** B 4
lūHospitalet de Llobregat **32** C 3
Lhünzê **48** E 5
Liancheng **49** K 5
Lianga **52** H 4
Lianhua Shan **49** J 5
Lianjiang **49** J 6
Lianxian **49** J 6
Lianyungang **49** K 4
Liaodong **49** L 3
Liaodong Wan **49** L 2
Liaoning **50** D 4
Liaoyang **50** D 4
Liaoyuan **50** E 4
Liard River **10** R 7
Liard River (River) **10** Q 6
Libby **18** C 2
Liberal **16** C 4
Liberec **36** D 2
Liberia **56** B 4
Libobo, Tanjung **52** H 6
Libreville **56** D 4
Libro Point **52** F 3
Libya **56** E 2
Libyan Desert **56** F 2
Licata **34** C 3
Lichinga **58** C 3
Lichuan (Hubei, China) **49** H 4
Lichuan (Jiangxi, China) **49** K 5
Lida **36** F 2
Lidzbark Warmiński **36** E 2
Liechtenstein **36** B 3
Liège **36** B 2
Liepāja **38** K 4
Lifou **59** F 6
Ligurian Sea **34** B 2
Lihue **50** E 4
Lijiang **48** G 5
Likasi **58** B 3
Likiep **59** F 2
Lillehammer **38** H 3
Lillestrøm **38** H 4
Lillooet **10** S 8
Lilongwe **58** C 3
Lima **24** D 4
Lima (Idaho, U.S.) **18** D 3
Lima (Ohio, U.S.) **14** C 2
Limassol **44** D 6
Limburg **36** B 2
Limerick **31** B 2
Limnos **34** E 3
Limoges **32** C 2
Limón **22** F 6
Limon **16** C 4
Limoux **32** C 3
Limpopo **58** C 4
Linares (Mexico) **20** E 3
Linares (Spain) **33** B 2
Lincoln (Illinois, U.S.) **14** B 2
Lincoln (Nebraska, U.S.) **16** D 3
Lincoln (U.K.) **28** D 3
Lincoln City **18** B 3
Lincolnshire Wolds **28** D 3
Line Islands **59** K 4
Linfen **49** J 3
Lingayen **52** G 2
Lingayen Gulf **52** G 2
Lingen **36** B 2
Lingga **52** C 6
Lingga, Kepulauan **52** D 6
Lingling **49** J 5
Lingshan **49** H 6
Lingshui **52** E 2
Linhai **49** L 5
Linhe **49** H 2
Linköping **38** J 4
Linkou **50** F 3
Lintao **49** G 3
Linton **16** C 2
Linxi **50** C 4
Linxia **49** G 3
Linyi **49** K 3
Linz **36** C 3
Lion, Golfe du **32** C 3
Lipa **52** G 3
Lipetsk **44** E 2

Lipova **36** E 3
Lipu **49** J 6
Lisboa **33** A 2
Lisbon **33** A 2
Lisburne, Cape **10** J 5
Lishu **50** D 4
Lishui **49** K 5
Liskeard **28** B 4
Liski **44** E 2
Lismore **60** J 5
Litang **49** H 6
Lithgow **60** J 6
Lithuania **38** K 4
Litoměřice **36** C 2
Litovko **50** G 3
Little Abaco Island **14** D 5
Little Andaman **47** G 6
Little Cayman **22** F 4
Little Colorado River **18** D 4
Little Desert National Park **60** G 7
Little Falls **16** E 2
Little Inagua Island **22** H 3
Little Minch **30** A 3
Little Missouri River **16** C 2
Little Nicobar **47** G 7
Little Rock **16** E 5
Little Sitkin Island **43** T 6
Littlefield **16** C 5
Littleton **18** E 4
Liuhe **54** A 2
Liuyuan **48** F 2
Liuzhou **49** H 6
Livengood **10** N 5
Liverpool (U.K.) **28** C 3
Liverpool Land **8** Gg 4
Liverpool Range **60** H 6
Livingston (U.S.) **18** D 2
Livingstone **58** B 3
Livny **44** E 2
Livorno **34** C 2
Lixian **49** J 5
Lizard Point **28** B 5
Ljubljana **36** C 3
Ljungby **38** H 4
Ljusdal **38** J 3
Llandovery **28** C 3
Llandudno **28** C 3
Llanelli **28** B 4
Llano River **16** C 5
Llanos **22** H 7
Lleida **32** C 3
Lleyn Peninsula **28** B 3
Lobito **58** A 3
Lobva **40** O 6
Lochboisdale **30** A 3
Lochinver **30** B 2
Lodeynoye Pole **40** H 5
Łódź **36** D 2
Lofoten **38** H 2
Logan **18** D 3
Logan, Mount **10** O 6
Logansport **14** B 2
Logashkino **42** O 2
Logroño **32** B 3
Loikaw **47** H 5
Loire **32** B 2
Lokan tekojärvi **38** L 2
Lokoja **56** D 4
Lokosovo **40** Q 5
Loks Land **8** Y 6
Lolland **36** C 2
Lom (Bulgaria) **34** E 2
Lom (Norway) **38** G 3
Loma Bonita **20** E 4
Lomblen **53** G 7
Lombok **53** F 7
Lomé **56** D 4
Lomond, Loch **30** B 3
Lompoc **18** B 5
Łomża **36** E 2
London (Canada) **14** C 2
London (U.K.) **28** D 4
Londonderry **31** C 1
Londonderry, Cape **60** D 2
Londrina **24** F 5
Lone Pine **18** C 4
Long Bay **14** D 4
Long Beach (California, U.S.) **18** C 5
Long Beach (Washington, U.S.) **18** B 2
Long Island (Bahamas) **22** H 3
Long Island (Canada) **8** V 8
Long Island (Papua New Guinea) **59** D 4
Long Kuyen **47** K 6
Long Lake **14** B 1
Longford (Ireland) **31** C 2
Longiram **52** F 6
Longjiang **50** D 3
Longlac **8** T 9
Longmont **18** E 3
Longnan **49** J 6
Longquan **49** K 5
Longreach **60** G 4
Longs Peak **18** E 3
Longview (Oregon, U.S.) **18** B 2
Longview (Texas, U.S.) **16** E 5
Longxi **49** G 3
Longyan **49** K 5
Longzhen **54** A 1
Longzhou **49** H 6
Lookout, Cape **14** D 4
Loop Head **31** A 2
Lop Buri **47** J 6
Lop Nor **48** E 2
Lop Nur **48** E 2
Lopatka **43** P 6
Lopatka, Mys **43** P 3
Loralai **46** B 2
Lorca **33** B 2
Lordsburg **18** E 5
Loreto (Baja California Sur, Mexico) **20** B 2
Loreto (Zacatecas, Mexico) **20** D 3
Lorient **32** B 2
Lorn, Firth of **30** A 3
Lorraine **36** B 3
Los Alamitos, Sierra de **20** D 2
Los Alamos **18** E 4
Los Angeles **18** C 5
Los Cuchumatanes, Sierra de **20** F 4
Los Huicholes, Sierra de **20** D 3
Los Mochis **20** C 2
Los Palacios **20** H 3
Los Reyes de Salgado **20** D 4
Los Teques **22** J 5
Los Testigos **22** K 5
Lošinj **34** C 2
Lost Trial Pass **18** D 2
Loubomo **58** A 2
Louga **56** B 3
Lougheed Island **10** V 3
Loughrea **31** B 2
Louisa **14** C 3
Louisiade Archipelago **60** J 2
Louisiana **16** E 5
Louisville **14** B 3
Loum **56** D 4
Louny **36** C 2
Loup River **16** C 3
Lourdes **32** B 3
Loushan **49** J 4
Louth (U.K.) **28** D 3
Lovech **34** E 2
Loveland **18** E 3
Lovell **18** E 3
Lovelock **18** C 3
Lovington **16** C 5
Lovozero **40** J 4
Low, Cape **8** T 6
Lowell **14** E 2
Lower California **20** B 2
Lower Hutt **62** B 3
Lower Lough Erne **31** C 1
Lower Red Lake **16** D 2
Lowestoft **28** E 3
Łowicz **36** D 2
Loyauté, Îles **59** F 6
Lualaba **58** B 2
Luūan **49** K 4
Luanda **58** A 2
Luang Prabang **47** J 5
Luanshya **58** B 3
Lubang Islands **53** F 3
Lubango **58** A 3
Lubao **58** B 2
Lubbock **16** C 5
Lübeck **36** C 2
Lubin **36** D 2
Lublin **36** E 2
Lubny **36** G 2
Lubuklinggau **52** C 6
Lubumbashi **58** B 3

Lucas, Lake **60** D 4
Luce Bay **28** B 2
Lucena (Philippines) **52** G 3
Lucena (Spain) **33** B 2
Lučenec **36** D 3
Lucera **34** D 2
Lucero **18** E 5
Lucknow **46** E 3
Luçon **32** B 2
Ludhiana **46** D 2
Ludington **14** B 2
Ludwigshafen **36** B 3
Lüeyang **49** H 4
Lufeng **49** K 6
Lugano **36** B 3
Lugo **33** A 1
Lugoj **36** E 3
Luhansŭk **44** E 3
Luimneach **31** B 2
Lukeville **18** D 5
Lukoyanov **40** K 6
Luleå **38** K 2
Luleälven **38** K 2
Lultin **43** U 3
Lumajangdong Co **48** C 4
Lumberton **14** D 4
Lumding **47** G 3
Lumsden **62** A 4
Lund **38** H 4
Lundu **52** D 5
Lundy **28** B 4
Lüneburg **36** C 2
Luninyets **36** F 2
Luobei **54** B 1
Luoding **49** J 6
Luohe **49** J 4
Luong Nam Tha **47** J 4
Luoxiao Shan **49** J 5
Luoyang **49** J 4
Luoyuan **49** K 5
Lupeni **36** E 3
Luqu **49** G 4
Lurgan **31** C 1
Lusaka **58** B 3
Lüshun **49** L 3
Lusk **16** C 3
Luton **28** D 4
Łutselkŭe **10** U 6
Lutsŭk **36** F 2
Luvua **58** B 2
Luwuk **52** G 6
Luxembourg **36** B 3
Luxi (Yunnan, China) **48** F 6
Luza **40** L 5
Luzern **36** B 3
Luzhou **49** H 5
Luzon **52** G 2
Luzon Strait **49** L 7
Lŭviv **36** E 3
Lycksele **38** J 3
Lyell Land **8** Ff 4
Lyepyelŭ **36** F 2
Lyme Bay **28** C 4
Lynchburg **14** D 3
Lyngdal **38** G 4
Lynx Lake **10** V 6
Lyon **32** C 2
Lysŭva **40** N 6
Lyudinovo **36** G 2
Maŭanshan **49** K 4
Maarianhamina **38** J 3
Maas **36** B 2
Maastricht **36** B 2
Mablethorpe **28** E 3
Mac. Robertson Land **63** Q 5
Macadam Plains **60** B 5
Macalpine Lake **10** W 5
Macapá **24** F 2
Macarena, Serranía de la **22** H 7
Macau **49** J 6
Macauley Island **59** H 7
Macclesfield **28** C 3
Macdonald, Lake **60** D 4
Macdonnell Ranges **60** E 4
Macedonia **34** E 2
Maceió **24** H 3
Macerata **34** C 2
Machala **24** C 3
Macheng **49** K 4
Machilīpatnam **46** E 5
Machiques **22** H 5
Ma-chuan Ho **48** D 5
Mackay **60** H 4
Mackay, Lake **60** D 4
Mackenzie King Island **10** U 3
Mackenzie Mountains **10** Q 6
Mackenzie River **10** Q 5
Mackinaw City **14** C 1
Macmillan Pass **10** R 6
Mâcon **32** C 2
Macon (Georgia, U.S.) **14** C 4
Macon (Mississippi, U.S.) **14** B 4
Macroom **31** B 2
Madagascar **58** D 3
Madang **59** D 4
Madau Island **59** E 4
Madawaska Highlands **8** V 9
Madeira (Portugal) **56** B 1
Madeleine, Îles de la **8** Y 9
Maden **35** H 5
Madera **18** B 4
Madhya Pradesh **46** D 4
Madison (Indiana, U.S.) **14** B 3
Madison (Wisconsin, U.S.) **14** B 2
Madison River **18** D 2
Madisonville (Kentucky, U.S.) **14** B 3
Madisonville (Texas, U.S.) **16** D 5
Madium **52** E 7
Madras (India) **46** E 6
Madras (Oregon, U.S.) **18** B 3
Madre de Chiapas, Sierra **20** F 4
Madre del Sur, Sierra **20** D 4
Madre Occidental, Sierra **20** C 2
Madre Oriental, Sierra **20** D 2
Madre, Laguna (Mexico) **20** E 3
Madre, Laguna (U.S.) **20** E 2
Madre, Sierra **53** G 2
Madrid **32** B 3
Madura **52** E 7
Madurai **46** D 7
Mae Sot **47** H 5
Maebashi **54** C 3
Maevatanana **58** D 3
Maéwo **59** F 5
Magadan **43** O 5
Magdagachi **42** J 6
Magdeburg **36** C 2
Magdelena, Isla (Mexico) **20** B 3
Magelang **52** E 7
Magerøya **38** L 1
Magnitogorsk **45** J 2
Magnolia **16** E 5
Magwe **47** H 4
Maha Sarakham **47** J 5
Mahābād **44** G 5
Mahạbalipuram **46** E 6
Mahābhārat Lek **46** E 3
Mahādeo Hills **46** D 4
Mahajanga **58** D 3
Maḥallāt **44** H 6
Mahanoro **58** D 3
Maharashtra **46** C 4
Mahasamund **46** E 4
Mahbunagar **46** D 5
Mahé **58** E 2
Mahesana **46** C 4
Mahetia **59** L 5
Mahia Peninsula **62** C 2
Mahilyow **36** G 2
Mahón **33** C 2
Mahuva **46** C 4
Maiana **59** G 3
Maicao **22** H 5
Maidstone **28** E 4
Maiduguri **56** E 3
Maikala Range **46** E 4
Maimana **45** K 5
Main Barrier Range **60** G 6
Main Channel **14** C 1
Maine **8** X 9
Maine, Gulf of **14** F 2
Mainland (Orkney, U.K.) **30** C 2
Mainland (Shetland, U.K.) **30** D 1
Maintirano **58** D 3
Mainz **36** B 2
Maio **56** A 3
Maitland **60** J 6
Maizuru **54** C 3
Majene **52** F 6
Majuro **59** G 3
Makalu **46** F 3
Makarov **50** H 3
Makarŭyev **40** K 6

Makassar **52** F 7
Makassar, Selat **52** F 7
Makat **44** H 3
Makedonia **34** E 2
Makemo **59** L 5
Makeni **56** B 4
Makgadikgadi Pan **58** B 4
Makhachkala **44** G 4
Makian **52** H 5
Makin **59** G 3
Makīnsk **45** M 2
Makiyivka **44** E 3
Makkovik **8** Z 7
Makó **36** E 3
Makrana **46** C 3
Maksimovka **54** C 1
Makurazuki **54** B 4
Makurdi **56** D 4
Mala, Punta **22** G 6
Malabar Coast **46** C 6
Malabo **56** D 4
Malacca, Strait of **52** B 5
Malad City **18** D 3
Maladzyechna **36** F 2
Málaga **33** B 2
Malaita **59** F 4
Malakāl **56** G 4
Malakula **59** F 5
Malang **52** E 7
Malanje **58** A 2
Mälaren **38** J 4
Malaspina Glacier **10** O 6
Malatya **35** H 5
Malawi **58** C 3
Malay Peninsula **52** B 4
Malaya **52** C 5
Malaya Kurilūskaya Grūada **54** D 2
Malaya Vishera **40** H 6
Malaybalay **52** H 4
Malaysia **52** D 4
Malbork **36** D 2
Malden **59** K 4
Maldives **46** C 7
Malé **46** C 8
Malea Atoll **46** C 8
Malegaon **46** C 4
Malheur Lake **18** C 3
Mali **56** C 3
Malin Head **31** C 1
Malinovoye Ozero **45** N 2
Mallaig **30** B 3
Mallawī **56** G 2
Mallery Lake **8** R 6
Mallorca **33** C 2
Mallow **31** B 2
Malmö **38** H 4
Maloelap **59** G 3
Malolos **53** G 3
Maloshuyka **40** J 5
Måløy **38** G 3
Malpelo, Isla del **22** F 7
Malta **34** C 3
Malta (U.S.) **18** E 2
Malta, Canale di **34** C 3
Maluku **53** H 6
Maluku, Laut **52** G 6
Malung **38** H 3
Malvan **46** C 5
Malyn **36** F 2
Malyy Lyakhovskiy, Ostrov **42** M 2
Malyy Taymyr, Ostrov **41** X 2
Malyy Yenisey **41** V 7
Mama **42** F 5
Mamburao **52** G 3
Mamonta, Poluostrov **41** R 3
Mamuju **52** F 6
Man **56** C 4
Man, Isle of **28** B 2
Manado **53** G 5
Managua **22** E 5
Manakara **58** D 4
Mananjary **58** D 4
Manapouri **62** A 4
Manas **48** D 2
Manas Hu **48** D 1
Manāslu **46** E 3
Manaus **24** F 3
Manavgat **35** D 6
Manawan **14** E 1
Manawoka **52** J 6
Manchester **28** C 3
Mandalay **47** H 4
Mandan **16** C 2
Mandioli **52** H 6
Mandla **46** E 4
Mandsaur **46** D 4
Mandvi **46** B 4
Mandya **46** D 6
Manfredonia **34** D 2
Mangaia **59** K 6
Mangalia **34** F 2
Mangalore **46** C 6
Mangareya **59** M 6
Mange **48** C 4
Manggar **52** D 6
Mangkalihat, Tanjung **52** F 5
Manglares, Cabo **22** G 7
Mangnai **48** E 3
Mangoky **58** D 4
Mangole **52** H 6
Mangshi **48** F 6
Manhattan **16** D 4
Manicouagan **8** X 8
Manicouagan, Réservoir **8** X 8
Manihi **59** L 5
Manihiki **59** J 5
Maniitsoq **8** Aa 5
Manila **52** G 3
Manipur **47** G 4
Manisa **35** B 5
Manistique **14** B 1
Manitoba **10** X 8
Manitoba, Lake **10** X 8
Manitou Springs **16** C 4
Manitoulin Island **8** U 9
Manitowoc **14** B 2
Manizales **22** G 6
Manja **58** D 4
Manjimup **60** B 6
Mankato **16** E 3
Manley Hot Springs **10** M 5
Manmad **46** C 4
Manna **52** C 6
Mannheim **36** B 3
Manning, Cape **10** S 3
Manokwari **52** J 6
Manono **58** B 2
Manpūojin **50** E 4
Manra **59** H 4
Manresa **32** C 3
Mansel Island **8** U 6
Mansfield (U.K.) **28** D 3
Mansfield (U.S.) **14** C 2
Manta **24** C 3
Manteo **14** D 3
Mantova **36** C 3
Manua Islands **59** J 5
Manuae **59** K 5
Manuangi **59** L 5
Manuel Benaivdes **20** D 2
Manui **52** G 6
Manukau **62** B 2
Manus Island **59** D 4
Manzanares **33** B 2
Manzanillo (Cuba) **22** G 3
Manzanillo (Mexico) **20** D 4
Manzhouli **50** C 3
Mao **22** H 4
Maoke, Pegunungan **53** K 6
Maoming **49** J 6
Mapaga **52** F 5
Mapimi, Bolsón de **20** D 2
Maple Creek **18** E 2
Maputo **58** C 4
Maqat **44** H 3
Mar del Plata **24** F 6
Mar Ionio **34** D 3
Marabá **24** G 3
Maracaibo **22** H 5
Maracaibo, Lago de **22** H 6
Maracay **22** J 5
Maradi **56** D 3
Marāgheh **44** G 5
Maramasike Ulawa **59** F 4
Marānd **44** G 5
Marathon (Canada) **14** B 1
Marathon (U.S.) **16** C 5
Marawi **52** G 4
Marbella **33** B 2
Marble Canyon **18** D 4
Marburg **36** B 2
Marcala **20** G 5
Mardān **45** M 6
Mardin **35** J 6

Maré **59** F 6
Mareeba **60** H 3
Marfa **16** C 5
Margai Caka **48** D 4
Margarita, Isla de **22** K 5
Margate **28** E 4
Margie **10** U 7
Margūilon **45** M 4
Maria (French Polynesia) **59** K 6
Maria (French Polynesia) **59** M 6
Maria Island **60** F 2
Maria Theresa Reef **59** K 7
Maria van Diemen, Cape **62** B 1
Mariana Islands **59** D 2
Marianao **20** H 3
Mariar **52** J 6
Marias River **18** D 2
Marías, Islas **20** C 3
Mariato, Punta **22** F 6
Maribor **36** D 3
Marie Byrd Land **63** W 4
Marie-Galante **22** K 4
Mariehamn **38** J 3
Marietta **14** C 4
Mariinsk **41** T 6
Marijampolė **36** E 2
Marūūina Horka **36** F 2
Marinduque **52** G 3
Marinette **8** T 9
Maringá **24** F 5
Marion (Illinois, U.S.) **14** B 3
Marion (Indiana, U.S.) **14** B 2
Marion (Iowa, U.S.) **16** E 3
Marion (Ohio, U.S.) **14** C 2
Marion Reef **60** J 3
Marion, Lake **14** C 4
Mariupolū **44** E 3
Marka **56** H 4
Markam **48** F 5
Mārkāpur **46** D 5
Markha **42** G 4
Markovo **41** T 5
Marlin **16** D 5
Marmara Denizi **35** C 4
Marmara, Sea of **34** F 2
Marmorilik **8** Aa 4
Maroantsetra **58** D 3
Marokau **59** L 5
Maros **52** F 6
Marotiri **59** L 6
Marovoay **58** D 3
Marquises, Archipel des **59** M 4
Marrakech **56** C 1
Marree **60** F 5
Marsala **34** C 3
Marseille **34** B 2
Marsh Harbour **14** D 5
Marsh Island **20** F 2
Marshall (Minnesota, U.S.) **16** D 3
Marshall (Texas, U.S.) **16** E 5
Marshall Islands **59** F 2
Marshalltown **16** E 3
Marshfield **16** E 3
Martapura (Indonesia) **52** C 6
Martapura (Indonesia) **52** E 6
Martigues **34** B 2
Martin **36** D 3
Martin (U.S.) **16** C 3
Martinez de la Torre **20** E 3
Martinique **22** K 5
Martinsburg **14** D 3
Martinsville **14** D 3
Marton **62** C 3
Martre, Lac la **10** T 6
Marutea **59** L 5
Marv Dasht **44** H 7
Mary **45** K 5
Mary River **8** V 4
Maryborough **60** J 5
Maryland **14** D 3
Marysville (California, U.S.) **18** B 4
Marysville (Kansas, U.S.) **16** D 4
Maryville **16** E 3
Masaka **58** C 2
Masalembu Besar **52** E 7
Masan **50** E 5
Masaya **22** E 5
Masbate **52** G 3
Masbate (Island) **52** G 3
Mascarene Islands **58** E 4
Mascota **20** D 3
Masela **52** H 7
Maseru **58** B 4
Mashhad **45** J 5
Masjed Soleymān **44** G 6
Maslyanskiy **40** Q 6
Mason City **16** E 3
Massachusetts **14** E 2
Massafra **34** D 2
Massawa **56** G 3
Massena **14** E 2
Massif Central **32** C 2
Massif du Makay **58** D 4
Massif du Tsaratanana **58** D 3
Masterton **62** C 3
Mastung **46** B 3
Masvingo **58** C 4
Mata **52** G 7
Matachewan **8** U 9
Matachic **20** C 2
Matadi **58** A 2
Matador **16** C 5
Matagalpa **20** G 5
Matagami **8** V 9
Matagorda Island **20** E 2
Mataiva **59** L 5
Matale **46** E 7
Matamoros (Mexico) **20** D 2
Matancita **20** B 2
Matane **8** X 9
Matanzas **22** F 3
Matara **46** E 7
Mataram **52** F 7
Mataró **32** C 3
Matata **62** C 2
Mātātīla Dam **46** D 3
Matehuala **20** D 3
Matera **34** D 2
Matheson **14** C 1
Mathura **46** D 3
Mati **52** H 4
Mātla **46** F 4
Matochkin Shar **40** N 3
Matosinhos **33** A 1
Matsudo **54** D 3
Matsue **54** B 3
Matsumoto **54** C 3
Matsuyama **50** F 6
Matsuzaki **54** C 4
Matterhorn (U.S.) **18** C 3
Mattoon **14** B 3
Matua, Ostrov **50** K 3
Maturín **22** K 6
Matylūka **41** T 5
Maug Islands **59** D 2
Mauganj **46** E 4
Maui **12** E 7
Mauke **59** K 6
Maumere **52** G 7
Mauna Kea **59** K 2
Maunoir, Lac **10** S 5
Maupihaa **59** K 5
Maupin **18** B 2
Maupiti **59** K 5
Maurice, Lake **60** E 5
Mauritania **56** B 3
Mauritius **58** E 3
Mauritius (Island) **58** E 4
Mawlaik **47** G 4
Maxcanú **20** G 3
May Pen **22** G 4
Maya **52** D 6
Maya Mountains **20** G 4
Mayaguana Island **22** H 3
Mayagüez **22** J 4
Mayāmey **45** J 5
Mayapán **20** G 3
Maykop **44** E 4
Maymyo **47** H 4
Mayn **43** S 4
Mayo **10** P 6
Mayotte (France) **58** D 3
Mayqayyng **45** N 2
Mayraira Point **52** G 2
Maysville **14** D 4
Mayya **42** K 4
Mazār-e Sharīf **45** L 5
Mazatenango **20** F 5
Mazatlán **20** C 3
Mazyr **36** F 2
Mbabane **58** C 4
Mbandaka **58** A 1
Mbanza-Ngungu **58** A 2
Mbeya **58** C 2

Mbuji-Mayi **58** B 2
McAlester **16** D 5
McAllen **20** E 2
McCamey **16** C 5
McCarthy **10** O 6
McComb **16** E 5
McCook **16** C 3
McDame **10** R 7
McDermitt **18** C 3
McGill **18** D 4
McGrath **43** Y 4
McKean Island **59** H 4
McKeesport **14** D 2
McKenzie Island **16** E 1
McKinney **16** D 5
McLarty Hills **60** C 3
McLeod Lake **10** S 8
MūClintock Channel **10** W 4
McPherson **16** D 4
McPherson Range **60** J 5
Mead, Lake **18** D 4
Meadow Lake **10** V 8
Meander River **10** T 7
Meath **31** C 2
Meaux **32** C 2
Medak **46** D 5
Medan **52** B 5
Medellūn **22** G 6
Medelpad **38** J 3
Medford **18** B 3
Medgidia **34** F 2
Medical Lake **18** C 2
Medicine Bow **18** E 3
Medicine Hat **10** U 8
Medina del Campo **33** B 1
Mediterranean Sea **33** C 2
Mednogorsk **45** J 2
Mednyy, Ostrov **43** R 6
Medvezhiy Yar **41** U 3
Medvezhūya, Gora **54** C 1
Medvezhūyegorsk **40** H 5
Meekatharra **60** B 5
Meeker **18** E 3
Meerut **46** D 3
Mega **52** J 6
Meghālaya **47** G 3
Megra **40** K 5
Mehanom, Mys **44** E 4
Mehar **46** B 3
Meighen Island **8** R 3
Meiktila **47** H 4
Meiningen **36** C 2
Meishan **49** G 4
Meißen **36** C 2
Meixian **49** K 6
Mekūelē **56** G 3
Meknès **56** C 1
Mekong (Cambodia) **47** K 6
Mekong (China) **48** F 4
Mekong, Mouths of the **47** K 7
Melaka **52** C 5
Melanesia **59** E 4
Melappālaiyam **46** D 7
Melbourne **60** G 7
Melcho Múzquiz **20** D 2
Melchor Ocampo **20** D 4
Melenki **40** K 6
Meleuz **40** N 7
Melitopolū **35** F 1
Melrose (U.S.) **18** D 2
Melun (France) **32** C 2
Melun (Myanmar) **47** G 4
Melville **10** W 8
Melville Island (Australia) **60** E 2
Melville Island (Canada) **10** U 3
Melville Land **8** Ee 2
Melville, Cape **60** G 2
Melville, Lake **8** Z 8
Mêmar Co **48** C 4
Memboro **52** F 7
Memmingen **36** C 3
Memphis **16** E 4
Mena (U.S.) **16** E 5
Mendoza **24** E 6
Menemen **35** B 5
Mengcheng **49** K 4
Mengzi **49** G 6
Menkere **42** H 3
Menominee **8** T 9
Menorca **33** C 2
Menshikova **50** G 2
Mentawei, Kepulauan **52** B 6
Mentekab **52** C 5
Mentese **35** C 6
Menzelinsk **40** M 6
Menzies **60** C 5
Meoqui **20** C 2
Meppen **36** B 2
Merano **36** C 3
Merced **18** B 4
Mercedes **24** E 6
Mercy, Cape **8** Y 6
Merefa **44** E 3
Mergui **47** H 6
Mergui Archipelago **47** H 6
Mérida (Mexico) **20** G 3
Mérida (Spain) **33** A 2
Mérida (Venezuela) **22** H 6
Mérida, Cordillera de **22** H 6
Meridian **14** B 4
Mérignac **32** B 3
Merke **45** M 4
Merkenes **38** J 2
Merredin **60** B 6
Merrill **14** B 1
Mersin **35** F 6
Mersing **52** C 5
Merthyr Tydfil **28** C 4
Mértola **33** A 2
Mertuyy **44** H 3
Merville Bugt **63** L 2
Merzifon **44** E 4
Mesabi Range **16** E 2
Mescalero **18** E 5
Meschede **36** B 2
Meseta de Chiapas **20** F 4
Mesolongi **34** E 3
Mesopotamia **44** F 5
Mesquite **16** D 5
Messerian **45** H 5
Messina **34** D 3
Messoyakna **41** R 4
Mestre **36** C 3
Metairie **16** E 5
Metapan **20** G 5
Meteghen **14** F 2
Metro **52** D 7
Metz **36** B 3
Meuse **36** B 3
Mexicali **18** C 5
Mexican Hat **18** E 4
Mexican Highlands **20** D 3
Mexico (Country) **20** D 3
México (Mexico) **20** E 4
México (State, Mexico) **20** E 4
Mexico (U.S.) **16** E 4
Mexico, Gulf of **20** F 3
Meyanobab **53** J 7
Meynopilūgyno **43** T 4
Mezcalapa, Río **20** F 4
Mezenū **40** K 4
Mezenskaya Guba **40** K 4
Mezhdurechensk **41** T 7
Mezhdurechenskiy **40** P 6
Mgachi **42** M 6
Mhow **46** D 4
Miami (Florida, U.S.) **14** C 5
Miami (Oklahoma, U.S.) **16** E 4
Miami Beach **14** C 5
Miandrivazo **58** D 3
Mianduhe **50** D 3
Mīāneh **44** G 5
Mianwali **46** C 2
Mianyang **49** G 4
Mianzhu **49** G 4
Michigan **14** B 2
Michigan City **14** B 2
Michigan, Lake **14** B 2
Michipicoten Bay **14** B 1
Michipicoten Island **14** B 1
Michoacán **20** D 4
Michurinsk **44** F 2
Micronesia, Federated States of **59** D 3
Midai **52** D 5
Middle Andaman **47** G 6
Middlesboro **14** C 3
Middlesbrough **28** D 2
Middletown **14** C 3
Midland (Michigan, U.S.) **14** C 2
Midland (Texas, U.S.) **16** C 5
Midleton **31** B 3
Midsayap **52** G 4
Midwest **18** E 3
Midyat **35** J 6
Mielec **36** E 2

Mieres **33** A 1
Mikhaylovka (Russia) **44** F 2
Mikkeli **38** L 3
Mikunū **40** M 5
Mikuni-sanmyaku **54** C 3
Miladummadulu Atoll **46** C 7
Milano **36** B 3
Milas **35** B 6
Milazzo **34** D 3
Mildura **60** G 6
Mile **49** G 6
Miles City **18** E 2
Milford **18** D 4
Milford Haven **28** B 4
Milford Sound **62** A 3
Mili **59** G 3
Milk River **18** E 2
Mill Island **8** V 6
Millau **32** C 3
Mille Lacs Lake **16** E 2
Milledgeville **14** C 4
Millennium Island **59** K 4
Millerovo **44** F 3
Millington **14** B 3
Millwood Lake **16** E 5
Milne Land **8** Ff 4
Milos **34** E 3
Milton Keynes **28** D 4
Milwaukee **14** B 2
Milwaukie **18** B 2
Milyatino **36** G 2
Min Shan **49** G 4
Min Xian **49** G 4
Mīnāū Ūabd Allāh **44** G 7
Minahasa Peninsula **52** F 5
Minamata **54** B 4
Minatitlán **20** F 4
Minbu **47** G 4
Mindanao **53** G 4
Mindelo **56** A 3
Minden **36** B 2
Minden (U.S.) **16** E 5
Mindon **47** G 5
Mindoro **53** G 3
Mineral Wells **16** D 5
Mineralūnyye Vody **35** K 2
Minerva Reefs North **59** H 6
Minerva Reefs South **59** H 6
Mingäcevir **44** G 4
Mingan **8** Y 8
Mingāora **45** M 6
Mingbuloq **45** K 4
Ming-Kush **45** M 4
Mingshui **50** E 3
Minigwal, Lake **60** C 5
Miniocoy **46** C 7
Minneapolis (Kansas, U.S.) **16** D 4
Minneapolis (Minnesota, U.S.) **16** E 3
Minnedosa **16** D 1
Minnesota **16** E 2
Minnesota River **16** D 3
Minot **16** C 2
Minqing **49** K 5
Minsin **47** H 3
Minsk **36** F 2
Minto **10** P 6
Minusinsk **41** U 7
Miraj **46** C 5
Miranda de Ebro **32** B 3
Miri **52** E 5
Mirnoye **41** T 5
Mirnyy **41** Y 5
Mirpur Khas **46** B 3
Mirzapur **46** E 3
Mishan **50** F 3
Misima Island **60** J 2
Miskitos, Cayos **22** F 5
Miskolc **36** E 3
Misoöl **52** H 6
Mişrātah **56** E 1
Mississippi **16** E 5
Mississippi Delta **20** G 2
Mississippi River **16** E 4
Missoula **18** D 2
Missouri **16** E 4
Missouri River **16** E 4
Mistissini **8** W 8
Mistissini, Lac **8** W 8
Mitchell (Australia) **60** H 5
Mitchell (U.S.) **16** D 3
Mitchelstown **31** B 2
Mithapur **46** B 4
Mithcell **61** G 3
Mithi **46** B 4
Mitiaro **59** K 5
Mitla **20** E 4
Mito **54** D 3
Miyake-jima **54** C 4
Miyako **54** D 3
Miyakonojō **50** F 6
Miyāni **46** B 4
Miyazaki **50** F 6
Mizen Head **31** B 3
Mizil **36** F 3
Mizoram **47** G 4
Mizusawa **54** D 3
Mjölby **38** J 4
Mjösa **38** H 3
Mladá Boleslav **36** C 2
Mljet **34** D 2
Mo i Rana **38** H 2
Moab **18** E 4
Moberly **16** E 4
Mobile **14** B 4
Mobile Bay **20** G 2
Mobridge **16** C 2
Moctezuma (Mexico) **20** C 2
Moctezuma (Mexico) **20** D 3
Modena **34** C 2
Modesto **18** B 4
Modowi **53** J 6
Moe **60** H 7
Moen-jo-dar **46** B 3
Mogdy **42** K 6
Mogocha **42** G 6
Mogoytuy **42** F 6
Moguqi **50** D 3
Mohammedia **56** C 1
Mohyliv Podilūskyy **36** F 3
Mojave **18** C 4
Mojave Desert **18** C 5
Mokokcghūng **47** G 3
Mokpūo **54** A 4
Molaly **45** N 3
Moldava **36** F 3
Molde **38** G 3
Moldova **36** F 3
Molfetta **34** D 2
Moline **16** E 3
Mollendo **24** D 4
Molokai **12** E 7
Molucca Sea **52** G 6
Moluccas **52** H 6
Mombasa **58** C 2
Mombetsu **54** D 2
Momskiy Khrebet **42** M 3
Mona, Canal de la **22** J 4
Monaco **34** B 2
Monadhliath Mountains **30** B 3
Monahans **16** C 5
Monarch Mountain **10** R 8
Monastir **34** C 3
Monchegorsk **40** H 4
Mönchen-Gladbach **36** B 2
Monclova **20** D 2
Moncton **8** Y 9
Mondego, Cabo **33** A 1
Mondy **41** W 7
Money Island **52** E 2
Monfalcone **36** C 3
Monforte de Lemos **32** B 3
Monforte de Lemps **33** A 1
Mong Cai **47** K 4
Mongers Lake **60** B 5
Monghyr **46** F 3
Mongolia **41** V 8
Monjes, Islas los **22** H 5
Monkey River **20** G 4
Mono Lake **18** C 4
Monreal del Campo **32** B 3
Monroe (Louisiana, U.S.) **16** E 5
Monroe (Michigan, U.S.) **14** C 2
Monroe (North Carolina, U.S.) **14** C 4
Monrovia **56** B 4
Montague Island **10** N 7
Montague, Isla **18** D 5
Montana (Bulgaria) **34** E 2
Montana (U.S.) **18** D 2
Montauban **32** C 3
Montceau-les-Mines **32** C 2
Mont-de-Marsan **32** B 3
Monte Albán **20** E 4
Monte Cristi **22** H 4

Montego Bay **22** G 4
Montélimar **32** C 3
Montemorelos **20** E 2
Montenegro **34** D 2
Monterūa **22** G 6
Monterey **18** B 4
Monterey Bay **18** B 4
Monterotondo **34** C 2
Monterrey **20** D 2
Montes Claros **24** G 4
Montevideo **24** F 6
Montgomery **14** B 4
Monticello **18** E 4
Montluçon **32** C 2
Montmagny **8** W 9
Monto **60** J 4
Montoro **33** B 2
Montpelier (Idaho, U.S.) **18** D 3
Montpelier (Vermont, U.S.) **14** E 2
Montpellier **32** C 3
Montréal **8** W 9
Montreal Lake **18** E 1
Montrose (U.K.) **30** C 3
Montrose (U.S.) **18** E 4
Monts Timétrine **56** C 3
Montserrat **22** K 4
Monywa **47** H 4
Monza **36** B 3
Moora **60** B 6
Moore, Lake **60** B 5
Moorea **59** K 5
Moorhead **16** D 2
Moose Jaw **10** V 8
Moosehead Lake **14** E 1
Moosomin **16** C 1
Moosonee **8** U 8
Mopti **56** C 3
Mora **38** H 3
Moradabad **46** D 3
Morales, Laguna **20** E 3
Moramanga **58** D 3
Moran **18** D 3
Morane **59** M 6
Moratuwa **46** D 7
Morava **36** D 3
Moray Firth **30** C 3
Morbi **46** C 4
Morden **16** D 2
Møre og Romsdal **38** G 3
Morecambe Bay **28** C 3
Moree **60** H 5
Morehead City **14** D 4
Morelia **20** D 4
Morelos **20** E 4
Moreni **35** A 2
Moresby **10** Q 8
Moreton Island **60** J 5
Morgan City **20** F 2
Morgantown **14** D 3
Mori (Japan) **54** D 2
Moriarty **18** E 5
Morioka **54** D 3
Morjärv **38** K 2
Morkoka **41** X 4
Morlaix **32** B 2
Mornington Island **60** F 3
Moro Gulf **52** G 4
Morocco **56** C 1
Morogoro **58** C 2
Moroleón **20** D 3
Morón **22** G 3
Morón de la Frontera **33** A 2
Morondava **58** D 4
Moroni **58** D 3
Morotai **52** H 5
Morozovsk **44** F 3
Morris **16** D 2
Morris Jesup, Kap **8** Dd 2
Mors **38** G 4
Morshansk **44** F 2
Mortlock Islands **59** E 3
Morwell **60** H 7
Moscow **18** C 2
Moses Lake **18** C 2
Mosjøen **38** H 2
Moskenesøy **38** H 2
Moskva **40** J 6
Mosquitia **20** G 5
Mosquitos, Golfo de los **22** F 6
Mossoró **24** H 3
Most **36** C 2
Mostaganem **56** D 1
Mostar **34** D 2
Mosul **44** F 5
Motala **38** J 4
Mothe **59** H 5
Motherwell **28** C 2
Motril **33** B 2
Motu Ko **59** J 5
Motu One **59** K 5
Motul **20** G 3
Motutunga **59** L 5
Mould Bay **10** T 3
Moulins **32** C 2
Moulmein **47** H 5
Moultrie **14** C 4
Moultrie, Lake **14** C 4
Moundou **56** E 4
Mount Airy **14** C 3
Mount Forest **14** C 2
Mount Gambier **60** G 7
Mount Isa **60** F 4
Mount Magnet **60** B 5
Mount Pleasant (Michigan U.S.) **14** C 2
Mount Pleasant (Utah, U.S.) **18** D 4
Mount Roskill **62** B 2
Mount Vernon (Illinois, U.S.) **14** B 3
Mount Vernon (Kentucky, U.S.) **14** C 3
Mount Vernon (Ohio, U.S.) **14** C 2
Mount Willoughby **60** E 5
Mountain Grove **16** E 4
Mountain Home **18** C 3
Moutong **53** G 5
Mouydir **56** D 2
Moyahua **20** D 3
Moūynoq **45** J 4
Moyo **52** F 7
Moyynty **45** M 3
Mozambique **58** C 3
Mozambique Channel **58** D 3
Mozdok **44** F 4
Mozhga **40** M 6
Mstislaw **36** G 2
Mtsensk **44** E 2
Mu Us Shamo **49** H 3
Muang Khammouan **47** J 5
Muang Khongxedon **47** K 5
Muang Loei **47** J 5
Muang Nan **47** J 5
Muang Pakxan **47** J 5
Muang Phayao **47** H 5
Muang Phrae **47** J 5
Muang Sing **47** J 4
Muang Xaignabouri **47** J 5
Muar **52** C 5
Muara **52** C 6
Muarabungo **52** C 6
Muaraenim **52** C 6
Muarajuloi **52** E 6
Muaratewe **52** E 6
Muck **30** A 3
Mudanjiang **50** E 4
Mudgee **60** H 6
Mufu Shan **49** J 5
Mufulira **58** B 3
Muğla **35** C 6
Muhu **38** K 4
Mui Bai Bung **47** J 7
Mukacheve **36** E 3
Mukden **50** D 4
Mukhen **54** C 1
Mukomuko **52** C 6
Mulaku Atoll **46** C 8
Mulaly **45** N 3
Mulan **50** E 3
Mulegé **20** B 2
Mulegé, Sierra de **20** B 2
Mulhacén **33** B 2
Mulhouse **36** B 3
Muling **54** B 2
Mull **30** B 3
Mullaittivu **46** E 7
Muller, Pegunungan **52** E 6
Mullewa **60** B 5
Multan **46** C 2
Mumbai **46** C 5
Mumra **44** G 3
Muna (Indonesia) **52** G 6
Muna (Russia) **42** H 3

München **36** C 3
Muncho Lake **10** R 7
Muncie **14** B 2
Munday **16** D 5
Munising **14** B 1
Munku-Sardyk, Gora **41** W 7
Munster **31** B 2
Münster **36** B 2
Muntok **52** D 6
Muonio **38** K 2
Muqdisho (Mogadishu) **56** H 4
Murakami **54** C 3
Murashi **40** L 6
Murchison River **60** B 5
Murcia **33** B 2
Murdo **16** C 3
Murfreesboro **14** B 3
Murmansk **40** H 4
Murom **40** K 6
Muroran **54** D 2
Muros **33** A 1
Muroto **54** B 4
Murray (Kentucky, U.S.) **14** B 3
Murray (River) **60** G 6
Murray (Utah, U.S.) **18** D 3
Murray Islands **59** D 5
Murray, Lake (U.S.) **14** C 4
Mururoa **59** M 6
Murwara **46** E 4
Muş **35** J 5
Musala (Indonesia) **52** B 5
Musan **50** E 4
Musgrave **60** G 2
Musgrave Ranges **60** E 5
Musina **58** B 4
Muskegon **14** B 2
Muskogee **16** D 4
Musoma **58** C 2
Musrakaman **52** F 6
Musselshell River **18** E 2
Muswellbrook **60** J 6
Mut **35** E 6
Mutoray **41** W 5
Mutsu **54** D 2
Mutsu-wan **54** D 2
Muzaffarnagar **46** D 3
Muzaffarpur **46** F 3
Muzhi **40** O 4
Muztaū Bīigi **45** P 3
Mwali (Mohéli) **58** D 3
Mwanza **58** C 2
Mwene Ditu **58** B 2
My Tho **47** K 6
Myadzyel **36** F 2
Myanaung **47** H 5
Myanmar **47** G 4
Myaungmya **47** G 5
Myingyan **47** H 4
Myitkyinā **47** H 3
Mykines **34** E 3
Mykolayiv **44** D 3
Mykonos **34** F 3
Mylius Erichsen Land **8** Ff 2
Mymensingh **47** G 4
Myndagayy **42** K 4
Mýrdalsjökull **38** B 3
Myrhorod **44** D 3
Myrtle Beach **14** D 4
Mys Shmidta **43** U 3
Mys Zhelaniya **40** P 2
Mysore **46** D 6
Myszków **36** D 2
Mytilini **34** F 3
Naalehu **12** E 8
Naas **31** C 2
Nabberu, Lake **60** C 5
Naberezhnyye Chelny **40** M 6
Nabeul **56** E 1
Nabire **53** K 6
Nābul **34** C 3
Nachuge **47** G 6
Nacozari **18** E 5
Nadiad **46** C 4
Nadu **46** D 6
Nadvirna **36** E 3
Nadym **40** Q 4
Naga **53** G 3
Naga Hills **47** G 3
Nagai Island **10** L 8
Nāgāland **47** G 3
Nagano **54** C 3
Nagaoka **54** C 3
Nagasaki **54** A 4
Nagaur **46** C 3
Nagda **46** D 4
Nagercoil **46** D 7
Nago **50** E 7
Nagoya **54** C 3
Nagpur **46** D 4
Nagqu **48** E 4
Nagykanizsa **36** D 3
Naha **50** E 7
Nahanni Butte **10** S 6
Nahanni National Park **10** R 6
Nahāvand **44** G 6
Naiman Qi **50** D 4
Nairn **30** C 3
Nairobi **58** C 2
Naissaar **38** K 4
Najafābād **44** H 6
Najin **54** B 2
Nakhodka **50** F 4
Nakhodka (Russia) **54** B 2
Nakhon Nayok **47** J 6
Nakhon Phanom **47** J 5
Nakhon Ratchasima **47** J 6
Nakhon Sawan **47** J 5
Nakhon Si Thammarat **47** H 7
Nakina **16** F 1
Nakuru **58** C 2
Nalayh **50** A 3
Nalūchik **44** F 4
Nallamalla Range **46** D 5
Nam Co **48** D 4
Nam Dinh **47** K 4
Namangan **45** M 4
Nameh **53** F 5
Namhkam **47** H 4
Namib Desert **58** A 3
Namibe **58** A 3
Namibia **58** A 4
Namjagbarwa Feng **48** F 5
Namlea **53** H 6
Nampa **18** C 3
Nampūo **50** E 5
Nampula **58** C 3
Namsos **38** H 3
Namtsy **42** J 4
Namu **59** F 3
Namwŏn **54** A 3
Nan Hai **47** K 7
Nan Hulsan Hu **48** F 3
Nanaimo **18** B 2
Nanam **50** E 4
Nanao **54** C 3
Nancha **50** E 3
Nanchang **49** K 5
Nancheng **49** K 5
Nanchong **49** H 4
Nanchuan **49** H 5
Nancowry **47** G 7
Nancy **36** B 3
Nanda Devi **46** D 2
Nānded **46** D 5
Nandurbār **46** C 4
Nandyāl **46** D 5
Nanfeng **49** K 5
Nānga Parbat **45** M 5
Nangatayap **52** E 6
Nangnim **54** A 2
Nangnim-sanmaek **54** A 3
Nangong **49** K 3
Nangpinch **52** E 6
Nanhua **48** G 5
Nanjing **49** K 4
Nanning **49** H 6
Nanpan Jiang **49** G 6
Nanping **49** K 5
Nansei-shotō **50** E 7
Nansen Land **8** Cc 2
Nantes **32** B 2
Nanton **18** D 1
Nantong **49** L 4
Nantucket Island **8** X 10
Nantucket Sound **14** E 2
Nanumea **59** G 4
Nanuque **24** H 4
Nanusa, Kepulauan **52** H 5
Nanxiong **49** J 5
Nanyang **49** J 4
Nanzhang **49** J 4
Nanzhao **49** J 4
Nao, Cabo de la **33** C 2
Napas **41** S 6
Napier **62** C 2
Naples **34** C 2

Naples (U.S.) **14** C 5
Napoli **34** C 2
Napuka **59** L 5
Naqadeh **35** L 6
Nara (Japan) **54** C 4
Naranjos **20** E 3
Narasapur **46** E 5
Narathiwat **47** J 7
Narayanganj **47** G 4
Narbonne **32** C 3
Nares Land **8** Bb 2
Narimanov **44** G 3
Närke **38** H 4
Naro-Fominsk **40** J 6
Narrabri **60** H 6
Narrandera **60** H 6
Narrogin **60** B 6
Narsaq **8** Bb 6
Narsimhapur **46** D 4
Narva **38** L 4
Narvik **38** J 2
Narūyan Mar **40** M 4
Naryn **45** N 4
Naryn Qum **44** G 3
Năsăud **36** E 3
Nashik **46** C 4
Nashta Rūd **44** H 5
Nashville **14** B 3
Näsijärvi **38** K 3
Nasīrābād (India) **46** C 3
Nasirābād (Pakistan) **46** B 3
Nassau **14** D 5
Nassau Island **59** J 5
Nässjö **38** H 4
Nastapoka, Isles **8** V 7
Næstved **38** H 4
Natal **24** H 3
Natashquan **8** Y 8
Natchez **16** E 5
Natchitoches **16** E 5
Nathorst Land **8** Ff 4
Natuna Besar **52** D 5
Natuna Besar, Kepulauan **52** D 5
Natuna Selatan, Kepulauan **52** D 5
Naturaliste, Cape **60** A 6
Nauru **59** F 4
Naūrzym **45** K 2
Naushki **41** X 7
Nava **20** D 2
Navahrudak **36** F 2
Navajo Dam **18** E 4
Naval Station **22** H 4
Navalmoral de la Mata **33** A 2
Navan **31** C 2
Navarin, Mys **43** T 4
Navarra **32** B 3
Navassa Island **22** G 4
Navoiy **45** L 4
Navojoa **20** C 2
Navolato **20** C 3
Navsari **46** C 4
Nawabshah **46** B 3
Naxçıvan **44** G 5
Naxçıvan (Azerbaijan) **35** L 5
Naxçıvan (Region) **44** G 5
Naxi **49** H 5
Naxos **34** F 3
Nayakhan **43** P 4
Nayarit **20** C 3
Nayoro **54** D 2
Nazarovo **41** U 6
Nazas **20** D 2
Nazca **24** D 4
Naze **50** E 7
Nazimovo **41** U 6
Ndjamena **56** E 3
Ndola **58** B 3
Neagh, Lough **31** C 1
Neale, Lake **60** D 4
Near Islands **43** S 6
Neblina, Pico de **22** J 7
Nebraska **16** C 3
Nebraska City **16** D 3
Nechako Plateau **10** S 8
Nechako Reservoir **10** R 8
Nedong **48** E 5
Needles **18** D 5
Needles Point **62** C 2
Neftegorsk **35** H 2
Nefteyugansk **40** Q 5
Negombo **46** D 7
Negonego **59** L 5
Negros **53** G 4
Nehe **50** D 3
Nei Mongol Zizhiqu **49** J 2
Neijiang **49** H 5
Neilton **18** B 2
Neiva **22** G 7
Nejanilini Lake **8** R 7
Nekemtē **56** G 4
Nekrasovka **54** C 2
Nelidovo **40** H 6
Nelūkan **42** L 5
Nellore **46** D 6
Nelūma **54** C 1
Nelson (Canada) **18** C 2
Nelson (New Zealand) **62** B 3
Nelson Island **43** W 4
Nelson River **10** X 8
Nelspruit **58** C 4
Nemiscau **8** V 8
Nemunas **38** K 4
Nemuro **54** E 2
Nenagh **31** B 2
Nenana **10** N 6
Nendo **59** F 5
Nenjiang **50** E 3
Nepa **41** X 6
Nepal **46** E 3
Nepalganj **46** E 3
Nephi **18** D 4
Nerchinsk **42** G 6
Nerekhta **40** K 6
Neryungri **42** H 5
Nesū **40** K 4
Neskaupstaður **38** C 2
Ness, Loch **30** B 3
Netherlands Antilles **22** J 5
Nettilling Lake **8** W 5
Neubrandenburg **36** C 2
Neuchâtel **36** B 3
Neumünster **36** B 2
Neuquén **24** E 6
Neustrelitz **36** C 2
Nevada (Missouri, U.S.) **16** E 4
Nevada (State, U.S.) **18** C 4
Nevada, Sierra **33** B 2
Nevada, Sierra (U.S.) **18** B 3
Nevelūsk **50** H 3
Never **42** H 6
Nevers **32** C 2
Nevinnomysk **44** F 4
Nevis **22** K 4
Nevşehir **35** F 5
Nevūyansk **40** O 6
New Albany **14** B 3
New Bedford **14** E 2
New Bern **14** D 3
New Braunfels **20** E 2
New Britain **59** E 4
New Brunswick **8** X 9
New Brunswick (U.S.) **14** E 2
New Castle **14** C 2
New Dehli **46** D 3
New England **14** F 2
New England Range **60** J 6
New Georgia **59** E 4
New Glasgow **8** Y 9
New Guinea **59** D 4
New Hampshire **14** E 2
New Hanover **59** E 4
New Haven **14** E 2
New Iberia **16** E 5
New Ireland **59** E 4
New Jersey **14** E 2
New Liskeard **14** D 1
New London **14** E 2
New Meadows **18** C 3
New Mexico **18** E 5
New Orleans **20** F 2
New Plymouth **62** B 2
New Providence Island **22** G 3
New Quay **28** B 3
New River **14** C 3
New Rockford **16** D 2
New Smyrna Beach **14** C 5
New South Wales **60** G 6
New Ulm **16** E 3
New Westminister **18** B 2
New York (State, U.S.) **14** D 2
New York (U.S.) **14** E 2
New Zealand **62** B 3
Newark (New Jersey, U.S.) **14** E 2
Newark (Ohio, U.S.) **14** C 2

Newark-on-Trent **28** D 3
Newberry **8** T 9
Newburgh **14** E 2
Newcastle (Australia) **60** J 6
Newcastle (Northern Ireland) **31** D 1
Newcastle (U.S.) **16** C 3
Newcastle upon Tyne **28** D 2
Newcastle Waters **60** E 3
Newcastle West **31** B 2
Newfoundland **8** Z 9
Newfoundland and Labrador **8** X 8
Newhaven **28** E 4
Newman **60** B 4
Newport (Arkansas, U.S.) **16** E 4
Newport (England, U.K.) **28** D 4
Newport (Oregon, U.S.) **18** B 3
Newport (Vermont, U.S.) **14** E 2
Newport (Wales, U.K.) **28** C 4
Newport (Washington, U.S.) **18** C 2
Newport Beach **18** C 5
Newquay **28** B 4
Newry (U.K.) **31** C 1
Newton **16** E 3
Newtown **28** C 3
Newtownabbey **28** B 2
Neyshābūr **45** J 5
Nezahualcóyotl **20** E 4
Ngamiland **58** B 3
Ngamring **48** D 5
Ngangerabeli Plain **58** C 2
Ngangla Ringco **48** C 4
Ngangzê Co **48** D 4
Ngau **59** G 5
Nggatokae Island **59** E 4
Nguru **56** E 3
Nha Trang **47** K 6
Niagara Falls **14** D 2
Niagara River **14** D 2
Niah **52** E 5
Niamey **56** D 3
Nianzishan **50** D 3
Nias **52** B 5
Niau **59** L 5
Nicaragua **22** E 5
Nicaragua, Lago de **22** E 5
Nice **34** B 2
Nichollūs Town **14** D 5
Nicobar Islands **47** G 7
Nicosia **44** D 5
Nido, Sierra del **20** C 2
Nidzica **36** E 2
Nienburg **36** B 2
Niğde **35** F 6
Niger **56** D 3
Niger (River) **56** C 3
Nigeria **56** D 4
Nihiru **59** L 5
Niigata **54** C 3
Niihama **54** B 4
Niihau **12** D 7
Niitsu **54** C 3
Nijmegen **36** B 2
Nikolayevsk **44** G 2
Nikolayevsk-na-Amure **42** M 6
Nikolūsk (Russia) **40** L 6
Nikolūsk (Russia) **44** G 2
Nikolski **43** W 6
Niksar **35** G 4
Nikšić **34** D 2
Nikumaroro **59** H 4
Nikunau **59** G 4
Nila **53** H 7
Nile **56** F 3
Niles **14** B 2
Nimach **46** C 4
Nimes **32** C 3
Nincheng **50** C 4
Nine Degree Channel **46** C 7
Ninety Mile Beach **60** H 7
Ningbo **49** L 5
Ningde **49** K 5
Ningdu **49** K 5
Ninghai **49** L 5
Ninghua **49** K 5
Ningjing Shan **48** F 4
Ningxia Huizu Zizhiqu **49** H 3
Ningxiang **49** J 5
Ninh Binh **47** K 4
Niobrara River **16** C 3
Niort **32** B 2
Nipāni **46** C 5
Nipigon **8** T 9
Nipigon, Lake **8** T 9
Nipissing, Lake **8** V 9
Nirmal **46** D 5
Niš **34** E 2
Nishinoūomote **54** B 4
Nistru **36** F 3
Nitchequon **8** W 8
Niterói **24** G 5
Nitra **36** D 3
Niuafoūou **59** H 5
Niuatoputapu **59** H 5
Niue Island **59** J 5
Niutao **59** G 4
Nizamabad **46** D 5
Nizhnekamsk **40** M 6
Nizhneudinsk **41** V 7
Nizhnevartovsk **41** R 5
Nizhniy Lomov **44** F 2
Nizhniy Novgorod **40** K 6
Nizhniy Tagil **40** N 6
Nizhnyaya Pesha **40** L 4
Nizhnyaya Poyma **41** V 6
Nizhnyaya Tunguska **41** U 5
Nizhyn **36** G 2
Njazidja (Grand Comore) **58** D 3
Nkayi **58** A 2
Nkongsamba **56** E 4
Nmai Hka **47** H 3
Noākhāli **47** G 4
Noatak National Reserve **10** L 5
Nobel **14** C 1
Nobeoka **54** B 4
Nogales **18** D 5
Noginsk **40** J 6
Noholoho **53** G 6
Noirmoutier, Île de **32** B 2
Nolinsk **40** L 6
Nombre de Dios **20** D 3
Nome **43** W 4
Nonacho Lake **10** V 6
Nonburg **40** M 4
Nong Khai **47** J 5
Nonoava **20** C 2
Nonouti **59** G 4
Nordenshelūda, Arkhipelag **41** U 2
Norderstedt **36** B 2
Nordfriesische Inseln **36** B 2
Nordhausen **36** C 2
Nordkapp **38** L 1
Nordkjosbotn **38** J 2
Nordostrundingen **8** Kk 2
Nord-Trøndelag **38** H 3
Nordvik **41** Y 3
Norfolk (Nebraska, U.S.) **16** D 3
Norfolk (Virginia, U.S.) **14** D 3
Norfolk Island **59** F 6
Norfork Lake **16** E 4
Norilūsk **41** T 4
Normal **14** B 2
Norman **16** D 4
Norman Wells **10** R 5
Normanby Island **60** K 3
Normandie **32** B 2
Normanton **60** G 3
Norrbotten **38** K 2
Norris Lake **14** C 3
Norrköping **38** J 4
Norrland **38** J 2
Norrtälje **38** J 4
Norseman **60** C 6
Norske Øer **8** Hh 3
North Adams **14** E 2
North Andaman **47** G 6
North Aulatsvik Island **8** Y 7
North Battleford **10** V 8
North Bay **8** V 9
North Belcher Islands **8** V 7
North Bend **18** B 3
North Canadian River **16** D 4
North Cape (New Zealand) **62** B 1
North Cape (Norway) **38** L 1
North Carolina **14** C 3
North Cascades National Park **18** B 2
North Channel (Canada) **14** C 1
North Channel (U.K.) **28** B 2
North Dakota **16** C 2
North Downs **28** D 4
North Fork Pass **10** P 6

North Geomagnetic Pole **8** X 3
North Island **62** B 2
North Kent Island **8** S 3
North Korea **50** F 4
North Lakhimpur **47** G 3
North Las Vegas **18** C 4
North Little Rock **16** E 5
North Magnetic Pole **10** V 3
North Minch **30** B 2
North Platte **16** C 3
North Platte River **16** C 3
North Rona **30** B 2
North Ronaldsay **30** C 2
North Saskatchewan **10** U 8
North Sea **38** F 3
North Slope **10** L 5
North Taranaki Bight **62** B 2
North Uist **30** A 3
North West Cape **60** A 4
North West Highlands **30** B 3
North York Moors **28** D 2
Northam **60** B 6
Northampton (U.K.) **28** D 3
Northeast Providence Channel **14** D 5
Northern Cook Islands **59** J 5
Northern Ireland **31** C 1
Northern Mariana Islands **59** D 2
Northern Territory **60** E 3
Northfield **16** E 3
Northway **10** O 6
Northwest Territories **10** S 6
Norton (U.S.) **14** C 3
Norton Sound **43** X 4
Norvegia, Cape **63** O 5
Norwalk **14** C 2
Norway **38** G 3
Norway (U.S.) **14** B 1
Norwegian Bay **8** S 3
Norwegian Sea **38** G 3
Norwich **28** E 3
Noshiro **54** D 2
Nosy Bé **58** D 3
Nosy Boraha **58** D 3
Nottawasaga Bay **14** C 2
Nottingham **28** D 3
Nottingham Island **8** V 6
Nouadhibou **56** B 2
Nouakchott **56** B 3
Nouméa **59** F 6
Nouvelle Calédonie **59** F 6
Nova Iguaçu **24** G 5
Nova Scotia **8** Y 10
Novara **36** B 3
Novaya Lyalya **40** O 6
Novaya Sibirū, Ostrov **42** O 1
Novaya Zemlya **40** M 3
Nové Zámky **36** D 3
Novhorod-Siversūkyy **36** G 2
Novi Ligure **34** B 2
Novi Pazar **34** E 2
Novi Sad **36** D 3
Novikovo (Russia) **54** D 1
Novo Hamburgo **24** F 5
Novoaltaysk **41** S 7
Novoanninskiy **44** F 2
Novobogatīnskoe **44** H 3
Novobureyskiy **54** A 1
Novocheboksarsk **40** L 6
Novocherkassk **44** F 3
Novodvinsk **40** K 5
Novohrad-Volynsūkyy **36** F 2
Novokuybyshevsk **44** G 2
Novokuznetsk **41** T 7
Novomoskovsk **44** E 2
Novorossiysk **44** E 4
Novorybnoye **41** X 3
Novosergiyevka **44** H 2
Novoshakhtinsk **44** E 3
Novosibirsk **41** S 6
NovosibirskoyeVodokhranil-ishche **41** S 7
Novotroitsk **45** J 2
Novoukrayinka **44** D 3
Novouzensk **44** G 2
Novovolynsūk **36** E 2
Novozybkov **36** G 2
Novvy Buh **44** D 3
Novvy Port **40** Q 4
Novyy **41** X 3
Novyy Bor **40** M 4
Novyy Oskol **44** E 2
Nowa Ruda **36** D 2
Nowa Sól **36** D 2
Nowgong **47** G 3
Nowogard **36** D 2
Nowy Sącz **36** E 3
Noyon **49** G 2
Nsukka **56** D 4
Nueces River **20** E 2
Nueltin Lake **8** R 6
Nueva Gerona **20** H 3
Nueva Rosita **20** D 2
Nueva San Salvador **20** G 5
Nuevo Casas Grandes **18** E 5
Nuevo Laredo **20** E 2
Nuevo Léon **20** D 2
Nuevo, Cayo **20** F 3
Nui **59** G 4
Nuiqsut **10** M 4
Nuka Hiva **59** M 4
Nukuūalofa **59** H 6
Nukufetau **59** G 4
Nukunono **59** H 4
Nukus **45** J 4
Nukutepipi **59** L 6
Nullarbor Plain **60** D 6
Numazu **54** C 3
Numbulwar Mission **60** F 2
Numfoor **52** J 6
Nunap Isua **8** Cc 7
Nunavut **8** R 5
Nungnak **10** L 5
Nunivak Island **43** W 4
Nunkun **45** N 6
Nuoro **34** B 2
Nurak **45** L 5
Nurakita **59** H 4
Nurlat **44** H 2
Nurmes **38** L 3
Nürnberg **36** C 3
Nushki **46** B 3
Nutak **8** Y 7
Nuuk **8** Aa 6
Nuussuaq **8** Z 4
Nyaingentanglha Feng **48** E 4
Nyaingentanglha Shan **48** D 5
Nyala **56** F 3
Nyandoma **40** K 5
Nyaunglebin **47** H 5
Nyazepetrovsk **40** N 6
Nyda **40** Q 4
Nyeboe Land **8** Z 2
Nyingchi **48** E 5
Nykøbing **36** C 2
Nyköping **38** J 4
Nyngan **60** H 6
Nyoman **36** E 2
Nyūregyháza **36** E 3
Nysa **36** D 2
Nyslott **38** L 3
Nystad **38** K 3
Nyurba **42** G 4
Nyuya **42** G 4
Nzérékoré **56** C 4
Nzwani (Anjouan) **58** D 3
Oahe Dam **16** C 3
Oahe, Lake **16** C 2
Oahu **12** E 7
Oak Ridge **14** C 3
Oakland **18** B 4
Oakley **16** C 4
Oakridge **18** B 3
Oakville **14** D 2
Oamaru **62** B 4
Oaxaca (Mexico) **20** E 4
Oaxaca (State, Mexico) **20** E 4
Obū **40** P 4
Oba **8** U 9
Oban (New Zealand) **62** A 4
Oban (U.K.) **30** B 3
Obanazawa **54** D 3
Obeh **45** K 6
Obi **53** H 6
Obi, Kepulauan **52** H 6
Obihiro **54** D 2
Obluchūye **50** F 3
Obninsk **40** J 6
Oborniki **36** D 2
Oboyanū **44** E 2
Obozerskiy **40** K 5
Obrenovac **34** E 2
Obshchiy Syrt **44** H 2
Obskaya Guba **40** Q 4
Ocala **14** C 5
Ocampo **20** C 2

Ocaña **22** H 6
Ocean City **14** D 3
Ochūamchūire **35** J 3
Ocher **40** M 6
Ockelbo **38** J 3
Oconee River **14** C 4
Ocotlán **20** D 3
Ocotlán de Morelos **20** E 4
Ocumare del Tuy **22** J 5
Odate **54** D 2
Odawara **54** C 3
Odemira **33** A 2
Ödemiş **34** F 3
Odendaalsrus **58** B 4
Odense **38** H 4
Oder **36** C 2
Odesa **44** D 3
Odessa **16** C 5
Odintsovo **40** J 6
Odra **36** C 2
Oelwein **16** E 3
Oeno Island **59** M 6
Offenbach **36** B 2
Ofu **59** H 5
Oga **54** C 3
Oga-hanto **54** C 2
Ōgaki **54** C 3
Ogallala **16** C 3
Ogbomoso **56** D 4
Ogden **18** D 3
Ogdensburg **14** D 2
Oglanly **44** H 5
Ogoron **42** J 6
Ogurjaly **44** H 5
Ohio **14** C 2
Ohio River **14** C 3
Ohrid **34** E 2
Ōita **54** B 4
Ojinaga **20** D 2
Oka **44** E 2
Okak Islands **8** Y 7
Okara **46** C 2
Okavango **58** A 3
Okaya **54** C 3
Okayama **54** B 4
Okazaki **54** C 4
Okeechobee, Lake **14** C 5
Okehampton **28** B 4
Okene **56** D 4
Okha **42** M 6
Okhotskoye More **43** N 5
Okinawa-jima **50** E 7
Oki-Shotō **54** B 3
Oklahoma **16** D 5
Oklahoma City **16** D 4
Oktyabrūsk **45** J 3
Oktyabrūskiy **44** H 2
Oktyabrūskoy Revolyutsii, Ostrov **41** V 2
Okulovka **40** H 6
Okushiri-tō **54** C 2
Ólafsvūk **38** A 3
Olanchito **20** G 4
Öland **38** J 4
Olathe **16** E 4
Olbia **34** B 2
Old Harbor **43** Z 5
Old Head of Kinsale **31** B 3
Oldenburg **36** B 2
Oldham **28** C 3
Olekma **42** G 6
Olekminsk **42** H 4
Olekminskiy Stanovik **42** G 6
Oleksandrivka **44** D 3
Olenegorsk **40** H 4
Olenek **41** Y 4
Olenek (River) **42** G 3
Oleniy, Ostrov **41** R 3
Oléron, Île dū **32** B 2
Oleśnica **36** D 2
Olevsūk **36** F 2
Olūga **54** C 2
Olhão **33** A 2
Öli Qoltyq Sory **44** H 3
Olinda **24** H 3
Olmaliq **45** L 4
Olochi **42** G 6
Olomouc **36** D 3
Olonets **40** H 5
Olosega **59** J 5
Olot **32** C 3
Olovyannaya **42** G 6
Oloyskiy Khrebet **43** Q 3
Olsztyn **36** E 2
Olteniţa **35** B 2
Olympia **34** E 3
Olympia (U.S.) **18** B 2
Olympic National Park **18** B 2
Olympus, Mount (U.S.) **18** B 2
Olyutorskiy **43** R 4
Olyutorskiy Poluostrov **43** S 4
Omū **41** R 6
Omagh **31** C 1
Omaha **16** D 3
Omarama **62** A 3
Omatako **58** A 4
Ometepec **20** E 4
Omiya **54** C 3
Omolon **43** P 3
Omoloy **42** K 3
Omsk **40** Q 7
Omsukchan **43** P 4
Omsukchanskiy Gory **43** O 4
Omura **54** A 4
Ōmuta **54** B 4
Omutninsk **40** M 6
Ondor Sum **49** J 2
Öndörhaan **50** B 3
Onega **40** J 5
Onega, Lake **40** J 5
OūNeill **16** D 3
Oneonta **14** D 2
Oneşti **36** F 3
Onezhskaya Guba **40** J 5
Onezhskoye, Ozero **40** J 5
Ongjin **50** E 5
Ongole **46** E 5
Onitsha **56** D 4
Ono-I-lau Island **59** H 6
Onomichi **54** B 4
Onon Gol **50** B 3
Onotoa **59** G 4
Onslow **60** B 4
Onslow Bay **14** D 4
Ontario **10** Y 8
Ontario (U.S.) **18** C 3
Ontario, Lake **14** D 2
Ontong Java **59** E 4
Oodnadatta **60** F 5
Ooldea **60** E 6
Oologah Lake **16** D 4
Opava **36** D 3
Opelousas **16** E 5
Opole **36** D 2
Opotiki **62** C 2
Opp **14** B 4
Oppdal **38** G 3
Oppland **38** G 3
Opportunity **18** C 2
Oputo **18** E 5
Oradea **36** E 3
Orai **46** D 3
Oral **44** H 2
Oran **56** C 1
Orange **58** A 4
Orange (Australia) **60** H 6
Orange (U.S.) **16** E 5
Orange Park **14** C 4
Orange Walk **20** G 4
Oranienburg **36** C 2
Ord River Dam **60** D 3
Ordos Plateau **49** H 3
Ordu **35** G 4
Örebro **38** J 4
Oregon **18** B 3
Oregon Inlet **14** D 3
Orekhovo-Zuyevo **40** J 6
Orel **44** E 2
Orem **18** D 3
Orenburg **40** N 7
Orestiada **34** F 2
Organ Pipe Cactus National Monument **18** D 5
Orgūn **45** L 6
Orhangazi **35** C 4
Orhei **36** F 3
Orhon Gol **41** W 8
Orick **18** B 3
Oriental, Cordillera (Colombia) **22** G 7
Orientale **58** B 1
Orillia **14** D 2
Orinoco, Rio **22** J 6
Orissa **46** E 5
Oristano **34** B 3
Oritz **20** B 2

Orivesi **38** L 3
Orizaba **20** E 4
Orizaba, Pico de **20** E 4
Orkanger **38** G 3
Orkney Islands **30** C 2
Orlando **14** C 5
Orléans **32** C 2
Ormoc **53** G 3
Örnsköldsvik **38** J 3
Orofino **18** C 2
Oroluk **59** E 3
Orona **59** H 4
Oroqen Zizhiqi **50** D 2
Oroville (California, U.S.) **18** B 4
Oroville (Washington, U.S.) **18** C 2
Orsa **38** H 3
Orsha **36** G 2
Orsk **45** J 2
Ortegal, Cabo **33** A 1
Ortigueira **33** A 1
Ortonville **16** D 2
Orulgan, Khrebet **42** J 3
Orūmīyeh **44** G 5
Oruro **24** E 4
Ōsaka **54** C 4
Osborne **16** D 4
Osceola **16** E 3
Osen **38** H 3
Osh **45** M 4
Oshakati **58** A 3
Oshawa **14** D 2
Oshkosh **14** B 2
Osijek **36** D 3
Osinniki **41** T 7
Osinovka **45** O 3
Oskaloosa **16** E 3
Oskarshamn **38** J 4
Öskemen **45** O 2
Oslo **38** H 4
Osmānābād **46** D 5
Osmaniye **35** G 6
Osnabrück **36** B 2
Osorno **24** D 7
Ossora **43** Q 5
Ostashkov **40** H 6
Östergötland **38** H 4
Östersjön **38** J 4
Östersund **38** H 3
Ostrava **36** D 3
Ostróda **36** D 2
Ostrogozhsk **44** E 2
Ostrołęka **36** E 2
Ostrov **38** L 4
Ostrów Mazowiecka **36** E 2
Ostrów Wielkopolski **36** D 2
Ōsumi-kaikyō **54** B 4
Ōsumi-shotō **54** B 4
Osuna **33** A 2
Oswego **14** D 2
Ōtake **54** B 4
Otaru **54** D 2
Otautau **62** A 4
Otranto **34** D 2
Ōtsu **54** C 3
Ottawa (Canada) **8** V 9
Ottawa (U.S.) **16** D 4
Ottawa Islands **8** U 7
Ottawa River **14** D 1
Ottenby **38** J 4
Ottumwa **16** E 3
Otway, Cape **60** G 7
Otwock **36** E 2
Ouachita Mountains **16** D 5
Ouaddaï **56** E 3
Ouagadougou **56** C 3
Ouahigouya **56** C 3
Ouargla **56** D 1
Ouarzazate **56** C 1
Oubangui **58** A 1
Oudtshoorn **58** B 5
Oujda **56** C 1
Oulu **38** L 3
Oulujärvi **38** L 3
Oumé **56** C 4
Ourense **33** A 1
Outer Hebrides **30** A 2
Ouvéa **59** F 6
Ouyen **60** G 7
Ovacık (Turkey) **35** E 6
Ovamboland **58** A 3
Oviedo **33** A 1
Ovruch **36** F 2
Owatonna **16** E 3
Owen Sound **14** C 2
Owen Stanley Range **59** D 4
Owensboro **14** B 3
Owo **56** D 4
Owosso **14** C 2
Owyhee **18** C 3
Owyhee River **18** C 3
Owyhee, Lake **18** C 3
Oxford (U.K.) **28** D 4
Oxford (U.S.) **14** B 4
Oymayakonskoye Nagorūye **42** M 4
Oyotung **42** N 2
Oyun Khomoto **42** L 3
Oyyl **44** H 3
Ozamiz **53** G 4
Ozark **14** B 4
Ozark Plateau **16** E 4
Ozarks, Lake of the **16** E 4
Ózd **36** E 3
Ozernoy, Zaliv **43** Q 5
Ozinki **44** G 2
Ozona **16** C 5
Ozurgetüi **44** F 4
Paamiut **8** Bb 6
Paarl **58** A 5
Pabna **47** F 4
Pachuca **20** E 3
Pacific Ocean **59** G 3
Padang **52** C 6
Padang (Island) **52** C 5
Padangpanjang **52** C 6
Padangsidempuan **52** B 5
Paderborn **36** B 2
Padova **36** C 3
Padrauna **46** E 3
Padre Island **20** E 2
Paducah **14** B 3
Paektu-San **50** E 4
Paeroa **62** C 2
Pag **34** C 2
Pagadian **53** G 4
Pagai Selatan **52** C 6
Pagai Utara **52** B 6
Pagan **59** D 2
Pagoda Point **47** G 5
Pagosa Springs **18** E 4
Paignton **28** C 4
Päijänne **38** L 3
Painan **52** C 6
Painesville **14** C 2
Painted Desert **18** D 4
Paisley **28** B 2
Pajala **38** K 2
Pak Phanang **47** J 7
Pakistan **46** B 3
Pakokku **47** H 4
Paks **36** D 3
Pakse **47** K 5
Pakuashipi **8** Z 8
Pala **56** E 4
Palana **43** P 5
Palanan Point **53** G 2
Palangkaraya **52** E 6
Palani **46** D 6
Palanpur **46** C 4
Palatka **43** O 4
Palau **59** C 3
Palau Islands **59** C 3
Palawan **53** F 4
Palawan Passage **53** F 4
Palayankottai **46** D 7
Paleleh **53** G 5
Palembang **52** C 6
Palencia **33** B 1
Palenque **20** F 4
Palermo **34** C 3
Palestine **16** D 5
Paletwa **47** G 4
Pālghāt **46** D 6
Pali **46** C 3
Palikir **59** E 3
Pālitāna **46** C 4
Pallasovka **44** G 2
Palliser, Cape **62** C 3
Palliser, Îles **59** L 5
Palm Springs **18** C 5
Palma **56** B 2
Palma de Mallorca **33** C 2
Palma Soriano **22** G 3
Palmas **24** G 3
Palmer **10** N 6

Palmerston **59** J 5
Palmerston (New Zealand) **62** B 4
Palmerston North **62** C 3
Palmira **22** G 7
Palopo **52** G 6
Palos, Cabo de **33** B 2
Palpetu, Tanjung **52** H 6
Palu **52** F 6
Pamekasan **52** E 7
Pamirs **45** M 5
Pamlico Sound **14** D 3
Pampa (U.S.) **16** C 4
Pampas **24** E 6
Pamplona **22** H 6
Pamplona-Iru-a **32** B 3
Panaji **46** C 5
Panama **22** G 6
Panama Canal **22** G 6
Panama City **14** B 4
Panamá, Golfo de **22** G 6
Panay **52** G 3
Pančevo **34** E 2
Pandharpur **46** D 5
Panevežys **38** K 4
Pangkadjene **52** F 6
Pangkalpinang **52** D 6
Pangnirtung **8** X 5
Pangutaran Group **52** F 4
Panipat **46** D 3
Panna **46** E 4
Panshi **50** E 4
Pantar **52** G 7
Pánuco **20** E 3
Pánuco, Río **20** E 3
Panxian **49** G 5
Pápa **36** D 3
Papa Westray **30** C 2
Papantla **20** E 3
Papar **52** F 4
Paparoa **62** B 2
Papeete **59** L 5
Papua New Guinea **59** D 4
Parabelū **41** S 6
Paracel Islands **52** E 2
Pāradwīp **46** F 4
Paragould **16** E 4
Paraguay **24** E 5
Parakou **56** D 4
Paramaribo **24** F 2
Paramushir, Ostrov **43** P 6
Paraná **24** F 6
Parang **52** G 4
Parangaba **24** H 3
Paraoa **59** L 5
Paray-le-Monial **32** C 2
Parbhani **46** D 5
Pardubice **36** D 2
Parengarenga Harbour **62** B 1
Parent **14** E 1
Parepare **52** F 6
Pariaman **52** C 6
Paricutín, Volcán **20** D 4
Parima, Sierra **22** K 7
Paris (France) **32** C 2
Paris (Illinois, U.S.) **14** B 3
Paris (Tennessee, U.S.) **14** B 3
Paris (Texas, U.S.) **16** D 5
Park Rapids **16** D 2
Parkano **38** K 3
Parker **18** D 5
Parkersburg **14** C 3
Parklākimidi **46** E 5
Parkland **18** B 2
Parma **34** C 2
Parnaíba **24** G 3
Pärnu **38** K 4
Paropamisus **45** K 6
Parramatta **60** J 6
Parras **20** D 2
Parras, Sierra de **20** D 2
Parry Islands **10** U 3
Parry, Kap **8** W 3
Partille **38** H 4
Partizansk **54** B 2
Pasadena **18** C 5
Pascagoula **14** B 4
Pashkovo **50** F 3
Passero, Capo **34** D 3
Passo Fundo **24** F 5
Pastavy **38** L 4
Pasto **22** G 7
Pasul Meste Cănis **36** F 3
Patagonia **24** D 7
Patan (India) **46** C 4
Patan (Nepal) **46** F 3
Paterna **33** B 2
Paterson **14** E 2
Pathankot **46** D 2
Pathfinder Reservoir **18** E 3
Patiala **46** D 2
Patmos **35** B 6
Patna **46** F 3
Patra **34** E 3
Pattani **47** J 7
Pattle Island **52** E 2
Patuākhāli **47** G 4
Patuca, Río **20** G 5
Pau **32** B 3
Paulatuk **10** S 5
Pauls Valley **16** D 5
Paungde **47** H 5
Pavla **36** B 3
Pavlodar **45** N 2
Pavlof Islands **43** X 6
Pavlohrad **44** E 3
Pavlovo **40** K 6
Pavlovsk **41** S 7
Pavlovskaya **35** H 1
Paxson **10** N 6
Payakumbuh **52** C 6
Payeti **52** G 7
Pay-Khoy, Khrebet **40** O 4
Paynes Find **60** B 5
Paysandú **24** F 6
Payson **18** D 3
Pazarcık **35** G 6
Pazardzhik **34** E 2
Peace Point **10** U 7
Peace River **10** T 7
Peach Springs **18** D 4
Peachland **18** C 2
Pearl River **14** B 4
Pearsall **20** E 2
Peary Land **8** Dd 2
Peawanuck **8** T 7
Peć **34** E 2
Pechenga **38** M 2
Pechora **40** N 4
Pechora (River) **40** M 4
Pechorskoye More **40** M 4
Pecos **16** C 5
Pecos Plains **16** C 5
Pecos River **16** C 5
Pécs **36** D 3
Pedriseña **20** D 2
Peel **28** B 2
Peera Peera Poolanno Lake **60** F 5
Pegasus Bay **62** B 3
Pegasus, Port **62** A 4
Pegu **47** H 5
Pegu Yoma **47** H 4
Peikang **49** L 6
Peipsi järv **38** L 4
Peipus, Lake **38** L 4
Peixian **49** K 4
Pejantan **52** D 5
Pekalongan **52** D 7
Pekanbaru **52** C 5
Pekin **14** B 2
Peking **49** K 3
Pelabuhanratu **52** D 7
Peleduy **42** F 5
Peleliu **59** C 3
Peleng **52** G 6
Pello **38** K 2
Pelly Crossing **10** P 6
Peloponnisos **34** E 3
Pelotas **24** F 6
Pemalang **52** D 7
Pematangsiantar **52** B 5
Pemba **58** D 3
Pemba Island **58** C 2
Pembina **16** D 2
Pembroke (Canada) **8** V 9
Pembroke (U.K.) **28** B 4
Peña Nevada, Cerro **20** E 3
Peñas, Cabo de **33** A 1
Pend Oreille Lake **18** C 2
Pend Oreille River **18** C 2
Pendleton **18** C 2
Penglai **49** L 3
Penida **52** F 7
Penmarcūh, Pointe de **32** B 2
Penn Hills **14** D 2

Pennines **28** C 2
Pennsylvania **14** C 2
Penny Ice Cap **8** X 5
Penobscot Bay **14** F 2
Peñón Blanco **20** D 3
Penong **60** E 6
Penrhyn **59** K 4
Penrith **60** J 6
Penrith (U.K.) **28** C 2
Pensacola **14** B 4
Pentecôte **59** F 5
Pentland Firth **30** C 2
Penza **44** F 2
Penzance **28** B 4
Penzhino **43** R 4
Penzhinskiy Khrebet **43** R 4
Peoria **14** B 2
Perabumulih **52** C 6
Percival Lakes **60** C 4
Pereira **22** G 7
Pereslavl-Zalesskiy **40** J 6
Pericos **20** C 2
Périgueux **32** C 2
Perija, Sierra de **22** H 6
Perlas, Laguna de **22** F 5
Permū **40** N 6
Pernik **34** E 2
Perote **20** E 4
Perpignan **32** C 3
Perry **14** C 4
Perry Bay **10** W 5
Perryton **16** C 4
Perryville **43** Y 5
Perth (Australia) **60** B 6
Perth (U.K.) **30** C 3
Perth-Andover **8** X 9
Peru **24** D 3
Perugia **34** C 2
Pervouralūsk **40** N 6
Pesaro **34** C 2
Pescara **34** C 2
Peschanyy Müyis **44** H 4
Peschanyy, Ostrov **42** G 2
Peshāwar **45** M 6
Pessac **32** B 3
Pestovo **40** J 6
Petacalco Bahía de **20** D 4
Petaluma **18** B 4
Petatlán **20** D 4
Petén Itzá, Lago **20** F 4
Petenwell Lake **16** E 3
Peter I Øy **63** X 5
Peterborough (Australia) **60** F 6
Peterborough (Canada) **14** D 2
Peterborough (U.K.) **28** D 3
Peterhead **30** D 3
Petermann Ranges **60** D 5
Petermanns Gletscher **8** Y 2
Petersburg (Virginia, U.S.) **14** D 3
Petitsikapau Lake **8** X 8
Peto **20** G 3
Petra Velikogo, Zaliv **50** F 4
Petrila **36** E 3
Petropavlovsk **40** P 7
Petropavlovsk-Kamchatskiy **43** P 6
Petrovsk **44** G 2
Petrovsk-Zabaykalūskiy **41** X 7
Petrozavodsk **40** H 5
Petukhovo **40** P 6
Pevek **43** S 3
Pforzheim **36** B 3
Phaliodi **46** C 3
Phaltan **46** C 5
Phan Rang **47** K 6
Phan Thiet **47** K 6
Phatthalung **47** J 7
Phenix City **14** B 4
Phetchabun **47** J 5
Phetchaburi **47** H 6
Phichit **47** J 5
Philadelphia **14** D 3
Philippi, Lake **60** F 4
Philippines **52** H 3
Phillipsburg **16** D 4
Philpots Island **8** V 4
Phitsanulok **47** J 5
Phnum Aôral **47** J 6
Phnum Pénh **47** J 6
Phoenix **18** D 5
Phoenix Islands **59** H 4
Phon **47** J 5
Phôngsali **47** J 4
Phu Vinh **47** K 7
Phuket **47** H 7
Phumĭ Chhuk **47** J 6
Piacenza **36** B 3
Piatra-Neamţ **36** F 3
Pichilingue **20** B 3
Pickering **28** D 2
Pickle Lake **10** Y 8
Pickwick Lake **14** B 3
Picos **24** G 3
Piedras Negras **20** D 2
Pieksämäki **38** L 3
Pielinen **38** L 3
Pierre **16** C 3
Pieštūany **36** D 3
Piet Retief **58** C 4
Pietermaritzburg **58** C 4
Piła **36** D 2
Pilas Group **53** G 4
Piloncillo Mountains **18** E 5
Pinar del Rio **20** H 3
Pincher Creek **18** D 2
Pine Bluff **16** E 5
Pine Bluffs **16** C 3
Pine Creek **60** E 2
Pine Falls **10** X 8
Pine Pass **10** S 7
Pine Point **10** U 6
Pine Ridge **16** C 3
Pinerolo **34** B 2
Pingdingshan **49** J 4
Pinghu **49** L 4
Pingjiang **49** J 5
Pingle **49** J 6
Pingluo **49** H 3
Pingnan **49** J 6
Pingquan **50** C 4
Pingtan **49** K 5
Pingtung **49** L 6
Pingvellir **38** A 3
Pingxiang (Guangxi,China) **49** J 5
Pingxiang (Jiangxi, China) **47** K 4
Pingyang **49** L 5
Pingyao **49** J 3
Pingyin **49** K 3
Pini **52** B 5
Pinjang **52** G 5
Pink Mountain **10** S 7
Pinnaroo **60** G 7
Pinos, Mount **18** C 5
Pinrang **52** F 6
Pinsk **36** F 2
Pinyug **40** L 5
Piombino **34** C 2
Pioner, Ostrov **41** U 2
Piotrków Trybunalski **36** D 2
Pipestone **16** D 3
Pipmuacan, Réservoir **8** W 9
Pir Panjal Range **45** M 6
Piracicaba **24** G 5
Pirot **34** E 2
Piru **52** H 6
Pisa **34** C 2
Pisco **24** D 4
Pishan **48** B 3
Pisté **20** G 3
Pitalito **22** G 7
Pitcairn Island **59** M 6
Piteå **38** K 2
Piteälven **38** K 2
Piteşti **35** A 2
Pit-Gorodoko **41** U 6
Pitt Island **10** Q 8
Pittsburg **16** E 4
Pittsburgh **14** C 2
Pittsfield **14** E 2
Piura **24** C 3
Pivdenyy Buh **36** F 3
Plainview **16** C 5
Plampang **53** F 7
Planalto do Mato Grosso **24** F 4
Plasencia **33** A 1
Plastun **54** C 2
Plateau du Djado **56** E 2
Platte **58** E 2
Platte River **16** D 3
Platteville **16** E 3
Plattsburgh **14** E 2
Plattsmouth **16** D 3
Plauen **36** C 2
Plavnikovye, Ostrova **41** S 3

Plavsk **44** E 2
Play Cu **47** K 6
Playa Azul **20** D 4
Pleasanton **20** E 2
Plenty, Bay of **62** C 2
Plentywood **16** C 2
Plesetsk **40** K 5
Pleven **34** E 2
Pligliang **49** H 3
Pljevlja **34** D 2
Płock **36** D 2
Plöckenpass **36** C 3
Ploieşti **35** B 2
Plovdiv **34** E 2
Plumridge Lakes **60** C 5
Plungė **38** K 4
Plymouth (U.K.) **28** B 4
Plzeň **36** C 3
Po (Italy) **34** C 2
Pobeda, Gora **42** N 3
Pobedino **54** D 1
Pocatello **18** D 3
Pocklington Reef **60** K 2
Pocono Mountains **14** D 2
Poços de Caldas **24** G 5
Podgorica **34** D 2
Podgornoye **41** S 6
Podgornyy **54** E 1
Podkagernoye **43** Q 4
Podkamennaya Tunguska **41** U 5
Podolūsk **40** J 6
Podosinovets **40** L 5
Podporozhūye **40** H 5
Podyuga **40** K 5
Pogibi **42** M 6
Pogranichnyy **50** F 4
Pūohang **54** A 3
Pohapei **59** E 3
Pohjanmaa **38** K 3
Point Baker **10** Q 7
Point Hope **10** J 5
Point Lake **10** U 5
Point Lay **10** K 5
Pointe-à-Pitre **22** K 4
Pointe-Noire **58** A 2
Poitiers **32** C 2
Poitou **32** B 2
Poivre Atoll **58** E 2
Pokaran **46** C 3
Pokhara **46** E 3
Pokhvistnevo **44** H 2
Pokrovka **54** B 2
Pokrovsk **42** J 4
Poland **36** D 2
Polatlı **35** E 5
Pol-e Khomri **45** L 5
Polesye **36** E 2
Polevskoy **40** O 6
Polewali **52** F 6
Pŏlgyo **54** A 4
Police **36** C 2
Poliny Osipenko **42** L 6
Pollāchi **46** D 6
Polohy **44** E 3
Polokwane **58** B 4
Polousnyy, Kryazh **42** L 3
Polson **18** D 2
Polunochnoye **40** O 5
Poluostrov Rybachiy **38** M 2
Poluy **40** P 4
Polyarnyy (Russia) **42** N 2
Polyarnyy Ural **40** O 4
Polysayevo **41** T 7
Pomona **18** C 5
Pompeyevka **54** B 1
Ponca City **16** D 4
Ponce **22** J 4
Pond Inlet **8** V 4
Pondicherry **46** D 6
Ponferrada **33** A 1
Ponoj **40** J 4
Ponta Grossa **24** G 5
Pontchartrain, Lake **16** E 5
Pontevedra **33** A 1
Pontiac **14** B 2
Pontianak **52** D 6
Poole **28** D 4
Poona **46** C 5
Popayán **22** G 7
Poplar Bluff **16** E 4
Popocatépetl, Volcán **20** E 4
Poprad **36** E 3
Poptún **20** G 4
Porbandar **46** B 4
Porcupine Plain **10** P 5
Porcupine River **10** O 5
Pordenone **36** C 3
Pori **38** K 3
Porirua **62** B 3
Porkkala **38** K 4
Porlamar **22** K 5
Porog **40** J 5
Poronaysk **50** H 3
Porreres **33** C 2
Porsgrunn **38** G 4
Port Adelaide **60** F 6
Port Alberni **18** B 2
Port Angeles **18** B 2
Port Arthur **49** L 3
Port Arthur (U.S.) **20** F 2
Port Augusta **60** F 6
Port Blair **47** G 6
Port Cartier **8** X 9
Port Chalmers **62** B 4
Port Charlotte **14** C 5
Port Elgin **14** C 2
Port Elizabeth **58** B 5
Port Ellen **30** A 4
Port Gentil **56** D 5
Port Graham **43** Z 5
Port Harcourt **56** D 4
Port Hard **10** R 8
Port Hedland **60** B 4
Port Heiden **43** Y 5
Port Hope Smith **8** Z 8
Port Huron **14** C 2
Port Jackson **62** C 2
Port Láirge **31** C 2
Port Laoise **31** C 2
Port Lavaca **20** E 2
Port Lincoln **60** F 6
Port Louis **58** E 3
Port Macquarie **60** J 6
Port Moller **43** X 5
Port Moresby **59** D 4
Port of Ness **30** A 2
Port of Spain **22** K 5
Port Ontario **14** D 2
Port Phillip Bay **60** G 7
Port Pirie **60** F 6
Port Sulphur **20** G 2
Port Talbot **28** C 4
Portadown **31** C 1
Portage la-Prairie **16** D 2
Portales **16** C 5
Port-au-Prince **22** H 4
Porterville **18** C 4
Portile de Fier **34** E 2
Portland (Aust.) **60** G 7
Portland (Maine, U.S.) **14** E 2
Portland (Washington, U.S.) **18** B 2
Portland, Bill of **28** C 4
Porto **33** A 1
Porto Alegre **24** F 6
Pôrto Santo **56** B 1
Porto Velho **24** E 3
Porto-Novo **56** D 4
Portoviejo **24** C 3
Portsmouth (New Hampshire, U.S.) **14** E 2
Portsmouth (Ohio, U.S.) **14** C 3
Portsmouth (U.K.) **28** D 4
Portsmouth (Virginia, U.S.) **14** D 3
Portsoy **30** C 3
Portugal **33** A 1
Posadas **24** F 5
Poso **53** G 6
Potenza **34** D 2
Potholes Reservoir **18** B 2
Pūotūi **35** J 3
Potomac River **14** D 3
Potosi **24** E 4
Potsdam **36** C 2
Pottstown **14** D 2
Povazská Bystrica **36** D 3
Powassan **14** D 1
Powder River **18** E 2
Powell River **18** B 2
Powell, Lake **18** D 4
Poyarkovo **54** A 1
Poza Rica de Hidalgo **20** E 3
Požarevac **34** E 2
Poznań **36** D 2

Pozoblanco **33** B 2
Prachuap Khiri Khan **47** H 6
Pradesh **46** D 2
Prague **36** C 2
Praha **36** C 2
Praia **56** A 3
Prairie du Chien **16** E 3
Praslin **58** E 2
Pratapgarh **46** C 4
Prato **34** C 2
Pratt **16** D 4
Praya **52** F 7
Prentice **16** E 2
Prenzlau **36** C 2
Preparis Island **47** G 6
Preparis South Channel **47** G 6
Prescott **18** D 5
Prescott Island **8** R 4
Presidente Prudente **24** F 5
Prešov **36** E 3
Presque Isle **14** F 1
Preston (U.K.) **28** C 3
Preston (U.S.) **18** D 3
Prestonburg **14** C 3
Prestwick **28** B 2
Pretoria **58** B 4
Preveza **34** E 3
Priangarskoye Plato **41** V 6
Pribilof Islands **43** W 5
Priboj **34** D 2
Příbram **36** C 3
Price **18** D 4
Prichard **14** B 4
Prieta, Sierra **18** D 5
Prievidza **36** D 3
Prilep **34** E 2
Primorskiy Kray **54** B 2
Primorsko-Akhtarsk **35** H 1
Prince Albert **10** V 8
Prince Albert National Park **10** V 8
Prince Charles Island **8** V 5
Prince Edward Island (Island) **8** Y 9
Prince Edward Island (Province) **8** Y 9
Prince George **10** S 8
Prince of Wales Island (Australia) **60** G 2
Prince of Wales Island (Canada) **8** R 4
Prince of Wales Island (U.S.) **10** Q 7
Prince of Wales, Cape **43** W 3
Prince Patrick Island **10** T 3
Prince Regent Inlet **8** S 4
Prince Rupert **10** Q 8
Princess Charlotte Bay **60** G 2
Princess Royal Island **10** R 8
Princeton (Canada) **18** B 2
Princeton (U.S.) **14** B 3
Príncipe **56** D 4
Prineville **18** B 3
Prinsesse Astrid Kyst **63** P 5
Prinsesse Ragnhild Kyst **63** P 5
Priozersk **40** H 5
Pripolyarnyy Ural **40** N 5
Priština **34** E 2
Privolzhskaya Vozvyshennostū **44** G 2
Priyutovo **44** H 2
Prizren **34** E 2
Proddatūr **46** D 6
Progreso **20** G 3
Prokhladnyy **35** K 3
Prokopūyevsk **41** T 7
Prokuplje **34** E 2
Proletarsk **44** F 3
Prome **47** H 5
Prosser **18** C 2
Prøven **8** Z 4
Provence **34** B 2
Providence **58** E 2
Providence (U.S.) **14** E 2
Providence, Cape **62** A 4
Providencia, Isla de **22** F 5
Provideniya **43** V 4
Provincetown **14** E 2
Provo **18** D 3
Prudhoe Bay **10** N 4
Pruszków **36** E 2
Pruzhany **36** E 2
Pryluki **36** G 2
Prypyatsū **36** F 2
Przemyśl **36** E 3
Pūsek **36** C 3
Pskov **38** L 4
Pucallpa **24** D 3
Pucheng **49** K 5
Puchūŏn **54** A 3
Pudasjärvi **38** L 2
Pudino **41** R 6
Pudops Dam **8** Z 9
Pudozh **40** J 5
Puebla (Mexico) **20** E 4
Puebla (State, Mexico) **20** E 4
Pueblo **16** C 4
Puente Alto **24** D 6
Puente-Genil **33** B 2
Puerto Ángel **20** E 4
Puerto Arista **20** F 4
Puerto Ayacucho **22** J 6
Puerto Baquerizo Moreno **24** C 3
Puerto Barrios **20** G 4
Puerto Cabello **22** J 5
Puerto Cabezas **20** H 5
Puerto Cortés **20** G 4
Puerto Cumarebo **22** J 5
Puerto Escondito **20** E 4
Puerto Juárez **20** G 3
Puerto la Cruz **22** K 5
Puerto Lempira **20** H 4
Puerto Libertad **20** B 2
Puerto Madero **20** F 5
Puerto Montt **24** D 7
Puerto Plata **22** H 4
Puerto Princesa **53** F 4
Puerto Rico **22** J 4
Puerto Vallarta **20** C 3
Puertollano **33** B 2
Pugachev **44** G 2
Puget Sound **18** B 2
Pukapuka (Cook Islands) **59** J 5
Pukapuka (French Polynesia) **59** M 5
Pukaruha **59** M 5
Pukchū ŏng **50** E 4
Puketeraki Range **62** B 3
Pula **34** C 2
Pulap **59** D 3
Pulau Penida **60** B 1
Puławy **36** E 2
Pullman **18** C 2
Pulupandan **52** G 3
Puluwat **59** D 3
Puncak Trikora **59** C 4
Pune **46** C 5
Punjab (India) **46** D 2
Punjab (Pakistan) **46** C 2
Puno **24** D 4
Punta Arenas **24** D 8
Punta Carreta **24** D 4
Punta Cristóbal **24** B 3
Punta Gorda (Belize) **20** G 4
Punta Prieta **20** B 2
Punto Fijo **22** H 5
Puper **52** J 6
Puqi **49** J 5
Pur **41** R 4
Purekkari neem **38** L 4
Puri **46** F 5
Purnea **46** F 3
Purtuniq **8** W 6
Purwakarta **52** D 7
Purwokerto **52** D 7
Pusan **50** E 5
Pushkin **40** H 6
Putaruru **62** C 2
Putian **49** K 5
Puting, Tanjung **52** E 6
Putla de Guerrero **20** E 4
Putorana, Plato **41** U 4
Putrajaya **52** C 5
Puttalan **46** D 7
Puttgarden **36** C 2
Puvirnituq **8** V 6
Puyang **49** J 3
Pwllheli **28** B 3
Pyandzh **45** L 5
Pyapon **47** H 5
Pyasina **41** T 3
Pyasino, Ozero **41** T 4
Pyatigorsk **44** F 4
Pyatistennoy **43** Q 3
Pyhäjärvi **38** L 3
Pyinmana **47** H 5

Pylos **34** E 3
Pūyŏngyang **50** E 5
Pyramid Lake **18** C 3
Pyrénées **32** B 3
Pyrgos **34** E 3
Pyryatyn **36** G 2
Pyu **47** H 5
Qaanaaq **8** X 3
Qabanbay **45** O 3
Qābis (Gabès) **56** D 1
Qafşah **56** D 1
Qaidam Pendi **48** E 3
Qala Nau **45** K 6
Qamashi **45** L 5
Qamdo **48** F 4
Qapshaghay **45** N 4
Qapshaghay Bögeni **45** N 4
Qaqortoq **8** Bb 6
Qarabutaq **45** K 3
Qaraghandy **45** M 3
Qaraghayly **45** N 3
Qaraqum **44** H 3
Qarataū **45** M 4
Qarataū Zhotasy **45** L 4
Qaratöbe **44** H 3
Qarazhal **45** M 3
Qarsaqbay **45** L 3
Qarshi **45** L 5
Qasigiannguit **8** Aa 5
Qaskeleng **45** N 4
Qaynar **45** N 3
Qazaqtyng Usaqshoqylyghy **45** J 3
Qazvīn **44** G 5
Qeqertarsuaq **8** Aa 5
Qeqertarsuaq (Island) **8** Aa 5
Qeshqantengiz **45** M 3
Qian Gorlos **50** D 3
Qianwei **49** G 5
Qianxi **49** H 5
Qiemo **48** D 3
Qijiang **49** H 5
Qijiaojing **48** E 2
Qikiqtarjuaq **8** Y 5
Qilian Shan **48** F 3
Qinūan **49** H 4
Qingdao **49** L 3
Qinggang **50** E 3
Qinghai **48** E 3
Qinghai Hu **48** F 3
Qinghe **48** E 1
Qingjiang **49** K 4
Qingyuan **49** J 6
Qinhuangdao **49** K 3
Qinling Shan **49** H 4
Qinzhou **49** H 6
Qionghai **47** L 5
Qionglai **49** G 4
Qiongshan **47** L 5
Qiqihar **50** D 3
Qitai **48** D 2
Qitaihe **54** B 1
Qiyang **49** J 5
Qom **44** H 6
Qomsheh **44** H 6
Qoūngūirot **45** J 4
Qoūqon **45** M 4
Qoraqoūl **45** K 5
Qoryooley **58** D 1
Qosköl **45** L 3
Qosshaghyl **44** H 3
Qostanay **45** K 2
Qotanqaraghay **45** P 3
Quan Dao Nam Du **47** J 7
Quang Ngai **47** K 5
Quanjyang **49** J 5
Quanzhou (Fujian, China) **49** K 6
Quanzhou (Guangxi,China) **49** J 5
QuūAppelle River **16** C 1
Quaqtaq **8** X 6
Quartu SantūElena **34** B 3
Quartzsite **18** D 5
Quatro Ciénegas **20** D 2
Qūchān **45** J 5
Québec **8** W 9
Québec (Canada) **14** E 1
Québec (State) **8** V 8
Queen Charlotte Islands **10** Q 8
Queen Elizabeth Islands **8** S 3
Queen Mary Land **63** S 5
Queen Maud Gulf **10** W 5
Queensland **60** F 4
Queenstown **58** B 5
Quelimane **58** C 3
Quemado **18** E 5
Querétaro (Mexico) **20** D 3
Querétaro (State, Mexico) **20** E 3
Quesnel **10** S 8
Quetta **46** B 2
Quezaltenango **22** D 5
Quezon City **52** G 3
Qui Nhon **47** K 6
Quibdó **22** G 6
Quilá **20** C 3
Quilon **46** D 7
Quilpie **60** G 5
Quimen **49** K 5
Quimper **32** B 2
Quincy **16** E 4
Quintana Roo **20** G 4
Quiriguá **20** G 4
Quitasueño, Banco **22** F 5
Quito **24** D 3
Qujing **49** G 5
Qulsary **44** H 3
Qumarlêb Jiuzhi **48** F 4
Qūrghonteppa **45** L 5
Qūs **56** G 2
Qusmurun Köli **45** K 2
Quxian **49** K 5
Qvareli **35** L 4
Qyzylorda **45** L 4
Raas Caseyr **56** J 3
Raas Xaafuun **56** J 4
Raasay, Sound of **30** A 3
Raba **53** F 7
Rabat **56** C 1
Rabaul **59** E 4
Râbniţa **36** F 3
Rach Gia **47** K 6
Racine **14** B 2
Rădăuţi **36** F 3
Radomsko **36** D 2
Radøy **38** F 3
Radviliškis **38** K 4
Radville **16** C 2
Rae-Edzo **10** T 6
Raevavae **59** L 6
Ragged Island Range **22** G 3
Ragusa **34** C 3
Rahīmyār Khān **46** C 3
Raiatea **59** K 5
Raichur **46** D 5
Raigarh **46** E 4
Rainy Lake **16** E 2
Raipur **46** E 4
Rāj Gangpur **46** E 4
Raj Nandgaon **46** E 4
Rajabasa **52** C 7
Rājahmundry **46** E 5
Rajanpur **46** C 3
Rājapālaiyam **46** D 7
Rajasthan **46** C 3
Rajkot **46** C 4
Rājmahal Hills **46** E 4
Rajshahi **47** F 4
Rakahanga **59** J 4
Rakaia **62** B 3
Rakitnoye **54** B 1
Raleigh **14** D 3
Raleigh Bay **14** D 4
Râmnicu Sărat **36** F 3
Râmnicu Vâlcea **36** E 3
Rampur **46** D 3
Ramree Island **47** G 5
Ramsey (Canada) **14** C 1
Ramsey (U.K.) **28** B 2
Ramsgate **28** E 4
Rāna Pratāp Sāgar **46** D 4
Rancagua **24** D 6
Ranchi **46** F 4
Randers **38** H 4
Rangaunu Bay **62** B 1
Ranger **16** D 5
Rangiroa **59** L 5
Rangkasbitung **52** D 7
Rangoon **47** H 5
Rangpur **47** F 3
Rangsang **52** C 5
Ranibennur **46** D 6
Rankin Inlet **8** S 6
Ranong **47** H 7
Ransiki **53** J 6
Rantau **52** C 5
Rantauprapat **52** B 5

Raohe **54** B 1
Raoul Island **59** H 6
Rapa **59** L 6
Raper, Cape **8** X 5
Rapid City **16** C 3
Raraka **59** L 5
Raroia **59** L 5
Rarotonga **59** K 6
Raūs Ajdīr **56** E 1
Rās Koh **46** B 3
Râs Timirist **56** B 3
Rasht **44** G 5
Rasskazovo **44** F 2
Rat Island **43** T 6
Ratak Chain **59** F 3
Ratangarh **46** C 3
Rath **46** D 3
Rathenow **36** C 2
Rathlin Island **31** C 1
Ratlam **46** D 4
Ratnagiri **46** C 5
Raton **16** C 4
Rattray Head **30** D 3
Rättvik **38** J 3
Raub **52** C 5
Rauma **38** K 3
Raumo **38** K 3
Raurkela **46** E 4
Rausu **54** E 2
Ravahere **59** L 5
Ravenna **34** C 2
Ravensthorpe **60** C 6
Rawaki **59** H 4
Rāwalpindi **45** M 6
Rawlinna **60** D 6
Rawlins **18** E 3
Rawson **24** E 7
Rāyadrug **46** D 6
Rāyagarha **46** E 5
Raychikhinsk **50** E 3
Raymond **18** B 2
Raymondville **20** E 2
Rayón **20** E 3
Rayong **47** J 6
Razgrad **34** F 2
Ré, Île de **32** B 2
Reading **28** D 4
Reao **59** M 5
Reata **20** D 2
Rebecca, Lake **60** C 6
Rebi **53** J 7
Reboly **40** H 5
Rebun-To **50** H 3
Rebun-to **54** C 1
Recherche, Archipelago of the **60** C 6
Rechna Doab **46** C 2
Rechytsa **36** G 2
Recife **24** H 3
Récifs Bampton **59** E 5
Red Bank **14** B 3
Red Basin **49** H 4
Red Bluff **18** B 3
Red Cloud **16** D 3
Red Deer **10** U 8
Red Deer River **10** U 8
Red Devil **43** Y 4
Red Lake **10** Y 8
Red Lake (Lake, Ontario, Canada) **16** E 1
Red Lodge **18** E 2
Red Oak **16** D 3
Red River (Canada) **16** D 2
Red River (U.S.) **16** C 5
Red Rock River **18** D 3
Red Sea **56** G 2
Red Wing **16** E 3
Redcliffe **60** J 5
Redding **18** B 3
Redditch **28** D 3
Redfield **16** D 3
Redlands **18** C 5
Redon **32** B 2
Redoubt Volcano **10** M 6
Redruth **28** B 4
Ree, Lough **31** B 2
Reef Islands **59** F 4
Reefton **62** B 3
Regensburg **36** C 3
Reggio di Calabria **34** D 3
Reggio nellū Emilia **34** C 2
Reghin **36** E 3
Regina **10** W 8
Reims **32** C 2
Reindeer Lake **10** W 7
Reine **38** H 2
Reinosa **33** B 1
Reitoru **59** L 5
Rekinniki **43** Q 4
Reliance **10** V 6
Rembang **52** E 7
Remontnoye **44** F 3
Rendsburg **36** B 2
Renfrew **14** D 1
Rengat **52** C 6
Renland **8** Ff 4
Renmark **60** G 6
Rennell Island **59** F 5
Rennes **32** B 2
Reno **18** C 4
Renton **18** B 2
Reo **52** G 7
Replot **38** K 3
Represa Boa Esperança **24** G 3
Represa Trés Marias **24** G 4
Republic **18** C 2
Republican River **16** D 4
Repulse Bay **8** T 5
Reşadiye **35** G 4
Reserve **18** E 5
Reshteh-ye Kūhhā-yeAlborz **44** H 5
Resistencia **24** E 5
Reşiţa **36** E 3
Resolution Island (Canada) **8** Y 6
Resolution Island (New Zealand) **62** A 4
Retalhuleu **20** F 5
Retkucha **43** S 3
Réunion (France) **58** E 4
Reus **32** C 3
Revda **40** N 6
Revelstoke **10** T 8
Revillagigedo Island **10** Q 7
Rewa **46** E 4
Rexburg **18** D 3
Rey **44** H 5
Rey, Isla del **22** G 6
Reyhanlı **35** G 6
Reykjavūk **38** A 3
Reynosa **20** E 2
Rēzekne **38** L 4
Rezh **40** O 6
Rhein **36** B 3
Rhinelander **14** B 1
Rhode Island **14** E 2
Rhodes **34** F 3
Rhondda **28** C 4
Rhône **32** C 3
Rhum **30** A 3
Riau, Kepulauan **52** C 5
Ribadeo **33** A 1
Ribe **38** G 4
Ribeirão Prêto **24** G 5
Richards, Cape **8** V 2
Richfield **18** D 4
Richland **18** C 2
Richmond (California, U.S.) **18** B 4
Richmond (New Zealand) **62** B 3
Richmond (Virginia, U.S.) **14** D 3
Riding Mountain National Park **10** W 8
Riesa **36** C 2
Rieti **34** C 2
Rīga **38** K 4
Riga, Gulf of **38** K 4
Riggins **18** C 2
Rigolet **8** Z 8
Rijeka **36** C 3
Riksgränsen **38** J 2
Riley **18** C 3
Rimatara **59** K 6
Rimini **34** C 2
Rimouski **8** X 9
Rinbung **48** D 5
Rinca **53** F 7
Ringsvassøy **38** J 2
Rio Amazonas **24** E 3
Río Beni **24** E 4
Rio Branco **24** E 4
Río Cuarto **24** E 6
Rio das Balsas **24** G 3
Rio de Janeiro **24** G 5
Rio de Oro **56** B 2
Río Gallegos **24** E 8

Rio Grande **24** F 6
Río Grande (Nicaragua) **20** G 5
Rio Grande (U.S.) **18** E 5
Río Lagartos **20** G 3
Rio Madeira **24** E 3
Río Madre de Dios **24** E 4
Río Negro **24** E 3
Rio Paraguai **24** F 4
Río Paraná **24** F 6
Rio Parnaíba **24** G 3
Rio Roosevelt **24** E 3
Río São **24** G 4
Rio Tapajós **24** F 3
Rio Teles Pires **24** F 4
Rio Tocantins **24** G 3
Río Ucayali **24** D 3
Ríoverde (Mexico) **20** D 3
Ripon **28** D 2
Rishiri-Tô **50** H 3
Ritzville **18** C 2
Riverside **18** C 5
Riverton (Canada) **16** D 1
Riverton (New Zealand) **62** A 4
Riverton (U.S.) **18** E 3
Rivière-du-Loup **8** X 9
Rivne **36** F 2
Rivoli **36** B 3
Rize **35** J 4
Rizhao **49** K 3
Roan Plateau **18** E 4
Roanne **32** C 2
Roanoke **14** D 3
Roanoke Rapids **14** D 3
Roanoke River **14** D 3
Roatán **20** G 4
Robeson Channel **8** Y 2
Robinson Ranges **60** B 5
Robstown **20** E 2
Roca Partida, Isla **20** B 4
Rochefort **32** B 2
Rochester (Minnesota, U.S.) **16** E 3
Rochester (New Hampshire, U.S.) **14** E 2
Rochester (New York, U.S.) **14** D 2
Rock Hill **14** C 4
Rock Island **16** E 3
Rock River **16** E 3
Rock Springs **18** E 3
Rockford **14** B 2
Rockhampton **60** J 4
Rockingham (U.S.) **14** D 4
Rocklands Reservoir **60** G 7
Rockport **20** E 2
Rockville **14** D 3
Rocky Mount **14** D 3
Rocky Mountain National Park **18** E 3
Rocky Mountains (Canada) **10** S 7
Rodeo (Mexico) **20** D 2
Rodeo (U.S.) **18** E 5
Rodez **32** C 3
Rodney, Cape **43** W 4
Rodos **34** F 3
Rodos (Greece) **35** C 6
Rodos (Island) **34** F 3
Rodos (Rhodes) Island **35** C 6
Rogaland **38** G 4
Rogers Peak **18** D 4
Rogue River **18** B 3
Rūohacha **22** H 5
Rohri **46** B 3
Rohtak **46** D 3
Roi Et **47** J 5
Roi Georges, Îles du **59** L 5
Rojo, Cabo (Mexico) **20** E 3
Røldal **38** G 4
Rolla (Missouri, U.S.) **16** E 4
Rolla (North Dakota, U.S.) **16** D 2
Rolvsøya **38** K 1
Roma (Australia) **60** H 5
Roma (Italy) **34** C 2
Roman **36** F 3
Romang **52** H 7
Romania **36** E 3
Romanovka **42** F 6
Rome (Georgia, U.S.) **14** B 4
Rome (Italy) **34** C 2
Rome (New York, U.S.) **14** D 2
Romny **36** G 2
Rømø **36** B 2
Roncador Reef **59** E 4
Roncador, Cayos de **22** F 5
Rondane **38** G 3
Rondonópolis **24** F 4
Rongan **49** H 5
Rongelap **59** F 2
Rongerik **59** F 2
Rongjiang **49** H 5
Rongxian (Guangxi,China) **49** J 6
Rongxian (Sichuan,China) **49** G 5
Rønne **38** H 4
Ronneby **38** H 4
Roquefort **32** B 3
Roraima **22** K 7
Røros **38** H 3
Rosamorada **20** C 3
Rosario (Argentina) **24** E 6
Rosario (Baja California Sur, Mexico) **20** B 2
Rosario (Sinaloa, Mexico) **20** C 3
Rosario, Bahía **18** C 5
Roscommon **31** B 2
Roscrea **31** C 2
Rose Island **59** J 5
Roseau **22** K 4
Roseburg **18** B 3
Rosenberg **20** E 2
Rosenheim **36** C 3
Rosetown **10** V 8
Roșiorii-de-Vede **34** F 2
Roskilde **38** H 4
Roslavlū **36** G 2
Roslyn **18** B 2
Ross River **10** Q 6
Rossan Point **31** B 1
Rossel Island **60** J 2
Rosslare **31** C 2
Rossoshū **44** E 2
Røst **38** H 2
Rostock **36** C 2
Rostov **40** J 6
Rostov-na-Donu **44** E 3
Roswell **16** C 5
Rota (Northern Mariana Islands) **59** D 2
Rota (Spain) **33** A 2
Rote **53** G 8
Rotorua **62** C 2
Rouen **32** C 2
Rousay **30** C 2
Rouyn **8** V 9
Rovaniemi **38** L 2
Rovigo **36** C 3
Rovnoye **44** G 2
Rowley Island **8** V 5
Roxas **53** G 3
Roxburgh **62** A 4
Roy **16** C 4
Royal Canal **31** C 2
Royal Tunbridge Wells **28** E 4
Royale, Isle **14** B 1
Royan **32** B 2
Rtishchevo **44** F 2
Ruacana Falls **58** A 3
Ruahine Range **62** C 3
Rubtsovsk **45** O 2
Ruby **10** L 6
Ruby Mountains **18** C 4
Rūd Sar **44** H 5
Rudbar **45** K 6
Rudkøbing **36** C 2
Rudnya **36** G 2
Rūdnyy **45** K 2
Rudyard **18** D 2
Rufino **24** E 6
Rugao **49** L 4
Rugby **16** C 2
Rügen **36** C 2
Ruhnu Saar **38** K 4
Ruiūan **49** L 5
Ruijin **49** K 5
Rumbek **56** F 4
Rumoi **54** D 2
Runan **49** J 4
Runaway, Cape **62** C 2
Rupat **52** C 5
Rupert **18** D 3
Rurutu **59** K 6
Ruse **34** F 2
Russell (Canada) **16** C 1
Russell (New Zealand) **62** B 2

Russell Island **8** R 4
Russell Islands **59** E 4
Russell Range **60** C 6
Russellville (Alabama, U.S.) **14** B 4
Russellville (Arkansas, U.S.) **16** E 4
Russia **41** R 5
Russkiy, Ostrov **41** U 2
Rustūavi **35** L 4
Rustenburg **58** B 4
Ruston **16** E 5
Ruteng **53** F 7
Ruthin **28** C 3
Rutland **47** G 6
Rutog **48** B 4
Ruzayevka **44** F 2
Ružomberok **36** D 3
Rwanda **58** C 2
Ryazanū **44** E 2
Ryazhskū **44** F 2
Rybinsk **40** J 6
Rybinskoye Vodokhranilishche **40** J 6
Rybnik **36** D 2
Ryegate **18** E 2
Rylūsk **36** G 2
Ryōtsu **54** C 3
Ryukyu Islands **50** E 7
Rzeszów **36** E 2
Rzhev **40** H 6
Sa Dec **47** K 6
Saarbrücken **36** B 3
Saaremaa **38** K 4
Saariselkä **38** L 2
Šabac **34** D 2
Sabadell **32** C 3
Sabah **52** F 5
Sabanalarga **22** G 5
Sabinas **20** D 2
Sabinas Hidalgo **20** D 2
Sabine River **16** E 5
Sable Island **8** Z 10
Sable, Cape **14** F 2
Sabzevār **45** J 5
Sacajawea Peak **18** C 2
Sachūŏn **54** A 4
Sachs Harbour **10** R 4
Saco **18** E 2
Sacramento **18** B 4
Sacramento Mountains **18** E 5
Sacramento River **18** B 3
Sacramento Valley **18** B 3
Sado **54** C 3
Sadovoye **44** F 3
Safāgis **34** C 4
Safford **18** E 5
Safi **56** C 1
Safronovo **40** L 4
Saga **54** B 4
Sagang **47** H 4
Sagar **46** D 4
Sagay **52** G 3
Saghyz **44** H 3
Saginaw **14** C 2
Saginaw Bay **14** C 2
Saglouc **8** V 6
Sagres **33** A 2
Sagua la Grande **22** F 3
Sagunto **33** B 2
Sagwon **10** N 5
Sahagun **22** G 6
Sahagún **33** A 1
Sahara **56** C 2
Saharanpur **46** D 3
Sahiwal **46** C 2
Sahrāū al Ḥajārah **44** F 6
Sahuaripa **20** C 2
Sahuayo **20** D 3
Saibai **59** D 4
Saigon **47** K 6
Saiki **54** B 4
Saimaa **38** L 3
Sain Alto **20** D 3
Saint Albans **14** E 2
Saint Albert **10** U 8
Saint Andrews **30** C 3
Saint Anthony **8** Z 8
Saint Augustine **14** C 5
Saint Austell **28** B 4
Saint Clair River **14** C 2
Saint Cloud **16** E 2
Saint Croix **22** K 4
Saint Davidūs Head **28** B 4
Saint Eustatius **22** K 4
Saint Francis **16** C 4
Saint François **58** E 2
Saint Francois Mountains **16** E 4
Saint George (Utah, U.S.) **18** D 4
Saint George, Cape **59** E 4
Saint Georgeūs **22** K 5
Saint Georgeūs Channel (U.K.) **31** C 3
Saint Helens **28** C 3
Saint Ignace **14** C 1
Saint Ignace Island **8** T 9
Saint John **14** F 1
Saint Johns **18** E 5
Saint Johnūs (Antigua and Barbuda) **22** K 4
Saint Johnūs (Canada) **8** Aa 9
Saint Johns River **14** C 4
Saint Johnsbury **14** E 2
Saint Joseph **58** E 2
Saint Joseph (U.S.) **16** E 4
Saint Joseph, Lake **10** Y 8
Saint Kitts **22** K 4
Saint Kitts-Nevis **22** K 4
Saint Lawrence **8** X 9
Saint Lawrence Island **43** V 4
Saint Lawrence, Gulf of **8** Y 9
Saint Louis **16** E 4
Saint Lucia **22** K 5
Saint Marks **14** C 4
Saint Martin **22** K 4
Saint Matthew Island **43** V 4
Saint Matthias Group **59** D 4
Saint Michael **43** X 4
Saint Paul (Minnesota, U.S.) **16** E 2
Saint Petersburg (U.S.) **14** C 5
Saint Petersburgh (Russia) **40** H 6
Saint Pierre **58** D 2
Saint Pierre et Miquelon **8** Z 9
Saint Stephen **14** F 1
Saint Thomas (Canada) **14** C 2
Saint Vincent and The Grenadines **22** K 5
SaintūAntioco, Isola di **34** B 3
Saint-Brieuc **32** B 2
Saint-Dié **36** B 3
Saint-Dizier **32** C 2
Saintes **32** B 2
Sainte-Therese **8** W 9
Saint-Étienne **32** C 2
Saint-Jean-sur-Richelieu **8** W 9
Saint-Jérôme **8** W 9
Saint-Malo **32** B 2
Saint-Malo, Golfe de **32** B 2
Saint-Nazaire **32** B 2
Saint-Quentin **32** C 2
Saipan **59** D 2
Sakai **54** C 4
Sakakawea, Lake **16** C 2
Sakarya **44** D 4
Sakata **54** C 3
Sakchu **54** A 2
Sakhalin **50** H 2
Sakht Sar **44** H 5
Säki **44** G 4
Saki **56** D 4
Sakon Nakhon **47** J 5
Sakti **46** E 4
Sal **56** A 3
Salamá **20** F 4
Salamanca **33** A 1
Salamanca (Mexico) **20** D 3
Salamat **56** F 3
Salamis **44** D 5
Salar de Uyuni **24** E 5
Salavat **40** N 7
Salayar **53** G 7
Saldus **38** K 4
Sale **60** H 7
Salekhard **40** P 4
Salem (Illinois, U.S.) **14** B 3
Salem (India) **46** D 6
Salem (Oregon, U.S.) **18** B 3
Salerno **34** C 2
Salerno, Golfo di **34** C 2
Salgótarján **36** D 3
Salgueiro **24** H 3
Salhus **38** G 3
Salida **18** E 4
Salihli **35** C 5

Salihorsk **36** F 2
Salina (Kansas, U.S.) **16** D 4
Salina (Utah, U.S.) **18** D 4
Salinas (U.S.) **18** B 4
Salinas de Hidalgo **20** D 3
Salinas Grandes **24** E 5
Salines, Cap de ses **33** C 2
Salisbury (Australia) **60** F 6
Salisbury (U.K.) **28** D 4
Salisbury Island **8** V 6
Salmon **18** D 2
Salmon River **18** C 2
Salmon River Mountains **18** C 3
Salon-de-Provence **34** B 2
Salūsk **44** F 3
Salt Fork **16** C 5
Salt Lake City **18** D 3
Salt River **18** D 5
Salta **24** E 5
Saltillo **20** D 2
Salto das Sete Quedas **24** F 5
Salton Sea **18** C 5
Sālūr **46** E 5
Salvador **24** H 4
Salvatierra **20** D 3
Salween **47** H 4
Salzburg **36** C 3
Salzgitter **36** C 2
Salzwedel **36** C 2
Sam Rayburn Reservoir **16** D 5
Samales Group **53** G 4
Samar **52** H 3
Samar Sea **52** G 3
Samara **44** H 2
Samarinda **52** F 6
Samarqand **45** L 5
Sambalpur **46** E 4
Sambas **52** D 5
Sambir **36** E 3
Samboja **52** F 6
Samburg **41** R 4
Samchūŏk **50** E 5
Samchūŏnpūo **50** E 6
Samoa **59** H 5
Samoa Islands **59** H 5
Samokov **34** E 2
Samos **34** F 3
Samothraki **34** F 2
Sampit **52** E 6
Samsang **48** C 4
Samsun **35** G 4
Samtredia **35** K 3
Samut Songkhram **47** H 6
San Agustin, Cape **53** H 4
San Andres Mountains **18** E 5
San Andrés Tuxtla **20** E 4
San Andrés y Providencia **22** G 5
San Angelo **16** C 5
San Antonio (U.S.) **20** E 2
San Antonio Bay **20** E 2
San Antonio, Cabo **22** F 3
San Benedetto del Tronto **34** C 2
San Benedicto, Isla **20** B 4
San Bernardino **18** C 5
San Bernardo **24** D 6
San Bernardo (Mexico) **20** B 2
San Blas **20** C 2
San Blas, Cape **14** B 6
San Borjas, Sierra de **20** B 2
San Buenaventura **20** D 2
San Carlos (Mexico) **20** E 3
San Carlos de Bariloche **24** D 7
San Clemente **18** C 5
San Clemente Island **18** C 5
San Cristobal **59** F 5
San Cristóbal (Dominican Republic) **22** H 4
San Cristóbal (Venezuela) **22** H 6
San Cristóbal de las Casas **20** F 4
San Diego **18** C 5
San Felipe (Mexico) **18** D 5
San Felipe (Mexico) **20** D 3
San Felipe (Venezuela) **22** J 5
San Fernando **22** K 5
San Fernando (Mexico) **20** E 3
San Fernando (Spain) **33** A 2
San Fernando de Apure **22** J 6
San Fernando(Philippines) **53** G 2
San Francisco (U.S.) **18** B 4
San Franciscó de Macoris **22** H 4
San Francisco del Oro **20** C 2
San Francisco del Rincón **20** D 3
San Gottardo, Passo del **36** B 3
San Hilario **20** B 3
San Ignacio (Belize) **20** G 4
San Ignacio (Mexico) **20** B 2
San Joaquin River **18** C 4
San Joaquin Valley **18** B 4
San Jorge Island **59** E 4
San Jorge, Bahía de **18** D 5
San Jose **53** G 2
San José (Costa Rica) **22** F 6
San José (Guatemala) **20** F 5
San José (U.S.) **18** B 4
San Jose de Buenavista **53** G 3
San Jose de Guanipa **22** K 6
San José del Cabo **20** C 3
San José, Isla **20** B 2
San Juan **24** E 6
San Juan de Guadalupe **20** D 3
San Juan del Norte, Bahūa de **22** F 5
San Juan del Río (Durango, Mexico) **20** D 3
San Juan del Río (Queretaro, Mexico) **20** E 3
San Juan Mountains **18** E 4
San Lázaro, Sierra de **20** B 3
San Lorenzo, Río **20** C 3
San Lucas (Mexico) **20** C 3
San Lucas, Cabo **20** B 3
San Luis **24** E 6
San Luis (Mexico) **20** B 2
San Luis de la Paz **20** D 3
San Luís Gonzaga, Bahía **18** D 5
San Luis Obispo **18** B 4
San Luis Peak **18** E 4
San Luis Potosí (Mexico) **20** D 3
San Luis Potosí (State, Mexico) **20** D 3
San Marcos (Mexico) **20** D 3
San Marcos (Mexico) **20** E 4
San Marcos (U.S.) **20** E 2
San Marino **34** C 2
San Miguel **22** E 5
San Miguel de Allende **20** D 3
San Miguel de Tucumán **24** E 5
San Miguel Islands **53** F 4
San Miguel Sola de Vega **20** E 4
San Nicolás (Mexico) **20** D 2
San Pablo (Philippines) **53** G 3
San Pédro **56** C 4
San Pedro (Mexico) **20** D 2
San Pedro Pochutla **20** E 4
San Pedro Sula **20** G 4
San Pietro, Isola di **34** B 3
San Quintín **18** C 5
San Quintín, Bahía de **18** C 5
San Rafael **24** E 6
San Rafael (Mexico) **20** D 2
San Remo **34** B 2
San Salvador **22** E 5
San Salvador (El Salvador) **20** G 5
San Salvador de Jujuy **24** E 5
San Salvador Island **22** G 3
San Severo **34** D 2
San Telmo **18** C 5
San Vicente (Mexico) **18** C 5
San Vincente **52** G 2
San Vito, Capo **34** C 3
Sanaga **56** E 4
Sanak Island **43** X 6
Sanana **53** H 6
Sanandaj **44** G 5
Sancti Spiritus **22** G 3
Sand **38** G 4
Sand Cay **46** C 6
Sand Hills **16** C 3
Sandagou **54** B 2
Sandakan **52** F 4
Sandane **38** G 3
Sandanski **34** E 2
Sanday **30** C 2
Sandbukt **38** K 2
Sandefjord **38** H 4
Sandıklı **35** D 5
Sandnes **38** G 4
Sandoway **47** G 5
Sandown **28** D 4
Sandoy **38** D 3
Sandstone (Australia) **60** B 5
Sandusky **14** C 2

Sandviken **38** J 3
Sandy Cape **60** J 4
Sandy Lake **10** Y 8
Sangamner **46** C 5
Sanger **18** C 4
Sanggau **52** E 5
Sangir **53** H 5
Sangir, Kepulauan **53** H 5
Sangiyn Dalay Nuur **41** V 8
Sangju **50** E 5
Sangli **46** C 5
Sangre de Cristo Mountains **18** E 4
Sanikiluaq **8** V 8
Sanjo **54** C 3
Sankt Gallen **36** B 3
Sankt Michel **38** L 3
Sankt Pölten **36** D 3
Sankt-Peterburg **40** H 6
Sankuru **58** B 2
Şanlıurfa **35** H 6
Sanlúcar de Barrameda **33** A 2
Sanmenxia **49** J 4
Sanming **49** K 5
Sannikova **42** L 2
Sanok **36** E 3
Santa Ana (El Salvador) **22** E 5
Santa Ana (Mexico) **18** D 5
Santa Ana (SolomonIslands) **59** F 5
Santa Ana (U.S.) **18** C 5
Santa Barbara (Mexico) **20** C 2
Santa Barbara (U.S.) **18** C 5
Santa Barbara Channel **18** B 5
Santa Catalina Island **18** C 5
Santa Clara **22** F 3
Santa Clara (Mexico) **20** C 2
Santa Clara los Gatos **18** B 4
Santa Cruz **24** E 4
Santa Cruz (U.S.) **18** B 4
Santa Cruz de la Palma **56** B 2
Santa Cruz de Tenerife **56** B 2
Santa Cruz Island **18** C 5
Santa Cruz Islands **59** F 5
Santa Elena, Cabo **22** E 5
Santa Fe **18** E 4
Santa Fé **24** E 6
Santa Inés, Bahía **20** B 2
Santa Isbel Island **59** E 4
Santa Margarita, Isla **20** B 3
Santa Maria **24** F 5
Santa Maria (U.S.) **18** B 5
Santa María del Oro **20** C 2
Santa María del Río **20** D 3
Santa Maria di Leuca,Capo **34** D 3
Santa María, Bahía de **20** C 2
Santa Maria, Laguna de **18** E 5
Santa Marta **22** H 5
Santa Rita (U.S.) **18** E 5
Santa Rosa **24** E 6
Santa Rosa (California, U.S.) **18** B 4
Santa Rosa (New Mexico, U.S.) **16** C 5
Santa Rosa de Copán **20** G 5
Santa Rosa Island **18** B 5
Santa Rosalía **20** B 2
Santai **49** H 4
Santander (Spain) **32** B 3
Santanghon **48** E 2
Santarém **24** F 3
Santee River **14** C 4
Santiago **24** D 6
Santiago (DominicanRepublic) **22** H 4
Santiago de Compostela **33** A 1
Santiago de Cuba **22** G 3
Santiago del Estero **24** E 5
Santiago do Cacém **33** A 2
Santiago Papasquiaro **20** C 2
Santiago, Río Grande de **20** D 3
Santo Antão **56** A 3
Santo Domingo (Dominican Republic) **22** J 4
Santo Domingo (Mexico) **20** B 2
Santos **24** G 5
Sany-Tash **45** M 5
São Carlos **24** G 5
São José do Rio Preto **24** F 5
São Luís **24** G 3
São Nicolau **56** A 3
São Paulo **24** G 5
São Tiago **56** A 3
São Tomé **56** D 4
São Tomé (Island) **56** D 5
São Tomé and Príncipe **56** D 4
Sapele **56** D 4
Sapporo **54** D 2
Sapulpa **16** D 4
Saqqaq **8** Aa 4
Saraburi **47** J 6
Sarajevo **34** D 2
Sarakhs **45** K 5
Sarangani **52** H 4
Sarangarh **46** E 4
Saransk **44** G 2
Sarapul **40** M 6
Sarapulūskoye **54** C 1
Sarasota **14** C 5
Saratov **44** G 2
Saravan **47** K 5
Sarawak **52** E 5
Sarayköy **35** C 6
Sardarshahr **46** C 3
Sardegna **34** B 3
Sardinia **34** B 3
Sargodha **46** C 2
Sarh **56** E 4
Sārī **44** H 5
Sarigan **59** D 2
Sarıkamış **35** K 4
Sarikei **52** E 5
Sariwon **50** E 5
Şarkısla **35** G 5
Şarköy **35** B 4
Sarnia **14** C 2
Sarny **36** F 2
Sarowbī **45** L 6
Sarqan **45** N 3
Sarych, Mys **44** D 4
Saryeh, Mys **44** D 4
Saryesik-Atyraū Qumy **45** N 3
Saryözek **45** N 4
Saryshaghan **45** M 3
Sāsarām **46** E 4
Sasebo **50** E 6
Saskatchewan **10** V 8
Saskatchewan River **10** W 8
Saskatoon **10** V 8
Saskylakh **41** Y 3
Sasovo **44** F 2
Sassari **34** B 2
Sassnitz **36** C 2
Sasyqköl **45** O 3
Sātāra **46** C 5
Sätbaev **45** L 3
Satna **46** E 4
Satpura Range **46** C 4
Satu Mare **36** E 3
Satun **47** J 7
Sauceda Mountains **18** D 5
Saucillo **20** C 2
Saudárkrókur **38** B 2
Sauk Centre **16** E 2
Sault Sainte Marie **8** U 9
Sault Ste Marie (Canada) **14** C 1
Saumarez Reef **60** J 2
Saumur **32** B 2
Saurimo **58** B 2
Sava **36** D 3
Savaii **59** H 5
Savannah **14** C 4
Savannah River **14** C 4
Savannakhet **47** J 5
Savanne **16** E 2
Savant Lake **16** E 1
Sāveh **44** H 5
Savona **34** B 2
Savonlinna **38** L 3
Savu **53** G 8
Sawāi Mādhopur **46** D 3
Sawankhalok **47** H 5
Sawhaj **56** G 2
Sawtooth Mountains **16** E 2
Sawu **60** C 2
Sayanogorsk **41** U 7
Sayaq **45** N 3
Sayat **45** K 5
Saydā **44** E 6
Sayram **45** L 4
Scammon Bay **43** W 4
Scarborough (U.K.) **28** D 2
Schaffhausen **36** B 3
Schell Creek Range **18** D 4

Schenectady **14** E 2
Schleswig **36** B 2
Schull **31** B 3
Schultz Lake **8** R 6
Schurz **18** C 4
Schwàbisch Hall **36** B 3
Schwedt **36** C 2
Schweinfurt **36** C 2
Schwerin **36** C 2
Sciacca **34** C 3
Scilly, Isles of **28** A 4
Scioto River **14** C 3
Scoresby Land **8** Gg 4
Scoresbysund **8** Gg 4
Scotland **30** C 3
Scott City **16** C 4
Scott Reef **60** C 3
Scott, Cape **60** D 2
Scottsbluff **16** C 3
Scottsdale (U.S.) **18** D 5
Scottsville **14** B 3
Scranton **14** D 2
Scugog, Lake **14** D 2
Scunthorpe **28** D 3
Sea Islands **14** C 4
Seabrook, Lake **60** B 6
Seaside **18** B 2
Seattle **18** B 2
Sebangka **52** C 5
Sebastián Vizcaíno, Bahía **18** D 6
Sebatik **52** F 5
Sebring **14** C 5
Sebuku **52** F 6
Sedalia **16** E 4
Sedanka Island **10** J 8
Seddon **62** B 3
Sedona **18** D 5
Sefrou **56** C 1
Segamat **52** C 5
Seget **52** J 6
Segezha **40** H 5
Ségou **56** C 3
Segovia **33** B 1
Seguam Island **43** V 6
Seguin **20** E 2
Segula Island **43** T 6
Sehwan **46** B 3
Seiland **38** K 1
Seinäjoki **38** K 3
Seine **32** C 2
Sekayu **52** C 6
Sekondi-Takoradi **56** C 4
Selaru **53** J 7
Selatan, Tanjung **52** E 6
Selawik Lake **10** K 5
Selawiko **10** K 5
Selbu **38** H 3
Selby **16** C 2
Selenge **41** W 8
Selennyakh **42** M 3
Selfoss **38** A 3
Selūgon **54** C 1
Selinunte **34** C 3
Selma (Alabama, U.S.) **14** B 4
Selma (California, U.S.) **18** C 4
Selvas **24** E 3
Selwyn Lake **10** W 6
Semarang **52** E 7
Semenovskiy, Ostrov **42** K 2
Semey **45** O 2
Semichi Islands **43** S 6
Semiluki **44** E 2
Semīozernoe **45** K 2
Semitau **52** E 5
Semīyarka **45** N 2
Semnān **44** H 5
Sendai (Japan) **54** B 4
Sendai (Japan) **54** D 3
Sendai-wan **54** D 3
Senegal **56** B 3
Senftenberg **36** C 2
Senigallia **34** C 2
Senja **38** J 2
Senneterre **8** V 9
Sens **32** C 2
Senta **36** E 3
Seoni **46** D 4
Seoul **50** E 5
Sepanjang **52** F 7
Sepasu **53** F 5
Sequoia National Park **18** C 4
Seram **53** H 6
Seramban **52** C 5
Serang **52** D 7
Serasan **52** D 5
Serb Republic **34** D 2
Serbia **34** E 2
Serbia and Montenegro **34** D 2
Serdobsk **44** F 2
Serebryansk **45** O 3
Şereflikoçhisar **35** E 5
Sergach **40** L 6
Sergeya Kirova, Ostrova **41** T 2
Sergino **40** P 5
Sergiyev Posad **40** J 6
Seria **52** E 5
Serifos **34** E 3
Serık **35** D 6
Sermersuaq **8** Z 3
Sermiligaaq **8** Dd 5
Sernovodsk **44** H 2
Sernyy Zavod **45** J 4
Serov **40** O 6
Serowe **58** B 4
Serpentine Lakes **60** D 5
Serpukhov **44** E 2
Serra do Mar **24** G 5
Serra do Paranapiacaba **24** F 5
Serra Geral **24** F 5
Serrana, Cayo de **22** F 5
Serranilla, Cayo de **22** G 4
Serres **34** E 2
Serro Duida **22** J 7
Sertavul Geçidi **44** D 5
Serui **53** K 6
Seryshevo **42** J 6
Seskarö **38** K 2
Sestao **32** B 3
Sestroretsk **40** H 5
Setana **54** C 2
Sète **32** C 3
Sete Lagoas **24** G 4
Setermoen **38** J 2
Setesdal **38** G 4
Sétif **56** D 1
Seto-naikai **54** B 4
Settat **56** C 1
Sette-Daban, Khrebet **42** L 4
Setúbal **33** A 2
Seul, Lac **10** Y 8
Sevastopolū **44** D 4
Severn **28** C 3
Severn River **10** Y 8
Severnaya Dvina **40** K 5
Severnaya Sosūva **40** O 5
Severnaya Zemlya **41** V 1
Severnoye **44** H 2
Severo-Baykalūskoye Nagorūye **42** F 5
Severodvinsk **40** J 5
Severo-Kurilūsk **43** P 6
Severomorsk **40** H 4
Severo-SibirskayaNizmennostū **41** T 3
Severo-Yeniseyskiy **41** U 5
Sevier Desert **18** D 4
Sevilla **33** A 2
Seward **10** N 6
Seward (Nebraska, U.S.) **16** D 3
Seychelles **58** E 2
Seydişehir **35** D 6
Seymchan **43** O 4
Seymour (U.S.) **14** B 3
Sfântu Gheorghe **35** A 2
Sfax **56** E 1
Shaanxi **49** H 3
Shabelē Wenz **56** H 4
Shache **48** B 3
Shachunūya **40** L 6
Shādegān **44** G 6
Shadrinsk **40** O 6
Shāhdol **46** E 4
Shahjahanpur **46** D 3
Shahpura (Madhya Pradesh, India) **46** E 4
Shahpura (Rajasthan,India) **46** C 3
Shahrak **45** K 6
Shahr-e Kord **44** H 6
Shāhrūd **45** J 5
Shaim **40** O 5
Shājāpur **46** D 4
Shakhtersk **50** H 3
Shakhtīnsk **45** M 3
Shakhty **44** F 3

Shalaurova **42** M 2
Shallāl as Sablūkah **56** G 3
Shalqar **45** J 3
Shamattawa **8** S 7
Shamokin **14** D 2
Shamrock **16** C 4
Shan **49** G 5
Shandan **49** G 3
Shandong **49** K 3
Shandong Bandao **49** K 3
Shang Xian **49** H 4
Shangcai **49** J 4
Shangcheng **49** K 4
Shanghai **49** L 4
Shanghang **49** K 5
Shangqiu **49** K 4
Shangrao **49** K 5
Shangzhi **50** E 3
Shannon (Kalaallit Nunaat) **8** Hh 3
Shannon (River, Ireland) **31** B 2
Shannon, Mouth of the **31** A 2
Shanshan **48** E 2
Shantarskiye Ostrova **42** L 5
Shantou **49** K 6
Shanxi **49** J 3
Shaoguan **49** J 6
Shaowu **49** K 5
Shaoxing **49** L 5
Shaoyang **49** J 5
Shar **45** O 3
Sharbaqty **45** N 2
Shark Bay **60** A 5
Sharūya **40** L 6
Shashi **49** J 4
Shaunavon **18** E 2
Shawinigan **14** E 1
Shawnee **16** D 4
Shchūchīnsk **45** M 2
Shchuchūye **40** O 6
Shebekino **44** E 2
Sheboygan **14** B 2
Shebunino **54** D 1
Sheffield (U.K.) **28** D 3
Sheffield (U.S.) **14** B 4
Shehong **49** H 4
Shekhupura **46** C 2
Shelagskiy, Mys **43** S 2
Shelburne **14** F 2
Shelby **18** D 2
Sheldon Point **43** X 4
Shelek **45** N 4
Shelikof Strait **43** Y 5
Shellharbour **60** J 6
Shemonaīkha **45** O 2
Shenandoah National Park **14** D 3
Shengxian **49** L 5
Shenkursk **40** K 5
Shenmu **49** J 3
Shenyang **50** D 4
Shepetivka **36** F 2
Shepparton **60** H 7
Sherard, Cape **8** U 4
Sherbrooke **14** E 1
Sherekhov **41** W 7
Sheridan **18** E 3
Sherlovaya Gora **42** G 6
Sherman **16** D 5
Sherman Station **14** F 1
Shetland Islands **30** D 1
Sheyenne River **16** D 2
Shibarghan **45** L 5
Shibata **54** C 3
Shidao **49** L 3
Shīeli **45** L 4
Shiguai **49** J 2
Shijiazhuang **49** J 3
Shikapur **46** D 6
Shikarpur **46** B 3
Shikoku **54** B 4
Shikotan, Ostrov **54** D 2
Shilka **42** G 6
Shilla **46** D 2
Shillong **47** G 3
Shilovo **44** F 2
Shimizu **54** C 3
Shimoga **46** D 6
Shimonoseki **54** B 4
Shin, Loch **30** B 2
Shingbwiyang **47** H 3
Shingū **54** C 4
Shinjo **54** D 3
Shiping **49** G 6
Shippagan **8** Y 9
Shipunovo **45** O 2
Shira **41** T 7
Shiranuka **54** D 2
Shirley Mountains **18** E 3
Shirokostan Poluostrov **42** M 2
Shīrvān **45** J 5
Shivpuri **46** D 3
Shiwan Dashan **49** H 6
Shizunai **54** D 2
Shizuoka **54** C 4
Shkodūr **34** D 2
Shmidta, Ostrov **41** U 1
Shmidta, Poluostrov **42** M 6
Shokalūskogo, Ostrov **40** Q 3
Sholapur **46** D 5
Sholaqqkorghan **45** L 4
Shoshone **18** D 3
Shoshone Peak **18** C 4
Shoshoni **18** E 3
Shostka **36** G 2
Shou Xian **49** K 4
Shouchang **49** K 5
Shouguang **49** K 3
Show Low **18** D 5
Shoyna **40** K 4
Shreveport **16** E 5
Shrewsbury **28** C 3
Shū **45** M 4
Shuangcheng **50** E 3
Shuangliao **50** D 4
Shuangyang **54** A 2
Shuangyashan **54** B 1
Shuguri Falls **58** C 2
Shuicheng **49** G 5
Shulan **50** E 4
Shule **48** B 3
Shumagin Islands **43** Y 5
Shumen **34** F 2
Shumerlya **40** L 6
Shumshu, Ostrov **43** P 6
Shuoxian **49** J 3
Shurab **45** M 4
Shūshtar **44** G 6
Shuya **40** K 6
Shuyak Island **43** Z 5
Shuyang **49** K 4
Shymkent **45** L 4
Si Racha **47** J 6
Siāhān Range **46** A 3
Siālkot **46** C 2
Siargao **52** H 4
Siau **52** H 5
Šiauliai **38** K 4
Sibay **45** J 2
Šibenik **34** D 2
Siberut **52** B 6
Sibi **46** B 3
Sibirskiye Uvaly **40** P 5
Sibirskoye **41** V 4
Sibirtsevo **54** B 2
Sibiryakova, Ostrov **41** R 3
Sibiu **36** E 3
Sibolga **52** B 5
Sibsagar **47** G 3
Sibu **52** E 5
Sibutu **52** F 5
Sibuyan **52** G 3
Sibuyan Sea **52** G 3
Sichuan **49** G 4
Sicilia **34** D 3
Sicilia, Canale di **34** C 3
Sicily **34** D 3
Siddhapur **46** C 4
Siddipet **46** D 5
Siderno **34** D 3
Sidi-Bel-Abbès **56** C 1
Sidney (Canada) **18** B 2
Sidney (Montana, U.S.) **16** C 2
Sidney (Nebraska, U.S.) **16** C 3
Siedlce **36** E 2
Siegen **36** B 2
Siena **34** C 2
Sieradz **36** D 2
Sierra Blanca **18** E 5
Sierra de Segura **33** B 2
Sierra Leone **56** B 4
Sierra Mojada **20** D 2
Sifnos **34** E 3
Sigep **52** B 6
Sighetu Marmației **36** E 3
Sighișoara **35** A 1

Sigli **52** B 4
Siglufjörður **38** B 2
Sigulda **38** K 4
Sihanoukville **47** J 6
Siirt **35** J 6
Sikar **46** D 3
Sikaram **45** L 6
Sikasso **56** C 3
Sikeston **14** B 3
Sikhote-Alinū **54** C 1
Sikkim **46** F 3
Siktyach **42** H 3
Silchar **47** G 4
Siletitengiz Köli **45** M 2
Silifke **35** E 6
Siliguri **46** F 3
Siling Co **48** D 4
Silistra **34** F 2
Siljan **38** H 3
Silkeborg **38** G 4
Sillem Island **8** W 4
Sillon de Talbert **32** B 2
Siloam Springs **16** E 4
Silvan **35** J 5
Silver City **18** E 5
Silverton (U.S.) **18** E 4
Simao **48** G 6
Simcoe, Lake **14** D 2
Simeulue **52** B 5
Simferopolū **44** D 4
Simla **46** D 2
Simojovel de Allende **20** F 4
Simplon Pass **36** B 3
Simpson Desert **60** F 4
Simpson Desert National Park **60** F 5
Simrishamn **38** H 4
Sinabang **52** B 5
Sinaloa **20** C 3
Sincelejo **22** G 6
Sinchūang **50** E 4
Sinchūang-ni **54** A 2
Sindjai **52** G 7
Sines, Cabo de **33** A 2
Singapore **52** C 5
Singaradja **52** F 7
Singkang **52** G 6
Singkawang **52** D 5
Singkep **52** C 6
Singö **38** J 3
Sīnnār **56** G 3
Sinoie, Lacul **35** C 2
Sinop **35** F 3
Sinpūo **54** A 2
Sintang **52** E 5
Sinŭiju **50** D 4
Sioux City **16** D 3
Sioux Falls **16** D 3
Sioux Lookout **16** E 1
Sipalay **52** G 4
Siping **50** D 4
Sipura **52** B 6
Siquijor **52** G 4
Sir Edward Pellew Group **60** F 3
Sira **46** D 6
Sirevåg **38** G 4
Sirohi **46** C 4
Sironj **46** D 4
Sirsa **46** D 3
Sisak **36** D 3
Sisaket **47** J 5
Siskiyou Mountains **18** B 3
Sisseton **16** D 2
Sissimiut **8** Aa 5
Sitapur **46** E 3
Sitka **10** P 7
Sitkalidak Island **10** M 7
Sittwe **47** G 4
Siuna **20** H 5
Sıvas **35** G 5
Siverek **35** H 6
Sivrihisar **35** D 5
Siwalik Range **46** D 2
Siwan **46** E 3
Sjælland **38** H 4
Skadovsūk **35** E 1
Skagerrak **38** G 4
Skagway **10** P 7
Skåne **38** H 4
Skardu **45** N 5
Skarodnaye **36** F 2
Skarżysko Kamienna **36** E 2
Skegness **28** E 3
Skeiðarárjökull **38** B 3
Skellefteå **38** K 3
Skellefteälven **38** J 2
Ski **38** H 4
Skibotn **38** K 2
Skien **38** G 4
Skikda **56** D 1
Skomvær **38** H 2
Skopelos **34** E 3
Skopje **34** E 2
Skövde **38** H 4
Skovorodino **42** H 6
Skowhegan **14** F 2
Skvyra **36** F 3
Skye **30** A 3
Skyros **34** E 3
Slamet, Gunung **52** D 7
Slantsy **38** L 4
Slatina **34** E 2
Slave River **10** U 6
Slavgorod **45** N 2
Slavnoye **54** E 1
Slavonski Brod **36** D 3
Slavuta **36** F 2
Slavyanka **54** B 2
Slavyansk-na Kubani **44** E 3
Sleeper Islands **8** U 7
Slettuheiði **38** B 2
Sligo **31** B 1
Sliven **34** F 2
Słolin **36** F 2
Slonim **36** F 2
Slough **28** D 4
Slovakia **36** D 3
Slovenia **36** C 3
Slovūūyansūk **44** E 3
Slozhnyy, Ostrov **41** T 2
Słupsk **36** D 2
Slutsk **36** F 2
Slyne Head **31** A 2
Slyudyanka **41** W 7
Småland **38** H 4
Smallwood Reservoir **8** Y 8
Smederevo **34** E 2
Smidovich **54** B 1
Smila **44** D 3
Smirnykh **50** H 3
Smith **10** U 7
Smiths Falls **14** D 2
Smokey Dome **18** D 3
Smokey Falls **8** U 8
Smoky Hill River **16** C 4
Smoky Hills **16** D 4
Smøla **38** G 3
Smolensk **36** G 2
Smolyan **34** E 2
Smythe, Mount **10** S 7
Snag **10** O 6
Snake River **18** C 3
Snake River Plain **18** D 3
Snow Mountain **18** B 4
Snowville **18** D 3
Snyder **16** C 5
Sobral **24** G 3
Soc Trang **47** K 7
Sochi **44** E 4
Société, Archipel de la **59** K 5
Society Islands **59** K 5
Socorro (U.S.) **18** E 5
Socorro, Isla **20** B 4
Sodankylä **38** L 2
Söderhamn **38** J 3
Södermanland **38** J 4
Södertälje **38** J 4
Soe **52** G 7
Sofia **34** E 2
Sofie Christensen Reef **59** L 8
Sofiya **34** E 2
Sofiysk **42** K 6
Sofporog **40** H 4
Sofronovo **40** J 6
Sōfu-gan **54** D 5
Sogamoso **22** H 6
Sogn og Fjordane **38** G 3
Sogndal **38** G 3
Soissons **32** C 2
Sŏjosŏn-man **49** L 3
Sokchūo **54** A 3
Söke **35** B 6
Sokhumi **44** F 4
Sokółka **36** E 2
Solano **52** G 2
Soldotna **43** Z 4

Solenoye **44** F 3
Solikamsk **40** N 6
Solū-Iletsk **44** H 2
Solimón, Punta **20** G 4
Solingen **36** B 2
Sollefteå **38** J 3
Solomon Islands **60** K 2
Solomon Sea **59** E 4
Solon **50** D 3
Solonchak Arys **45** L 3
Solway Firth **28** C 2
Soma **35** B 5
Somalia **56** H 4
Sombor **36** D 3
Sombreretè **20** D 3
Somerset **14** C 3
Somerset Island **8** S 4
Somoto **20** G 5
Son La **47** J 4
Son Tay **47** K 4
Sønderborg **36** B 2
Søndre Strømfjord **8** Aa 5
Sonepur **46** E 4
Song Cau **47** K 6
Song Ma **47** J 4
Songhua Hu **50** E 4
Songhua Jiang **54** A 1
Songjiang **49** L 4
Songkhla **47** J 7
Sŏngnam **54** A 3
Songnim **50** E 5
Sonmiani Bay **46** B 3
Sonneberg **36** C 2
Sonoita **18** D 5
Sonora (Mexico) **20** B 2
Sonora (U.S.) **16** C 5
Sonora, Río **20** B 2
Sonoran Desert **18** D 5
Sonqor **44** G 6
Sonsonate **22** E 5
Sonsorol Islands **52** J 4
Sopka Shiveluch **43** Q 5
Sopot **36** D 2
Sopron **36** D 3
Sor Kajdak **44** H 4
Sorada **46** E 5
Sorang **45** M 3
Sorel **8** W 9
Soria **32** B 3
Sörmjöle **38** J 3
Soroca **36** F 3
Sorocaba **24** G 5
Sorochinsk **44** H 2
Sørøya **38** K 1
Sorsele **38** J 2
Sorsogon **52** G 3
Sortavala **40** H 5
Sortland **38** J 2
Sør-Trøndelag **38** H 3
Sŏsan **54** A 3
Sosnogorsk **40** M 5
Sosnovo-Ozerskoye **42** F 6
Sosnowiec **36** D 2
Sosūva **40** O 6
Sotsial **45** N 3
Soudan **60** F 4
Souk Ahras **34** B 3
Sŏul **50** E 5
Soulac-sur-Mer **32** B 2
Souris (Manitoba, Canada) **16** C 2
Sousa **24** H 3
South Africa **58** A 5
South Andaman **47** G 6
South Aulatsivik Island **8** Y 7
South Australia **60** E 6
South Bend (Indiana, U.S.) **14** B 2
South Bend (Washington, U.S.) **18** B 2
South Carolina **14** C 4
South China Sea **47** K 7
South Dakota **16** C 3
South Downs **28** D 4
South East Cape **60** H 8
South East Point **60** H 7
South Georgia (U.K.) **24** H 8
South Island **62** A 3
South Korea **50** F 5
South Lake Tahoe **18** C 4
South Molton **28** C 4
South Platte River **16** C 3
South Ronaldsay **30** C 2
South Saskatchewan River **18** D 1
South Shields **28** D 2
South Sioux City **16** D 3
South Stradbroke Island **60** J 5
South Taranaki Bight **62** B 2
South Uist **30** A 3
Southampton **28** D 4
Southampton Island **8** T 6
Southend **10** W 7
Southend-on-Sea **28** E 4
Southern Alps **62** A 3
Southern Cook Islands **59** K 5
Southern Cross **60** B 6
Southern Indian Lake **8** R 7
Southern Uplands **28** B 2
Southport (Australia) **60** J 5
Southport (U.K.) **28** C 3
Southport (U.S.) **14** D 4
Southwest Cape **62** A 4
Sovetskaya Gavanū **50** H 3
Sovetskiy **40** L 6
Spain **33** B 2
Spanish Fork **18** D 3
Spanish Town **22** G 4
Sparks **18** C 4
Spartanburg **14** C 4
Sparti **34** E 3
Spartivento, Capo **34** B 3
Spassk-Dalūniy **54** B 2
Spearfish **16** C 3
Spencer **16** D 3
Spencer Gulf **61** F 6
Spencer, Cape **60** F 7
Spenser Mountains **62** B 3
Spey **30** C 3
Split **34** D 2
Spokane **18** C 2
Spooner **16** E 2
Springdale (U.S.) **16** E 4
Springer **16** C 4
Springfield (Colorado, U.S.) **16** C 4
Springfield (Conneticut, U.S.) **14** E 2
Springfield (Illinois, U.S.) **14** B 3
Springfield (Missouri, U.S.) **16** E 4
Springfield (Oregon, U.S.) **18** B 3
Springfield (Tennessee, U.S.) **14** B 3
Springsure **60** H 4
Spurn Head **28** E 3
Squamish **18** B 2
Squillace, Golfo di **34** D 3
Srebrenica **34** D 2
Sredinnyy Khrebet **43** P 6
Sredne Sibirskoye Ploskogorūye **41** W 4
Srednekolymsk **43** O 3
Sremska Mitrovica **34** D 2
Sretensk **42** G 6
Sri JayawardenepuraKotte **46** E 7
Sri Kālahasti **46** D 6
Sri Lanka **46** E 7
Srīkākulam **46** E 5
Srinagar **45** M 6
Staaten River National Park **60** G 3
Stack Skerry **30** B 2
Stade **36** B 2
Stafford **28** C 3
Stakhanov **44** E 3
Stallworthy, Cape **8** S 2
Stalowa Wola **36** E 2
Stamford **14** E 2
Standerton **58** B 4
Stanke Dimitrov **34** E 2
Stanley **24** F 8
Stanley (U.S.) **16** C 2
Stanovoy Khrebet **42** H 5
Stanovoye Nagorūye **42** F 5
Stanthorpe **60** J 5
Stara Planina **34** E 2
Stara Zagora **34** F 2
Staraya Russa **40** H 6
Starbuck Island **59** K 4
Stargard Szczeciński **36** D 2
Staritsa **54** D 1
Starobilūsūk **44** E 3
Starodub **36** G 2
Starogard Gdański **36** D 2

Start Point **28** C 4
Staryy Oskol **44** E 2
State College **14** D 2
Statesboro **14** C 4
Statesville **14** C 3
Staumnes **38** A 2
Staunton **14** D 3
Stavanger **38** G 4
Stavropolū **44** F 3
Stavropolka **45** L 2
St-Denis **58** E 4
Steenstrup Gletscher **8** Z 3
Stefansson Island **10** V 4
Steinbach **16** D 2
Steinkjer **38** H 3
Stendal **36** C 2
Stephenville (U.S.) **16** D 5
Stepnyak **45** M 2
Sterling **16** C 3
Sterlitamak **40** N 7
Ste-Thérèse **14** E 1
Steubenville **14** C 2
Stevenage **28** D 4
Stevens Point **14** B 2
Stewart Crossing **10** P 6
Stewart Island **62** A 4
Stewart River **10** P 6
Steyr **36** C 3
St-Georges (Canada) **14** E 1
Stillwater **16** D 4
Štip **34** E 2
Stirling (Australia) **60** B 6
Stirling (U.K.) **30** C 3
Stirling Range **60** B 6
Stirling Range National Park **60** B 6
St-Jean-sur-Richelieu **14** E 1
St-Léonard **14** F 1
St-Louis **56** B 3
Stockholm **38** J 4
Stockport **28** C 3
Stockton **18** B 4
Stockton Plateau **16** C 5
Stockton-on-Tees **28** D 2
Stoke-on-Trent **28** C 3
Stokksnes **38** C 3
Stolbovoy, Ostrov **42** L 2
Stonehaven **30** C 3
Stora Lulevatten **38** J 2
Stora Sjöfallet **38** J 2
Storavan **38** J 2
Stord **38** F 4
Store Bælt **38** H 4
Store Koldewey **8** Hh 3
Store Sotra **38** F 3
Storlien **38** H 3
Stornoway **30** A 2
Storstrømmen **8** Gg 3
Storuman **38** J 2
Stowbtsy **36** F 2
Strabane **31** C 1
Strait of Magellan **24** E 8
Stralsund **36** C 2
Strand **58** A 5
Stranraer **28** B 2
Strasbourg **36** B 3
Stratford (Canada) **14** C 2
Stratford (New Zealand) **62** B 2
Stratford (U.S.) **16** C 4
Stratford-upon-Avon **28** D 3
Strathbogie **30** C 3
Strathspey **30** C 3
Strathy Point **30** B 2
Straubing **36** C 3
Streaky Bay **60** E 6
Strelka (Russia) **41** U 6
Strelka (Russia) **43** O 4
Strelka-Chunya **41** W 5
Streymoy **38** D 3
Stronsay **30** C 2
Stroud **28** C 4
Strumica **34** E 2
Stryy **36** E 3
Stuart Bluff Range **60** E 4
Stuart Island **43** X 4
Sturgeon Lake **16** E 2
Sturt Desert **60** G 5
Sturt National Park **60** G 5
Stutterheim **58** B 5
Stuttgart **36** B 3
Suai **53** H 7
Subi Besar **52** D 5
Subotica **36** D 3
Suceava **36** F 3
Suchumi **44** F 4
Sucre **24** E 4
Sudak **35** F 2
Sudan **56** F 3
Sudbury **8** U 9
Sudd **56** G 4
Suðuroy **38** D 3
Suess Land **8** Ff 4
Sugoy **43** P 4
Sühbaatar (Mongolia) **50** A 2
Sühbaatar (Mongolia) **50** B 3
Suhl **36** C 2
Suibin **54** B 1
Suichang **49** K 5
Suide **49** J 3
Suihua **50** E 3
Suileng **50** E 3
Suining **49** H 4
Suir **31** C 2
Suixi **49** K 4
Suiyang **54** B 2
Suizhong **50** D 4
Suizhou **49** J 4
Sujawal **46** B 4
Sukabumi **52** D 7
Sukadana **52** D 6
Sukagawa **54** D 3
Sukaraja **52** E 6
Sukhana **42** G 3
Sukhona **40** K 6
Sukhothai **47** H 5
Sukkertoppen **8** Aa 5
Sukkur **46** B 3
Sula **38** F 3
Sula Islands **52** H 7
Sula Sgeir **30** A 2
Sula, Kepulauan **52** G 6
Sulaiman Range **46** B 3
Sulawesi **52** F 6
Sule Skerry **30** B 2
Sulincheen **49** H 2
Sulphur **16** E 5
Sulphur Springs **16** D 5
Sulu Archipelago **52** F 5
Sulu Sea **52** F 4
Sumalē **56** H 4
Sumatera **52** C 6
Sumatra **52** C 6
Sumba **53** F 8
Sumbawa **52** F 7
Sumbawa Besar **52** F 7
Sumburgh Head **30** D 2
Sumedang **52** D 7
Sumenep **52** E 7
Sumisu-jima **54** D 4
Summer Lake **18** B 3
Summit Lake **10** S 7
Šumperk **36** D 3
Sumqayit **44** G 4
Sumter **14** C 4
Sumy **36** G 2
Sun Valley **18** D 3
Sunbury **14** D 2
Sunchŭŏn **54** A 4
Sunchŭon (North Korea) **50** E 5
Sunderland **28** D 2
Sundsvall **38** J 3
Sungai Kolok **47** J 7
Sungai Petani **52** C 4
Sungaidareh **52** C 6
Sungalguntung **52** C 5
Sungurlu **35** F 4
Sunndalsøra **38** G 3
Sunshine **60** G 7
Suntar **42** G 4
Suntar Khayata, Khrebet **42** L 4
Sunwu **54** A 1
Sunyani **56** C 4
Suomi **38** L 3
Suomussalmi **38** L 3
Suonenjoki **38** L 3
Suoyarvi **40** H 5
Superior (Montana, U.S.) **18** D 2
Superior (Wisconsin, U.S.) **16** E 2
Superior, Lake **16** E 2
Sūr **44** E 6
Surabaya **52** E 7
Surakarta **52** E 7
Surat **46** C 4
Surat Thani **47** H 7
Suratgarh **46** C 3

Surgut **40** Q 5
Suriapet **46** D 5
Surigao **52** H 4
Surin **47** J 6
Suriname **24** F 2
Surovikino **44** F 3
Surskoye **44** G 2
Surtsey **38** A 3
Sürüç **35** H 6
Surulangun **52** C 6
Survey Pass **10** M 5
Susanville **18** B 3
Suşehri **35** H 4
Susitna River **10** M 6
Susquehanna **14** D 2
Susurluk **35** C 5
Sutherland **30** B 2
Sutton (West Virginia, U.S.) **14** C 3
Sutwik Island **43** Y 5
Suva **59** G 5
Suvadiva **46** C 8
Suvorov **59** J 5
Suwa **54** C 3
Suwałki **36** E 2
Suwannee River **14** C 4
Suwanose-jima **50** F 7
Suwaydah **35** H 7
Suwon **50** E 5
Suzhou **49** L 4
Suzu **54** C 3
Svappavaara **38** K 2
Svatove **44** E 3
Svay Riĕng **47** K 6
Svealand **38** H 4
Sveg **38** H 3
Svendborg **38** H 4
Sverdlovsk **40** O 6
Sverdrup Islands **10** W 3
Sverdrup, Ostrov **41** R 3
Svetlaya **54** C 1
Svetlograd **44** F 3
Svetlyy (Russia) **42** G 5
Svir **40** H 5
Svirsk **41** W 7
Svistov **34** F 2
Svobodnyy **42** J 6
Svyatoy Nos, Mys (Russia) **40** J 4
Svyetlahorsk **36** F 2
Swain Reefs **60** J 4
Swains Island **59** H 5
Swan Hill **60** G 7
Swan Range **18** D 2
Swan River **10** W 8
Swansea **28** B 4
Swaziland **58** C 4
Sweden **38** H 3
Sweet Home **18** B 3
Sweetwater **16** C 5
Sweetwater River **18** E 3
Świecie **36** D 2
Swift Current **10** V 8
Swift River **10** Q 6
Swindon **28** D 4
Świnoujście **36** C 2
Switzerland **36** B 3
Syanno **36** F 2
Sydney (Australia) **60** J 6
Sydney (Canada) **8** Y 9
Syeverodonetsūk **44** E 3
Syktyvkar **40** M 5
Sylacauga **14** B 4
Sylhet **47** G 4
Sylt **36** B 2
Syngyrli, Mys **44** H 4
Syracuse (Kansas, U.S.) **16** C 4
Syracuse (New York, U.S.) **14** D 2
Syria **44** E 5
Syriam **47** H 5
Syrian Desert **44** E 6
Syros **34** E 3
Syverma, Plato **41** U 4
Syzranū **44** G 2
Szczecin **36** C 2
Szczecinek **36** D 2
Szczyrno **36** E 2
Szeged **36** E 3
Székesfehérvár **36** D 3
Szekszárd **36** D 3
Szentes **36** E 3
Szolnok **36** D 3
Szombathely **36** D 3
Taasiilaq Ammassalik **8** Dd 5
Tabasará, Serranía de **22** F 6
Tabasco **20** F 4
Tabasco y Campeche, Llanosde **20** F 4
Taber **18** D 2
Tabiteuea **59** G 4
Tablas **52** G 3
Table Rock Lake **16** E 4
Tabor **42** O 2
Tabora **58** C 2
Tabory **40** O 6
Tabrīz **44** G 5
Tacámbaro **20** D 4
Tacheng **48** C 1
Tacloban **52** G 3
Tacna **24** D 4
Tacoma **18** B 2
Tacuarembó **24** F 6
Tacurong **52** G 4
Tadoule Lake **8** R 7
Tūaebaek-Sanmaek **54** A 3
Taegu **50** E 5
Taej n **50** E 5
Taejŏn **54** A 3
Taenga **59** L 5
Tafahi **59** H 5
Taft **52** H 3
Taganrog **44** E 3
Tagula Island **60** J 2
Tagum **52** H 4
Tahan, Gunong **52** C 5
Tahanea **59** L 5
Tahe **50** D 2
Tahiti **59** L 5
Tahkuna nina **38** K 4
Tahoe, Lake **18** B 4
Tahoua **56** D 3
Tahulandang **52** H 5
Tahuna **52** H 5
Tai Hu **49** K 4
Taiaro **59** L 5
Taibai Shan **49** H 4
Tūaichung **49** L 6
Taihape **62** C 2
Taihu **49** K 4
Taikang **49** J 4
Tailai **50** D 3
Tūainan **49** L 6
Tūaipei **49** L 6
Taiping **52** C 5
Taishan **49** J 6
Tūaitung **49** L 6
Taivalkoski **38** L 2
Taiwan **49** L 6
Taiwan Haixia **49** K 6
Taiyuan **49** J 3
Taizhou **49** K 4
Taj Mahal **46** D 3
Tajikistan **45** L 5
Tajito **18** D 5
Tajo, Rūo **33** B 2
Tajrīsh **44** H 5
Tajumulco, Volcán **20** F 4
Tak **47** H 5
Takalar **52** F 7
Takamatsu **54** B 4
Takaoka **54** C 3
Takapuna **62** B 2
Takara-jima **50** E 7
Takasaki **54** C 3
Takengon **52** B 5
Takhli **47** J 5
Takijuk Lake **10** U 5
Takikawa **54** D 2
Takla Landing **10** R 7
Takla Makan **48** C 3
Taklimakan Shamo **48** C 3
Takume **59** L 5
Takutea **59** K 5
Tala **20** D 3
Talagbetutu **52** C 6
Talaimannar **46** D 7
Talak **56** D 3
Talamanca, Cordillera de **22** E 5
Talara **24** C 3
Talas **45** M 4
Talaud, Kepulauan **52** H 5
Talavera de la Reina **33** B 2
Talca **24** D 6
Talcahuano **24** D 6
Tālcher **46** F 4

Taldyqorghan **45** N 3
Talence **32** B 3
Talghar **45** N 4
Taliabu **52** G 6
Taliquin **45** L 5
Taliwang **52** F 7
Talkeetna **10** M 6
Tallahassee **14** C 4
Tallinn **38** K 4
Tallulah **16** E 5
Talūmenka **45** O 2
Talnakh **41** T 4
Talūne **44** D 3
Talok **52** F 5
Talovka **44** G 4
Taloyoak **8** S 5
Talsi **38** K 4
Talu **52** B 5
Taluk **52** C 6
Taluma **42** H 5
Tam Ky **47** K 5
Tama Abu Range **52** F 5
Tamale **56** C 4
Tamar **28** B 4
Tamaulipas **20** E 3
Tamaulipas, Llanos de **20** E 2
Tamazunchale **20** E 3
Tambacounda **56** B 3
Tambalan **52** F 5
Tambalan, Kepulauan **52** D 5
Tambov **44** F 2
Tamiahua, Laguna de **20** E 3
Tamil **46** D 6
Tammerfors **38** K 3
Tampa **14** C 5
Tampa Bay **14** C 5
Tampere **38** K 3
Tampico **20** E 3
Tamsagbulag **50** C 3
Tamuín **20** E 3
Tamworth **60** J 6
Tana **58** C 2
Tana (Norway) **38** L 2
Tūana Haykū **56** G 3
Tanabe **54** C 4
Tanaga Island **43** U 6
Tanahbala **52** B 6
Tanahgrogot **52** F 6
Tanahjampea **52** G 7
Tanahmasa **52** B 6
Tanama **41** R 3
Tanami Desert Wildlife Sanctuary **60** D 3
Tanana **10** M 5
Tanchūōn **54** A 2
Tandag **52** H 4
Tandil **24** F 6
Tando Adam **46** B 3
Tando Muhammad Khan **46** B 3
Tandsjöborg **38** H 3
Tanega-shima **54** B 4
Tanga **58** C 2
Tanga (Russia) **42** F 6
Tanger **56** C 1
Tangerang **52** D 7
Tanggu **49** K 3
Tanggula Shan **48** E 4
Tanggula Shankou **48** E 4
Tanghe **49** J 4
Tangmai **48** F 4
Tangra Yumco **48** D 4
Tangshan **49** K 3
Tangwanghe **50** E 3
Tangyin **49** J 3
Tangyuan **50** E 3
Tanimbar, Kepulauan **52** J 7
Tanjang Karossa **60** B 1
Tanjona Bobaomby **58** D 3
Tanjona Masoala **58** D 3
Tanjona Vilanandro **58** D 3
Tanjona Vohimena **58** D 4
Tanjungbalai **52** B 5
Tanjungpandan **52** D 6
Tanjungpinang **52** C 5
Tanjungredep **52** F 5
Tanjungselor **52** F 5
Tānk **46** C 2
Tankovo **41** T 5
Tanna **59** F 5
Tännäs **38** H 3
Tannu Ola, Khrebet **41** U 7
Tanţā **56** G 1
Tantoyuca **20** E 3
Tanzania **58** B 2
Taoūan **50** D 3
Tūaoyūan **49** L 5
Tapachula **22** D 5
Tapaktuan **52** B 5
Tappahannock **14** D 3
Tapul Group **53** G 4
Taqtabrod **45** L 2
Tara **40** Q 6
Tara Vai **59** M 6
Tarābulus (Lebanon) **44** E 6
Tarābulus (Tripoli) **56** E 1
Tarahumara, Sierra **20** C 2
Tarakan **53** F 5
Taranto **34** D 2
Taranto, Golfo di **34** D 2
Tararua Range **62** C 3
Taraz **45** M 4
Tarbes **32** C 3
Tarcoola **60** E 6
Tardoki-Yani, Gora **54** C 1
Taree **60** J 6
Târgu Jiu **36** E 3
Târgu Mureş **36** E 3
Tarija **24** E 5
Tarko-Sale **41** R 5
Tarlac **53** G 2
Tärnaby **38** J 2
Tarnobrzeg **36** E 2
Tarnów **36** E 3
Taroom **60** H 5
Tarpon Springs **14** C 5
Tarragona **32** C 3
Tarrassa **32** C 3
Tarsus **35** F 6
Tart **48** E 3
Tartu **38** L 4
Tartus **44** E 6
Tarutung **52** B 5
Taseyevo **41** U 6
Tash-Kömür **45** M 4
Tashkurgan **45** L 5
Tashtagol **41** T 7
Tashtyp **41** T 7
Tasiilap Karra **8** Ee 5
Tasiilaq **8** Dd 5
Tasikmalaja **52** D 7
Taşköprü **35** F 4
Tas-Kystaby, Khrebet **42** M 4
Tasman Bay **62** B 3
Tasman Peninsula **60** H 8
Tasman Sea **60** K 7
Tasmania (Island) **60** G 8
Tasmania (State) **60** G 8
Tassili nūAjjer **56** D 2
Tas-Tumus **42** J 4
Tata **36** D 3
Tatabánya **36** D 3
Tatarsk **41** R 6
Tatarskiy Proliv **50** H 3
Tatau **52** E 5
Tataurovo **41** X 7
Tathlina Lake **10** T 6
Tatnam, Cape **8** S 7
Tatry **36** D 3
Tatta **46** B 4
Tatvan **35** K 5
Tau **59** J 5
Tauere **59** L 5
Taunggyi **47** H 4
Taunton **28** C 4
Taupo **62** C 2
Taupo, Lake **62** C 2
Taurag **38** K 4
Tauranga **62** C 2
Taurus **35** D 6
Tavas **35** C 6
Tavastehus **38** K 3
Tavda **40** P 6
Taveuni **59** H 5
Tavoy **47** H 6
Tavşanli **35** C 5
Tawas City **14** C 2
Tawau **52** F 5
Tawitawi Group **52** F 4
Taxco de Alarcón **20** E 4
Tay **30** C 3
Tay Ninh **47** K 6
Tay, Loch **30** B 3
Tayga **41** T 6
Taygonos, Mys **43** P 4
Taygonos, Poluostrov **43** Q 4
Taylor **43** X 3

Taylorville **14** B 3
Taymyr, Ozero **41** W 3
Taymyr, Poluostrov **41** U 3
Taypaq **44** H 3
Tayshet **41** V 6
Taz **41** S 5
Taza **56** C 1
Tazovskiy **41** R 4
Tazumal **22** E 5
Tūbilisi **35** L 4
Te Anau, Lake **62** A 3
Te Araroa **62** C 2
Te Awamutu **62** C 2
Te Kao **62** B 1
Te Puia **62** C 2
Teapa **20** F 4
Tébessa **56** D 1
Tebingtinggi **52** B 5
Tecate **18** C 5
Tecomán **20** D 4
Tecuala **20** C 3
Tecuci **36** F 3
Tees **28** C 2
Tegal **52** D 7
Tegucigalpa **22** E 5
Tegulūdet **41** T 6
Tehrān **44** H 5
Tehuacán **20** E 4
Tehuantepec **20** E 4
Tehuantepec, Golfo de **20** E 4
Tehuantepec, Istmo de **20** F 4
Tejen **45** K 5
Tejo **33** A 2
Tekeli **45** N 4
Tekirdağ **34** F 2
Tekokota **59** L 5
Tūelavi **35** L 4
Telegraph Creek **10** Q 7
Telemark **38** G 4
Telford **28** C 3
Teller **43** W 3
Tellicherry **46** D 6
Telmen Nuur **41** V 8
Teloloapan **20** E 4
Telšiai **38** K 4
Teluk Anson **52** C 5
Telukdalem **52** B 5
Téma **56** C 4
Tematangi **59** L 6
Temax **20** G 3
Tembenchi **41** V 4
Tembilahan **52** C 6
Tembisa **58** B 4
Tembleque **33** B 2
Temirtau **41** T 7
Temirtaū **45** M 2
Temoe **59** M 6
Tempe **18** D 5
Temple **16** D 5
Temryuk **35** G 2
Temuco **24** D 6
Ten Degree Channel **47** G 7
Tenāli **46** E 5
Tenasserim **47** H 6
Tenerife **56** B 2
Tengchong **48** F 5
Tenggara, Kepulauan **52** H 7
Tengger Shamo **49** G 3
Tengiz Köli **45** L 2
Tengxian (Guangxi, China) **49** J 6
Tengxian (Shandong,China) **49** K 3
Tennant Creek **60** E 3
Tennessee **14** B 3
Tennessee River **14** B 4
Tenojoki **38** L 2
Tenosique **20** F 4
Teocaltiche **20** D 3
Teófilo Otoni **24** G 4
Teotihuacan **20** E 4
Tepa **53** H 7
Tepache **20** C 2
Tepan **52** C 6
Tepic **20** D 3
Tepoca, Bahía de **18** D 5
Tequila **20** D 3
Teramo **34** C 2
Terek **44** F 4
Terempa **52** D 5
Teresina **24** G 3
Teressa **47** G 7
Términos, Laguna de **20** F 4
Termiz **45** L 5
Ternate **52** H 5
Terney **54** C 1
Terni **34** C 2
Ternopilū **36** F 3
Terpeniya, Mys **50** H 3
Terpeniya, Zaliv **54** D 1
Terrace **10** R 8
Terrace Bay **14** B 1
Terracina **34** C 2
Terre Adélie **63** T 5
Terre Haute **14** B 3
Terrebonne Bay **20** F 2
Teruel **32** B 3
Teshekpuk Lake **10** M 4
Teskey Ala-Too **45** N 4
Teslin Lake **10** Q 6
Tete **58** C 3
Tetiaroa **59** L 5
Tétouan **56** C 1
Tetovo **34** E 2
Tevriz **40** Q 6
Texarkana **16** E 5
Texas (U.S.) **16** C 5
Texas City **20** F 2
Teykovo **40** K 6
Teywarah **45** K 6
Teziutlán **20** E 4
Tezpur **47** G 3
Thai Nguyen **47** K 4
Thailand **47** H 5
Thailand, Gulf of **47** J 6
Thal **45** M 6
Thal Desert **46** C 2
Thames (New Zealand) **62** C 2
Thames (U.K.) **28** D 4
Thāne **46** C 5
Thanh Hoa **47** K 5
Thanjāvūr **46** D 6
Thar Desert **46** C 3
Thasos **34** E 2
Thaton **47** H 5
Thayetmyo **47** H 5
The Fens **28** D 3
The Gambia **56** B 3
Thedford **16** C 3
Thermaïkos Kolpos **34** E 2
Thermopilal **34** E 3
Thermopolis **18** E 3
Thessalia **34** E 3
Thessaloniki **34** E 2
Thetford **28** E 3
Thetford Mines **8** W 9
Thief River Falls **16** D 2
Thiès **56** B 3
Thika **58** C 2
Thiladummathi Atoll **46** C 7
Thimbu **47** F 3
Thimphu **47** F 3
Thionville **36** B 3
Thira **34** F 3
Thirsk **28** D 2
Thomastown **31** C 2
Thomasville (Alabama, U.S.) **14** B 4
Thomasville (Georgia, U.S.) **14** C 4
Thompson **8** R 7
Thompson Falls **18** C 2
Thon Buri **47** J 6
Thongwe **47** H 5
Thonze **47** H 5
Thraki **34** F 2
Three Forks **18** D 2
Three Hummock Island **60** G 8
Three Kings Islands **62** B 1
Three Pagodas Pass **47** H 5
Throssell, Lake **60** C 5
Thule **8** X 3
Thunder Bay **8** T 9
Thunder Bay (Canada) **14** B 1
Thunder Bay (U.S.) **14** C 2
Thung Song **47** H 7
Thurso **30** C 2
Thy **38** G 4
Tian Shan **48** B 2
Tiandong **49** H 6
Tianjin **49** K 3
Tianjun **48** F 3
Tianmen **49** J 4
Tianshui **49** H 4
Tianyang **49** H 6
Tibesti **56** E 2

Tibet **48** C 4
Tiburón, Isla **20** B 2
Ticul **20** G 3
Tieli **50** E 3
Tieling **50** D 4
Tientsin **49** K 3
Tierra Blanca **20** E 4
Tierra Colorada **20** E 4
Tifton **14** C 4
Tigalda Island **43** X 6
Tighina **36** F 3
Tigilū **43** P 5
Tigris **44** F 6
Tigris, River **35** J 7
Tijuana **18** C 5
Tikal **20** G 4
Tikamgarh **46** D 4
Tikanlik **48** D 2
Tikhoretsk **35** J 2
Tikhvin **40** H 6
Tikopia **59** F 5
Tiksi **42** J 2
Tilburg **36** B 2
Tillamook **18** B 2
Tillanchong **47** G 7
Tilos **34** F 3
Timagami, Lake **14** C 1
Timanskiy Kryazh **40** L 4
Timaru **62** B 3
Timashevsk **35** H 2
Timiskaming **8** V 9
Timiskaming, Lac **14** D 1
Timişoara **36** E 3
Timmins **8** U 9
Timon **60** C 1
Timor **52** H 7
Timor Sea **53** H 8
Timpton **42** J 5
Tinaca Point **52** G 4
Tindivanam **46** D 6
Tinian **59** D 2
Tinos **34** F 3
Tinsukia **47** H 3
Tioman **52** C 5
Tipperary (Ireland) **31** B 2
Tipton, Mount **18** D 4
Tiquisate **20** F 5
Tiranë **34** D 2
Tiraspol **36** F 3
Tire **34** F 3
Tiree **30** A 3
Tirol **36** C 3
Tirreno, Mare **34** C 3
Tiruchchirappalli **46** D 6
Tiruneveli **46** D 7
Tirupati **46** D 6
Tirūvottiyūr **46** E 6
Tisa **36** E 3
Tisza **36** E 3
Tiszántú **36** E 3
Titlāgarh **46** E 4
Titograd **34** D 2
Titusville **14** C 5
Tivoli **34** C 2
Tizi Ouzou **56** D 1
Tizimin **20** G 3
Tkvarcheli **44** F 4
Tlalnépantla **20** E 4
Tlapa de Comonfort **20** E 4
Tlapacoyan **20** E 4
Tlaxcala **20** E 4
Tlemcen **56** C 1
Toamasina **58** D 3
Toba Kākar Range **46** B 2
Tobago **22** K 5
Tobermory (Canada) **8** U 9
Tobermory (U.K.) **30** A 3
Tobolū **40** P 6
Tobolūsk **40** P 6
Tobyl **45** K 2
Tobyl (River) **45** K 2
Tobylzhan **45** N 2
Tocopilla **24** D 5
Todos Santos **20** B 3
Tofino **18** A 2
Togian, Kepulauan **52** G 6
Togo **56** D 4
Togtoh **49** J 2
Tok **10** O 6
Tokat **44** E 4
Tokelau Islands **59** H 4
Tokmok **45** N 4
Tokoroa **62** C 2
Toksun **48** D 2
Tokuno-shima **50** E 7
Tokushima **54** B 4
Tōkyō **54** C 3
Tôlañaro **58** D 4
Toledo (Spain) **33** B 2
Toledo (U.S.) **14** C 2
Toledo Bend Reservoir **16** E 5
Toledo, Montes de **33** A 2
Toliara **58** D 4
Toliary **58** D 4
Tolstoy, Mys **43** P 5
Toluca **20** E 4
Tolūyatti **44** G 2
Tom **41** S 6
Tomah **16** E 3
Tomakomai **54** D 2
Tomar **33** A 2
Tomari **54** D 1
Tomaszów Mazowiecki **36** E 2
Tomatlán **20** C 4
Tombigbee River **14** B 4
Tombouctou **56** C 3
Tomdibuloq **45** K 4
Tomelloso **33** B 2
Tomini, Teluk **52** G 6
Tomkinson Ranges **60** D 5
Tommot **42** J 5
Tomsk **41** S 6
Tonasket **18** C 2
Tondano **52** G 5
Tonekābon **44** H 5
Tonga **59** H 5
Tonga Trench **59** H 6
Tongariro National Park **62** C 2
Tongatapu **59** H 6
Tongatapu Group **59** H 6
Tongbei **50** E 3
Tongchuan **49** H 3
Tonghai **49** G 6
Tonghe **50** E 3
Tonghua **50** E 4
Tongjan **50** F 3
Tongjiang **50** F 3
Tongjiang (Heilongjiang, China) **54** B 1
Tongjoson-man **54** A 3
Tongliao **50** D 4
Tongling **49** K 4
Tongren **49** H 5
Tongxiam **49** K 3
Tūongyŏng **54** A 4
Tongyu **50** D 4
Tongzi **49** H 5
Tonichí **20** C 2
Tonk **46** D 3
Tonkin, Gulf of **47** K 5
Tonopah **18** C 4
Tonstad **38** G 4
Tooele **18** D 3
Toowoomba **60** J 5
Topeka **16** D 4
Topki **41** T 6
Topolobampo **20** C 2
Topozero, Ozero **40** H 4
Toppenish **18** B 2
Torbalı **35** B 5
Torbat-e Ḩeydarīyeh **45** J 5
Torbat-e Jām **45** K 5
Töre **38** K 2
Torgau **36** C 2
Toribulu **52** F 6
Torino **36** B 3
Tori-shima **54** D 4
Torneå **38** K 2
Torneälven **38** K 2
Torneträsk **38** K 2
Tornio **38** K 2
Tornionjoki **38** K 2
Toronto **14** D 2
Toropets **40** H 6
Toros Dağları **35** D 6
Torquay **28** C 4
Torre del Greco **34** C 2
Torrelavega **33** B 1
Torremolinos **33** B 2
Torrens, Lake **60** F 6
Torrent **33** B 2
Torreón **20** D 2
Torres Strait **59** D 5
Torrevieja **33** C 2
Torrington **16** C 3
Torsby **38** H 3

Tórshavn **38** D 3
Tortola **22** K 4
Tortolì **34** B 3
Tortosa **32** C 3
Tortue, Île de la **22** H 3
Toruń **36** D 2
Torzhok **40** H 6
Tosa-shimizu **54** B 4
Tosa-wan **54** B 4
Toscana **34** C 2
Toshkent **45** L 4
Toson Hu **48** F 3
Tosya **35** F 4
Totūma **40** K 6
Totonicapan **20** F 5
Tottori **54** B 3
Touggourt **56** D 1
Touliu **49** L 6
Toulon **34** B 2
Toulouse **32** C 3
Toungoo **47** H 5
Touraine **32** C 2
Touri-án, Cabo **33** A 1
Tours **32** C 2
Tovuz **35** L 4
Towada **54** D 2
Towanda **14** D 2
Townsend **18** D 2
Townshend Island **60** J 4
Townsville **60** H 3
Towson **14** D 3
Toyama **54** C 3
Toyohashi **54** C 4
Toyota **54** C 3
Tqvarchūeli **44** F 4
Trabzon **35** H 4
Trafalgar, Cabo **33** A 2
Trail **18** C 2
Traill Ø **8** Gg 4
Tralee **31** B 2
Tralee Bay **31** A 2
Trang **47** H 7
Trangan **52** J 7
Transantarctic Mountains **63** Y 4
Transylvania **36** E 3
Trapani **34** C 3
Traralgon **60** H 7
Trarza Ouarâne **56** B 3
Traverse City **14** B 2
Třebíc **36** D 3
Tremonton **18** D 3
Trenčūn **36** D 3
Trent **28** C 3
Trento **36** C 3
Trenton (Missouri, U.S.) **16** E 3
Trenton (New Jersey, U.S.) **14** E 2
Tres Arroyos **24** E 6
Tres Picos **20** F 4
Tres Zapotes **20** E 4
Treviso **36** C 3
Trevose Head **28** B 4
Triángulos, Arrecifes **20** F 3
Trichur **46** D 6
Trier **36** B 3
Trieste **36** C 3
Trikala **34** E 3
Trincomalee **46** E 7
Trinidad **24** E 4
Trinidad (California, U.S.) **18** B 3
Trinidad (Colorado, U.S.) **16** C 4
Trinidad (Cuba) **22** F 3
Trinidad (Trinidad and Tobago) **22** K 5
Trinidad and Tobago **24** F 1
Trinity Islands **43** Z 5
Trinity River **16** D 5
Tripoli **34** E 3
Tripura **47** G 4
Trivandrum **46** D 7
Trobriand Islands **59** E 4
Trois-Rivières **8** W 9
Troitsko-Pechorsk **40** N 5
Troitskoye **45** O 2
Troitskoye (Russia) **54** C 1
Trollhättan **38** H 4
Troms **38** J 2
Tromsø **38** J 2
Trona **18** C 4
Trondheim **38** H 3
Trout Lake **10** S 6
Troy **14** B 4
Troyan **34** E 2
Troyes **32** C 2
Trubchevsk **36** G 2
Trujillo **24** D 3
Trujillo (Honduras) **20** G 4
Trujillo (Venezuela) **22** H 6
Truro (Canada) **8** Y 9
Truro (U.K.) **28** B 4
Truth or Consequences **18** E 5
Tsentralūno Tungusskoye Plato **41** W 5
Tsetserleg **41** W 8
Tshikapa **58** A 2
Tsiigehtchic **10** Q 5
Tsimlyansk **44** F 3
Tsingtao **49** L 3
Tsipanda **42** L 5
Tsipikan **42** F 6
Tsiroanomandidy **58** D 3
Tūskhinvali **35** K 3
Tsu **54** C 4
Tsuchiura **54** D 3
Tsugaru-Kaikyō **54** C 2
Tsuruga **54** C 3
Tsuruoka **54** C 3
Tsushima **50** E 6
Tsuyama **54** B 3
Tual **52** J 7
Tuam **31** B 2
Tuamot, Îles **59** L 5
Tuanake **59** L 5
Tuangku **52** B 5
Tuapse **44** E 4
Tuba City **18** D 4
Tuban **52** E 7
Tubbataha Reefs **52** G 4
Tübingen **36** B 3
Tubruq **56** F 1
Tubuai **59** L 6
Tubuai Islands **59** K 6
Tucson **18** D 5
Tucumcari **16** C 4
Tucupita **22** K 6
Tudela **32** B 3
Tudmur **44** E 6
Tuguegarao **52** G 2
Tugur **42** L 6
Tui **33** A 1
Tukangbesi, Kepulauan **52** G 7
Tuktoyaktuk **10** Q 5
Tukums **38** K 4
Tukuringra, Khrebet **42** H 6
Tula **44** E 2
Tula (Mexico) **20** E 3
Tulancingo **20** E 3
Tulare **18** C 4
Tulcea **36** F 3
Tulūchyn **36** F 3
Tüledi Araldary **44** G 3
Tulemalu Lake **10** W 6
Tulita **10** R 6
Tullahoma **14** B 3
Tully **60** H 3
Tulsa **16** D 4
Tuluksak **43** X 4
Tulum **20** G 3
Tulun **41** W 7
Tulungagung **52** E 7
Tumaco **22** G 7
Tumany **43** P 4
Tumbes **24** C 3
Tumen **54** A 2
Tumkūr **46** D 6
Tunceli **35** H 5
Tungkang **49** L 6
Tungku **52** F 4
Tungsten **10** R 6
Tūnis **56** D 1
Tunis, Golfe de **34** C 3
Tunisia **56** D 1
Tunja **22** H 6
Tunugayualok Island **8** Y 7
Tununak **43** W 4
Tunxi **49** K 5
Tuotuo He **48** E 4
Tupelo **14** B 4
Tupik **42** G 6
Tuquan **50** D 3
Tura (India) **47** G 3
Tura (Russia) **41** W 5
Turakh **42** H 2
Turan **41** U 7
Turana, Khrebet **42** K 6
Turbaco **22** G 5

Turbo **22** G 6
Turda **36** E 3
Turek **36** D 2
Türgen Uul **41** U 8
Tŭrgovishte **35** B 3
Turgutlu **34** F 3
Turhal **35** G 4
Turinsk **40** O 6
Turiy Rog **54** B 1
Tŭrkistan **45** L 4
Tŭrkmenabat **45** K 5
Tŭrkmenbashi **44** H 4
Turkmenistan **45** J 5
Türkoğlu **35** G 6
Turks and Caicos Islands **22** H 3
Turks Islands **22** H 3
Turku **38** K 3
Turneffe Islands **20** G 4
Turnu-Măgurele **34** E 2
Turpan **48** D 2
Turukhan **41** S 4
Turukhansk **41** T 4
Tuscaloosa **14** B 4
Tutavev **40** J 6
Tuticorin **46** D 7
Tuttle Creek Lake **16** D 4
Tuttut Nunaat **8** Ff 4
Tutuala **52** H 7
Tutuila **59** H 5
Tuvalu **59** H 4
Tuvana-i-ra **59** H 6
Tuxpán **20** C 3
Tuxpan **20** E 3
Tuxtepec **20** E 4
Tuxtla Gutiérrez **20** F 4
Tuy Hoa **47** K 6
Tuyen Quang **47** K 4
Tuymazy **44** H 2
Tuz Gölü **35** E 5
Tūz Khurmātū **44** F 6
Tuzla **34** D 2
Tverū **40** J 6
Tweed **28** C 2
Twin Falls (U.S.) **18** D 3
Twin Islands **8** U 8
Twins, The **62** B 3
Twisp **18** B 2
Two Harbors **16** E 2
Tyatino **54** E 2
Tybee Island **14** C 4
Tygda **42** J 6
Tyler **16** D 5
Tym **41** S 5
Tynda **42** H 5
Tyne **28** D 2
Tynset **38** H 3
Tyrma **42** K 7
Tyrnavos **34** E 3
Tyrrhenian Sea **34** C 3
Tysnesøy **38** F 4
Tyssedal **38** G 3
Tyukalinsk **40** Q 6
Tyumen **40** P 6
Tyung **42** G 3
Tzucacab **20** G 4
Ua Pou **59** M 4
Uashat **8** X 8
Uaxactún **20** G 4
Ube **54** B 4
Úbeda **33** B 2
Uberaba **24** G 4
Uberlândia **24** G 4
Ubon Ratchathani **47** J 5
Uchiura-Wan **54** D 2
Udachnyy **41** Y 4
Udaipur **46** C 4
Uddevalla **38** H 4
Udgīr **46** D 5
Udine **36** C 3
Udokan **42** G 5
Udokan, Khrebet **42** G 5
Udon Thani **47** J 5
Udskaya Guba **42** L 6
Udupi **46** C 6
Udzha **42** G 2
Ueda **54** C 3
Uekuli **52** G 6
Uele **58** B 1
Uelen **50** D 3
UelūKal **43** U 3
Uelzen **36** C 2
Ufa **40** N 7
Uganda **58** C 1
Ugashik **43** Y 5
Uglegorsk **50** H 3
Uglich **40** J 6
Ugolūnyye Kopi **43** T 4
Uig **30** A 3
ŪUiha **59** H 5
Uiju **50** D 4
Uinta Mountains **18** D 3
Uitenhage **58** B 5
Ujae **59** F 3
Ujelang **59** F 3
Ujjain **46** D 4
Ujung Pandang **52** F 7
Ukhta **40** M 5
Ukiah (California, U.S.) **18** B 4
Ukiah (Oregon, U.S.) **18** C 2
Ukraine **36** F 3
Ukrainka **41** R 6
Ulaanbaatar **50** A 3
Ulakhan-Bam, Khrebet **42** L 5
Ulakhan-Chistay, Khrebet **42** M 3
Ulan Ul Hu **48** E 4
Ulan-Burgasy, Khrebet **41** X 7
Ulan-Ude **41** X 7
Ulchin **54** A 3
Uleåborg **38** L 3
Ulgal **50** C 3
Ulhāsnagar **46** C 5
Uliastal **50** C 3
Ullapool **30** B 3
Ullared **38** H 4
Ullersuaq **8** W 3
Ulm **36** B 3
Ulsan **54** A 3
Ulster **31** C 1
Ulu **42** J 4
Ulunga **54** C 1
Ulunkhan **42** F 6
Ulūyanovsk **44** G 2
Ulytaū **45** L 3
Umanū **44** D 3
Uman **53** K 6
Umboi **59** D 4
Umeå **38** K 3
Umeälven **38** J 3
Umiat **10** M 5
Umm Durmān (Omdurman) **56** F 3
Umnak Island **43** W 6
Umtata **58** B 5
Unadilla **14** C 4
Unalakleet **43** X 4
Unalaska Island **43** W 6
Unelja **36** G 2
Unga **43** X 5
Ungava Bay **8** X 7
Ungava, Péninsule dū **8** V 6
Unimak Island **43** X 5
Union City **14** B 3
United Kingdom **28** D 2
United States of America **16** C 4
University City **16** E 4
Unst **30** D 1
Upata **22** K 6
Upernavik **8** Z 4
Upington **58** B 4
Upolu **59** H 5
Upolu Point **12** E 7
Upper Arlington **14** C 2
Upper Hutt **62** C 3
Upper Klamath Lake **18** B 3
Upper Lough Erne **31** C 1
Upper Red Lake **16** D 2
Uppland **38** J 3
Uppsala **38** J 4
Urak **42** M 5
Urakawa **54** D 2
Ural Mountains **40** N 7
Uralovka **42** J 6
Uralūsk **44** H 2
Uralūskiy Gory **45** J 2
Uranium City **10** V 7
Urbino **34** C 2
Urdzhar **45** O 3
Urenū **40** L 6
Urengoy **41** R 4
Urfa **44** E 5
Urgal **42** K 6
Urganch **45** K 4
Urla **35** B 5
Uroteppa **45** L 5
Ursuq Ash Shuyūkh **44** G 6
Uruapan **20** D 4

Uruguay **24** F 6
Ürümqi **48** D 2
Uryupinsk **44** F 2
Urzhum **40** L 6
Urziceni **35** B 2
Uşak **35** C 5
Ushakova, Ostrov **41** R 1
Üsharal **45** O 3
Ushki, Zaliv **43** N 5
Üshtöbe **45** N 3
Ush-Urekchen, Khrebet **43** Q 3
Üsküdar **34** F 2
Usmanū **44** E 2
Usolūye-Sibirskoye **41** W 7
Ussuri **54** B 2
Ussuriysk **54** B 2
Ustū-Ilimsk **41** W 6
Ustū-Ilimskoye Vodokhranil-ishche **41** W 6
Üstirt **44** H 4
Ustū-Ishim **40** Q 6
Ustū-Kamchatsk **43** Q 5
Ustū-Kara **40** P 4
Ustū-Katav **40** N 7
Ustū-Khayryuzovo **43** P 5
Ustū-Kulom **40** M 5
Ustū-Kut **41** X 6
Ustū-Labinsk **44** E 3
Ustū-Maya **42** K 4
Ustū-Milū **42** K 5
Ustū-Muya **42** G 5
Ustū-Nera **42** M 4
Ustū-Omchug **43** N 4
Ustū-Padenūga **40** K 5
Ustū-Penzhino **43** R 4
Ustū-Port **41** S 4
Ustū-Sopochnoye **43** P 5
Ustū-Tatta **42** K 4
Ustū-Tsilūma **40** M 4
Ustū-Tsima **40** M 4
Ustū-Urgal **42** K 6
Ustū-Usa **40** N 4
Ustū-Vaga **40** K 5
Ustū-Voyampolka **43** P 5
Usu **48** C 2
Usulután **22** E 5
Usumacinta, Río **20** F 4
Utah **18** D 4
Utah Lake **18** D 3
Utica **14** D 2
Utirik **59** F 2
Utrecht **36** B 2
Utsunomiya **54** C 3
Uttar Pradesh **46** D 3
Uttaradit **47** J 5
Utupua **59** F 5
Uuldza **50** B 3
Uummannaq (Kalaallit Nunaat) **8** Aa 4
Uummannaq (Kalaallit Nunaat) **8** Cc 6
Üüreg Nuur **41** U 8
Uusikaupunki **38** K 3
Uva **40** M 6
Uvalde **20** E 2
Uvarovo **44** F 2
Uvdal **38** G 3
Uvs Nuur **41** U 7
Uwajima **54** B 4
Uxmal **20** G 3
Uyedineniya, Ostrov **41** S 2
Uzbekistan **45** K 4
Uzhhorod **36** E 3
Uzhur **41** T 6
Užice **34** D 2
Uzlovaya **44** E 2
Uzunköprü **35** B 4
Vaal **58** B 4
Vaal Dam **58** B 4
Vaasa **38** K 3
Vác **36** D 3
Vacaria **24** F 5
Vache, Île-à **22** H 4
Vadodara **46** C 4
Vaduz **36** B 3
Vágar **38** D 3
Vaghena Island **59** E 4
Vaiaku **59** G 4
Vakh **41** S 5
Valachia **34** E 2
Valday **40** H 6
Valdayskaya Vozvyshennostū **40** H 6
Valdez **10** N 6
Valdivia **24** D 6
Val-dūOr **8** V 9
Valdosta **14** C 4
Vale of White Horse **28** D 4
Valence **32** C 3
Valencia (Spain) **33** B 2
Valencia (Venezuela) **22** J 5
Valentine **16** C 3
Valera **22** H 6
Valga **38** L 4
Valjevo **34** D 2
Valladolid (Mexico) **20** G 3
Valladolid (Spain) **33** B 1
Valle **38** G 4
Valle de la Pascua **22** J 6
Valle de Zaragoza **20** C 2
Valle Hermoso **20** E 2
Valletta **34** C 3
Valley City **16** D 2
Valley Station **14** B 3
Valleyfield **14** E 1
Valmiera **38** L 4
Valparaiso **20** D 3
Valparaíso **24** D 6
Vals, Tanjung **53** K 7
Valuyki **44** E 2
Van **35** K 5
Van Buren **16** E 4
Van Dieman, Cape **60** E 2
Van Diemen Gulf **60** E 2
Van Gölü **35** K 5
Van Horn **16** C 5
van Rees, Pegunungan **53** K 6
Van Wert **14** C 2
Vanadzor **35** L 4
Vanavara **41** W 5
Vancouver **18** B 2
Vancouver Island **10** R 8
Vandalla **14** B 3
Vanderbijlpark **58** B 4
Vanderhoof **10** S 8
Vanderlin Island **60** F 3
Vänern **38** H 4
Vänersborg **38** H 4
Vangunu Island **59** E 4
Vanikoro Islands **59** F 5
Vankarem **43** U 3
Vanna **38** J 1
Vanna Levu **59** G 5
Vannatu **61** K 3
Vannes **32** B 2
Vansittart Island **8** U 5
Vanua Lava **59** F 5
Vanuatu **59** F 5
Vārānasi **46** E 3
Varangerhalvøya **38** L 1
Varaždin **36** D 3
Varberg **38** H 4
Vardø **40** H 3
Värmland **38** H 4
Varna **34** F 2
Varna (Bulgaria) **35** B 3
Värnamo **38** H 4
Varnenski Zaliv **35** C 3
Varsinais Suomi **38** K 3
Varzuga **40** J 4
Vasa **38** K 3
Vaşac **36** E 3
Vasai **46** C 5
Vaslui **36** F 3
Vasta **44** G 3
Västerås **38** J 4
Västerbotten **38** J 3
Västergötland **38** H 4
Västervik **38** J 4
Västmanland **38** J 4
Vasylūkiv **36** G 2
Vasyugan **41** R 6
Vatican City State **34** C 2
Vatnajökull **38** B 3
Vatoa **59** H 5
Vatomandry **58** D 3
Vatra Dornei **36** F 3
Vättern **38** H 4
Vaughn **18** E 5
Vavaūu Group **59** H 5
Vavuniya **46** E 7
Vawkavysk **36** E 2
Växjö **38** H 4
Vaygach **40** N 3
Vega **38** H 2
Vejle **38** G 4

Veles **34** E 2
Velikaya Kema **54** C 1
Velikiy Ustyug **40** L 5
Velikiye-Luki **40** H 6
Veliko Tŭrnovo **34** F 2
Velikonda Range **46** D 5
Vellore **46** D 6
Velūsk **40** K 5
Vendinga **40** L 5
Vendôme **32** C 2
Venetie **10** N 5
Venezia **36** C 3
Venezuela **24** E 2
Venezuela, Golfo de **22** H 5
Venice, Gulf of **36** C 3
Ventspils **38** K 4
Ventura **18** C 5
Venustiano Carranza **20** F 4
Veracruz (Mexico) **20** E 4
Veracruz (State, Mexico) **20** E 3
Veraval **46** C 4
Verde River **18** D 4
Vereeniging **58** B 4
Vereshchagino **40** M 6
Verkhneangarskiy Khrebet **41** X 6
Verkhneimbatskoye **41** T 5
Verkhnevilyuysk **42** H 4
Verkhniy Ufaley **40** O 6
Verkhnyaya Amga **42** J 5
Verkhnyaya Salda **40** O 6
Verkhnyaya Toyma **40** K 5
Verkhoturūye **40** O 6
Verkhoyansk **42** K 3
Verkhoyanskiy Khrebet **42** J 3
Vermilion Bay **16** E 2
Vermont **14** E 2
Vernal **18** E 3
Vernon (Canada) **10** T 8
Vernon (U.S.) **16** D 5
Vero Beach **14** C 5
Veroia **34** E 2
Verona **36** C 3
Versailles **32** C 2
Veshenskaya **44** F 3
Vest-Agder **38** G 4
Vesterålen **38** H 2
Vestfjorden **38** H 2
Vestmannaeyjar **38** A 3
Vestvågøy **38** H 2
Vesūyegonsk **40** J 6
Vétaoundé **59** F 5
Vetlanda **38** J 4
Vevelstad **38** H 2
Vezhūydor **40** M 5
Viana do Castelo **33** A 1
Viangchan **47** J 5
Vibo Valentia **34** D 3
Viborg **38** G 4
Vic **32** C 3
Vicenza **36** C 3
Vichuga **40** K 6
Vichy **32** C 2
Vicksburg **16** E 5
Victoria **58** E 2
Victoria (Australia) **60** G 7
Victoria (Canada) **18** B 2
Victoria (Malaysia) **52** F 4
Victoria (U.S.) **20** E 2
Victoria de las Tunas **22** G 3
Victoria Island **10** U 4
Victoria River Downs **60** E 3
Victoria Strait **10** W 5
Victorias **52** G 3
Victoriaville **14** E 1
Victorville **18** C 5
Videle **35** A 2
Vidin **34** E 2
Vidisha **46** D 4
Vidra **34** F 2
Viedma **24** E 7
Viejo, Cerro (Mexico) **18** D 5
Vienna **36** D 3
Vienna (U.S.) **14** C 3
Vienne **32** C 2
Vientiane **47** J 5
Vieques, Isla de **22** K 4
Vierzon **32** C 2
Viesca **20** D 2
Viet Triu **47** K 4
Vietnam **47** K 5
Vigan **52** G 2
Vigo **33** A 1
Vihari **46** C 2
Vijayawāda **46** E 5
Vikhorevka **41** W 6
Vikna **38** H 3
Vila **59** F 5
Vila Real **33** A 1
Vila Real **33** B 2
Vilalba **33** A 1
Vilanova i la Geltrú **32** C 3
Vila-real **32** B 3
Vilhelmina **38** J 3
Viliga-Kushka **43** P 4
Viljandi **38** L 4
Vilūkitskogo, Ostrov **41** R 3
Vilūkitskogo, Proliv **41** W 2
Villa Ahumada **18** E 5
Villa Coronado **20** C 2
Villa de Cos **20** D 3
Villa Flores **20** F 4
Villa Frontera **20** D 2
Villa Hidalgo **20** D 2
Villa María **24** E 6
Villa Ocampo (Mexico) **20** C 2
Villa Union **20** C 3
Villach **36** C 3
Villahermosa **20** F 4
Villaldama **20** D 2
Villavicencio **22** H 7
Ville de Reyes **20** D 3
Villeurbanne **32** C 2
Villmanstrand **38** L 3
Villupuram **46** D 6
Vilnius **36** F 2
Vilye **36** F 2
Vilyuy **42** G 4
Vilyuyskoye Plato **41** X 4
VilyuyskoyeVodokhranilishche **41** X 5
Viña del Mar **24** D 6
Vinaròs **32** C 3
Vincennes **14** B 3
Vindhya Range **46** C 4
Vineland **14** D 3
Vinh **47** K 5
Vinh Loi **47** K 7
Vinkovci **36** D 3
Vinnytsya **36** F 3
Virac **52** G 3
Viramgam **46** C 4
Virden **16** C 2
Virgin Islands **22** J 4
Virginia (Minnesota, U.S.) **16** E 2
Virginia (State, U.S.) **14** D 3
Virginia Beach **14** D 3
Virginia Falls **10** R 6
Virudunager **46** D 7
Visalia **18** C 4
Visayan Sea **52** G 3
Visby **38** J 4
Viscount Melville Sound **10** U 4
Viseu **33** A 1
Viseul de Sus **36** E 3
Vishakhapatnam **46** E 5
Visnagar **46** C 4
Vistula **36** D 2
Viterbo **34** C 2
Viti Levu **59** G 5
Vitim **42** G 5
Vitimskoye Ploskogorūye **42** F 6
Vitória **24** H 5
Vitória da Conquista **24** G 4
Vitoria-Gasteiz **32** B 3
Vitsyebsk **40** H 6
Vittoria **34** C 3
Vittorio Veneto **36** C 3
Vivi **41** V 5
Vizcaíno, Desierto de **20** B 2
Vizcaíno, Sierra **20** B 2
Vize, Ostrov **41** R 2
Vizianagaram **46** E 5
Vūk **38** B 3
Vladikavkaz **35** L 3
Vladimir **40** K 6
Vladivostok **54** B 2
Vlorū **34** D 2
Vojvodina **36** D 3
Volga **44** G 3
Volgo-Balt Kanal **40** J 5
Volgodonsk **44** F 3
Volgograd **44** F 3
Volkhov **40** H 6
Volnovakha **44** E 3
Volochanka **41** U 3

Volodymyr-Volynsūkyy **36** E 2
Vologda **40** J 6
Volos **34** E 3
Volūsk **44** G 2
Volzhsk **40** L 6
Volzhskiy **44** F 3
Vongping **48** F 5
Voranava **36** F 2
Voreioi Sporades **34** E 3
Vorkuta **40** O 4
Vormsi **38** K 4
Voronezh **44** E 2
Voronina, Ostrov **41** U 2
Võru **38** L 4
Voss **38** G 3
Vostochno-Sibirskoye More **43** P 2
Vostochnyy (Russia) **54** D 1
Vostochnyy Sayan **41** U 7
Vostok Island **59** K 5
Votkinsk **40** M 6
Voyvozh **40** N 5
Vozhgora **40** L 5
Voznesensūk **44** D 3
Vozrozhdeniya **45** J 3
Vozvrashcheniye **54** D 1
Vrangelya, Ostrov **43** T 2
Vranje **34** E 2
Vratsa **34** E 2
Vryburg **58** B 4
Vsetūn **36** D 3
Vsevolozhsk **40** H 6
Vukovar **36** D 3
Vung Tau **47** K 6
Vyatka **40** L 6
Vyatskiye Polyany **40** M 6
Vyazūma **40** H 6
Vyborg **38** L 3
Vyksa **40** K 6
Vyselki **35** H 2
Vyshniy Volochek **40** H 6
Vysokiy, Mys **42** N 1
Vysokogorsk **54** C 2
Vytegra **40** J 5
W nsan **50** E 5
Wa **56** C 4
Wa Keeney **16** D 4
Wabash River **14** B 3
Waboden **10** X 8
Wabowden **10** X 8
Waco (U.S.) **16** D 5
Waconda Lake **16** D 4
Wad Madanī **56** G 3
Wadi Drâa **56** B 2
Wādī Sawbā **56** G 4
Wadley **14** C 4
Wadsworth **18** C 4
Wagga Wagga **60** H 7
Wagin **60** B 6
Wagon Mound **16** C 4
Wagoner **16** D 4
Wāh Cantonment **45** M 6
Wahai **52** H 6
Wahiawa **12** E 7
Wahpeton **16** D 2
Waiau **62** B 3
Waibeem **52** J 6
Waigeo **52** J 5
Waija **52** H 6
Waikato **62** C 2
Waikouaiti **62** B 4
Waimate **62** B 3
Wainwright **10** K 4
Waiotira **62** B 2
Waipara **62** B 3
Wairau **62** B 3
Wairoa **62** C 2
Waitaki **62** B 3
Waitara **62** B 2
Waitemata **62** B 2
Waiwo **52** J 6
Wakasa-wan **54** C 3
Wakatipu, Lake **62** A 4
Wakayama **54** C 4
Wakema **47** H 5
Wakkanai **50** H 3
Wałbrzych **36** D 2
Wałcz **36** D 2
Waldport **18** B 3
Wales (U.K.) **28** C 3
Wales (U.S.A.) **43** W 3
Wales Island **8** T 5
Walker Lake **18** C 4
Wall **16** C 3
Walla Walla **18** C 2
Wallaceburg **14** C 2
Wallaroo **60** F 6
Wallis and Futuna **59** H 5
Wallis, Îles **59** H 5
Walsall **28** D 3
Walsenburg **16** C 4
Walt Disney World **14** C 5
Walterboro **14** C 4
Waltershausen Gletscher **8** Ff 4
Walvis Bay **58** A 4
Wanaka **62** A 3
Wanaka, Lake **62** A 3
Wandel Sea **8** Gg 2
Wanganui **62** C 2
Wangaratta **60** H 7
Wangiwangi **52** G 7
Wangkui **50** E 3
Wangqing **54** A 2
Wanneroo **60** B 6
Wanning **47** L 5
Wanxian **49** H 4
Wanyuan **49** H 4
Warangal **46** D 5
Warburton Range **60** D 5
Ward **62** B 3
Ware **10** R 7
Waren **53** K 6
Warin Chamrap **47** J 5
Warm Springs **18** C 4
Warming Land **8** Aa 2
Warner Mountains **18** B 3
Warner Peak **18** C 3
Warner Robins **14** C 4
Warren (U.S.) **14** C 2
Warri **56** D 4
Warrington **28** C 3
Warrnambool **60** G 7
Warrumbungle Range **60** H 6
Warsaw **36** E 2
Warszawa **36** E 2
Warwick **60** J 5
Wasatch Range **18** D 3
Wasco **18** C 4
Wasgomuwa National Park **46** E 7
Wash, The **28** E 3
Washburn Lake **10** V 4
Washim **46** D 4
Washington (Indiana, U.S.) **14** B 3
Washington (Maryland, U.S.) **14** D 3
Washington (North Carolina, U.S.) **14** D 3
Washington (State, U.S.) **18** B 2
Washington Court House **14** C 3
Washington Land **8** X 2
Wasior **52** J 6
Waskaganish **8** V 8
Waspán **20** H 5
Watampone **52** G 6
Waterbury **14** E 2
Waterford **31** C 2
Waterloo (U.S.) **16** E 3
Waterton Lakes National Park **18** D 2
Watertown (New York, U.S.) **14** D 2
Watertown (South Dakota, U.S.) **16** D 3
Watertown (Wisconsin, U.S.) **14** B 2
Waterville **8** X 10
Watford City **16** C 2
Watrous (U.S.) **16** C 4
Watson Lake **10** R 6
Watts Bar Lake **14** C 3
Watubela, Kepulauan **52** J 6
Waukara, Gunung **52** F 6
Waukarlycarly, Lake **60** C 4
Waukegan **14** B 2
Waukesha **14** B 2
Wausau **14** B 2
Wave Hill **60** E 3
Waverly **16** E 3
Wāw **56** F 4
Wawa **8** U 9
Way, Lake **60** C 5
Waycross **14** C 4
Wayland **14** C 3
Wayne **14** C 3

Webster **16** D 2
Webster City **16** E 3
Weda **52** H 5
Weh **52** B 4
Wehē **56** H 4
Wei He **49** J 4
Weichang **50** C 4
Weiden in der Oberpfalz **36** C 3
Weifang **49** K 3
Weihai **49** L 3
Weinan **49** H 4
Weirton **14** C 2
Weiser **18** C 3
Weishan Hu **49** K 4
Weißwasser **36** C 2
Wejherowo **36** D 2
Welkom **58** B 4
Wellesley Islands **60** F 3
Wellington (Kansas, U.S.) **16** D 4
Wellington (Nevada, U.S.) **18** C 4
Wellington (New Zealand) **62** B 3
Wells **18** D 3
Wellsboro **14** D 2
Wellton **18** D 5
Wels **36** C 3
Wenatchee **18** B 2
Wenchang **47** L 5
Wendeng **49** L 3
Wendover **18** D 3
Wenling **49** L 5
Wenshan **49** G 6
Wentworth **60** G 6
Wenzhou **49** L 5
Weri **52** J 6
Weslaco **20** E 2
Wessel Islands **60** F 2
Wessel, Cape **60** F 2
West Allis **14** B 2
West Bend **14** B 2
West Bengal **46** F 4
West Cape Howe **60** B 7
West Memphis **16** E 4
West Palm Beach **14** C 5
West Plains **16** E 4
West Point **14** B 4
West Virginia **14** C 3
West Wyalong **60** H 6
West Yellowstone **18** D 3
Westbrook **14** E 2
Wester Ross **30** B 3
Western Australia **60** B 4
Western Ghāts **46** C 5
Western Port **60** G 7
Western Sahara (Morocco) **56** B 2
Weston **14** C 3
Weston-super-Mare **28** C 4
Westport **62** B 3
Westray **30** C 2
Westree **14** C 1
Westwood **18** B 3
Wetar **52** H 7
Wetzlar **36** B 2
Wewak **59** D 4
Wexford **31** C 2
Weyburn **16** C 2
Weymouth **28** C 4
Whakatane **62** C 2
Whale Cove **8** S 6
Whalsay **30** D 1
Whangarei **62** B 2
Whapmagoostui **8** V 7
Wharton Lake **10** W 6
Wheatland **16** C 3
Wheeler Peak (Nevada, U.S.) **18** D 4
Wheeler Peak (New Mexico, U.S.) **18** E 4
Wheeling **14** C 2
White Butte **16** C 2
White Island **8** T 5
White River **8** T 9
White River (Arkansas, U.S.) **16** E 5
White River (Indiana, U.S.) **14** B 3
White River (Ontario, Canada) **14** B 1
White River (South Dakota, U.S.) **16** C 3
White Sulphur Springs **18** D 2
White Volta **56** C 4
Whitecourt **10** T 8
Whitefish Bay **14** C 1
Whitefish Point **14** B 1
Whitehaven **28** C 2
Whitehorse **10** P 6
Whitewater Bay **14** C 5
Whitney **14** D 1
Whitsunday Island **60** H 4
Whittier **10** N 6
Whiyby **28** D 2
Wholdaia Lake **10** V 6
Whyalla **60** F 6
Wibaux **16** C 2
Wichita **16** D 4
Wichita Falls **16** D 5
Wick **30** C 2
Wickenburg **18** D 5
Wickham, Cape **60** G 7
Wicklow **31** C 2
Wicklow Head **28** B 3
Wicklow Mountains **31** C 2
Wien **36** D 3
Wiener Neustadt **36** D 3
Wiesbaden **36** B 2
Wight, Isle of **28** D 4
Wilbur **18** C 2
Wilcannia **60** G 6
Wilhelm II Land **63** R 5
Wilhelmshaven **36** B 2
Wilkes Barre **14** D 2
Willamette River **18** B 3
Willapa Bay **18** A 2
Willard **18** E 5
Willcox **18** E 5
Willemstad **22** J 5
Williams **18** D 4
Williams Lake **10** S 8
Williamsburg (Kentucky, U.S.) **14** C 3
Williamsburg (Virginia, U.S.) **14** D 3
Williamsport **14** D 2
Willis Group **60** J 3
Williston (U.S.) **16** C 2
Williston Lake **10** S 7
Willow Bunch **18** E 2
Willows **18** B 4
Wilmington (New Jersey, U.S.) **14** D 3
Wilmington (North Carolina, U.S.) **14** D 4
Wilson **14** D 3
Wilson Lake **14** B 4
Wilson, Cape **8** U 5
Wilsonūs Promontory National Park **60** H 7
Wiluna **60** C 5
Winchester (U.K.) **28** D 4
Winchester (U.S.) **14** C 3
Wind River **18** E 3
Wind River Range **18** E 3
Windermere **28** C 2
Windhoek **58** A 4
Windorah **60** G 5
Window Rock **18** E 4
Windsor (Ontario, Canada) **14** C 2
Windsor (U.K.) **28** D 4
Windsor Forest **14** C 4
Windsor Locks **14** E 2
Windward Islands (Caribbean) **22** K 5
Windward Islands (French Polynesia) **59** K 5
Winfield (Alabama, U.S.) **14** B 4
Winfield (Kansas, U.S.) **16** D 4
Winnebago, Lake **14** B 2
Winnemucca **18** C 3
Winnfield **16** E 5
Winnipeg **16** D 2
Winnipeg, Lake **10** X 8
Winnipegosis, Lake **10** W 8
Winnipesaukee, Lake **14** E 2
Winona **16** E 3
Winslow **18** D 4
Winslow Reef **59** H 4
Winston-Salem **14** C 3
Winter Park **14** C 5
Winton **60** G 4
Winton (New Zealand) **62** A 4
Wisconsin **16** E 2
Wiseman **10** M 5
Wisła **36** D 2
Wismar **36** C 2

Witbank **58** B 4
Witney **28** D 4
Wittenberg **36** C 2
Wittenberge **36** C 2
Włocławek **36** D 2
Wokam **52** J 7
Woking **28** D 4
Wolf Creek **18** D 2
Wolf Point **18** E 2
Wolf Rock **28** B 5
Wolfsberg **36** C 3
Wollaston Forland **8** Gg 4
Wollaston Lake **10** W 7
Wollongong **60** J 6
Wolseley **16** C 1
Wolverhampton **28** C 3
Wonju **54** A 3
Wŏnsan **54** A 3
Wood Buffalo National Park **10** U 7
Woodland **18** B 4
Woodlark Island **59** E 4
Woods, Lake **60** E 3
Woods, Lake of the **16** D 2
Woodstock (Canada) **14** F 1
Woodstock (U.S.) **14** E 2
Woodville **16** E 5
Woodward **16** D 4
Woomera **60** F 6
Worcester **58** A 5
Worcester (U.K.) **28** C 3
Worcester (U.S.) **14** E 2
Wordie Gletscher **8** Gg 4
Workington **28** C 2
Worland **18** E 3
Worthing **28** D 4
Worthington **16** D 3
Wosi **52** H 6
Wosu **52** G 6
Wotho **59** F 2
Wotje **59** G 3
Wotu **52** G 6
Wowoni **52** G 6
Woy Woy **60** J 6
Wozrojdeniye Orol **45** J 3
Wrangell **10** Q 7
Wrangell Mountains **10** O 6
Wrangell Saint Elias National Park **10** O 6
Wrangell, Cape **43** S 6
Wrath, Cape **30** B 2
Wrexham **28** C 3
Wright Patman Lake **16** D 5
Wrigley **10** S 6
Wrocław **36** D 2
Wu Shan **49** J 4
Wuchang (Heilongjiang, China) **50** E 4
Wuchang (Hubei, China) **49** J 4
Wuchuan **49** J 6
Wuda **49** H 3
Wudu **49** G 4
Wugang **49** J 5
Wuhai **49** H 3
Wuhan **49** J 4
Wuhu **49** K 4
Wuji Shan **49** K 5
Wulff Land **8** Aa 2
Wuling Shan **49** H 5
Wumeng **49** G 5
Wunnummin Lake **8** T 8
Wuppertal **36** B 2
Wuqing **49** K 3
Würzburg **36** B 3
Wutai Shan **49** J 3
Wutunghliao **49** G 5
Wuwei (Anhui, China) **49** K 4
Wuwei (Gansu, China) **49** G 3
Wuxi **49** L 4
Wuyiling **54** A 1
Wuyuan **49** H 2
Wuzhong **49** H 3
Wuzhou **49** J 6
Wye **28** C 3
Wyndham **60** D 3
Wyoming (Michigan, U.S.) **14** B 2
Wyoming (State, U.S.) **18** E 3
Wyperfeld National Park **60** G 7
Xaidulla **48** B 3
Xam Nua **47** J 4
Xankändı **44** G 5
Xanthi **34** E 2
Xayar **48** C 2
Xenia **14** C 3
Xi Jiang **49** J 6
Xiachengzi **54** B 2
Xiachuan Dao **49** J 6
Xiaguan **48** G 5
Xiamen **49** K 6
Xiūan **49** H 4
Xiangfan **49** J 4
Xiangtan **49** J 5
Xianju **49** L 5
Xianyang **49** H 4
Xiaogan **49** J 4
Xiaojin **49** G 4
Xiapu **49** L 5
Xiawa **50** D 4
Xichang **49** G 5
Xicoténcati **20** E 3
Xigaze **48** D 5
Ximiao **48** G 2
Xin Barag Youqi **50** C 3
Xinūanjiang Shuiku **49** K 5
Xinchang **49** L 5
Xing Xian **49** J 3
Xinghai **48** F 3
Xinghe **49** J 2
Xinging **54** A 1
Xingren **49** H 5
Xingtai **49** J 3
Xingyi **49** G 5
Xinhua **49** J 5
Xinhui **49** J 6
Xining **49** G 3
Xinjiang Uygur Zizhiqu **48** C 3
Xinjin **49** L 3
Xinmin **54** A 1
Xinning **49** J 5
Xinwen **49** K 3
Xinxiang **49** J 3
Xinyang **49** J 4
Xiqing Shan **49** G 3
Xiushui **49** J 5
Xiuwu **49** J 3
Xiuyan **50** D 4
Xixiang **49** H 4
Xizang Zizhiqu **48** C 4
Xoūjayli **45** J 4
Xouhil **20** G 4
Xuanhan **49** H 4
Xuanhua **50** C 4
Xuanwei **49** G 5
Xuchang **49** J 4
Xuguit Qi **50** D 3
Xupu **49** J 5
Xuwen **49** J 6
Xuyong **49** H 5
Xuzhou **49** K 4
Yaūan **49** G 4
Yablonovyy Khrebet **42** F 6
Yabuli **54** A 2
Yadgir **46** D 5
Yahyalı **35** F 5
Yailang **48** G 4
Yakima **18** B 2
Yakumo **54** D 2
Yaku-Shima **50** E 6
Yaku-shima **54** A 4
Yakutal **10** P 7
Yakutsk **42** J 4
Yala **52** C 4
Yalatorovsk **40** P 6
Yalong Jiang **49** G 4
Yalta **44** D 4
Yalta (Ukraine) **35** F 2
Yamagata **54** D 3
Yamaguchi **54** B 4
Yamal, Poluostrov **40** P 3
Yam-Alinū, Khrebet **42** K 6
Yambo **22** G 7
Yambol **34** F 2
Yamdena **52** J 7
Yamethin **47** H 4
Yamma Yamma, Lake **60** G 5
Yamoussoukro **56** C 4
Yamzho Yumco **48** E 5
Yana **42** L 2
Yanūan **49** H 3
Yancheng **49** L 4
Yang Xian **49** H 4
Yangchun **49** J 6
Yanggao **49** J 2
Yangiyoūl **45** L 4
Yangjiang **49** J 6
Yangliuqing **49** K 3

Yangôn **47** H 5
Yangquan **49** J 3
Yangtze Kiang **48** F 4
Yangxin **49** K 5
Yangzhou **49** K 4
Yanji **54** A 2
Yankton **16** D 3
Yano-Indigirskaya Nizmennostū **42** M 3
Yanov Stan **41** S 4
Yanqing **50** C 4
Yanshou **50** E 3
Yantai **49** L 3
Yanyuan **49** G 5
Yanzhou **49** K 3
Yaoundé **56** E 4
Yap Islands **59** C 3
Yapen **53** K 6
Yaqui, Río **20** C 2
Yaransk **40** L 6
Yardimei Burnu **44** D 5
Yaren **59** F 4
Yarensk **40** L 5
Yarlung Zangbo Jiang **47** F 3
Yarmouth **14** F 2
Yaroslavlū **40** J 6
Yartsevo (Russia) **41** U 5
Yasawa Group **59** G 5
Yashkulū **44** G 3
Yasun Burnu **35** G 4
Yathkyed Lake **8** R 6
Yatsushiro **54** B 4
Yavatmāl **46** D 4
Yawata-hama **54** B 4
Yaxchilán **20** F 4
Yaxian **47** K 5
Yaya **41** T 6
Yazd **45** H 6
Yazoo City **16** E 5
Yazoo River **16** E 5
Ye **47** H 5
Yecheng **48** B 3
Yedinka **54** C 1
Yefremov **44** E 2
Yegorūyevsk **40** J 6
Yekaterinburg **40** O 6
Yelabuga **40** M 6
Yelanū **44** F 2
Yelets **44** E 2
Yelizarovo **40** P 5
Yelizovo **43** P 6
Yell **30** D 1
Yellow Sea **49** L 3
Yellowhead Pass **10** T 8
Yellowknife **10** U 6
Yellowstone Lake **18** D 3
Yellowstone National Park **18** D 3
Yellowstone River **16** C 2
Ýelöten **45** K 5
Yelūsk **36** F 2
Yenangyaung **47** G 4
Yenisey **41** T 5
Yeniseysk **41** U 6
Yeniseyskiy Kryazh **41** T 5
Yeniseyskiy Zaliv **41** R 3
Yeo Lake **60** C 5
Yeovil **28** C 4
Yerbogachen **41** X 5
Yerevan **44** F 4
Yerköy **44** D 5
Yermitsa **40** M 4
Yermo **20** D 2
Yerofei-Pavlovich **42** H 6
Yershov **44** G 2
Yertsevo **40** K 5
Yeşilhisar **35** F 5
Yeşilırmak **35** G 4
Yessey **41** W 4
Yeu, Île dū **32** B 2
Yevpatoriya **35** E 2
Yevreyska Avtonomnaya Oblastū **54** B 1
Yeysk **35** H 1
Yiūan **50** E 3
Yibin **49** G 5
Yibug Caka **48** D 4
Yichang **49** J 4
Yichun (Heilongjiang, China) **50** E 3
Yichun (Jiangxi, China) **49** J 5
Yidu (Hubei, China) **49** J 4
Yidu (Shandong, China) **49** K 3
Yilan **50** E 3
Yıldızeli **35** G 5
Yin Shan **49** H 2
Yinchuan **49** H 3
Yingkou **50** D 4
Yining **48** C 2
Yirshi **50** C 3
Yishan **49** H 6
Yitong **50** E 4
Yitulihe **50** D 2
Yixian **50** D 4
Yiyang (Hunan, China) **49** J 5
Yiyang (Jiangxi, China) **49** K 5
Yizhang **49** J 5
Ymer Ø **8** Gg 4
Yogyakarta **52** E 7
Yokohama **54** C 3
Yokosuka **54** C 3
Yokote **54** D 3
Yonago **54** B 3
Yonaguni-shima **49** L 6
Yonezawa **54** D 3
Yongchang **49** G 3
Yongchuan **49** H 5
Yongdeng **49** G 3
Yonghung **54** A 3
Yŏngju **50** E 5
Yongxiu **49** K 5
Yonkers **14** E 2
York (Nebraska, U.S.) **16** D 3
York (Pennsylvania, U.S.) **14** D 3
York (U.K.) **28** D 3
York Factory **8** S 7
York, Cape **60** G 2
Yorke Peninsula **60** F 6
Yorkshire Wolds **28** D 3
Yorkton **10** W 8
Yoro **20** G 4
Yosemite National Park **18** B 4
Yoshkar-Ola **40** L 6
Yŏsu **50** E 6
Youngstown **14** C 2
Youyi Feng **41** T 8
Yozgat **35** F 5
Yreka **18** B 3
Yrghyz **45** K 3
Ysyk-Köl **45** N 4
Ytterhogdal **38** H 3
Ytyk-Kyuyelū **42** K 4
Yū Shan **49** L 6
Yūanlin **49** L 6
Yuanping **49** J 3
Yuanqu **49** J 3
Yūbari **54** D 2
Yucatán **20** G 3
Yucatan Peninsula **20** G 3
Yucatán, Canal de **20** G 3
Yuci **49** J 3
Yueqing **49** L 5
Yuexi **49** G 5
Yueyang **49** J 5
Yugorskiy Poluostrov **40** O 4
Yugo-Tal **43** O 3
Yukhnov **44** E 2
Yukogirskoye Ploskogorūye **43** O 3
Yukon **10** P 5
Yukon Flats **10** N 5
Yukon Flats National Monument **10** N 5
Yukon Plateau **10** P 6
Yukon River (Canada) **10** P 6
Yukon River (U.S.) **43** X 4
Yukon Territory **10** P 5
Yuli **48** D 2
Yulin (Guangxi, China) **49** J 6
Yulin (Shaanxi, China) **49** H 3
Yuma (Arizona, U.S.) **18** D 5
Yuma (Colorado, U.S.) **16** C 3
Yumen **48** F 3
Yumenzhen **48** F 2
Yun Xian **49** J 4
Yunaska Island **43** V 6
Yuncheng **49** J 3
Yunkai Dashan **49** J 6
Yunnan **49** G 6
Yunxiao **49** K 6
Yurga **41** S 6
Yushan **49** K 5
Yushkozero **40** H 5
Yushu **50** E 4
Yutian **48** C 3
Yuxi **49** G 6

Yuxian **49** J 3
Yuyao **49** L 4
Yuzhno Muyskiy Khrebet **42** F 5
Yuzhno-Aleksandrovka **41** V 6
Yuzhno-Sakhalinsk **54** D 1
Yuzhnyy Anyuyskiy Khrebet **43** Q 3
Zabol **45** K 6
Zabrze **36** D 2
Zabūrūnūe **44** H 3
Zacapa **20** G 5
Zacápu **20** D 4
Zacatecas (Mexico) **20** D 3
Zacatecas (State, Mexico) **20** D 3
Zacatepec **20** E 4
Zachodnyaya Dzvina **38** L 4
Zadar **34** D 2
Zafra **33** A 2
Zagreb **36** D 3
Zahlah **44** E 6
Zakamensk **41** W 7
Zakopane **36** D 3
Zakynthos **34** E 3
Zalaegerszeg **36** D 3
Zalari **41** W 7
Zambeze **58** C 3
Zambezi **58** B 3
Zambia **58** B 3
Zamboanga **52** G 4
Zambonga Peninsula **52** G 4
Zambrów **36** E 2
Zamora **33** A 1
Zamora de Hidalgo **20** D 4
Zanesville **14** C 3
Zanjān **44** G 5
Zanulūye **40** L 5
Zanzibar **58** C 2
Zanzibar Island **58** C 2
Zaoyang **49** J 4
Zaozhuang **49** K 4
Zapadno-Sibirskaya Ravnina **40** O 5
Zapadnyy Sayan **41** T 7
Zapala **24** D 6
Zaporizhzhya **44** E 3
Zara **35** G 5
Zaragoza **32** B 3
Zaragoza (Mexico) **20** D 2
Zarasai **38** L 4
Zárate **24** F 6
Zarghūn Shahr **45** L 6
Zaria **56** D 3
Żary **36** D 2
Zāskār Mountains **45** N 6
Zatoka Gdańska **38** J 4
Zatoka Pomorska **36** C 2
Zavitinsk **42** J 6
Zavodoukovsk **40** P 6
Zavūyalova, Ostrov **43** N 5
Zaysan **45** O 3
Zduńska Wola **36** D 2
Zeitz **36** C 2
Zelenodolūsk **40** L 6
Zelenogorsk **38** L 3
Zelenokumsk **44** F 4
Zenica **34** D 2
Žepa **34** D 2
Zestapūoni **35** K 3
Zeya **42** J 6
Zeya (River) **42** J 6
Zeyskoye Vodokhranilishche **42** J 6
Zgorzelec **36** D 2
Zhalaghash **45** K 3
Zhalpaqtal **44** G 3
Zhangaözen **44** H 4
Zhangaqala **44** G 3
Zhangatas **45** L 4
Zhangbei **49** J 2
Zhangguangcai Ling **50** E 4
Zhangjiakou **49** J 2
Zhangpu **49** K 6
Zhangwu **50** D 4
Zhangye **48** G 3
Zhangzhou **49** K 6
Zhänibek **44** G 3
Zhanjiang **49** J 6
Zhaoan **49** K 6
Zhaodong **54** A 1
Zhaodong Hulan **50** E 3
Zhaoguang **54** A 1
Zhaojue **49** G 5
Zhaoqing **49** J 6
Zhaotong **49** G 5
Zhaoxing **54** B 1
Zhaoyuan **50** E 3
Zhaozhou **54** A 1
Zharkent **45** N 4
Zhashkiv **44** D 3
Zhaysang Köli **45** O 3
Zhayylma **45** K 2
Zhayyq **44** H 3
Zhejiang **49** L 5
Zhelezīnka **45** N 2
Zheleznogorsk **44** E 2
Zheleznogorsk-Ilimskiy **41** W 6
Zhenghe **49** K 5
Zhengzhou **49** J 4
Zhenjiang **49** K 4
Zhenlai **50** D 3
Zhenning **49** H 5
Zhenxiong **49** G 5
Zhenyuan **49** H 5
Zherdevka **44** F 2
Zhetiqara **45** K 2
Zhezkazgan **45** L 3
Zhigalovo **41** W 7
Zhigansk **42** H 3
Zhigulevsk **44** G 2
Zhijiang **49** H 5
Zhmerynka **36** F 3
Zhob **46** B 2
Zhodzina **36** F 2
Zholymbet **45** M 2
Zhong Xian **49** H 4
Zhongshan **49** J 6
Zhongwei **49** H 3
Zhongxiang **49** J 4
Zhosaly **45** K 3
Zhou Shan Dao **49** L 4
Zhou Shan Quandao **49** L 4
Zhoukouzhen **49** J 4
Zhovtnevoye **44** D 3
Zhujiang Kou **49** J 6
Zhukovka **36** G 2
Zhumadian **49** J 4
Zhuolu **50** C 4
Zhuoxian **49** K 3
Zhushan **49** J 4
Zhuzhou **49** J 5
Zhytomyr **36** F 2
Zibo **49** K 3
Zielona Góra **36** D 2
Zigong **49** G 5
Zihuatanejo **20** D 4
Zile **44** E 4
Žilina **36** D 3
Zima **41** W 7
Zimatlán de Alvaréz **20** E 4
Zimbabwe **58** B 3
Zinder **56** D 3
Zitácuaro **20** D 4
Ziyang **49** G 4
Zlatoust **40** N 6
Zlín **36** D 3
Zmeinogorsk **45** O 2
Znamenka (Kazakhstan) **45** N 2
Znamenka (Ukraine) **44** D 3
Znojmo **36** D 3
Zonguldak **35** D 4
Zrenjanin **36** E 3
Zuera **32** B 3
Zugdidi **44** F 4
Zujevka **40** M 6
Zunyi **49** H 5
Zürich **36** B 3
Zvolen **36** D 3
Zwickau **36** C 2
Zwolle **36** B 2
Zyryanka **43** O 3
Zyryanovsk **45** O 3
Żywiec **36** E 3

Maps of the World

Contents

Map no

THE WORLD
Legend 2–3
World, political; population; time zones 4–5

NORTH AMERICA
North America, political 6
Canada 7
Eastern Canada 8–9
Western Canada 10–11
USA 12–13
Eastern USA 14–15
Central USA 16–17
Western USA 18–19
Mexico 20–21
Central America and Caribbean 22

SOUTH AMERICA
South America, political 23
South America 24–25

EUROPE
Europe, political 26
British Isles 27
England and Wales 28–29
Scotland 30
Ireland 31
France 32
Spain and Portugal 33
Italy and The Balkans 34

Map no.

EUROPE (*Ctd.*)
Turkey 35
Central Europe 36–37
Scandinavia and The Baltic 38

ASIA
Asia, political 39
Northern Russia 40–41
Eastern Russia 42–43
Asia, Southwestern 44–45
India and Southeast Asia 46–47
Central Asia and China 48–49
Japan and East Asia 50–51
East Indies 52–53
Japan 54

AFRICA
Africa, political 55
Northern Africa 56–57
Southern Africa 58

AUSTRALIA
Oceania 59
Australia 60–61
New Zealand 62

POLAR REGIONS
Polar Regions 63

The World, Oceans 64

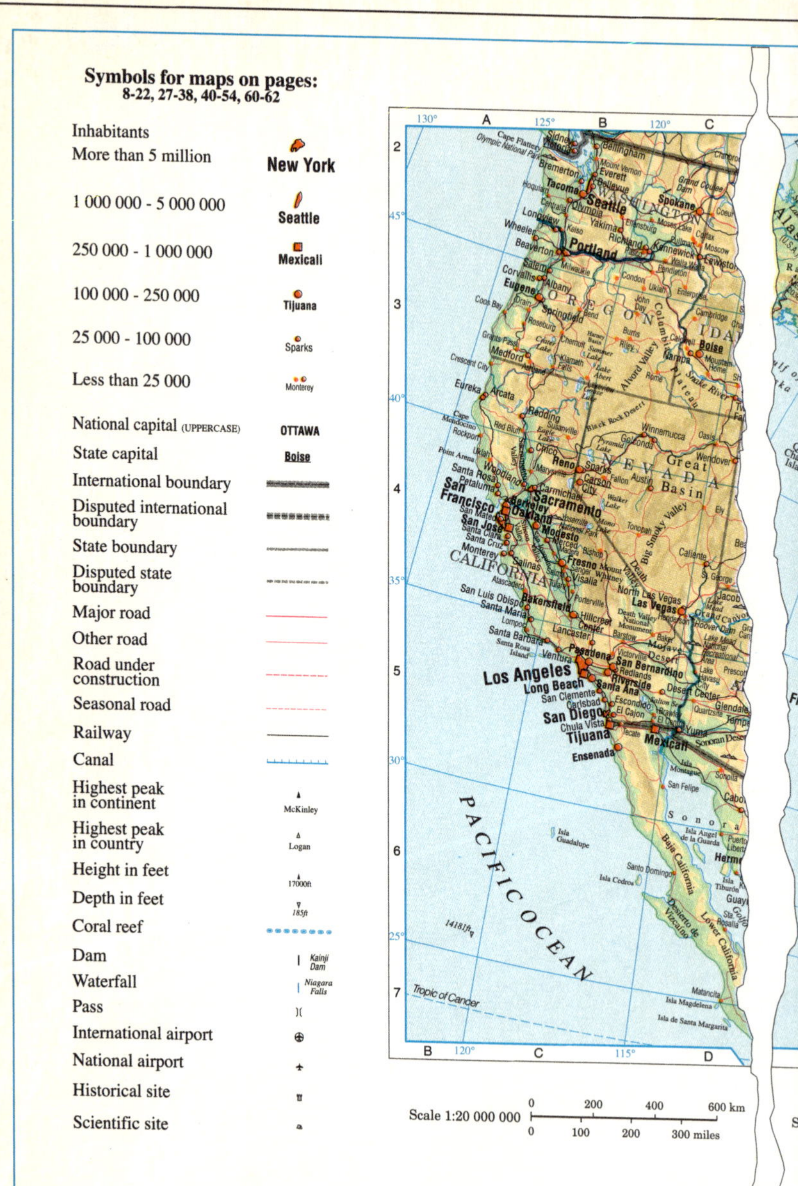

Symbols for maps on pages:
8-22, 27-38, 40-54, 60-62
Inhabitants
More than 5 million
New York
1 000 000 - 5 000 000
Seattle
250 000 - 1 000 000
Mexicali
100 000 - 250 000
Tijuana
25 000 - 100 000
Sparks
Less than 25 000
Monterey
National capital (UPPERCASE)
OTTAWA
State capital
Boise
International boundary
Disputed international boundary
State boundary
Disputed state boundary
Major road
Other road
Road under construction
Seasonal road
Railway
Canal
Highest peak in continent
McKinley
Highest peak in country
Logan
Height in feet
17000ft
Depth in feet
185ft
Coral reef
Dam
Kainji Dam
Waterfall
Niagara Falls
Pass
International airport
National airport
Historical site
Scientific site
WASHINGTON
OREGON
CALIFORNIA
NEVADA
Great Basin
PACIFIC OCEAN
Seattle
Portland
San Francisco
Sacramento
Oakland
San Jose
Los Angeles
Long Beach
San Diego
Tijuana
Mexicali
Las Vegas
Boise
Reno
Fresno
Tropic of Cancer
Scale 1:20 000 000
0 200 400 600 km
0 100 200 300 miles

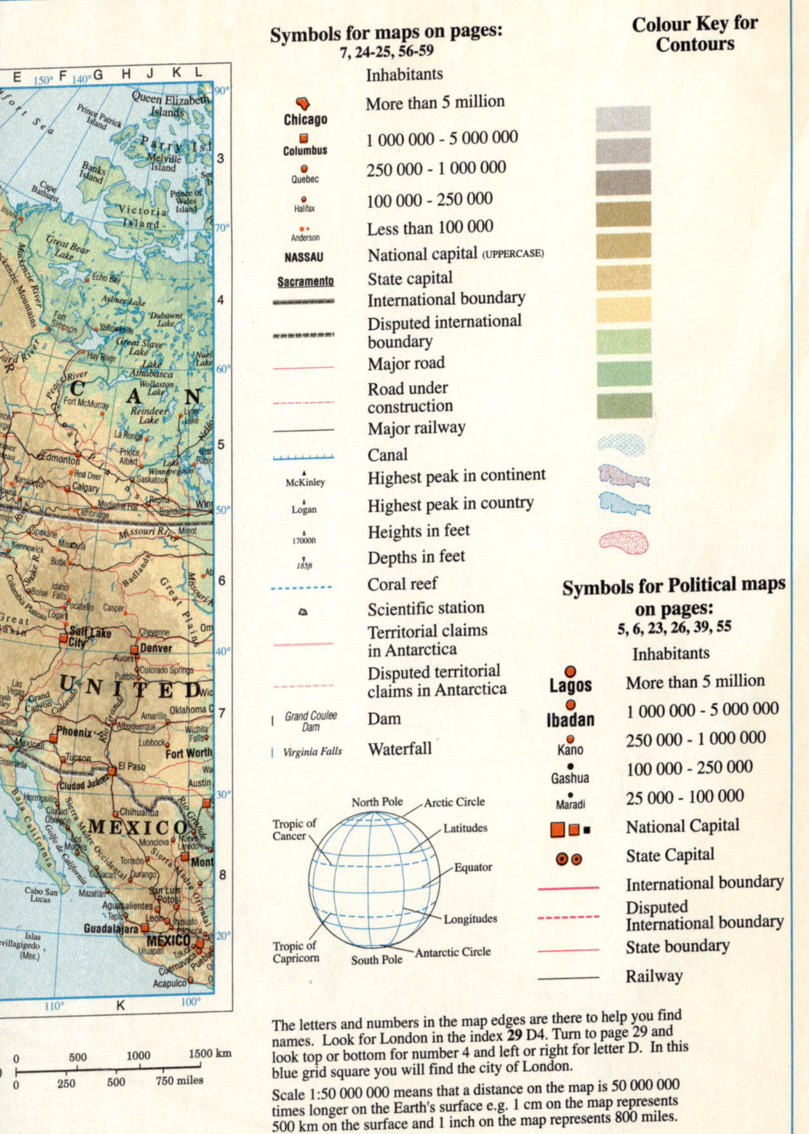
Symbols for maps on pages:
7, 24-25, 56-59
Inhabitants
Chicago
More than 5 million
Columbus
1 000 000 - 5 000 000
Quebec
250 000 - 1 000 000
Halifax
100 000 - 250 000
Anderson
Less than 100 000
NASSAU
National capital (UPPERCASE)
Sacramento
State capital
International boundary
Disputed international boundary
Major road
Road under construction
Major railway
Canal
McKinley
Highest peak in continent
Logan
Highest peak in country
17000ft
Heights in feet
185ft
Depths in feet
Coral reef
Scientific station
Territorial claims in Antarctica
Disputed territorial claims in Antarctica
Grand Coulee Dam
Dam
Virginia Falls
Waterfall
Colour Key for Contours
Symbols for Political maps on pages:
5, 6, 23, 26, 39, 55
Inhabitants
Lagos
More than 5 million
Ibadan
1 000 000 - 5 000 000
Kano
250 000 - 1 000 000
Gashua
100 000 - 250 000
Maradi
25 000 - 100 000
National Capital
State Capital
International boundary
Disputed International boundary
State boundary
Railway
North Pole
Arctic Circle
Tropic of Cancer
Latitudes
Equator
Longitudes
Tropic of Capricorn
South Pole
Antarctic Circle
The letters and numbers in the map edges are there to help you find names. Look for London in the index 29 D4. Turn to page 29 and look top or bottom for number 4 and left or right for letter D. In this blue grid square you will find the city of London.
Scale 1:50 000 000 means that a distance on the map is 50 000 000 times longer on the Earth's surface e.g. 1 cm on the map represents 500 km on the surface and 1 inch on the map represents 800 miles.
0 500 1000 1500 km
0 250 500 750 miles

The World Political

• National capital
International boundary

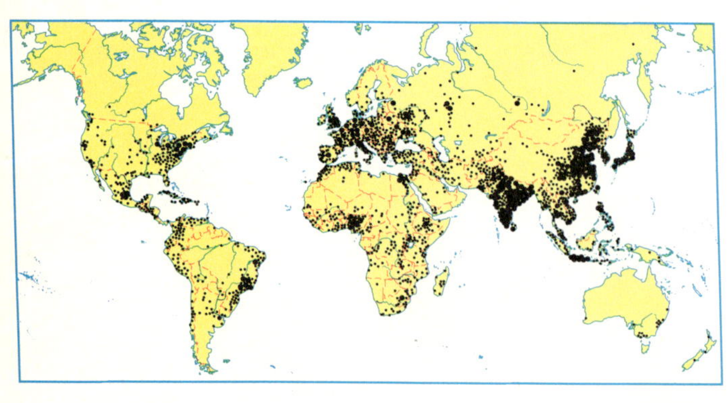

POPULATIO

• 10 million inhabitan
· 1 million inhabitan

The density of popul varies over the Earth's surface. Some parts sparsely populated bec of geographical condit high mountains, hot de or cold tundra. Compar maps on pages 8-9,1 Some parts are der populated due to good conditions, economica physically convenient f big cities, as well as reasons such as religi ethnic grouping. Popul growth is mainly centre the already densely populated areas.

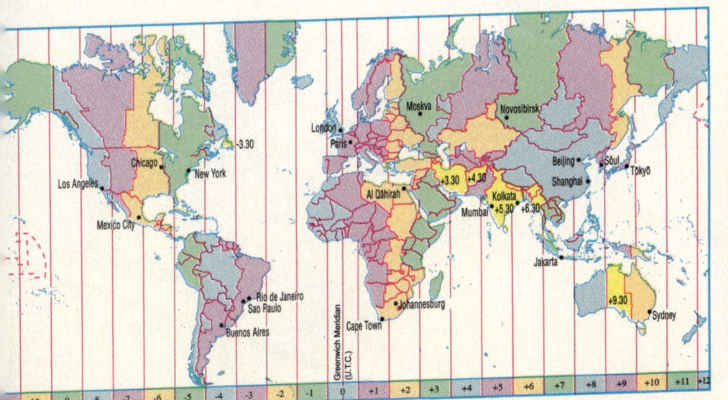
Moskva
Novosibirsk
London
Paris
-3.30
Chicago
New York
Los Angeles
Mexico City
Beijing
Sŏul
Tōkyō
Shanghai
+3.30
+4.30
Al Qāhirah
Kolkata
+5.30
+6.30
Mumbai
Jakarta
Rio de Janeiro
São Paulo
Buenos Aires
Cape Town
Johannesburg
+9.30
Sydney
Greenwich Meridian (U.T.C.)
-10 -9 -8 -7 -6 -5 -4 -3 -2 -1 0 +1 +2 +3 +4 +5 +6 +7 +8 +9 +10 +11 +12

TIME ZONES

The Earth spins around its axis anticlockwise and completes one turn every 24 hours. As the world rotates it is day on the part facing the Sun and night on the side in shadow. As shown on this map, we have divided the Earth into 24 standard time zones. They are based upon lines of longitude at 15 degree intervals but mainly follow country or state boundaries. You can compare times around the world by using the map. For example; when it is 12 noon in London it is 5 hours earlier in New York or 7 am.

North America Political

ARCTIC OCEAN
Beaufort Sea
Brooks Range
ALASKA (U.S.A.)
Alaska Range
Bering Strait
Norton Sound
Bristol Bay
Gulf of Alaska
Anchorage
Fairbanks
Juneau
YUKON TERRITORY
Whitehorse
NORTHWEST TERRITORIES
NUNAVUT
Great Bear Lake
Great Slave Lake
Yellowknife
Banks Island
Victoria Island
Queen Elizabeth Islands
Parry Islands
Devon Island
Baffin Island
Baffin Bay
Davis Strait
Hudson Bay
Hudson Strait
James Bay
Foxe Basin
Labrador Sea
CANADA
BRITISH COLUMBIA
ALBERTA
SASKATCHEWAN
MANITOBA
ONTARIO
QUÉBEC
LABRADOR
NEWFOUNDLAND
Rocky Mountains
Vancouver
Victoria
Edmonton
Calgary
Regina
Saskatoon
Winnipeg
Lake Winnipeg
Churchill
Toronto
Ottawa
Montréal
Québec
Gulf of St. Lawrence
Halifax
St. John's
PACIFIC OCEAN
NORTH ATLANTIC OCEAN
UNITED STATES
Seattle
Portland
San Francisco
Sacramento
Los Angeles
San Diego
Salt Lake City
Las Vegas
Phoenix
Denver
Minneapolis
Chicago
Detroit
Indianapolis
St. Louis
Kansas City
Dallas
Houston
San Antonio
New Orleans
Atlanta
Charlotte
Miami
Tampa
Orlando
Jacksonville
Washington DC
Philadelphia
New York
Boston
Pittsburgh
Columbus
Gulf of Mexico
Bermuda (U.K.)
Saragasso Sea
THE BAHAMAS
Havana
CUBA
JAMAICA
HAITI
DOMINICAN REPUBLIC
Port-au-Prince
Santo Domingo
PUERTO RICO (U.S.A.)
Caribbean Sea
MEXICO
Mexico City
Monterrey
Guadalajara
Tijuana
Golfo de California
Tropic of Cancer
BELIZE
GUATEMALA
HONDURAS
EL SALVADOR
NICARAGUA
COSTA RICA
PANAMA
COLOMBIA
Bogotá
VENEZUELA
Caracas
GUYANA
SURINAME
ECUADOR
Quito
PERU
Lima
BOLIVIA
La Paz
BRAZIL
Brasília
Manaus
Belém
Equator
Îles Marquises
FRENCH POLYNESIA (Fr.)

ARCTIC OCEAN
Beaufort Sea
Labrador Sea
Davis Strait
Baffin Bay
Hudson Bay
Hudson Strait
Foxe Channel
James Bay
Ungava Bay
Gulf of Alaska
Gulf of Boothia
Amundsen Gulf
Lancaster Sound
Viscount Melville Sound
Gulf of St Lawrence
Gulf of Maine
Queen Elizabeth Islands
North Magnetic Pole
Parry Islands
Melville Island
Bathurst Island
Devon Island
Ellesmere Island
Banks Island
Victoria Island
Prince of Wales Island
Baffin Island
Prince Charles Island
Southampton Island
Coats Island
Mansel Island
Belcher Islands
Akimiski Island
Cape Bathurst
Cape Tatnam
Cape Henrietta Maria
Cape Bauld
KALAALLIT NUNAAT (GREENLAND) (Den.)
Kong Christian IX Land
Kong Christian X Land
Kong Frederik VI Kyst
Arctic Circle
ICELAND
REYKJAVIK
NUUK (GODTHÅB)
Nunap Isua (Kap Farvel)
Iqaluit
Péninsule d'Ungava
Labrador
Schefferville
Happy Valley-Goose Bay
Newfoundland
St John's
Île d'Anticosti
Prince Edward I.
Cape Breton I.
St-Pierre et Miquelon (Fr.)
Sable Island
Halifax
Moncton
Charlottetown
Sydney
CANADA
UNITED STATES
Alaska (U.S.A.)
Brooks Range
Point Barrow
Yukon Flats
Fairbanks
Inuvik
Mackenzie Mountains
Klondike Plateau
Yukon Plateau
Yukon River
Whitehorse
Mount Logan
Juneau
Alexander Archipelago
Queen Charlotte Islands
Prince Rupert
Coast Mountains
Rocky Mountains
Mackenzie River
Great Bear Lake
Takijuk Lake
Horn Plateau
Fort Simpson
Virginia Falls
Liard River
Yellowknife
Great Slave Lake
Hay River
Alexandra Falls
Peace River
Lake Athabasca
Elizabeth Falls
Fort McMurray
Aberdeen Lake
Dubawnt Lake
Baker Lake
Nueltin Lake
Churchill
Port Nelson
Reindeer Lake
Lynn Lake
Southern Indian Lake
Gillam
Churchill Lake
La Ronge
Gods Lake
Severn River
Norway House
Island Lake
Lake Winnipeg
Lake Winnipegosis
Lake Manitoba
Lac Seul
Lake Nipigon
Albany River
Moosonee
Prince George
Edmonton
Red Deer
Calgary
Prince Albert
Saskatoon
Regina
Moose Jaw
Medicine Hat
Lethbridge
Brandon
Winnipeg
Kamloops
Kelowna
Port Hardy
Vancouver Island
Vancouver
Victoria
Cape Flattery
Seattle
Olympia
Mount Vernon
Tacoma
Portland
Spokane
Grand Coulee Dam
Kennewick
Columbia Plateau
Harney Basin
Eugene
Medford
Coast Range
Boise
Idaho Falls
Twin Falls
Pocatello
Missoula
Butte
Fort Peck Dam
Fort Peck Lake
Missouri River
Minot
Bismarck
Lake Oahe
Oahe Dam
Rapid City
Sioux Falls
Grand Forks
Valley City
Duluth
St Cloud
Minneapolis
St Paul
La Crosse
Wausau
Green Bay
Manitowoc
Madison
Milwaukee
Lake Michigan
Grand Rapids
Flint
Thunder Bay
Lake Superior
Lake Huron
Timmins
Matachewan
Detroit
London
Erie
Brampton
Hamilton
Toronto
Oshawa
Buffalo
Rochester
Syracuse
OTTAWA
Montréal
Québec
La Tuque
Chicoutimi
Port-Cartier
Uashat
Rimouski
St Lawrence
Appalachian Mountains
Albany
Springfield
Hartford
Yonkers
New Haven
Bridgeport
Newark
New York
Providence
Boston
Concord
Portsmouth
Portland
Saint John

Scale 1: 3 600 000

0 500 1000km

0 300 600miles

Eastern Canada

Greenland Sea
Kalaallit Nunaat (Greenland)
Kong Christian IX Land
Kong Christian X Land
Peary Land
Wandel Sea
Lincoln Sea
North Pole
International Date Line
Arctic Circle
Ellesmere Island
Devon Island
Baffin Bay
Davis Strait
Baffin Island
Parry Islands
Victoria Island
ARCTIC OCEAN
NUNAVUT

Scale 1: 23 000 000

0 250 500km
0 150 300miles

CANADA
Hudson Bay
Labrador Sea
Hudson Strait
Ungava Bay
James Bay
ATLANTIC OCEAN
QUÉBEC
ONTARIO
MANITOBA
NEWFOUNDLAND & LABRADOR
NOVA SCOTIA
Newfoundland
Cape Breton Island
Gulf of Saint Lawrence
Île d'Anticosti
MICHIGAN
WISCONSIN
MINNESOTA
IOWA
INDIANA
OTTAWA
Montréal
Québec
Toronto
Chicago
Detroit
Boston
Winnipeg
Thunder Bay
Halifax
St John's
Minneapolis
Cleveland
Milwaukee

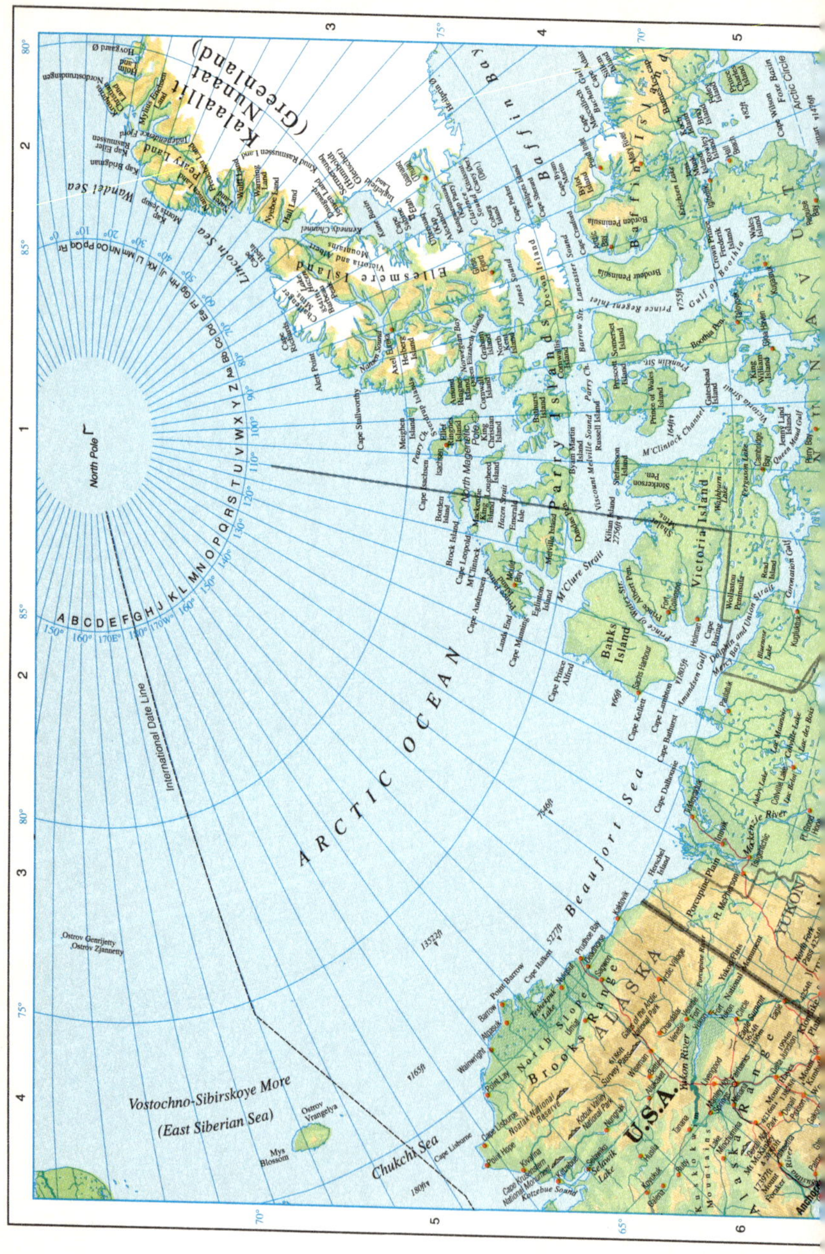
ARCTIC OCEAN
Beaufort Sea
Chukchi Sea
Vostochno-Sibirskoye More
(East Siberian Sea)
Ostrov Vrangelya
International Date Line
North Pole
Kalaallit Nunaat (Greenland)
Lincoln Sea
Wandel Sea
Ellesmere Island
Baffin Bay
Baffin Island
Parry Islands
Banks Island
Victoria Island
Devon Island
Somerset Island
Prince of Wales Island
M'Clintock Channel
M'Clure Strait
Viscount Melville Sound
Lancaster Sound
Gulf of Boothia
Amundsen Gulf
ALASKA
U.S.A.
Brooks Range
North Slope
YUKON
Mackenzie River
Porcupine Plain
Kotzebue Sound
Cape Lisburne
Point Hope
Point Barrow
Barrow
Wainwright
Prudhoe Bay
Herschel Island
Arctic Circle

Scale 1: 23 000 000

0 250 500km

0 150 300miles

C A N A D A
UNITED STATES
Hudson Bay
PACIFIC OCEAN
Gulf of Alaska
BRITISH COLUMBIA
ALBERTA
SASKATCHEWAN
MANITOBA
ONTARIO
NORTH DAKOTA
SOUTH DAKOTA
MONTANA
WYOMING
IDAHO
WASHINGTON
OREGON
CALIFORNIA
NEBRASKA
MINNESOTA
IOWA
WISCONSIN
Vancouver
Victoria
Seattle
Portland
Calgary
Edmonton
Regina
Saskatoon
Winnipeg
Minneapolis
St Paul
Thunder Bay
Vancouver Island
Queen Charlotte Islands
Alexander Archipelago

PACIFIC OCEAN
Vancouver Island
Vancouver
Victoria
Seattle
Tacoma
Spokane
Portland
Eugene
Salem
Medford
Calgary
Lethbridge
Saskatoon
Regina
BRITISH COLUMBIA
ALBERTA
SASKATCHEWAN
C
A
WASH
OREGON
IDAHO
Boise
MONTANA
Great Falls
Missoula
Butte
Billings
Bismarck
NORTH
SOUTH
Rapid City
WYOMING
Casper
Cheyenne
ROCKY MOUNTAINS
NEVADA
Great Basin
Reno
Carson City
Salt Lake City
Ogden
Provo
UTAH
NEBRAS
Denver
Aurora
Boulder
Colorado Springs
Pueblo
COLORADO
Grand Junction
San Francisco
Oakland
Sacramento
San Jose
Modesto
Fresno
CALIFORNIA
Bakersfield
Las Vegas
Los Angeles
Long Beach
Pasadena
San Bernardino
Riverside
Santa Ana
San Diego
Tijuana
Ensenada
Mexicali
ARIZONA
Phoenix
Mesa
Tucson
Flagstaff
Colorado Plateau
NEW MEXICO
Santa Fe
Albuquerque
Amarillo
Lubbock
El Paso
Ciudad Juárez
UNITE
Hermosillo
Chihuahua
Ciudad Obregón
Los Mochis
Culiacán
Mazatlán
Durango
Torreón
Saltillo
Tepic
San Luis Potosí
MEXICO
Baja California
Golfo de California
Lower California
Tropic of Cancer
Hawaiian Islands
Kauai
Oahu
Honolulu
Hawaii
Hawaii (U.S.A.)
Scale 1: 25 640 000
RUSSIA
Koryakskiy Khrebet
International Date Line
Bering Sea
Aleutian Islands (U.S.A.)
Alaska (U.S.A.)
Brooks Range
Alaska Range
Anchorage
Gulf of Alaska
Mackenzie Mountains
Scale 1: 52 630 000

Scale 1: 22 115 000

0 200 400 600 800 1000km

0 100 200 300 400 500 600miles

ONTARIO
QUÉBEC
NEW BRUNSWICK
WISCONSIN
MICHIGAN
MISSOURI
STATES
ATLANTIC OCEAN
Gulf of Mexico
Gulf of Maine
Lake Superior
Lake Michigan
Lake Huron
Thunder Bay
Duluth
St. Paul
Milwaukee
Green Bay
Grand Rapids
Chicago
Detroit
Toledo
Cleveland
Lansing
Ann Arbor
Gary
South Bend
Fort Wayne
Davenport
Peoria
Springfield
Indianapolis
Dayton
Columbus
Cincinnati
Louisville
Lexington
Evansville
St. Louis
Kansas City
Independence
Springfield
Memphis
Nashville
Knoxville
Chattanooga
Huntsville
Birmingham
Atlanta
Augusta
Macon
Columbus
Montgomery
Jackson
Shreveport
Little Rock
Baton Rouge
New Orleans
Mobile
Pensacola
Tallahassee
Jacksonville
Daytona Beach
Orlando
Tampa
St. Petersburg
Fort Myers
Fort Lauderdale
West Palm Beach
Hialeah
Miami
Savannah
Charleston
Columbia
Charlotte
Greensboro
Winston-Salem
Durham
Raleigh
Fayetteville
Wilmington
Norfolk
Virginia Beach
Portsmouth
Richmond
Charleston
Pittsburgh
Youngstown
Akron
Canton
Erie
Buffalo
Rochester
Syracuse
Albany
Scranton
Allentown
Harrisburg
Baltimore
WASHINGTON
Philadelphia
Trenton
Newark
New York
Yonkers
Bridgeport
New Haven
Hartford
Springfield
Providence
Boston
Portland
Toronto
Hamilton
Kitchener
London
Windsor
Oshawa
OTTAWA
Montréal
Québec
Sherbrooke
Fredericton
Saint John
Halifax
Timmins
Sudbury
Atlantic City
DELAWARE
NEW JERSEY
MARYLAND
ARKANSAS
LOUISIANA
Beaumont
Galveston
Lafayette
Pinar del Rio
LA HABANA (HAVANA)
Matanzas
CUBA
Santa Clara
Cienfuegos
Camagüey
Holguín
Santiago de Cuba
Guantánamo
THE BAHAMAS
NASSAU
Freeport
Yucatan Peninsula
Mérida
Cancún
Tropic of Cancer
Indias Occidentales (West Indies)
Cayman Islands (U.K.)

Eastern USA

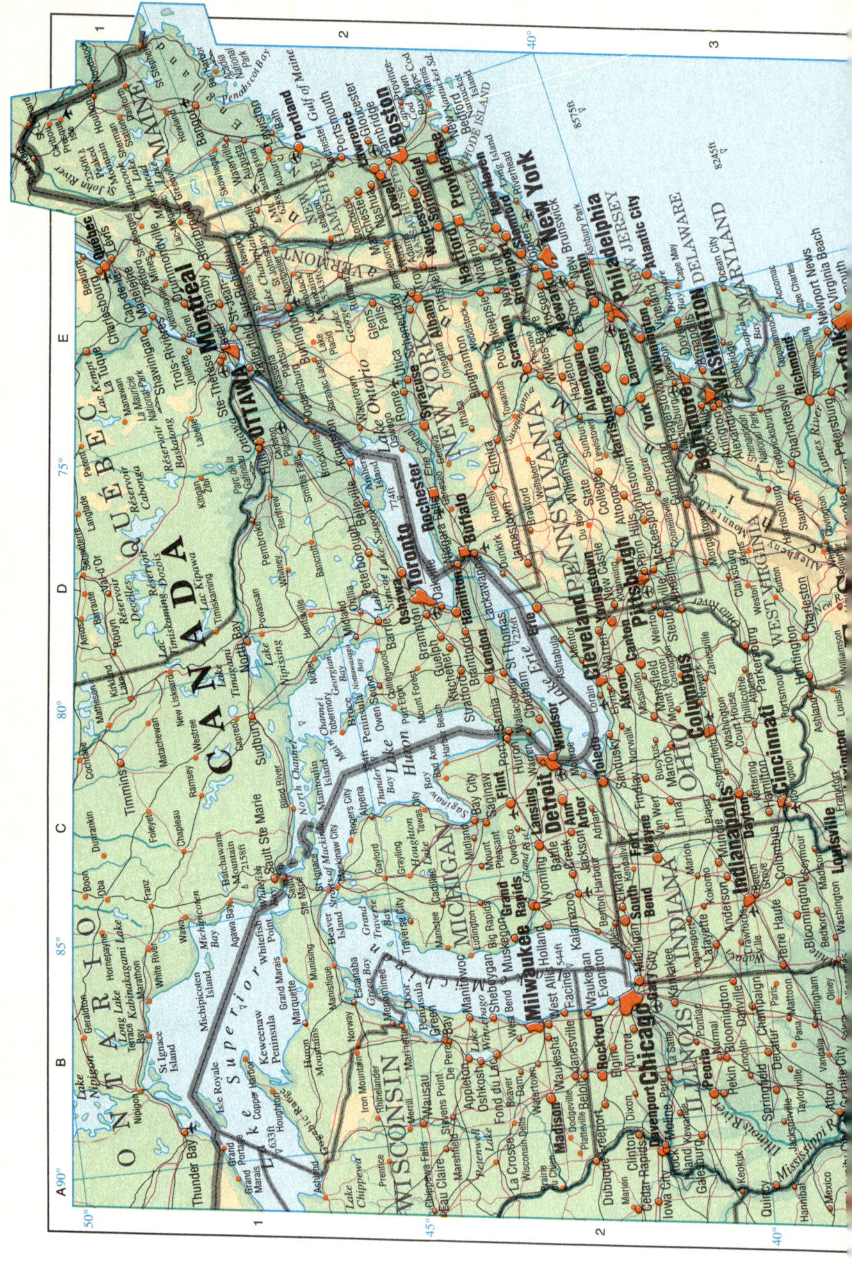
CANADA
QUEBEC
ONTARIO
MAINE
NEW HAMPSHIRE
VERMONT
MASSACHUSETTS
RHODE ISLAND
CONNECTICUT
NEW YORK
NEW JERSEY
PENNSYLVANIA
DELAWARE
MARYLAND
WEST VIRGINIA
VIRGINIA
OHIO
INDIANA
ILLINOIS
MICHIGAN
WISCONSIN
OTTAWA
WASHINGTON
Montreal
Quebec
Toronto
Boston
New York
Philadelphia
Baltimore
Pittsburgh
Cleveland
Detroit
Chicago
Milwaukee
Buffalo
Rochester
Columbus
Cincinnati
Indianapolis
Louisville
Portland
Providence
Hartford
Albany
Syracuse
Richmond
Lake Superior
Lake Michigan
Lake Huron
Lake Erie
Lake Ontario
Georgian Bay
Gulf of Maine
Thunder Bay
Sault Ste Marie
Sudbury
Hamilton
London
Windsor
Toledo
Akron
Dayton
Fort Wayne
South Bend
Grand Rapids
Lansing
Flint
Madison
Rockford
Peoria
Springfield
Newark
Trenton
Atlantic City
Harrisburg
Scranton
Erie
Dover
Annapolis
Norfolk
Newport News
Virginia Beach
Charleston
Huntington
Ohio River
Mississippi River
Illinois River
A
B
C
D
E
1
2
3
50°
45°
40°
75°
80°
85°
90°

Scale 1: 11 500 000

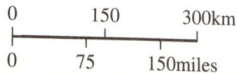

0 150 300km

0 75 150miles

Central USA

Sacle 1: 11 500 000

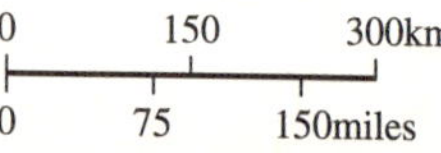
0
150
300km
0
75
150miles

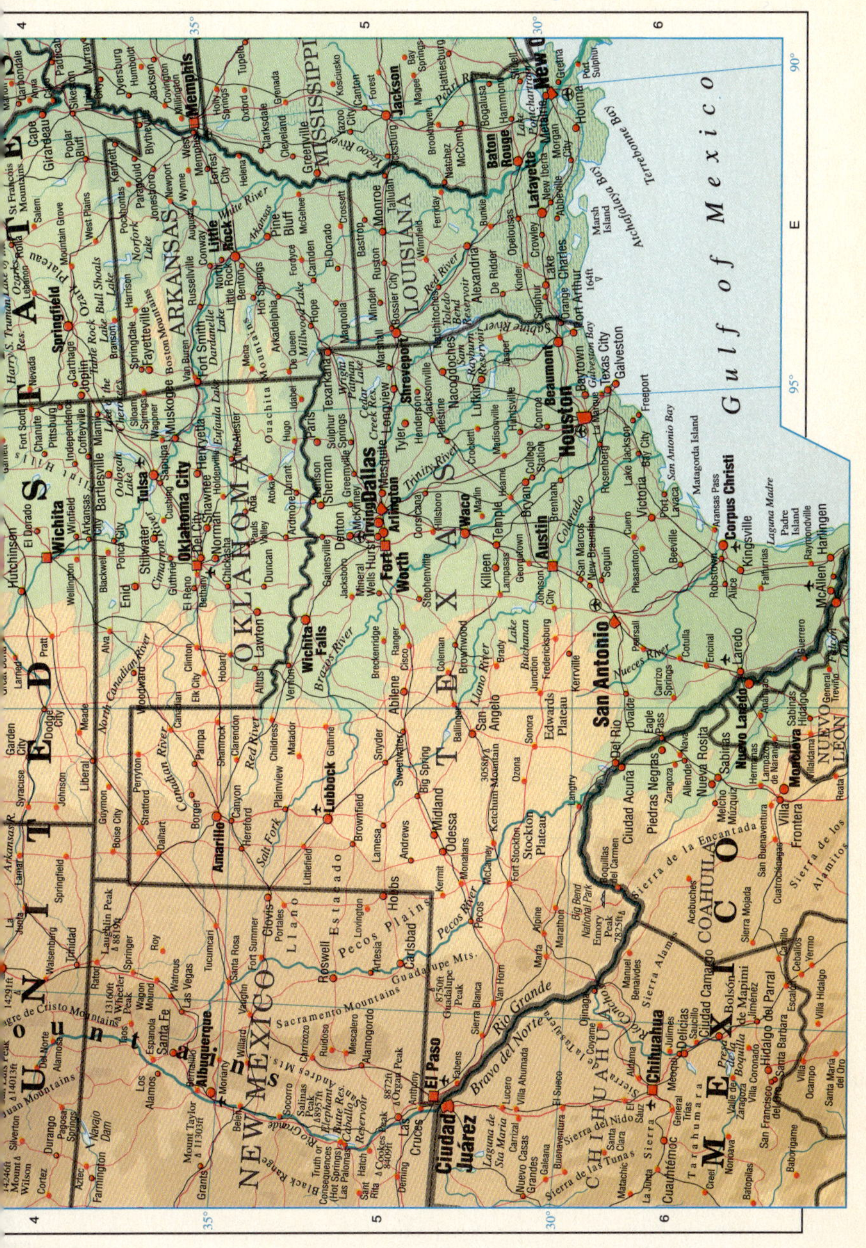
UNITED STATES
MEXICO
Gulf of Mexico
NEW MEXICO
OKLAHOMA
TEXAS
ARKANSAS
LOUISIANA
MISSISSIPPI
CHIHUAHUA
COAHUILA
NUEVO LEÓN
Memphis
Little Rock
Springfield
Wichita
Tulsa
Oklahoma City
Amarillo
Lubbock
Albuquerque
Santa Fe
El Paso
Ciudad Juárez
Chihuahua
Dallas
Fort Worth
Arlington
Irving
Waco
Austin
San Antonio
Houston
Beaumont
Shreveport
Jackson
Baton Rouge
Lafayette
Corpus Christi
Laredo
Nuevo Laredo
Monclova
Wichita Falls
Abilene
Midland
Odessa
Galveston
Rio Grande
Red River
Pecos River
Brazos River
Colorado
Sacramento Mountains
Guadalupe Mts.
Llano Estacado
Pecos Plains
Edwards Plateau
Stockton Plateau
Ouachita Mountains
Ozark Plateau
Boston Mountains
Sierra Madre
Matagorda Island
Padre Island
Laguna Madre
Terrebonne Bay
Atchafalaya Bay
Galveston Bay
San Antonio Bay
4
5
6
35°
30°
95°
90°
E

Scale 1: 11 500 000

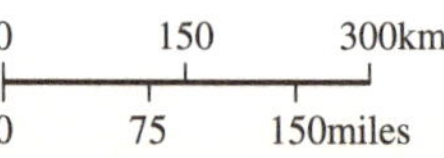
0
150
300km
0
75
150miles

UNITED STATES
NEW MEXICO
ARIZONA
MEXICO
SONORA
CHIHUAHUA
BAJA CALIFORNIA NORTE
BAJA CALIFORNIA SUR
PACIFIC OCEAN
Golfo de California
Colorado Plateau
Painted Desert
Sonoran Desert
Sacramento Mountains
Guadalupe Mts.
Sangre de Cristo Mountains
San Juan Mountains
Black Range
Sierra Madre Occidental
Sierra Tarahumara
Sierra de San Borjas
Sierra Vizcaíno
Sierra de la Giganta
Desierto de Vizcaíno
Rio Grande
Bravo del Norte
Gila River
Salt River
Little Colorado R.
Rio Yaqui
Rio Sonora
Rio Conchos
Los Angeles
Long Beach
San Diego
Tijuana
Ensenada
Mexicali
Las Vegas
Bakersfield
Santa Barbara
Riverside
San Bernardino
Pasadena
Palm Springs
Phoenix
Mesa
Scottsdale
Tucson
Flagstaff
Yuma
Nogales
Albuquerque
Santa Fe
El Paso
Ciudad Juárez
Roswell
Carlsbad
Las Cruces
Chihuahua
Hermosillo
Guaymas
Ciudad Obregón
Los Mochis
Navojoa
Delicias
Hidalgo del Parral
Cuauhtémoc
Death Valley
Grand Canyon
Lake Mead
Hoover Dam
Salton Sea
Channel Islands
Santa Catalina Island
San Clemente Island
Isla Cedros
Isla Guadalupe (Mex.)
Isla Tiburón
Isla Angel de la Guarda
Los Alamos
Gallup
Farmington
Durango
Lordsburg
Deming
Alamogordo
Douglas
Agua Prieta
Caborca
Puerto Libertad
Santa Rosalía
Mulegé
Loreto
San Felipe
San Quintín
Punta Eugenia
4
5
6
B
C
35°
30°
25°
115°
120°

B
110°
C
105°
D
1
2
3
4
5
30°
25°
20°
15°
San Diego
Tijuana
Mexicali
Ensenada
El Centro
Sonoran Desert
ARIZONA
Tucson
Organ Pipe Cactus National Monument
NEW MEXICO
El Paso
Ciudad Juárez
Las Cruces
Roswell
Lubbock
Carlsbad
Hobbs
Midland
Odessa
Big Spring
Pecos
Stockton Plateau
Nogales
Agua Prieta
Caborca
Hermosillo
SONORA
Guaymas
Empalme
Ciudad Obregón
Navojoa
Los Mochis
Culiacán
SINALOA
Mazatlán
CHIHUAHUA
Chihuahua
Delicias
Ciudad Camargo
Hidalgo del Parral
Cuauhtémoc
Bolsón de Mapimí
COAHUILA
Monclova
Saltillo
Torreón
Gómez Palacio
DURANGO
Durango
Sierra Madre Occidental
Mexican Highlands
ZACATECAS
Zacatecas
Fresnillo
MÉXICO
Aguascalientes
León
Guadalajara
JALISCO
NAYARIT
Tepic
Puerto Vallarta
Manzanillo
COLIMA
Colima
MICHOACÁN
Uruapan
Morelia
Acapulco
BAJA CALIFORNIA NORTE
BAJA CALIFORNIA SUR
Baja California
Lower California
Golfo de California
Isla Tiburón
Isla Angel de la Guarda
Isla Cedros
Santa Rosalía
Loreto
La Paz
Cabo San Lucas
San José del Cabo
Isla Magdelena
Tropic of Cancer
Islas Marías
Islas Revillagigedo (Mex.)
Isla San Benedicto
Isla Roca Partida
Isla Socorro
PACIFIC OCEAN

Scale 1: 14 720 000

0 200 400km

0 100 200miles

E
F
G
H
95°
90°
85°
1
2
3
4
5
30°
25°
20°
15°
ARKANSAS
MISSISSIPPI
ALABAMA
GEORGIA
LOUISIANA
FLORIDA
U N I T E D S T A T E S
Dallas
Fort Worth
Arlington
Shreveport
Jackson
Montgomery
Columbus
Macon
Savannah
Birmingham
Houston
Beaumont
Austin
Baton Rouge
Lafayette
New Orleans
Biloxi
Mobile
Pensacola
Tallahassee
Jacksonville
Tampa
St Petersburg
Lakeland
Corpus Christi
Matamoros
Gulf of Mexico
LA HABANA (HAVANA)
Marianao
CUBA
Pinar del Río
Canal de Yucatán
YUCATÁN
Mérida
Cancún
Yucatan Peninsula
Campeche
CAMPECHE
QUINTANA ROO
Bahía de Campeche
TABASCO
Ciudad del Carmen
Coatzacoalcos
Minatitlán
Villahermosa
BELIZE
Belize
Ciudad Madero
Tampico
Poza Rica de Hidalgo
VERACRUZ
Jalapa Enríquez
Veracruz
Orizaba
OAXACA
Oaxaca
CHIAPAS
Tuxtla Gutiérrez
Golfo de Tehuantepec
GUATEMALA
Guatemala
HONDURAS
San Pedro Sula
TEGUCIGALPA
SAN SALVADOR
Santa Ana
San Miguel
EL SALVADOR
NICARAGUA
Mississippi Delta
Dry Tortugas

22 Central America and Caribbean

ATLANTIC OCEAN
Sargasso Sea
Tropic of Cancer
Gulf of Mexico
Caribbean Sea
PACIFIC OCEAN
UNITED STATES
MEXICO
CUBA
THE BAHAMAS
JAMAICA
HAITI
DOMINICAN REPUBLIC
BELIZE
GUATEMALA
HONDURAS
EL SALVADOR
NICARAGUA
COSTA RICA
PANAMA
COLOMBIA
VENEZUELA
GUYANA
BRAZIL
ANTIGUA AND BARBUDA
ST KITTS AND NEVIS
DOMINICA
ST LUCIA
BARBADOS
ST. VINCENT AND THE GRENADINES
GRENADA
TRINIDAD AND TOBAGO
Indias Occidentales (West Indies)
Antillas Mayores (Greater Antilles)
Antillas Menores (Lesser Antilles)
Turks and Caicos Islands
Netherlands Antilles
LA HABANA (HAVANA)
NASSAU
PORT-AU-PRINCE
SANTO DOMINGO
KINGSTON
MÉXICO
GUATEMALA
TEGUCIGALPA
SAN SALVADOR
MANAGUA
SAN JOSÉ
PANAMÁ
BOGOTÁ
CARACAS
Miami
Houston
New Orleans
Monterrey
Acapulco
Mérida
Santiago de Cuba
Maracaibo
Medellín
Cali
Barranquilla
Cartagena
Valencia
San Juan

Scale 1: 30 670 000

0 500 1000km

0 300 600miles

BRAZIL
COLOMBIA
VENEZUELA
PERU
BOLIVIA
PARAGUAY
URUGUAY
ARGENTINA
CHILE
ECUADOR
GUYANA
SURINAME
FRENCH GUIANA (Fr.)
Caribbean Sea
PACIFIC OCEAN
SOUTH ATLANTIC OCEAN
Tropic of Capricorn
Equator
Brasília
Rio de Janeiro
São Paulo
Salvador
Belém
Manaus
Fortaleza
Recife
Bogotá
Caracas
Quito
Lima
La Paz
Sucre
Asunción
Buenos Aires
Montevideo
Santiago
Georgetown
Paramaribo
Cayenne
Falkland Islands (Islas Malvinas) (U.K.)
South Georgia (U.K.)
Patagonia
Cabo de Hornos (Cape Horn)

Scale 1: 35 937 500

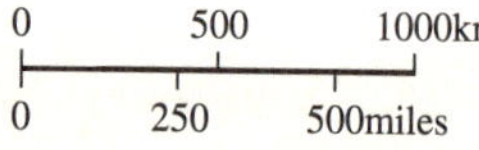
0
500
1000km
0
250
500miles

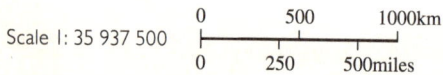

PACIFIC OCEAN
ATLANTIC OCEAN
Tropic of Capricorn
PARAGUAY
ASUNCIÓN
URUGUAY
MONTEVIDEO
ARGENTINA
BUENOS AIRES
La Plata
Mar del Plata
Rosario
Santa Fé
Córdoba
San Miguel de Tucumán
Bahía Blanca
Pampas
CHILE
SANTIAGO
Valparaíso
Viña del Mar
Concepción
Talcahuano
Temuco
Valdivia
Osorno
Puerto Montt
Isla de Chiloé
Antofagasta
Desierto do Atacama (Atacama Desert)
Mendoza
Rio de Janeiro
São Paulo
Santos
Campinas
Curitiba
Porto Alegre
Lagoa dos Patos
Lagoa Mirim
Golfo San Matías
Golfo de San Jorge
Gran Altiplanicie Central
Strait of Magellan
Punta Arenas
Rio Gallegos
Isla Grande de Tierra del Fuego
Cape Horn
Falkland Islands (Islas Malvinas) (U.K.)
Stanley
South Georgia (U.K.)
Archipiélago Juan Fernández (Chile)
Galapagos Islands (Islas Galápagos) (Ecu.)
Equator
Isla Isabela
Isla Fernandina
Isla Santa Cruz
Isla San Cristóbal
Isla Santa María
Scale 1: 13 300 000

KALAALLIT NUNAAT
(GREENLAND)
(Denmark)
Ittoqqortoormiit
(Scoresbysund)
Denmark Strait
Arctic Circle
ICELAND
Reykjavík
Akureyri
Seyðisfjörður
Vestmannaeyjar
Surtsey
Jan Mayen
(Norway)
FØROYAR
Faroe Islands
(Den.)
Tórshavn
Shetland Is.
Orkney Is.
Hebrides
Rockall
(U.K.)
Norwegian
Sea
NORTH
ATLANTIC
OCEAN
NORWAY
Bergen
Stavanger
Ålesund
Trondheim
Namsos
Mo i Rana
Bodø
Narvik
Tromsø
Hammerfest
Nordkapp
Vardø
Kirkenes
Oslo
Hamar
SWEDEN
Kiruna
Haparanda
Luleå
Skellefteå
Umeå
Östersund
Gävle
Stockholm
Örebro
Göteborg
Malmö
Gotland
Öland
FINLAND
Rovaniemi
Kemi
Oulu
Kuopio
Vaasa
Tampere
Turku
Helsinki
UNITED
KINGDOM
Edinburgh
Manchester
Liverpool
Birmingham
London
Southampton
IRELAND
Dublin
Cork
North
Sea
DENMARK
Århus
Copenhagen
NETHER-
LANDS
Amsterdam
Rotterdam
BELGIUM
Brussels
LUX.
FRANCE
Paris
Brest
Bordeaux
Toulouse
Lyon
Marseille
Nice
Strasbourg
Bay of Biscay
SPAIN
Madrid
Bilbao
Zaragoza
Barcelona
Valencia
Murcia
Sevilla
Palma
Mallorca
AND.
PORTUGAL
Lisbon
Porto
Strait of Gibraltar
GIBRALTAR
(U.K.)
Tanger
Oran
Algiers
Constantine
Tunis
ALGERIA
TUNISIA
MOROCCO
Mediterranean
Sea
Corsica
Sardinia
Sicily
Messina
MALTA
Valletta
GERMANY
Hamburg
Berlin
München
SWITZ.
Bern
AUSTRIA
Vienna
LIECH.
ITALY
Milano
Rome
Napoli
VAT.
S.M.
SLOVENIA
Ljubljana
CROATIA
Zagreb
B.-H.
Sarajevo
YUGOSLAVIA
Belgrade
ALB.
Tiranë
MACE.
GREECE
Athens
Crete
CZECH REP.
Prague
SLOVAKIA
Bratislava
HUNG.
Budapest
POLAND
Łódź
Warsaw
Kraków
ROMANIA
Bucharest
MOL.
Chisinau
BULG.
Sofia
TURKEY
İstanbul
Bursa
İzmir
Ankara
Konya
Adana
CYPRUS
Nicosia
SYRIA
Halab
Al Mawşil
Euphrates
IRAN
Tehran
Tabriz
Kirkūk
GEORGIA
Tbilisi
ARMENIA
Yerevan
AZERBAIJAN
Baku
Black Sea
Sea of Azov
Yalta
Simferopol'
Odesa
UKRAINE
Kiev
Kharkiv
Dnipropetrovs'k
Donets'k
BELARUS
Minsk
Homyel'
Vitsyebsk
LITHUANIA
Vilnius
LATVIA
Riga
ESTONIA
Tallinn
RUSSIA
Baltic
Sea
Moscow
Sankt-Peterburg
Novgorod
Tver'
Yaroslavl'
Kostroma
Ivanovo
Smolensk
Bryansk
Kursk
Orel
Tula
Lipetsk
Voronezh
Rostov-na-Donu
Krasnodar
Groznyy
Volgograd
Saratov
Penza
Saransk
Ul'yanovsk
Samara
Sterlitamak
Ufa
Orenburg
Kazan'
Nizhniy Novgorod
Vologda
Rybinsk
Kirov
Glazov
Perm'
Kotlas
Syktyvkar
Ukhta
Pechora
Nar'yan Mar
Vorkuta
Amderma
Indiga
Mezen'
O. Kolguyev
Arkhangel'sk
Severnaya Dvina
Onega
Belomorsk
Petrozavodsk
Xonosha
White Sea
Murmansk
Kola
Peninsula
Kandalaksha
Ural Mountains
Volga
Don
KAZAKHSTAN
Zheyyq
Atyrau
Astrakhan'
Aktau
Caspian Sea
Arctic Circle
60°
45°
30°
15°E
0°
15°W

A
B
C
D
E
F
G
H
12°
10°
8°
6°
4°
2°
0°
1
2
3
4
5
6
60°
58°
56°
54°
52°
ATLANTIC OCEAN
Shetland Islands (U.K.)
Unst
Fetlar
Yell
Ronas Hill 1476ft
St Magnus Bay
Papa Stour
Mainland
Whalsay
Foula
Lerwick
Bressay
Sumburgh Head
Fair Isle
North Rona
Sula Sgeir
Sule Skerry
Stack Skerry
Westray
Rousay
Papa Westray
North Ronaldsay
Sanday
Stronsay
Orkney Islands (U.K.)
Mainland
Hoy
Kirkwall
Pentland Firth
South Ronaldsay
Duncansby Head
Thurso
Wick
Butt of Lewis
Cape Wrath
Strathy Point
Ben Hope 3041ft
Flannan Islands
Stornoway
Isle of Lewis
North Minch
Outer Hebrides
Sound of Harris
Little Minch
St Kilda
North Uist
South Uist
Barra
Ullapool
North West Highlands
Loch Shin
Moray Firth
Skye
Kyle of Lochalsh
Inverness
Loch Ness
Kinnaird Head
Rattray Head
SCOTLAND
Aberdeen
Monadhliath Mountains
Ben Macdui 4294ft
Dee
Glas Maol 3505ft
Grampian Mountains
Ben Nevis 4408ft
Loch Tay
Tay
Sea of the Hebrides
Rhum
Eigg
Muck
Coll
Tiree
Iona
Mull
Inner Hebrides
Firth of Lorn
Colonsay
Jura
Islay
Loch Lomond
Loch Fyne
Perth
Dundee
North Sea
Stirling
Glenrothes
Alloa
Dunfermline
Firth of Forth
Kirkcaldy
Fife Ness
Glasgow
Edinburgh
Paisley
Motherwell
Kilmarnock
Arran
Kintyre
Sound of Jura
Firth of Clyde
Ayr
Southern Uplands
Tweed
Merrick 2765ft
Cheviot Hills
The Cheviot 2676ft
UNITED KINGDOM
Dumfries
Hadrian's Wall
Malin Head
Bloody Foreland
Aran Island
Errigal Mountain 2467ft
Rathlin I.
Lough Foyle
Londonderry
Ballymena
Rossan Point
Lavagh More 2211ft
NORTHERN IRELAND
Larne
North Channel
Donegal Bay
Ulster
Lower Lough Erne
Lough Neagh
Newtownabbey
Bangor
Belfast
Erris Head
Downpatrick Head
Upper Lough Erne
Achill Head
Lough Conn
Clew Bay
Mourne Mountains 2795ft
Dundalk (Dún Dealgan)
Dundalk Bay
Slyne Head
Connaught
Lough Ree
Meath
Lough Corrib
Galway (Gaillimh)
Galway Bay
Aran Islands
Hags Head
Royal Canal
Grand Canal
IRELAND (EIRE)
DUBLIN (BAILE ÁTHA CLIATH)
Dún Laoghaire
Shannon
Leinster
Wicklow Mountains
Wicklow Head
Loop Head
Mouth of the Shannon
Kerry Head
Tralee Bay
Limerick (Luimneach)
Munster
Mount Leinster 2612ft
Suir
Blackwater
Waterford (Port Láirge)
Dingle Bay
Carrauntoohil 3414ft
Cork (Corcaigh)
Rosslare
Carnsore Point
Dursey Island
Caha Mountains
Bantry Bay
Mizen Head
Old Head of Kinsale
Clear Island
Celtic Sea
Irish Sea
Isle of Man
Carmel Head
Anglesey
Holyhead
Caernarfon Bay
Snowdon 3559ft
Braich y Pwll
Cardigan Bay
Cahore Point
St George's Channel
Fishguard
St David's Head
Scotland
Blyth
Newcastle-upon-Tyne
South Shields
Sunderland
Tyne
Durham
Hartlepool
Middlesbrough
Darlington
Tees
Solway Firth
Carlisle
Workington
Whitehaven
Lake District
Scafell Pike
Windermere
Pennines
Scarborough
Bridlington
Bridlington Bay
Douglas
Barrow-in-Furness
Lancaster
Morecambe Bay
Fleetwood
Blackpool
Harrogate
York
Leeds
Halifax
Bradford
Preston
Blackburn
Huddersfield
Kingston-upon-Hull
Liverpool
Birkenhead
Bolton
Oldham
Manchester
Sheffield
Grimsby
Spurn Head
Humber
Colwyn Bay
Chester
Macclesfield
Chesterfield
Mansfield
Lincoln
Wrexham
Crewe
Stoke-on-Trent
Nottingham
Boston
The Wash
Grantham
Shrewsbury
Stafford
Derby
Trent
Wolverhampton
Walsall
Leicester
ENGLAND
King's Lynn
Norwich
WALES
Dudley
Birmingham
Coventry
Peterborough
Great Yarmouth
Lowestoft
Cambrian Mountains
Wye
Severn
Great Malvern
Worcester
Northampton
Bury St Edmunds
Banbury
Hereford
Bedford
Cambridge
Ipswich
Cheltenham
Felixstowe
Harwich
Clacton-on-Sea
Llanelli
Rhondda
Merthyr Tydfil
Gloucester
Oxford
Luton
Colchester
Swansea
Port Talbot
Newport
Harlow
Chelmsford
Basildon
Cardiff
Bristol
Bath
Swindon
LONDON
Thames
Slough
Reading
Southend-on-Sea
Barry
Bristol Channel
Windsor
Chatham
Lundy
Weston-super-Mare
Aldershot
Guildford
Canterbury
Ramsgate
Hartland Point
Exmoor 1705ft
Bridgwater
Basingstoke
Taunton
Salisbury
Winchester
Crawley
Folkestone
Dover
Pas de Calais
Calais
Bude Bay
Yeovil
Southampton
Worthing
Brighton
Hastings
Channel Tunnel
Cap Gris Nez
Trevose Head
Tamar
Bodmin Moor 1375ft
Dartmoor 2027ft
Exeter
Bournemouth
Poole
Newport
Portsmouth
Isle of Wight
Bexhill
Eastbourne
Strait of Dover
Boulogne-sur-Mer
Weymouth
Torquay
Lyme Bay
Bill of Portland
Penzance
Plymouth
Land's End
Start Point
Isles of Scilly
Wolf Rock
Lizard Point
Bishop Rock
English Channel (La Manche)
FRANCE

Scale 1: 7 670 500

0 100 200km

0 50 100miles

Scale 1: 3 835 250

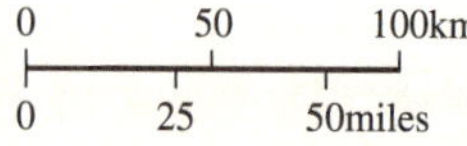
0
50
100km
0
25
50miles

ENGLAND
WALES
FRANCE
LONDON
Norwich
Great Yarmouth
Lowestoft
King's Lynn
Thetford
Bury St Edmunds
Ipswich
Felixstowe
Harwich
Clacton-on-Sea
Colchester
Chelmsford
Southend-on-Sea
Margate
Ramsgate
Basildon
Chatham
Canterbury
Dover
Folkestone
Channel Tunnel
Maidstone
Royal Tunbridge Wells
Hastings
Bexhill
Eastbourne
Brighton
Newhaven
Worthing
Bognor Regis
Crawley
Guildford
Woking
Windsor
Slough
Reading
High Wycombe
Aldershot
Basingstoke
Winchester
Portsmouth
Southampton
Eastleigh
Isle of Wight
Newport
Sandown
Peterborough
The Fens
Ely
Great Ouse
Cambridge
Stevenage
Harlow
Bedford
Luton
Milton Keynes
Aylesbury
Northampton
Leicester
Birmingham
Coventry
Walsall
Telford
Wolverhampton
Dudley
Redditch
Stratford-upon-Avon
Banbury
Oxford
Witney
Thames
Vale of White Horse
Cotswold Hills
Swindon
Cheltenham
Worcester
Severn
Leominster
Great Malvern
Hereford
Gloucester
Stroud
Bristol
Bath
Weston-super-Mare
Salisbury
Bournemouth
Poole
Dorchester
Weymouth
Bill of Portland
Yeovil
Taunton
Bridgwater
Exmoor
South Molton
Exeter
Torquay
Paignton
Start Point
Dartmoor
Okehampton
Plymouth
Barnstaple
Bideford
Tamar
Bodmin Moor
Liskeard
St Austell
Truro
Falmouth
Newquay
Redruth
Helston
Penzance
Land's End
Lizard Point
Wolf Rock
Trevose Head
Bude
Bude Bay
Hartland Point
Lundy
Lyme Bay
Newtown
Builth Wells
Black Mountains
Brecon
Wye
Llandovery
Merthyr Tydfil
Rhondda
Newport
Cardiff
Barry
Port Talbot
Swansea
Llanelli
Carmarthen
Aberystwyth
Cardigan Bay
New Quay
Cardigan
Fishguard
St David's Head
Milford Haven
Pembroke
Bristol Channel
St George's Channel
Rosslare
Carnsore Point
English Channel (La Manche)
Strait of Dover (Pas de Calais)
Calais
Cap Gris Nez
Boulogne-sur-Mer
Abbeville
Blangy-sur-Bresle
Neufchâtel-en-Bray
Marseille-en-Beauvaisis
Dieppe
Rouen
Seine
Yvetot
Bolbec
Pont-Audemer
Fécamp
Cap d'Antifer
Le Havre
Ouistreham
Caen
Baie de Seine
Bayeux
Isigny
Périers
St-Pierre-Église
Pointe de Barfleur
Cherbourg
Cap de la Hague
Valognes
Barneville-Carteret
Alderney
Sark
Guernsey
St Peter Port
Jersey
St Helier
Channel Islands (U.K.)
Isles of Scilly
Hugh Town
Bishop Rock

Scotland

A
B
C
D
8°
6°
4°
2°
2
3
4
58°
56°
60°
Sula Sgeir
North Rona
Sule Skerry
Stack Skerry
Fair Isle
Papa Westray
Westray
North Ronaldsay
Sanday
Rousay
Stronsay
Mainland
Kirkwall
Orkney Islands (U.K.)
Hoy
South Ronaldsay
Pentland Firth
Shetland Islands (U.K.)
Unst
Ronas Hill 1476ft
Fetlar
Yell
Mainland
Whalsay
Lerwick
Bressay
Sumburgh Head
1
2
Butt of Lewis
Port of Ness
Cape Wrath
Strathy Point
Flannan Islands
Outer Hebrides
Carloway
Stornoway
Cromer
Isle of Lewis
North Minch
Durness
Ben Hope 3041ft
Thurso
Duncansby Head
John o'Groat's
Caithness
Wick
Sutherland
Lochinver
Loch Shin
Helmsdale
Sound of Harris
North Uist
Little Minch
Sound of Raasay
Ullapool
Brora
Dornoch
Easter Ross
Moray Firth
Uig
Skye
South Uist
Wester Ross
North West Highlands
Dingwall
Kyle of Lochalsh
Lochboisdale
Broadford
Nairn
Elgin
Portsoy
Fraserburgh
Kinnaird Head
Rattray Head
Inverness
Strathspey
Spey
Keith
Strathbogie
Peterhead
Loch Ness
Barra
Rhum
Mallaig
Eigg
Glen Mor
Fort Augustus
Monadhliath Mountains
SCOTLAND
Aberdeen
4294ft
Ben Macdui
Dee
Muck
Sea of the Hebrides
Fort William
Ben Nevis 4408ft
Cairngorm Mtns
Braemar
Glas Maol 3505ft
Stonehaven
Coll
Tobermory
Grampian Mountains
Tiree
Montrose
Forfar
Mull
Iona
Oban
Loch Tay
Tay
Arbroath
Perth
Dundee
North Sea
Firth of Lorn
Loch Lomond
Inveraray
Colonsay
Jura
Glenrothes
St Andrews
Fife Ness
Inner Hebrides
Loch Fyne
Argyll
Stirling
Alloa
Islay
Greenock
Dunfermline
Kirkcaldy
Firth of Forth
Dumbarton
Glasgow
Edinburgh
Port Ellen
Sound of Jura
Paisley
East Kilbride
Motherwell
Kintyre
Firth of Clyde
Kilmarnock
Berwick-upon-Tweed
Arran
Southern Uplands
Galashiels
Tweed
Campbeltown
Rathlin I.
Prestwick
Ayr
Jedburgh
Hawick
North Channel
Lough Foyle
Coleraine
Girvan
UNITED KINGDOM
Merrick 2765ft
2676ft The Cheviot
Cheviot Hills
NORTHERN IRELAND
Ballymena
Larne
Dumfries
Castle Douglas
Hadrian's Wall
Blyth
Stranraer
Lough Neagh
Newtownabbey
Gatehouse of Fleet
Newcastle-upon-Tyne
Tyne
South Shields
Luce Bay
Solway Firth
Carlisle
Bangor
Belfast
ENGLAND
Durham
Sunderland
Portadown
Lurgan
Penrith
Armagh
Downpatrick
Isle of Man
Whitehaven
Workington
Tees
Hartlepool
Lake District

Scale 1: 3 584 550

0 50 100km
0 25 50miles

ATLANTIC OCEAN
Islay
Port Ellen
Sound of Jura
Kintyre
Arran
Firth of Clyde
Campbeltown
Malin Head
Rathlin Island
Carndonagh
Bloody Foreland
Buncrana
Errigal Mountain 2467ft
Lough Foyle
Coleraine
Aran Island
Letterkenny
Londonderry
Ballymena
Larne
Stranraer
NORTHERN IRELAND
Lavagh More 2211ft
Strabane
Rossan Point
Donegal
Ulster
Antrim
Newtownabbey
Omagh
Cookstown
Lough Neagh
Bangor
Belfast
Donegal Bay
Lower Lough Erne
Ballygawley
Portadown
Lurgan
Downpatrick Head
Erris Head
Enniskillen
Bangor Erris
Sligo
Armagh
Downpatrick
Ballina
Collooney
Upper Lough Erne
Newry
Newcastle
Achill Head
Lough Conn
Foxford
Boyle
Carrick-on-Shannon
Cavan
2795ft Mourne Mountains
Castlebar
Clew Bay
Dundalk (Dún Dealgan)
Bailieborough
Dundalk Bay
Claremorris
Longford
Aasleagh
Ballinrobe
Connaught
Roscommon
Meath
Drogheda (Droichead Átha)
Navan
Clifden
Slyne Head
Tuam
Lough Ree
Irish Sea
Lough Corrib
Athlone
Carmel Head
Royal Canal
Kinnegad
DUBLIN (BAILE ÁTHA CLIATH)
Galway (Gaillimh)
Grand Canal
Galway Bay
Dún Laoghaire
Aran Islands
Loughrea
IRELAND (EIRE)
Bray
Kildare
Hags Head
Ennistimon
Shannon
Lough Derg
Port Laoise
Ennis
Roscrea
Wicklow
Wicklow Head
Leinster
Nenagh
Kilkee
Durrow
Carlow
Wicklow Mountains
Limerick (Luimneach)
Arklow
Loop Head
Kilkenny
Mouth of the Shannon
2612ft Mount Leinster
Gorey
Kerry Head
Newcastle West
Tipperary
361ft
Tralee Bay
Thomastown
Cahore Point
Munster
Cahir
Suir
Enniscorthy
Tralee
Barrow
Clonmel
Wexford
Rosslare
Mitchelstown
Mallow
Waterford (Port Láirge)
Carnsore Point
Killarney
Blackwater
Dingle Bay
3411ft Carrauntoohill
Dungarvan
St George's Channel
Cahersiveen
Macroom
Cork (Corcaigh)
Fishguard
Kenmare
Midleton
St David's Head
Caha Mountains
Bandon
Dursey Island
Bantry
Kinsale
Milford Haven
Bantry Bay
Schull
Old Head of Kinsale
Pembroke
Mizen Head
Clear Island
420ft
Celtic Sea
8157ft
A B C D
1 2 3
10° 8° 6°
54° 52°

Scale 1: 3 835 250

0 50 100km

0 25 50miles

France

A
B
C
D
1
2
3
WALES
Rhondda
Swansea
Cardiff
Newport
Bristol
Bristol Channel
Hartland Point
U.K.
Exeter
Plymouth
Southampton
Bournemouth
Brighton
Portsmouth
Eastbourne
Isle of Wight
Oxford
Reading
LONDON
Cambridge
Colchester
Ipswich
Clacton-on-Sea
Southend-on-Sea
Ramsgate
Canterbury
Crawley
Dover
Hastings
Lizard Point
English Channel (La Manche)
Strait of Dover/Pas de Calais
'S-GRAVENHAGE (THE HAGUE)
Rotterdam
AMSTERDAM
Haarlem
Leiden
Utrecht
Tilburg
Eindhoven
Antwerpen
Brugge
Oostende
Vlissingen
BELGIUM
BRUXELLES
Leuven
Gent
Liège
Namur
Charleroi
Düsseldorf
Köln
Bonn
Aachen
Maastricht
Münster
Wuppertal
Koblenz
Wiesbaden
Dunkerque
Calais
Boulogne-sur-Mer
Lille
Roubaix
Tournai
Douai
Arras
Lens
Mons
Cambrai
Maubeuge
Abbeville
Dieppe
Fécamp
Amiens
St-Quentin
Charleville-Mézières
LUXEMBOURG
Trier
Kaiserslautern
Saarbrücken
Ludwigshafen
Karlsruhe
Cherbourg
Le Havre
Rouen
Beauvais
Compiègne
Soissons
Laon
Reims
Guernsey
Channel Islands (U.K.)
Jersey
Sillon de Talbert
Golfe de St-Malo
Granville
Caen
Normandie
Évreux
Versailles
PARIS
Creil
Île de France
Épernay
Meaux
Châlons-en-Champagne
Metz
Nancy
Strasbourg
Brest
Saint-Brieuc
Saint-Malo
Le Mont-Saint-Michel
Bretagne
Quimper
Lorient
Pointe de Penmarc'h
Île de Groix
Quiberon
Belle-Île
Vannes
Saint-Nazaire
Rennes
Laval
Le Mans
Alençon
Dreux
Chartres
Étampes
Corbeil-Essonnes
Melun
Troyes
Sens
Saint-Dizier
Chaumont
Épinal
Colmar
Mulhouse
Belfort
Orléans
Vendôme
Sologne
Blois
Tours
Angers
Saumur
Nantes
Cholet
Île de Noirmoutier
Île d'Yeu
La Roche-sur-Yon
Bressuire
Touraine
Vierzon
Bourges
Auxerre
Avallon
Morvan
Nevers
Dijon
Besançon
Dole
Beaune
Le Creusot
Chalon-sur-Saône
Mâcon
Châtellerault
Poitiers
Niort
Luçon
Île de Ré
Île d'Oléron
La Rochelle
Rochefort
Royan
Pointe de la Coubre
Soulac-sur-Mer
Saintes
Angoulême
Châteauroux
Montluçon
Moulins
Montceau-les-Mines
Vichy
Roanne
FRANCE
Limoges
Clermont-Ferrand
Lyon
Villeurbanne
Vienne
Saint-Étienne
Bourg-en-Bresse
Genève
Lausanne
SWITZERLAND
BERN
Chambéry
Grenoble
Torino
ITALY
Bay of Biscay
Bordeaux
Mérignac
Pessac
Arcachon
Bègles
Périgueux
Brive-la-Gaillarde
Grotte de Lascaux
Bergerac
Dordogne
Aurillac
Massif Central
Le Puy-en-Velay
Annonay
Privas
Valence
Montélimar
Langon
Garonne
Agen
Cahors
Rodez
Mende
Millau
Côte d'Argent
Roquefort
Mont-de-Marsan
Armagnac
Montauban
Albi
Castres
Cévennes
Alès
Nîmes
Avignon
Arles
Montpellier
Toulouse
Biarritz
Bayonne
Anglet
Dax
Pau
Tarbes
Lourdes
Carcassonne
Limoux
Béziers
Sète
Narbonne
Salon-de-Provence
Aix-en-Provence
Aubagne
Marseille
La Seyne-sur-Mer
Toulon
Hyères
Martigues
Provence
Digne-les-Bains
Nice
Cannes
Antibes
Fréjus
Cap Camarat
Côte d'Azur
Golfe du Lion
Perpignan
Cap de Creus
Pyrénées
ANDORRA
Pic d'Estats 9676ft
Pico de Aneto 11165ft
Santander
Bilbao
Barakaldo
Irún
Donostia-San Sebastián
Vitoria-Gasteiz
Pamplona-Iruña
Navarra
Logroño
Miranda de Ebro
Burgos
Calahorra
Tudela
Soria
Zaragoza
Huesca
Lleida
Figueres
Girona
Vic
Manresa
Terrassa
Granollers
Sabadell
Mataró
Barcelona
l'Hospitalet de Llobregat
Costa Brava
Mediterranean Sea
Reus
Tarragona
Vilanova i la Geltrú
Costa Dorada
Tortosa
Teruel
Vinaròs
Costa del Azahar
SPAIN
Calatayud
Guadalajara
Alcalá de Henares
MADRID
Cuenca
Aranjuez
Castilla La Mancha

Scale 1: 8 214 500

0 100 200km

0 50 100miles

FRANCE
SPAIN
PORTUGAL
ALGERIA
ANDORRA
Bay of Biscay
Mediterranean Sea
Islas Baleares (Balearic Islands) (Sp.)
Costa del Azahar
Costa Brava
Costa Dorada
Costa Blanca
Costa del Sol
Costa Verde
Cordillera Cantábrica
Pyrénées
Sistema Ibérico
Sistemas Béticos
Sierra Nevada
Sierra de Gredos
Montes de Toledo
La Mancha
Andalucía
Algarve
Tierra de Campos
Estrecho de Gibraltar (Strait of Gibraltar)
Golfo de Cádiz
MADRID
LISBOA (LISBON)
Barcelona
Valencia
Sevilla
Zaragoza
Bilbao
Málaga
Murcia
Córdoba
Granada
Valladolid
Palma de Mallorca
Porto
Coimbra
Salamanca
Toledo
Alicante
Cartagena
Almería
Cádiz
Gibraltar (U.K.)
Ceuta (Sp.)
Tanger
AL JAZĀ'IR (ALGIERS)
Toulouse
Marseille
Perpignan
Montpellier
Mallorca
Menorca
Eivissa
Formentera
Rio Ebro
Rio Tajo
Rio Duero
Rio Guadiana
Guadalquivir
Rio Júcar

Scale 1: 8 214 500

0 100 200km

0 50 100miles

Italy and The Balkans

AUSTRIA
HUNGARY
ROMANIA
MOLDOVA
BULGARIA
TURKEY
GREECE
ALBANIA
MACEDONIA
SERBIA & MONTENEGRO
BOSNIA HERZEGOVINA
CROATIA
SLOVENIA
SWITZERLAND
ITALY
TUNISIA
ALGERIA
MALTA
MONACO
SAN MARINO
VATICAN CITY STATE
Carpathian Mountains
Black Sea
Adriatic Sea
Mare Tirreno (Tyrrhenian Sea)
Mar Ionio (Ionian Sea)
Aegean Sea
Ligurian Sea
Mediterranean Sea
Corse (Corsica) (Fr.)
Sardegna (Sardinia) (It.)
Sicilia (Sicily) (It.)
Kyklades (Cyclades)
Voreioi Sporades
Ionioi Nisoi
Canale di Sicilia
Canale di Malta
Strait of Bonifacio
Sea of Marmara
BUCURESTI (BUCHAREST)
BUDAPEST
BEOGRAD (BELGRADE)
SOFIYA (SOFIA)
ATHINA (ATHENS)
ROMA (ROME)
Napoli (Naples)
Firenze (Florence)
WIEN (VIENNA)
BRATISLAVA
ZAGREB
LJUBLJANA
SARAJEVO
SKOPJE
TIRANE
CHISINAU
TUNIS
BERN
VADUZ
VALLETTA
Istanbul
Thessaloniki
Izmir
Marseille
Milano
Torino
Genova
Venezia
Bari
Palermo
Messina
Catania
Cagliari
Varna
Constanta
Burgas

Scale 1: 12 523 000

0 200 400km

0 100 200miles

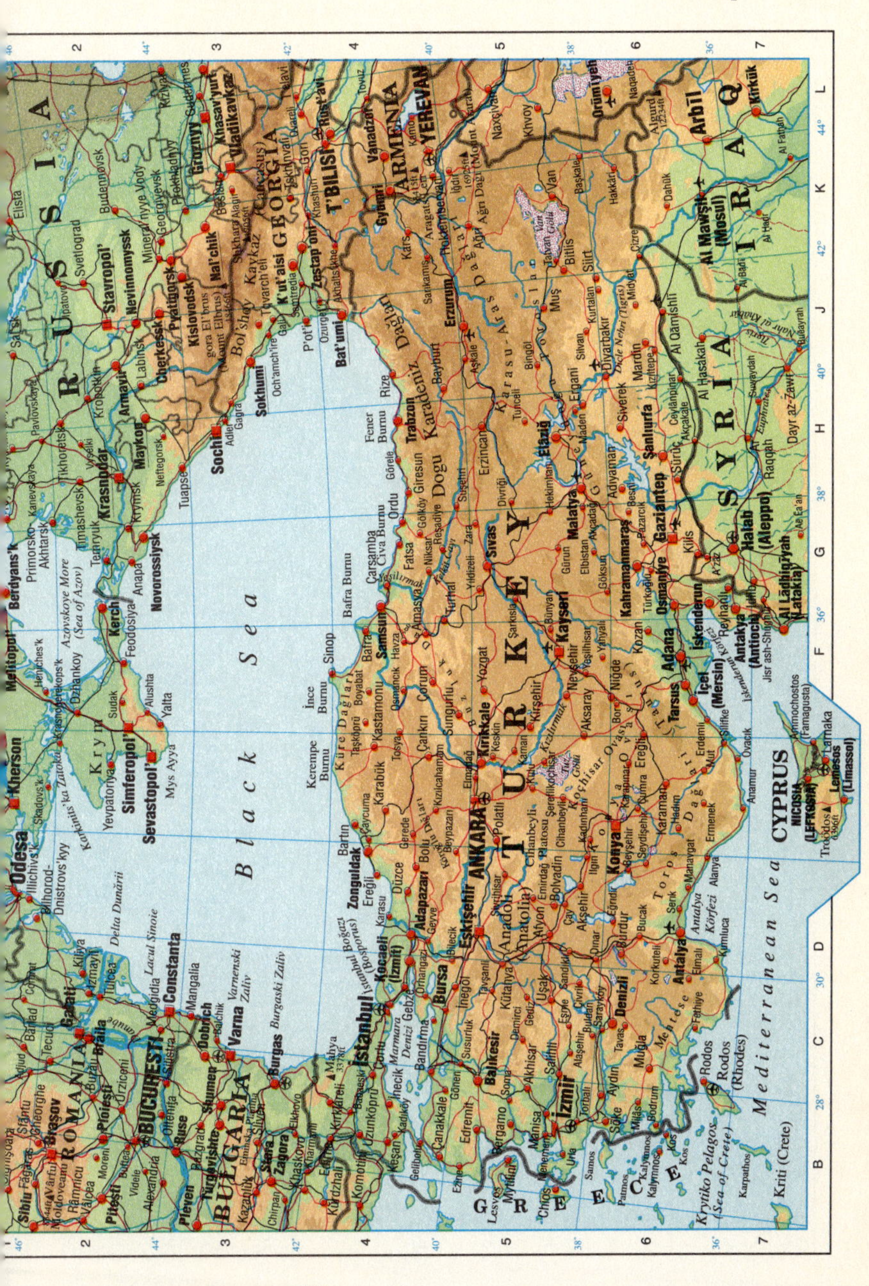
TURKEY
Black Sea
Mediterranean Sea
RUSSIA
GEORGIA
ARMENIA
SYRIA
IRAQ
CYPRUS
BULGARIA
ROMANIA
GREECE
ANKARA
İstanbul
İzmir
Bursa
Adana
Konya
Antalya
Kayseri
Samsun
Trabzon
Erzurum
Sivas
Malatya
Gaziantep
Diyarbakır
Van
Eskişehir
T'BILISI
YEREVAN
NICOSIA (LEFKOSIA)
Halab (Aleppo)
BUCUREŞTI
Odesa
Sevastopol'
Simferopol'
Krasnodar
Sochi
Varna
Burgas
Constanta
Kriti (Crete)
Rodos (Rhodes)
Marmara Denizi
Lake Van

Scale 1: 11 322 900

0 150 300km

0 75 150miles

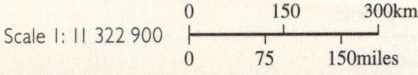

A
B
C
D
5°
10°
15°
55°
50°
45°
1
2
3
4
North Sea
DENMARK
SWEDEN
NETHERLANDS
BELGIUM
LUXEMBOURG
GERMANY
FRANCE
SWITZERLAND
LIECHT.
AUSTRIA
CZECH REPUBLIC
SLOVENIA
CROATIA
ITALY
SAN MARINO
Östersjön (Baltic Sea)
Helgoländer Bucht
Frisian Islands
Gulf of Venice
The Alps
Jylland
Ålborg
Århus
Odense
KØBENHAVN (COPENHAGEN)
Malmö
Helsingborg
Bornholm (Den.)
Rügen
Kiel
Hamburg
Bremen
Hannover
BERLIN
Szczecin
Poznań
Gdańsk
AMSTERDAM
'S-GRAVENHAGE (THE HAGUE)
Rotterdam
Utrecht
Antwerpen
BRUXELLES
Liège
Düsseldorf
Köln
Bonn
Dortmund
Essen
Bielefeld
Münster
Magdeburg
Leipzig
Dresden
Halle
Erfurt
Kassel
Frankfurt am Main
Wiesbaden
Mainz
Mannheim
Saarbrücken
Karlsruhe
Stuttgart
Nürnberg
Würzburg
Regensburg
München
Augsburg
Strasbourg
Metz
Nancy
Reims
Dijon
Besançon
Mulhouse
Basel
Zürich
BERN
Luzern
Lausanne
Genève
Lyon
Villeurbanne
Saint-Étienne
Grenoble
PRAHA (PRAGUE)
Plzeň
Brno
WIEN (VIENNA)
Linz
Salzburg
Innsbruck
Graz
LJUBLJANA
ZAGREB
Rijeka
Trieste
Venezia
Verona
Milano
Torino
Genova
Bologna
Firenze
Ferrara
Parma
Bergamo
Brescia
Padova
Ravenna
Rimini
Wrocław
Chemnitz

Scale 1: 92 000 000

0 150 300km

0 75 150miles

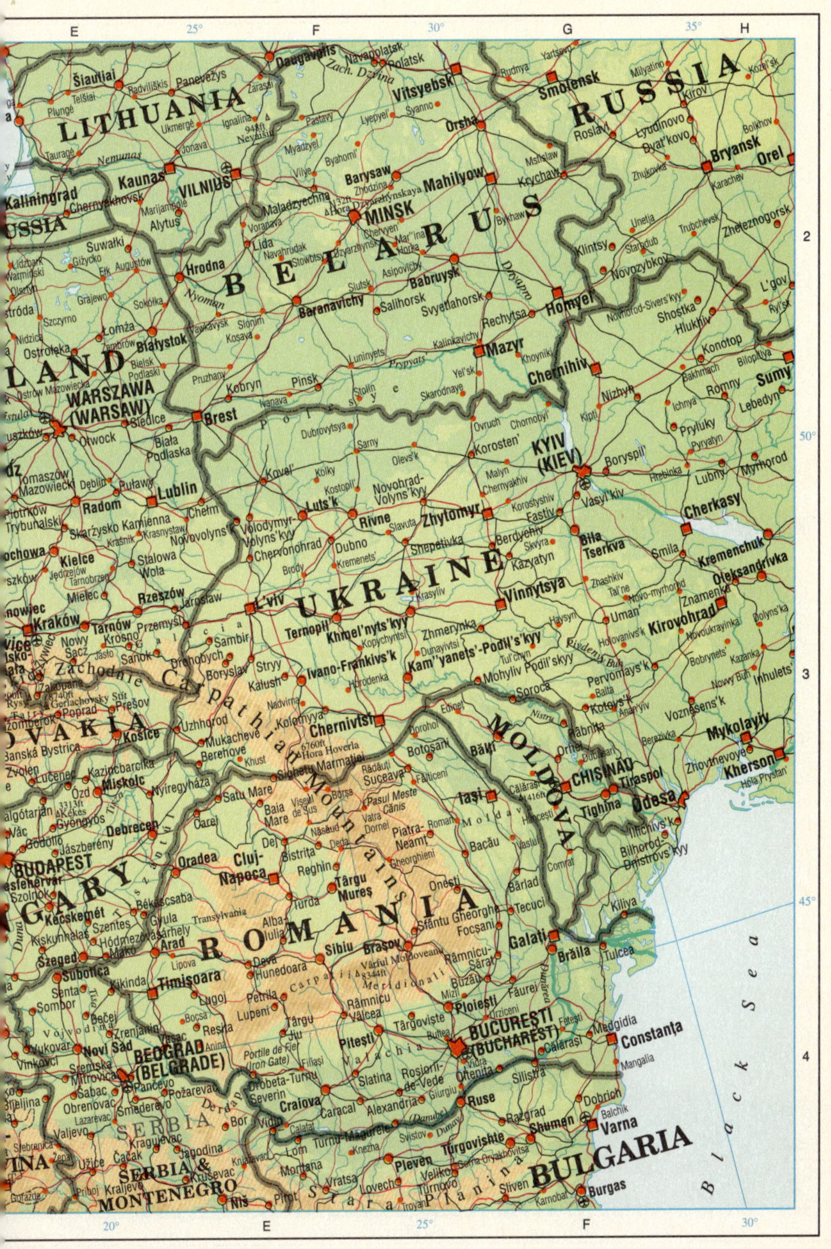
LITHUANIA
BELARUS
RUSSIA
UKRAINE
MOLDOVA
ROMANIA
BULGARIA
SERBIA &
MONTENEGRO
Black Sea
Carpathian Mountains
Vilnius
Kaunas
Šiauliai
Kaliningrad
Daugavpils
Vitsyebsk
Smolensk
Orsha
Mahilyow
Barysaw
MINSK
Hrodna
Baranavichy
Babruysk
Homyel'
Mazyr
Pinsk
Brest
Bryansk
Orel
Chernihiv
Sumy
KYIV
(KIEV)
Zhytomyr
Rivne
Luts'k
L'viv
Ternopil'
Khmel'nyts'kyy
Vinnytsya
Cherkasy
Kirovohrad
Mykolayiv
Kherson
Odesa
CHIŞINĂU
Tiraspol
Chernivtsi
Iaşi
Galaţi
Brăila
Constanţa
BUCUREŞTI
(BUCHAREST)
Ploieşti
Braşov
Sibiu
Cluj-Napoca
Oradea
Timişoara
Craiova
Piteşti
Ruse
Varna
Burgas
Pleven
Shumen
BEOGRAD
(BELGRADE)
Novi Sad
Subotica
Szeged
Debrecen
Miskolc
Košice
Kraków
Tarnów
Rzeszów
Lublin
Radom
Kielce
WARSZAWA
(WARSAW)
Białystok
Brest
Kecskemét
BUDAPEST
Kiliya
Izmayil
Sevastopol
Zaporizhzhya

Greenland Sea
ICELAND
REYKJAVÍK
Vatnajökull
Hofsjökull
Langjökull
Mýrdalsjökull
Arctic Circle
Scale 1: 12 500 000
Streymoy
Fugloy
Vágar
Eysturoy
Tórshavn
Sandoy
Suðuroy
Faroe Islands
(Den.)
Scale 1: 10 345 000
Norwegian Sea
Barents Sea
North Sea
Skagerrak
Kattegat
Gulf of Bothnia
Gulf of Finland
Östersjön (Baltic Sea)
NORWAY
SWEDEN
FINLAND
SUOMI
RUSSIA
ESTONIA
LATVIA
LITHUANIA
BELARUS
POLAND
DENMARK
NETHERLANDS
Nordkapp
North Cape
Lofoten
Vesterålen
Tromsø
Murmansk
Trondheim
Bergen
Stavanger
OSLO
Göteborg
STOCKHOLM
Uppsala
Gotland
Öland
HELSINKI
(HELSINGFORS)
TALLINN
RĪGA
VILNIUS
MINSK
Kaliningrad
KØBENHAVN
(COPENHAGEN)
Malmö
Bornholm
Hamburg
BERLIN
WARSZAWA
(WARSAW)
Gdańsk
AMSTERDAM
Oulu (Uleåborg)
Tampere (Tammerfors)
Turku (Åbo)
Umeå
Luleå
Sundsvall
Kiruna
Åland

Scale 1: 14 375 000

0 200 400km

0 100 200miles

ARCTIC OCEAN
PACIFIC OCEAN
Greenland Sea
Norwegian Sea
Barents Sea
Kara Sea
Laptev Sea
East Siberian Sea
Bering Sea
Sea of Okhotsk
Sea of Japan
South China Sea
Arabian Sea
Bay of Bengal
Andaman Sea
Caspian Sea
Black Sea
Red Sea
Banda Sea
Celebes Sea
Sulu Sea
RUSSIA
Siberia
VERKHOYANSK RANGE
Cherskogo Range
Stanovoy Range
Chukot Range
Koryak Range
Franz Josef Land
Novaya Zemlya
Svalbard
MONGOLIA
Gobi Desert
CHINA
KAZAKHSTAN
UZBEKISTAN
TURKMENISTAN
KYRGYZSTAN
TAJIKISTAN
AFGHANISTAN
PAKISTAN
INDIA
NEPAL
SRI LANKA
MALDIVES
IRAN
IRAQ
SAUDI ARABIA
YEMEN
OMAN
KUWAIT
JORDAN
SYRIA
LEBANON
ISRAEL
TURKEY
CYPRUS
JAPAN
NORTH KOREA
SOUTH KOREA
TAIWAN
PHILIPPINES
VIETNAM
LAOS
THAILAND
CAMBODIA
MYANMAR (BURMA)
MALAYSIA
SINGAPORE
INDONESIA
PALAU
FEDERATED STATES OF MICRONESIA
MICRONESIA
NORTHERN MARIANA ISLANDS (U.S.A.)
EGYPT
LIBYA
SUDAN
CHAD
NIGER
NIGERIA
ALGERIA
MALI
ETHIOPIA
SOMALIA
CENTRAL AFRICAN REPUBLIC
CAMEROON
TUNISIA
FINLAND
SWEDEN
NORWAY
DENMARK
UNITED KINGDOM
FRANCE
SPAIN
ITALY
GERMANY
POLAND
UKRAINE
BELARUS
ESTONIA
LATVIA
LITHUANIA
ROMANIA
GREECE
Moscow
Beijing
Tokyo
Delhi
Mumbai
Kolkata (Calcutta)
Chennai
Karachi
Tehran
Baghdad
Riyadh
Kabul
Manila
Jakarta
Singapore
Shanghai
Istanbul
Cairo
Bering Strait
O. Sakhalin
Kuril'skiye Ostrova
0°
15° E
30°
45°
60°
75°
90°
150° W

Scale 1: 20 815 000

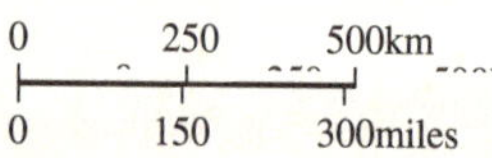
0 250 500km
0 150 300miles

Severnaya Zemlya
Ostrov Komsomolets
Ostrov Oktyabr'skoy Revolyutsii
Ostrov Bol'shevik
Ostrov Pioner
Ostrov Vize
Ostrov Dlinnyy
Ostrova Sergeya Kirova
Arkhipelag Nordenshel'da
Proliv Vil'kitskogo
Ostrov Malyy Taymyr
More Laptevykh
(Laptev Sea)
Ostrova Dunay
Ostrov Bol'shoy Begichev
Ostrov Peschanyy
Anabarskiy Zaliv
Khatangskiy Zaliv
Poluostrov Taymyr
Gory Byrranga
Ozero Taymyr
Severo-Sibirskaya Nizmennost'
Dikson
Khatanga
Tiksi
Kharaulakhskiy Khrebet
Lena
Olenek
Anabar
Verkhoyanskiy Khrebet
Arctic Circle
Anabarskoye Ploskogor'ye
Plato Putorana
Noril'sk
Talnakh
Dudinka
Yenisey
Igarka
Sredne Sibirskoye Ploskogor'ye
Vilyuyskoye Plato
Vilyuy
Mirnyy
Vilyuyskoye Vodokhranilishche
Nizhnyaya Tunguska
Podkamennaya Tunguska
Tsentral'no Tungusskoye Plato
Turukhansk
Urengoy
Tarko-Sale
RUSSIA
Yartsevo
Angara
Ust'-Ilimsk
Ust'-Kut
Bratsk
Bratskoye Vodokhranilishche
Krasnoyarsk
Kansk
Achinsk
Tomsk
Novosibirsk
Kemerovo
Novokuznetsk
Barnaul
Biysk
Abakan
Irkutsk
Angarsk
Ozero Baykal
Ulan-Ude
Severo-Baykal'skoye Nagor'ye
Stanovoye Nagor'ye
Vostochnyy Sayan
Kyzyl
Tannu Ola
Altay
MONGOLIA
ULAANBAATAR
Hangayn Nuruu
Hövsgöl Nuur
Aqsū
70°
65°
60°
55°
50°
4
5
6
7
8

More Laptevykh
(Laptev Sea)
RUSSIA
CHINA
MONGOLIA
Severo-Sibirskaya Nizmennost'
Plato Putorana
Sredne Sibirskoye Ploskogor'ye
Verkhoyanskiy Khrebet
Khrebet Cherskogo
Khrebet Suntar Khayata
Aldanskoye Nagor'ye
Stanovoy Khrebet
Stanovoye Nagor'ye
Yablonovyy Khrebet
Vitimskoye Ploskogor'ye
Khrebet Dzhugdzhur
Tsentral'no Tungusskoye Plato
Viluyskoye Plato
Arctic Circle
Ozero Baykal
Lena
Olenek
Vilyuy
Aldan
Amur
Noril'sk
Yakutsk
Ulan-Ude
Chita
Blagoveshchensk
Komsomol'sk na-Amure
Nikolayevsk-na-Amure
Tiksi
Mirnyy
Neryungri
Tynda
Svobodnyy
Ust'-Ilimsk
Ust'-Kut
Verkhoyansk
Shantarskiye Ostrova
Ostrov Bol'shoy Lyakhovskiy
Ostrov Kotel'nyy
Ostrov Bennetta
HEILONGJIANG
NEI MONGOL ZIZHIQU
70°
65°
60°
55°
50°
90°
95°
100°
105°
110°
115°
120°
125°
130°
135°
140°
145°
150°
155°
A
B
C
D
E
F
G
H
J
K
L
M
N
O
P
3
4
5
6
7

Scale 1: 20 444 700

0 250 500km

0 150 300miles

Asia, South-Westerm

MOSKVA
BELARUS
MINSK
POLAND
WARSZAWA (WARSAW)
SLOVAKIA
HUNGARY
ROMANIA
BUCUREŞTI
MOLDOVA
CHIŞINĂU
UKRAINE
KYIV
BULGARIA
SOFIYA (SOFIA)
Istanbul
Black Sea
GEORGIA
T'BILISI
ARMENIA
YEREVAN
AZERBAIJAN
BAKI
TURKEY
ANKARA
Anadolu (Anatolia)
Kaspiyskoye More (Caspian Sea)
Mediterranean Sea
CYPRUS
LEFKOSIA (NICOSIA)
SYRIA
DIMASHQ (DAMASCUS)
LEBANON
BAYRUT (BEIRUT)
ISRAEL
Tel Aviv-Yafo
YERUSHALAYIM (JERUSALEM)
JORDAN
'AMMAN
IRAQ
BAGHDĀD
Syrian Desert
SAUDI ARABIA
EGYPT
AL QĀHIRAH (CAIRO)
AL KUWAYT (KUWAIT)
KUWAIT
TEHRĀN
Volgograd
Rostov-na-Donu
Odesa
Sevastopol'
Astrakhan'
Makhachkala
Tabrīz
Halab (Aleppo)
Al Mawşil (Mosul)
Al Başrah (Basra)
Euphrates
Tigris
The Gulf

Scale 1: 20 390 650

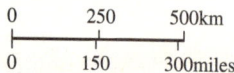

0 250 500km

0 150 300miles

KAZAKHSTAN
UZBEKISTAN
KYRGYZSTAN
TAJIKISTAN
AFGHANISTAN
PAKISTAN
INDIA
CHINA
XINJIANG UYGUR ZIZHIQU
Taklimakan Shamo (Takla Makan)
Kunlun Shan
Tian Shan
Hindu Kush
Pamirs
Himalayas
Karakoram Range
Paropamisus
Aral'skoye More (Aral Sea)
Balqash Köli
Ysyk-Köl
Yekaterinburg
Chelyabinsk
Kurgan
Omsk
Magnitogorsk
Pavlodar
Semey
Barnaul
Novoaltaysk
Rubtsovsk
Öskemen
ASTANA
Qaraghandy
Temirtau
Kokshetaū
Qostanay
Rūdnyy
Orsk
Petropavlovsk
Almaty (Alma-Ata)
BISHKEK
Ürümqi
Taraz
Shymkent
Qyzylorda
Aral
TOSHKENT
Namangan
Andijon
Osh
Farg'ona
Nukus
Urganch
Samarqand
Buxoro
Qarshi
DUSHANBE
AŞGABAT (ASHKHABAD)
Türkmenabat
Mary
Mashhad
Herat
KĀBUL
Kandahār
Quetta
ISLAMABAD
Rawalpindi
Peshawar
Lahore
Faisalabad
Gujranwala
Multan
Amritsar
Ludhiana
NEW DELHI
Delhi
Jaipur
Agra
Jodhpur
Ajmer
Bikaner
Srinagar
Kermān
Kashi
Hotan
Aksu
Yining

AFGHANISTAN
PAKISTAN
NEPAL
INDIA
SRI LANKA
MALDIVES
Arabian Sea
INDIAN OCEAN
Tropic of Cancer
Kandahār
Quetta
Peshāwar
ISLAMABAD
Rawalpindi
Srinagar
Lahore
Amritsar
Multan
Faisalabad
Karachi
Hyderabad
Sukkur
New Delhi
Delhi
Jaipur
Agra
Jodhpur
Bikaner
Ahmadābād
Vadodara
Rajkot
Surat
Indore
Bhopal
Ujjain
Jabalpur
Nagpur
Kanpur
Lucknow
Allahabad
Varanasi (Benares)
Patna
KATHMANDU
Mumbai (Bombay)
Pune (Poona)
Aurangabad
Nasik
Thane
Sholapur
Hyderabad
Kolhapur
Vishakhapatnam
Vijayawada
Bangalore
Mysore
Mangalore
Calicut
Cochin
Coimbatore
Madurai
Trivandrum
Tiruchchirappalli
Salem
Chennai (Madras)
Jaffna
Trincomalee
Kandy
COLOMBO
Galle
Laccadive Islands
LAKSHADWEEP
Kavaratti
Nine Degree Channel
Eight Degree Channel
Scale 1: 30 120 000

Scale 1: 20 360 750

0 250 500km

0 150 300miles

CHINA
QINGHAI
SICHUAN
GANSU
SHAANXI
HUBEI
HUNAN
GUIZHOU
YUNNAN
GUANGXI ZHUANGZU ZIZHIQU
ARUNACHAL PRADESH
ASSAM
NAGALAND
MANIPUR
TRIPURA
MIZORAM
MYANMAR (BURMA)
LAOS
THAILAND
CAMBODIA (KAMPUCHEA)
VIETNAM
MALAYSIA
INDONESIA
Chengdu
Chongqing
Kunming
Xian
Wuhan
Changsha
Guiyang
Nanning
Guilin
Lhasa
Mandalay
YANGON (RANGOON)
Moulmein
Pegu
HA NOI
Haiphong
Hue
Da Nang
VIANGCHAN (VIENTIANE)
Chiang Mai
BANGKOK (KRUNG THEP)
PHNUM PENH
Ho Chi Minh (Saigon)
Qui Nhon
Nha Trang
Hainan Dao
Beibu Wan (Gulf of Tonkin)
Gulf of Thailand
Andaman Sea
Nan Hai (South China Sea)
Andaman Islands (India)
Nicobar Islands (India)
Port Blair
Ten Degree Channel
Preparis South Channel
Sumatera (Sumatra)
Banda Aceh
Strait of Malacca
George Town
Ipoh
Kota Bharu
Hat Yai
Paracel Islands
Irrawaddy
Salween
Mekong
95°
100°
105°
110°
115°
30°
25°
20°
15°
10°
G
H
J
K
L
2
3
4
5
6
7

KYRGYZSTAN
BISHKEK
Almaty (Alma-Ata)
Taraz
Andijon
Osh
Tian Shan
Ürümqi
Altay Shan
Kashi
Taklimakan Shamo (Takla Makan)
XINJIANG UYGUR ZIZHIQU
Altun Shan
Kunlun Shan
Qaidam Pendi
Karakoram Range
Srinagar
JAMMU AND KASHMIR
Jammu
XIZANG ZIZHIQU (TIBET)
Nyaingentanglha Shan
Tanggula Shan
Lhasa
CHINA
QINGHAI
NEPAL
KATHMANDU
Himalaya
BHUTAN
THIMPHU
ARUNACHAL PRADESH
NEW DELHI
Delhi
Lucknow
Kanpur
Allahabad
Varanasi (Benares)
Patna
INDIA
Nagpur
Bhopal
Jabalpur
Kolkata (Calcutta)
Bhubaneshwar
Cuttack
DHAKA (DACCA)
BANGLADESH
Chittagong
Mouths of the Ganges
Bay of Bengal
MYANMAR (BURMA)
Mandalay
Sittwe
Tropic of Cancer

Scale 1: 20 422 850

0 250 500km

0 150 300miles

105°
H
110°
J
115°
K
120°
L
125°
M
130°
N
ULAANBAATAR
OLIA
Dundgovĭ
Gobi Desert
Erenhot
NEI MONGOL ZIZHIQU
Huhhot
Jining
Baotou
Harbin
Changchun
Jilin
Shenyang
Fushun
Anshan
RUSSIA
Vladivostok
NORTH KOREA
P'YŎNGYANG
SŎUL (SEOUL)
Inch'ŏn
Taegu
Pusan
SOUTH KOREA
Sea of Japan
BEIJING (PEKING)
Tianjin (Tientsin)
Dalian
Shijiazhuang
Taiyuan
Baoding
Tangshan
Qinhuangdao
Datong
Zhangjiakou
Chengde
Jinan
Qingdao (Tsingtao)
Huang Hai (Yellow Sea)
Zhengzhou
Luoyang
Kaifeng
Xi'an
Xianyang
Lanzhou
HEBEI
SHANXI
SHAANXI
HENAN
SHANDONG
JIANGSU
ANHUI
HUBEI
HUNAN
JIANGXI
ZHEJIANG
FUJIAN
GUANGDONG
GUIZHOU
NINGXIA HUIZU ZIZHIQU
GUANGXI ZHUANGZU ZIZHIQU
HAINAN
Nanjing
Shanghai
Hangzhou
Ningbo
Wenzhou
Hefei
Wuhan
Nanchang
Changsha
Chongqing
Chengdu
Guiyang
Kunming
Nanning
Guilin
Guangzhou
Shantou
Xiamen
Fuzhou
Kowloon
Victoria
Hong Kong
MACAU
Zhanjiang
Haikou
Hainan Dao
Dong Hai (East China Sea)
Nan Hai (South China Sea)
Taiwan Haixia (Formosa Strait)
TAIWAN (FORMOSA)
T'AIPEI
Kaohsiung
Bashi Haixia
Luzon Strait
PHILIPPINES
VIETNAM
HA NOI
Haiphong
Beibu Wan (Gulf of Tonkin)
Bo Hai (Gulf of Chihli)
1
4
5
6
7
30°
25°
20°
G
105°
H

RUSSIA
MONGOLIA
JAPAN
NORTH KOREA
SOUTH KOREA
Sea of Japan
Gobi Desert
Sakhalin
Kuril'skiye Ostrova
Stanovoy Khrebet
Yablonovyy Khrebet
Sikhote-Alin
Amur
Honshu
Hokkaido
TOKYO
Yokohama
Nagoya
Osaka
Kyoto
Sapporo
Hakodate
Aomori
Sendai
Niigata
Kanazawa
Vladivostok
Nakhodka
Khabarovsk
Komsomol'sk na-Amure
Blagoveshchensk
Harbin
Qiqihar
Changchun
Jilin
Shenyang
Fushun
Anshan
Dalian
P'YONGYANG
SEOUL (SOUL)
Inch'on
Ch'ongjin
Hamhung
Wonsan
BEIJING (PEKING)
Tianjin
Tangshan
Zhangjiakou
Datong
Baotou
Hohhot
Chita
Ulan-Ude
ULAANBAATAR
Yakutsk
Tynda
Neryungri
Ozero Baykal
Yin Shan
NEI MONGOL

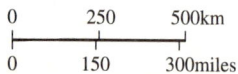

Scale 1: 20 572 350

0 250 500km

0 150 300miles

CHINA
Shanghai
Dong Hai
(East China Sea)
Nansei-shotō (Ryukyu Islands)
Okinawa-jima
Naha
Tropic of Cancer
PACIFIC
OCEAN
TAIWAN
(FORMOSA)
T'AIPEI
Kaohsiung
Hong Kong
Kowloon
Victoria
Guangzhou
(Kanton)
Bashi Haixia
Luzon Strait
PHILIPPINES
Luzon
Quezon City
Nan Hai
(South China Sea)
Hainan Dao
VIETNAM
HA NOI
Haiphong
Da Nang
Wuhan
Hangzhou
Nanjing
Kyūshū
Kagoshima
Nagasaki

LAOS
THAILAND
MYANMAR (BURMA)
CAMBODIA (KAMPUCHEA)
VIETNAM
CHINA
MALAYSIA
SINGAPORE
BRUNEI
Hainan Dao
Chiang Mai
Chiang Rai
Luang Prabang
VIANGCHAN (VIENTIANE)
YANGON (RANGOON)
Pegu
Bassein
Mawlamyine
Mouths of the Irrawaddy
BANGKOK (KRUNG THEP)
Thon Buri
Nakhon Ratchasima
Ubon Ratchathani
Angkor Wat
PHNUM PENH
Ho Chi Minh (Saigon)
Da Nang
Hue
Qui Nhon
Nha Trang
Gulf of Thailand
Beibu Wan (Gulf of Tonkin)
Andaman Sea
Mergui Archipelago
Nan Hai (South China Sea)
Phuket
Hat Yai
Songkhla
George Town
Kota Bharu
Ipoh
Kuantan
KUALA LUMPUR
PUTRAJAYA
Johor Bharu
Strait of Malacca
Malaya
Banda Aceh
Medan
Pekanbaru
Padang
Jambi
Palembang
Sumatera (Sumatra)
Kepulauan Mentawai
Bengkulu
Kuching
Pontianak
Kalimantan
Sarawak
Banjarmasin
Kepulauan Natuna Besar
Kepulauan Natuna Selatan
Kepulauan Lingga
Kepulauan Riau
Pangkalpinang
Bangka
Belitung
Equator
INDIAN OCEAN
Laut Jawa (Java Sea)
Jawa (Java)
JAKARTA
Bandung
Semarang
Yogyakarta
Surakarta
Surabaya
Malang
Madura
Christmas Island (Austr.)
Scale 1: 20 444 700
0 250 500km
0 150 300miles

125°
H
130°
J
135°
K
3
10°
4
5°
5
0°
6
5°
7
10°
8
Dalupiri
Camiguin
Fuga
Mayraira Point
Claveria
San Vincente
Laoag
Aparri
Batac
Tuguegarao
Vigan
Palanan Point
Ilagan
Luzon
San Fernando
Baguio
Dagupan
Lingayen
Baler
Cabanatuan
Tarlac
Gapan
Angeles
Quezon City
Malolos
MANILA
Santa Cruz
Calagua Islands
Catanduanes
Daet
San Pablo
Virac
Lipa
Lucena
Naga
Legaspi
PHILIPPINES
Sorsogon
Lubang Islands
Batangas
Marinduque
Calapan
Burias
Samar
16733ft
Mamburao
Sibuyan Sea
Masbate
Mindoro
Tablas
Sibuyan
Samar Sea
Catbalogan
Busuanga
Masbate
Visayan Sea
Tacloban
34122ft
Calamian Group
Kalibo
Roxas
11484ft
Panay
Cadiz
Ormoc
33ft
Libro Point
Victorias
Leyte
San Jose de Buenavista
Iloilo
Bacolod
Cebu
Dinagat
35435ft
Surigao
Siargao
Dumaran Island
Pulupandan
Bohol
Tagbilaran
Cagayan Islands
Sipalay
Negros
Siquijor
Camiguin
Butuan
Puerto Princesa
Cavili
18295ft
Dumaguete
Cagayan de Oro
Bislig
Arena
Dipolog
Ozamiz
Iligan
Malaybalay
Palawan
Sulu Sea
Pagadian
Marawi
Mindanao
Tagum
Baganga
Bugsuk Island
Bancoran
Zamboanga Peninsula
Davao
San Miguel Islands
Cotabato
Digos
Cape San Agustin
Kagayan de Sulu Island
Zamboanga
Moro Gulf
Koronadal
General Santos (Dadiangas)
Pilas Group
Basilan
9840ft
Basilan City
Kalsong
Pangutaran Group
Jolo
Samales Group
20342ft
Tinaca Point
Sarangani
Sandakan
Tawitawi Group
Tapul Group
Kepulauan Nanusa
Kepulauan Kawio
Karakelong
16077ft
Kawalusu
Kepulauan Talaud
Lahad Datu
Sulu Archipelago
Sibutu
Tahuna
Sangir
Tawau
Sebatik
Celebes Sea
Hapo
Morotai
Siau
5578ft
18111ft
Tarakan
Tahulandang
Kepulauan Sangir
Galela
Biaro
Akelamo
Equator
15171ft
15093ft
Halmahera
Manado
Doro
Biak
Tondano
Ternate
Waigeo
Walbeem
Manokwari
Tanjung Kandi
Boroko
Laut Maluku (Molucca Sea)
Makian
Puper
Gunung Kwoka
Numfoor
Weda
Mega
9843ft
Rensiki
Yapen
Tanjung Mangkalihat
Pinjang
Paleleh
Gorontalo
Gebe
Gag
Teluk Cendrawasih
Kasiruta
Waiwo
Seget
Wasior
Moutong
Bacan
Wosi
Tanjung Libobo
Mapaga
Kepulauan Togian
12796ft
Mandioli
Damar
Kafiau
33ft
Len Malaäs
Inanwatan
Teluk Tomini
Kepulauan Obi
Misoöl
Samarinda
Toribulu
Luwuk
Fluk
Obi
Mariar
7216ft
Peleng
Taliabu
Mangole
Maluku (Moluccas)
Nabire
Pegunungan Maoke
New Guinea
Palu
10260ft Gunung Waukara
Poso
Bongka
Sanana
Wahai
Bula
4593ft
Weri
Pegunungan Charles Louis
Puncak Jaya
16503ft
Samboja
Balikpapan
Uekuli
Kepulauan Sula
Boano
Piru
10023ft
Gunung Binaiya
Amahai
Ibonma
Modowi
Uman
Sulawesi (Celebes)
Wosu
Kepulauan Banggai
Tanjung Palpetu
Namlea
Buru
Seram (Ceram)
Gorong
Kepulauan Watubela
Adi
Bukit Gandadiwata
Wotu
18701ft
Ambon
Manawoka
A
Mamuju
Palopo
Labengke
Kepulauan Banda
I
Kepulauan Kai
Wokam
10086ft
Manui
Tual
Komfane
Kobroor
Polewali
Noholoho
Kendari
S
Majene
Pinrang
Wowoni
Kai Besar
Kepulauan Aru
Parepare
Pangkadjene
Singkang
Kolaka
Trangan
Watampone
E
Buton
Laut Banda (Banda Sea)
24411ft
Makassar
N
Muna
Wangiwangi
Ujung Pandang (Makassar)
Maros
Sindjai
Kabaena
Kepulauan Tukangbesi
Nila
Takalar
Banteng
Baubau
Tanjung Vals
Bulukumba
Yamdena
Kalukalukuang
Jeneponto
Selayar
Binongko
Kepulauan Tenggara
Damar
Kepulauan Tanimbar
8859ft
Kepulauan Babar
Romang
Tepa
Selaru
Kalaotoa
Wetar
Kisar
Masela
1378ft
Tanahjampea
Lesser Sunda Islands
Kepulauan Leti
Kalao
Alor
Atauro
Tutuala
Laut Flores (Flores Sea)
Flores
Larantuka
Kalabahi
DILI
EAST TIMOR
10827ft
Laut Arafura (Arafura Sea)
Cape Wessel
Reo
Mata
Pantar
Moyo
Raba
Rinca
Labuhanbadjo
Maumere
Lomblen
Wessel Islands
Sumbawa Besar
Ruteng
Badjawa
Endeh
Kefamenanu
Suai
Plampang
Soe
Cape Croker
Croker Island
Elcho Island
Sumbawa
Memboro
Payeti
Timor
180ft
Cape Van Diemen
Melville Island
Van Diemen Gulf
Frederick Hills
9515ft
Kupang
Timor Sea
Bathurst Island
Sumba
Savu
Rote
Darwin
Arnhem Land
Numbulwar Mission
Charles Point
Ashmore Reef
Hibernia Reef
Cape Scott
Pine Creek
AUSTRALIA
Northern Mariana Islands (U.S.A.)
FED. STATES OF MICRONESIA
Kayangel Islands
PALAU
KOROR
Peleliu
22311ft
Sonsorol Islands
PACIFIC OCEAN

A
B
C
D
E
F
130°
135°
140°
145°
150°
1
2
3
4
45°
40°
35°
CHINA
RUSSIA
NORTH KOREA
SOUTH KOREA
JAPAN
HEILONG JIANG
JILIN
YEVREYSKA A. O.
PRIMORSKIY KRAY
Sea of Japan
PACIFIC OCEAN
Dong Hai
(East China Sea)
Hokkaidō
Honshū
Shikoku
Kyūshū
Cheju-do (S.Korea)
UNDER RUSSIAN ADMINISTRATION CLAIMED BY JAPAN
Khabarovsk
Yuzhno-Sakhalinsk
Vladivostok
Nakhodka
Ussuriysk
Jiamusi
Mudanjiang
Jixi
Hegang
Yichun
Shuangyashan
Ch'ŏngjin
Hamhŭng
Wŏnsan
Kaesŏng
SŎUL
Sŏngnam
Taejŏn
Taegu
Pusan
Kwangju
Chŏnju
Ulsan
Cheju
Wakkanai
Asahikawa
Sapporo
Otaru
Obihiro
Kushiro
Tomakomai
Muroran
Hakodate
Aomori
Hachinohe
Hirosaki
Akita
Morioka
Sendai
Yamagata
Niigata
Fukushima
Kōriyama
Iwaki
Hitachi
Mito
Utsunomiya
Maebashi
Nagano
Toyama
Kanazawa
Fukui
TŌKYŌ
Chiba
Kawasaki
Yokohama
Yokosuka
Shizuoka
Hamamatsu
Nagoya
Toyota
Okazaki
Gifu
Kyōto
Ōsaka
Kōbe
Nara
Sakai
Wakayama
Okayama
Kurashiki
Fukuyama
Hiroshima
Tottori
Matsue
Yamaguchi
Shimonoseki
Kita-Kyūshū
Fukuoka
Sasebo
Nagasaki
Kumamoto
Ōita
Miyazaki
Kagoshima
Matsuyama
Takamatsu
Tokushima
Kōchi
Ostrov Urup
Ostrov Iturup
Ostrov Shikotan
Tatarskiy Proliv
Tsugaru-Kaikyō
Ōsumi-kaikyō
Izu-shotō
Tane-ga-shima
Yaku-Shima
Fuji-san
Sado
Oki-Shotō

Scale 1: 14 375 000

0 200 400km

0 100 200miles

15°
0°
15°
30°
45°
Brest
Paris
FRANCE
Strasbourg
Bratislava
Budapest
HUNG.
ROMANIA
MOL.
Chisinau
Donets'k
Rostov-na-Donu
Krasnodar
Atyrau
Astrakhan
AUSTRIA
SWITZ.
SLOVENIA
Zagreb
CROATIA
Belgrade
Bucharest
Odesa
Sea of Azov
Simferopol'
Bordeaux
Bay of Biscay
Lyon
Milano
Toulouse
Nice
Marseille
Corsica
ITALY
Rome
VAT.
S.M.
B.-H.
Sarajevo
YUGO-SLAVIA
BULG.
Sofia
Black Sea
Istanbul
Grozny
Zhangaözen
Caspian Sea
GEORGIA
T'bilisi
ARMENIA
Yerevan
AZERBAIJAN
Baku
Bilbao
AND.
Zaragoza
Porto
Madrid
SPAIN
Valencia
Barcelona
Palma
Mallorca
Napoli
Sardinia
Tirana
ALB.
MACE.
GREECE
Izmir
Bursa
Ankara
TURKEY
Adana
Tabriz
Lisbon
PORTUGAL
Sevilla
Málaga
Murcia
Messina
Sicily
Valletta
MALTA
Athens
Crete
Konya
Halab
SYRIA
Al Mawsil
Tehran
Strait of Gibraltar
GIBRALTAR (U.K.)
Tanger
Rabat
Fès
Meknès
Oran
Algiers
Constantine
Tunis
TUNISIA
Mediterranean Sea
Nicosia
CYPRUS
Beirut
LEBANON
ISRAEL
Damascus
Kirkuk
Baghdad
Qom
IRAN
Funchal
Madeira (Port.)
Casablanca
MOROCCO
Marrakech
Atlas Mountains
Touggourt
Béchar
Tripoli
Misratah
Sirte
Banghazi
Tubruq
Alexandria
Cairo
Port Said
Suez
Amman
JORDAN
Jerusalem
IRAQ
Al Basrah
Esfahan
Islas Canarias (Sp.)
Gran Canaria
Agadir
Tindouf
ALGERIA
Adrar
Ain Salah
LIBYA
Sabhã
Ghãt
Libyan Desert
EGYPT
Nile
Luxor
Aswan
Lake Nasser
Red Sea
KUWAIT
Kuwait
BAHRAIN
Manama
QATAR
Riyadh
Al Madinah
El Aaiún
WESTERN SAHARA
Tropic of Cancer
(Occupied by Morocco)
F'dérik
Taoudenni
Tamanrasset
Sahara
Tummo
Al Khufrah
Tibesti
Wadi Halfa
Delgo
Nubian Desert
Kareima
Port Sudan
Jiddah
Makkah
SAUDI ARABIA
MAURITANIA
Nouakchott
MALI
NIGER
Bilma
Faya (Largeau)
Jizan
Sénégal
Tombouctou
Bourem
Agadez
CHAD
Omdurman
Khartoum
ERITREA
Massawa
Asmara
San'a
YEMEN
Al Hudaydah
Al Mukalla
Dakar
SENEGAL
Banjul
THE GAMBIA
Bamako
Mopti
BURKINA FASO
Ouagadougou
Niamey
Maradi
Kano
Gashua
Lake Chad
Abéché
N'Djamena
Nyala
SUDAN
Gonder
DJIBOUTI
Djibouti
Adan
Bissau
GUINEA
Conakry
Freetown
SIERRA LEONE
Monrovia
LIBERIA
Yamoussoukro
CÔTE D'IVOIRE
Abidjan
Tamale
GHANA
TOGO
BENIN
Accra
Lomé
Porto-Novo
NIGERIA
Ibadan
Lagos
Abuja
CAMEROON
Yaoundé
CENTRAL AFRICAN REPUBLIC
Bangui
Wau
Juba
ETHIOPIA
Addis Ababa
Berbera
SOMALIA
Ogaden
Gulf of Guinea
Malabo
EQUATORIAL GUINEA
SÃO TOMÉ & PRÍNCIPE
São Tomé
Libreville
GABON
CONGO
Bondo
Bumba
Kisangani
UGANDA
Kampala
KENYA
Mogadishu
Equator
Annobon (Pagalu) (Eq. Guinea)
Mbandaka
DEM. REP. OF CONGO (ZAIRE)
RWANDA
Kigali
Lake Victoria
Nairobi
Kismaayo
Brazzaville
Kinshasa
BURUNDI
Bujumbura
TANZANIA
Dodoma
Mombasa
Zanzibar I.
Dar es Salaam
Amirante Islands
SEYCHELLES
Farquhar Islands
CABINDA (Ang.)
Matadi
Kananga
Lake Tanganyika
Ascencion (U.K.)
Luanda
Malanje
Kamina
ANGOLA
Lake Nyasa
COMOROS
Moroni
Antsirañana
Lobito
Huambo
Luena
Lubumbashi
Kitwe
Ndola
MALAWI
Lilongwe
Namibe
Lubango
Mongu
ZAMBIA
Lusaka
Nampula
Blantyre
Mozambique Channel
Antalaha
Mahajanga
Maevatanana
Antananarivo
St. Helena (U.K.)
Cunene
Zambezi
Lake Kariba
Harare
ZIMBABWE
Bulawayo
MADAGASCAR
Morombe
Fianarantsoa
Tropic of Capricorn
Walvis Bay
Windhoek
BOTSWANA
MOZAMBIQUE
NAMIBIA
Gaborone
Pretoria
Maputo
SWAZILAND
Mbabane
Keetmanshoop
Johannesburg
SOUTH ATLANTIC OCEAN
Orange
Maseru
LESOTHO
Durban
SOUTH AFRICA
INDIAN OCEAN
Cape Town
Cape of Good Hope
Port Elizabeth
Tristan da Cunha (U.K.)
Gough Island (U.K.)

ATLANTIC OCEAN
PORTUGAL
SPAIN
MOROCCO
ALGERIA
Western Sahara (Morocco)
MAURITANIA
MALI
NIGER
SENEGAL
THE GAMBIA
GUINEA-BISSAU
GUINEA
SIERRA LEONE
LIBERIA
CÔTE D'IVOIRE
GHANA
TOGO
BENIN
BURKINA FASO
NIGERIA
CAMEROON
EQUATORIAL GUINEA
GABON
TUNISIA
SÃO TOMÉ AND PRÍNCIPE
Canary Islands (Sp.)
Madeira (Port.)
Tropic of Cancer
Equator
Gulf of Guinea
Bight of Benin
Ivory Coast
Grain Coast
Sahara
Hoggar
Tassili n'Ajjer
Monts Timétrine
Plateau du Djado
Aïr
Talak
Fezzan
Haut Atlas
RABAT
ALGIERS
TUNIS
DAKAR
BAMAKO
NOUAKCHOTT
NIAMEY
OUAGADOUGOU
ABUJA
ACCRA
LOMÉ
PORTO-NOVO
CONAKRY
FREETOWN
MONROVIA
YAOUNDÉ
MALABO
LIBREVILLE
SÃO TOMÉ
CAPE VERDE
PRAIA
Scale 1: 26 140 000

Scale 1: 30 585 400

0 500 1000km

0 300 600miles

TURKEY
Izmir
Konya
Adana
Gaziantep
Kayseri
ATHINA
Kriti (Crete)
CYPRUS
NICOSIA
LEBANON
BEYROUTH (BEIRUT)
SYRIA
Halab (Aleppo)
DIMASHQ (DAMASCUS)
ISRAEL
Tel Aviv-Yafo
YERUSHALAYIM (JERUSALEM)
'AMMĀN
JORDAN
IRAQ
BAGHDĀD
Al Mawşil (Mosul)
Al Başrah (Basra)
Syrian Desert
IRAN
Eşfahān
Shīrāz
Kermān
Zagros
KUWAIT
AL KUWAYT (KUWAIT)
The Gulf
BAHRAIN
AL MANĀMAH
QATAR
AD DAWḨAH (DOHA)
ABŪ ZABY (ABU DHABI)
U.A.E.
Dubayy
SAUDI ARABIA
AR RIYĀḌ (RIYADH)
An Nafūd (The Great Nefud)
Ad Dahnā'
Najd
Ḥijāz
Al Madīnah (Medina)
Makkah (Mecca)
Jiddah
Aṭ Ṭā'if
Ar Rub' al Khālī
YEMEN
ŞAN'Ā'
Al Mukallā
Gulf of Aden
Red Sea
Al Iskandarīyah (Alexandria)
AL QĀHIRAH (CAIRO)
Būr Sa'īd (Port Said)
As Suways (Suez)
Al Jīzah (Giza)
EGYPT
Aswān
Lake Nasser
Libyan Desert
Al Kufrah
Aş Şaḩrā' al Janūbīyah
Būr Sūdān (Port Sudan)
Nile
Umm Durmān (Omdurman)
AL KHARṬŪM (KHARTOUM)
SUDAN
Al Fāshir (El Fasher)
Al Ubayyid (El Obeid)
Nyala
Kassalā
ERITREA
ASMARA
Massawa
DJIBOUTI
ĀDĪS ABEBA
ETHIOPIA
Lake T'ana Hayk'
Dirē Dawa
Hārer
SOMALIA
MUQDISHO (MOGADISHU)
Kismaayo
Sudd
Juba
Lake Turkana
KENYA
NAIROBI
Mombasa
Kilimanjaro
UGANDA
KAMPALA
Lake Victoria
RWANDA
KIGALI
BURUNDI
BUJUMBURA
Lake Tanganyika
TANZANIA
DODOMA
Dar es Salaam
Zanzibar
Pemba Island
Zanzibar Island
INDIAN OCEAN
CENTRAL AFRICAN REPUBLIC
DEM. REP. OF THE CONGO
Kisangani
Congo
Kananga
Mbuji-Mayi

CAMEROON
GABON
CONGO
DEM. REP. OF THE CONGO
UGANDA
KENYA
RWANDA
BURUNDI
TANZANIA
ANGOLA
ZAMBIA
MALAWI
ZIMBABWE
MOZAMBIQUE
NAMIBIA
BOTSWANA
SWAZILAND
LESOTHO
SOUTH AFRICA
MADAGASCAR
PACIFIC OCEAN
INDIAN OCEAN
Mozambique Channel

MAURITIUS
Scale 1: 40 650 000

SEYCHELLES
Scale 1: 41 670 000

MADAGASCAR
Scale 1: 33 330 000

Scale 1: 31 947 000

0
500
1000km
0
300
600miles

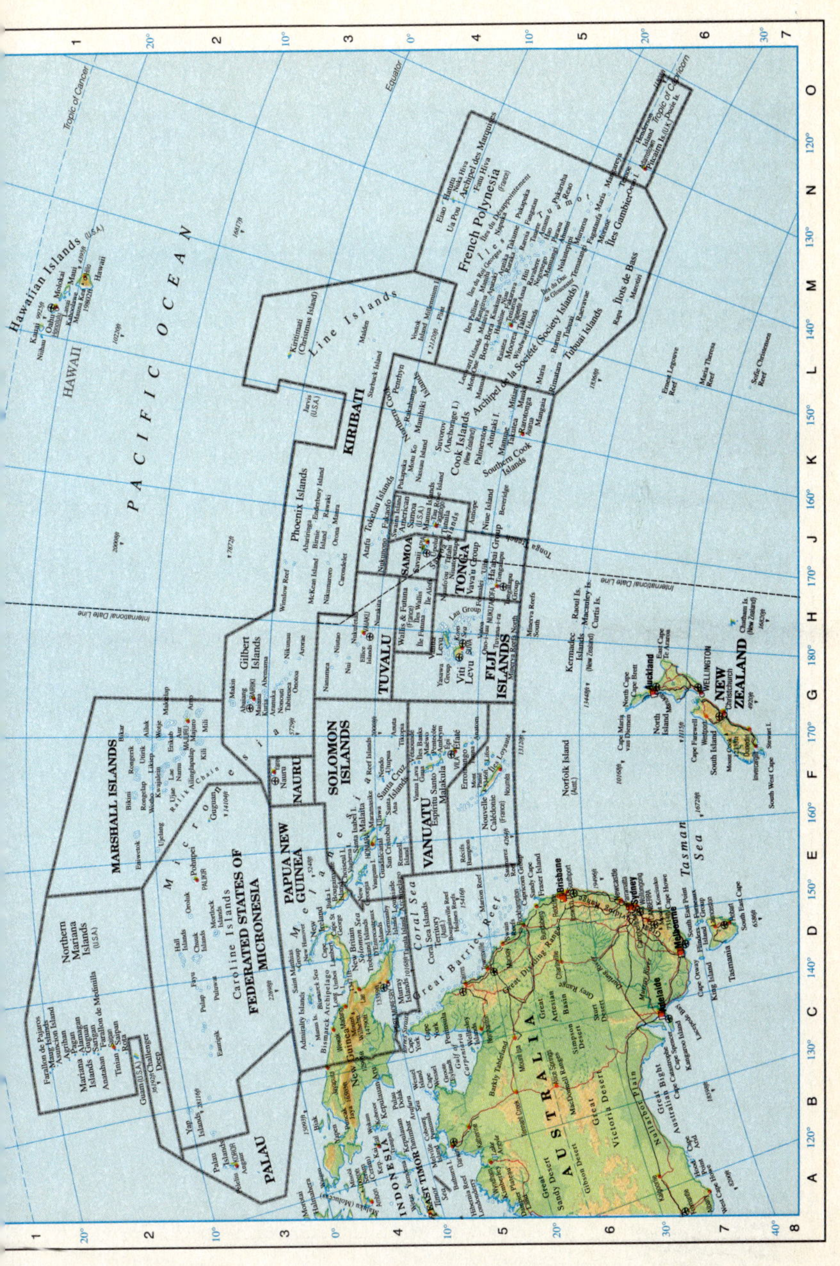
PACIFIC OCEAN
Hawaiian Islands (U.S.A.)
HAWAII
Line Islands
KIRIBATI
Phoenix Islands
Gilbert Islands
MARSHALL ISLANDS
Northern Mariana Islands (U.S.A.)
FEDERATED STATES OF MICRONESIA
Caroline Islands
PALAU
PAPUA NEW GUINEA
NAURU
SOLOMON ISLANDS
TUVALU
SAMOA
TONGA
FIJI ISLANDS
VANUATU
Nouvelle Calédonie (France)
Cook Islands
French Polynesia (France)
Pitcairn Is. (U.K.)
Tropic of Capricorn
Tropic of Cancer
Equator
International Date Line
Coral Sea
Tasman Sea
Great Barrier Reef
AUSTRALIA
Great Sandy Desert
Gibson Desert
Great Victoria Desert
Simpson Desert
Great Dividing Range
Nullarbor Plain
Great Australian Bight
Tasmania
NEW ZEALAND
North Island
South Island
WELLINGTON
Auckland
Christchurch
Brisbane
Sydney
Melbourne
Adelaide
Kermadec Islands (New Zealand)
Norfolk Island (Aust.)
Chatham Is. (New Zealand)
INDONESIA
EAST TIMOR
Timor Sea
Gulf of Carpentaria
Arafura Sea
Bismarck Archipelago
New Britain
New Ireland
Solomon Sea
Tonga Trench
Mariana Islands
Guam (U.S.A.)
Challenger Deep

Scale 1: 74 149 700

0 1000 2000km

0 600 1200miles

INDONESIA
Timor Sea
Bali
Sumbawa
Sumba
Timor
Kupang
Rote
Sawu
INDIAN OCEAN
Ashmore Reef
Hibernia Reef
Scott Reef
Bonaparte Archipelago
Cape Londonderry
Cape Scott
Joseph Bonaparte Gulf
Bathurst Island
Melville Island
Darwin
Van Diemen Gulf
Arnhem Land
Katherine
Pine Creek
Daly Waters
Newcastle Waters
Tennant Creek
Adele Island
Buccaneer Archipelago
Cape Lévêque
Dampier Land
Broome
Derby
King Leopold Ranges
Kimberley Plateau
Halls Creek
Fitzroy Crossing
Wyndham
Kununurra
Ord River Dam
Lake Argyle
Drysdale River National Park
Eighty Mile Beach
Port Hedland
Dampier
Barrow Island
North West Cape
Onslow
Great Sandy Desert
McLarty Hills
Tanami Desert Wildlife Sanctuary
Lake Gregory
Lake Lucas
Lake Hazlett
Lake Mackay
Percival Lakes
Lake Dora
Lake Auld
Lake Waukarlycarly
Chichester Range National Park
Hamersley Range
Hamersley Range National Park
Newman
Lake George
Lake Disappointment
Lake Macdonald
Gibson Desert
W E S T E R N A U S T R A L I A
N O R T H E R N T E R R I T O R Y
A U S T R A L I A
Macdonnell Ranges
Alice Springs
Finke Gorge National Park
Lake Amadeus
Ayers Rock-Mount Olga National Park
Kulgera
Petermann Ranges
Musgrave Ranges
Tropic of Capricorn
Barlee Range
Collier Ranges National Park
Kennedy Range National Park
Robinson Ranges
Carnarvon
Gascoyne Junction
Macadam Plains
Shark Bay
Lake Gregory
Lake Nabberu
Lake Buchanan
Lake Gillen
Lake Carnegie
Baker Lake
Meekatharra
Wiluna
Lake Way
Lake Darlot
Lake Throssell
Yeo Lake
Great Victoria Desert
Serpentine Lakes
Lake Dey-Dey
Lake Maurice
Everard Range
Mt Willoughby
Cue
Lake Austin
Sandstone
Mount Magnet
Laverton
Leonora
Lake Carey
Lake Barlee
Lake Ballard
Menzies
Lake Minigwal
Lake Rebecca
Plumridge Lakes
Great Victoria Desert Nature Reserve
Kalbarri National Park
Geelvink Channel
Houtman Abrolhos
Mullewa
Geraldton
Dongara
Mongers Lake
Paynes Find
Lake Moore
Lake Deborah West
Lake Deborah East
Kalgoorlie
Coolgardie
Lake Lefroy
Lake Cowan
Lake Dundas
Norseman
Southern Cross
Merredin
Northam
Stirling
Wanneroo
Perth
Fremantle
Gosnells
Armadale
The Johnston Lakes
Lake Grace
Narrogin
Wagin
Ravensthorpe
Fitzgerald River National Park
Stirling Range National Park
Bunbury
Busselton
Cape Naturaliste
Augusta
Cape Leeuwin
Manjimup
Denmark
Albany
West Cape Howe
Cheyne Bay
Bremer Bay
Hood Point
Esperance
Cape Arid
Archipelago of the Recherche
Cape Arid National Park
Balladonia
Nullarbor Plain
Hampton Tableland
Rawlinna
Forrest
Eucla Motel
Ooldea
Great Australian Bight
Tarcoola
Penong
Streaky Bay
Anxious Bay
S O U T H

Scale 1: 20 909 300

0 300 600km

0 150 300miles

PAPUA NEW GUINEA
SOLOMON ISLANDS
VANUATU
Coral Sea
Coral Sea Islands Territory (Aust.)
Great Barrier Reef
Nouvelle Calédonie (Fr.)
QUEENSLAND
NEW SOUTH WALES
VICTORIA
AUSTRALIAN CAPITAL TERRITORY
CANBERRA
Brisbane
Sydney
Melbourne
Adelaide
Newcastle
Wollongong
Tasman Sea
Bass Strait
TASMANIA
Hobart
Launceston
Great Dividing Range
Great Artesian Basin
Cape York Peninsula
Fraser Island
Flinders Island
King Island
Furneaux Group

A
170°
B
175°
C
1
2
3
4
35°
40°
45°
Three Kings Islands
Cape Maria van Diemen
North Cape
Parengarenga Harbour
Te Kao
Rangaunu Bay
Awanui
Kaitaia
Cape Brett
Russell
Kawakawa
Whangarei
Waiotira
Dargaville
Needles Point
Hauraki Gulf
Great Barrier Island
Paparoa
Kaipara Harbour
Port Jackson
Colville Channel
Helensville
East Coast Bays
Takapuna
Mount Roskill
Waitemata
Auckland
Manukau
Thames
Bay of Plenty
Cape Runawa
Te Araroa
East Cape
North Island
Paeroa
Tauranga
Matata
Whakatane
Hamilton
Te Awamutu
Putaruru
Te Puia
Opotiki
Albatross Point
Tokoroa
Kawerau
Rotorua
Waikato
Awakino
Lake Taupo
Taupo
Huiarau Range
North Taranaki Bight
Tongariro National Park
Wairoa
Gisborne
New Plymouth
Makorako 5665ft
Mahia Peninsula
Cape Egmont
Waitara
Ruapehu 9174ft
Hawke Bay
Mount Egmont 8259ft
Stratford
Eltham
Napier
Hawera
Taihape
Cape Kidnappers
South Taranaki Bight
Hunterville
Hastings
Wanganui
Ruahine Range
Tasman Sea
Marton
Palmerston North
Dannevirke
Cape Farewell
Levin
Cook Strait
Collingwood
Durville Is.
Abel Tasman National Park
Tasman Bay
Tararua Range
Castlepoint
Motueka
Porirua
Masterton
The Twins 5989ft
Upper Hutt
Karamea Bight
Red Hill 5871ft
Nelson
Lower Hutt
Mount Owen 6150ft
Richmond
WELLINGTON
Blenheim
Cape Palliser
Westport
Seddon
Cape Campbell
Buller
Spenser Mts
Wairau
Ward
Reefton
Mount Travers 7669ft
Manakau 8561ft
Greymouth
Kaikoura Range
Kaikoura
Hokitika
Waiau
South Island
NEW ZEALAND
Cheviot
Harihari
Southern Alps
Rakaia
Waipara
Mount Arrowsmith 9168ft
Pegasus Bay
Christchurch
Mount Cook 12333ft
Banks Peninsula
Canterbury Plains
Haast
Akaroa
Jackson Head
Ashburton
Mount Aspiring 9958ft
Canterbury Bight
Omarama
Timaru
Milford Sound
Lake Wanaka
Waitaki
Waimate
Wanaka
Lake Te Anau
Oamaru
Alexandra
Doubtful Sound
Fiordland National Park
Lake Wakatipu
Hampden
Roxburgh
Palmerston
Waikouaiti
Resolution Island
Manapouri
Clutha
Lumsden
Port Chalmers
Dunedin
Winton
Cape Providence
Otautau
Gore
Balclutha
4920ft
Riverton
Invercargill
Foveaux Strait
Bluff
Mount Anglem 3214ft
Oban
Stewart Island
Port Pegasus
Southwest Cape

0 150 300km

0 75 150miles

Seattle
Vancouver
Fairbanks
Mt McKinley 20303ft
Alaska (U.S.A.)
Yukon River
Bering Strait
Prudhoe Bay
Barrow
Chukchi Sea
Ostrov Vrangelya
East Siberian Sea
Arctic Circle
Khrebet Cherskogo
CHINA
Yakutsk
RUSSIA
Verkhoyansk
Lena
Sredne Sibirskoye Ploskogor'ye
Siberia
Ozero Baykal
Irkutsk
Tiksi
Novosibirskiye Ostrova
More Laptevykh
Mys Chelyuskin
Poluostrov Taymyr
12461ft
PACIFIC OCEAN
NORTH AMERICA
ASIA
EUROPE
ATLANTIC OCEAN
Mackenzie River
Inuvik
Great Bear Lake
Beaufort Sea
Banks Is.
ARCTIC OCEAN
International Date Line
Victoria Is.
Parry Is.
Lake Winnipeg
CANADA
Churchill
Queen Elizabeth Is.
North Magnetic Pole (1988)
North Pole
Severnaya Zemlya
Norilsk
Yenisey
Zapadno-Sibirskaya Ravnina
Novosibirsk
Southampton Is.
Hudson Bay
Foxe Basin
Baffin Island
Ellesmere Is.
Nares Strait
Geomagnetic North Pole
Qaanaaq (Thule)
Melville Bugt
Baffin Bay
Kap Morris Jesup
Peary Land
17122ft
Franz Josefs Land (Rus.)
Mys Zhelaniya
Kara Sea
Ob'
Omsk
Hudson Strait
Iqaluit
KALAALLIT NUNAAT
Greenland (Den.)
Nordostrundingen
Nordaustlandet
Novaya Zemlya
5209ft
Vorkuta
Upernavik
Greenland Sea
Svalbard (Nor.)
Barents Sea
5304ft
Ural Mountains
KAZAKHSTAN
Labrador
Davis Strait
Ilulissat
Bjørnøya (Nor.)
North Cape
Yekaterinburg
Nuuk (Godthåb)
Murmansk
Chelyabinsk
Happy Valley-Goose Bay
Labrador Sea
12494ft
Tasiilaq (Ammassalik)
12136ft
Denmark Strait
Jan Mayen Is. (Nor.)
3862ft
Arkhangel'sk
Narvik
NORWAY
SWEDEN
FINLAND
Newfoundland
NORTH ATLANTIC OCEAN
Nunap Isua (Kap Farvel)
Norwegian Sea
Saint John's
ICELAND
REYKJAVÍK
Nizhniy Novgorod
Samara
SOUTH ATLANTIC OCEAN
Scotia Sea
South Orkney Is. (U.K.)
INDIAN OCEAN
Falkland Islands (Islas Malvinas) (U.K.)
Stanley
Isla Grande de Tierra del Fuego
ARGENTINA
Strait of Magellan
Punta Arenas
Ushuaia
Cape Horn
CHILE
South Shetland Is.
Bellingshausen (Rus.)
Esperanza (Arg.)
Marambio (Arg.)
Weddell Sea
Palmer (U.S.A.)
Larsen Ice Shelf
Antarctic Peninsula
Vernadsky (Ukraine)
Drake Passage
Rothera (U.K.)
Palmer Land
San Martín (Arg.)
4190ft
Mount Jackson
Alexander Island
UNITED KINGDOM
ARGENTINA
Halley (U.K.)
Coats Land
Belgrano II (Arg.)
Berkner Island
Ronne Ice Shelf
Filchner Ice Shelf
Neumayer (Ger.)
Kap Norvegia
SANAE (S.A.)
NORWAY
Maitri (India)
Novolazarevskaya (Rus.)
Prinsesse Martha Kyst
Prinsesse Astrid Kyst
Kronprinsesse Märtha Kyst
Prinsesse Ragnhild Kyst
Syowa (Japan)
Molodezhnaya (Rus.)
Enderby Land
3180ft
Dronning Maud Land
Dome Fuji (Japan)
Mac. Robertson Land
Mawson (Austr.)
10998ft
Mount Menzies
Lambert Glacier
Amery Ice Shelf
Zhongshan (China)
Davis (Austr.)
Ingrid Christensen Coast
Queen Astrid Coast
King Leopold and Queen Astrid Coast
West Ice Shelf
3660ft
Mount Hawks
Polar Plateau
9158ft
East Antarctica
17187ft
Bellingshausen Sea
Vinson Massif 16859ft
Ellsworth Mountains
Ellsworth Land
South Pole
Amundsen-Scott (USA)
2800ft
Wilhelm II Land
Mirny (Rus.)
Davis Sea
Peter I Øy
9912ft
9233ft
Transantarctic Mountains
West Antarctica
Abbot Ice Shelf
Shackleton Ice Shelf
SOUTH PACIFIC OCEAN
Queen Mary Land
9804ft
Queen Maud Mts
Mount Kirkpatrick
14852ft
14255ft
14064ft
South Geomagnetic Pole (1995)
Knox Coast
Cape Poinsett
Marie Byrd Land
Walgreen Coast
Amundsen Sea
Greenpeace (International)
Getz Ice Shelf
4181ft
Rockefeller Plateau
Ross Ice Shelf
Roosevelt Is.
3491ft
Wilkes Land
Casey (Austr.)
Sabrina Coast
AFRICA
SOUTH AMERICA
ATLANTIC OCEAN
INDIAN OCEAN
PACIFIC OCEAN
AUSTRALIA
Scott Base (N.Z.)
McMurdo (U.S.A.)
Mount Erebus 12794ft
Victoria Land
FRANCE
Terre Adélie
Antarctic Circle
Ross Sea
Dumont d'Urville (Fr.)
South Magnetic Pole (1995)
Cape Adare
13645ft
George V Land
NEW ZEALAND
Scott Is.
Balleny Is.
AUSTRALIA
Dumont d'Urville Sea
A B C D E F G H J K
N O P Q R S T U V W
150° W 180° 150° E 120° 90° 60° 30° W 0° 30° E
45° S 30° W 0° 30° E 60° 90° 120° 60° S 150° W 180° 150° E 60° S
75°

Scale 1: 62 726 750

0 1000 2000km

0 500 1000miles

Underwater landscapes

Topography of the ocean floor can be divided into two distinct features: the continental margins and the deep sea basins.
The character of the ocean basin depends on the extent to which sediments mask the crust and also the degree of volcanic activity.
The sediments may be either pelagic or terrigenous. The latter are brought down by turbidity currents which are avalanches of silt and sand from the continental shelf. These powerful currents can cut channels in the continental shelf such as the Hatteras Canyon off North America and transport material thousands of kilometres.
On the continental shelf, sediments are affected by waves, tidal currents and changes in sea level.

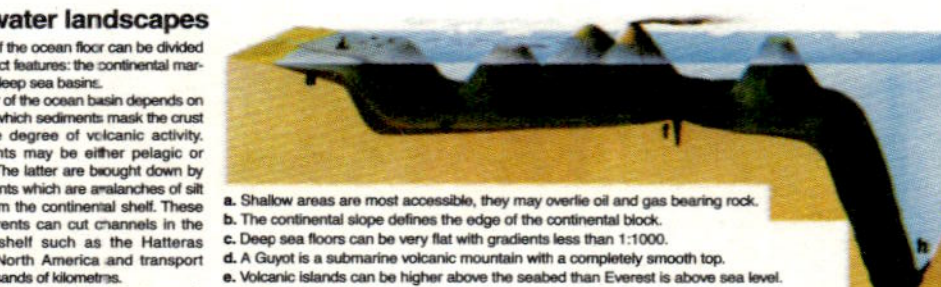

a. Shallow areas are most accessible, they may overlie oil and gas bearing rock.
b. The continental slope defines the edge of the continental block.
c. Deep sea floors can be very flat with gradients less than 1:1000.
d. A Guyot is a submarine volcanic mountain with a completely smooth top.
e. Volcanic islands can be higher above the seabed than Everest is above sea level.
f. Mid ocean ridges. New oceanic crust is formed along these.
g. Atolls are extinct volcanoes which have been colonized by coral.
h. Deep sea trenches. Oceanic crust is destroyed under neighbouring plates.

Seabed treasures

In the deeper sea regions mineral exploitation has concentrated on manganese nodules. These lumps grow at rates of between 3-8 mm, .25 in each million years, and they are valuable for the copper, nickel and cobalt they contain. Granules vary in size and may be up to 150 mm, 6 ins in diameter.
On the continental shelves and near coastal regions placer deposits are often commercially viable. They consist of heavy mineral particles which have been weathered from locally occuring ore bodies and deposited on beaches and in estuaries. Gold is extracted from placer deposits off Alaska.

- Moderate coverage of manganese nodules
- Extensive coverage of manganese nodules
- Nodules with >1.8% nickel and copper
- Nodules with >1% cobalt
- Nodules with >35% manganese
- Placer deposits

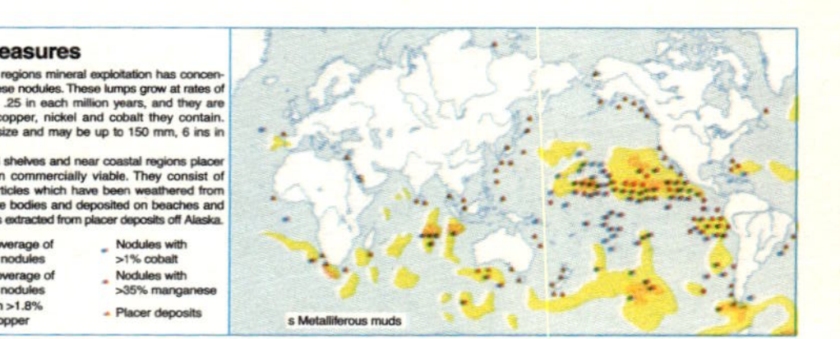
s Metalliferous muds